The Battle of Jutland

This is a major new account of the Battle of Jutland, the key naval battle of World War I in which the British Grand Fleet engaged the German High Seas Fleet off the coast of Denmark in 1916. Beginning with the building of the two fleets, John Brooks reveals the key technologies employed from ammunition, gunnery and fire control to signalling and torpedoes as well as the opposing commanders' tactical expectations and battle orders. In describing Jutland's five major phases, he offers important new interpretations of the battle itself and how the outcome was influenced by technology, as well as the tactics and leadership of the principal commanders, with the reliability of their own accounts of the fighting reassessed. The book draws on contemporary sources, which have been rarely cited in previous accounts, from the despatches of both the British and German formations to official records, letters and memoirs.

After a career in computing and telecommunications, John Brooks obtained his doctorate from the Department of War Studies, King's College London. Now an independent scholar, he is the author of *Dreadnought Gunnery and the Battle of Jutland: The Question of Fire Control* (2005).

Cambridge Military Histories

Edited by
HEW STRACHAN, Chichele Professor of the History of War, University of Oxford and Fellow of All Souls College, Oxford
GEOFFREY WAWRO, Professor of Military History, and Director of the Military History Center, University of North Texas

The aim of this series is to publish outstanding works of research on warfare throughout the ages and throughout the world. Books in the series take a broad approach to military history, examining war in all its military, strategic, political and economic aspects. The series complements Studies in the Social and Cultural History of Modern Warfare by focusing on the 'hard' military history of armies, tactics, strategy and warfare. Books in the series consist mainly of single-author works – academically rigorous and groundbreaking – which are accessible to both academics and the interested general reader.

A full list of titles in the series can be found at:
www.cambridge.org/militaryhistories

The Battle of Jutland

John Brooks

CAMBRIDGE UNIVERSITY PRESS

CAMBRIDGE
UNIVERSITY PRESS

University Printing House, Cambridge CB2 8BS, United Kingdom

One Liberty Plaza, 20th Floor, New York, NY 10006, USA

477 Williamstown Road, Port Melbourne, VIC 3207, Australia

314-321, 3rd Floor, Plot 3, Splendor Forum, Jasola District Centre, New Delhi - 110025, India

79 Anson Road, #06-04/06, Singapore 079906

Cambridge University Press is part of the University of Cambridge.

It furthers the University's mission by disseminating knowledge in the pursuit of
education, learning and research at the highest international levels of excellence.

www.cambridge.org
Information on this title: www.cambridge.org/9781316604502

First published 2016
Reprinted 2016
First paperback edition 2018

A catalogue record for this publication is available from the British Library

Library of Congress Cataloging in Publication data
Brooks, John, 1942– author.
The Battle of Jutland / John Brooks.
Cambridge : Cambridge University Press, 2016. | Series: Cambridge military
histories | Includes bibliographical references and index.
LCCN 2016014668 | ISBN 9781107150140 (hardback)
LCSH: Jutland, Battle of, 1916. | BISAC: HISTORY / Military / General.
LCC D582.J8 B76 2016 | DDC 940.4/56–dc23
LC record available at http://lccn.loc.gov/2016014668

ISBN 978-1-107-15014-0 Hardback
ISBN 978-1-316-60450-2 Paperback

Again for Anne
without whom this book would not have been possible
with my love and thanks

Contents

Figures

Tables

Map

Preface

The literature on the Battle of Jutland is immense; Rasor's 1992 annotated bibliography runs to 528 items.[1] Yet, in the course of my earlier research and writing on fire control in the dreadnought era, I found that, to understand British gunnery and tactics during the battle, I needed to go back to the *fons et origo*, directly or indirectly, of so much of what has been written about Jutland from a British perspective: namely the despatches (often with supporting charts) submitted by flag officers and by the commanding officers of major ships, flotillas, even individual destroyers. Their great value lies in their immediacy and authenticity. Most were written within a few days of returning to harbour, each addressed to the author's superior officer. Because they were required promptly, there was little or no opportunity for more senior commanders to influence their contents.[2] Thus a typical despatch described the events and observations that were recorded or remembered as most important by the author and his subordinates, with little regard for what might later prove significant to the wider picture. Of course, a despatch was unlikely to include anything explicitly discreditable to its author or openly critical of his superiors (though we shall encounter single instances of both). Even so, these despatches are indispensable as contemporary, personal reports of the battle as experienced by those that were there. My previous book *Dreadnought Gunnery and the Battle of Jutland* concentrated mainly on the gun actions between heavy ships during the daylight hours. Now, in this study, I hope to use these same sources and the same methodology in describing, for all the formations present, the course of the battle during daylight on 31 May 1916 and onwards through the night to the morning of 1 June.

In 1920, the great majority of the British Jutland despatches, together with a selection of gunnery reports and a comprehensive list of signals, were published by command as the *Official Despatches with Appendices* (Cmd. 1068). The value of this collection has not always been recognised; Captain

[1] Eugene Rasor, *The Battle of Jutland. A Bibliography* (Westport, CT: Greenwood Press, 1992), pp. 63–170.
[2] See Chapter 7 for *Lion*'s turn through a complete circle.

Roskill described it as 'an indigestible, unanalysed and in some important respects incomplete mass of material'.[3] In fact, the only significant matter that was expurgated refers either 'solely to personnel, recommendations *i.e.*, in no way bearing on the course of the action' or to fire control equipment and methods that remained secret;[4] fortunately, these missing passages can be consulted if needed in the original typed documents preserved in the National Archives.[5] It is true that, as Andrew Gordon states, the despatches are 'riddled with inconsistencies and conflicts'.[6] Given that they were written as records of individual experiences very soon after an action that was plagued with poor visibility, this is only to be expected. But this gives them their authenticity and they contain much information that appears nowhere else. However, they must be used critically and it is incumbent on all historians drawing on them to state clearly which despatches are the basis for their narrative and conclusions. The text of the *Official Despatches* is now available online, and many readers may wish to download a copy in order to check specific citations.

In addition to the despatches themselves, this account makes use of other sources which are either nearly contemporary with the battle or date from the post-war years when participants' memories were still fresh.[7] ADM 137 (the files of the Historical Section of the Committee of Imperial Defence at TNA) contains additional material about Jutland itself as well as the wider war. The Beatty Papers (in the National Maritime Museum) contain several important reports which, had they not been withheld, would probably have been included in the *Official Despatches*. The Jellicoe Papers (in the British Library and online) also contain some unpublished reports, while the four volumes, published by the Navy Records Society, of the papers of the two admirals contain a wealth of material, including that relating to the post-war Jutland Controversy. In 1919, Jellicoe published *The Grand Fleet 1914–1916* and in 1921 Fawcett and Hooper brought out their collection of the 'personal experiences of sixty officers and men of the British Fleet' who fought at Jutland. In 1923, Sir Julian Corbett's five chapters on the battle appeared in the third volume of the official British history, though they provided few references to his sources. In contrast, the Dewar brothers' suppressed *Naval Staff Appreciation* (1922) and their 'de-venomised' *Admiralty Narrative* (1924) contain many references to the *Official Despatches* and also to some other sources that are now probably lost; Jellicoe's dissenting appendix to the

---

[3] Stephen Roskill, *Admiral of the Fleet Earl Beatty. The Last Naval Hero: An Intimate Biography* (New York: Athenium, 1981), p. 323.

[4] *Battle of Jutland ... Official Despatches with Appendices*, Cmd.1068 (London: HMSO, 1920), pp. 54 and 381 and, e.g. pp. 77 and 126.

[5] ADM 137/301–2.

[6] Andrew Gordon, *The Rules of the Game. Jutland and British Naval Command* (London: John Murray, 1996), p. 539.

[7] Full source details, including those available on the Web, are in the Bibliography.

Admiralty Narrative and his appendix for an unpublished revised edition of his book provide further insights into some of his important decisions. The Harper *Record*, eventually published in 1927, was in large measure a summary of the *Official Despatches* but it also contains some additional information.[8] The series of Staff College lectures on Jutland prepared in 1929–30 by Captains Bertram Ramsay and John Godfrey have also been consulted. Of more recent publications, the account of the battle by Nigel Steel and Peter Hart (2003) quotes extensively from the recollections of the battle that are held by the Imperial War Museum; those that were set down soon after the battle have been used here where they provide additional contemporary insights. Many other relevant modern publications are listed in the Bibliography. These works include the third volume of Arthur Marder's *From the Dreadnought to Scapa Flow* and John Campbell's *Jutland. An Analysis of the Fighting*; the latter must be treated critically but the author's deep knowledge of ships' structures and the effects of shell hits remains indispensable.

Because of this study's emphasis on British primary sources, it has a point of view that, at least to some extent, is closer to the British than the German ships. Even so, it requires a reliable German perspective on the battle. In the early 1920s, little was available to the British authors then writing about Jutland other than the despatch of the German commander-in-chief Admiral Scheer and his memoir of 1920. In contrast, the works of these British writers, and the *Official Despatches* that underpinned them, were published while the German official historian, Captain Otto Groos, was still preparing his account of Jutland; this was published in 1925 and a translation was completed in the following year, though only for official use within the Royal Navy. Since Groos could also consult the despatches of German ships and formations, he claimed, with some justification, that he was able 'for the first time to present an account based on official information *from both sides*'.[9] Perhaps partly because of this, his work was some two-and-a-half times the length of Corbett's account, giving detailed descriptions of the movements and actions of the German ships. Thus Groos's *German Official Account* provides the necessary German point of view for this book (though his concluding attempts to claim an unqualified German victory have been discounted). While the British translation that has been cited here has not, to my knowledge, been published, it was the basis for V E Tarrant's *Jutland. The German Perspective* (1995) which provides

---

[8] For the history of these publications, see A Temple Patterson (ed.) *The Jellicoe Papers. Volume II, 1916–1935* (Navy Records Society, 1968), pp. 399–404, Bryan Ranft (ed.) *The Beatty Papers, Volume II 1916–1927* (Aldershot: Scholar Press for the Navy Records Society, 1993), pp. 417–28, Roskill, Ch. 15 and Gordon, Ch. 24.

[9] Captain O Groos (trans. Lieut-Cmdr. W T Bagot), *The Battle of Jutland (The German Official Account)* (Naval Staff, Admiralty, 1926), p. iv, original emphasis.

extended quotations and summarises the remainder of the text. In addition to Scheer's memoir, another important early German source is the book by Commander Georg von Hase, the gunnery officer of the battlecruiser *Derfflinger*; this was published in English in 1921 as *Kiel and Jutland* and is particularly informative about German gunnery methods.

Both official histories were published with a considerable number of detailed charts, though the German set has proved to be the more influential, because it was evidently the basis of the charts that were prepared by Captain John Creswell RN to accompany Marder's volume on Jutland.[10] The resemblance between the two sets is too close to be coincidental; compare, for example, the tracks of the two battlecruiser forces on Marder's Chart 4 with those on the German Charts 4 and 5, redrawn for Tarrant's book as Figs. 17 and 18. However, the historical accuracy of these detailed charts, which show the movements of many ships, large and small, is questionable. They are doubtless helpful in gaining an overall impression of the progress of the battle. But, as Andrew Gordon had demonstrated so convincingly in *The Rules of the Game*, even the track charts of just one formation, the British 5th Battle Squadron, are too inaccurate and inconsistent to be reconcilable.[11] How Captains Groos and Creswell went about the daunting task of unifying the navigational information from two complete fleets is unrecorded and, to me, impossible to imagine. For the simple charts that illustrate this book, I have preferred, as with the text, to go back to the immediate aftermath of the battle, specifically to the charts that accompanied the despatches from the senior commanders, Jellicoe, Beatty and Scheer. For each phase of the battle, the tracks of the British and German flagships are redrawn together on the same scale to show the relative move-ments of the two sides. But no adjustments have been made to eliminate any apparent inconsistencies, so that readers can decide for themselves whether they can be resolved.

The Battle of Jutland was a grave disappointment to the British people, who had expected that, if only the German fleet could be brought to action, the Royal Navy would win an annihilating victory in the tradition of Nelson. Because of the Admiralty's bald initial communiqué, there was even some delay before the public accepted that, despite the British losses, the outcome had been a strategic victory; after a brief excursion, the German High Sea Fleet had withdrawn hastily to its harbours, leaving the Grand Fleet's dominance of most of the North Sea essentially unchanged. But the price of strategic victory had been no less than a tactical defeat.[12] The British forces were considerably stronger – 151 British and 99 German ships were present while, type for type, British

---

[10] Arthur Marder, *From the Dreadnought to Scapa Flow. Vol. III. Jutland and After* (Oxford, 1978), pp. xi–xii. The German charts are acknowledged as only one of Creswell's sources.
[11] Gordon, Ap. II.   [12] *FDSF III*, Ch. 6.

ships fired heavier broadsides. Yet they suffered many more casualties – 6,768 British killed and wounded compared with 3,058 German. Of major vessels, Britain lost three battlecruisers and three armoured cruisers, Germany one battlecruiser and one predreadnought battleship, though only Germany also lost light cruisers, four in all.[13] This book has two principal objectives. The first is to try to identify and explain the many reasons for this striking disparity, including the significant differences in technology and tactics and in leadership and command. The second objective is to provide a detailed and substantiated account of the whole battle as experienced by all formations from the squadrons of dreadnoughts to the flotillas of destroyers. To avoid a work of inordinate length, I am not attempting a critique of the existing literature. Instead, as in my last book, I am returning to the contemporary and near-contemporary sources that have been discussed earlier; throughout, my aim is to identify clearly the sources on which my narrative and conclusions are based. My best hope is that, by taking this approach, I can construct a new, source-based foundation on which further research can build with confidence. Readers will doubtless find some of my interpretations less convincing than others, but I hope that they will always be able to identify my sources as a starting point for their own investigations.

In the narrative chapters, the text is interspersed with tables which list the signals that are relevant to the events being described. These signals are, I believe, indispensable since they capture so much of the essence of each episode – its temporal sequence, the exchanges of reports and orders passing between commanders and subordinates, navigational details like courses and speeds, and tactical manoeuvres. The format of these tables for both British and German signals is the same as that used in the *Official Despatches* for British signals (though with simplified punctuation); note that the left-hand column contains the time of despatch of British signals but the time of receipt of German signals, and that the German sources identify signals *not* sent by wireless as 'Visual'. For consistency with the original sources, these signal times and the times in the text are given using a 12-hour clock followed by 'am' or 'pm';[14] however, again as in the originals, signal times-of-origin use a 24-hour format. All times are expressed in Greenwich Mean Time. In both navies in World War I, with only a few exceptions, courses and bearings were expressed by means of the 32 magnetic compass points and this convention has been retained; also, I hope that, like me, most readers find that, say, SWbyW has an immediate significance that 223° True does not. For brevity, in the text and tables squadrons and flotillas are identified simply by a number and two or

---

[13] N J M Campbell, *Jutland, an Analysis of the Fighting* (London: Conway Maritime Press, 1986), pp. 338–41.

[14] A slight change from the originals, made to avoid ambiguity, is that '12' always means the hour after noon, '0' the hour after midnight.

three letters for the formation type. Arabic numerals are used for British units and Roman for German while the letters follow national conventions: for example, 12DF for the British 12th Destroyer Flotilla but XIITF for the German XII Torpedo-boat Flotilla.

To keep the footnotes as brief as possible, frequently referenced sources are identified by short mnemonics, e.g., *OD* for *Official Despatches*, *GF* for Jellicoe's *The Grand Fleet*. The full citations can be found against the mnemonics, listed alphabetically, in the first part of the Bibliography. Other cited published works are identified in the footnotes by the names of their authors plus, if needed for multiple works by the same author, an abbreviated title; full details are in Section III of the Bibliography.

Acknowledgements

I am most grateful to Professor Sir Hew Strachan for inviting me to write a full account of the Battle of Jutland and for his patience and unfailing support as this book has slowly taken shape. I have been exceedingly fortunate in the friendship, encouragement and advice over many years of Professor Andrew Lambert and Dr Ruddock Mackay. My writing labours have been regularly and convivially punctuated by meetings with Stephen McLaughlin and John Roberts; Steve has been exceptionally generous in sharing the fruits of his archival research, and John's expert advice on the design and performance of ships has been indispensable. I am indebted to Rear-Admiral James Goldrick RAN for his guidance on the operational challenges facing the opposing navies in the North Sea in 1914–18. And I must also thank all those who have so kindly provided me with references and copies of published and unpublished works and with much-valued advice on naval and ordnance matters, particularly Keith Allen, Byron Angel, Professor Ian Buxton, Kent Crawford, Simon Harley, Stuart Haller, William Jurens, Laszlo Kiss, Tony Lovell, Nathan Okun, William O'Neill, David Ramsay, Ed Rudnicki and Matthew Seligmann. If my memory or record-keeping has let me down, I send my sincere apologies to anyone whose name should have been included here. I must add that, if I have misunderstood or misinterpreted any of the invaluable information that I have been sent, I alone am responsible. I must express my gratitude to the late William Schleihauf for inviting me to join the Fire Control Group (FCG) in 2001; many of those listed earlier are members, and it has been a pleasure to be able to learn from the group's expertise in so many aspects of naval warfare. Lastly, I wish to thank the editors – Michael Watson, Rosalyn Scott and Claire Sissen at the Cambridge University Press and Aishwariya Ravi at Integra Software Services – for the advice and guidance that has taken this book from first submission to final publication.

1   Building the battlefleets

The Battle of Jutland, fought on 31 May and 1 June 1916, was the only action in World War I between the massed fleets of Great Britain and Germany. The two fleets had been built during the naval competition between the two countries that is often known as the 'dreadnought race'. But, though the dreadnought battleships and battlecruisers were the most striking elements of the two fleets, the competition also extended to the other warships types – particularly light cruisers and destroyers – that, by 1916, had been integrated into these 'grand battlefleets'.[1] This introductory chapter traces the course of this Anglo-German competition from its beginning in the 'predreadnought' era to the eve of the battle itself, focussing on three specific aspects: first, the numbers of vessels of the four types (and also submarines) that were authorised and built under each yearly programme; second, the fluctuations in the British margin of numerical superiority; and, third, the technical characteristics of the warships constructed by the rival navies. All three aspects are summarised in the tables accompanying the text. To allow ready comparisons, the tables are organised by programme years (in both Britain and Germany extending from April of one year to March of the next), with completions as well as authorisations being counted in each programme year.[2]

After the passing of the Naval Defence Act of 1889,[3] the first two ships of the *Majestic* class, authorised as part of the programme for the financial year 1893–94, established the characteristics of the British battleships for the next ten years: a primary armament of four 12in guns in two centre-line turrets, a secondary broadside battery of twelve 6in, an anti-torpedo-boat armament of 12pdr guns and, in the main, a speed of 18 knots. Up to the programme of 1900–01, twenty-nine vessels of this type had been authorised. They were followed for the next three programme years by the eight battleships of the *King Edward VII* class, which mounted 4-12in and 4-9.2in in turrets and also 10-6in and 14-12pdr. The two *Lord Nelsons* for 1904–05 reverted to three

---

[1] Brooks, 'Battle-Fleet Tactics', p. 183.
[2] The most comprehensive source for British and German programme years is *War Vessels and Aircraft. British and Foreign. Part II, Quarterly Return ... October 1915*, ADM 186/15.
[3] Marder, *Anatomy*, pp. 105–7.

calibres – 4-12in, 10-9.2in in turrets and 24-12pdr. By the end of the programme year 1904–05, thirty-nine of these battleships (which would soon be
known as 'predreadnoughts') had been authorised and thirty-one completed,
while all thirty-nine had been completed before the end of 1908–09. From
1896, France embarked on a major programme of armoured cruiser construction; by 1906, she had laid down nineteen of these large vessels, which were
faster than battleships but with thinner armour.[4] Once French intentions
became clear, Britain responded decisively, as she had throughout the nine-
teenth century to foreign challenges;[5] beginning with the six *Cresseys* of the
1897–98 programme, thirty-five British armoured cruisers were authorised and
twenty completed by the end of 1904–05 with all thirty-five in service by the
end of 1908–09.

In 1890, the young Emperor Wilhelm II, who had already shown an active
interest in naval affairs, dismissed Chancellor Bismarck and thereafter pursued
his intent to provide Germany with a navy that matched her growing status as a
world power. Between 1894–95 and 1900–01, Germany authorised the construction of five each of the *Kaiser Friedrich III* and *Wittelsbach* classes.
Compared with foreign predreadnoughts (including those being built in
Britain), they were as well protected while, although their turret guns were of
only 24cm (9.4in) calibre, they were quick-firers (QF); they also had a heavier
secondary battery of 18-15cm (5.9in). In the same period, Germany also laid
down three armoured cruisers. In June 1897, Rear-Admiral Alfred Tirpitz was
appointed State Secretary of the Imperial Navy Office, a post he retained for the
next nineteen years. His first Navy Law of 1898 established an annual construction rate of three large ships while the Amendment (*Novelle*) of 1900
specified that in most years construction would commence of two battleships,
one large cruiser, six light cruisers and one division of six torpedo boats. This
programme was justified by Tirpitz's 'risk-theory' (*Risikogedanke*); this was
founded on the hope that the German battlefleet, if it could be increased to two-
thirds of the whole British fleet, would be strong enough to threaten Britain
with the loss of the battlefleet that she would be able to deploy in home waters.[6]
Alternatively expressed, Germany's aim was to reduce Britain's numerical
margin in battleships to not more than 50%. Under the laws, five battleships
each of the *Braunschweig* and *Deutschland* classes were authorised in the years
between 1901–02 and 1905–06, together with a further five armoured cruisers.
In these last two predreadnought battleship classes, the turret gun calibre was

---

[4] Except where stated otherwise, characteristics of British and French ships are from *CAWFS
1860–1905* and *1906–21*.
[5] A Lambert (ed.), *Steam Warship*, pp. 9 and 12. Beeler, pp. 208–9.
[6] Seligmann *et al.* (eds.), pp. 8, 67, 75–80 and 82; the editors of this invaluable compilation of
primary sources for *The Naval Route to the Abyss* provide incisive introductions to each phase of
the naval race. Herwig, pp. 25–8 and 32–9.

increased to 28cm (11in) (also QF) and the heavier secondary battery mounted 14-17cm (6.7in).[7] Thus between Britain and Germany, the final numerical ratios were 39:20 for predreadnoughts and 35:8 for armoured cruisers, a British margin of 164% for all heavy ships; clearly, Tirpitz's aim of a margin of no more than 50% was at best a distant prospect.

While Britain remained superior in battleships and armoured cruisers, Germany was already establishing a lead in two types of lighter vessels that would, in time, become vital components of the battlefleet – light cruisers and ocean-going destroyers. The first of the ten light cruisers of the *Gazelle* class had been designed in 1896 as a single type capable of the many duties performed by small cruisers; all but *Gazelle* herself were designed for 21½ knots. They were followed in the four years 1902–06 by seven *Bremens* and four *Königsbergs*. Britain, on the other hand, continued to lay down third-class cruisers – none were capable of more than 20 knots – until the programme years 1902–04, in which four *Gems* (22 knots, except for the 22½-knot *Amethyst*, which was turbine-powered) and eight *Scouts* were authorised (all twelve were reclassified as light cruisers in 1913). The 25-knot *Scouts* had a three-knot advantage over the contemporary *Bremens*, but their endurance was poor and in service they were used as flotilla cruisers to lead destroyers (Tables 1.1 and 1.2).[8]

The Imperial German Navy was also an innovator in surface torpedo vessels. The boats of the *S90* class were designed for a new role, to work with the fleet, and were accordingly given raised forecastles so that they could continue to operate in rough seas; forty-two were laid down between 1898 and 1905, though there was a gradual increase in displacement over this period. Their success was recognised in Britain, where the Admiralty had also accepted the need for more seaworthy destroyers. The outcome was the 25½-knot *River* class, with raised forecastles and heavier scantlings than in previous British designs; thirty-four were built in the three programmes from 1901 to 1904. In comparison with the *S90s* (which the Germans classified as large torpedo-boats rather than destroyers), the *Rivers* were bigger, nominally slower and more heavily gunned: though they carried two rather than three torpedo tubes. But, as Tables 1.3 and 1.4 show, Germany, due to her earlier start, had established a significant lead in completed destroyers that were capable of operating in the wider North Sea, either with the fleet or independently.[9]

As soon as France and America achieved some successes with submarines, the Admiralty moved decisively, in the three years 1901–04 ordering from

---

[7] Except where stated otherwise, characteristics of German ships are from Gröner Vol. I (surface vessels) and Vol. II (U-boats).

[8] McBride, '"Scout" Class', p. 274. Rear-Admiral J de Robeck, 'History of "Attentive" Class', 1912, in 'Flotilla Scouts, Cruisers & Depôt Ships [etc.]' in ADM 1/8273.

[9] Herwig, pp. 14–15 and 28–9. Lyon, pp. 15–16. March, pp. 72–3. *CAWFS 1860–1905*, pp. 99–100, 262 and 264–5 and *1906–21*, p. 164. Friedman, *Destroyers*, pp. 86–93.

Vickers five 'Holland' boats to a licensed American design, thirteen 'A'-class boats (still largely experimental) and then eleven of the 'B' class. Apart from *A13*, all these boats had petrol engines and, although the *B*-class were larger than contemporary designs abroad, they were best suited to coastal defence roles. In contrast, due to Tirpitz's opposition to submarine warfare, Germany's first submarine, *U1*, also of the coastal type, was not laid down until 1904; this and other early U-boats were powered by kerosene engines.[10]

Fisher's construction scheme

When Admiral Sir John Fisher became First Sea Lord on 20 October 1904, he had already assured the First Lord, Lord Selborne, that his proposals for new construction, redistributing the Fleet, scrapping ineffective ships and making more efficient use of the Navy's manpower would yield 'a great reduction in the Navy Estimates'. Construction would 'be absolutely restricted to four types of ship being all that modern fighting necessitates': battleships and armoured cruisers (both with uniform armament), large fast destroyers and submarines.[11] Fisher and the expert committee advising him considered several armaments for the new 21-knot battleship but they soon settled on all-12in. For a time, a 9.2in calibre was considered sufficient for the armoured cruiser to fight 'a similar class to herself'. But again, by December, all-12in was preferred, together with a speed of 25 knots. A Committee on Designs was then formed to produce more detailed proposals; it was they who extended Fisher's assertion that 'Battleship and Armoured Cruiser are approximating to each other' to the conclusion that her 12in armament '*makes the Armoured Cruiser all the more qualified to lie in the line of battle if required to do so*' (emphasis in original).[12]

The Committee made the momentous decision that both battleship and armoured cruiser should be powered by steam turbines. In choosing deck layouts, they decided that the battleship would have ten guns in five turrets – two wing turrets and three on the centre line giving a broadside fire of eight guns. To support the boat derrick, they stepped the battleship's single tripod mast abaft the fore funnel. As a result, the fire control top would prove unduly liable to smoke interference; fortunately, this mistake was not repeated in the two-masted armoured cruisers. The armoured cruiser would have eight guns, the two turrets amidships being arranged slightly *en échelon* between the

---

[10] Brown, *Grand Fleet*, pp. 78–81. Herwig, pp. 38–9.   [11] Mackay, pp. 306–11.

[12] *Naval Necessities. Proposals Affecting Policy, Administrative Reform and Types of Fighting Vessel*, Admiralty, 21 October 1904 (but not printed until November), p. 62, FISR 8/4. *Report of the Committee on Designs* (London, 1905), pp. 33 and 41, FISR 8/4. Brooks, '*Dreadnought*', pp. 162–3; this section is largely based on this paper, which questions whether Fisher's dreadnought policy should be seen as 'a stroke of genius'.

second and third funnels; this permitted limited arcs (about 30°) of across-deck fire if the damage to the decks from blast was accepted. The Committee also decided that the latest 12pdr guns would be satisfactory for the anti-torpedo-boat armament, though the armoured cruisers were completed with the 4in weapons that became standard for this purpose. With space restricted in the superstructures, in both designs some of these guns were mounted without shields on the turret tops, where the gun crews were completely exposed; while shields were liable to explode any shells hitting directly, they at least provided some protection against splinters. Despite Fisher's preference for the armoured cruiser type, priority was given to building a single battleship, the *Dreadnought*, as quickly as possible under the 1905–06 programme. She was launched amid extensive publicity orchestrated by Fisher in February 1906, and commissioned in readiness for her first, experimental cruise in December 1906. The three *Invincible*-class battlecruisers (to use the term that was officially adopted in 1911) were laid down under the same programme in February–April 1906 and completed between June 1908 and March 1909.[13]

Given Britain's great preponderance in armoured cruisers and with three *Invincibles* already under construction, there was no reason to lay down any more battlecruisers in the next two programme years. But in each of these years, three dreadnought battleships were authorised, the *Bellerophon* class in 1906–07 and the similar *St Vincent* class in 1907–08. The turret layout was the same as in *Dreadnought*. But her successors had two tripod masts, the foremast being stepped ahead of the funnels and the anti-torpedo-boat guns were 4in. *Dreadnought*'s main armour belt (between the lower and middle deck) was 11in in thickness but 10in in the subsequent battleship classes with 12in guns. In all, the middle-to-main deck armour was 8in thick but the sides between the main and upper decks were unarmoured. In *Dreadnought* and the *Invincibles*, protection against underwater hits by torpedoes and mines was limited to internal longitudinal bulkheads abreast the cordite magazines and shell rooms; this arrangement was retained in all later battlecruisers. But the *Bellerophons* were fitted with continuous longitudinal bulkheads that protected not only the magazines and shell rooms but the engine and boiler rooms as well; this feature was then repeated in the *St Vincent* class and also in *Neptune* of the 1908–09 programme.[14]

Destroyers and submarines

Fisher began his time as First Sea Lord by declaring that '[a]ny intermediate type of cruiser . . . is utterly useless . . . One armoured cruiser [of the new type]

---

[13] Roberts, *Dreadnought*, pp. 9–17 and 28–30 and *Battlecruisers*, pp. 19–25 and 96–7. See also Parkes, p. 494 and Rüger, pp. 79–81.

[14] *CAWFS 1906–21*, pp. 22–3. Roberts, *Dreadnought*, p. 32 and *Battlecruisers*, p. 109. Burt, pp. 69–70, 85 and 128–9. Parkes, *passim* for armour details.

would overtake and gobble them up one after the other.'[15] He promptly cancelled the orders for four additional cruisers of the *Gem* class and no small cruisers were laid down in Britain in the three years 1904–07. He also put a stop to the anticipated orders under the 1904–05 estimates for an improved design developed from the *River* class, proposing instead a new type of 900 tons with 4in guns and a speed of 36 knots. Even had this been technically feasible, the cost would have been prohibitive. More realistic requirements were set out in November 1904 when the specialist firms that built torpedo craft were asked to tender for destroyers armed with three 12pdr guns that would burn oil fuel for a speed of 33 knots. The brief to the Committee on Designs further stipulated two torpedo tubes and a displacement of about 600 tons for what was described as an ocean-going destroyer 'to accompany Fleets in all weathers . . . to any part of the world'. But the tenders received had evidently established that only a few could be afforded, since the Committee was instructed to consider also a small coastal destroyer of about 250 tons carrying two 12pdrs and three tubes at 26 knots. They were also informed that the Board had decided to build one 36-knot experimental vessel.[16]

The 'ocean-going' destroyer was developed as the turbine-powered *Tribal* class. Their displacement climbed to 850 tons and more: while at between £130,000 and £141,000, they cost much more than the last batch of the *River* class (£72,500–81,000). Only five, two and five *Tribals* respectively were built in the three programme years 1905–08, the final seven being given a heavier gun armament of two 4in. The first of the class did not join the fleet until April 1908; thus no new destroyers were commissioned in 1906–08 and only four in the following year. Their speed trials led to much legal dispute and, even when they did reach 33 knots, it was at the expense of high fuel consumption. They were not good sea boats, their endurance was poor, and throughout the War, they served as part of the Dover Patrol; thus they fell far short of the ocean-going fleet destroyers imagined by Fisher.

The coastal destroyers were at first named after insects and known as the *Cricket* class; twelve were ordered in each of the years 1905–08. They too were turbine-powered and oil-fuelled (they were nicknamed the 'oily-wads'), but they lacked beam and were too lightly built to undertake destroyer duties. After the trials of the first two in 1906, they were reclassified as torpedo boats numbered *TB1-TB36* and employed only in coastal patrol and local defence flotillas. Thus they added nothing to the Royal Navy's strength of destroyers capable of operating on the enemy's coast or with the fleet. The large destroyer

[15] *Naval Necessities* (see note 12), p. 39.
[16] *CAWFS 1860–1905*, p. 84. Friedman, *Destroyers*, pp. 93–6. *Naval Necessities*, p. 27. March, pp. 84–7. *Committee on Designs* (see note 12), pp. 33–4.

Swift was built to meet Fisher's demands for a 36-knot vessel but, despite her high displacement and cost and prolonged experiments, she barely exceeded 35 knots. She was used as a flotilla leader, but she was too frail for service in northern waters, and in 1915 she too joined the Dover Patrol.[17]

With the *B*-class, Britain established a lead in submarine design and construction. As First Sea Lord, Fisher, already a submarine enthusiast, was prepared to commit to an extended production run of *C*-class boats; thirty-eight were authorised in the four years from 1905–06, and all had been commissioned before the end of 1910. They were little different from the *B*-class, though Fisher was convinced that even these small coastal types were capable of playing a major part in the defence of British coasts and harbours against invasion. However, even in 1904 the need had been recognised for a substantially larger 'overseas' type that could operate for some days on an enemy coast. Though delayed in part by negotiations to break Vickers's monopoly of submarine construction, and probably also by the time needed to develop a satisfactory diesel engine, the prototype *D1* was ordered in 1906 and she ran her trials in late 1908. *D2* was built under the programme for 1908–09 and the rest of the class (*D3–D8*) under that for 1909–10, the last for which Fisher was responsible as First Sea Lord.[18] Thus, while at first he had no option but to build coastal submarines, he was also responsible for the first British class of submarines capable of offensive operations.

Tirpitz's response

At the turn of 1904–05, the German naval attaché in London reported on Vickers's proposals for an all-10in gunned battleship and on British intentions to increase the capabilities of the battleships of the 1905–06 programme.[19] The latter intelligence may have been influenced by an article in the *Daily Mail* for 30 December 1904.

The British Admiralty's reply in this friendly competition with our possible ally [the USA] will be a ship carrying ten 12in. guns and displacing 17,000 to 18,000 tons.

  She will be able to destroy any battleship now afloat or as yet designed with consummate ease, firing as she will a broadside of seven 850lb. shells.[20]

This implies (incorrectly) that three guns were mounted on each side in single turrets. But the report may have had some influence on the German design

[17] *CAWFS 1906–21*, pp. 71–3. Brown, *Warrior to Dreadnought*, p. 195. March, pp. 70–1 and 85–95. Friedman, *Destroyers*, pp. 102–11.

[18] Mackay, pp. 297–303. *CAWFS 1906–21*, p. 87. *Quarterly Return, October 1915* (see note 2), pp. 29–30. Brown, *Grand Fleet*, pp. 80–3. N Lambert, *Fisher*, pp. 154–7 and 182.

[19] *FDSF I*, p. 57. Seligmann *et al.* (eds.), p. 156.

[20] Press cutting with Narbeth to DNC, 30 December 1904 in Ship's Cover 213/12, *Dreadnought*, NMM.

study of March 1905 (Project c) for a small all-big-gun battleship of 15,400 tons with eight 11in guns in two dual centre-line turrets and two single turrets on each side; it also mounted eight 6.7in in casemates.[21] Tirpitz was deeply disturbed when more accurate information on *Dreadnought* reached Germany in the summer of 1905 (her chief characteristics were published in *Engineering* for 26 May 1905). Previously he had been opposed to an increase in displacement beyond the capacity of existing infrastructure. He now realised that, rather than permit any further decline in the relative fighting power of his capital ships, he had no choice but to respond to Fisher's initiative, despite the high costs of bigger ships and the enlargement of fixed works, including the Kiel Canal, to accommodate them. On 22 September, Tirpitz chaired the meeting that agreed the principal characteristics of what would be Germany's first dreadnought battleships, the 18,570-ton *Nassau* class.[22] They mounted six dual 11in turrets, two on the centre line and two each side, but, despite the additional turret, their broadside of eight heavy guns was no greater than *Dreadnought*'s and their reciprocating engines gave them a speed of only 19 knots. But they had a substantial secondary battery of 12–5.9in, and they were better protected.

Dreadnought herself was launched, with great fanfares, in February 1906. In Germany, the *Flottenverein* was criticising Tirpitz for the inferior quality of existing ships, while the Moroccan crisis had heightened the sense of rivalry with Britain. Thus there was little opposition when in May 1906 the Reichstag passed a further *Novelle* under which the construction tempo remained at two battleships and one armoured cruiser per annum despite the considerable increase in the cost of dreadnought battleships.[23] Because of the time required to produce the radically new designs, no German capital ships were actually laid down in 1906 but, between June and August 1907, all four *Nassau*-class battleships were started. And Britain was not the only country capable of building rapidly. Thus the tempo of German completions barely faltered. *Nassau* and *Westfalen* commissioned and began their trials in October and November 1909, though they did not join the fleet until the following May; the trials of *Rheinland* and *Posen* began in April and May 1910, and they both entered service in September 1910.[24] The characteristics of *Blücher*, the first German armoured cruiser with a uniform main armament, were also decided at the meeting of 22 September 1905, but she was not laid down until February 1907, and she also commissioned in October 1909. Her design was too far advanced to change when news of the 12in guns of the *Invincible* class reached

---

[21] Seligmann *et al.* (eds.), pp. 156 and 165–9.
[22] Herwig, pp. 57–8. *IDNS*, p. 58. Epkenhans, "'Opportunity'", p. 84. Seligmann *et al.* (eds.), pp. 157 and 172–5. Kelly, pp. 256–7.
[23] Herwig, p. 59. Seligmann *et al.* (eds.), pp. 157–9.
[24] Gröner I, pp. 23–4. *CAWFS 1906–21*, p. 145. Herwig, pp. 59–60.

Germany and she was built with twelve 8.3in guns arranged as in the *Nassau*. Unlike the British ships, she also had a secondary battery, of eight 5.9in: but, with a maximum belt thickness of 7.1in, her protection was little better than previous armoured cruisers. In contrast, during the design of Germany's first 'battlecruiser', *Von der Tann* of the 1907–08 programme, it was accepted, despite Tirpitz's initial opposition but with the Kaiser's support, that she must be capable of fighting in the battle line. Hence at 9.8in, her belt was only fractionally less than the 10in thickness fitted to contemporary British battleships. Her eight turret guns were 11in pieces, with the two midships turrets *en échelon* before and abaft the second funnel; this arrangement allowed them to fire across the deck over arcs of 125°. She too had the usual German secondary battery, in her case of ten 5.9in guns. She was the first German capital ship powered by turbines for a design speed of 24.75 knots.[25] In the *Invincibles*, which displaced almost 2,000 tons less than *Von der Tann*, Fisher had accepted the mediocre protection of previous armoured cruisers in order to obtain high speed and mount a uniform armament of heavy guns. Now, in a future conflict with Germany, British battlecruisers could expect to face German ships of the same class that, by British standards of protection, were fast battleships.

By May 1907, the Imperial Navy Office concluded that the latest designs of foreign dreadnoughts, not only British but American and Japanese, would necessitate further increases in displacement and cost for the ships of the German programme of 1908–09. To meet this rise in expenditure, a new amendment was needed. With the public mobilised by the Navy League in favour of naval expansion and an expectation of majority support in the Reichstag, in September Tirpitz seized the opportunity 'to make hay while the political and military sun shines'. On 18 November 1907, a new bill was published which increased the tempo of dreadnought construction for the next four years (1908–09 to 1911–12) to three battleships and one battlecruiser per annum; though it would then reduce to one of each in later years. The cost ceilings for both types were also substantially increased. The *Novelle* was passed by the Reichstag in March 1908 with a substantial majority.[26] The first three battleships of the *Helgoland* class, laid down for 1908–09 under the new law, were the first German dreadnoughts with 12in guns but the six turrets, arranged as in the *Nassaus*, could only deliver a broadside of eight guns. Although the *Helgolands* still had reciprocating engines, they were designed for 20.5 knots, a performance that could only be obtained by an increase in displacement of almost 4,000 tons over the *Nassaus*; they also displaced nearly

[25] Herwig, pp. 44–5. Gröner I, pp. 53–4. *CAWFS 1906–21*, pp. 150–2. Staff, *1914–18*, pp. 3 and 5–6 and Burt, pp. 11–15.
[26] Seligmann *et al.* (eds.), pp. 164 and 226–31. Herwig, pp. 63–4.

3,000 tons more than HMS *Neptune* of the same year. In 1909–10, Germany began a fourth *Helgoland* and the first two ships of the *Kaiser* class; another three *Kaisers* followed in 1910–11 (Tables 1.5 and 1.6). The new class were the first German battleships driven by turbines, which gave them a design speed of 21 knots. They mounted ten 12in guns in three centre-line turrets, the after pair arranged for superfiring; the two amidships turrets were positioned *en échelon* as in *Von der Tann* allowing across-deck firing over 120° arcs. Their armour, with a maximum thickness of 13.8in, established a standard of protection that would never be matched by British dreadnought battleships but these advances required a further displacement increase of almost 2,000 tons. In the *König* class, of which the first three were built under the programme for 1911–12, all turrets were on the centre line, for the first time allowing the full main armament to fire without restriction on either broadside.

Germany laid down three battlecruisers in the three years 1908–11 (Tables 1.7 and 1.8). Like *Von der Tann*, they were all turbine-powered and they were protected almost as well as contemporary British battleships. They retained the 11in gun but mounted ten of them, the extra two in a superfiring turret aft; the two turrets amidships were *en échelon*, as in *Von der Tann* and the *Kaisers*. The last of the three, *Seydlitz*, was, at 26.5 knots, a knot faster than *Moltke* and *Goeben* and her armour more than an inch thicker. She was followed in 1911–12 by *Derfflinger*; she had similar protection and the same speed, but mounted eight 12in guns, all on the centre line. Like all German dreadnoughts, battleships and battlecruisers, these ships had continuous longitudinal torpedo bulkheads.[27]

In the four years 1902–06, Germany had laid down light cruisers at the rate (almost three per annum) authorised by the 1900 amendment. But, for 1906–07, perhaps because it was known that Britain had stopped building this type of vessel or because of the financial demands of Germany's dreadnoughts, the rate of construction was cut to an average of two per annum; this rate was then regularised by the 1908 amendment for the years up to 1916–17.[28] Although turbines had been tried in earlier classes, they were first fitted uniformly in the *Kolberg* class (1907–09); these ships, which were bigger than their predecessors, had twelve rather than ten 4.1in guns and a speed of 25.5 knots. The next class, the *Magdeburgs*, was delayed by the design of their new longitudinal frame system so that all four were not started until 1910–11. They were designed for 27 knots with, for the first time, mixed coal and oil firing. They carried the larger 50cm torpedo and were given a cut-down quarterdeck to serve as a mine deck with a capacity of 120 mines;[29] these features were repeated in

[27] Staff, *1914–18*, p. 7 *et seq.* Campbell, p. 20.   [28] Seligmann *et al.* (eds.), pp. 75–7 and 233.
[29] *CAWFS 1906–21*, p. 159. Brown, *Grand Fleet*, pp. 70–1 for longitudinal framing.

subsequent classes. The following *Karlsruhe* and *Graudenz* classes (1911–13) were similar though they were the last German light cruisers to mount 4.1 in guns.

Until 1905–06, Germany authorised six destroyers for each year but in 1906–07 the annual rate of production doubled from six to twelve; this was then maintained until 1913–14. Turbines were fitted as standard from 1908–09, giving design speeds of 32 knots or more, though speeds in service were substantially less.[30] German destroyers in general had fewer, lighter guns (two 3.5in were standard from 1907–08 until three were fitted for 1913–14) and more torpedoes than their British contemporaries. They also displaced less, a difference that became particularly marked in 1911–13, when, as a result of requests from the German fleet, displacement was cut to obtain greater man-oeuvrability. However, the first trials revealed a serious loss of seaworthiness[31] and, from 1913–14, displacement was increased to nearer British tonnages; at the same time, the change was made to oil firing, while these larger boats had six torpedo tubes plus two reloads. From 1911–12 onwards, German destroyers were also equipped to carry eighteen, later twenty-four, mines.

Germany did not complete her first experimental coastal submarine, *U1*, until December 1906 because of Tirpitz's refusal to create 'a museum of experiments'. She was followed by three more experimental boats and then, up to the commissioning of *U18* in November 1912, by a series of designs of similar displacement to the British *D*-class. But, because of problems in developing suitable lightweight diesel engines, all were powered by kerosene (paraffin) engines; the yellow–white fumes and noise from their exhausts made them dangerously conspicuous on the surface. The change to true diesels began in 1910 with the order for *U19* but, as will be described later, she and her successors did not begin to enter service until 1913.[32]

Britain changes course

An early sign of concern that Fisher's construction policy was not meeting the Royal Navy's needs for light craft can be detected in the 1907–08 programme. Although this included the last twelve 'coastal destroyers' (by then classed as torpedo boats) and five *Tribals*, it also authorised the construction of *Boadicea*, a small 25-knot light cruiser mounting only six 4in guns. This did not compare well with the ten or twelve 4.1in guns carried by her German contemporaries; but at least she restarted light cruiser building after a gap of three years. In April 1907, Admiral Lord Charles Beresford was appointed Commander-in-Chief of the Channel Fleet. He was soon bombarding the Admiralty with criticisms of

---

[30] Gröner I, p. ix.   [31] *CAWFS 1906–21*, pp. 164 and 167. Gröner I, p. 76.
[32] Herwig, pp. 86–8. *CAWFS 1906–21*, pp. 173–6. Gröner II, pp. 3–7.

Fisher's policies, including the construction of dreadnoughts – 'we start at scratch with that type of ship'. In December 1907, he complained of a dangerous shortage of unarmoured (light) cruisers and destroyers that were capable of operating on the German coast.[33] Not without cause – by March 1908, Germany would have commissioned twenty light cruisers and sixty seaworthy destroyers compared with twelve and thirty-four respectively by Britain.[34] However, the Sea Lords had already recognised the growing deficiencies in modern light cruisers and destroyers. In June 1907, they approved an initial outline of the 1908–09 programme for which 'our efforts should be directed to the provision of Cruisers – a coming want'; it included five 'improved Boadiceas' armed with ten 4in guns (nothing bigger was then considered necessary), as well as twelve new destroyers 'with superior endurance and sea-keeping qualities to the most recent German destroyers'. As for armoured ships, it was considered that a single battleship and two armoured cruisers with eight 9.2in guns (in effect, small battlecruisers) would suffice.[35]

On 3 October, the British naval attaché in Berlin completed a report describing the expected acceleration in German construction, though this did not discourage Fisher from assuring the diners at the Lord Mayor's Banquet on 9 November: 'Sleep quiet in your beds.' And, despite the publication of the *Novelle* on 18 November, the Cabinet remained determined on a further reduction of naval expenditure. Fisher himself was prepared to cut the battleship and one of the armoured cruisers from the programme, though he proposed increasing the number of light cruisers to ten; evidently he no longer doubted their usefulness. But the reduction in capital ships was too much for the other Sea Lords. Their threat of resignation persuaded Fisher to sign a joint memorandum which insisted that, in view of recent German declarations, Britain's minimum programme for 1908–09 must contain one battleship, one armoured cruiser, six light cruisers and sixteen destroyers. However, the memorandum declared that the right course would be to lay down two battleships rather than one, and it also predicted that, depending on the rapidity of German shipbuilding, a programme of five battleships a year might be necessary in subsequent years.[36] Even the simplest calculation, based on Germany's stated intentions, could justify such conclusions; if the minimum programme were to be accepted, by March 1909 Britain's lead in authorised true dreadnoughts (excluding the 9.2in gunned armoured cruiser as no more than a match for

---

[33] *FDSF I*, pp. 91 and 96–7. His complaint about shortage of light vessels was repeated in June 1908 – Mackay, p. 400.

[34] The Royal Navy also had many second- and third-class cruisers that had preceded the *Gems*, but only the two 21-knot *Challengers* had a nominal speed of more than 20 knots: *CAWFS 1860–1905*, p. 79.

[35] *Navy Estimates Committee. Report upon Navy Estimates for 1908–9*. Admiralty, November 1907, pp. 6, 13–14 and 19, FISR 8/11. Mackay, p. 387. Brown, *Grand Fleet*, pp. 60–1.

[36] Mackay, pp. 383–5 and 387–92.

Blücher) would be just 11:9. The cabinet refused to authorise more than the minimum programme, though the battlecruiser as built would have eight 12in guns. *Indefatigable*'s midships turrets were ahead and astern of her middle funnel, giving them cross-deck firing arcs of about 70°. But otherwise she was little different from the *Invincibles*, notably in her 6in belt armour; in both classes, this only extended from the lower to the main deck. However, nothing was then known about the protection of the *Von der Tann*, let alone of *Moltke*, so no one in Britain yet realised that they, unlike their British counterparts, were armoured to withstand the fire of their own kind.[37] Even with a full-sized battlecruiser in the British programme for 1908–09, the ratio of authorised dreadnoughts was still 12:9. Because Britain cut its building rate when Germany increased hers, in dreadnoughts Germany had been allowed, albeit unknowingly, to surpass the 3:2 (12:8) ratio that was her undeclared target for capital ships.

Neptune, the battleship of the British 1908–09 programme, also had two midships turrets *en échelon*, arranged as in *Indefatigable* to give similar across-deck firing arcs; she had one fore turret and two after turrets, one superfiring over the other.[38] The light cruisers and destroyers initiated a real effort to make up for the small numbers that had been built during Fisher's earlier years as First Sea Lord. Of the six cruisers, one, *Bellona*, was a repeat *Boadicea*. However, the remaining five, of the new *Bristol* class, were larger than their German contemporaries, the *Kolbergs*, and were armed with two 6in as well as ten 4in guns. With the sixteen 27-knot destroyers of the *Beagle* class, the Royal Navy reverted to the pre-Fisher emphasis on seaworthiness rather than extreme speed; they also carried the new 21in 'heater' torpedo. However, while they retained turbine propulsion, they were coal-fired, because facilities for refuelling with coal were more widely available than for oil.[39]

Once the estimates for 1908–09 had been accepted, discussions began in May 1908 on the following year's programme. The Admiralty proposed four dreadnoughts with two more if necessary: though Churchill and Lloyd George insisted that four would be ample. But, in October, troubling intelligence was received that Germany had already placed orders for two battleships that were part of the next year's programme; this was some fourteen months before the commencement of the British ships of the same year. Yet, even if Germany did not advance her whole building programme, under the 1908 *Novelle*, by the end of 1911–12, Germany would have laid down a total of twenty-one dreadnoughts while, as the Sea Lords recognised, by that time older ships would gradually fall out of the reckoning so that 'only Dreadnoughts will count as line

---

[37] Burt, pp. 106–7. Parkes, pp. 492 and 513. Roberts, *Battlecruisers*, pp. 28–9 and 99–102.
[38] Burt, pp. 126–7 shows an arc of 63°.
[39] *CAWFS 1906–21*, pp. 51 and 73–4. Brown, *Grand Fleet*, pp. 68–9.

of battle ships'. They concluded that nothing less than eight dreadnoughts must be laid down in 1909–10 to ensure that Britain could 'maintain the command of the sea in a war with Germany'. Some of their arithmetic was unduly alarmist; the Admiralty calculated that, by the end of 1911–12, Germany would have *completed* seventeen dreadnoughts.[40] But, after Britain's construction rate had been allowed to fall behind Germany's in 1908–09, there could be no doubt that a large programme in 1909–10 was essential. Asquith obtained the Cabinet's agreement for four dreadnoughts with a further four if they proved necessary and, at the insistence of the Sea Lords, a footnote was added to the naval estimates as a commitment to the 'footnote four'. In the debate on the estimates on 16 March 1909, comparisons were based only on British and German strengths and only in terms of dreadnoughts. Although the government's case was accepted in Parliament, the debate touched off a major crisis with demands that 'We want eight, and we won't wait.' However, in April, intelligence was received that Austria planned to construct three or four dreadnoughts; this plan quickly led to Italy laying down her first dreadnought. On 26 July, the First Lord, Reginald McKenna, informed the House that, in view of these developments in the Mediterranean, the footnote four would be built – though they would not be laid down until April 1910 – and that this would not prejudice the programme for 1910–11.[41]

The construction of dreadnoughts by other navies greatly complicated the application of the long-standing two-power standard. In April 1909, the Controller, John Jellicoe, first proposed that a much simpler standard (though one that would not be made public until 1912) would be for Britain to aim for a 60% margin in dreadnoughts over Germany alone.[42] By this criterion, the large programme of 1909–10 was clearly only the beginning. In terms of dreadnoughts laid down, the small programme of 1908–09 had allowed the margin to plummet to only 33% (Table 1.9); the 14% margin in battleships alone was even narrower. The 1909–10 programme would only increase the margin to 54% while, if Germany did no more than adhere to her announced plans, by the end of 1911–12, Britain would need to lay down a further thirteen dreadnoughts to pass the 60% margin.

When the German estimates for 1909–10 became available to the Admiralty in December 1908, the increased costs were taken to indicate either that their building rate was speeding up or, as Jellicoe, the Controller, correctly deduced, that their latest designs were 'vastly more powerful than our later ships'. By March 1909, Fisher declared that '4 of the German Dreadnoughts are of 22,000 tons and that cruiser H [*Goeben*] will surpass the *Indomitable*'.[43] In fact, as

---

[40] Seligmann *et al.* (eds.), pp. 349–5, 363 and 371. *FDSF I*, p. 155.

[41] *FDSF I*, pp. 151–6 and 159–71. See also Sondhaus, pp. 210–11.

[42] *FDSF I*, pp. 183–5. *IDNS*, pp. 190–1.

[43] *FDSF I*, p. 153. *JP I*, pp. 13–14. Roberts, *Battlecruisers*, p. 32.

we have already seen, the increase to more than 22,000 tons had been made the year before with the *Helgolands*, though, in weight of broadside and speed, they were inferior to their contemporary, *Neptune*. But the three 21-knot *Kaisers* of the 1909–10 programme were the first German battleships with turbines and they had the same turret layout as *Neptune* and *Hercules* and *Colossus*, the first two battleships of the new British programme. They were laid down earlier than usual, in July 1909. Two aspects of their design were retrograde steps. They reverted to the *Dreadnought* arrangement of stepping a single mast abaft the fore funnel, where its fire control top was liable to smoke interference. And, also like *Dreadnought*, they did not have continuous long-itudinal bulkheads, just longitudinal screens close to magazines and shell rooms. These features would be repeated in all the 1909–10 dreadnoughts.[44] But in other respects the later ships were considerably more powerful, not least because they would mount the heavier 13.5in gun. The battleship *Orion*, laid down in November 1909, carried ten of them in five centre-line turrets. Her lower belt was an inch thicker than her predecessors and she also had an 8in armour strake between the main and upper deck (as did the next two battleship classes). However, despite Fisher's protestations, her speed remained at 21 knots. The battlecruiser *Lion*, which was laid down in September 1909, was a new embodiment of Fisher's preferred type; if he had had his way, all eight ships would have been like her. Whereas previous battlecruisers had displaced slightly less than their battleship contemporaries, *Lion* was almost 4,000 tons heavier than *Orion*; she also cost 10% more than the battleship and 36% more than her predecessor, *Indefatigable*. She carried eight 13.5in guns in four centre-line turrets and was designed for 28 knots. Her protection was a sig-nificant improvement on the first generation of British battlecruisers; she had a 9in waterline belt between the lower and main deck and a 6in armour strake between the main and upper deck (battlecruisers did not have a middle deck). But this was still inferior to that of *Moltke* and *Goeben*. The 'footnote four' were laid down at the very beginning of the next programme year: three more *Orions* in April 1910 and the battlecruiser *Princess Royal* in May. All the ships of the 1909–10 programme suffered from smoke interference to the fire-control tops on their single masts, but it was worse in the battlecruisers. Before *Lion* and *Princess Royal* could enter service, their original tripod masts had to be replaced by pole masts stepped ahead of the fore funnels.[45]

The 1909–10 programme again increased the construction rates for light cruisers and destroyers. As in 1908–09, it included two types of light cruiser, both with improved armament. The two small *Blondes* mounted ten 4in guns,

---

[44] *CAWFS 1906–21*, p. 26. Brooks, 'Mast and Funnel', pp. 43–4. Burt, pp. 138 and 195. Parkes, pp. 519 and 521–2.

[45] Roberts, *Battlecruisers*, pp. 32 and 103. Sumida, *IDNS*, Tables 16 and 17. *CAWFS 1906–21*, pp. 28–9. Brooks, 'Mast and Funnel', pp. 44–6.

while, in the four larger *Weymouths*, the mixed calibres of the *Bristols* was replaced with a uniform armament of eight 6in. The programme also included the twenty-strong *Acorn* class of 27-knot destroyers. Being oil-fuelled, they were smaller and less expensive than the coal-fired *Beagles*, but even so they were better armed, with two 4in and two 12pdr guns. Thus, when the shortage of light cruisers and destroyers was raised during the Beresford Enquiry in the summer of 1909, the First Lord could argue that future requirements for modern vessels were already being provided for.[46]

After Fisher reluctantly retired from the Admiralty in January 1910, the Board agreed to programmes of four battleships and one battlecruiser in each of the next two years, although this would only increase the British margin over Germany in dreadnoughts laid down to 43%. However, in June 1910, two more battlecruisers, to be called *Australia* and *New Zealand* after the dominions that would pay for them, were laid down. In design, they were little different from the *Indefatigable*, which was already outclassed when her construction started in February 1909. But *Australia* was built to be the flagship of the Royal Australian Navy, in which role her prospective opponents were likely to be enemy cruisers operating against the Empire's trade routes. At first, *New Zealand* was also intended for service in eastern waters but, upon her completion in 1912, she was presented to the Royal Navy.[47] Yet, even if both ships are counted, the British dreadnought margin was no more than 52%. Four battleships of the *King George V* class and the battlecruiser *Queen Mary* were built under the 1910–11 programme proper. Both designs were similar to those of the previous year, and both had to be modified to step a pole mast ahead of the fore funnel. Five light cruisers were also laid down, two of the smaller *Actives* and three larger *Chathams* of an improved design. Both were half a knot faster than their immediate predecessors but were otherwise similar. The programme also authorised the largest class of destroyers built in peacetime, the twenty-three *Acherons*. The fourteen built to the standard Admiralty design were repeats of the 27-knot *Acorns*, but in addition there were nine 'specials' with speeds up to 32 knots. The programme also included the first six submarines of the *E*-class, which were enlarged and improved versions of the overseas *D*-type.[48]

In Autumn 1910, concerns about the dreadnought strength of the Triple Alliance led to demands for six dreadnoughts for 1911–12, but Lloyd George insisted on five. The 1911–12 dreadnoughts were the four *Iron Duke* battleships and the battlecruiser *Tiger*. In them, the 4in anti-torpedo-boat guns mounted in the superstructure were replaced by batteries of 6in guns in casemates. It seems that many officers still believed in the value of a hail-of-fire from 6in guns

---

[46] *FDSF I*, pp. 196–7.   [47] *FDSF I*, pp. 179, 205, 213–15 and 219. *CAWFS 1906–21*, pp. 26–7.
[48] Brooks, 'Mast and Funnel', pp. 46–8. *CAWFS 1906–21*, pp. 53–4, 75 and 87–8.

against enemy battleships, especially if they were encountered at short ranges in poor visibility. But the increase in calibre was principally required to stop large modern destroyers, preferably before they could fire the new 'heater' torpedoes from ranges as long as 8,000 yards. Since such attacks were now to be expected during fleet actions, the 6in guns were behind 6in armour as protection against fire, secondary as well as primary, from enemy battleships.[49] In the *Iron Dukes*, as in the previous *King George V* class, longitudinal bulkheads protected engine rooms as well as magazines against underwater hits but the protection for the boiler rooms depended on massed coal bunkers; however, in *Tiger*, as in previous British battlecruisers, only the magazines had longitudinal screens.[50] By the time the new dreadnoughts were completed, the designs had been modified so that they had full tripod masts stepped well ahead of the funnels. In another change to the deck layout, both *Tiger*'s after turrets were positioned abaft her three funnels, so Q as well as X turret could fire directly astern. It was hoped that *Tiger* would make 30 knots with her boilers on overload, though this objective added further to her great cost – £2.59 million, compared with £2.04 M for an *Iron Duke* – but her best trial speed, albeit on a shallow course, was just over 29 knots.[51]

The 1911–12 programme for light cruisers and destroyers was a little smaller than that for 1910–11, but it was still sufficient to ensure that, by the end of the programme year, Britain had overtaken Germany, though only just, in the numbers of these vessels laid down. It included the final *Active* and three larger *Birminghams*, the latter mounting an additional 6in gun. The twenty destroyers of the *Acasta* class were a marked advance on previous classes in displacement, speed (29 knots) and armament (three 4in guns and two additional torpedoes as reloads). There was an even greater contrast with their German contemporaries, which were barely more than half the displacement of the new British boats. British submarine construction continued with a further five members of the *E*-class, in which *E9* and later boats, while retaining two beam and one stern torpedo tubes, were given a second bow tube.[52] By the end of 1911–12, Britain had commissioned forty-nine coastal submarines of the *B* and *C* classes and seven of the overseas *D*-class. Excluding the experimental *U1–U4*, Germany had commissioned nine U-boats but, while they were similar to the *D*-class in displacement, all were powered by the unsatisfactory kerosene engines.

---

[49] *FDSF I*, pp. 216–19. Kerr, pp. 47–9. Brown, *Grand Fleet*, p. 42. Brooks, 'Battle-Fleet Tactics', pp. 187–92.

[50] Parkes, pp. 519, 521–2, 539 and 548–9. Burt, p. 197. Roberts, *Battlecruisers*, pp. 105 and 109.

[51] Brooks, 'Mast and Funnel', p. 50. Roberts, *Battlecruisers*, pp. 36–8, 79 and 81. *IDNS*, Tables 16 and 17.

[52] *CAWFS 1906–21*, p. 88. Brown, *Grand Fleet*, p. 83.

Last peacetime programmes

From 1909–10 onwards, the large British programmes left no doubt that the country had both the will and the financial and industrial resources to over-match Germany not only in dreadnoughts but in light cruisers, destroyers and, though less immediately, in submarines. In the latter half of 1911, the Second Moroccan Crisis gave Tirpitz and the Emperor the opportunity to press for an increase in the rate of dreadnought construction beyond the two *per annum* permitted after 1911–12 by the 1908 *Novelle*. At the start of 1912, they were proposing three additional ships over the next six years with a 3:2:3:2:3:2 tempo. This objective was revealed to the British by the German Chancellor, Bethmann Hollweg, while, in his discussions with Lord Haldane, Tirpitz for the first time proposed the 3:2 ratio in dreadnoughts that had continued to be his 'guiding star'. On 18 March, Churchill, in his first speech to Parliament on the naval estimates as First Lord, publicly acknowledged that British policy aimed at a 60% margin over Germany, and he announced that Britain would pursue either a 4:3:4:3:4:3 programme or a 5:4:5:4:5:4 one if the *Novelle* was enacted. As authorised by the Reichstag, the amendment actually authorised a 2:3:2:2:3:2 tempo. On 18 July, Parliament was informed that the British six-year programme would be 4:5:4:4:4:4;[53] without counting *Australia*, by 1917–18, Britain would have laid down fifty-six dreadnoughts to Germany's thirty-five, a British margin of exactly 60%. Despite the failure of the Haldane Mission, diplomatic relations between Britain and Germany actually improved once their new naval programmes had been determined. Both sides had been much more candid than previously about the objectives of their naval construction programmes;[54] each now knew the margin sought by the other; and that the difference was, at 10%, not very great. Following the British slowdown in 1908–09 and Germany's supreme effort in 1908–12, by the end of 1911–12, with the British margin in authorised dreadnoughts at 52%, Tirpitz was less than one ship away from his 3:2 objective – or, if *Australia* was discounted, he had surpassed it. But it was now clear that Britain would not allow her margin to shrink any further, and in February 1913, before a Reichstag committee, Tirpitz declared his acceptance of the British 16:10 standard.[55]

In accordance with the 1912 *Novelle*, Germany laid down two dreadnoughts in 1912–13, the final *König*-class battleship and the battlecruiser *Lützow*; the latter was similar to her predecessor, *Derfflinger*, though she carried larger 60cm torpedoes. As in previous years, two light cruisers and twelve destroyers were also started, both classes being similar to the designs of the year before. However, there was a marked acceleration in submarine construction; probably, four diesel-powered overseas boats were started in 1911–12, but

[53] *FDSF I*, pp. 272–86. Seligmann *et al.* (eds.), pp. 319–21.   [54] *FDSF I*, pp. 286–7.
[55] *FDSF I*, p. 311. Seligmann *et al.* (eds.), p. 399.

seventeen in the two years 1912–14.[56] In 1913–14, the last complete programme before the outbreak of war, Germany laid down the authorised three
dreadnoughts, the battlecruiser *Hindenburg* (generally similar to the *Lützow*)
and two *Bayern*-class battleships, though none was completed in time for
Jutland. The battleships mounted eight 15in and fourteen 5.9in guns; for the
first time, there were no smaller guns for defence against destroyer attacks. At
22 knots, the *Bayerns* were a knot faster than their predecessors, but their
maximum armour thickness remained the same. The 1914–15 programme
initially comprised the battleship *Sachsen* (similar to the *Bayerns*) and the
battlecruiser *Mackensen*; the latter would have been armed with eight 13.8in
guns. During the War, three more *Mackensens* and one more *Sachsen* were
started, but no ship of either class had been completed when the War ended.[57]
For her 1913–14 programme, Germany laid down two light cruisers,
Wiesbaden and *Frankfurt*; they were larger than previous classes and were
armed with eight 5.9in guns and two additional torpedo tubes. They were the
last purely German designs to be completed before the Battle of Jutland but, at
the beginning of the War, Germany also took over two cruisers being built for
Russia; though somewhat smaller, *Pillau* and *Elbing* also mounted eight 5.9in.
For the twelve *V25*-class destroyers, Germany reverted to a larger and more
seaworthy type which was also the first to be fuelled only by oil. Their design
then became the mainstay of the wartime emergency programme. With the
usual German emphasis on torpedo armament, they had six torpedo tubes and
two reloads; the majority, including all that had been commissioned by May
1916, mounted three 3.5in guns.

In 1912–13 Britain laid down the four fast battleships of the *Queen Elizabeth*
class, armed with eight 15in guns and (in service) fourteen 6in. Their main belts
between the lower and main decks were 13in at the waterline but tapered to 8in
below and 6in above, while the main-to-upper belt was also 6in thick. They
reintroduced continuous longitudinal bulkheads as protection against underwater hits. The *Queen Elizabeths* were fuelled only by oil; it was hoped that
they would reach 25 knots on overload power, but their best speed in service
was 24 knots. Fisher gave his enthusiastic support to the decisions to adopt the
new and untried 15in gun and oil fuel, though, true to his long-standing
preference, he wanted them used in a 30-knot battlecruiser which he called
the *Non-Pareil*.[58] Oil alone was also the fuel for the light cruisers of the same
programme. With German light cruisers continuing to mount 4.1in guns, the
Royal Navy did not need any more of the larger cruisers fully armed with 6in,
but it was still very short of small, fast, light cruisers that could work with, and

[56] Estimated from build years and launch dates in Gröner II, pp. 7–9.
[57] Gröner I, pp. 28–30 and 57–8.
[58] Burt, pp. 284–6. *CAWFS 1906–21*, pp. 33–4. Parkes, pp. 563–4. Mackay, p. 435. *IDNS*,
pp. 258–60.

also oppose, the latest destroyers. Thus the cruiser programme for the year comprised the eight ships of *Arethusa* class. They mounted two 6in and six 4in guns; their double thickness of side plating proved capable of resisting German 4.1in shells, and they were powered by destroyer-type machinery. This enabled *Arethusa* to reach 29 knots on overload power during her curtailed trials at the beginning of the War. The destroyers for 1912–13 were the 22 boats of the *Laforey* class. Like the preceding *Acastas*, they were 29-knot boats armed with three 4in guns. They also mounted a pair of the new twin torpedo tubes; thus, in action, they would have four torpedoes immediately available, just like the contemporary German boats. (They also had fittings to stow and lay four mines, but it seems that they were never actually used.)[59]

At the end of 1912, the Federated Malay States undertook to pay for a fifth battleship of the *Queen Elizabeth* class; *Malaya* would be laid down in May 1913. However, she would not be counted towards the 60% margin and, in his speech on the 1913–14 estimates on 26 March 1913, Churchill announced that the programme would include five new battleships.[60] These became the *Revenge* class, of which *Revenge* herself and *Royal Oak* would be completed in time for Jutland. Like the *Queen Elizabeths*, they mounted eight 15in guns and were fitted with continuous longitudinal bulkheads, but the protective deck was a deck higher and the main belt was a uniform 13in in thickness. They were designed for 21 knots and, initially, it was intended that they would revert to mixed coal and oil firing. Continuing the adherence to the six-year programme announced in 1912, the initial estimates for 1914–15 included three more *Revenge*-class battleships and one fast battleship, an improved version of the *Queen Elizabeth* class to be called *Agincourt*. However, beginning in December 1913, consideration was given to the possibility of substituting submarines and other torpedo craft for one or even two of these battleships – though, if two, the British margin in authorised dreadnoughts would have been reduced to 57% (54% without *Malaya*). No final decision had been taken by the outbreak of the War,[61] but preliminary work on two of the battleships was then suspended and the other two ships, one of them *Agincourt*, were cancelled. When Fisher returned as First Sea Lord in October 1914, he insisted that the five *Revenge*-class battleships, already under construction, should be converted for oil firing only, and that the two suspended ships, already named *Renown* and *Repulse*, should be built rapidly as 32-knot battlecruisers with six 15in guns and armour no thicker than that in the *Invincibles*.[62] Fortunately, neither ship was completed in time to face German battlecruisers at Jutland.

[59] *CAWFS 1906–21*, pp. 55 and 76. Brown, *Grand Fleet*, pp. 65–6.
[60] *FDSF I*, pp. 312–14 and 321.   [61] Bell, pp. 46–7; cf. N Lambert, *Fisher*, pp. 296–303.
[62] Roberts, *Battlecruisers*, pp. 46–50 and 126. McBride, 'Armageddon', pp. 61–2. *CAWFS 1906–21*, pp. 35–6 and 38–9. Parkes, p. 584.

The light cruisers of the 1913–14 programme were the six *Carolines* and two *Calliopes*, the last two having more efficient geared turbines. Being somewhat larger than the *Arethusas*, all eight were less cramped and had more stability; their two 6in guns were both mounted aft while, of their eight 4in, two were placed side-by-side on the forecastle (later in the War, they were replaced by another 6in).[63] The original programme also contained sixteen destroyers of the *M*-class; they had the same armament as the *Laforeys*, but, at Churchill's insistence, they were much faster – though the standard Admiralty design could only make the design speed of 34 knots at light load. Later, three of the class were cancelled in favour of the first two flotilla leaders of the *Lightfoot* class; these were large destroyers with extra accommodation for a flotilla's Captain (D) and his staff, with the additional advantage that they would release urgently needed light cruisers for other duties.[64]

By the end of 1913–14, the last peacetime programme year, Britain's margin in authorised dreadnoughts was 62%, though only if both *Australia* and *Malaya* were counted. In completed dreadnoughts, the margin, though still falling, was 59% without *Australia*. But, in his speeches on the 1913–14 estimates, Churchill had declared for the first time that a 50% margin in dreadnoughts would suffice in home waters. On the eve of the declaration of war, each country had commissioned one more battleship, so the global dreadnought ratio was 29:18, a satisfactory British margin of 61%. But three British battlecruisers and one German were stationed in the Mediterranean while *Australia* remained in the Pacific. Thus the British margins in home waters were 47% for all dreadnoughts, but only 43% for battleships. Hence the after-effects of the British slowdown and German acceleration in 1908–09 were still being felt, notably in the battleship margin. For light cruisers and destroyers, the consequences of Fisher's early programmes was that Britain had barely established equality with Germany; on 31 July 1914, the completion ratios were 34:33 for light cruisers, 143:133 for destroyers – though, as will be discussed shortly, Britain had a higher proportion of more modern designs. In submarine construction, Britain's early lead in overseas submarines, gained by Fisher, had not been maintained due to unsuccessful efforts to develop a fleet submarine and to the need to place orders for small submarines to encourage other firms to compete with Vickers. At the beginning of the War, eighteen boats of the *D* and *E* classes had been commissioned, whereas, although Germany's first eighteen U-boats had been powered by kerosene engines, she was now constructing true diesel-powered overseas submarines,

[63] *CAWFS 1906–21*, pp. 56–8. Brown, *Grand Fleet*, p. 66.
[64] *CAWFS 1906–21*, pp. 76–7. *Moorsom*'s trial speed from John Roberts.

of which the eleventh was commissioned on 1 August 1914. Both navies then started large war programmes based on pre-war designs (*E12* and *U43*).[65]

Wartime accessions

As soon as war broke out, Britain seized two battleships that were on the point of being delivered to Turkey; these became the *Erin* (ten 13.5in guns) and the extraordinary *Agincourt* (fourteen 12in in seven turrets). A powerful battleship under construction for Chile was also purchased and, as *Canada* (ten 14in guns), she joined the Fleet in September 1915.[66] It is a sign of Britain's capacity for warship building that, despite having laid down forty-two dreadnoughts in the nine years from 1905–06 to 1913–14, she still had slips available for foreign orders. By March 1915, *Goeben* had been transferred to Turkey, *Audacious* (and also the semi-dreadnought *Blücher*) has been sunk and *Australia* had joined the Grand Fleet, but *Inflexible* and the recently completed *Queen Elizabeth* were at the Dardanelles. Both sides had also rushed ships to completion, so that Britain had thirty-three dreadnoughts (twenty-four battleships and nine battlecruisers) with the Grand Fleet, while the High Seas Fleet had twenty-one (seventeen battleships and four battlecruisers). This gave a satisfactory dreadnought British margin of 57%, but the battleship margin (41%) was still short of Churchill's 50%. However, Germany was actually worse off, since she also had to take account of the four dreadnoughts of the Russian Baltic Fleet.[67] By the eve of Jutland, her position had deteriorated further. All British dreadnoughts were then in home waters, and the Royal Navy had commissioned another seven battleships. In contrast, Germany had added only one more dreadnought to her fleet, the battlecruiser *Lützow*. Thus the ratios had increased to 42:22 in dreadnoughts, 32:17 in battleships and 10:5 in battlecruisers. Britain's dreadnought margin, however calculated, was now potentially overwhelming.

Counting from the German *Gazelles* of 1896–1902 and the British *Gems* and *Scouts* of 1902–04, Britain had only just drawn ahead (by one) in commissioned light cruisers at the beginning of the War. Yet initially, only nine – by November, twelve – of the thirty-four could be allocated to the Grand Fleet itself.[68] Thereafter, the numbers steadily improved. By 31 May 1916, the six *Carolines*, two *Calliopes* and four *Cambrians* – the last were repeat *Calliopes* from the 1914–15 programme – had been completed. Also, two light cruisers built for Greece were taken over in 1915 and named *Birkenhead* and *Chester*;

---

[65] N Lambert, *Fisher*, pp. 154–7, 182 and 221–34. Gröner II, pp. 4–9. *CAWFS 1906–21*, p. 88. Brown, *Grand Fleet*, p. 83.

[66] *CAWFS 1906–21*, pp. 36–8.

[67] *CAWFS 1906–21*, pp. 25, 27, 30, 34, 151–2 and 302–3. Roberts, *Battlecruisers*, p. 123.

[68] *GF*, pp. 18–19. *JP I*, p. 85.

they were armed with ten 5.5in guns that could fire more rapidly than the standard British 6in.[69] Germany, by contrast, did not complete any of the cruisers laid down in 1914–15 in time for Jutland. By then, she had commissioned thirty-nine light cruisers compared with fifty-five by Britain. But, again, Germany's situation was worse than the bare numbers suggest. Because she started earlier and Fisher had stopped British light cruisers construction for three years, Germany had a greater proportion of older ships; if only turbine-powered cruisers were counted, then the ratio was 44:19 in Britain's favour. Furthermore, Germany effectively lost fifteen cruisers before Jutland, of which six were turbine-powered; Britain lost three, two with turbines.[70] Thus on the eve of Jutland, the ratios of light cruisers were 52:24 for all types and 42:12 for those with turbines.

When the War began, Britain had just nosed ahead in the number of completed destroyers. Both countries took over boats that had been built or designed for other navies: Britain from Greece, Chile and Turkey; Germany from Argentina. Germany also built four large destroyers of the *B97* class around four sets of powerful machinery that had been intended for Russia, then four more to the same design. Both also expanded their 1914–15 programmes into large wartime emergency programmes based on designs already being built; an additional five *Lightfoot*-class flotilla leaders were included in the British orders.[71] By the eve of Jutland, Germany had commissioned 193 seaworthy destroyers since introducing the type with the *S90* class, and Britain had commissioned 221 since the *Rivers*. However, because Britain started later and her construction rate was reduced while Fisher's *Tribals* and *Crickets* were being built, Britain had a greater margin in more modern boats – if only turbine-powered boats are counted, the ratio was 188:124. As with light cruisers, Britain's losses had also been lighter; 8:27 in all types, 5:16 in those with turbines.[72] Thus, just prior to the Battle of Jutland, the ratios of surviving commissioned boats stood at 213:166 for all types, 183:108 for those with turbines; the corresponding British margins were thus 28% and 69% respectively. Between the beginning of the War and the eve of Jutland, Germany completed sixty destroyers to Britain's seventy-eight; thus, unlike in dreadnoughts and light cruisers, Germany's wartime destroyer construction rate had not fallen much behind Britain's. Yet, while it had not been enough to make up for the greater German losses nor for her higher proportion of older designs, in destroyers Britain's superiority was not as commanding as it was in other types

[69] *CAWFS 1906–21*, pp. 56–9.
[70] Light cruiser losses from Gröner I, pp. 101–9 (German) and *CAWFS 1860–1905*, p. 85 and *1906–21*, pp. 53 and 55 (British). The German total includes *Breslau*.
[71] *CAWFS 1906–21*, pp. 77–80 and 169. Gröner I, pp. 78–81.
[72] Destroyer losses from Gröner I, pp. 169–79 and 185 (German) and *CAWFS 1860–1905*, pp. 99–100 and *1906–21*, pp. 74–6 and 78 (British).

of warship. Tirpitz had evidently continued to sustain the branch in which he had made his name in the 1880s.[73]

Overall, Germany did not lose the naval competition with Britain decisively until well after the War began. Only Britain was able to take over three foreign battleships. But the main explanation for her superiority just before Jutland was that she was able to complete so many of the vessels that had been authorised before the War, as well as to sustain large emergency war programmes, especially for light cruisers and destroyers. None of this was the case for Germany, except in the construction of destroyers and submarines, though her position was undermined by her more serious losses of smaller vessels.

Comparisons

Dreadnoughts

For the *Revenge* and *Bayern* classes of 1913–14, British and German designs converged on very similar combinations of armament, speed and protection; both allocated just less than 32% of displacement to vertical and horizontal armour.[74] But, until then, in general German battleships and battlecruisers were better protected than their British counterparts. This is most evident in a comparison of the maximum thicknesses of the main (waterline) belts and in the extent of side armour which, in all German classes, protected the secondary batteries as well as the sides beneath them. Secondary batteries were only fitted in the later British classes and, because the guns were closer together, their armour was less extensive. However, while the British battleships with 12in guns had no side armour between the main and upper decks, this was corrected in subsequent classes, to the extent that the 8in upper armour in the *Orion*, *King George V* and *Iron Duke* classes was thicker than the 7.1in of the *Kaisers* and *Königs*.[75] German battlecruisers were almost as well armoured as their battleships, whereas the protection of the *Invincible* and *Indefatigable* classes was inadequate in thickness and extent while the *Lions* and *Tiger* still compared poorly with their German contemporaries.[76] Continuous longitudinal bulkheads were designed into all German dreadnoughts but were omitted in all British battlecruisers and in too many battleships.

Until the *Bayern*-class battleships, the Germans preferred to mount guns of lesser calibre in their turrets; thus the guns themselves and their shells were lighter, though their muzzle velocities were greater. The British 12in 50-calibre guns introduced in the *St Vincent* class (Marks XI and XII) increased muzzle

---

[73] Herwig, pp. 15 and 33.   [74] Parkes, pp. 588–91.
[75] Gröner I, pp. 26–7 for 180mm (7.1in) upper belts.
[76] Roberts, *Battlecruisers*, pp. 99–109 and Staff, *passim*, for battlecruiser armour.

velocities, but this reduced both accuracy and barrel life.[77] These problems were avoided and greater penetration and larger bursting charges were obtained by the calibre increase to 13.5in in the *Orions* and *Lions*. However, German turret and barbette armour was thicker and, until the British 1911–12 programme, only German ships had secondary batteries. Also, the *Nassau* and *Helgoland* classes bore the weight of six turrets but could still only fire eight guns on each broadside. The *Invincibles* were the first dreadnoughts with the midships turrets *en échelon*, but the cross-deck firing arcs were so restricted that they were effectively limited to six-gun broadsides. The *Indefatigables* and the three British battleships with a similar midships layout were less restricted, though the firing arcs were no more than 70°. After them the turrets of British dreadnoughts were all on the centre line, though (apart from *Tiger*) the midships (Q) turret was necessarily limited to firing arcs of 120° on either side. Germany adopted the *en échelon* layout for her first four battlecruisers and the *Kaisers* but with firing arcs of 120° that largely avoided the tactical restrictions inherent in the similar British designs.

After *Dreadnought* showed the way, all British dreadnoughts were powered by turbines. Germany has some experience of turbine propulsion in light cruisers and destroyers but Tirpitz, unlike Fisher, would not at first risk its widespread adoption. Both the *Nassau* and *Helgoland* classes were given heavier reciprocating engines, so that the former were only capable of 19 knots and the latter's large increase in displacement was due in part to an increase in design speed to 20.5 knots. However, the German navy was less conservative in choosing the lighter small-tube boilers, even though their 'performance dropped off more rapidly with use and they required more frequent cleaning and repair'. These disadvantages compared with the large-tube boilers in British ships were acceptable in a fleet that was built for operations in the North Sea, whereas the Royal Navy had to equip its ships for extended periods at sea, including, if necessary, operations around the globe. German machinery spaces were more congested and the boilers were forced to a greater extent than in British ships.[78] German hull construction was also lighter. In general, stresses greater by 10%–20% were accepted while some plating was much lighter; this may have saved weight but it necessitated elaborate scarphing and riveting, which added to both cost and building time.[79] Gary Staff's comparative tables show significant variations in the distribution of weights, expressed as percentages of total displacement, between different German and British battlecruiser classes. But, with certain exceptions, two

---

[77] Hodges, pp. 61–2, 122 and 124.
[78] Roberts, *Battlecruisers*, pp. 72–4. Brown, *Grand Fleet*, pp. 25 (comparison of machinery in *Tiger* and *Hindenburg*) and 50. For battlecruiser maximum trial speeds and power outputs, compare Roberts, *Battlecruisers*, pp. 80–1 and Gröner I, pp. 53–6.
[79] Brown, *Grand Fleet*, p. 50. Parkes, p. 591.

conclusions are clear and they probably are applicable to battleships as well. The percentages for the armament were little different, probably because the weight saving from the lighter German guns was offset by the heavier turrets and barbettes and by the secondary batteries. And the lower German tonnages allocated to the hull and machinery allowed the weight of armour to be about 10% greater than in the British ships.[80]

The *Nassau* and *Helgoland* classes were barely adequate responses to *Dreadnought* and the following British classes. But, with the *Kaisers* and *Von der Tann*, Germany began to produce excellent, distinctive designs that, compared with their British contemporaries, accepted some sacrifice in turret gun power, boiler reliability, crew space and hull strength to obtain superior protection above and under water. Unlike some British classes, none were hampered by restricted firing arcs. German battlecruisers were really fast battleships whereas, in British ships of the same nominal type, Fisher's demands for high speed were met by sacrificing protection, notably in the *Invincibles* and *Indefatigables* with their limited displacements.

Light cruisers

Germany invented the small, fast, multipurpose light cruiser and then built them at a steady pace with gradual increases in displacement and speed. Although a few single ships were powered by turbines, the *Kolbergs* of 1907–09 were the first all-turbine class; they also increased the armament from ten to twelve 4in. The next class, the delayed *Magdeburgs* of 1910–11, introduced longitudinal framing, a structural armour belt, mixed coal and oil firing and facilities for mine-laying. But gun calibre was not increased to 5.9in until the *Wiesbaden* class of 1913–14.

After the hiatus imposed by Fisher, construction of light cruisers began again in Britain in 1907–08 with the small and inadequate *Boadiceas*, though these were followed by the better-armed *Blondes* and *Actives*. However, having started with vessels that were smaller than their German contemporaries, in 1908–09, Britain began a series of larger light cruiser classes which, after the initial *Bristols*, had a uniform armament of 6in guns. All these vessels had mixed firing and turbines, while the *Chathams* of 1910–11 were given a structural armour belt. After fifteen of these larger light cruisers had been authorised without any reaction from Germany, construction was switched to smaller cruisers with a mixed 4in and 6in armament, a thicker armoured belt and oil firing. More efficient geared turbines were first fitted in the *Calliope* class and then became standard in British light cruisers (though it appears that

---

[80] Staff, *1914–18*, pp. 6 and 38.

the second *Karlsruhe*, commissioned in August 1916, was the only German vessel completed during the War with geared turbines).[81]

Germany started building light cruisers earlier, adopted turbines rather slowly and persisted with designs that mounted the 4.1in gun. Britain restarted construction of the type after turbine propulsion was well established, soon increased the annual building rate and adopted the larger 6in gun five years before the first German class with the 5.9in. By 1916, the Royal Navy had many more light cruisers, particularly of more recent construction, while Germany had only four ships with 5.9in guns.

Destroyers

Germany was also an innovator in the design of torpedo vessels, building the first that were sufficiently seaworthy to accompany the battlefleet. They and their successors were described as 'high seas torpedo-boats', and, while it is at times convenient to use the term 'destroyer' for German as well as for British boats, the different nomenclature is a reminder that German designs carried more torpedoes, the British a heavier gun armament – with the exception of the wartime *B97*-class, German boats were also smaller. Before Fisher became First Sea Lord, both countries built large classes with reciprocating engines (except for one boat in each class with turbines). As with light cruisers, Germany then continued with steady development, from 1906–07 building twelve boats each year. The programme for 1908–09 introduced mixed firing and turbines in all vessels, similar designs following for the next two years. The smaller boats built under the 1911–13 programmes lacked seaworthiness.[82] Their successors swung back to higher displacements, introduced oil-only firing and added a third 3.5in gun, two more torpedo tubes (six in all) and a second reload.

Fisher's obsession with speed led in the *Tribals* to poor seaworthiness, inadequate range and excessive cost, while the small *Crickets* were no substitute for proper destroyers. While the early adoption of turbines and oil fuel in both classes provided valuable experience of both technologies, the sixteen *Beagles* of 1908–09 reverted to a more robust hull design and (for the last time) to coal firing. Thereafter, classes of twenty or more oil-fired, turbine-powered destroyers were built with gradual increases in displacement, speed and armament. Also, in 1913–14, Britain introduced a larger type – the flotilla leader, an innovation that was not followed by Germany.

As we shall see, all the destroyers that fought at Jutland were turbine-powered. But, whereas all the British boats were oil-fired, two of the German flotillas still had to contend with mixed coal-and-oil firing and (with the

---

[81] Gröner I, pp. 113 and 186.   [82] *CAWFS 1906–21*, pp. 164 and 167. Gröner I, p. 76.

exception of one vessel) were formed from the boats numbered *V1* to *S24*, which were too small to be fully effective.

Jellicoe and the Grand Fleet

Prior to his appointment as Commander-in-Chief Grand Fleet in August 1914, Admiral Sir John Jellicoe held several positions of direct influence over the designs of British warships, culminating between October 1908 and December 1910 in his appointment as Third Sea Lord and Controller, the Board member ultimately responsible for all the Navy's material.[83] Thus he oversaw the large programme of 1909–10 which introduced the 13.5in gun, more extensive side armour but also more limited protection against underwater hits. Yet, in July 1914, when he already expected that he would soon be leading Britain's battlefleet, he was expressing serious reservations about the fighting qualities of its dreadnoughts. The First Lord, Winston Churchill, had just written a note on the relative strengths of the British and German dreadnought fleets in 1917; by considering only weight of broadside, Churchill had reached a favourable conclusion. But Jellicoe (then still Second Sea Lord) responded by insisting that 'the only really fair method of comparison . . . is that of displacement' and that, on approximately the same displacement, a greater weight of broadside must lead to corresponding disadvantages. Consequently, British battleships had 'much inferior protection on the side, for the gun positions, conning towers, internally against torpedo explosion, and in some cases inferior speed'. Having compared the British and German designs year by year, he concluded that

far from the British ships showing a superiority the exact opposite is the case and assuming equality in design it is highly dangerous to consider that our ships as a whole are superior or even equal fighting machines.

For battlecruisers, Jellicoe was prepared to accept that, in terms of displacement, the later British ships and the earlier German ones were superior to their contemporaries. But in his year-by-year comparisons, he concluded that all the German ships were better – in some cases, far better – protected.[84]

By October 1914, Jellicoe's anxieties must have been increased by rumours that the Germans might be regunning the *Kaiser* and *König* classes with heavier pieces; an Admiralty conference concluded that, even though there was no evidence, the *Königs* might have been completed with 14in guns. Then, in March 1915, Jellicoe learned that a gunner from the *Blücher* had mentioned that *Lützow* and *Hindenburg* would have 38cm (15in) guns. Showing his readiness to assume the worst, in a letter to the Admiralty Jellicoe concluded

[83] Patterson, *Jellicoe*, pp. 39–41 and 44. Winton, p. 110.
[84] Seligmann *et al.* (eds.), pp. 478–83 with Churchill's scathing marginal comments.

as almost certain that the same gun would rearm the *Königs*.[85] Subsequently, neither possibility was accepted by the Admiralty's Intelligence Division; their *Quarterly Return* for October 1915 listed both *Lützow* and the *Königs* with 12in guns.[86] Yet alarming rumours about the latest German battlecruisers, though unsupported by the intelligence returns, persisted in the Fleet. In February 1916, Beatty wrote to the Prime Minister, Asquith, stating his belief that *Lützow* and *Hindenberg* and the following two battlecruisers would have 15in or even, possibly, 17in guns; for good measure, he added that the first two were already in service and that the next two would be added 'this year, and possibly at an early date', though he then admitted that 'our information is practically nil'. Beatty was also concerned about the speeds of his own ships, declaring that the three *Invincibles* (plus the three *Indefatigables* if the Germans left the *Von der Tann* in harbour) 'can never get into action if the enemy decides not to permit them to'. And Beatty complained about the delays in the construction of *Repulse* and *Renown*, informing Asquith that he had left the Commander-in-Chief 'perturbed and despondent about the delays in new construction'.[87]

As well as fears about the quality of his ships, from the start of his appointment Jellicoe had serious concerns about their numbers. These became acute in November 1914 after the Grand Fleet's squadron of predreadnoughts (the *King Edward VII* class forming the 3BS) had been assigned temporarily to the Channel Fleet, three battlecruisers had been detached to deal with von Spee's squadron while two more remained in the Mediterranean. In conveying his concerns to the Admiralty, Jellicoe insisted that the 'German fleet will obviously select its own moment for moving into the North Sea and will be at full strength' but that his own forces would inevitably be reduced by the necessity for regular refitting. Jellicoe correctly attributed sixteen dreadnought battleships to the High Seas Fleet and, by ignoring the imminent arrival of *Benbow* and *Emperor of India*, he gave his own strength as twenty-one. Of these, he assumed that two would be under refit giving a meagre margin of 19%, much less than the pre-war target of 50%. (Fortunately, the 3BS were about to rejoin him, though they would be stationed at Rosyth.) In battlecruisers, both sides had the same number in the North Sea but, due to refitting, Jellicoe saw this as a probable inferiority of one. He also anticipated 'a certain inferiority of five light cruisers' though this figure took no account of the heavier 6in armament of six of his own ships and included eight older German ships which Jellicoe himself listed with speeds of only 20–22 knots. Jellicoe had better reasons for concern about destroyers since the four flotillas

[85] 'Rearmament of German Warships' in ADM 137/1909, ff. 118 and 131–7.
[86] *Quarterly Return, October 1915*, (see note 2) pp. 103 and 105.
[87] *BP I*, pp. 282–6. *JP I*, pp. 205 and 207–10 (the bracket on p. 208 should not embrace *Derfflinger*). *War Vessels and Aircraft … Monthly Return, February 1916*, p. 29 in ADM 186/22.

of the Grand Fleet were divided, two with the battlefleet itself and two making up Commodore Tyrwhitt's Harwich Force. Jellicoe declared that, in the event of a major action between the fleets, there was 'a very great probability' that a junction with the Harwich force would not happen and that he would then face an inferiority of 'about 30 T.B.D.'s'. To reach this number, he assumed that, of the surviving destroyer in the series *G137* to *G197* and *V1* to *S36* (ninety-five in total), sixty-six would be with the High Seas Fleet, the rest in the Baltic; this implied that, of the forty destroyers attached to the Grand Fleet, four would be unavailable. However, if most of the forty-one boats with the Harwich Force joined him, his inferiority would be more than cancelled out. Yet on 4 December, Jellicoe chose to ignore the demands of the Baltic, noting that the 'latest return gives at least eight German flotillas in the North Sea, a total of 88 boats'; in *The Grand Fleet* he stated that, as far as he knew, the number of 'German destroyers probably attached to the High Seas Fleet' then remained at eighty-eight until May 1916.[88]

After the turn of the year, Jellicoe's situation would improve steadily. The year 1915 saw the arrival of *Canada* and the first three battleships of the *Queen Elizabeth* class; on 24 August, the latter became the nucleus of the 5th Battle Squadron (5BS) commanded by Rear-Admiral Hugh Evan-Thomas. By May 1916, the two remaining ships of the squadron had been commissioned, while the first two battleships of the *Revenge* class were also completed. Thus, despite the loss of *Audacious*, the British battle fleet then consisted of the fleet flagship, *Iron Duke*; three battle squadrons of 21-knot (or better) dreadnought battleships, each of eight ships; and the five 24-knot fast battleships of the 5BS.[89] *Dreadnought* herself was under refit, but neither she nor the predreadnoughts were needed with the main battlefleet; the seven survivors of the *King Edward VII* class had already left Rosyth for Sheerness on 29 April 1916, and *Dreadnought* joined them later as their new flagship.[90]

After the mining of *Amphion* on 6 August 1914, the Royal Navy lost no more light cruisers until the early months of 1916. Even after German surface forces had been swept from the trade routes, some 'Town'-class light cruisers were retained overseas, but the majority, and all the smaller classes of light cruiser, were concentrated in the North Sea. In February 1915, the British scouting forces were formed into the Battle Cruiser Fleet (BCF) under the command of the newly promoted Vice-Admiral Sir David Beatty. By the end of the month, nine battlecruisers, including *Australia*, were in home waters, while *Inflexible* would join them after repairs in June. The BCF was also given three light-cruiser squadrons, each of four ships: two squadrons of 'Towns' and one

[88] Goldrick, pp. 158 and 173–4. *JP I*, pp. 83–7 and 102. *GF*, p. 254.
[89] *CAWFS 1906–21*, pp. 31–8. *GF*, p. 157.
[90] *FDSF II*, p. 433. Roberts, *Dreadnought*, pp. 22–3 (she rejoined the Grand Fleet in May 1918).

squadron of ships of the *Arethusa* and *Caroline* classes. In June 1915, as more light cruisers of the 'C' classes were commissioned, two further squadrons were formed. The 4LCS was created to work closely with the battlefleet, and by the close of 1915 it had grown to six ships. In addition, as previously, four or five of the oldest light cruisers were attached to individual battle squadrons or to the fleet flagship, while *Fearless* and the new light cruisers *Castor* and *Champion* led three of the flotillas. The 5LCS was formed as part of the Harwich Force; by January 1916, the squadron was five strong, and in addition *Undaunted* led a flotilla. Between February and April, *Arethusa* was sunk while four more of Tyrwhitt's light cruisers were badly damage, but repairs and the transfer of *Carysfort* from the 4LCS had restored his total to five by 31 May.[91]

Until February 1915, Jellicoe had to make do with two flotillas, the 2DF of the *Acorn* (*H*) class and the 4DF of the *Acasta* (*K*) class, each of twenty boats. By July 1915, as the latest *M*-class boats were allocated to Tyrwhitt's force, the transfer of *Fearless* and the 1DF (comprising the majority of the *Acheron* or *I* class) increased the strength of the destroyers in Northern waters to sixty-five.[92] Towards the end of 1915, as the first *Repeat-M* class were completed, the 11DF and 12DF were formed as parts of the battle fleet; by January 1916, their strengths were fifteen and five respectively. However, the total fleet destroyer strength, at sixty-six, had hardly changed, partly, it seems, because six boats from the 2DF had been transferred to the Mediterranean. As more *Repeat-Ms* were commissioned, the 13DF was also formed to work with the BCF, while, in the Spring of 1916 the remainder of the 2DF (its *H*-class boats were the oldest with the fleet) was sent to Devonport. The net result was that the Grand Fleet destroyers, now in five flotillas, numbered seventy-four by 1 April and eighty by 31 May. Sixty-nine of them (86%) took part in the battle itself, 'an unusually large proportion' according to Jellicoe.[93] On the eve of Jutland, the nominal strength of the two Harwich Force flotillas was forty boats though, as we shall see, eight were then with Grand Fleet.[94]

The Intelligence Division of the Admiralty supplied information on foreign war vessels and formations in a *Monthly Return*, supplemented by a *Quarterly Return* giving detailed technical data ship by ship, where they were known; as the circulation lists in the returns show, they were widely distributed to senior officers, not least to both Jellicoe and Beatty. They provided accurate information on the numbers, characteristics and organisation of German capital ships,

---

[91] *CAWFS 1906–21*, pp. 50–9. *GF*, pp. 135–6 and 149. Roberts, *Battlecruisers*, p. 122. Corbett, pp. 54 and 414.

[92] Of the other three members of the *I* class, *Oak* was attached to *Iron Duke*, *Firedrake* and *Lurcher* to the Harwich submarine flotillas.

[93] *GF*, pp. 136 and 254. *CAWFS 1906–21*, pp. 74–80. Corbett, pp. 262 and 320. *GFBOs III*, XXI.7, XXIII (p. 40) and XXVII.10.

[94] For more detail on the Harwich flotillas, see: *GF*, pp. 18–20; March, p. 122; Goldrick, pp. 250 and 254; *CAWFS 1906–21*, pp. 77–8 and Corbett, pp. 54, 128, 261–2 and 305.

confirming that, following the completion of the *König* class, only *Lützow* joined the High Seas Fleet before Jutland and that the German scouting forces were led by the five battlecruisers of the ISG. The German battlefleet was listed as the flagship, *Friedrich der Grosse* and three battle squadrons, each of eight ships – two of dreadnoughts and one of predreadnoughts. The Intelligence Division also kept reasonably accurate track of the completions and war losses of German light cruisers. Of the surviving turbine-powered light cruisers, two remained unallocated in the returns for 1916 and nine were shown as forming the IISG, though two were designated as leaders of destroyers. The twelfth, *Stettin*, was the flagship of the IVSG, which also contained five older light cruisers with reciprocating engines. Wrongly, *Pillau* and *Elbing* were thought to have 5.1in guns.[95]

The information on German destroyers was less precise in certain details. Though quite accurate for boats up to *S24* and for the ex-Argentine *G101-G104*, the *Quarterly Return* for October 1915 underestimated both the displacement and armament of *V25-S36*, which it gave as 660 tons, 2–8.8cm guns and '4(?)' torpedo tubes. It gave only the bare ship numbers for *G37-V48* and *V99-V100*, while *S49-G95* and six of the *B97* class were not mentioned at all.[96] *S49-G95* were still the most notable omissions from the *Monthly Return* for May 1916 (corrected to 30 April). However, from November 1915, the *Monthly Returns* had included the remark: 'About 15 additional Destroyers are believed to be now available and others probably approaching completion'. At that date, only ten unrecorded boats had actually been commissioned, so German destroyer strength was then slightly overestimated. But, between November 1915 and April 1916, a further seventeen destroyers were completed. Since the final return before Jutland also listed three new destroyers for the first time, the '15 additional' figure had become insufficient, though only be nine. As for the individual flotillas of the High Seas Fleet equipped with destroyers displacing more than 500 tons (i.e. those numbered *G137* and upwards), prior to November 1915, they were listed in the *Monthly Returns* as comprising two flotillas of boats with reciprocating engines (twenty-two at full strength) and five flotillas (fifty-five boats) powered by turbines. Subsequently, a sixth turbine-powered flotilla was added and the two with reciprocating engines were re-equipped; thus the final return before Jutland stated correctly that all eighty-eight fleet destroyers were turbine-powered.[97]

We have seen that the number of destroyers with the Grand Fleet itself reached sixty-five in the second half of 1915. Yet the 'Destroyer Addendum' of October 1915 to the *Grand Fleet Battle Orders* warned the fleet that, in

---

[95] *War Vessels and Aircraft ... Monthly Returns* for January, April, July and November 1915 (in ADM 186/12–14) and February and May 1916 (in ADM 186/22–23).

[96] *Quarterly Return, October 1915*, pp. 108–15; this is the only *Quarterly Return* in ADM 186.

[97] *Monthly Returns, passim.* Gröner I, pp. 178–81, 184–5 and 188. Tarrant, pp. 259–60.

destroyers, 'the German preponderance may be as great as two to one', though the addendum did not explain how this alarming prediction was consistent with the statement two pages later that 'the Germans will have at least eight flotillas *viz.* eighty eight boats', let alone with the information in the intelligence returns. In January 1916, when three new Grand Fleet flotillas were being formed, both statements were omitted from the superseding 'Destroyer Instructions'.[98] Yet the influx of new destroyers and light cruisers did nothing to reduce Jellicoe's concerns; in the same month, he wrote to Balfour, the First Lord, to express his dissatisfaction with increasing delays in completing repairs and 'the fact that new ships are slowly (but *very* slowly) dribbling in' (emphasis in original). He insisted that 'we know well that the Germans are increasing the number of their light cruisers'; that 'in spite of the immense number [of destroyers we] laid down fifteen months ago we are not relatively so strong compared to Germany as we were then; certainly not in home waters'; and that 'we *know* that the Germans have added many new boats'. Balfour responded:

You tell me that ... the Germans are increasing the number of their light cruisers and destroyers ... but we have no authentic information of this kind ... other than the Quarterly Return, which does not suggest any large augmentation in either of these classes.

In reply, Jellicoe claimed that his remarks were based on the return, but the only examples he cited were the few vessels taken over by Germany from foreign powers at the beginning of the war. Despite the contrary intelligence in the returns, his pessimistic view was evidently unshakeable; in February, he wrote to the First Sea Lord, Jackson: 'I only wish I could exchange half-a-dozen battleships for half their value in light cruisers and destroyers.'[99] At least by then he was satisfied with the strength of his battle line.

Should Jellicoe have been, as Beatty described him, 'so perturbed and despondent' about his relative strengths in light cruisers and destroyers? Although the Battle of the Dogger Bank had demonstrated that a junction was possible between forces from Harwich and Rosyth,[100] he was justified in doubting that the same favourable circumstances would be repeated. If not, then a first encounter would probably be between the BCF alone and the I and II SGs. Beatty had a nominal 10:5 advantage in battlecruisers and an even greater preponderance in weight of fire, surely enough to make up for the weak protection of six of his ships. The light cruiser ratio would be between 12:7 and 12:11, depending on whether the two German light cruisers unallocated in the British returns were with the IISG (though they might be in the Baltic) and on whether the two destroyer leaders engaged with the rest of the IISG. Yet, Beatty had seven ships with uniform 6in or 5.5in armament, whereas the IISG was thought to possess, at most, two with 5.9in

---

[98] *GFBOs III*, 'Destroyer Addendum', 1/10/15, II.5 and II.24 (ff. 335 and 337) and 'Destroyer Instructions', January 16, XXIX and XXX.
[99] *JP I*, pp. 199–200, 205–6, 218 and 225–6.   [100] Goldrick, pp. 250–4.

and two with 5.1in. If less than overwhelming, Beatty had an adequate superiority. However, such strength as the IISG possessed was the result of the weakness of the IVSG, which accompanied the battlefleet; it had only six older light cruisers, just one with turbines. In contrast, with the Grand Fleet, Jellicoe had at least thirteen modern light cruisers. If Jellicoe was despondent about light cruisers, it was only because he chose to ignore the information about German vessels in the intelligence returns.

When comparing destroyer strengths in November 1914, Jellicoe was prepared to allow that almost a third of the enemy boats might be in the Baltic; however, the intelligence returns gave no explicit indications of which vessels were serving there, which perhaps partially excuses Jellicoe's subsequent tacit assumption that all available enemy destroyers might be encountered in the North Sea. In November 1914, he only counted German boats of more than 500 tons but, less than a month later, his claim that the 'latest return gives at least eight German flotillas in the North Sea' was correct only if he included at least one flotilla with older, smaller boats.[101] The reported German numbers had not changed when Jellicoe issued the 'Destroyer Addendum' to the *Grand Fleet Battle Orders* (the *GFBOs*) in October 1915, when, according to the intelligence returns, Germany had only seven flotillas (seventy-seven boats) that were effective opponents for the sixty-five modern destroyers with the Grand Fleet. Thus, to arrive at the 2:1 ratio, Jellicoe appears to have assumed, first, that Germany would be prepared to withdraw every modern destroyer from the Baltic – and also from Flanders – before an operation by the battlefleet; second, that every German boat would be present; and, third, that only thirty-eight of the sixty-five British boats (58%) might be available – this figure could increase to 68% if the Germans fielded eight flotillas. As he had done before, Jellicoe would have argued that Germany could choose her moment, whereas the British flotillas were much more frequently at sea. But the available intelligence told him that Germany relied on at least two flotillas with more unreliable reciprocating engines and that her destroyers were generally smaller – those numbered between *V1* and *S24* especially so – and were therefore more prone to damage whenever they put to sea. On balance, the average British availability was probably somewhat worse than the German figure, but Jellicoe's assumption that it might be 58%–68% of the German figure carried pessimism to extremes. However, he provided at least some encouragement to his flotillas, assuring them in his October 'Destroyer Addendum' that, although they must expect to be outnumbered, they could meet a torpedo attack 'with superior force composed of high speed and good gun power, both of which are possessed by our destroyers'.[102]

---

[101] *Monthly Return*, January 1915 is the earliest found in ADM 186; it suggests (pp. 32–3) that the eighth flotilla was the IVDF, with boats displacing 325 tons.

[102] *GFBOs III*, 'Destroyer Addendum', II.5.

In their efforts to claim a greater share of naval resources, both Jellicoe and Beatty probably exaggerated somewhat the inadequacies of their ships and numbers. But the pervasive pessimism in their communications and their willingness to believe the worst, even without any corroboration from the intelligence returns, suggests that they were prey to genuine and potentially demoralising fears. In the 'Destroyer Addendum' of October 1915, Jellicoe even allowed his alarmist estimate of destroyer numbers to be circulated to the whole Fleet. Jellicoe had been closely involved in the design of the fleet that he now led. But his technical knowledge of his dreadnoughts only added to his pessimistic inclination to dwell on their inferior protection rather than on their superior gun power. To make the best of ships that had been built deliberately to emphasise offensive over defensive qualities, the Grand Fleet needed leaders with a confident attacking spirit. Beatty, despite his limited success at the Dogger Bank, seemed to have that spirit. But there are few signs of it in Jellicoe's writings after he became Commander-in-Chief. In Chapter 3, we shall examine how his apprehensions influenced the battle orders that were in force at Jutland. But first, in the next chapter, we shall consider some key technologies that bear on both the expectations of action and how the battle came to be fought.

Notes on the tables

For both counties, each programme year is from April to the following March. These years are used for both the numbers of vessels authorised and the number completed/commissioned. In the characteristics tables, the year for each class is the first year in which its construction was authorised.

Data for British vessels are from *CAWFS 1860–1905* and *1906–1921* except that completion dates for destroyers are from Admiralty War Staff, Intelligence Division, *Quarterly Return, October 1915*, ADM 186/15. Data for German vessels are mainly from Gröner I. However, for capital ships, this work's commissioning dates are for commencement of trials; completion dates for full commissioning are from *CAWFS 1906–1921*.

Displacements are normal, average or design (not deep load) and are expressed in tons. Conversions from tonnes (by multiplying by 0.9842) are rounded to the nearest 10 tons (except for destroyers).

In the tables of characteristics, light grey shading is used for British ships, dark grey for German.

Tables to Chapter 1

Table 1.1. *Light cruiser programmes*

Programme year	British				German[8]			
	Authorised		Totals all classes		Authorised		Totals all classes	
	Class or ship	No.	Authorised	Completed[2]	Class or ship	No.	Authorised	Completed[2]
1896–1902					Gazelles	10	10	7
1902–03	Gem class	2	6		Bremens	3	13	8
	Scouts[1]	4						
1903–04	Gem class	2	12		Bremens	2	15	11
	Scouts[1]	4						
1904–05			12	4	Bremens	2	18	13
					Königsberg	1		
1905–06			12	12	Königsbergs[9]	3	21	15
1906–07			12	12	Dresdens	2	23	17
1907–08	Boadicea[2]	1	13	12	Kolbergs[10]	2	25	20
1908–09	Bellona[2]	1	19	12	Kolbergs[10]	2	27	22
	Bristols	5						
1909–10	Blondes	2	25	14				24
	Weymouths	4						
1910–11	Actives	2	30	20	Magdeburgs[11]	4	31	26
	Chathams[3]	3						
1911–12	Fearless[4]	1	34	25	Karlsruhes	2	33	27
	Birminghams	3						

1912–13	*Arethusas*	8	42	30	*Graudenz*	2	35	31
1913–14	*Carolines*	6	50	32	*Wiesbadens*	2	37	33
	Calliopes	2						
1914–15	*Cambrians*	4	58	45	*Pillaus*[12]	2	43	36
	Centaurs[5]	2			*Königsbergs ii*[5]	4		
	Birkenheads[6]	2						
1915–May 1916	*Caledons*[7]	4	62	55	*Cölns*[13]	10	53	39

Notes

1 Of the *Adventure, Forward, Pathfinder* and *Sentinel* classes.
2 Both *Boadicea* class; programme years verified from *Quarterly Return, October 1915.*
3 *Melbourne* and *Sidney* built for Royal Australian Navy in British yards not included; they joined the 2LCS after Jutland.
4 *Active* class.
5 None completed before Jutland.
6 Built for Greece, purchased in early 1915.
7 Ordered in December 1915; none completed before Jutland.
8 German programme years, with some interpolations, from *War Vessels, British and Foreign. Part II Quarterly Return, October 1915,* ADM 186/15. The programme years in *Conway's 1906–21* correspond with the 'official design' years in Gröner, both being a year in advance of those in the table.
9 *Stuttgart* assumed to be in the 1905–06 programme.
10 Assumes *Kolberg* and *Mainz* in 1907–08 programme, *Cöln* and *Augsburg* in 1908–09.
11 Delayed by design of new longitudinal frame system.
12 Taken over from Russia.
13 Ten laid down in 1915–15, seven launched in 1916–18, two completed in 1918.

Table 1.2. *Light cruiser characteristics*

First year	Class or ship	No. in class	Displacement (design) tons	Machinery			Armour (max)		Guns	Torpedo tubes	Mines
				Engines	Fuel	Speed knots (design)	Deck	Belt			
	Gazelles	10	2,600–2,660	Recip.	Coal	21.5[1]	25mm (1in)		10–10.5cm (4.1in)	2–45cm (17.7in)	
1896	*Bremens*	7	3,230	Recip.[2]	Coal	22[2]	35mm (1.4in)		10–10.5cm	2–45cm	
	Gem class	4	3,000	Recip.[3]	Coal	21.75[3]	2in		12–4in	2–18in	
1902–03	*Scouts*	8	2,640–2,900	Recip.	Coal	25	⅝–¾in	2in[4]	10–12pdr (3in)	2–18in	
1904–05	*Könisbergs*	4	3,340–3,420	Recip.[5]	Coal	23[5]	30mm (1.2in)		10–10.5cm	2–45cm	
1906–07	*Dresden Emden*	1 1	3,610	Turbine Recip.	Coal	24 23.5	30mm		10–10.5cm	2–45cm	
1907–08	*Kolbergs*	4	4,290	Turbine	Coal	25.5[6]	40mm (1.6in)		12–10.5cm	2–45cm	
	Boadiceas	2	3,300	Turbine	Coal (oil)	25	1in		6–4in	2–18in	
1908–09	*Bristols*	5	4,800	Turbine	Coal (oil)	25	2in		2–6in; 10–4in	2–18in	
1909–10	*Blondes*	2	3,350	Turbine	Coal (oil)	24.5	1.5in		10–4in	2–21in	
	Weymouths	4	5,250	Turbine	Coal (oil)	25	2in		8–6in	2–21in	
1910–11	*Actives*	3	3,440	Turbine	Coal (oil)	25	1in		10–4in	2–21in[7]	
	Chathams	3	5,400	Turbine	Coal (oil)	25.5	1.5in	2in	8–6in	2–21in	
	Magdeburgs	4	4,460–4,500	Turbine	Coal (oil)	27	40mm	60mm (2.4in)	12–10.5cm	2–50cm (19.7in)	120

1911–12	*Karlsruhes*	2	4,820	Turbine	Coal (oil)	27.8	40mm	60mm	12–10.5cm	2–50cm	120
	Birminghams	3	5,440	Turbine	Coal (oil)	25.5	1.5in	2in	9–6in	2–21in	
	Arethusas	8	3,750	Turbine	Oil	28.5	1in	3in	2–6in: 6–4in	4–21in	
1912–13	*Graudenz*	2	4,830	Turbine	Coal (oil)	27.5	40mm	60mm	12–10.5cm	2–50cm	8
	Wiesbadens	2	5,100	Turbine	Coal (oil)	27.5	40mm	60mm	8–15cm (5.9in)	4–50cm	120
1913–14	*Carolines*	6	4,219	Turbine	Oil	28.5	1in	3in	2–6in: 8–4in	4–21in	
	Calliopes	2	4,228	Turbine[9]	Oil	28.5	1in	4in	2–6in: 8–4in	2–21in	
	Cambrians	4	4,320	Turbine[9]	Oil	28.5	1in	3in	2–6in: 8–4in	2–21in	
1914–15	*Pillaus*	2	4,320	Turbine	Coal (oil)	27.5	80mm (3.1in)		8–15cm	2–50cm	120
	Birkenhead	2	5,185–5,235	Turbine	Coal (oil)	25.5	1.5in	2in	10–5.5in	2–21in	
	Chester				Oil[1]	26.5					

Notes

1 *Gazelle* 19.5 knots.
2 *Lübeck* turbines, speed 22.5 knots.
3 *Amethyst* turbines, speed 22.5 knots.
4 *Foresight, Forward, Pathfinder* and *Patrol* only.
5 *Stettin* turbines, speed 24 knots.
6 *Mainz* 26 knots.
7 A majority of reference books (but not *CAWFS 1906–21*) states that the *Blondes* had 18in and the *Actives* 21in torpedoes
8 Gröner I, p. 109 appears to state that *Regensburg* only was fitted to carry 120 mines later in the War.
9 Geared turbines.

Table 1.3. *Destroyer programmes*

Programme year	British				German			
	Authorised		Totals all classes		Authorised		Totals all classes	
	Class or ship	No.	Authorised	Completed	Class or ship	No.	Authorised	Completed
1898–1901					*S90-S107*	18	18	10
1901–04	*Rivers (E)*	34	34	9	*G108-S125*	18	36	30
1904–05			34	18	*S126-S131*	6	42	35
1905–06	*Tribals (F)* (*Crickets*[1] *Swift*	5 12) 1	40	34	*G132-G136* *G137*	5 1	48	42
1906–07	*Tribals* (*Crickets*[1]	2 12)	42	34	*S138-S149*	12	60	47
1907–08	*Tribals*[2] (*Crickets*[1]	5 12)	47	34	*V150-V161*	12	72	60
1908–09	*Beagles (G)*	16	63	38	*V162-G173*	12	84	72
1909–10	*Acorns (H)* *Rivers (E)*[3]	20 2	85	48	*G174-V185*	12	96	82
1910–11	*Acherons (I)*	23	108	77	*V186-G197*	12	108	92
1911–12	*Acastas (K)*[4]	20	128	95	*V1-G12*	12	120	110
1912–13	*Laforeys (L)*	20	148	112	*S13-S24*	12	132	125
1913–14	*Ms* *Lightfoots*	13 2	163	135	*V25-S36*	12	144	132

1914–15	Repeat Ms (1st–4th orders)[5]	70	253	163	G37-V48[12]	12	204	147
	Medeas[6]	4			S49-V84[12]	36		
	Laforeys (L)[7]	2			B97-V100	4		
	Arno[8]	1			B109-B112	4		
	Talismans[9]	4			G101-G104[13]	4		
	Lightfoots[10]	5						
	Faulknors[10]	4						
April 1915–May 1916	Repeat Ms (5th order)[11]	20	273	221	G85-G95[12]	11	215	193

Notes

[1] Built as coastal destroyers but reclassified as torpedo boats; they are not included in the totals.
[2] Assumes *Maori* completed in 1909–10.
[3] *Test* and *Stour* purchased as replacements for *Blackwater* and *Gala*.
[4] Assumes *Lynx* completed in 1913–14.
[5] 1st–4th orders placed in September 1914–February 1915.
[6] Purchased from Greece.
[7] *Lassoo* and *Lochinvar* ordered from Beardmore as repeat *L*-class.
[8] Built for Portugal by Ansaldo, purchased in March 1915. Similar to *E*-class but with 4-12pdr.
[9] May have been ordered initially for Turkey; Admiralty order November 1914.
[10] Ordered by Chile, purchased in August–September 1914.
[11] 5th order placed in May 1915.
[12] Wartime mobilisation programmes, authorisation dates uncertain.
[13] Ordered by Argentina, seized on outbreak of war.

Table 1.4. Destroyer characteristics

First year	Class or ship	No. in class	Displacement tons	Machinery			Guns	Torpedo		Mines
				Engines[1]	Fuel	Speed knots (design)		Tubes	Reloads	
1898–99	*S90–G136*	47	305–405	Recip.[1]	Coal	27–28	3-5cm[2] (1.97in)	3-45cm (17.7in)	2	
1901–02	*Rivers (E)*	36	550–590	Recip.[3]	Coal	25.5	1-12pdr (3in) 3-6pdr (2.2in)	2-18in		
	G137	1	571	Turbine	Coal	30	1-8.8cm (3.5in): 3-5.2cm (2.05in)	3-45cm	2	
1905–06	*Tribals (F)*	12	850–1,090	Turbine	Oil	33	3-12pdr or 2-4in[4]	2-18in		
	Crickets	36	225–255	Turbine	Oil	26	2-12pdr	3-18in		
	Swift	1	2,170	Turbine	Oil	35	4-4in	2-18in		
1906–07	*S138–S149*	12	525	Recip.	Coal	30	1-8.8cm: 3-5.2cm	3-45cm	1	
1907–08	*V150–160*	11	549	Recip.	Coal	30	2-8.8cm	3-45cm	1	
	V161	1	606	Turbine	Coal	32	2-8.8cm	3-45cm	1	
1908–09	*V162–G173*	12	629–689	Turbine	Coal + oil	32	2-8.8cm	3-45cm	1	
	Beagles (G)	16	945	Turbine	Coal	27	1-4in: 3-12pdr	2-21in		

1909–10	*Acorns (H)*	20	772	Turbine	Oil	27	2–4in: 2–12pdr	2–21in		
	G174-V185	12	640–689	Turbine	Coal + oil	32	2–8.8cm	4–50cm (19.7in)	1	
1910–11	*V186-G197*	12	650–655	Turbine	Coal + oil	32	2–8.8cm	4–50cm	1	
	Acherons (I)	23	778	Turbine	Oil	27–32	2–4in: 2–12pdr	2–21in		
1911–12	*Acastas (K)*	20	1,072	Turbine	Oil	29	3–4in	2–21in	2	
	V1-G12	12	560–564	Turbine	Coal + oil	32	2–8.8cm	4–50cm	1	18
1912–13	*S13-S24*	12	559	Turbine	Coal + oil	32.5	2–8.8cm	4–50cm	1	18
	Laforeys (L)	22	965–1,010	Turbine	Oil	29	3–4in	4–21in		
	Ms	103	850–1,055	Turbine	Oil	34–35	3–4in	4–21in		
1913–14	*Lightfoots*	7	1,440	Turbine	Oil	34.5	4–4in	4–21in		
	V25-S36	12	789–799	Turbine	Oil	33.5	3–8.8cm	6–50cm	2	24
	G37-G95	59	815–945	Turbine	Oil	33.5–34.5	3–8.8cm or 3–10.5cm (4.1in)[5]	6–50cm	2	24
1914–15	*B97 class*	8	1,329–1,352	Turbine	Oil	36–36.5	4–8.8cm	6–50cm	2	24
	G101-G104	4	1,098	Turbine	Oil	33.5	4–8.8cm	6–50cm	2	24
	Medeas	4	1,007–1,040	Turbine	Oil	32	3–4in	4–21in		
	Talismans	4	1,098	Turbine	Oil	32	5–4in	4–21in		
	Faulknors	4	1,610	Turbine	Coal + oil	31	6–4in	4–21in		

Notes

[1] *S125* (1903–04) turbines, speed 28 knots.

[2] *G132-G134* and *G136* 3–5.2cm (2in). *G135* 1–8.8cm (3.5in), 2–5.2cm.

[3] *Eden* (1901–02) turbines.

[4] Five 1905–06 boats 3–12pdr (3in), remaining seven 2–4in.

[5] *G49-G59*, *V67-V81* and *G85-91* 3–8.8cm. *S60-66*, *V82-V84* and *G92-G95* 3–10.5cm (4.1in) none commissioned by May 1916.

Table 1.5. *Dreadnought battleship programmes*

Programme year	British				German			
	Authorised		Totals all classes		Authorised		Totals all classes	
	Class or ship	No.	Authorised	Completed	Class or ship	No.	Authorised	Completed
1905–06	Dreadnought	1	1					
1906–07	Bellerophons	3	4	1	Nassaus[5]	2	2	
1907–08	St Vincents	3	7	1	Nassaus	2	4	
1908–09	Neptune	1	8	2	Helgolands	3	7	
1909–10	Colossus	2	14	6	Helgoland	1	10	
	Orions[1]	4			Kaisers	2		
1910–11	King George Vs	4	18	8	Kaisers	3	13	4
1911–12	Iron Dukes	4	22	12	Königs	3	16	7
1912–13	Queen Elizabeths	4	26	16	König	1	17	10
1913–14	Malaya[2]	1	32	19	Bayern[6]	2	19	13
	Revenges[3]	5						
1914–15	Agincourt	3	35	26	Sachsens[7]	2	21	17
	Erin							
	Canada[4]							
1915– May 1916			35	33			21	17

Notes

[1] *Monarch*, *Conqueror* and *Thunderer* were laid down in April 1910.
[2] *Queen Elizabeth* class, laid down in October 1913.
[3] Three completed by May 1916, two present at Jutland.
[4] *Agincourt* and *Erin* taken over from Turkey, *Canada* purchased from Chile.
[5] *Nassau* and *Westfalen* were laid down in July and August 1907 and commissioned for trials in October and November 1909, respectively.
[6] Neither ship was completed in time for Jutland.
[7] Neither ship was completed.

Table 1.6. *Dreadnought battleship characteristics*

First year	Class or ship	No. in class	Displacement tons	Machinery		Speed knots (design)	Belt armour (max.)	Guns			Torpedo tubes (beam)
				Engines	Fuel			Turret	Secondary	Anti-torpedo	
1905–06	*Dreadnought*	1	18,110	Turbine	Coal (oil)	21	11in	1–12in		27–12pdr (3in)	5(4)–18in
1906–07	*Bellerophons*	3	18,800	Turbine	Coal (oil)	20.75	10in	10–12in		16–4in	3(2)–18in
	Nassaus	4	18,570	Recip.	Coal	19	300mm (11.8in)	12–28cm (11in)	12–15cm (5.9in)	16–8.8cm (3.5in)	6(4)–45cm (17.7in)
1907–08	*St Vincents*	3	19,560	Turbine	Coal (oil)	21	10in	10–12in		20–4in	3(2)–18in
	Neptune	1	19,680	Turbine	Coal (oil)	21	10in	10–12in		16–4in	3(2)–18in
1908–09	*Helgolands*	4	22,450	Recip.	Coal	20.5	300mm	12–30.5cm (12in)	14–15cm	14–8.8cm	6(4)–50cm (19.7in)
1909–10	*Colossus*	2	20,225	Turbine	Coal (oil)	21	11in	10–12in		16–4in	3(2)–21in
	Orions	4	22,200	Turbine	Coal (oil)	21	12in	10–13.5in		16–4in	3(2)–21in
	Kaisers	5	24,330	Turbine	Coal (oil)	21[1]	350mm (13.8in)	10–30.5cm	14–15cm	8–8.8cm	5(4)–50cm
1910–11	*King George Vs*	4	23,000	Turbine	Coal (oil)	21	12in	10–13.5in		16–4in	3(2)–21in
1911–12	*Iron Dukes*	4	25,000	Turbine	Coal (oil)	21	12in	10–13.5in	12–6in		4(4)–21in
	Königs	4	25,390	Turbine	Coal (oil)	21	350mm	10–30.5cm	14–15cm	6–8.8cm	5(4)–50cm
1912–13	*Queen Elizabeths*	5	27,500	Turbine	Oil	25	13in	8–15in	14–6in		4(4)–21in
	Revenge	5	28,000	Turbine	Oil	23	13in	8–15in	14–6in		4(4)–21in
1913–14	*Bayerns*	2	28,080	Turbine	Coal (oil)	22	350mm	8–38cm (15in)	16–15cm		5(4)–60cm
1914–15	*Agincourt*	1	27,500	Turbine	Coal (oil)	22	9in	14–12in	20–6in	10–3in	3(2)–21in
	Erin	1	22,780	Turbine	Coal (oil)	21	12in	10–13.5in	16–6in		4(4)–21in
	Canada	1	28,600	Turbine	Coal (oil)	22¾	9in	10–14in	16–6in		4(4)–21in

Notes
[1] *Prinzregent Luitpold* 20 knots – cruising diesel and centre shaft not fitted.

Table 1.7. *Battlecruiser programmes*

Programme year	British				German			
	Authorised		Totals all classes		Authorised		Totals all classes	
	Class or ship	No.	Authorised	Completed	Class or ship	No.	Authorised	Completed
1905–06	*Invincibles*	3	3					
1906–07			3					
1907–08			3		*Von der Tann*	1	1	
1908–09	*Indefatigable*	1	4	3	*Moltke*	1	2	
1909–10	*Lions*[1]	2	6	3	*Goeben*[3]	1	3	
1910–11	*Australias*[2]	2	9	4	*Seydlitz*	1	4	1
	Queen Mary	1						
1911–12	*Tiger*	1	10	4	*Derfflinger*	1	5	2
1912–13				7	*Lützow*	1	6	3
1913–14				9	*Hindenburg*[4]	1	7	4
1914–15	*Renowns*[4]	2	13	10	*Mackensens*[5]	4	11	5
	Courageous[4]	1						
1915–May 1916	*Glorious*[4]	1	15	10			11	6
	Furious[4]	1						

Notes
[1] *Princess Royal* was laid down in May 1910.
[2] Laid down June 1910. *New Zealand* was a gift to the Royal Navy. *Australia* was ordered as the flagship for Royal Australian Navy, joined the Grand Fleet in February 1915.
[3] Nominally transferred to Turkey in August 1914.
[4] None of these ships was completed before Jutland.
[5] None of these ships was completed.

Table 1.8. *Battlecruiser characteristics*

First year	Class or ship	No. in class	Displacement (design) tons[2]	Machinery			Belt armour (max.)	Guns				Torpedo tubes (beam)
				Engines	Fuel	Speed knots (design)		Turret	Secondary	Anti-torpedo		
1905–06	*Invincibles*	3	17,250	Turbine	Coal (oil)	25	6in	8–12in	10–15cm (5.9in)	16–4in		5(4)–18in
1907–08	*Von der Tann*	1	19,060	Turbine	Coal	24.75	250mm (9.8in)	8–28cm (11in)	10–15cm (5.9in)	16–8.8cm (3.5in)		4(2)–45cm (17.7in)
1908–09	*Indefatigables*	3	18,750	Turbine	Coal (oil)	25	6in	8–12in		16–4in		2(2)–18in
1908–09	*Moltkes*	2	22,620	Turbine	Coal	25.5	270mm (10.6in)	10–28cm	12–15cm	12–8.8cm		4(2)–50cm (19.7in)
1909–10	*Lions*	2	26,350	Turbine	Coal (oil)	28	9in	8–13.5in		16–4in		2(2)–21in
1909–10	*Queen Mary*	1	27,000	Turbine	Coal (oil)	28	9in	8–13.5in		16–4in		2(2)–21in
1910–11	*Seydlitz*	1	24,590	Turbine	Coal	26.5	300mm (11.8in)	10–28cm	12–15cm	12–8.8cm		4(2)–50cm
1911–12	*Tiger*	1	28,500	Turbine	Coal (oil)	28	9in	8–13.5in	12–6in			4(4)–21in
1911–12	*Derfflinger*	1	26,180	Turbine	Coal (oil)	26.5	300mm	8–30.5cm (12in)	12–15cm	4–8.8cm		4(2)–50cm
1912–13	*Lützow*	1	26,180	Turbine	Coal (oil)	26.5	300mm	8–30.5cm	14–15cm			4(2)–60cm (23.6in)
1913–14	*Hindenburg*	1	26,520	Turbine	Coal (oil)	27	300mm	8–30.5cm	14–15cm			

Table 1.9. *British margins*

Programme year	Battleship numbers				Dreadnoughts numbers[1]				British margins (per cent)[2]			
	Authorised		Completed		Authorised		Completed		Battleships		All dreadnoughts	
	British	German	British	German	British	German	British	German	Authorised	Completed	Authorised	Completed
1905–06	1				4							
1906–07	4	2	1		7	2	1		100		250	
1907–08	7	4	1		10	5	1		75		100	
1908–09	8	7	2		12	9	5		14		33	
1909–10	14	10	6		20	13	9		40		54	
1910–11	18	13	8	4	27	17	12	5	38	100	59	140
1911–12	22	16	12	7	32	21	16	9	38	71	52	78
1912–13	26	17	16	10	36	23	23	13	53	60	57	77
1913–14	32	19	19	13	42	26	28	17	68	46	62	65
1914–15	35	21	26	17	48	32	36	22	67	53	50	64
1915–May' 16	35	21	33	17	50	32	43	23	67	94	56	87

Notes

[1] Totals for dreadnought battleships and battlecruisers.

[2] The British margin is the fraction (expressed as a percentage) by which the British numerical strength exceeds the German; for example, in 1909–10, the British had completed twelve dreadnoughts, the Germans had completed nine; thus the ratio was 1:33 and the margin was 33%.

2   Technologies

The ships of the 'grand battlefleets' that met at Jutland embodied many of the advanced technologies of their day in their hulls, armour, machinery and armament. Four of these technologies are of particular significance to the course and outcome of the battle:

- signalling, the means of communication between commanders which extended from the centuries-old flag-signalling to the latest developments in electricity and wireless;
- fire control, the system of special instruments that enabled ships' guns to hit their targets at ranges of eight miles or more;
- ammunition, particularly the limitations of British armour-piercing (AP) shells and the handling of the British propellant, cordite;
- torpedoes, especially the running properties of the latest weapons, the threats they posed to a battle line and how these might be avoided.

Signalling

In 1906, the Admiralty issued a new *Signal Manual* and accompanying *Signal Book*. With amendments, these two handbooks then remained in use until they were superseded – in detail but not in principles – by the *General Signal Book 1915*, which was in force at Jutland.[1] For centuries, flags were at the heart of naval signalling, not only because they remained an effective method of communicating between ships but because they determined the 'language' of signals. In the Royal Navy, signals were made using flags (mostly rectangular, a few triangular or swallow-tailed burgees) and pendants (narrow, tapered banners). By 1915, there were:

- twenty-six flags for the letters of the alphabet;
- ten numeral flags;

---

[1] The 1906 *Signal Manual* (ADM 186/658) explained the signalling system and the *Fleet Signal Book* (ADM 186/657) specified signals in detail. Both functions were served by the *General Signal Book 1915* (ADM 186/699).

- ten numeral pendants; and
- ten special pendants and thirteen special flags.[2]

The standard signals for manoeuvring and action were not spelt out letter by letter but were expressed as short 'codes', each code corresponding to a 'hoist' of just a few flags or pendants. A small number of signals could be made using just a single flag; for example, the 5 flag alone was a general signal to the whole fleet to 'Open fire'; the H flag was a general destroyer recall. Other important signals were almost as brief; the 1 flag superior to (i.e. hoisted above) the A flag (signal '1A') reformed the fleet in line-ahead on the same course, maintaining a constant speed, by means of turns to starboard. The two-letter codes were given a large repertoire of standard meanings; for example, in the 1906 *Signal Book*, AA to BS were for action signals and OD to PZ for use in exercises.

An order intended for a specific formation within a fleet was 'addressed' by hoisting a 'distinguishing signal' superior to the order itself; thus 'H 3Pdt.' (H flag, 3 pendant) addressed the 3rd Destroyer Flotilla. Also, some orders needed to be qualified by additional information. For example, a pendant ordering an alteration of course was hoisted superior to a two-letter compass code; the code CL (Charlie London) for SEbyE was part of Jellicoe's famous Jutland deployment signal. Thus signals conveying orders had a standard compact format:

- an optional 'distinguishing signal', omitted from general signals to the whole fleet: for a major formation, a flag and a pendant;
- for the order code: one pendant or flag, one pendant and one (rarely two) flags, or two (rarely three) flags; and
- optional qualifying information, typically one or two letter or numeral flags.

While suitable for the prompt communication of action and manoeuvring orders, these *Signal Book* codes were not sufficient for all the less urgent information that had to be conveyed between the ships of a fleet. This need was met by the *Vocabulary Signal Book*. A signal of this type was sent as a sequence of three-letter codes, each code standing either for individual words (often in various alternative forms), or for longer phrases.[3] Only when the vocabulary book failed to provide the required words or phrases was it necessary to spell out some parts of a signal letter by letter. In the War, these were enciphered by means of a simple transposition alphabet: and then broken into three-letter groups.[4]

'The Size 1 flags issued to capital ships were big: the rectangular ones 11 feet by 9 feet.' But, even in good visibility, five miles was too far for signalling only

---

[2] *GSB 1915*, Plates I and II.

[3] For example, *Vocabulary Signals for the Use of His Majesty's Fleet*, London 1908, ADM186/655; these vocabulary codes, not the *Signal Book* (*pace* Gordon, pp. 183 and 362), were the direct descendents of Home-Popham's Vocabulary Code. See also Kent, pp. 5–7 and Pl.I.

[4] *Addendum No. 3 to Vocabulary Signal Book (1913)*, 14 October 1914 in ADM186/671. These groups were prefixed and followed by any two of twelve special distinguishing code groups.

by flags[5] and the *Grand Fleet Signal Orders* insisted that, whenever flag signals were difficult to distinguish, they must be repeated by alternative means[6] (to be described shortly). Furthermore, one ship could not make flag signals to another that was directly downwind of the apparent wind (the 'wind-you-feel' on the signalling ship due to the combined effects of the actual wind and its own motion). Funnel smoke also streamed in this direction but the solution lay, as in the days of sail, in the use of repeating ships stationed where their repeats of the flagship's signals could be clearly seen.

A few signals, like the 5 flag for 'Open fire', were acted upon 'as soon as seen'. But the majority were not 'made executive', that is, put into effect, until the flagship had received confirmation that they had been received and understood by all the intended recipients. The procedure, slightly simplified, was that a ship answered a signal by hoisting the Answering Pendant (white and red): 'at the dip' when the signal was first seen, then 'close up' as soon as it was understood. However, if the ship was responsible for repeating the signal to others, it hoisted the signal itself, initially at the dip, and close up when it had been answered by all the ships for which this 'repeating ship' was responsible. Answering pendants and repeats were kept flying until the flagship made the signal executive by hauling it down (after which all ships hauled down their pendants and repeats, thereby freeing the halyards for further signal). If no repeating ships were in position and the fleet was in single line-ahead, all ships repeated the Admiral's signal up and down the line from the flagship, initially at the dip and then close up as this same response carried back along the line from ships further from the Admiral.[7] When in command of the Mediterranean Fleet of eleven battleships in 1895, Admiral Sir Michael Culme-Seymour insisted that:

Even in a large fleet the time for the signal leaving the deck to the time it is hauled down should not average more than from thirty to sixty seconds.[8]

By the early years of the twentieth century, while flag signalling had been developed to a high state of efficiency, it was by no means the only form of visual communication. Mechanical semaphores or simple hand flags could be used to send signals as letters, numbers and a few special control signs. Alternatively, letters and numbers could also be sent by Morse code, these signals being flashed by, among others, searchlights and arc lamps with shutters, and truck flashing lamps.[9] But the point to emphasise is that signals sent by semaphore or flashed in Morse were essentially in the same form as flag signals – with the minor qualification that, when sending by semaphore or

---

[5] Gordon, p. 70. Kent, p. 51.   [6] *Grand Fleet Signal Orders*, section 4, ADM 137/266.
[7] *GSB 1915*, pp. 328–33 including the rules governing how, in a large fleet, divisional guides acted as repeating ships.
[8] Quoted in Gordon, p. 304.   [9] *Signal Manual*, 1906, pp. 42–4 and 94–104.

Morse, some character sequences were reserved to stand for the numeric and special pendants[10] and the special flags. Of course, semaphore and flashing were better suited to the longer routine signals encoded using the vocabulary book. Flag signals remained the principal means for manoeuvring the fleet and conveying orders in action, though semaphore or flashing provided alternative means of repeating flag signals, or sending them over greater distances than were practicable by flags. In good visibility in northern waters, the large truck semaphores could be read at a distance of eight to ten miles, while the searchlights and arc lamps could be read to the horizon.[11]

By 1906, wireless telegraphy (W/T) was already making communication by Morse code possible over distances far beyond the limits of visual contact. By 1907, two standard designs of W/T set had been developed: to use their later designations, the Type 1 was a high-power 14KW (kilowatt) set that was fitted in dreadnoughts and armoured cruisers; other ships larger than destroyers received the 1½KW Type 2. Both types were provided with at least six wavebands (then known as 'waves' or 'tunes'), and their operating ranges were, respectively, 500 and 100 miles. *Vernon* then went on to design sets operating at 1 to 1¼KW on shorter wavelength over ranges from 5 to 50 miles; these were the Type 4 for destroyers and the Type 3 and Type 9 auxiliary sets for, respectively, battleships and all types of cruiser (battlecruisers to light cruisers). The auxiliary sets were particularly suitable as yet another alternative to flags for repeating manoeuvring and action signals.

Because of its broadcast nature, W/T required special control procedures to identify the sender and ensure that recipients were ready to receive. The necessary control sequences were appended to the beginning and end of each wireless message, but the signal itself remained in the standard visual signal format. From 1907, further procedures were introduced to prevent individual 'tunes' from becoming congested with too many competing signals. In the fleet, wireless guardships monitored each tune and passed on signals to the flagship by visual means or on the 'Admiral's wave'. However, until the beginning of the War, communication by W/T remained rather ponderous compared with visual methods.[12] But, after the formation of the Grand Fleet, new equipment – particularly buzzers between wireless offices and bridges – were introduced to speed up the communication of signals within ships. And procedures were refined so that, when appropriate, general signals could be broadcast from the flagship without answering delays. At the end of 1914, a new *Grand Fleet Battle Order* (*GFBO*) informed the fleet that, in action (when wireless silence was no longer necessary):

---

[10] For example, the letters PT preceded the pendant number: *GSB 1915*, pp. 324–7 and 335–40.

[11] Kent, pp. 244 and 249.

[12] Hezlett, Chapters II and III, particularly pp. 63–4, 71–5 and 294–8.

Where practicable, the Admiral will make manoeuvring and action signals by W/T as well as by visual.

By the time of Jutland, there was no qualification:

The Admiral will make manoeuvring and action signals by W/T as well as by visual.[13]

After the War, Jellicoe wrote that:

in 1916 I could handle the Battle Fleet by wireless with as much ease and rapidity as by visual signals. At the beginning of the War ten minutes to a quarter of an hour would elapse before I could be sure that all ships had received a manoeuvring wireless signal addressed to the whole battle Fleet. By 1916, the time rarely exceeded two to three minutes.[14]

However, while short manoeuvring and action signals could be received throughout the whole Fleet in a few minutes, the longer – and less urgent – messages that were encoded using the *Vocabulary Book* or transposition codes took longer. As Jellicoe also recollected, for 'reports emanating from the bridge of a ship':

A considerable interval is bound to elapse; this included the time taken to write out the report, transmit it to the wireless office or signal bridge, code it, signal it, decode it on board the receiving ship, write it out and transmit it to the bridge. The interval is greater with wireless than with visual signals.[15]

Manoeuvring signals

Having examined the means of relaying signals, we can now consider the 'purport' of some of the most important, beginning with manoeuvring signals. These formed a major part of the *Signal Book* and were used to order a fleet to assume one of a selection of standard formations, and to alter course while in such formations. The simplest fleet formations were in single line, the most important being line-ahead. However, fleets were organised into divisions so that they could be disposed as distinct groups in more complex formations.

---

[13] *GFBO*, 'XXIII. Signals in Action' (19 December 1914) in ADM137/288. See also *Wireless Instructions 1915*, Admiralty 1915, pp. 105–9, ADM 186/682 and *GFBOs III*, XII(a).

[14] *GF*, p. 48. He added: 'This great improvement was due to new methods introduced, as well as to incessant practice in harbour'. Gordon, p. 354 asserts that 'formated ships could not be synchronously manoeuvred by non-visual means [including W/T] until the 1940s'. This was doubtless the case in 1907 but not during the War. Both the *Wireless Instructions 1915* (see note 13) pp. 78 and 105–9 and the *Grand Fleet Cruising Disposition, Organisation and Instructions for Manoeuvring by W/T* (bound in *General Signal Book 1915*, ADM 186/699) describe how manoeuvring orders were executed synchronously by W/T at the termination of a five-second 'dash' contained in a special 'Executive' signal.

[15] *GF*, p. 202. Gordon, pp. 355 and 644 n. 69, implies that these greater delays applied also to manoeuvring signals. This leads him to conclude that Jellicoe's claim that manoeuvring signals could be received in two to three minutes 'must be taken with a very large pinch of salt' and that such times were only achieved in the harbour practices.

The usual cruising formation was in divisions in line-ahead, columns disposed abeam i.e. the divisional columns in line-ahead were on parallel courses with the leading ships of each column – known as the guides – all on beam bearings. (Columns might also be disposed quarterly – 'in quarter-line' – with the guides on a line-of-bearing abaft the beam of the guide of the foremost column.)

Each division constituted a distinct unit that could be manoeuvred independently, but frequently the whole fleet would be manoeuvred together by general signals. Course changes were ordered by one of three pendants (Fig. 2.1). If the turn was to a point of the compass, the appropriate pendant was hoisted superior to one or two alphabetical flags specifying the compass point.[16] Alternatively, the turn could be specified as a number of points, expressed by one or two numeral flags; if the pendant was superior, the turn was to starboard: if inferior, to port.

Blue Pendant (blue with a white spot) signified 'alter course together'. All ships turned together when the signal was made executive, maintaining a constant speed through the turn. This was an 'equal-speed' manoeuvre which preserved the compass bearings and distances between all ships in the fleet.

9 Pendant (white, red spot) signified 'alter course, the leading ships together, the rest in succession'. This meant that the leading ships of each divisional column turned together when the signal was hauled down, thus preserving the compass bearings between them. Then, in each division, the following ships turned one after the other so that, on completion of the manoeuvre, their relative bearings from the leading ship were preserved.[17] This too was an 'equal-speed' manoeuvre. Usually, the ships in individual divisional columns would be in line-ahead, which meant that the following ships turned so that they could follow in the wake of the leader.

Compass Pendant (red, white spot) signified that the whole fleet must turn onto the new course while preserving the order and formation of its columns, i.e. relative bearings and distances were preserved. Put simply, after a Compass Pendant turn, the fleet would be in the same formation as before the turn but on the new course. If the fleet was, as usual, in columns of divisions, the columns towards which the turn was made reduced speed, while those on the outside of the turn increased their speeds; this was, therefore, an 'unequal-speed' manoeuvre. If the fleet was in single line-ahead, the leading ship simply turned first and all the rest followed, altering course in succession as they reached the same turning point.[18]

---

[16] The compass rose was divided into 32 points (N, NbyE, NNE, NEbyN, NE and so on). While the two-letter code allowed for a further subdivision into quarter-points, courses and bearings were almost always specified in whole points.

[17] A relative bearing was measured from the course of the ship taking the bearing.

[18] *GSB 1915*, pp. 14, 17 and 32.

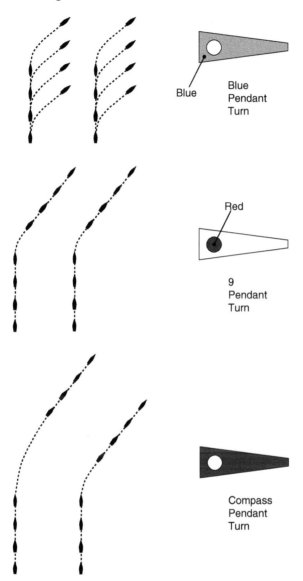

Figure 2.1 Turning pendants

The signals that ordered a fleet to take up one of the standard formations, while at the conclusion of the manoeuvre preserving the course of the fleet, were equally brief – normally only a pendant and a flag or two flags (though a third flag was sometimes needed for the little-used 'quarter-line' formations).

This was possible because each signal specified only the final formation and was the same regardless of the starting formation. The signals made with a pendant were called 'forming and disposing' or 'unequal-speed' signals. They made no assumptions at all about the initial formation of the fleet and it was expected that each divisional commander would chose the courses and speeds best designed to assume the specified formation safely. For example, the signal '2Pdt. A' ordered the fleet to form in divisions (2Pdt) in line-ahead (A), columns disposed abeam to port (number pendant superior) of the column containing the 'guide of the fleet'. The 1915 *Signal Book* required only four pages to describe the full repertoire of eighteen distinct forming-and-disposing signals.[19]

In contrast, no less than seventy-two pages were needed to describe the 'equal-speed' signals made with two or three flags.[20] Yet the number of distinct equal-speed signals was the same as the number of the 'unequal-speed signals'. However, the difference was that the equal-speed signals were provided for use when the fleet was already in one standard formation and the admiral wished to reform as rapidly as possible in a different formation on the same course. Thus, each page of this large section of the *Signal Book* described precisely how the ships of a fleet could move from one standard formation to another, specifying, in words and by diagram, what turns were required of each ship, and when they should be made. For example, signal 'A1' ordered a fleet to reform in single line-ahead by means of turns to port, 1A by turns to starboard. The execution of this and all other equal-speed manoeuvres depended on the columns being separated by a distance equal to their length; this distance was called 'manoeuvring distance'.

Unequal-speed manoeuvres could in general be executed with smaller course changes but they took longer, the time depending on the margin of speed between the slowest and fastest divisions. In contrast, the time required for equal-speed manoeuvres was shorter and predictable in advance. Andrew Gordon has criticised the '*Signal Book* goose-step' as 'the manoeuvring system by which British fleet tactics were hamstrung for more than forty years',[21] a description that seems to apply most closely to the large number of predefined equal-speed manoeuvres. But, as we have seen, the equal-speed manoeuvres were no more than part of the complete system. And, given that, in many cases, these manoeuvres could be executed in more than one way, precise descriptions were essential to ensure that each ship knew precisely how and when it should make its turns. However, some of the standard formations – those in line-abreast come to mind – were becoming less and less relevant as battle ranges

---

[19] *GSB 1915*, pp. 170–3. Further explanatory instructions for unequal and equal speed signals were at pp. 306–9.
[20] *GSB 1915*, pp. 175–245.   [21] Gordon, pp. 582 and 599, also 185–6 and 586.

increased though, on the other hand, the more unfamiliar a manoeuvre, the greater was the need for step-by-step instructions for its execution. Despite at least one attempt to reduce the number of equal-speed signal variants, the full *repertoire* was retained in both the 1906 and 1915 signal books.[22]

Developments in signalling

In November 1907, Captain Cuthbert Hunter of the protected cruiser *Edgar* submitted a proposal for a new system of enemy reporting based on position square charts, though a competing system devised by Captain H E Purey-Cust was adopted after comparative trials in 1908.[23] Meanwhile, on 15 February 1908, Hunter submitted a comprehensive critique of the existing signalling codes as unsuited to the chaotic conditions of battle, though it is noteworthy that his criticisms did not extend to the equal-speed signals. Hunter concluded that the only solution was a wholesale reconstruction of the *Signal Book* and he submitted a complete new book of his own to show how this might be done. On 13 March, Captain Allan Everett, the Superintendent of the Signal Schools, admitted candidly 'that war or battle requirements are not the prime considerations of the existing code'. But he pointed out that the battle signals lacking in the present books could be introduced simply by assigning them to the unused codes 00 to 99 represented by pairs of numeral flags. Hunter, accepting that half a loaf was better than no bread, quickly submitted an addendum to his first proposal; this nominated the most important of his action signals for assignment to these numeric codes.[24] His proposed new book and addendum were printed and circulated to fleet commanders. Admirals Beresford and Battenberg (Channel and Atlantic Fleets) supported wholesale changes, but the majority opinion favoured revising the present books and introducing new action signal codes. Seventy-six new Action Signals were included in the 1910 addenda to the signal books and manual.[25]

Nor did the influence of Hunter's proposals end there. From 1912, a Signal Committee, presided over successively by Rear-Admiral Richard Peirse and

[22] Vice-Admiral Lord Charles Beresford, 'Notes on Signal Paper', 19 December 1904 with anonymous *Memorandum to Committee for Considering the Simplification and Improvement of the Present System of Signalling in the Fleet*, FP 4217 in FISR 5/10. See also Gordon, p. 345 and pp. 356–7 for the troubled gestation of the 1906 edition.

[23] For the record of the Hunter and Cust codes, see 'Position Square Charts ...' in ADM 1/7987. See also Gordon, p. 358, though this implies that the Hunter code was adopted.

[24] Captain Cuthbert Hunter RN, *A Criticism on the Present Signal Book, with Suggestions for Its Revision*, printed 6/08, copies in 'Captain Cuthbert Hunter's Criticism of the Signal Book and Proposed New Signal Book' Vol. I (ADM 116/1068) and Vol. II (ADM 116/1069). Further copies in ADM 186/661 and ADM 186/663. Gordon, pp. 359–61.

[25] Correspondence and reports in ADM 116/1068. '*Action Signals*, 1910 for insertion in *Fleet Signal Book*' in ADM 116/1069. Gordon does not mention the 1910 *Action Signals* addendum and concludes that Hunter 'failed' (p. 362).

Captain Sidney Fremantle, set about a comprehensive revision of all the signal books. By 1913, new books had been completed, the Action Signals in particular showing Hunter's influence.[26] In August 1914, the worldwide distribution of the new books had just begun but, as Fremantle recalled:

> It was considered on the outbreak of war that the partial introduction of a complete set of books, with which many of the officers and men concerned were unfamiliar, would be likely to cause much confusion.[27]

Hence the old *Signal Book* with its amendments remained in use until the promulgation of the *General Signal Book 1915*.[28] While still not the wholesale reorganisation demanded by Hunter, the new book consolidated the many changes and improvements that had been accumulated since 1906. The final word on the fully developed British signalling system of World War I can be left to the American Commander Holloway Frost, who wrote in 1936:

> We must heartily commend the visual signalling system of the Grand Fleet. We particularly like the laconic wording and the great rapidity with which despatches were sent from ship to ship. Radio communication was also very rapid and errors were kept to a very small percentage.[29]

Deployment signals

By the early years of the twentieth century, the Royal Navy accepted that the battlefleet would fight in line, even though it was recognised that this formation was tactically unwieldly.[30] In the usual close order spaced at two cables (400 yards) stem to stem,[31] a line of ten predreadnoughts proceeding at 15 knots required almost eight minutes to alter course in succession. The disadvantage of the single line during the preliminary phase of the battle, when two fleets manoeuvred for position as they approached each other, had been clearly shown during the 1901 combined manoeuvres.

Beresford approached in single line ahead, but Wilson approached in columns of divisions disposed abeam, which was his cruising formation. As soon as he sighted Beresford, he signalled a line of bearing for his guides of divisions, which was at right angles to the bearing of the 'enemy'. When Beresford started to lead his fleet round to engage Wilson, the latter formed line of battle in a few minutes in that direction, and

---

[26] For final proofs of the *Fleet Signal Book, Volume I* and the *Signal Manual* (London, 1913), see ADM 186/669 and 670. Related correspondence is in 'Signal Books 1912–1914' in ADM 1/8274.
[27] Fremantle, p. 170.   [28] *GSB 1915, passim.*   [29] Kent, p. 55.
[30] McLaughlin, 'Equal Speed', pp. 122–5 and 'Battle Lines', pp. 3–5.
[31] *Signal Manual 1906*, p. 56.

held an enormous tactical advantage until Beresford's line had finished crawling round their turning point.[32]

A year later, Fisher concluded that: 'Everything points to our golden rule to get our line of battle *"in one single line at right angles to the direction of the enemy when he is sighted"* . . .'.[33] When in command of the Home Fleet from 1909 to 1911, Admiral Sir William May conducted a series of tactical investigations from which he concluded, like Fisher, that 'the advantage will lie with the Fleet that can most readily form single line ahead at right angles to the line joining the centres of the two Fleets'.[34] As Wilson had demonstrated in 1901, the most flexible approach formation was in columns in line-ahead, disposed abeam at manoeuvring distance. But, after sighting the enemy, it was then necessary to deploy the fleet quickly into single line. The simplest case was if the enemy was encountered directly ahead, when the deployment could be ordered by 9 Pendant; all the guides turned together through eight points (90°), the ships in each column then following their guides in succession. For divisions of four ships at 15 knots, this would take just over three minutes, irrespective of the number of divisions (Fig. 2.2). But, as in 1901, the enemy fleet might not be directly ahead. In that case and time permitting, the line-of-bearing of the column guides could be adjusted so that it was at right angles to the enemy's bearing; this was ordered by means of a 'Forming and Disposing' signal.[35] Then once again the deployment could be ordered by 9 Pendant, with the new course lying along the previous line-of-bearing of the guides.

May's exercises had shown that, due to faulty reporting of the enemy's position or the need to make allowances for the directions of sun, sea and wind, the guides' line-of-bearing might not be correctly aligned for a 9 Pendant deployment. The solution was then for the wing division that would lead the fleet (called the 'column of direction') to turn directly onto the optimum course; the other divisions turned twice, the first turns to reach the course of the column of direction and the second to follow in its wake. Such manoeuvres could only be ordered with several hoists from the standard *Signal Book*. May's remedy was to define a new significance for two of the number pendants. The 8 Pendant, when hoisted superior to a numeric flag, ordered the column of direction to turn the number of points indicated. The ships of the other columns turned onto the guides' line-of-bearing, then turned again to follow in the wake of the leading division (Fig. 2.2). This was an equal-speed manoeuvre requiring that the columns be at manoeuvring distance. May also defined a similar signal using the 6 Pendant for forming line when the columns were at less than

[32] Dreyer, p. 50.   [33] Marder, *Fear God I*, p. 251; original emphasis.
[34] Admiral Sir William May, *Notes on Tactical Exercises. Home Fleet. 1909–1911*, pp. 19–20 (also 240 and 441–2), Eb012, AL.
[35] *GSB 1915*, pp. 172–3 for signals.

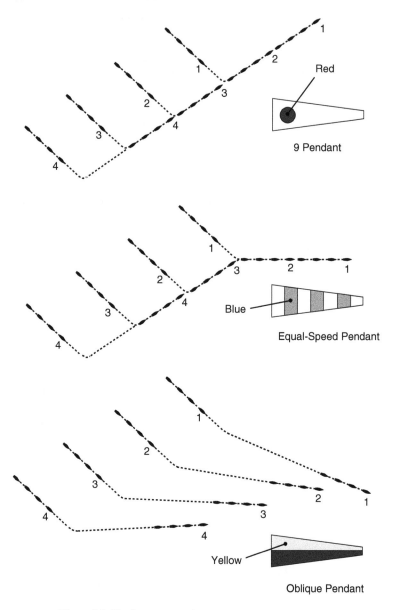

Figure 2.2 Deployment pendants

manoeuvring distance; this ordered a necessarily more protracted unequal-speed manoeuvre. He suggested that the 6 Pendant would also be preferable if, when sighted, the enemy proved to be on quite a different bearing from that assumed when setting the line-of-bearing of the guides.[36] Even before the completion of either of these manoeuvres, all the columns were more or less in line, with unobstructed arcs of fire at the enemy; but the line would have one or more bends, stationary points through which all ships initially astern of them would have to pass one by one. This handed the enemy an opportunity to concentrate his fire on these stationary points, a recognised but unavoidable danger.[37]

By 1913, perhaps a year earlier, the temporary significance attached by May to the 6 and 8 Pendants had been superseded by the introduction of two special deployment pendants, the Equal Speed Pendant (white and blue vertical stripes) and the Oblique Pendant (divided horizontally, yellow above red). Their definitions had also been revised and extended so that the column that would lead the fleet was identified explicitly. The extent of the turn to be made by the 'column of direction' was specified either by a numeral flag (or flags) indicating a number of points; or by two alphabetic flags representing a compass code. When numeral flags were used, if the pendant was hoisted superior, the *starboard* column turned to *starboard* to lead the fleet; if inferior, the *port* column turned to *port*. Whereas, if the turn was ordered using a compass code, the column that would lead the fleet was that nearest to the indicated compass point.[38] The definitions remained essentially unchanged when both deployment pendants were incorporated in the *General Signal Book 1915*.[39]

German signals

In January 1915, the Naval Intelligence Department circulated translations of four 'German Fleet Orders', which were probably among the trove of secret publications recovered from the *Magdeburg*.[40] One of the translations was of the *Manoeuvring Instructions for the Fleet 1914*, the German Navy's equivalent of the British *General Signal Book*. This shows that the Royal Navy was not alone in preferring that fleet manoeuvres be fully specified. The *Manoeuvring Instructions* also laid down standard fleet formations

---

[36] May, *Tactical Exercises* (see note 34), pp. 432–9. May described only one form of each hoist, with the pendant superior; he appears to have assumed that the direction of the turn would be self-evident from the tactical situation.

[37] May, *Tactical Exercises*, p. 21. Action signal '43' signified 'Concentrate on the enemy's ships as they come to the turn': *GSB 1915*, p. 62 and *Action Signals*, 1910 (see note 25).

[38] 'My War Orders and Dispositions', f. 4, JMSS 49012 (pencil amendment). *Handbook of Signalling*, London 1913, Plate I, ADM 186/667 (which, unlike the other 1913 books, remained in circulation). Admiralty, '1913 Edition of Signal Books', 24 April 1914 and telegram to C.-in -C. India, 27 October 1914 in 'Signal Books 1912-1914' in ADM 1/8274. *Fleet Signal Book I*, 1913, pp. 23–5.

[39] *GSB 1915*, pp. 17–18 and 32.

[40] Goldrick, *Before Jutland*, pp. 105, 185 and 187. Beesly, p. 7.

(including line-ahead, line-abreast and columns variously disposed) and instructions and diagrams for altering course and formation. For these purposes, the Germans made greater use of unequal-speed manoeuvres, but each was described in detail so that it was clear how it should be executed.

The Germans were if anything more emphatic than the British about the need to form a single battle line. The preface to the *Manoeuvring Instructions* began:

> Single line is the only useful formation for battleships. The aim of the 'manoeuvring instructions' is to establish the best means for the organization and handling of this formation.[41]

To this end, the instructions specified flag signals and manoeuvres for forming single line on any course from several 'preparatory' (approach) and cruising formations; these signals served much the same purpose as the British signals made with the Equal Speed and Oblique Pendants. The simpler preparatory formations were of squadrons in line-ahead disposed abeam or on a line of bearing at 'column intervals', i.e. at manoeuvring distance in British terminology. There were also 'deep preparatory formations' with two squadrons abreast in the lead at column intervals and a third and a possible fourth squadron (usually predreadnought squadrons) following astern; a 'fleet cruising formation' was similar, except that the columns were spaced at the standard 'ship interval' in line-ahead of two cables.[42]

The German signal book contained signals corresponding to the British Compass, Blue and 9 Pendants,[43] as well as others both with and without direct British equivalents. It also included special signals for use in action that were limited to one or at most two flags or 'elements' and were made only by the Commander-in-Chief. These always made both with flags and by auxiliary wireless ('Z') set but were only made executive by hauling down the flag signal. Every ship repeated each action signal by flags and obeyed it as soon as it was understood and it had been repeated (or answered if it could not be repeated) by neighbouring ships or columns.[44] Certain action signals ordered ships to follow in the wake of the leader and to turn in succession or together. An 'action turn about' (*Gefechtkehrtswendung*) onto an opposite course could be ordered with a single Green or Red flag; this reversed the order of the whole fleet. These flags could also be used if the columns were disposed quarterly, i.e. with the guides on a line-of-bearing at an angle to their initial course; in this case, the turn was only to a course corresponding to this line-of-bearing. Also,

[41] *Manoeuvring Instructions for the Fleet*, Berlin, 3 February 1914, p. vi translated in 'German Fleet Orders', ADM 186/17.

[42] *Ibid.*, pp. 14–18 and 30–4.   [43] *Ibid.*, pp. 35 and 42–5.

[44] 'Tactical Order No. 2: Signal Orders during and after an Action' in *German Tactical Orders*, January 1915, pp. 11–12 in 'German Fleet Orders' (see note 41). 'Regulations concerning Signalling during and after an Action' in *German Navy Tactical Orders*, April 1920, p. 68, ADM 186/55.

an action turn together (*Gefechtswendung*) to any compass point would be ordered with a flag (Ä-D) and a numeral pendant (0–7). Rules defining which ship (or ships) turned first were laid down so that they could be made in action even if the fleet was in a curved or broken line. A *Gefechtskehrtwendung* was initiated by the rear ship (about to lead the van) commencing its turn while simultaneously hauling down the signal; as soon as the next ship saw the signal being hauled down, it turned and hauled down its own hoist, and so on successively along the line.[45]

The German signal flags and pendants were, of course, quite different in design from their British equivalents representing individual letters and numbers. The formats of German signals were also different and give the impression of being more *ad hoc* and less systematic. Yet their purports were often similar in their general intentions, while their meanings were conveyed just as laconically.

British gunnery

In May 1916, the majority of 12in-gunned dreadnoughts still relied on a developed version of the fire control system that had first been installed in *Dreadnought* herself. A new instrument that was first supplied in production form in 1912 was the Evershed target indicator, the pointers of which showed the turret trainers and rangefinder operators how to find and hold the target designated by the gunnery control officer. All these ships were fitted with Barr & Stroud (B&S) 9-foot coincidence rangefinders. A ship's principal rangefinder was in the fire control top (the fore-top in two-masted ships) on an Argo gyro-stabilised rangefinder mounting; the power training of this mounting appears to have been its best feature. Following a decision pushed through at the start of the War, each turret also had a 9-foot rangefinder on its roof, protected by an armoured hood.[46] Each control top was also provided with one or more of the instruments called Dumaresqs after their inventor. This instrument was set with own ship's speed and the enemy's course and speed; then, when the dial was rotated so that its sighting vanes were aimed at the target, two values vital to accurate shooting could be read from the dial. The first was the 'range-rate' (also called the 'rate of change of range'); expressed in yards-per-minute, it was a measure of how rapidly the range was increasing or decreasing. The second was the 'speed-across' (also known as the 'Dumaresq deflection'); expressed in knots to left or right, it indicated the

---

[45] *Manoeuvring Instructions*, pp. 35–40 and 45–8. 'Tactical Order No. 5: An Action turn together in the formation column line-ahead, disposed quarterly', 17 April 1914 in 'Tactical Orders for the High Sea Fleet, 1914' (typed translation) ADM 137/4326; for a later version, see *JP I*, p. 253 and *German Navy Tactical Orders* (1920) (see note 44), p. 64. See also *GOA*, p. 114.

[46] *DGBJ*, pp. 40–1, 50–2, 85 and 92–4. Brooks, 'Mast and Funnel', pp. 40–4.

apparent speed of the target across the line-of-sight extending from the firing ship to the target. By applying corrections for range and for wind across the range, the speed-across was converted into the deflection set on the gunsights; this and other corrections built into the sight were intended to ensure that the gun was 'aimed off' from the line-of-sight by the correct angle required to hit. By keeping the Dumaresq's sighting vanes on the target, the instrument continued to indicate the latest range-rate and speed-across as the target's bearing changed. Later and more elaborate Dumaresqs, notably the Mark VI, were also able to keep the range-rate and speed-across – if not exactly, to a good approximation – as own ship altered course.[47]

Ranges, range-rate and enemy bearing were transmitted electrically to the transmitting station (the TS) from which fire was controlled. British transmitters and receivers were of the 'step-by-step' type; each electric pulse from the transmitter caused the receiver to increment or decrement its displayed value by one step, e.g. by 25 yards on a range receiver. While usually reliable, if action damage caused electrical problems, a receiver could get 'out-of-step' with its transmitter. It was then necessary to realign both at a prearranged starting value; realignment was also necessary if receivers had to be switched from one group of transmitters to another, e.g. if the primary fire control position was put out of action.[48]

The TS was the location of the ship's range predictor or 'range-clock'; in the 12in-gunned dreadnoughts this was the Vickers Clock, named after its maker. This clockwork-powered instrument had a large dial with, originally, a single hand indicating the range on a scale around the dial's circumference. Provided it was set regularly with the latest range-rate from the Dumaresq, the Vickers Clock provided a prediction of the changing range while any range corrections were easily applied by rotating the scale, relative to the dial and hand. By 1913, the Vickers Clock was fitted with a second hand mounted frictionally on the shaft carrying the first hand. The first indicated the predicted true range of the target from the firing ship. The second showed the gun range to be set on the sights: that is, the true range as corrected for wind along the range, atmospheric density, propellant temperature and the change in range during the time-of-flight of the shells.[49] From the TS, the gun range and the corrected deflection were transmitted by step-by-step instruments to the turrets. In the early dreadnoughts, range and deflection had to be read from the receivers and then set on the dials of the gunsights. But, beginning with *Indefatigable, Colossus* and *Hercules*, the receivers were incorporated into follow-the-pointer (FTP) sights; as the name suggests, to keep his sight set, each sight-setter had only to rotate the body of the receiver to keep its pointer opposite a fixed index. Firing the

[47] *DGBJ*, Ch. 2 for the principles of long-range gunnery, pp. 24–5, 42–3 and 52–3 for Dumaresqs.
[48] *DGBJ*, pp. 41–2 and 46–7.   [49] *DGBJ*, pp. 25–7, 43, 53–5 and 62.

guns in more-or-less simultaneous salvos depended on the guns being aimed continuously, i.e. on the gunlayers and turret trainers working their hydraulic elevating and training controls to keep the sights continuously on the target. Although this had not been possible when *Dreadnought* first entered service, steady improvements in hydraulic controls and training engines ensured that by 1911–12, continuous aim was possible in most sea states.

In the TSs of the majority of these older dreadnoughts, simple, manually worked plotting boards were provided to make a plot of the rangefinder ranges, as received from aloft and from the turrets, against time – hence its name, a time-and-range plot. In some ships, a second manual board was used to plot target bearings against time.[50] (The methods of fire control that depended on time-and-range and time-and-bearing plots are described in a following section.)

The dreadnought classes with 13.5in guns continued to rely on the B&S 9-foot rangefinder. In the *Orion*-class battleships, the principal rangefinder on its Argo mount was in the top, but in all the rest of these battleships and battlecruisers it was placed under an armoured revolving hood on top of the conning tower; this hood became known as the 'Argo tower'. *Queen Mary*, the *King George V* class and later ships were built with a rangefinder on each turret and, by the time of Jutland, these had been fitted in the *Orions* and *Lions*. The first ships fitted with longer 15-foot rangefinders were the *Queen Elizabeth* class, followed by the *Revenge* class; as well as the turret rangefinders, the main rangefinder (on a B&S mounting) was located in a larger armoured hood on the gun control tower atop the conning tower (as described later, this hood also housed a director sight).[51] Some of the dreadnoughts built under the programmes of 1909–10 and 1910–11 received the first production model of Dreyer fire control table, which was later called the Dreyer Table Mark III. The first was probably installed in *Monarch* around the end of 1912, the remaining four from the order placed with Elliott Brothers going to *Lion, Princess Royal, Thunderer* and *King George V*. The table had electrically driven time-and-bearing and time-and-range plotters. When first delivered, they automatically recorded the target ranges and bearings taken at the Argo rangefinder mounting; later, the range plotter was adapted so that the ranges from the other rangefinders could be plotted manually. As the plots progressed, the plotted points developed into bands across the paper, the slope of each band being proportional to the rate of change of observed range or bearing. Hence these plotters were also termed 'rate plotters' and each was provided with a rotating disc with parallel wires to measure the rate.

---

[50] *DGBJ*, pp. 32–5, 41, 44–7 and 59–61.
[51] *DGBJ*, pp. 50–1. Brooks, 'Mast and Funnel', pp. 44–57.

In the Mark III table, two electrically driven variable-speed drives acted as range and bearing clocks. And the table was equipped with a modified Dumaresq Mark VI coupled electrically to a receiver for the ship's Anschütz gyrocompass so that it could be adjusted automatically for alterations in own ship's course. However, the setting of rates derived from the Dumaresq on the two clocks was done manually. As well as the rate discs, the Mark III tables introduced two other important features that appeared in all subsequent Dreyer tables. The first was that the range plot was equipped with a pencil that automatically plotted the clock range; thus the range predicted by the clock could be constantly compared with ranges measured by the rangefinder. The second was that a differential gearbox enabled ballistic or spotting corrections to be added to the clock range to generate the gun range; gun range was then transmitted to the turrets (and later to the director sight) by means of follow-the-pointer transmitters.[52]

In 1912, Arthur Pollen's Argo Company supplied the prototype of a new type of range-and-bearing clock for trials in the battleship *Orion*. In the same year the Admiralty also ordered five more Argo Clocks Mark IV for comparative tests against the Dreyer Tables Mark III (the prototype was purchased later). Each clock was a mechanical *tour-de-force* which, on steady courses, predicted target ranges and bearings entirely automatically. But, if own ship altered course, its clock had to be switched into a different operating mode in which target bearings were set manually.[53] Argo also supplied a prototype rate plotter to *Orion* but this all-Argo installation remained unique. Even before the final rupture between Pollen and the Admiralty, it had been decided that the other Argo clocks would be coupled to Dreyer-type rate plotters; this combination became knows as the Dreyer Table Mark II, which was fitted in *Conqueror, Ajax, Centurion, Audacious* and *Queen Mary*.[54] By 1918, *Orion* was listed as having a Dreyer Table Mark II but it is probable that she still had her Argo rate-plotter at Jutland.[55]

The Dreyer Table Mark IV, the first of which was installed in *Iron Duke*, introduced an entirely new design of Electrical Dumaresq. This still adjusted automatically for alterations of course but its electrical two-axis follower now

---

[52] *DGBJ*, pp. 159–66.

[53] Assuming that 'helm-free' meant a system that is operated identically whether courses were steady or altering, only the Dreyer Table Mark III was 'helm-free', but it was not automatic. The Argo clock was automatic, but only on steady courses.

[54] *DGBJ*, pp. 92, 95–8 and 166–8 in which I reached very different historical and technical conclusions from those of Professor Jon Sumida in *IDNS*. His *ad hominem* review essay of *DGBJ* did not challenge these conclusions, by which I stand here: see 'Gunnery, Procurement, and Strategy in the *Dreadnought* Era', *Journal of Military History*, 69 (October 2005), pp. 1179–87 and my response, *ibid.*, p. 70 (January 2006), pp. 195–200.

[55] *Orion* is not in the February 1916 list of 'Ships in which Dreyer's Fire Control is fitted or is being fitted': DRYR 2/1.

Table 2.1. *Dreyer Table allocation*

Mark I (other ships uncertain)	Mark III	Mark II with Argo Clock Mark IV	Mark IV	Mark IV*
(*Dreadnought*)	*Monarch*	*Conqueror*	*Iron Duke*	*Canada*
Bellerophon	*Thunderer*		*Benbow*	
Vanguard		*Ajax*	(*Emperor of India*)	*Barham*
	King George V	*Centurion*	(*Queen Elizabeth*)	*Warspite*
Marlborough		(*Audacious*)		*Valiant*
				Malaya
	Lion	*Queen Mary*	*Tiger*	
	Princess Royal			*Revenge*
				Royal Oak

enabled it to set the rates on the electric rate and bearing clocks automatically as well.[56] The ranges from multiple rangefinders (including those from the Argo mounting) were now plotted (by perforating the paper) using a device called the Brownrigg keyboard. As delivered, the Mark IV could plot ranges up to 17,000 yards whereas the succeeding Mark IV*, which was otherwise similar, could plot ranges as high as 20,000 yards. These limits were later extended to 25,000 and 28,000 yards respectively, though how many tables were modified in time for Jutland is not known.[57] On the eve of Jutland, a few 12in-gunned ships had been re-equipped with a Dreyer Table Mark I, though the number is uncertain. Only *Bellerophon* mentioned a Mark I table in her reports after the battle, whereas it appears that *New Zealand* and *Indomitable* still relied on manual plotting boards, as perhaps did *Invincible* and *Indefatigable*. Despite its number, the Mark I was a later model designed in 1915 as a simpler mechanical table for those ships without an integrated fire control table – though it was also supplied to *Marlborough*, probably because, when she was completed, there were not enough Mark IV tables available. The Mark I was a simpler mechanical design incorporating a special Dumaresq (the Mark VI*), a modified Vickers Clock as its range-clock and a time-and-range plotter that was hand-cranked. Nonetheless, it had the characteristic features of the more elaborate Dreyer table: a rate-measuring disc, a Brownrigg keyboard, automatic plotting of clock range, a spotting differential to generate gun range and follow-the-pointer transmission.[58] The allocation of the different marks of Dreyer table up to the eve of Jutland is summarised in Table 2.1. Ships not present at the battle are in brackets.

[56] Thus the Mark IV (and the similar Marks IV* and V) were both automatic and helm-free.
[57] *DGBJ*, pp. 168–73.
[58] *DGBJ*, pp. 175–7; the Dumaresq was not connected to the gyro-compass. In principle, but probably only rarely in practice, ships with the Dreyer Table Mark I could make a time-and-bearing plot with a manual plotting board.

Range-finder accuracy

The range-taker at a British coincidence range-finder used one eye to view a target image that was split horizontally into two equal halves; the range adjustment head caused one half-image to move horizontally relative to the other. The range-taker endeavoured to position the split so that it cut through some distinct vertical features of the target's image, masts being particularly suited to his purpose. He then worked the range adjustment until the parts of these features in the lower and upper images were exactly in line. Anyone with adequate eyesight could obtain ranges of a sort with a coincidence range-finder. But, before the war, the Admiralty was slow to accept the need to train range-takers properly and the rating of range-taker was not introduced until July 1914. Subsequently, their training depended on the initiative of individual squadrons and standards seemed to have varied considerably. Battle experience from the Falklands and the Dogger Bank had taught that, at long ranges, ranges from range-finders were likely to be few and inaccurate. In 1915, Frederic Dreyer was Captain of *Orion* in the 2nd Battle Squadron (2BS); he feared that, because of these discouraging results and the emphasis in the recent 'Gunnery Addendum' to the *GFBOs* on opening fire without waiting to plot ranges, range-finding practice would be neglected.[59] While he continued to encourage the training of range-takers – 'a tedious business requiring great patience and persistence' – he did not expect his efforts to have much impact outside his own squadron.[60] At long ranges, even the 2BS was none too accurate. During the long-range firing practice held on 2 August 1915, when the average opening range was 16,500 yards, the 'average initial error in range was, for the battleships [six of the eight, including *Orion*, being from the 2BS], a little over 800 yards; no less than five ships were more than 1,200 yards in error'. Jellicoe – who had noted similar errors after the earlier practice of 24 December 1914 – concluded that 'at very long ranges our 9-ft. rangefinders are outranged'. Dreyer's response was that:

An inspection of a few of the Rangefinder Plots of the Fleet leads one to believe that excellent results can be obtained roughly speaking up to 15,000 yards in clear weather, and good results from 15,000 to 17,000 yards and fair above that.[61]

However, in view of the Dreyer Tables' dependence on accurate ranges for their plots, he was a less than disinterested inspector. Dreyer's own range-finder expert in *Orion* was of the view that, with the 9-foot range-finder, range-takers

---

[59] *DGBJ*, pp. 20, 52 and 225–6.

[60] Draft letter, Dreyer to unnamed recipient, 26 March 1915 in DRYR 1/3.

[61] Orders and remarks on target practices held 2 August 1915, ADM 137/2020, ff. 120 and 208 (some of the five may have been cruisers, which also took part in the practice) and 24 December 1914, ADM 137/2019, f. 27. Frederic Dreyer, 'A Few Notes on the Determination of the Most Advantageous Range ...', n.d. but September 1915 in Jellicoe MSS, Add. 49012, f. 82.

required 'considerable skill and patience' to obtain accurate ranges even at 10,000 yards and that the instrument was 'scarcely adequate' at 20,000 yards; useful ranges might be obtained at this long range by men with above-average eyesight but only after thorough training.[62] For the majority, 15,000–17,000 yards was probably the limit for obtaining fairly accurate ranges.

Methods of control

The principles of fire control were essentially the same whether a ship was equipped with manual plotters or a fire control table. As soon as a target was sighted, its true range, course and speed were estimated visually, though the estimated range was needed only until the first range-finder ranges were taken. Estimated course and speed were set on the Dumaresq[63] to obtain initial values of range-rate and speed-across and, from the latter, the gun deflection. The range-clock was then started, having been set with these first values of true range and range-rate; the initial ballistic corrections were applied to the clock-range in the manner of a spotting correction to obtain the gun-range. Clock-range and gun-range then changed together according to the latest range-rate read from the Dumaresq. The *GFBOs* in force at Jutland insisted that:

It must be clearly understood that under no circumstances is fire to be withheld for the purposes of obtaining a 'plot'; it should not even be delayed for rangefinder ranges if there is the smallest possibility of disadvantage resulting from delay.[64]

Thus, if fire had to be opened at once, most reliance had to be placed on observing the fall of shot and applying corresponding corrections to hit and then keep on hitting the target (this process of 'spotting' will be described shortly).

However, in many tactical situations, not least when the enemy was sighted in good visibility at long range, range-finder ranges and target bearings could be taken regularly before it was necessary to open fire; these ranges and bearings were recorded on manual plotting boards or on the rate plots of the Dreyer Tables. As soon as a few ranges had been plotted, an initial mean (average) range for the plotted points could be estimated by eye; this 'mean rangefinder range of the moment' was compared with the clock-range and, if they did not agree, the clock could be adjusted ('tuned') accordingly. As range plotting continued, the plot developed as a band of points. The mean range-finder ranges from moment to moment provided the best available indication of

---

[62] Lieutenant J W Rivett-Carnac, 'Notes on Rangefinders ...' in ADM 137/466. The range-finder's range scales were non-uniform; one division represented 100 yards at 10,000 yards but 400 yards at 20,000 yards.
[63] Or the functionally equivalent dials and linkage of the Argo Clock Mark IV.
[64] *GFBOs III*, XIV.8.

the true-range of the target, while the slope of the notional line through these mean values measured the range-rate. Also, if the plotted range-rate differed from the range-rate that was read from the Dumaresq and set on the range-clock, the disparity could be corrected by adjusting the Dumaresq.

In those ships equipped to plot bearings, the plot of observed bearings yielded a bearing-rate, which was then converted to an equivalent speed-across. Now both range-rate and speed-across from the plots could be compared with the values from the Dumaresq; using a procedure known as a 'cross-cut', the instrument was worked 'in reverse' to obtain new and better values of enemy speed and course that were more in accordance with the observed values recorded on the plots. Once the Dumaresq settings had been corrected by a cross-cut, its future values of range-rate and speed-across were more accurate than before – and hence the predicted values of range and bearings obtained from the clocks also followed the observed values more closely.[65] Thus, if time permitted, plotting enabled the fire control operators to set their Dumaresqs and clocks as accurately as possible before opening fire. If they were successful, the opening salvos would fall close to the target and only a few spotting corrections to deflection, range and perhaps range-rate would be necessary to start hitting. However, at any time the target might alter course, thereby 'throwing out' the rates previously obtained; if possible, plotting then continued until new rates could be measured from the plots.

This method of control, which became known later as 'rate control', was devised in 1911 and 1912 for use with manual plotting boards and particularly with the Dreyer-pattern rate plotters of the fire control tables Marks III and II although, at that time, the ships in service had few turret range-finders.[66] Thus, especially if the range was long or the visibility unfavourable, ranges might be few in number and scattered on the range plot. Nonetheless, the method was designed to make the best of the ranges that could be obtained. Even so, in difficult conditions for ranging, the opening deflection, range and range-rate might be only approximate, in which case large spotting corrections would then be needed to hit and keep on hitting the target.

During 1913, the ships of the *King George V* class, with range-finders on all five turrets, joined those of the *Orion* class in the 2BS. In all these ships, as we have seen, the ranges from the main Argo range-finder were plotted automatically and those from the turrets manually. In 1913, the 2BS developed a new method of control called 'range-finder control'. This was best suited to short-to-medium ranges in good visibility, when their many range-finders could take numerous accurate ranges which, when recorded on the time-and-range plot,

---

[65] If no bearing plot was made, the corrected range-rate could be used to correct either the Dumaresq's target course or speed – normally the former – but not both.

[66] *DGBJ*, pp. 61–4 and 159–66.

gave an essentially continuous indication of the mean range-finder range. The gun range was then tuned to follow the changes in the mean plotted range, with relatively little reliance on the range clock or, once hitting was established, on spotting.[67] But range-finder control had developed from the previous method that had been devised before the ranges from many range-finders had been available. In November 1913, this older method was described as 'the alternative system *i.e. maintaining the Range by means of the Rate*'; by 1915, it had been named 'rate control'.[68] Unlike range-finder control, rate control was suited to long ranges, poor visibility or both, when range-finder ranges were more likely to be few and inaccurate.[69] But it must also be emphasised that the two were not mutually exclusive and that elements of both were used together. The *Manual of Gunnery 1915* insisted that 'when using range-finder control, the rate must always be kept working in case a change ... to rate control becomes necessary' and that, in rate control 'Usually the range-finders are used ... as a check on the clock'.[70]

Aiming, firing and spotting

Before the introduction of the director, in each turret the guns were aimed continuously by the gunlayers and the turret trainer; this was known as 'individual laying' or simply as 'gunlayers'. When the firing gong was sounded, all the guns in the salvo, normally one gun in each turret, could fire almost together – though there might be small time differences as each layer made final fine adjustments to his aim.[71] Firing began with 'deliberate salvos', i.e. the fall of each salvo was spotted and the corrections applied before firing the next salvo. If the opening deflection was wrong, the deflection was corrected first until the salvos were falling on the line-of-sight, usually either short of or over the target. Then large spotting corrections (typically up or down 800 yards) were made until the salvos either straddled or, more likely, 'crossed the target' (one salvo over, the next short, or *vice versa*). Since the shots in a salvo were spread by between 200

---

[67] *DGBJ*, pp. 167–8 based on 'Remarks on Rangefinder Control', Enclosure No. I to *Home Fleet General Order No. 14*, 5 November 1913, DRAX 1/9 and *MoG III 1915*, pp. 17–18.

[68] Enclosure No. I (see note 67, original emphasis). *MoG III 1915*, p. 6.

[69] The later sources for rate control are *HFGO 14* (see note 67), pp. 2–4 and *MoG III 1915*, pp. 7–9 and 11–17.

[70] *MoG III 1915*, p. 6. Although *DGBJ*, pp. 163–4 and 167–8 describes rate control, Brooks, 'Preparing for Armageddon', pp. 11–12 gives it due emphasis, both as a term and a method. This paper questions the conclusions in Sumida, 'Matter of Timing' and 'Expectation' that Jellicoe embraced range-finder control as a means of fighting a brief action at short range. See also McLaughlin, 'Battle Lines', pp. 8–12.

[71] *MoG III 1915*, pp. 10–11. In a 'ripple salvo', the guns were fired in sequence beginning with the leeward gun to avoid the risk of smoke interference but, by 1915, ripples were discouraged since 'it must cause loss of time'.

and 400 yards, the object of spotting was to straddle, i.e. for one or two shots to fall short of the target so that there was a good probability that other shots in the salvo would hit. Once the target had been crossed, the next spotting correction was half the previous one (e.g. 400 yards) in the opposite direction. And, if this did not straddle, the next correction was halved again (e.g. 200 yards), its direction being determined by whether or not the target had been crossed again. Thus the sizes of the corrections were predetermined, only the direction being decided from observations of the fall of shot. This spotting procedure was known as 'working a bracket', the bracket being continued only until the target was straddled. If in rate-control, then, provided that the range-rate set on the range clock was correct, subsequent salvos would continue to straddle. But, if the rate was incorrect, the salvos would drift off the target, in which case further corrections for both range and range-rate were ordered.[72]

Once the target had been straddled consistently, the rate of fire could be increased in one of two ways. The first was to fire 'rapid salvos', preferably at a steady rate, without waiting to correct the range of one salvo by spotting the previous one; each salvo was still spotted but the correction was applied not to the next salvo but to a later one. Alternatively, rapid salvos were fired as 'double gun salvos' in which two salvos were fired in quick succession after which both were spotted before firing the next double. The second way to increase the firing rate was by 'rapid independent', in which guns were loaded, aimed and fired as rapidly as possible by the individual turrets. If continuous aim was possible then, after loading, each gun was quickly 'on' the target, ready to fire; hence 'rapid independent' was capable of the maximum rate of fire.[73] However, the irregular firing was liable to interfere with ranging, aiming and spotting. Yet, while this interference was probably more severe at longer ranges, rapid independent was not limited to shorter ranges; after the Battle of the Dogger Bank, when the range from Beatty's flagship *Lion* was never less than 14,825 yards, her Captain Chatfield regretted that the 'mistake made was in not at once going into rapid independent and putting forth our whole volume of fire'.[74] Also:

Independent [as distinct from rapid independent] fire may be obligatory in bad weather, during smoke interference, or if the enemy's fire is accurate, more especially if the director system cannot be employed.[75]

[72] For example, the order 'UP 200, OPEN 100' increased the range by 200 yards and the range-rate by 100 yards/min. For brackets, see *DGBJ*, pp. 21–2, 27 and 63–4.
[73] *GFBOs I*, 'Gunnery Addendum', March 1915, p. 1. *MoG III 1915*, pp. 9–11. *Spotting Rules 1916*, November 1916, pp. 4–5 in Ja011, AL.
[74] *BP I*, p. 231.
[75] *MoG III 1915*, p. 10 – which used the terms 'gunlayers' salvos' and 'gunlayers' independent' when aiming and firing was by the individual turret crews.

Although the later marks of Dumaresq, including those in the Dreyer tables, were designed to keep the rates even when own ship was altering course, this capability was most useful in keeping the rates while manoeuvring prior to opening fire. It was generally accepted that, once action was imminent and after firing began, changes of course, especially large turns, were to be avoided as far as possible, because of the ill effects of heel, vibration and rapid changes of target bearing on aiming and firing and also on the taking of ranges and bearings. Both British and German sources emphasised what Admiral Chatfield described as 'that steady course which is so important to gunnery', while the German 'Hints for Battle' insisted:

Every leader, every Captain and every navigating officer must bear in mind that even the best gunlayer cannot shoot, unless the ship maintains a steady course.[76]

The British director

The director system enabled all guns to follow the aim of a director sight; this sight was mounted aloft in all ships while, in 15in-gunned ships, a second director sight was located in the armoured hood above the conning tower. In the British Scott/Vickers system of World War I, each 'director sight' was in effect a dummy gun and gunsight with its own layer and trainer. Gun range and deflection were transmitted to the director sight, while the director sight transmitted gun elevation and turret training angles to the turrets; in the turrets, the layers and trainers worked their hydraulic controls to follow the pointers of the elevation and training receivers. The director layer fired all guns in a simultaneous salvo with an electric trigger; as with individual laying, director salvos could be deliberate, rapid or doubles. In August 1914, six of the eight modern dreadnoughts of the 2BS had directors.[77] But, as more directors entered service, it became apparent that 'it is more difficult to handle a director well than it is to lay a gun'. In January 1915, Jellicoe insisted that 'under no conditions will the director layer be successful unless the director layer is thoroughly efficient as a layer [and] works his training wheel with discretion'. Thus the man in the layer's seat was both the layer and the trainer. He attempted to train continuously, even though: 'If the director is kept constantly "on" for line the turrets have difficulty in following their pointers'.[78] It was recognised that 'Director layers cannot fire exactly to order but must take their

---

[76] Chatfield, p. 142 and also p. 134. *German Tactical Orders, January 1915*, p. 7 in 'German Fleet Orders'. *DGBJ*, pp. 28–9.

[77] Brooks, 'Scott and the Director', pp. 161–70.

[78] *GFG&TOs*, p. 32. Jellicoe, 'Remarks on the Use of Director Firing ...', 18 January 1915, ADM 137/2019, ff. 60 and 62. It seems that the trainer's main duty was to slew the director rapidly when changing target or when own ship altered course.

opportunities ... whilst except under unfavourable conditions, gunlayers are able to fire within a brief interval of the fire gong'. This suggests that the director layer set the director to a fixed elevation, then trained continuously while waiting for the ship's roll to bring his telescope cross-wires 'on' for elevation. (At the Dogger Bank, in a calm sea, *Tiger*'s director layer fired on the upward roll to increase the motion of the ship.)[79] But, in August 1915, Jellicoe remained concerned that:

[W]ith an inefficient layer, the director is slow and inaccurate, and, probably, much inferior to gunlaying ... the success or failure of the director system depends practically entirely on the efficiency of the layer and the degree of perfection to which the guns' crews have been drilled to follow the director pointers.[80]

Because of the director's elevated position and ability to fire simultaneous salvos, it had clear advantages over individual laying, particularly at extreme ranges, in bad visibility and light or when the turret sights were obscured by spray or smoke; its simultaneous salvos were particularly helpful when ships were firing in concentration at a single target.[81] But, in good conditions for turret gunlaying, director firing was likely to be slower. At the Battle of Jutland, all British dreadnoughts, except *Erin* and *Agincourt*, were fitted with directors.

Beginning in 1912, Evershed target indicators were delivered first to the 12-inch gunned dreadnoughts (except *Neptune, Australia* and *New Zealand*) and, once the war started, priority was given to the latest ships with 15-inch armament. At Jutland, of dreadnoughts with 13.5in guns, only *Lion, Princess Royal, Queen Mary, Orion, Conqueror, King George V* and *Centurion* had Evershed installations.[82] In all ships with these instruments, the director sight was fitted with an Evershed receiver to ensure that it too was trained on the designated target. If ships without the Evershed gear wished to resort to individual laying, their directors could still serve as target indicators; but, if the director should be damaged in action – which, as we shall see, happened in *Tiger* during the battle – they had to resort to their B&S bearing receivers, which merely displayed the target bearing, without any facility for following pointers.

Ranges and firing rates

When the visibility was limited, the range for opening fire was that at which the enemy was sighted. But, in good visibility, the C-in-C could choose the ranges

---

[79] *GFG&TOs*, pp. 51 and 65.

[80] Jellicoe, 'Remarks on full calibre firing ...', 30 August 1915, ADM 137/2020, f. 210.

[81] Jellicoe, 'Director Firing' (see note 78), ff. 60 and 62. *MoG III 1915*, p. 10.

[82] Admiralty, Gunnery Branch, *Handbook of Fire Control Instruments, 1914*, pp. 30–42, ADM 186/191. 'Details of Bearing Indicators. Main Armament' with 'Gunnery Information ... action of 31st May 1916', 12 June 1916, ADM 1/8460/149. *Queen Mary* was probably fitted with an Evershed in the first half of 1915.

for deployment, opening fire and continuing the action in accordance with his tactical preferences. In the *GFBOs* in force at Jutland, in favourable weather, Jellicoe expected to deploy at 18,000–20,000 yards but 'it is not intended . . . to open fire at a greater range than 18,000 yards unless the enemy does so earlier . . . Ships must, however, be *ready* to open fire at extreme range'.

As for action ranges:

In weather of good visibility, the range should be between 15,000 and 10,000 yards; the latter being reached as the enemy's fire is overcome; in the *early* stages of the action I do not desire to close the range much inside 14,000 yards.[83]

In the summer of 1915, when the battle orders already read as just quoted, Frederic Dreyer recommended opening at 15,000 yards and then closing in, all guns bearing to 13,500 yards, a range that would 'enable us to get good Rangefinder Ranges and increase our hits by supporting Spotting'.[84] But Captain Roger Backhouse of Jellicoe's staff considered that: 'Under good conditions for spotting, I think 15000 yards a good range for battle; under bad conditions, it might come down to 9 or 10000'. Since he thought that it would be wise to assume that the German torpedo range was now 10,000 yards, he added: 'If there were no destroyer torpedoes I sh$^{\underline{d}}$ suggest a fighting range to 10000 to 12000 yards in good weather as decisive results would follow quicker'. Backhouse concluded: 'I think the Battle orders are correct as now written'.[85]

In a memorandum on director firing dated 18 January 1915, Jellicoe insisted:

It cannot be too strongly emphasised that volume of accurate fire is the object to be aimed at . . . (Three salvos per minute is reported to be the German rate of fire as soon as the range is established.)

The March 'Gunnery Addendum' to the *GFBOs* repeated this emphasis, adding: '"Lion's" experience in the action of 24th January showed conclusively the value of rapid fire as a means of preventing fire in reply' – though Chatfield's report stated that, at the end, *Seydlitz* and *Derfflinger* were each firing at about two salvos per minute.[86] Despite its general emphasis on rapidity, the addendum was careful to set firing rates according to circumstances. For ranges of 10,000 yards and upwards, it stipulated that fire should be opened with deliberate salvos, i.e. applying spotting corrections from one salvo before firing the next; expected salvo intervals for 13.5in guns were then fifty seconds at 18,000 yards, forty seconds at 12,000 yards. Immediately the range had been found by straddling the target – or even beforehand if the enemy's rate

---

[83] *GFBOs III*, VII. 5 and 7 and XIV.1 (original emphasis).
[84] *GFBOs I*, 'Gunnery Addendum' (20 March 1915), pars. I.9 and VI and 'Battle Tactics' (12 March 1915), par. 4. Dreyer, 'A Few Notes' (see note 61), f. 82.
[85] Backhouse's submission to C.-in-C., 14 September 1915 in JMSS 49012, ff. 94–5.
[86] Jellicoe, 'Director Firing', f. 61. 'Gunnery Addendum', 20 March 1915 (see note 84), par. I.9. *BP I*, p. 232.

of fire was faster – the rate of fire was to be increased, either by using independent or rapid salvos, since 'it is otherwise impossible to develop a high rate of fire at long range'.

[I]n the ordinary course, two salvos per minute from 12-inch and larger calibre guns should give a sufficient rate of fire at long ranges, but the interval between salvos can be decreased to about twenty seconds as the range and time of flight decrease and hitting becomes better established.

... In all cases, unless it is *certain* that hits are being obtained, ships using rapid fire ... should frequently check for a short time at a lower rate of fire. This ... is certainly *essential* when using independent firing.

... When range of visibility is less than 10,000 yards, ships must be prepared to open rapid fire from the outset ... *The only safe rule is to get short and spot 'up'*.[87]

When new 'Gunnery Instructions' were incorporated in the *GFBOs* in December 1915, the last two exhortations remained, as did that which urged 'At all ranges, the early development of *accurate rapid fire* is the object to be kept in view'. But all explicit figures for firing rates were omitted.[88] Perhaps this change had been made because practice had established that the earlier rates were too ambitious for some ships; evidently, it was now accepted that accuracy must not be sacrificed to arbitrary standards of rapidity. As we shall see, this important lesson may not have been taken to heart in the Battle Cruiser Fleet.

Before the War, British battle practices were at ranges of about 8,000–9,000 yards, though some special firings are known at ranges up to 16,000 yards. But, in November and December 1914, the Grand Fleet held its first long-range practices at 15,000 yards and more. After a hiatus in the early months of 1915, fleet firing practices at towed targets became routine. With full charges, the ranges (with only one exception) were from 15,000 to 18,000 yards. However, to limit barrel wear, a greater proportion of firings (in the ratio 68:39) were with reduced charges at 10,000–13,000 yards: but, due to the steeper trajectories, the required accuracy of gun ranges was much the same. Thus these practices tested the fleet's abilities to fire at the long ranges expected at the beginning of an action in good visibility. Nonetheless, on 20 December 1915, Jellicoe ordered a special practice by *Iron Duke* with the object of confirming that the pre-war standards of shooting at ranges of less than 10,000 yards – the ranges that might be expected in poor visibility – were being maintained.[89]

Projectiles

For heavy turret guns, British ships were supplied with three natures of explosive-filled shell: APC (armour-piercing capped), CPC (common pointed

---

[87] 'Gunnery Addendum' (20 March 1915) pars. 6–10 (original emphases).
[88] *GFBOs III*, pars. XIV, 1–9.   [89] *DGBJ*, pp. 66–70. Brooks, 'Armageddon', pp. 7–9.

capped) and HE (high explosive). On striking armour plate, the mild-steel 'soft' cap was intended to limit the initial impact stress on the hard point of the shell so that it could bore into the plate and, if possible, penetrate right through. Normal (perpendicular) impact was most favourable for complete penetration whereas, at the more oblique angles to be expected at longer range and in action, the shell case was more likely to break up without holing the plate. The design of the British caps varied considerably from supplier to supplier and from the small solid caps of the 12in to several different forms of hollow cap for 13.5in and greater calibres. Ideally, an armour-piercing shell should penetrate right through the plate before its delayed-action fuse, triggered by the impact with the plate, detonates the filling well inside the enemy vessel under attack. However, the British shells fell short in several respects. The heat treatment for hardening the APC shells made them too brittle and so more likely to shatter on impact.[90] Also, the fillers were unsuitable for the purpose. APC was filled with the high explosive lyddite (picric acid), its weight about 3% of the whole shell. CPC shells were larger with thinner walls, their cavity containing about 9% by weight of black powder. Both fillers exploded spontaneously due to the shock of impact on thicker plates, the effect being more rapid in the case of lyddite. Thus, even if the shell body remained intact as it penetrated, lyddite exploded as it was still going through the plate while a CPC shell might go on a few feet further.[91] Nonetheless there could still be a substantial effect close to the rear of the plate, due to the explosion itself and to flying fragments of shell and armour plate. If the plate was too thick the shell would break up without penetrating at all; but at least it could be relied upon to explode outside, perhaps buckling the plate and its supports. Thus the fuses (which were screwed into the bases of both APC and CPC shells) were not even necessary when attacking thick plate; their principal functions were to prevent prematures and to burst a shell after it passed through thinner plate (1in or greater). However, the fuses had no special delay element, so they could initiate bursts anywhere from five to eighteen feet in the rear of thinner plate. Well before the War, these less-than-ideal properties of the British APC and CPC were understood and seem to have been accepted without any active attempts to remedy them. The large HE shells had the thinnest walls and were filled with about 13% by weight of lyditte, while

---

[90] Campbell, pp. 342–3, 345 and 386. *MoG I 1915*, p. 156. *Final Report of the President, Projectile Committee, 1917*, Pls. I–IV, ADM 186/166. *Reports of the Shell Committee, 1917 and 1918*, p. 155, ADM 186/169. *Technical History and Index. TH29, Ammunition for Naval Guns*, p. 43, AL.

[91] 'Choice of Projectiles in Action' with minute by DNO, 3 November 1911 in 'Important Questions dealt with by DNO ... Vol. I – 1912', f. 118, AL. 12in APC had been filled initially with black powder but by March 1916 if not September 1915 they were being refilled with lyddite, a process that appears to have been largely completed before Jutland: Jellicoe's memos of 3 September 1915 and 2 March 1916 in ADM 137/2020, f. 233 and /2021, f. 265; *MoG I 1915*, p. 163; *GFG&TOs*, p. 166 printed 6 July 1916.

their nose fuses were intended to detonate the filler even on non-armour plate. Their powerful explosive effect could open up light structures and cause extensive damage and injuries from blast and from the small, fast-moving fragments produced as they burst.[92]

In March 1914, the Admiralty informed the C-in-C, Admiral Callaghan, of experimental firings with 13.5in Light APC and CPC against 10in KC plate at 20° to the normal; at striking velocities equivalent to a range of 10,000 yards, both penetrated and burst while going through the plate; a similar result was obtained by a 13.5in Heavy APC round at normal incidence at an equivalent 9,900 yards. But the 'Gunnery Amendment' to the *GFBOs* of March 1915 claimed that: 'At 20,000 yards 13.5-inch (heavy) A.P. shell filled lyddite will penetrate sixteen inches of armour, 13.5-inch (light) about fourteen inches', and that these shells were 'effective at all ranges' (though not stated explicitly, these figures must refer to normal impact). It accepted that these shells had 'much greater penetration' than 12in, though it still declared that 12in APC could 'penetrated belt armour at more than 11–12,000 yards'. It instructed ships with guns of 13.5in and larger calibre guns to open fire with APC or CPC shell; those with 12in guns with CPC or HE. This recommendation was repeated in the *GFBOs* in force at Jutland but not the extravagant claims for penetration at the longest ranges; instead, officers were referred to the current *Manual of Gunnery 1915*.[93] They may have been disconcerted to find that their heavy shells, both APC and CPC, were subjected to proof testing only at normal impact and at striking velocities equivalent to much less than expected battle ranges (13.5in Heavy rounds partly excepted, see table). And, in all cases, the proof tests did not assess performance at the oblique impacts that were always experienced on vertical plate at long range, and would be increased further when the enemy's course was not perpendicular to the line-of-fire. Perhaps to allay concerns, the manual also contained graphical perforation diagrams showing the conditions 'under which capped A.P. shell may reasonably [*sic*] be expected to perforate K.C. armour when attacked normally and at 30°'. As Table 2.2 shows, the predictions in these diagrams were considerably more optimistic for normal incidence while the equivalent range limits for oblique attack were almost the same as for proof testing at normal. The diagrams also implied that all 12in and 13.5in APC could penetrate 8in plate at normal at maximum range, as could both types of 13.5in at 30°; however, at this oblique angle, the 12in shells were limited to 14,100 or 15,300 yards (Mark X and XI guns, respectively). The equivalent ranges at proof were considerably longer

[92] *MoG I 1915*, p. 167. Secretary to C.-in-C., Home Fleets, 20 March 1914, 'Important Questions Dealt with by DNO ... Vol. III – 1914', f. 292, AL. 'Choice of Projectiles' (see note 91), ff. 119–20.

[93] Secretary to C.-in-C., 1914 (see note 92), ff. 293–4. *GFBOs I*, 'Gunnery Addendum', V (20 March 1915). *GFBOs III*, VII.6 and XVII.2 (December 1915).

Table 2.2. *British proof tests and predicted perforation properties*

| Gun and shell | CPC proof at normal | | APC proof at normal | | APC perforation diagrams, 12in plate | |
	Plate thickness	Range yards	Plate thickness	Range yards	Range at normal	Range at 30°
12in Mk X	9in	12,300	12in	7,350	8,570	7,300
12in Mk XI	9in	13,500	12in	8,450	10,200	8,400
13.5in Light	10in	14,200	12in	8,750	14,000	9,300
13.5in Heavy	10in	20,500	12in	11,400	16,400	11,400
15in	12in	22,800	15in	8,900		

for CPC than for APC but the plates were thinner and, to be accepted, it was only required 'that some portion of the shell must pass through the plate'. The earlier 'Gunnery Addendum' concluded that CPC 'have nearly as good penetration as A.P. shell filled lyddite ... and their much larger burster [makes them] thoroughly effective at any range'.[94]

In late 1910, towards the end of his time as Controller, Jellicoe had been well aware of the deficiencies of British 12in APC and had requested the Ordnance Board to consider a new design capable of carrying its burster through armour plate when striking obliquely. However, as he recalled, 'the matter was not sufficiently pressed'.[95] It is unlikely that, when he returned to the Admiralty as Second Sea Lord, he did not know of the modest test results then being obtained with 13.5in shells. He signed both the 'Gunnery Amendment' and the later gunnery *GFBOs*, though it seems incredible that he believed the claims in the former; perhaps his main object was to reassure the Fleet about its projectiles. As a gunnery officer, Jellicoe should have recognised the disparity in the *Manual of Gunnery* between the conditions of proof and the performance claimed by the perforation diagrams, but the latter were the best guide he had on how his ships' shell would behave under battle conditions of oblique impact. They indicated that, in electing to fight the early stages of an action at not much inside 14,000 yards, he was imposing a range at which British APC and CPC had little chance of penetrating the thickest German armour in main belts and on turret faces (typically 300–350mm or 11.8–13.8in). At that range, the angle of descent of a 13.5in heavy shell was 12°[96] so, even when the enemy course was not perpendicular to the line-of-flight, it appeared that both APC and CPC has a reasonable prospect of holing battleship upper belts (which Jellicoe

[94] *MoG I 1915*, pp. 154–6 and Pls. 21–3. *GFBOs I*, 'Gunnery Addendum', V (20 March 1915).
[95] *JP I*, p. 14. JMSS, 49038, ff. 211–12.
[96] Admiralty, Gunnery Branch, *Range Tables ... Vol. I, 1918*, p. 149, ADM 186/236.

believed were 9in thick) and casemate (7¾in) armour[97] and then bursting when some way through the plates. He could also expect that the blast and splinters from CPC and HE would cause significant structural damage and injury to personnel, thereby disrupting command and control and creating the desired confusion in the enemy's ships.

Cordite

The propellant used in British guns was called cordite, a mixture mainly of the explosives nitrocellulose and nitroglycerine. The full charge for a heavy turret gun consisted of four cartridges, each cartridge being a cylindrical silk bag filled with cords (sticks) of cordite; attached to one end was an igniter, a flat bag of black powder protected by a tear-off disc of thin board. The cartridges for each turret were stored in brass cases, two per case, in the cordite magazines at the bottom of each turret, just above the shell rooms. In supplying cordite to the guns, the lids were taken off the magazine cases, the bare cartridges removed and passed through the open magazine door to what was called the handing room. There the tear-off discs were removed before the cartridges were loaded into the system of hoists that took them through a working chamber to the turret gunhouse. The hoists provided a degree of protection against the effects of hits but were not completely flashproof.[98]

While cordite was not as inflammable as gunpowder, it was known that one 6in cartridge burning in the enclosed space of an ammunition trunk 'will explode a similar cartridge when at 2½ feet distance . . . but will not necessarily do this when at 8½ feet distance'. However, no lessons were drawn about the concomitant danger from bare cartridges for heavy guns in a turret handing room. It was also well recognised that cordite gradually deteriorated after manufacture to the point that it could ignite spontaneously; and that the remedy was regular inspection controlled by accurate record-keeping of the histories of every manufactured lot. Suspect lots were classified as 'first use' and, if not expended, were supposed to be landed after no more than 18 months on board.[99] However, before Jutland two large ships – the predreadnought *Bulwark* on 26 November 1914 and the armoured cruiser *Natal* on 30 December 1915 – were destroyed by cordite explosions. The first may have started in a pile of some thirty bare 6in charges left in an ammunition passage. The enquiry into the second disaster, which did not report until September 1916, concluded:

---

[97] For Jellicoe's information on German ships (that for *Kaiser* is used here) see diagrams accompanying his comments to the 1SL dated 14 July 1914 in ADM 116/3091. See also *GF*, pp. 200–1.

[98] See Chapter 10 for details and sources.

[99] *MoG I 1915*, pp. 144 and 150–2. *GFG&TOs*, p. 154.

On the whole the cordite on board was getting old ... and ... the magazine records were in an incomplete state. Some of the 'First Use' and 'Fire First' cordite ... was ... neither tested, fired nor returned for over 20 months from the date of its receipt.

After *Vanguard's* cordite also blew up on 9 July 1917, the subsequent enquiry concluded that it was still the case that 'explosives were not treated with sufficient respect in seagoing ships'.[100] This verdict seems to apply even more to the period up to the Battle of Jutland, in particular, as we shall now find, in the battlecruisers.

The Battle Cruiser Fleet

Tiger's shooting at the Dogger Bank was conspicuously inaccurate, though there were extenuating circumstances; as her Captain, Henry Pelly, recalled: 'I don't think we had ever fired our big guns at a moving target when we were called upon to attack the enemy on January 24'. However, after a formal enquiry into her fighting efficiency, Beatty concluded that Pelly had 'not given that assistance and guidance to his Gunnery Lieut^n which is so essential'. However, Lieutenant Evan Bruce-Gardyn had already attracted Fisher's ire and only he was relieved of his appointment. Beatty, despite regarding Pelly as 'a little bit of the nervous excitable type', took no further action, declaring 'I am all against change; it is upsetting and inclined to destroy confidence'.[101]

The accuracy and rapidity at long range of the German fire at the Dogger Bank action left a strong impression on *Lion's* Captain Chatfield.

It is certain that Battle Cruisers, and probably Battleships, may have to open fire at much greater ranges than 15,000 yards, and that rapid fire will be employed by the enemy at 18,000, which must be answered by rapid fire.

Beatty's emphasis, while showing a surprisingly complacent view of his ships' gunnery, was quite different.

The Falkland Is. fight, and 24th January, have proved that hits can be made without difficulty [*sic*] at 19 or 20000 yards, but this range is not decisive and the percentage of hits is too small.
    ... we <u>must</u> try and get in closer without delay. Probably 12,000 to 14,000 yards would suit us well, this being outside the effective range of enemy's torpedoes and 6" guns.[102]

---

[100] *Technical History and Index, TH24, Storage and Handling of Explosives in Warships*, pp. 53 and 62, AL.
[101] Goldrick, pp. 263 and 298–301. Pelly, p. 157. Beatty to Jellicoe, 5 March 1915 in JMSS 49008, f. 24v.
[102] *BP I*, pp. 234 and 225.

These divergent views on fighting ranges would have an important bearing on their next encounter with Hipper's battlecruisers.

Chatfield concluded that, once *Lion*'s fire had ignited big fires in *Seydlitz*'s after turrets: 'The mistake made was in not at once going into rapid independent'. He insisted: 'That *rapidity of fire* is essential. The difficulties in controlling it are nothing compared to the disadvantages that ensue once the enemy's volume of shorts is greater than your own.' He continued:

> Salvos when gunlaying [aiming and firing independently] are impracticable, as, owing to interference with aim, the rate of fire becomes a minimum … Directors must fire rapid double salvos as soon as the range is found.[103]

As we have seen, his report influenced the greater emphasis on rapid fire in the March 1915 'Gunnery Addendum' to the *GFBOs*. However, Battle Cruiser Order (BCO) 17, 'Rate of Fire' (printing date 15 June 1915) went even further, insisting that ships with both 13.5in and 12in guns should expect to attain a firing rate of three rounds per turret per minute under favourable conditions. It concluded that:

> Under most conditions interference [due to smoke, spray, motion, etc.] is best met by the use of Independent. Under other conditions the best results might be obtained by firing salvoes.

Furthermore, this order, unlike the 'Gunnery Addendum', stipulated a single intended firing rate, without qualification concerning either range, or whether or not the target has already been straddled.[104] The emphasis (both in this BCO and Chatfield's remarks) on independent fire even suggests that Beatty's ships were attempting to fire rapidly from the moment they opened fire, despite the difficulties of spotting straddles.[105] While the exact system of rapid fire adopted in the BCF remains uncertain, the results were undoubtedly poor. In November 1915, Jellicoe wrote to Beatty:

> I am afraid you must have been very disappointed at *Lion* and *Tiger*'s battle practice results. I can't understand how a control officer of experience could have made such a blunder as that made by *Lion*'s … I fear the rapidity ideas were carried to excess in one case (*Queen Mary* I think). Also the RF operators were bad. It is most difficult for you to give them proper practice I know.

---

[103] *BP I*, pp. 231–2.

[104] BCO 17, 'Rate of Fire' printed 15 June 1915 in DRAX 1/3. The required firing rate meant that, *on average*, each turret gun fired once every 40 seconds. Compare this with the statement that 'An average rate of loading for 13.5 B.L. Guns – using due precautions and proper precision – is 35 seconds'.

[105] After the Dogger Bank, Chatfield recommended (*BP I*, p. 232): 'The main object when opening fire must not be to straddle but to obtain a big *volume of fire* short and then work it up by small "ups" till hitting commences' (original emphases) and that 'Fairly reliable corrections for all ranges are; "down, 1,000"; or "up, 200"'.

In reply, Beatty admitted his disappointment but did not show much concern.

> Yes indeed it was a terrible disappointment the battle practice of *Lion* and *Tiger* ...
>
> The 'Tiger's' R.F. operators were bad which primarily accounted for her result ... the other 3 were not bad but undoubtedly as you say we could do with much more practice at sea ... I do not think you will be let down by the gunnery of the battle-cruisers when our day comes.
>
> ...
>
> I should very much like to have a yarn with you on the subject of Rapidity of Fire. I feel very strongly on the subject and think we should endeavour to quicken up our firing ... The Germans certainly <u>do</u> fire 5 to our own 2.

Jellicoe responded on 23 November:

> I ... am very glad you think all will be well ...
>
> I am all for rapidity of fire, but my only fear is that ships may break into rapid fire *too soon*, as *Queen Mary* I think did. It's all right even if not hitting *if short* but no use *if over*.[106]

He does not seem to have pressed the issue further with Beatty. But, as we have already noted, when the *GFBO* gunnery instructions were revised in the following month, they abandoned any attempt to define specific rates of fire. Yet BCO 17 was not withdrawn and it was still in force at the time of Jutland. The surviving evidence suggests that the combination of excessive rapidity and limited opportunities for practice seriously compromised the standards of gunnery in the BCF. One officer recalled that 'their reputation for gunnery was very very shaky indeed', while:

> An officer posted to *Invincible* reported back to *Barham*'s first-lieutenant that 'he was shocked by the standard of inefficiency he encountered'.[107]

In the last months before Jutland, Lieutenant Stephen King-Hall recorded in his diary a collective view that 'the Battle Cruisers' shooting was rotten' and that ships from the Forth visiting Scapa for practice found that: 'The Battle Cruisers' name up here is mud, owing to the inefficiency of their gunnery and the general casualness and lack of concentration with which they appear to treat the war'.[108] This testimony is particularly damning since King-Hall was an officer in *Southampton*, one of the BCF's own light cruisers. Perhaps some of the battlecruisers had improved by 31 May, but on the 7th, Beatty wrote to Jellicoe:

---

[106] *JP I*, pp. 188–9. JMSS 49008, ff. 67–9. At the Dogger Bank, the three leading German ships fired 976 rounds, their British opposite numbers 869: Campbell, *Battlecruisers*, pp. 24, 44 and 50. Perhaps Beatty's 5:2 ratio was based on *Lion*'s experience of the concentrated fire of *Seydlitz* and *Moltke*.

[107] Gordon, pp. 30 and 51.   [108] Louise King-Hall, pp. 436 and 488.

I am sending you the results of the recent firing. The *Tiger's* was as usual unsatisfactory.[109]

Although Beatty was at last considering a replacement, Captain Pelly was still in command when, as Beatty and so many others had anticipated so eagerly, their day came.

In a battlecruiser striving to fire at the maximum rate of three rounds per turret per minute, twelve cordite propellant charges per minute, each weighing 74lb, had to be supplied from a magazine to its handing room.[110] Since, prior to Jutland, no flash-tight scuttles were fitted in the heavy magazine doors, the rapid passage of men and cartridges left no alternative but to leave the doors open.[111] There was also a temptation for the magazine crew to anticipate demand by removing the lids from cordite cases, taking cartridges out of the cases, and stacking cartridges in readiness both inside the magazine and in the handing room, thereby adding further to the number of unprotected cartridges exposed to flash from hits on any part of the turret structure. When, in June 1915, Chief Gunner Alexander Grant was hastily appointed to *Lion* after his predecessor had been court-martialled and dismissed, he found that all these dangerous practices had been followed during her actions in the Heligoland Bight and at the Dogger Bank. He was able to insist, once he had demonstrated that no delay resulted, that:

– only one magazine (of up to four serving a turret) should be in use at a time during action
– during lulls in the action, the magazine door should be closed and clipped
– charges should not be taken from their cases until required (he did not state whether he banned the premature removal of lids, though this seems likely)
– not more than one full charge should be in the handing room – this was presumably in addition to the two full charges in the hoppers from which charges could be tipped into the cordite hoists.[112]

However, Grant's authority did not extend beyond the flagship, while no BCO was issued to impose his rules in other battlecruisers; if bad practices had been tolerated previously in *Lion*, they were probably still being followed in much of the BCF at the time of Jutland.

The immediate reason for Alexander Grant's appointment was that his predecessor had allowed *Lion's* cordite to get into such a chaotic state that a large percentage of cases had different batch numbers marked on each case, its two lids and the two cartridges inside. Thus it was no longer possible to carry

[109] *BP I*, p. 308.
[110] Campbell, *Jutland*, pp. 371–2 and 378. N Lambert, '"Bloody Ships"', pp. 34–7.
[111] *JP II*, p. 97.
[112] Alexander Grant, 'H.M.S. *Lion*, 1915-16' in Susan Rose (ed.) *The Naval Miscellany Vol. VII* (NRS, 2008) pp. 384–90.

out systematic tests on different batches so that, should any batch have deteriorated, it could be removed before it became dangerous. Since it led to a court-martial, this was probably an extreme case. But, when Grant first went aboard, the gunnery officer, Lieutenant-Commander Gerald Longhurst, assured him that the cordite had all been put right: and, when Grant set about solving the problem (which required that the magazines were entirely restocked with cordite), Longhurst's immediate comment was: 'Well, you are not going to make a noise about it'. Grant's view was that, partly because cordite was a much safer explosive than gunpowder, the precautions for handling it had become 'considerably relaxed, even I regret to say, to a dangerous degree throughout the Service'.[113] This widespread indifference may be enough to explain why Longhurst, who had the final responsibility for the flagship's magazines, retained his position when the gunner was dismissed. But this episode also seems to be another instance of the casualness endemic in the BCF and of the reluctance of its senior commanders to get rid of incompetent officers.

In particular, historians have wondered at Beatty's willingness to overlook the inadequacies of his flag lieutenant. Ralph Seymour was not a fully qualified signals officer and, during the action after the Scarborough Raid, he made a serious mistake in addressing a signal to Beatty's light cruisers. Yet he retained his position and has been widely blamed for the signals at the end of the Battle of the Dogger Bank which contributed to the escape of three German battlecruisers.[114] However, the despatches of Beatty and his second-in-command, Rear-Admiral Moore, both accepted that the two signals 'Compass Pendant, NE' and 'AF – attack the enemy rear' flew together briefly before one or the other was hauled down. If the first, the joint signal meant 'Course NE to attack the enemy rear'; if the second, 'Attack the enemy rear bearing NE'. Beatty also stated that his object had been to cut off the already-damaged *Blücher* from the other battlecruisers; at the time, she bore NEbyE from the British line and throughout the action had been the rear enemy ship. *Lion* subsequently hoisted the action signal '74 – close nearer the enemy' but this did not change the object of the attack. By the time that it was apparent from *Lion* that it was no longer necessary to cut off *Blücher* and that Moore should renew the pursuit of the main German force, he was beyond signalling reach. Since the three signals were chosen by Beatty with advice from his flag-commander,[115] it is not at all clear how or indeed if Seymour was at fault; even if the first two were not hauled down in the intended order, there was no

[113] Grant (see note 112), pp. 384, 386 and 388.
[114] E.g. *FDSF II*, pp. 140 and 162–3 and Roskill, pp. 60, 103 and 113–14.
[115] *BP I*, pp. 207–8 and 217–20. Admiralty, *Naval Staff Monograph No. 12*, p. 222 (ADM 186/610). *Signal Book 1906*, p. 29. For the recent definitive account, see Goldrick, *Before Jutland* esp. pp. 275–8 and 293.

significant difference in their meaning. Beatty kept Seymour on after the Dogger Bank and, indeed, for the remainder of the War.

German gunnery

Fire control

At Jutland, all the German dreadnoughts relied on 3-metre Zeiss stereoscopic range-finders.[116] A range-taker viewed the target with both eyes, each eye receiving an image from one of the objectives at the ends of the instrument; thus he saw a single view of the target in greatly exaggerated perspective depth. The optics of the range-finder also projected into this view a *Wandermarke* in the form of small marks arranged in the form of a St Andrew's cross. As the range-taker adjusted the range head, the *Wandermarke* appeared to him to move nearer or further away. To find the range, he had to position the centre of the *Wandermarke* at the same apparent distance as the target. Unlike the coincidence range-finder, the stereoscopic range-finder did not depend on any exact alignments, horizontally or vertically, so it could obtain ranges even if the target was almost shrouded in smoke. However, stereoscopic range-finders could only be used by those with good stereoscopic vision, and even they required rigorous selection and training; German range-takers using the 3-metre Zeiss did not qualify if their errors exceeded 400 metres at 20,000 metres.[117] Thus German range-takers were better trained than their British counterparts and, while strictly comparative figures have not been found, it is probable that in use the Zeiss 3-metre range-finder was as accurate at 20,000 yards as the B&S 9-foot instrument at about 16,000 yards. (The good shooting at long range of the 5BS during the Run to the South suggests that their B&S 15-foot range-finders were at least as accurate as the Zeiss 3-metre.) Each German turret range-finder was mounted below the armoured roof with prismatic objectives protruding through it. A second type, on which particular reliance was placed, rotated above the roof of each armoured control tower; extension tubes brought the images down to eyepieces in the tower, where the range-taker was located.

The fire of German dreadnoughts was normally directed from the fore control position, an armoured tower in the rear of the conning tower, though there was a reserve armoured position aft, and small spotting tops on the masts. Orders from the control officers were passed by telephone and voice pipe to the transmitting stations beneath the armoured deck and from there gunnery data and orders were transmitted to the turrets. Early German fire control systems used electrical

---

[116] This section is based on *DGBJ*, pp. 221–4 with additional information from the sources cited here.
[117] Admiralty, Gunnery Branch, *Handbook of Stereoscopic Rangefinders 1919*, pp. 4–6 and 8, ADM 186/237.

step-by-step transmitters and receivers, which operated with DC (direct current). But in 1906, the firm of Siemens & Halske demonstrated what seems to have been the world's first system of AC (alternating current) data transmission. This type of instrument would later be given the generic name 'synchro'; as it implies, they were synchronous devices in which the receiver or receivers always rotated in synchronism with the transmitter. Thus receivers did not get 'out-of-step' and, if receivers were switched from one transmitter to another, they immediately assumed the same position as the newly connected transmitter. After testing and incorporating the new receivers into follow-the-pointer sights, in 1913 the German Navy placed a large order with Siemens & Halske to equip twenty-one battleships and five battlecruisers.[118] In the War, these synchronous AC instruments were used throughout the German fire control system.[119]

The part of the system that transmitted ranges from the various range-finders to the control positions was known as the *Basis Gerät*. From 1908, range-rate was obtained from the *EU-Anzeiger*, while a separate instrument indicated deflection corrected for wind, etc.; both embodied the same principles as the British Dumaresq. At Jutland, *Derfflinger* had also been provided with a more elaborate rate instrument which, like the Dumaresq, kept both range-rate and deflection; this was probably the device called the *EU/SV-Anzeiger*, which appears to have kept the rates approximately through a turn (as did the British Mark VI Dumaresq). It seems that these instruments were set with visual estimates of enemy course and speed to obtain initial values of deflection and range-rate. And that, while deflection was then corrected by spotting, a better value for range-rate was subsequently obtained from the range-finder ranges (as will be described shortly). The German Navy introduced its first range clock in 1912, when it would have been set for rate from the *EU-Anzieger*; this clock may have been the *Aw-Geber C.12* Elevation Telegraph. However, the development of German range clocks remains uncertain. British intelligence reports mention an early model having a drum with a spiral range scale and a more recent type with a circular range dial and a boss for setting spotting corrections. In his post-war book, Georg von Hase, the gunnery officer of the battlecruiser *Derfflinger*, describes an 'elevation telegraph' connecting to follow-the-pointer turret sights, and a range clock '[o]n the elevation telegraph'. But two successive paragraphs are contradictory as to whether range or elevation was transmitted to the turrets.[120] Reports by the US Navy of the German system at

[118] Georg Siemens, *History of the House of Siemens Vol. I* (Freiburg/Munich: Karl Alber, 1957) pp. 264–7. P L Taylor, *Servomechanisms* (London: Longmans, 1960), pp. 32–4.

[119] Reports from 1921 in 'Fire Control System. German Navy', Register 13826, File R-3-C, NARA.

[120] Lautenschläger, p. 135. Naval Staff, Intelligence Department, *German Gunnery Information Derived from the Interrogation of Prisoners of War*, October 1918 (C.B.01481), p. 16, Ca 0108, AL. von Hase, pp. 82–3.

the end of the war include a description of an *Aufsatztelegraph* (sight telegraph) that incorporated both a range clock, based on a variable-speed drive, and transmitters; when in direct fire (as opposed to full director fire), the latter transmitted ranges,[121] so this was probably also the case with earlier equipment.

Between the Dogger Bank and Jutland, the Germans introduced an instrument which displayed the ranges received from up to eight range-finders and, by electrical means, calculated the mean range of all those ranges that were considered valid – the officer in charge could switch out of the calculation any range-finder giving anomalous results. He also reported 'the change of range per minute calculated from the difference of the range-finder readings'.[122] Thus this instrument, called the '*Mittlungs Apparat*' in British intelligence reports, provided an alternative value for range-rate to that obtained from the *EU-Anzeiger* and a mean range-finder range to compare with the predicted range from the range-clock. However, when repeatedly altering course, the German Navy seems to have relied less on its rate instruments and clocks and more on its stereoscopic range-finders. After Jutland, *Seydlitz* reported that:

The electric clock was used only in the first part of the engagement [the Run to the South]; afterwards the movements of the ship were so frequent and sudden that regular shooting by electric clock was impossible. Firing was continued in connection with the ... Basisgerat ... in [the] forward gun control tower.[123]

Thus in these conditions the Germans used a form of range-finder control.

All the German dreadnoughts at Jutland, except *Westfalen* and *Rheinland* (*Nassau*-class),[124] were fitted with a periscopic training director in each control position that transmitted accurate training angles to follow-the-pointer receivers in the turrets. This *Richtungsweiser* combined the functions of the Evershed and the training part of the director in the British system. One model was designated *Rw-Geber C.13*, while *Derfflinger* had a new model called the *C/XVII* (or *C.17?*); this had better optics and a supplementary training sight in the fore-top for use if the main sight below could not see the target. However, while the turrets could be trained by director, gun laying remained in the hands of the turret layers, who were taught to lay continuously and who preferred to fire themselves after the fire gong had sounded; as would be

---

[121] US Naval Attaché, Berlin, 'Germany. Ordnance. Fire Control', 13 April 1921 (with diagrams) in 'Fire Control, German Navy' (see note 119).

[122] von Hase, p. 132. A later 'Range Averaging and Rate Instrument' had a second range pointer driven by a variable-speed drive; to obtain the range-rate, this pointer's rate of rotation was adjusted to match that of the mean range pointer. 'Germany. Ordnance. Fire Control' (see note 121).

[123] *Seydlitz*, 'General Experience' in 'Jutland, Later Reports', f. 272, ADM 137/1644.

[124] Campbell, p. 367.

expected, after Jutland several British observers described the German salvos as rapid ripples. Thus German ships could only shoot at targets that were visible from their turrets.

Accounts by the gunnery officers of *Derfflinger, Von der Tann* and *Lützow* all indicate that German dreadnoughts found their targets by firing and spotting single salvos, correcting the sight settings before firing the next; *Von der Tann* began against *Indefatigable* by firing a *Gabel* (fork), the first two range corrections being (in British terminology) '8 Up', '4 Down'.[125] This was very similar to a British bracket; however, while attempts to estimate the distance over were forbidden, German spotters were trained to estimate the distance of salvos short of the target so that their 'forks' could be adjusted accordingly. Spotting was assisted by electric 'hit-indicators', which sounded buzzers in the top, control and TS when the salvo was due to fall; however, these seem to have been far from reliable. Once their target had been straddled with about 25% of shots falling short, German ships fired a burst of rapid, unspotted salvos – interspersed when the range was short enough with salvos from the secondary guns – until inevitably, the target was lost and they had to revert to single, spotted salvos. Usually, salvos were fired by one gun in each turret, though *Lützow*'s salvos were fired alternatively by her fore and aft pairs of turrets.[126]

Ranges

In August 1910, the British naval attaché in Berlin reported that German 'battle practice is carried out at moving targets, at ranges up to 10,000 metres'.[127] No further information on German practices seems to have been obtained until near the end of 1914, when British naval intelligence somehow obtained full details of German practices conducted in 1912–13; they were translated and circulated to senior officers in December 1914. Between April and July 1913, nearly all the fully worked up battleships and battlecruisers carried out practices in which speeds were 12–16 knots; the ranges were from 12,250 to 16,000 yards; rates reached 325 yards per minute; and the targets were three old battleships, moored in line. Some ships made only one hit from thirty-six rounds fired but, under less demanding conditions, others obtained over 10%. In addition, the rates of fire per turret gun equate to salvos fired every 27–43 seconds, intervals which are consistent with breaking into rapid fire once the target had been straddled. Satisfactory hitting was also achieved with the

---

[125] von Hase, pp. 145–7. For *Von der Tann*, see Mahrholz, pp. 53–4. Staff, *World War One*, pp. 45 and 276. Mahrholtz's spotting orders were '8 zurück' and '4 vor'; German ranges were expressed in hectometres of 100m.

[126] Paschen, p. 33. Staff, *World War One*, pp. 234, 272 and 275.

[127] Captain H Heath, 'Report 27/10', 6 August 1910 in Seligmann (ed.) *Naval Intelligence*, p. 264.

secondary batteries at average opening ranges of about 11,700 yards, 10,700 yards at the close. Thus, when hostilities began, the German Navy had given most of its heavy ships an opportunity for practice at long ranges, and to observe the effects of their fire falling on and around actual ship targets.[128]

British commanders were also provided with translations of *German Tactical Orders*, which appear to have been written between August and November 1914. They declared: 'There are no reasons for us to *open fire* at ranges over 13,200 yards, unless the enemy should force us to open before, by himself opening fire at greater ranges.' But an earlier paragraph insisted that: 'A long action at *great ranges* is not to our advantage. We must ... attempt to get as soon as possible within ranges of from 8,800 to 6,600 yards to make use of our strong medium calibre armament and of our torpedoes.'[129] However, by the time the translation was circulated in January 1915, the German ability to fire accurately at long ranges had already been demonstrated during the Battle of the Falkland Islands and it would soon be confirmed at the Battle of the Dogger Bank, when *Lion* was immobilised even though the *minimum* range she recorded was 14,825 yards. Thus, in commenting on the German *Tactical Orders*, Frederic Dreyer concluded that: 'The experience of the War must have shown the Germans that they had little or no hope in clear weather of getting their Battle Line to so close a range as 8,800 to 6,600 yards from the Grand Fleet'[130] while Jellicoe's battle orders show that he had no intention of allowing them to make the attempt.[131]

Ammunition

German capital ships with 11in guns carried only base-fused armour-piercing capped (APC) shells, whereas those with 12in guns were provided with 70% APC, the rest being an uncapped, base-fused shell with twice the weight of burster, which Campbell describes as semi-armour-piercing (SAP). In both types, the burster comprised TNT blocks, protected from impact by cardboard-disc separators and, in the head of the cavity, a wooden block and felt discs. The base fuses were delayed-action; against unarmoured targets, the SAP would burst 2–6 metres behind the impacted plate. Like the British AP shell, the German AP was of nickel steel and the nose was hardened, though not to the same extent so the case was less brittle; in both types, the nose was covered by a hollow mild-steel cap. In test firings, the German 11in AP penetrated 280mm

---

[128] Admiralty War Staff, Intelligence Division, *Germany. Results of Firing Practices, 1912–13*, December 1914, pp. 14–15, 24–7, 34–5 and 44–53, ADM 137/4799. *DGBJ*, pp. 223–4. Seligmann, 'German Preference', pp. 38–41 and 44.

[129] *German Tactical Orders. January 1915*, pp. 5–6 in 'German Fleet Orders'.

[130] *DGBJ*, p. 220. Dreyer, 'A Few Notes', (see note 16) f. 85.

[131] *GFBOs III*, VII.6: compare with Addendum No. 5, printed 12 September 1914 in *JP I*, p. 63.

(11in) of armour at 10,000 metres and 200mm (7.9in) at 12,000 metres; the 12in AP 345mm (13.6in) at 10,000 metres, 305mm (12in) at 12,000 metres.[132]

German RP C/12 propellant contained less nitroglycerine than cordite and it was better stabilised. Three quarters of a full charge remained in a brass cartridge case, the remainder in a silk bag; a single black-powder igniter was in the case underneath the charge. Yet, despite these apparent advantages compared with British charges, at the Dogger Bank *Seydlitz* suffered a very serious fire of no less than sixty-two full charges that burned out her two after turrets; on the other hand, the fire did not develop into an explosion.[133] Despite observing this catastrophe from a distance and some other indirect warnings, the Royal Navy remained largely indifferent to the dangers of fire and explosion in its turrets and cordite magazines.

Torpedoes

The principal torpedoes in use at the time of Jutland were the 21in British Mark II**** and the 50cm (19.7-in) German G7**. Both could be set for high-speed (HS) and long-range (LR) running, while some British ships had been issued with torpedoes having an extreme-range (ER) setting. The maximum running distances of these weapons at different settings are given in Table 2.3.[134]

If an attack on a single target was to succeed, the torpedo had to be fired on a collision course, i.e. on the course that enabled it to cross the target's course just as the target reached the crossing point. In the Royal Navy, torpedoes were aimed by a sighting instrument called a Torpedo Director, which, if set accurately for target course and speed, calculated the angle to aim off from the line-of-bearing to the target at the moment of firing. (The director was also set with the target range at the moment of firing in order to confirm that the torpedo

Table 2.3. *Torpedo characteristics*

Setting	British 21in Mark II****	German 50cm G7**
HS	4,200 yards at 44–45 knots	5,450 yards at 35 knots
LR	10,750 yards at 28–29 knots	10,950 yards at 28–28.5 knots
ER	c. 17,000 yards at 18 knots	

[132] Campbell, p. 345. Staff, *World War One*, pp. 17 and 208 (though impact angle and source unstated).
[133] Campbell, pp. 373–4 and 377–8.
[134] Campbell, p. 400. Only *Lützow* had the new 60cm H8 running to 15,300 yards at 30 knots: Staff, *1914–18*, p. 36.

could reach its target in less than its maximum running range.)[135] But a hit also depended on the target maintaining this same course and speed during the running time of the torpedo. Also, with the target bringing every gun to bear in order to break up an attack, the difficulties of both accurately estimating enemy course and speed and precisely aiming the torpedo were considerable. By 1916, the Royal Navy's view was that any hits on single ships at long range were merely flukes and that single ships should not be attacked at ranges greater than 1,500 yards; this was close enough to allow a substantial margin of error but such attacks were too dangerous except for submarines by day (unless the visibility was exceptionally bad) and for destroyers by night.[136]

Fortunately for the effectiveness of the torpedo as a weapon, its main use in a fleet action was for attacking not single ships but battle lines. During the day in adequate visibility, flotillas had to face a rapid and effective fire from the enemy line and, in such circumstances, were not expected to close within a gun range of less than 7,000 yards; thus their torpedoes had to be set for LR. If only to prevent wild shots, it was still worth aiming with the torpedo director at a selected target ship using the estimated course and speed of the enemy battle line. But the real object was to 'brown'[137] with torpedoes that part of the enemy line containing the nominal target; then the maximum probability of a hit was determined simply by the ratio of the average length of a ship to the distance between ships in the line. Heavy ships, about 600ft or one cable long, were spaced in close order at 2½ cables so this hit probability was 2:5 (40%).[138] However, this was attainable only if the ships in the line obligingly took no avoiding action when they sighted the approaching torpedoes (of which more below). Similar considerations applied to night attacks but flotillas could hope to approach to much shorter ranges before being illuminated by searchlights and coming under fire; thus they could set their torpedoes for HS running.

As well as last-minute manoeuvres to avoid torpedoes near the end of their runs, the ships of a battle line could turn away from attackers as soon as they launched their torpedoes; if the turns-away were bold enough, they could ensure that the torpedoes were evaded altogether.[139] To counter such turns, both the British and German navies preferred to fire torpedoes only if, assuming that the enemy held his course, the torpedoes reached his line after running no more than 75% of their maximum range, i.e. with a range

---

[135] www.dreadnoughtproject.org/tfs/index.php/Torpedo_Director. It has been assumed that the German Navy had instruments embodying the same principles.
[136] Admiralty, Gunnery Branch, *Handbook of Torpedo Control, 1916*, June 1917, ADM 186/381, pp. 82–3.
[137] *Fire into the brown*, let fly into a covey without singling out a bird. *Concise Oxford Dictionary*.
[138] *Torpedo Handbook 1916* (see note 136), pp. 83 and 86.
[139] To distinguish the two types of turn, those made as torpedoes were launched are here described as 'evading'; turns made as the torpedoes approached are termed 'avoiding'.

margin of at least 25%.[140] To preserve this margin while not closing to a gun range of less than 7,000 yards, it was necessary to fire from well ahead of the target; the *Handbook of Torpedo Control 1916* recommended that, for day-time attacks:

a position four points on the bow of the leading ship, or . . . that part of the line selected as the target, at a range of 7,000 yards with 10,000-yard torpedoes . . . may be taken as ideal . . . but on any bearings between three and six points on the enemy's bow, 25 per cent. inside the extreme firing range, are positions which give reasonable prospects of success, although the chances of the enemy avoiding the attack by an alteration of course away are increased as the range increases.[141]

This handbook was not issued until 1917 but the torpedo memorandum appended to the *GFBOs*, dated 1 May 1916, asked for a range margin of 30%–40% to allow for the enemy turning away and for attacks to be delivered from at least 30° before the beam of the leading enemy ship, i.e. from not more than about 5½ points on the enemy bow.[142]

These recommendations can be checked by calculations based on triangles of velocity; because they are directly applicable to the principal torpedo attack by German destroyers on the Grand Fleet at Jutland, these calculations have been based on the properties of the German torpedoes though, when set for LR, the performance of British torpedoes was very similar. If it is assumed that the attackers correctly estimated the target's course and speed (taken to be 17 knots), then the calculated range margin remained in excess of 25% even if the torpedoes were fired from a position as much as 8,700 yards distant, six points on the target's bow. However, the range margin diminished rapidly as the bearing of the firing position increased. If the attackers were directly on the target's beam (eight points on the bow), even if the firing range was reduced to 7,000 yards, the range margin was barely 20%.[143] And, if at this same firing range, the attacker was more than one point abaft the beam, the target was beyond the maximum running range of the torpedo. These results illustrate why a ship under attack turned away. To counter such evasive action, the attacker could adjust his aim on the assumption that the target would indeed turn away;[144] even so, the range margin was still reduced while, if the turn-away was large enough, the torpedo could run out of fuel before it reached the target.

So far, we have considered the simple case of a destroyer attack from well ahead on the enemy's leading ships, when the torpedo firing range and the range

---

[140] *Handbook 1916*, p. 85 (25%). *German Tactical Orders*, January 1915, p. 7 in ADM 186/17 (25%–30%).

[141] *Handbook 1916*, p. 85.

[142] *GFBOs III*, 'Attack Plans. General Remarks' with memorandum of 1 May 1916, ff. 341–2.

[143] The calculated values are rounded to the nearest 100 yards or compass point to avoid any impression that torpedoes could be aimed with precision.

[144] By altering the target course set on the Torpedo Director: *Handbook 1916*, pp. 84–5.

for defensive gun fire from the target were much the same. However, a less favourable situation for the attackers arose if, on approaching the enemy line, they found themselves already on the beam of the enemy's leading ships or even of ships further along the line. Thus the attackers were exposed to gunfire from these enemy ships at the shortest possible gun range, yet the attackers were poorly placed to make a torpedo attack on the very ships that could do them most damage by gunfire. In these circumstances, the attackers had two imperatives. The first was to ensure that they did not go too close to the ships from which they were on beam bearings. The British limit was not less than 7,000 yards; although an explicit figure has not been found in German sources, during their daylight torpedo attack at Jutland, their destroyers fired at ranges of 6,600–7,700 yards, so they seem to have adopted similar limits. Assuming a minimum perpendicular distance of 7,000 yards between the enemy line and its attackers, further calculation establishes that the attacks would be most effective if the target selected was a ship from which the attacking destroyer bore five points on the bow. This would maximise both the range margin and the amount of the turn-away that would be necessary to evade the torpedoes completely. In fact, the same five-point bearing was also optimal even if the perpendicular distance was greater, although beyond 8,200 yards, the range margin was less than 25%. In the limiting case, the perpendicular distance equalled the maximum torpedo running range. Then the torpedo had to be fired along the perpendicular; it could just reach a target that held its course, though with no range margin whatsoever. All these considerations also applied to torpedo fire between two battle lines on parallel courses; a firing ship would best select a target from which it bore five points on the bow, i.e. a target bearing three points abaft its own beam. But at expected ranges between capital ships, the range margins of LR torpedoes would have been small at best. Hence the need for ER torpedoes though, since they travelled so slowly, they were easier to avoid if they were sighted at the end of their run.

Attackers hoped that, by securing an adequate range margin, their torpedoes would reach the target ships even if the latter turned away. The object of each ship under attack was, if possible, to turn away far enough to evade all torpedoes, whatever the range margin. But it had to take account not only of torpedoes fired accurately at itself but of other torpedoes fired, accurately or not, at *any* ship in the line. If the turn-away was insufficient, there was always a possibility that, among the torpedoes fanning out from an attacking flotilla, there was one that would hit on the new course. To be safe, the turn-away had to be greater than that required to intercept any such torpedo just as it ran out of fuel; this ensured that the target ship passed ahead of all possible torpedoes before they stopped. This was not feasible if a daylight attack were pressed home to a suicidally short firing range – 4,400 yards or less for a German G7** set for LR. But if a flotilla closed to a perpendicular distance of not less than

7,000 yards from the enemy line, calculations establish that a turn-away of less than 3½ points was sufficient to evade all possible torpedoes. If the perpendicular distance was 8,000 yards, a turn-away of less than 2½ points was enough. (The same figures apply to torpedoes fired between two parallel battle lines.) Thus if flotillas fired their torpedoes from distances that gave them a reasonable prospect of survival, the ships under attack could be certain that, if their turns-away were bold enough, they could evade entirely the torpedoes fired at them; this was no small advantage. However, it must be emphasised that, once a ship had turned away, it had to hold its course for the running time of the attacking torpedoes (about 11½ minutes for the G7**). If it turned back too soon, it was once again in danger of crossing a torpedo track at the wrong moment.

If a daytime torpedo attack was to be evaded safely, the turn-away had to be made quickly, as soon as the attackers were seen to launch their torpedoes. For this purpose, the *GFBOs* defined a special use of the Preparative flag; when hoisted singly, it directed all the subdivisions of the battlefleet (of two ships in the normal daytime organisation) to turn away together by two points.[145] Also, two instruments were designed early in the War to make the necessary predictions without the need for calculations; an example of the 'Bunbury Enemy Torpedo Calculator' was under trial in *Iron Duke* at Jutland and was used during the battle.[146] This instrument embodied the same principles used in calculating the turns-away quoted above.

In daylight, ships under attack also had a chance of avoiding torpedoes when their tracks became visible in the last minutes of their run. The most dangerous were those that were converging at a constant relative bearing, a sure sign that they were on a collision course. If such a torpedo was approaching from a quarter, it was best to turn away onto a roughly similar course; otherwise to turn towards it so that it passed ahead. If the relative bearing was changing, it was advisable to turn such that this bearing changed more rapidly in the same sense. A counter to these avoiding turns was as recommended in Jellicoe's *GFBO* torpedo memorandum:

To increase the chance of hitting, the maximum number of torpedoes should be fired in attack, providing conditions are favourable.[147]

Then, while avoiding one torpedo, a ship was more likely to stray into the path of another.

A night torpedo attack with torpedoes on HS settings posed severe problems for both sides.[148] For the attackers, judging target course, speed and distance

---

[145] *GFBOs III*, IX: see further in Chapter 3.
[146] See www.dreadnoughtproject.org/tfs/index.php/Bunbury_Enemy_Torpedo_Calculator and www.dreadnoughtproject.org/tfs/index.php/Crace_Enemy_Torpedo_Calculator. *GF*, p. 229.
[147] 'Memorandum', 1 May 1916 (see note 142). *Handbook 1916*, p. 83.
[148] An attack in misty weather by day had many of the same difficulties.

would have been difficult, especially if they were illuminated by searchlights and subjected to intense fire from the secondary batteries of the enemy line; their best chance was a browning attack aimed at ships well away from either end of the line, the torpedoes to be fired from as close a range as possible. On the other side, the targets could see only those attackers that were actually illuminated by searchlights, so would find it hard to judge the moment when torpedoes were being fired and hence the timing and extent of turns-away. They also had little prospect of seeing any torpedoes as they approached. If British destroyers firing HS torpedoes could close to a firing range of 2,600 yards, their targets could not evade the torpedoes with certainty. But, at a firing range of 3,500 yards, they could do so by turning away at least 9 points from the line-of-bearing – though, for example, this would require an actual turn of 5 points if the attack was made from 4 points on the bow.[149] The *GFBOs* anticipated that, if attacked from ahead from one side, 'the enemy would turn in the direction to place the destroyers abaft the beam'.[150] The night attack plan therefore recommended that, if a flotilla was in a position to attack from ahead, its four divisions should divide into two groups to attack on both the port and starboard bows of the enemy van. Either the enemy would be forced to hold his course or his turn-away from one destroyer group would create better opportunities for the other.

---

[149] The calculations assume a German fleet speed of 16 knots.
[150] 'Attack Plans. General Remarks' (see note 142).

3   Orders for battle

By the time of Jutland, the *Grand Fleet Battle Orders* ran to some seventy-six pages containing thirty sections of text and diagrams and a few supplementary memoranda. For the first two weeks of the War, the Grand Fleet had operated under the orders issued to the Home Fleets by Jellicoe's predecessor as C-in-C, Admiral Sir George Callaghan, and, indeed, many of the *Home Fleet General Orders* remained in force long afterwards.[1] But, on 18 August, Jellicoe issued his first *GFBOs* and these were followed by five further addenda, the printed version of No. 5 being dated 12 September 1914.[2] Thereafter, new and amended battle orders and addenda continued to flow from the flagship, although some orders remained little changed even on the eve of the battle. In his post-war memoir, Jellicoe confirmed that he had modelled the early *GFBOs* on the 'War Orders' that he had written in 1912 when in command of the 2nd Division of the Home Fleet. And he revealed much of his character as a commander in declaring his intention that, in his battle orders,

The tactics to be pursued by the different units of the Fleet in action under all conceivable conditions were provided for as far as possible.[3]

This chapter will examine the key expectations and concerns which shaped the development of the *GFBOs* between August 1914 and May 1916. It will consider Jellicoe's profound concerns about the several distinct threats posed by torpedoes and mines, as well as the limited scope he allowed his squadron commanders for independent action. It will also explore how far Beatty's *Battle Cruiser Orders* (*BCOs*) differed in spirit and substance from the *GFBOs*. And, lastly, it will describe how the *GFBOs* reveal the nature of the distinct phases of the battle that Jellicoe expected to fight and the roles in battle of the different classes of ships that came under his command.

---

[1] Home Fleet General Orders . . . 15 May 1914 . . . to 1 October 1916, ADM 137/260.
[2] *GFBOs I, e*xcerpts in *JP I*, pp. 52–63.   [3] *GF*, p. 43.

Underwater threats

From the first weeks of his appointment as C-in-C, Jellicoe was preoccupied with threats from underwater weapons, though initially he was principally concerned that, in a fleet action, the Germans would drop mines and mount massed destroyer attacks. He anticipated that, if he deployed first, the Germans might then deploy onto an opposite course. His intended response to this move changed during August 1914 as his conviction deepened that the Germans might lay mines in their wake. At first, he was prepared to allow the flag officer leading the British line to follow round the enemy rear, provided he exercised great caution. But, by the end of the month, Jellicoe has concluded that:

I have every reason to suppose that the Germans will make use of mines if they can do so ... I am consequently averse to crossing their track.

Thus, if the Germans turned onto an opposite course, he intended the fleet to turn quickly by divisions onto the same course, the predreadnoughts of the 3BS keeping out of the way as the dreadnoughts passed on the engaged side, then falling in again at the rear. The vice-admiral commanding the van of the original deployment was not allowed to circle the enemy rear without orders or even to turn inwards by more than two points.[4]

GFBOs issued in December 1914 and February 1915 warned that, when chased, 'German men-of-war drop mines astern. This actually occurred when "Breslau" was being chased by "Gloucester"', that is, during the pursuit of the Goeben. In fact, although Breslau (of the Magdeburg class and so equipped for minelaying) 'kept crossing the Gloucester's course as though to drop mines ... Captain Kelly did not flinch [and] steamed on undisturbed'. The same orders also referred to confidential intelligence 'that the Germans have practiced [sic] a tactical retreat with the object of drawing an enemy across mines laid by destroyers, as well as across a line of submarines'.[5] Yet these expectations were not borne out in the Battle of the Dogger Bank. When the M-class destroyers were ordered forward to report the retreating enemy, Meteor's captain observed the German destroyers 'as closely as possible to see whether they were dropping mines. I could see no splashes'.[6] Furthermore, the German Destroyer Tactics (also translated and circulated in January 1915) left no doubt of the German reluctance to burden their destroyers with mines in action.

---

[4] JP I, pp. 57 and 63. GFBOs I, 14 (18 August 1914); Add. 2 (31 August 1914) sect. IV and Add. 5, pars. 7–9 and 13B (12 September 1914).

[5] GFBO, XIX (6 December 1914), ADM 137/288. GFBOs I, XII (23 February 1915). Corbett I, p. 66.

[6] [Report of] Action ... 24 January 1915, p. 17, ADM 137/1943.

Destroyers employed in mining operations are greatly prejudiced in their use as destroyers during the period they are equipped with mines. They should therefore only be employed in mining operations in exceptional circumstances.[7]

The Jutland *GFBOs* accepted that it was fairly certain that Germans would not lay mines from 'ships which are intended to take part in a gun action unless they can be laid from such ships before they come under fire'. Yet the same section continued to prohibit circling the enemy's rear.

The menace of mines dropped from fighting ships is minimised by avoiding the waters passed over by such vessels. For this reason it would be unwise to circle the rear of the enemy's Battlefleet should deployment take place on opposite courses ... the Vice-Admiral at our van is not to circle the enemy's rear unless directed to do so.[8] (Emphasis in original)

In his 1912 'War Orders and Dispositions' for the 2nd Division of the Home Fleet, Jellicoe had insisted that the priority of destroyers with the fleet was to attack the enemy line with torpedoes, while the accompanying light cruisers were to prevent the attack of the enemy's torpedo craft on the British battle line.[9] But, when he took over the command of the Grand Fleet, apart from the four small light cruisers attached to the battle squadrons as repeating ships (*Boadicea* and her sisters), the Grand Fleet possessed only the four 6in-gunned ships of the 1st Light Cruiser Squadron (1LCS), strengthened by *Falmouth* and *Liverpool*.[10] In accordance with the War Plans, only two flotillas, the 2DF and 4DF, were attached to the Grand Fleet; the 1DF and 3DF of, respectively, the *Acheron* and *Laforey* classes, were based at Harwich.[11] Although the Admiralty assured Jellicoe: 'You may rely on having the Harwich Flotillas with you before fleets meet', Addendum 2 (31 August) to the *GFBOs* reversed the offensive priorities that he had laid down in 1912.

It is probable that the German battlefleet will be accompanied by large numbers of destroyers [which] we may expect ... to attack immediately an opportunity occurs.
It is impressed on all destroyer officers that their primary duty is to stop the German destroyers by engaging them in close action.[12]

This acceptance that destroyers must act defensively was probably unavoidable. Given the Royal Navy's global commitments at the beginning of the war, Jellicoe had no immediate prospect of acquiring more light cruisers, while Addendum 4 (4 September) establishes that he expected the 1LCS to be fully occupied, in company with the battlecruisers, in dealing with German cruisers.[13]

[7] *Destroyer Tactics, January 1915*, p. 59 in 'German Fleet Orders', ADM 186/17.
[8] *GFBOs III*, VII.13 (December 1915).   [9] Brooks, 'Battle-Fleet Tactics', p. 193. *JP I*, p. 25.
[10] *GF*, pp. 19, 24 and 70–1. *GFBOs I*, 15 (18 August 1914).
[11] *GF*, pp. 19–20. Goldrick, p. 28.   [12] *JP I*, pp. 51–2 and 60.
[13] *GFBOs I*, Add. 4, 'Duties of Cruisers', 3 (4 September 1914). *JP I*, pp. 64–5. See further Brooks, 'Battle-Fleet Tactics', pp. 200–1.

Traps

Another pressing problem for Jellicoe was how to avoid submarine and mine traps prepared by the enemy. His apprehensions about underwater attacks were soon reinforced by the sinking off Harwich of the three elderly armoured cruisers *Aboukir, Hogue* and *Cressy* on 22 September 1914. Then, on 15 October, the Grand Fleet lost the protected cruiser *Hawke*, torpedoed by the same U-boat, *U9*, while reports of submarines near an entrance to Scapa Flow, or even inside, convinced the C-in-C that he must seek a temporary base to the west. Unfortunately, his move was observed by another U-boat; its report enabled the Germans to lay the minefield that claimed the new battleship *Audacious* on 27 October.[14] Three days later, he wrote to the Admiralty:

The Germans have shown that they rely to a very great extent on submarines, mines and torpedoes, and there can be no doubt whatever that they will endeavour to make the fullest use of these weapons in a fleet action ... it is evident that the Germans cannot rely ... upon having their full complement of submarines and minelayers present ... unless the battle is fought in waters selected by them and in the Southern area of the North Sea ... My object will therefore be to fight the fleet action in the Northern portion of the North Sea.[15]

Thereafter, he remained averse to venturing into the Heligoland Bight. He feared that the 'submarine menace both before action, during passage south, and during action will be our great trouble' and that 'sooner or later we shall be lured out over a trap of mines or submarines'. He was all too aware of the strategic consequences should he make a mistake.

It only requires the fleet to be inadvertently taken over one minefield for a reversal to take place in the relative strength of the British and German fleets. The existence of the Empire is at once in the most immediate and grave danger.

He was worried that the Germans would use their battlecruisers to decoy the BCF well down into the Heligoland Bight. There, especially, he expected them to prepare submarines and mine traps; consequently, he would be obliged, despite loss of time, to manoeuvre them off their chosen ground. He also expected that, close to their bases, the Germans would send out 'an immense force of destroyers', much greater than his own; presumably, he expected them to make use of their many older boats that were best suited to coastal waters. And his operations would be curtailed by the endurance of his own destroyers, which prevented the fleet from keeping at sea for more than about 2½ days.[16] In 1916, the Admiralty urged Jellicoe to adopt a more active policy of heavily supported air raids on the German coast (of which more in the next chapter). But, in a private letter to Beatty of 11 April, the C-in-C declared that

---

[14] *GF*, Chapters IV and V. Goldrick, pp. 126–32 and 138–41.   [15] *JP I*, p. 75.
[16] Correspondence from March 1915 to April 1916 in *JP I*, pp. 152, 165, 168, 175–6, 202 and 233.

our policy should be to engage them *not* in a position close to their minefields, and therefore close to their SM, TBD and aircraft bases, but to accept the position that we must wait until they give us the chance in a favourable position.

And, in a memorandum to the First Sea Lord, Admiral Sir Henry Jackson, Jellicoe warned:

So long as the High Seas Fleet is confined to its harbours ... it is not ... wise to risk unduly the heavy ships of the Grand Fleet, particularly if the risks come, not from the High Seas Fleet itself, but from such attributes [*sic*] as mines and submarines ... any real disaster to our heavy ships lays the country open to invasion and also gives the enemy the opportunity of passing commerce destroyers out of the North Sea.[17]

As well as worrying about the risk of the Grand Fleet straying across a prepared minefield or line of submarines, Jellicoe was also exercised about the Germans laying traps in a fleet action. In Addendum 2 to the early *GFBOs* (dated 31 August 1914) he warned the Fleet: 'It is probable that the German battlefleet will be accompanied by large numbers of destroyers, many of which will carry a few mines, and possibly minelayers and submarines too.' In his important letter to the Admiralty of 30 October, what had seemed probable was assumed as certain.

If ... the enemy battlefleet were to turn away from the advancing Fleet, I should assume that the intention was to lead us over mines and submarines, and should decline to be so drawn.

His proposed safeguard would 'consist in moving the battlefleet at very high speed to a flank before deployment takes place or the gun action commences': though he also added that 'I should feel that after an interval of high speed manoeuvring I could safely close'. He directed Their Lordships' attention 'to the alteration of pre-conceived ideas on battle tactics which are forced upon us by the anticipated appearance in a fleet action of submarines and minelayers'. On 1 November, the Secretary of the Admiralty informed him that 'My Lords ... approve your views and desire to assure you of their full confidence in your contemplated conduct'.[18] (Jellicoe would make specific reference to this correspondence in his secret despatch after the Battle of Jutland.)

Not everyone in the Admiralty agreed with Jellicoe. In commenting on the C-in-C's letter, Sir Arthur Wilson saw 'great practical difficulties in bringing submarines into effective action ... They may accompany the fleet on the surface until the enemy is sighted, but they must dive before they come under fire, and then they will almost certainly be left behind.'[19] Nonetheless, a fear of

[17] *BP I*, pp. 302–3. *JP I*, p. 232. [18] *JP I*, pp. 60, 75–7 and 79.
[19] Wilson, 'Remarks on ... letter of 30th October, 1914', 22 November 1914, f. 143, ADM 137/995.

submarines accompanying German surface vessels was prevalent from the beginning of the War. At the Battle of the Heligoland Bight (28 August), on three occasions Beatty's ships took avoiding action following unconfirmed submarine sightings, in one case of three boats attacking together.[20] Beatty claimed that, near the end of the Dogger Bank action, he had personally sighted a periscope and that his eight-point turn was made to avoid mines that might be dropped by Hipper's destroyers; yet the Admiralty knew that there were no submarines in the vicinity,[21] while, as we have seen, there were no indications that any German ships dropped mines. Nonetheless, when amended *GFBOs* were issued in March 1915, they gave the vice-admiral in the van full discretion to act should submarine or destroyer attacks be mounted from the enemy van or from ahead or should there be any threat of minelaying ahead of the British line.[22] And, as already noted, these orders also anticipated that the Germans might make a tactical retreat in order to draw the British fleet over mines laid by destroyers or across a line of submarines.

The dangers posed by submarines and minelaying became the principal preoccupation of the tactical exercises held during 1915, and also of a war game played out aboard *Benbow*, under the direction of Vice-Admiral Sir Doveton Sturdee, in June of that year. The game assumed a German fleet of three battle squadrons and five scouting groups, accompanied by five mine-layers of the *Niobe* class[23] and ten destroyer flotillas, with eighteen submarines on the flanks advancing at fleet speed; as in subsequent exercises, it was assumed that they could make 16 knots on the surface.[24] The slow 21.5-knot German minelayers did not influence the course of the action while, when the German forces retired, mines laid by destroyers were avoided by the pursuing British battlecruisers. After the game, Jellicoe, probably with the German *Destroyer Tactics* in mind, questioned whether their destroyers carrying mines would risk coming under gunfire. German destroyer attacks were also considered to have been countered successfully by British destroyers (60 in all) and light cruisers. The German submarines proved a greater threat, being credited with sinking three armoured cruisers on the approach and a battleship on deployment. Further British losses were avoided by the

[20] *BP I*, pp. 123, 125 and 130–1.

[21] Naval Staff Monograph, *Dogger Bank*, p. 215 n. 9, ADM 186/610.

[22] *GFBOs I*, VI.7 (12 March 1915).

[23] The British intelligence returns overstated the number of older German light cruisers that had been converted to minelaying – of the *Gazelle* class, which included *Niobe*, only *Arcona* was so equipped. *Cf.* Admiralty War Staff, Intelligence Division, *Quarterly Return, October 1915*, pp. 106–7, ADM 186/15 and Gröner I, p. 101.

[24] 'Tactical Fleet Exercises … 1915-16', ff. 92, 146 and 157, ADM 137/1958. The *Quarterly Return* (pp. 118–19) gave the approximate speeds of *U21-U35* as 17–18 knots surfaced, 11–12 knots submerged; the actual speeds were 15.4–16.7 knots and 9.5–10.3 knots, respectively (Gröner I, pp. 4 and 6).

battleships running over two other groups of submarines. Jellicoe's narrative of the game was almost entirely concerned with the early phases of the action and the problems posed by the submarines and destroyers and, once the two fleets had opened fire on parallel courses, the exercise was concluded.[25]

The same preoccupation with the manoeuvring phase of battle and the threats from underwater weapons is found in the conduct of the fleet tactical exercises held at sea during 1915. The series began in March, while in June, the squadrons representing the High Seas Fleet were ordered to close the range and then turn away to create the opportunity for a destroyer attack and to lure the British over a minefield. However, in his remarks on the exercise, Jellicoe acknowledged the 'difficulty of laying mines ahead of the fleet', though he also warned that the German battlefleet might deploy away from Heligoland 'to afford minelayers and submarines an opportunity for getting into position unobserved, turning later so as to draw the British fleet over the mines or submarines'.[26] The next major exercise took place on 3 September, the German fleet being instructed to refuse action, with the object of attacking with submarines, destroyers or mines. However, the deployment was at only 12,000 yards, after which both fleets made two sixteen-point turns. Jellicoe concluded that the risk of attack by submarines with the enemy fleet was greatly increased when a deployment at less than 18,000 yards was followed by closing courses in the next hour.[27]

In the exercise on 3 November, the German fleet was supposed to be accompanied by six submarines in two groups on the beam and ahead; those ahead reached a position to attack but only because the speed of the British fleet was just 13½ knots.[28] The exercise of 2 December returned once more to the problem of a German fleet attempting to draw the British over a submarine and mine trap. The former's cruisers laid a minefield astern, while eight submarines were imagined in its vicinity. However, the British sighted the minelayers, avoided the minefield and did not follow when the Germans turned away. Also, owing to the differences in reckoning, the position of the minefield could not be plotted with sufficient certainty to assess its effect. The exercise ended with a German attack as an exercise in fire control but, as previously, Jellicoe's remarks drew no tactical lessons on how an enemy might be defeated by gunfire.[29]

Thus the experience gained in 1915 did little to substantiate concerns about the tactical use of mines and submarines by the Germans. In the June war game, submarines were judged to have made effective attacks. But, in actual exercises

[25] 'Tactical Exercises' (see note 24), ff. 45–6, 56–61 and 64.
[26] 'Tactical Exercises', ff. 8–10 and 28 and 39. *GF*, pp. 137 and 146.
[27] 'Tactical Exercises', ff. 92 and 111–12. *GF*, pp. 150 and 158.
[28] 'Tactical Exercises', ff. 118–19, 140–1 and 146. *GF*, pp. 161 and 163.
[29] 'Tactical Exercises', ff. 155, 157, 170 and 186–91. *GF*, pp. 165–6.

at sea, even though the submarines were imaginary, they were only successful in favourable circumstances. The exercises also demonstrated the difficulties of tactical minelaying ahead and of setting traps with mines and submarines when retreating. Jellicoe himself recognised 'the danger one runs by laying a minefield in action or just before it',[30] and also that the German destroyers carrying mines (he could have included the light cruisers as well) would avoid a gun action. And yet, when revised *GFBOs* were issued in December 1915 and January 1916, they still warned that:

> The possibility of the enemy having prepared a submarine or mine area with intention to manoeuvre us over it must always be present to the mind of the Commander-in-Chief and may largely influence his tactics.

Also that the Germans would almost certainly attempt to use submarines in a fleet action 'if our fleet can be made to conform to their plan'.[31] It seems that the previous year's work had done nothing to lessen Jellicoe's apprehensions.

> Exercises at sea and exercises on the Tactical Board shew that one of the most difficult movements to counter on the part of the enemy is a 'turn away' of his line of battle, either in succession or otherwise. The effect of such a turn (which may be for the purpose of drawing our fleet over mines or submarines) is obviously to place us in a position of decided disadvantage as regards attacks by torpedoes fired either from ships or destroyers ... It may be expected that I shall not follow a decided turn of this nature shortly after deployment.[32]

It is difficult to explain why British commanders were so certain that the Germans would use mines and submarines in a fleet action. While the losses of *Audacious* to a mine and of three armoured cruisers to a single submarine had been alarming demonstrations of the potency of underwater weapons, they had not happened in battle. Captured documents and other intelligence provided no explicit indications that these weapons would be employed in action. The intelligence returns on German light cruisers and destroyers, though vague on details, did report that many of these vessels were fitted for minelaying but Jellicoe himself appreciated the dangers of carrying mines under fire. The highest surface speed attributed to German submarines was equal to the maximum speed of the predreadnoughts that were, necessarily, part of the German battlefleet. Thus in calm weather the surfaced submarines might have been able to keep up with the fleet at its normal cruising speed: but, in most sea states, they would have slowed up the whole force. Furthermore, once the submarines had dived to reach attacking positions ahead, they would have been in considerable danger of being run down by their own surface ships as the fleet deployed.

---

[30] *JP I*, p. 191.   [31] *GFBOs III*, XXIV.3–4 (January 1916).
[32] *GFBOs III*, VII.8–9 (December 1915).

Apprehensions in the Grand Fleet may well have been heightened for the very reason that they were not based on experience. The first minelayer suitable for working with the fleet was the *Abdiel*, a converted flotilla leader that was completed only in March 1916.[33] In 1915, both Jellicoe and Beatty pressed for a submarine flotilla to be placed under the C-in-C's direct command. In November 1915, the Admiralty agreed to the establishment of the 11th Submarine Flotilla (11SF) at Blyth in Northumberland.[34] Jellicoe intended that its boats would be able to join the Grand Fleet prior to a fleet action in the middle or southern parts of the North Sea. Yet Jellicoe's own estimate of the sea-going speed of the available submarines did not exceed 12 knots (he did not expect even the new 19½-knot *J*-class, then building, to make more than 16 knots); the *GFBO* for the 11SF gave no guidance as to how the submarines could keep position between joining the fleet and encountering the enemy.[35]

Thus, from Jellicoe down, Grand Fleet commanders had no practical experience of working submarines with the battlefleet and very little of minelayers. Also, none of them had served in such vessels themselves. Some, like Sturdee, had begun their careers in torpedo boats,[36] which might have helped in appreciating the practicalities of minelaying, but the submarine service was too new for most senior commanders to have formed a realistic view of its capabilities and limitations. Such unfamiliarity probably lay behind the tendency to underestimate the real problems with these weapons systems, which then led to an unwarranted dread of their perceived ability to strike from the depths without warning and with devastating effect.

Destroyer torpedo attacks

As the winter of 1914 approached, Jellicoe's concerns about numbers increased further. Having been ordered to detach eight of his boats to join the 3rd Battle Squadron at Rosyth, on 4 December he warned the Admiralty that he could not count on having more than thirty-two destroyers with the Grand Fleet and that, without enough destroyers and light cruisers to counter a German attack, 'the only course left to me is the objectionable and difficult one of turning the battle fleet away when the attack takes place'.[37] This intention was soon provided for by the introduction of special signals in the *GFBOs*. By December 1914, the 'Preparative' flag, when hoisted singly, signified that the whole battlefleet should turn away together in subdivisions by two points; the manoeuvre was to be repeated each time the signal was made. At first, this signal was to be obeyed as soon as seen, but, by December 1915, when hauled

---

[33] *CAWFS 1906–21*, p. 77.   [34] *FDSF III*, pp. 7–8. *JP I*, p. 179.
[35] *GFBOs III*, XXVI (10 March 1916). *CAWFS 1906–21*, pp. 90–1.
[36] *ODNB*, 'Sturdee, Doveton'.
[37] *JP I*, pp. 93–4 and 102. See also Brooks, 'Battle-Fleet Tactics', pp. 201–2 and *FDSF II*, p. 154.

down. 'Leading Ship of Subdivisions should sound their syrens [*sic*] as they turn.'[38]

As the numbers of light cruisers and destroyers in the Grand Fleet increased during 1915, Beatty felt able to revert to the views on destroyer priorities that he had first expressed forcibly in 1913. In August, he wrote to Jellicoe: 'I am a very firm believer in getting our T.B.D. attack with the *torpedo* in first, which would place them admirably for frustrating a counter attack of enemy craft.' The same offensive spirit also appeared in a letter to Beatty from Rear-Admiral Horace Hood, commander of the 3rd Battle Cruiser Squadron, which the former recommended to the Commander-in-Chief. But Jellicoe would not accept its arguments 'for the reason that I consider the German Fleet will be in great numerical preponderance in destroyers (probably at least double our number) whilst ship for ship, the German destroyers carry nearly twice as many torpedoes as are carried by our own vessels'. Thus the Destroyer Addendum of October 1915 continued to emphasise that the primary duty of the destroyers was 'to stop the German destroyers by engaging them in close action' and it even repeated Jellicoe's fear that, in destroyers, 'the German preponderance may be as great as two to one'. But after it was issued, Jellicoe did concede that, if the 10DF of *M*-class destroyers were working with the BCF in the van, they should make an early attack on the head of the enemy line.[39]

In January 1916, somewhat amended 'Destroyer Instructions' were incorporated in the main text of the *GFBOs* and remained in force at Jutland. The warning that German destroyers might outnumber the British by two-to-one was omitted. If the British battlecruisers and cruisers were in a commanding position to prevent a German destroyer attack on the British van, the destroyers stationed there were permitted to mount a torpedo attack with cruiser support. However, the principal instructions remained essentially defensive.

Unless the conditions are clearly very favourable and enable our light-cruisers to deal effectually with the German destroyers, it is impressed on all destroyer officers that their primary duty is to stop the German destroyers[,] engaging them in close action before they can fire their torpedoes, and that torpedo attack on the German battlefleet is secondary to gun attack on their destroyers.

The next-but-one paragraph gave some encouragement to offensive action.

It must, however, be understood that our flotillas are not to miss a favourable opportunity for successful attack on the enemy's battlefleet, particularly on the ships of the 'Dreadnought' type.

---

[38] *GFBOs I*, XVII (21 November 1914, 6 December 1914 and 23 February 1915), X (23 March 1915) and *GFBOs III*, IX (December 1915). For turns other than two points, numeral flags were hoisted inferior. Quote from *GSB 1915*, p. 20.

[39] *JP I*, p. 178. Brooks, 'Battle-Fleet Tactics', pp. 196–7 and 203–4 citing 'Tactical Questions', ff. 20–8, ADM 137/1966. *GFBOs III*, 'Destroyer Addendum', II.4–5 (1 October 1915).

But such opportunities were to be taken only under cover of low visibility, without risk of heavy losses, with certainty that the torpedoes would cross the enemy's track, and provided that an attack would not create an opening for the enemy's destroyers to counterattack.[40] With so many qualifications, these new instructions probably did little to change the defensive habits of mind which had been instilled in British destroyer commanders since the first weeks of the War. As new flotillas were being created, in April 1916 the Grand Fleet's destroyers were reorganised under the newly appointed Commodore (F) James Hawksley with his broad pendant in *Castor*, although he still retained his previous responsibilities as Captain (D) of the 11DF. Thus he had no time before the Battle of Jutland to exercise his new command or, even if he had been so minded, to develop more offensive tactics.[41]

Jellicoe and command

During August and September 1914, while anti-submarine and other defences were being belatedly prepared for the main fleet bases of Scapa Flow, Cromarty and Rosyth, the Grand Fleet was continually at sea. This gave Jellicoe opportunities for regular exercises in battle tactics, including deployment into line of battle. In his fifth addendum to the early *GFBOs*, he concluded that:

As the result of the experience gained recently in handling large fleets, [the] Commander-in-Chief cannot be certain of controlling the movements of even 20 ships under conditions of fast steaming with much funnel smoke; with the noise of battle and smoke of bursting shell added, the practicality of exercising general control will be still further reduced.

But, while granting discretionary powers to his vice-admirals to manoeuvre their squadrons independently, Jellicoe also insisted that the battlefleet should keep together and conform to his movements.[42] These conflicting intentions remained in the Jutland *GFBOs*.

The Commander-in-Chief controls the whole Battlefleet *before* deployment and *on* deployment except in the case of low visibility [when the line of battle would be formed immediately, usually on the wing column nearest the enemy]. He cannot be certain, *after* deployment, of being able to control the movements of three battle squadrons ...

It therefore becomes necessary to decentralise command to the fullest extent possible, and the Vice-Admirals commanding squadrons have discretionary power to manoeuvre the divisions independently whilst conforming generally to the movements of the Commander-in-Chief and complying to his known intentions ...

---

[40] *GFBOs III*, XXX.1–4 (January 1916) with original underlining.
[41] Corbett, pp. 318–19. www.dreadnoughtproject.org/tfs/index.php/James_Rose_Price_Hawksley.
[42] *GF*, Chapters IV and V. *GFBOs I*, Add. 5, 2–5 in *JP I*, pp. 61–2.

In all cases the ruling principle is that the *'Dreadnought'* fleet as a whole keeps together, attempted isolated attacks on a portion of the enemy line being avoided as liable to lead to the isolation of that division which attempts the movement and so long as the fleets are engaged on approximately similar courses, the squadrons should form one line of battle.

... The Fleet is to be guided generally by the movements of the division led by the Commander-in-Chief, which ... must therefore be very carefully watched ... Signals may either be indistinguishable or they may take too long to get through a large fleet. This does not mean that they will not be made, but the movement signalled may be commenced before the executive is given. It is hoped that difficulties in signalling will be largely overcome by the use of wireless telegraphy.[43] (Emphasis in original)

Thus Jellicoe hoped that W/T would allow him to continue controlling the whole battlefleet, while his insistence that it should keep together in one line of battle left his vice-admirals precious little scope for exercising their 'discretionary powers of manoeuvre'. Since 1910, action signal 13 had been available to order that: 'As soon as fire is opened, the Senior Officers of Divisions will take charge of their divisions and act independently in accordance with Admiral's instructions';[44] however, the *GFBOs* provide no hint of any circumstances in which Jellicoe might have let his divisional (or squadron) commanders off the leash by making this signal.

The Jutland *GFBOs*, while recognising that initially the fleets might deploy in opposite directions, continued to forbid the vice-admiral at the van from circling the enemy rear without an explicit order. Action signals 02 and 21 were redefined (see below) for turning the divisions of fleet in rapid succession onto the same course as the enemy, thus restoring the tactical situation to that assumed everywhere else in the *GFBOs*. Jellicoe declared:

Action on approximately similar courses will be one of the underlying objects of my tactics [b]ecause it is the form of action likely to give decisive results.

Once the battlefleets were engaged:

Until the enemy is beaten by gunfire, it is ... my intention to keep outside torpedo range of the enemy's battle line ... with the two vans approximately abeam and the fleets on parallel courses, our van could afford to be at a shorter range than our rear ... with a view to obtaining decisive results with gunfire and for the purpose of firing their torpedoes, but not being followed to that close range by our centre or rear.

This was the only passage that discussed how an action might develop – except that the van squadron was required to repel attacks from ahead by destroyers or submarines or take action against minelaying ahead of the line, while the vice-admiral commanding the rear squadron was expected to deal with a German

---

[43] *GFBOs III*, VII.1–4 (December 1915) – extracts from the Jutland *GFBOs* in *JP I*, pp. 243–53.
[44] *GFBOs III*, XII.1 (December 1915). *GSB 1915*, p. 59.

divisional attack on his part of the line.[45] There were no instructions for different tactical situations that might arise after the lines had been formed – an obvious case being that in which one side crossed the 'T' of the other. Thus, even if Jellicoe achieved this tactical ideal, his divisional admirals had no guidance on how to exploit the opportunity; perhaps he thought it too unlikely to be worth detailed consideration.

Apart from the provisions for the whole fleet to reduce the range gradually to 10,000 yards and for the van to edge inwards to a closer range still, the battle orders say nothing more on how a decisive victory might be won. Jellicoe's orders for the selection of targets read:

The two main principles to remember are:

(i) No ship of the enemy in a position to inflict damage should be unfired at.
(ii) Fire at your opposite number.

In discussing concentration, the *GFBOs* recommended that concentration in pairs gave the best results. But the only detailed example of fire distribution assumed that, while the Germans would be in full strength, the Grand Fleet would be short of two *Queen Elizabeths* and three dreadnoughts,[46] that is, it would have one ship fewer than its opponent at full strength. Thus, although Jellicoe acknowledged his superiority in the power of individual ships and the number of dreadnoughts, his orders contain no guidance on how to achieve a decisive concentration of fire on a part of the enemy line. Apparently, Jellicoe just assumed that the Germans would be willing to fight it out broadside to broadside until overwhelmed by the heavier fire from the British line. He provided no guidance to his commanders on how to act should the Germans decline to be so obliging. Having declared that he would control the whole fleet both before and during deployment, he alone assumed the responsibility for preventing a reluctant German fleet from evading action. But, even if he succeeded, the Germans might later, under a heavy, long-range fire, seek to break off the action by turning away. But then Jellicoe's main concern was not how to make the most of the superiority he had won, but how to avoid the perceived dangers from mine and torpedo attacks that he expected would cover the German withdrawal. It is no exaggeration to state that his battle orders were not principally about securing victory with his preferred weapon, the heavy gun: but about avoiding serious losses from the underwater weapons that caused him so many apprehensions.

In March 1916, the battlefleet's own fast division, the 5BS, reached its full strength of five *Queen Elizabeth*-class battleships.[47] Yet this powerful force was given only limited scope for independent action, though it is unlikely that its Rear-Admiral Commanding, Hugh Evan-Thomas, would have kicked

[45] *GFBOs III*, VII.12–15 (December 1915).   [46] *GFBOs III*, VII.15, XV.1, 6 and 9.
[47] *CAWFS 1906–21*, pp. 33–4.

against such restrictions. He had served with Jellicoe as a young officer and remained a close personal friend and admirer. And in 1917 Herbert Richmond found that Evan-Thomas was no supporter of divided tactics.

He takes the view that any separation [of the line] is dangerous because an analysis of the P.Z.s [tactical exercises] done during the time experiments were made shows that for *once* that the squadronal attack succeeded, it was beaten five or so times.[48]

In cruising dispositions, the 5BS was positioned well ahead of the battlefleet but, on encountering the enemy, Evan-Thomas was expected to rejoin the battlefleet in a position that, if practicable, Jellicoe would himself order – either at the van or rear of the battle line or as a fast division some four or five miles ahead. Yet RAC 5BS was given little guidance on how a fast division should proceed. The only identified opportunity was if both the British and German battlecruisers were absent, when the 5BS was to seek a commanding position from which to attack the enemy van and to support attacks by British armoured and light cruisers and destroyers. Otherwise, if in the van or rear, the 5BS was little more than an extension of the main battle line – unless ordered otherwise, they were a part of the battle line for purposes of fire distribution.[49]

In contrast to the detailed orders to Evan-Thomas, Jellicoe allowed Beatty, as vice-admiral commanding the BCF (VAC BCF), to 'act as he considers necessary' in carrying out his general instructions. Prior to meeting the enemy, the BCF's battlecruisers and light cruisers were to drive in the enemy's light forces. Then, the battlecruisers' primary function was the destruction of the enemy battlecruisers – unless the latter were absent or had already been destroyed, when the BCF was to serve as a fast division of the battlefleet.[50] Yet cooperation with the 5BS, especially when it too was acting as a fast division, was not mentioned. One is left with the impression that, on the eve of Jutland, Jellicoe and his staff had still not decided how to employ their most powerful battleships to battle-winning effect (as we shall see, in the battle itself the problem had been taken out of their hands).

While VAC BCF and, to a lesser extent, RAC 5BS were authorised to manoeuvre their squadrons independently, the freedom of action of the vice-admirals commanding the squadrons in the battle line proper was, in practice, much more restricted. These restraints were in part a reflection of Jellicoe's

---

[48] Gordon, pp. 39–40. Marder, *Portrait*, pp. 262–3. The experiments were conducted by Admiral Sir William May when C-in-C, Home Fleets, 1909–11 and described in his *Notes on Tactical Exercises. Home Fleet. 1909–1911*, pp. 19–20, 240 and 441–2, Eb012, AL. Of twelve exercises described on pp. 266–328 (Exercises I–VIII) and 362–410 (Exercises XI–XIV), only four divisional attacks were judged to have fired as many rounds or a greater number of rounds as their opponents in single line. This albeit simple measure suggested that, in practice, divided attack did not often realise its theoretical advantages.

[49] *GFBOs III*, V.1–5 and 9 and XV.5(a) (December 1915).

[50] *GFBOs III*, XXIV.6–7 (January 1916).

inherent centralising instincts; Rear-Admiral Duff of the 4BS agreed with Sturdee's predecessor[51] that 'the Fleet is very badly run. The Staff in the *Iron Duke* is far too large, which prevents decentralisation, and takes all initiative and authority out of the hands of the Vice Admirals.'[52] However, another factor was that Jellicoe had serious reservations about the abilities of these same vice-admirals, who by the end of 1915 were Sir Cecil Burney (1BS), Sir Martyn Jerram[53] (2BS) and Sir Doveton Sturdee (4BS).

Burney, who was also second-in-command of the Grand Fleet, and Jellicoe were old friends from their days as midshipmen and were part of the 'Malta clique' that surrounded Admiral Sir Michael Culme-Seymour. Burney had a good record as a commander of squadrons and fleets,[54] though Fisher damned him as 'lachrymose' and 'dismal' and declared to Jellicoe 'I don't understand how you all value him'. After he had been six months with the Grand Fleet, Jellicoe still considered Burney 'first-rate', not least as a handler of fleets, when in good health. But he was often ill, which made him depressed, pessimistic and overcautious. Yet Jellicoe thought these traits were no bad thing.

In my view it is desirable to have an admiral as Commander-in-Chief who realises the dangers of submarines and mines to a fleet and will not rush blindly at the enemy fleet ... Burney's caution will therefore be of use.[55]

This comment says as much about Jellicoe's cast of mind as it does about the man who would take over the Grand Fleet if Jellicoe were incapacitated or his flagship disabled.

Jerram took over the command of the 2BS in December 1915 from the ailing Vice-Admiral Sir George Warrender. Before the war, Jerram had been in command on the China station and, just before hostilities commenced, he had followed Admiralty instructions by moving his main force from the vicinity of Tsingtau to Hong Kong, even though he correctly foresaw that this would allow the escape of the *Emden*. He subsequently wished that he had disobeyed the order,[56] but probably such a display of independence would not have recommended him to Jellicoe. Even before Jerram's appointment, Jellicoe had doubted that he had the necessary experience and, by April 1916, concluded that Jerram 'has not a tithe of the fleet experience of Burney'. Jerram, unlike his predecessor, never visited Jellicoe unless sent for. Yet it seems that he should have tried harder to learn from the C-in-C; when in early 1916 Jellicoe had been able to arrange a fleet battle exercise, he judged that Jerram 'did not do too well'.[57]

[51] Vice-Admiral Sir Douglas Gamble: *GF*, p. 19.   [52] *FDSF II*, p. 11.
[53] T H M Jerram is often named as Martyn (*ODNB: FDSF III*, p. 42) but as Thomas in *OD*, p. 43.
[54] *JP I*, p. 212. Gordon, pp. 300–1. *ODNB*, 'Burney, Cecil'.
[55] *JP I*, pp. 116–17, 167 and 177–8. Jellicoe's chief-of-staff, Madden, thought Burney should have been replaced: *FDSF II*, pp. 440–1.
[56] *GF*, p. 167. *ODNB*, 'Jerram, Martyn'. Halpern, pp. 72–4.
[57] *JP I*, pp. 177 and 241. 'Tactical Exercises', f. 238.

Jerram was unusual in not having specialised in the 'material' branches like gunnery or torpedo; he began his career as a navigator. And, in their formative years as junior officers, both Jerram and Burney had spent considerable periods in boys' training ships and establishments.[58] It seems that the latter experience in particular would have inclined both to accept without question the habits of command of 'a Service which gave tremendous power to the autocrat, left little initiative to the subordinate [and in which c]entralisation was carried to its extreme'.[59] A striking example of such autocrats who were also compliant subordinates is that 'great martinet', Rear-Admiral Sir Robert Arbuthnot. During the Scarborough raid on 16 December 1916, his flagship *Orion* sighted a German force of light cruisers and destroyers. His flag-captain, Frederic Dreyer, put her guns on the leading cruiser but Arbuthnot refused his request to open fire. 'No, not until the Vice-Admiral signals "Open fire" or his flagship fires'; shortly afterwards, the enemy was blotted out by a rain squall.[60] When the battle fleet deployed, either Burney's or Jerram's squadron would be in the van; neither, it seems, would have had much appetite for independent action or for departing from a strict interpretation of the *GFBOs*.

The vice-admiral of the 4BS, which, with the flagship, formed the centre divisions of the battle line, was of a different stamp entirely. Sturdee had the invaluable experience of having fought a major gunnery action at the Falkland Islands. He was a materialist who had specialised in torpedoes and, as a young officer, had shown considerable intellectual ability as a prize-winning essayist. He had unorthodox views on tactics and was the only Grand Fleet commander who continued to advocate divided (i.e. divisional) tactics.[61] In September 1915 he proposed a new approach formation in which the Grand Fleet would, just before engaging the enemy, divide into two large divisions, each manoeuvred independently by its admiral. He claimed that 'dividing the fleet can force a fight on advantageous terms' and that there was no risk of one division being isolated and overpowered. But Captain Roger Backhouse of Jellicoe's staff questioned Sturdee's assumptions, namely that the Germans would have no battlecruisers and that they would either delay obvious deployments or deploy in the wrong directions; however, he did recommend that Sturdee's ideas should be tried out on the Tactical Board.[62]

In fact, Jellicoe seems to have gone one better even though, in the previous August, he had described Sturdee as 'full of fads'. For the tactical exercises held in October and November 1915, which were intended to explore

[58] *ODNB* entries.
[59] 'Pre-War Tactics', January 1929 in Captain J H Godfrey RN, 'Jutland', Royal Navy Staff College, Greenwich, 1930, AL. See also *FDSF II*, pp. 19–20.
[60] Dreyer, pp. 75 and 103–4.   [61] *ODNB*, 'Sturdee, Doveton'. Gordon, p. 41.
[62] F C D Sturdee, 'Dispositions for the "Approach"', 10 September 1915 (ff. 56–60) and Backhouse to C.-in-C. 12 September 1915 (ff. 89–93) in JMSS. 49012.

the use of the new 5BS as a fast division, Sturdee was given command of the 'British' forces (the 'enemy' force was under Burney). Jellicoe's memorandum on the November exercise analysed the cruiser actions but merely remarked that 'the tactics of the battlefleets have been discussed by the Commander-in-Chief with the flag officers'.[63] This reluctance to be more specific may well signify an unwillingness to criticise his admirals in a document that was widely circulated, so we do not know who was most at fault. However, Sturdee remained suspect, and not only in Jellicoe's eyes. When discussing a possible replacement for Burney as VAC 1BS, the C-in-C insisted:

I should never feel safe with his [Sturdee's] command of the most important squadron and leading the van ... and I know the other flag officers hold the same views.

Three days later, he added that Sturdee's 'tactical notions are against all our ideas'. Jellicoe had also been angered by the dissention in the fleet caused by Sturdee's continuing insistence that, in action, Blue Pendant turns were preferable to those by 9 Pendant. But, even if Sturdee was at times 'an unruly subordinate', his tactical ideas do seem to have been valued by Jellicoe; in his secret despatch after Jutland, the C-in-C singled out Sturdee for his assistance in studying how to counter a turn-away by the enemy – even if, the despatch added: 'There is no real counter.'[64]

Battlecruiser orders

In March 1913, Rear-Admiral David Beatty hoisted his flag in *Lion* as commander of the 1st Battle Cruiser Squadron (1BCS).[65] Just a month later, he wrote out his initial views on the 'Functions of a Battle-Cruiser Squadron', while by July, he had clarified his ideas sufficiently to issue his first set of 'Battle Orders'.[66] In action with heavy cruisers, 'The order of battle, unless chasing, will be in single line ahead.' And, doubtless to minimise delays in executing his orders, Beatty warned that his ships must be prepared for him to haul down a signal before all had repeated it 'close up'. In pursuing a retreating fleet, the battlecruisers would manoeuvre in line-abreast or quarter-line and open out considerably when within torpedo range. If used as a fast division, they should be prepared to attack either the enemy's van (when a chief object would be 'to pour in a steady fire with long range torpedoes') or his rear (when a sharp look-out for enemy submarines would be essential). They should also expect to defend against attacks by enemy torpedo craft and cruisers, and to

---

[63] *JP I*, p. 177. 'Tactical Exercises', ff. 118–19, 139–41 and 146–7.
[64] *JP I*, pp. 241–2. *FDSF III*, pp. 31–3. Gordon, p. 34. *OD*, p. 3.
[65] Roberts, *Battlecruisers*, pp. 122–3. Roskill, pp. 59–60.
[66] 'Functions of a Battle-Cruiser Squadron', 5 April 1913 and 'Confidential Battle Orders', 17 July 1913 in *BP I*, pp. 59–64 and 73–5. *Navy List, July 1913.*

protect and support the British flotillas. In his April draft, Beatty had emphasised that his captains 'to be successful must possess in a marked degree:
initiative, resource, determination, and no fear of accepting responsibility'.
In his battle orders, he repeated: 'Much must be left to the initiative and
judgement of Captains.' But the specific examples he then gave concerned
concentration of fire, avoiding torpedoes, and small alterations of course and/or
bearing to facilitate the firing of guns and torpedoes or to avoid smoke or
backwash. Captains were warned not to haul out of line by more than one point
'lest they hamper the squadron when turning in succession', and that 'no
movement must mask the fire of other ships, or in any way inconvenience
them from a manoeuvring point of view'. Thus, by insisting on preserving the
integrity of the line, Beatty left little scope for bold initiatives.

On the formation of the Battle Cruiser Fleet in February 1915, Beatty's
earlier orders were reissued, in some cases with consolidated amendments, as
the first of the series of *Battle Cruiser Orders* (*BCOs*). The first five derived
from his pre-war orders and, while BCO 3, 'Battle orders', repeated that 'Much
must be left to the initiative and judgement of Captains', it still gave the same
rather limited scope for independent action once line had been formed.
Similarly, the revised text of BCO 1, 'General Principles' insisted that
'Orders issued by signal frequently indicate the Admiral's intentions or requirements; they may have to be obeyed literally by some ships and not by others'.
But if, for example, an order specified a course for the Admiral and ships near
him, all that was allowed was that 'More distant ships may find a *slightly* [my
emphasis] different course will better suit their requirements'.[67]

On the other hand, Beatty granted considerable freedom to individual ships if
they were spread and the enemy was then sighted. BCO 4 (the text unchanged
since July 1913) insisted that 'a sudden alteration of course by [one] ship . . .
being an almost certain indication of an enemy having been sighted . . . should
be acted upon immediately . . . All ships that *may* be required to support must
proceed to do so until they know definitely that they will not be required.' Each
captain was to use his discretion in ensuring that he placed his ship to support
her consorts. This did not require all ships to be in close order – indeed, close
order was to be avoided if heavy smoke on the engaged side might mask the
guns of ships astern – but ships near one another were nonetheless expected to
form line roughly at right angles to the bearing of the enemy. As far as possible,
all this was to be done without signal, while 'absence of a signal . . . usually
denotes that the Admiral relies on each ship to take whatever action may be
necessary without waiting to be told'. In selecting enemy ships to attack,
captains were to be guided by the principle (found in BCO 2) that:

---

[67] BCOs 1–5 in *BP I*, pp. 250–9.

If hostile battle-cruisers are present they must form the objective of our battle-cruisers ... We should engage with sufficient strength to annihilate them ... If there are no battle-cruisers with the enemy fleet, our B.C.F. will act as a fast division of the Grand Fleet.

When light cruisers first came under Beatty's direct orders in December 1914, he demanded that their captains too must cultivate 'those qualities which Cruiser work specially requires' and that they must realise that 'all orders issued by me are to be read as INSTRUCTIONS indicating my requirements and intentions'.[68] However, in BCO 8, which probably dates from the second quarter of 1915,[69] there was a significant change in what the battlecruisers could expect after the enemy had been sighted.

On closing to engage the enemy, the tactics of the Battle Cruisers will be in accordance with my Battle Orders *and as directed by signal at the time.* The Light Cruisers will probably not receive *detailed* orders by signal. [My emphases]

It appears that Beatty had concluded that he would need to direct his enlarged force of battlecruisers by signal as they closed, and the order even implies that his directions might be detailed. Yet the earlier BCO 4, which envisaged closing without signals, remained in force. However, in other respects, Beatty persisted in his efforts to keep signalling to a minimum. By March 1915 at the latest, he had defined a special significance for the Blue Pendant as a means of turning his ships together as quickly as possible. The pendant was hoisted singly at the yardarm towards which the turn would be made; helms were put over when the pendant was dipped and righted when it was hauled down. Jellicoe, who, as we have seen, was averse to Blue Pendant turns anyway, thought 'with the large number of ships you have it will be a little dangerous' and too like George Tryon's 'action principles'.[70] Beatty seems to have taken some account of Jellicoe's history lesson; the reissued BCO 21 of March 1916 stipulated: 'Blue Pendant singly is never to be used when there are more than five ships in the line' and that 'such turns will never exceed 8 points'.

In the *BCOs*, Beatty stated his expectations that his light cruiser captains 'must first gain information and report it fully' and 'Keep the Admiral informed of everything important'. Also: 'They are expected to use their own initiative in moving to carry out the Admiral's requirements and taking the offensive whenever opportunity permits'.[71] As encouragement, Beatty informed them in BCO 9:

I wish to impress on Light Cruiser Captains the great extent to which the German Cruiser Screen has now been reduced in strength.

---

[68] BCO 6 (first printed 27 December 1914). All BCOs are in DRAX 1/3. The single numbering sequence as used here was introduced with BCO 32 (6 February 1916).

[69] BCO 8 refers to the 'recent increase in strength' of the BCF.

[70] Jellicoe to Beatty, 2 March 1915, BTY 13/21. Gordon, Ch. 10 and App. V.

[71] BCOs 6, 7 (probably early 1915) and 8.

It now had at most three armoured cruisers in support, while, of the light cruisers, only four had guns greater than 4.1in and only twelve were capable of more than 23 knots. This confident assessment contrasts with the *GFBOs* gloomy prediction (unsubstantiated by the intelligence returns): 'The Germans have probably added to their fleet a considerable number of light cruisers armed with a heavier gun than the 4.1 inch.' Beatty even saw offensive opportunities in the anticipated German mining tactics that were behind so many of the defensive precautions in the *GFBOs*.

particularly as the German Light Cruisers may carry a deck cargo of mines, I consider it will be generally desirable to press them continuously and as hard as possible ... if the enemy lay mines ... it is far better they should be laid during a hasty retreat in sight of our ships.[72]

Beatty's rule for his light cruiser captains was:

When in touch with the enemy, they can never be wrong
 (i) In shadowing a superior force;
 (ii) In endeavouring to destroy an equal or inferior force.[73]

Thus all vessels under his command were left in no doubt that he intended to take the offensive whenever there was a good prospect of annihilating his opponents.

The Jutland battle orders

The *GFBOs* were detailed tactical orders addressed to all ships of the Grand Fleet: battleships and battlecruisers, armoured and light cruisers, destroyers, minelayers and submarines. But, implicitly, they also reveal Jellicoe's assumptions about the distinct phases of the battle as it would develop between his forces and those of the High Seas Fleet. In the interests of brevity, some aspects of the *GFBOs* have been omitted where they have no relevance to the battle as fought – for example, those provisions referring to the 3BS and the older German predreadnoughts of the IV and V BSs, all of which were absent.

Organisations

The formation of the battlefleet, around which all other forces orbited, was defined by the organisation of the three battle squadrons and the fleet flagship into divisions and subdivisions (two subdivisions per division); normally, divisions were the units in which the fleet was manoeuvred. By 1916, only

---

[72] BCO 9 (*Prinz Adalbert*, sunk 23 October 1915, was not one of the listed armoured cruisers). *GFBOs III*, XXIV(d) (January 1916).
[73] BCO 6.

two organisations were in force. Organisation No. 5 was that usually adopted when cruising in daylight and it was assumed without further orders after deployment for action. Each division was formed of four ships:
- the 1st and 2nd Division from the 2BS, the squadron flagship, *King George V*, leading the 1st Division;
- the 3rd and 4th Divisions from the 4BS, the fleet flagship, *Iron Duke*, leading the 3rd Division; and
- the 5th and 6th Divisions from the 1BS, the squadron flagship, *Marlborough*, leading the 6th Division.

The 5BS formed the 7th Division but was not normally part of the battlefleet for manoeuvring purposes. Organisation No. 2 was the usual one for cruising at night; the 1st, 2nd and 3rd Divisions comprising, respectively, the 2BS, the 4BS and *Iron Duke*, and the 1BS; the 5BS was then the 4th Division.

Though not strictly part of these organisations, each battle squadron had an attached cruiser to act as its repeating ship – *Bellona, Boadicea, Blanche* and *Blonde* to the 1, 2, 4 and 5BSs, respectively.

Cruising orders

During the day, the battlefleet's usual cruising order – formed with signal 'LT1' – was in Organisation No. 5: six divisions, each in line astern, the divisions disposed abeam, 11 cables apart, that is, 5½ miles between the outer (wing) divisions. The antisubmarine screen was formed by the 4, 11 and 12 DFs while it was hoped that there would be enough destroyers to screen the 5BS as well; the 13DF screened the battlecruisers. Other cruising orders were laid down for use when destroyers were absent or in thick weather.[74]

The remainder of the fleet were positioned, mostly ahead of the battlefleet, according to one of the 'Cruising Dispositions' specified in the *GFBOs*. If the BCF was absent, the Grand Fleet advanced during the day in Disposition I (signal 'LS1'), led by a screening line of armoured cruisers. The *GFBOs* assumed that up to 13 armoured cruisers would be available from four cruiser squadrons; they would be placed abeam in six groups, labelled A–D, F and G from port to starboard; each group was ten miles from its neighbours in clear weather and not less than five miles in poor visibility. A and G were formed respectively by the 7CS and the 3CS, B and C from the 2CS and D and F from the 1CS. Ten miles astern of the cruiser line came the 5BS and *Blonde*. The 4LCS, in single line-abreast at a spacing of one to two miles, were six miles further astern, zigzagging across the front of the battleship columns as an advanced submarine screen and lookout; *Boadicea* and *Bellona* were on each

---

[74] *GFBOs III*, II(a), XXI.7 and XXVII.10 (January 1916). Unless indicated otherwise, the Jutland *GFBOs III* are dated December 1915.

flank, about nine miles from the flagship. The 4LCS was at most four miles ahead of the battleships, but not less than three miles in order to leave room for the screening destroyers. *Blanche, Campania* (the battlefleet's seaplane and balloon carrier) and any minelayers brought up the rear, five miles astern of the battleships.

If the BCF was with the battlefleet, the advance was in Disposition V (signal 'LS5'). It was led by the twelve light cruisers of the 1, 3 and 2 LCSs, in that order from port to starboard; they were in pairs up to ten miles, and not less than five miles, apart. The battlecruisers were ten miles astern of the light cruisers and five miles ahead of a line of armoured cruisers; the latter were organised in squadrons disposed abeam at separations of ten miles in good visibility. Their line was five miles in advance of the 5BS; the remainder of the fleet was then positioned as ordered by 'LS1'.[75]

Thus, in both dispositions, the advanced cruiser screen was 50 miles wide in good weather, and not less than 25 miles wide. In 'LS1', the armoured cruisers were at most 20 miles ahead of the battlefleet, but in 'LS5', the BCF's light cruisers were up to 30 miles in advance. Any 'LS' disposition signal could be qualified by a numeric hoist that specified a lesser distance from the advanced screen to the battlefleet; all other distances were then reduced in proportion, though no further than the minima already noted. Two compass signals hoisted inferior to the disposition signal could also place the centres of the screens at some other bearing than right ahead and specify the line-of-bearing of the vessels in each screening line. Furthermore, the 'Cruiser Instructions' in the *GFBOs* contained an additional eight dispositions for advancing or retiring, with or without the BCF, by day or night or after action, but they did not apply to the tactical situations encountered at Jutland.[76]

Both Jellicoe and Beatty repeatedly expressed their concerns that German Zeppelins working with their fleet as scouts could obtain early information on British whereabouts and dispositions. The *GFBOs* assumed that, in good visibility, the fleet might be sighted from the air at a distance of 50 miles and that this would 'enable the enemy to dispose his submarines and minelayers to the best advantage'. In April 1916, new orders were issued for an advanced line of three armoured or light cruisers positioned 40 miles ahead of the battlefleet to give advanced warning of Zeppelins. However, in its absence (which was the case at Jutland), the wing ships of the cruiser screen were exhorted to take 'energetic steps' to drive off airships, though it was also recognised that their anti-aircraft armament needed strengthening.[77]

---

[75] *GFBOs III*, XX (21 April 1916) and XXI.6 and Dispositions I and V.

[76] *GFBOS III*, XXI.2 and Dispositions II–IV, V–X.

[77] *JP I*, pp. 168, 172, 174–5, 178 and 207. *GFBOs III*, XXI.19–21 and XXII.22–3 (both 2 April 1916).

The approach

When cruising, the cruisers of the advanced screen were required to clear the path of the fleet of any merchantmen that might report it. If possible the cruisers were to close and examine such vessels, though boarding would be left to any accompanying destroyers.[78] However, the principal task of the cruiser lines was to look out for and make contact with the enemy fleet.

If our battle cruiser fleet is not in company with the fleet it is probable that it will be employed as an advanced force in order to gain touch with the enemy earlier than would otherwise be the case.

However, apart from this statement, little distinction was made in the *GFBOs* between the BCF operating independently and its being disposed as the advanced guard of the fleet. In either event, if the BCF's light cruisers first made contact with the enemy, they were to use their high speed to maintain touch with a superior force or to engage an equal or inferior one (this echoes Beatty's expectations in the *BCOs*). But, whichever line of cruisers first gained touch, the ships on the flanks were not to be drawn inwards to seek action; their primary duties were, first, to protect the flanks of the battlefleet from mine-layers and submarines, driving in all enemy ships that might conceal submarines: and, second, to outflank the enemy's screen. The BCF's light cruisers, supported by the battlecruisers, were also to push home their reconnaissance and drive in the enemy's light forces, thereby denying him knowledge of the British fleet. This might then result in the whole of the BCF becoming engaged with the German scouting groups, but:

This would be very much to our advantage, as every ship of the enemy accounted for before the battlefleets meet will simplify the situation.

Alternatively:

Prior to deployment, the battle-cruisers, in the absence of German vessels of this class, could drive in all enemy light vessels and give us . . . full information as to the enemy's battlefleet, whilst denying him knowledge of ours.[79]

When the enemy was reported, *Campania*, if not already ordered to a position in rear of the cruiser screen, was required to proceed to the front at her full 21-knot speed – this was demanding for her elderly engines. She would then use her kite balloon for reconnaissance. But the primary duty of her seaplanes (reflecting yet again the oft-repeated apprehensions about under-water attack) was to scout for submarines and to attack them with bombs. The seaplanes were to scout in the direction of the enemy's fleet only if no

---

[78] *GFBOs III*, XXII.12–14 (2 April 1916).
[79] *GFBOs III*, XXII.(1) and 3 and XXIV.4, 7 and 9 (January 1916).

submarines had been seen. If fast seaplanes were aboard, they were to be used to attack any reported Zeppelins.[80]

Despite their 'comparatively low speed ... compared with ships of later types',[81] the armoured cruisers were to engage the enemy's armoured and light cruisers, including any of the latter that may have evaded the BCF. If the BCF's ships became fully engaged with the enemy's advanced forces, the British armoured cruisers, with support from the 5BS, were required to push on to gain touch with the enemy's battlefleet.[82]

The orders on enemy reporting read:

In clear weather there should be no difficulty as to the part played by the cruisers ... It is of great importance that all cruisers should plot the position of the enemy's ships as they are sighted or reported ... a correct plot is vitally important in thick weather.

... Ships having to make a report of sighting or of movements of the enemy must pass the message to the Admiral as well as to their own senior officer.

These paragraphs appear in a section of the *GFBOs* which defines the duties of all three types of cruiser (battle, armoured and light) 'when employed to screen and look out for the battlefleet'.[83] However, in the text, 'cruiser' alone usually means 'armoured cruiser'. Yet these are the only orders concerning enemy reporting during the critical phase when the two fleets were approaching each other. Whatever their precise scope and intention, it is certain that they do *not* state, emphatically and clearly, the vital necessity during the approach of keeping the C-in-C informed of all enemy sightings and movements, and of doing so under all conditions, not just in thick weather.

At the end of the approach, the two battlefleets would be in sight of one another and, the *GFBOs* assumed, 'reports of the enemy's movements are no longer necessary' – though with a familiar exception:

Cruisers and light-cruisers both before and after deployment must keep the sharpest look-out for submarines and must report their presence immediately to the Commander-in-Chief.

The 5BS was expected to rejoin the battlefleet in time for deployment. Other ships, including those of the BCF, not already engaged with the enemy would also fall back with the intention, as far as possible, of taking up their predefined deployment positions. If as intended the two inner squadrons of armoured cruisers (the 2CS and 1CS) were leading the outer battleship divisions, each squadron would be well placed to fall back into a position close to the nearest flank of the battlefleet. Whereas, both before and after deployment, the wing squadrons (the 3CS and 7CS) were required to scout widely on the flanks 'to

---

[80] *GFBOs III*, XXII.10 (2 April 1916). *CAWFS 1906–21*, p. 66.

[81] Of those at Jutland, 23 knots except the 22-knot *Hampshire: CAWFS 1860–1905*, pp. 71–3.

[82] *GFBOs III*, V.4 and XXII.4.   [83] *GFBOs III*, XXII.5–6.

prevent mines being laid in the path or probable path of the battlefleet' and to intercept submarines operating on the surface; the squadron finding itself in the rear after deployment was to watch for minelayers 'even at considerable distance in rear of the German battlefleet'.[84] The C-in-C would also order the destroyers of the battlefleet screen to take up positions on the flanks of the battleship columns that would enable them to gain their positions in the van and rear of the battle line as the battleships deployed.[85] The fleet then waited for the flagship to signal the deployment.

Deployment

The orders for the deployment of the Grand Fleet assumed without qualification that both battlefleets would fight in single line-ahead, either on similar courses or perhaps initially for a short time on roughly opposite courses. From information in captured German documents (circulated in translation as the O.X.O. papers), the main German line was expected to be formed of the I, II (more modern predreadnoughts) and III BSs, with the ISG ahead on the engaged bow and eight destroyer flotillas positioned initially along the whole length of the line on its disengaged side. The British line would be formed by deploying the battlefleet from its cruising and approach formation of divisional columns into one line, with the divisions either in numerical order or its reverse. Thus the line would be led by either Jerram's or Burney's flagship, with the fleet flagship near the centre. As the battlefleet deployed, in accordance with the *GFBO* 'Deployment Diagram', the remaining vessels of the fleet would go to positions along two lines-of-bearing inclined inwards towards the enemy; one extended forwards from the van battleship at two to three points from right ahead, the other rearwards from the rear line battleship at two points from right astern.[86]

The *GFBOs* also assumed that the battleships of the High Seas Fleet would approach in columns. Unless they deployed first, Jellicoe intended to deploy at a range of 18,000–20,000 yards. He hoped that he would be able to deploy first, since his whole line could then concentrate fire on the leading ships (perhaps the leading pairs) of the German columns.[87] There were a number of considerations determining the moment for deployment, and the course and dispositions to be adopted. If the Germans deployed away from Heligoland, it was assumed that they would later turn about. Ideally, each enemy ship should end up slightly abaft the beam of its British opponent. In clear weather, the gunnery

---

[84] *GFBOs III*, XXII.4, XXIII and XXIV.9.

[85] *GFBOs III*, V.4–5 and XXIV.5 and 8 and XXVIII.(1) (both January 1916) and 'Modifications to . . . Diagrams', 7 April 1916.

[86] *GFBOs III*, VII.13–14 and (XXIII) (unnumbered as printed but number confirmed in XXIV.13). *German Tactical Orders*, January 1915, p. 10 in 'German Fleet Orders', ADM 186/17.

[87] *GFBOs III*, VII.5 and XV.12–15.

advantage lay with the fleet in the leeward position, especially if the wind was on the bow. But in weather throwing up spray, the windward position was better. Either way, gunnery advantage might have to be given up in order to get to the eastward, intercept the enemy and force him to a decisive action before he could gain his own waters. 'Our superiority in the power of individual ships, or in the number of ships of the "Dreadnought" type, might warrant such a sacrifice.' The most likely moment for an attack by submarines accompanying the German fleet was at the end of the approach or on deployment.[88]

The Battlefleet will be deployed by Oblique pendant, by Equal Speed manoeuvring signal, by Equal Speed pendant, or by Forming and Disposing signal, according to the bearing of the enemy's centre relative to the course of the Fleet and the time available.

However, further instructions were provided only for deployment by Oblique Pendant – perhaps because it was the preferred method, and also because it could not be carried through successfully unless each column adopted the correct course and speed. An exhaustive report prepared by the navigating officer of *King George V* tabulated courses and speeds for six columns for many combinations of initial column spacings and final courses; for the usual spacing of 11 cables and a speed of 18 knots, the time to complete the manoeuvre was about 30 minutes.[89] Compare this with a time of less than four minutes for all columns to turn into line by 9 Pendant or Equal Speed Pendant. However, this was not the end of the Equal Speed Pendant manoeuvre; about another 18 minutes would be needed before all ships were on the final course. Even so, in that time, no ship masked the fire of its consorts, which was not the case in a deployment by Oblique Pendant. Thus the latter method was unsuited to rapid deployments when the enemy would soon be within range.[90]

Jellicoe was well aware that the time available for deployment might be short and that it might have to commence without waiting for the deployment signal to be repeated and answered by the whole battlefleet. George Tryon would surely have approved his orders for such situations. The flagship would hoist the deployment signal but it would then at once turn as necessary, sounding one or two short blasts on the siren to indicate a turn to starboard or port; commanders of columns would themselves turn as soon as possible, their flagships repeating the siren signal at short intervals until it was repeated in adjacent columns. Once the actual deployment signal had been read, courses could be corrected as necessary. Using the siren was clearly most appropriate (and safest) for an equal speed deployment, since for most columns the initial turn was predetermined. But in low visibility the enemy fleet might be sighted on

[88] *GFBOs III*, VII.15 and VIII.2–3 and XXIV.3–4 (January 1916) and XXVI.5 (10 March 1916).
[89] *GFBOs III*, VI.(1)–2 and VII.(1). 'Tables for use when deploying by Oblique Pendant', 24 February 1916 in JMSS 49011, f. 162.
[90] Dreyer, pp. 159–61. McLaughlin, 'Equal Speed', pp. 131–2.

a beam bearing such that there would be no choice but to form line as quickly as possible on the nearest wing column; in that case, course and speed would be decided by the commander of the wing column and signalled with accompanying warning siren blasts.[91]

As the other battle squadrons were forming line, the 5BS made its own way to its deployment position. If practicable, the C-in-C would order it either to form well ahead of the battlefleet as a fast division, or to take a position in the van or rear of the battle line. But, if RAC 5BS did not receive explicit orders and the BCF was present, he was to go to the rear if the fleets deployed on opposite courses, or if both fleets deployed away from Heligoland (in which case the Germans were expected to reverse course later). Otherwise, he was to go to the van. The armoured cruisers of the 1CS and 2CS, the light cruisers and the destroyer flotillas would also do their best to take up their assigned positions on the Deployment Diagram, further out on the lines of bearing. When the range between the two battle lines was 18,000 yards, the vessels in the van were also required to keep outside an arc of 15,000-yard radius centred on the leading enemy battleship. However, the *GFBOs* accepted that the diagram could be no more than a guide, and that commanders would have to use their initiative in taking up position – subject to the general principles that, usually, the greater strength was required in the van, and that their smoke must not interfere with the fire of the battlefleet.[92]

The simplified schematic below is based on the Deployment Diagram but is not to scale; the enemy battle line was to starboard. The more advanced formations (A to E) comprised the battlecruisers (the three squadrons are shown separately) and the light vessels on their bows. The presence of the 5LCS and 10DF depended on their joining the battlefleet in time from Harwich. A second group of light vessels were positioned ahead of the 5BS. Although the battlecruisers were pushed forward as far as possible without losing their guns' bearings on the ISG, the gap between them and the 5BS was still too small to allow this second group to be in one line. Thus these light cruiser and destroyer flotillas would move out in turn to attack, with the armoured cruiser squadron at F moving as necessary so as not to hamper them. At the rear of the line, the first position (M) was occupied by the 5BS if present, but, if not, the remaining forces moved up one position.

The three attached light cruisers were to take their positions one mile on the disengaged beams of the flagships of the 2nd, 3rd and 5th Divisions while the minelayer's station was further out, 'where no danger exists from the enemy's fire'.[93]

---

[91] *GFBOs III*, VI.3–4.
[92] *GFBOs III*, V.5–10 (XXIII) and 'Deployment Diagram' and XXIV.5, 8 and 15 (January 1916).
[93] *GFBOS III* (XXIII) and 'Deployment Diagram' and IV.3 (19 April 1916) and XXIV.16 (January 1916).

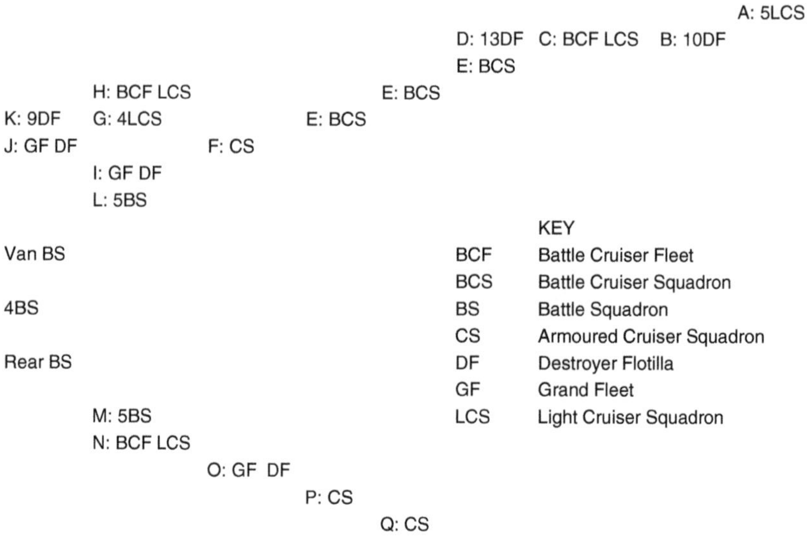

```
                                                                    A: 5LCS
                                            D: 13DF  C: BCF LCS   B: 10DF
                                            E: BCS
            H: BCF LCS                 E: BCS
K: 9DF    G: 4LCS                 E: BCS
J: GF DF              F: CS
        I: GF DF
        L: 5BS
                                            KEY
Van BS                           BCF    Battle Cruiser Fleet
                                 BCS    Battle Cruiser Squadron
4BS                              BS     Battle Squadron
                                 CS     Armoured Cruiser Squadron
Rear BS                          DF     Destroyer Flotilla
                                 GF     Grand Fleet
        M: 5BS                   LCS    Light Cruiser Squadron
        N: BCF LCS
             O: GF  DF
                 P: CS
                    Q: CS
```

Figure 3.1 Deployment diagram

Action

Battle squadrons

The aim of the battlefleet is the destruction of the enemy's battleships [while the] duty of preventing interference with our battlefleet belongs to vessels of generally similar type to those of the enemy which require to be dealt with.[94]

As we have seen, Jellicoe's tactical objective was to achieve action on approximately similar courses – since this was likely to give the most decisive results – with the battlefleet in single line in close order. Single line-ahead was easiest for station keeping and (as noted in another echo of Tryon's principles) it was the only formation in which course could be altered without signal. But such a turn in succession by the whole fleet took a long time: almost 22 minutes at 18 knots. It also created too marked a bend in the line at the fixed turning point; this point could then be concentrated on by the enemy while each ship passed through it in turn. Thus Jellicoe's intention was normally to turn the battlefleet in divisions by 9 Pendant. In case the two fleets deployed initially on opposite courses, special action signals were defined for turning the whole fleet by divisions in rapid succession, commencing with the rearmost division; signal '21' turned the ships towards the enemy, '02' away. These signals were to 'be obeyed as soon as seen. The Leading Ship of each Division is to turn directly the Leading

---

[94] *GFBOs III*, XXIV.1 (January 1916).

Ship of the Division astern is seen to have commenced to turn.'[95] Compared with a German 'action-turn-together', these manoeuvres took longer but the guides of each division, normally their flagships, remained the same. The battle orders did not discuss the possibility that the enemy (who might not be similarly inhibited about crossing his opponent's wake) could circle the British rear.

As already noted, the vice-admirals commanding squadrons were given limited discretionary powers to manoeuvre their squadrons independently, though Jellicoe expected that he himself would control the movements of the 4BS in the centre of the line. In Organisation No. 5, with its four-ship divisions, the same powers were extended to the rear-admirals of the 2nd and 5th Divisions, unless directed otherwise by the C-in-C or their vice-admirals. But Sturdee, though VAC 4BS and leader of the 4th Division, was tied more firmly to Jellicoe's coat-tails; his division was required to conform generally to the movements of the C-in-C's 3rd Division 'unless any contrary directions are given'. The vice-admiral leading the van was required to adjust his course and speed to the best advantage of the whole line, subject to Jellicoe's general intentions on battle ranges and, towards the end of the action, to lead the van divisions to a shorter range without being in danger from torpedoes fired from the enemy line. The vice-admiral at the rear was expected to act independently should the German mount divisional attacks, in conjunction with the 5BS if they had formed astern of him.[96] If at the rear, RAC 5BS was to engage the rear of the enemy and to frustrate any attempt at a turn-away movement. If in the van when the BCF was absent, the primary duty of the 5BS was to attack the enemy battlecruisers. But if they too were absent, the 5BS was to seek a commanding position from which itself to attack the enemy van and to support attacks by British armoured and light cruisers and destroyers[97] – this appears to have been its greatest opportunity to act independently as a fast division.

Jellicoe's apprehensions about the dangers from mines and torpedoes, which we have encountered again and again, permeated the *GFBOs*. He insisted that he would not follow a turn-away by the enemy line-of-battle shortly after deployment because he anticipated that it would be made for the purpose of taking the British fleet over submarines. But he anticipated that, throughout an action, to follow such a turn-away would risk attack from torpedoes fired by retreating battleships and destroyers, or being drawn over mines or submarines. He also warned that the fleet must expect massed attacks by German flotillas supported by light cruisers and that, if these could not be contained by the British light forces (of which more later), the fleet would have to be turned away in subdivisions by means of the Preparative flag to evade the torpedoes.

---

[95] *GFBOs III*, VII.10, 13 and 14 and VIII.1. *GSB 1915*, pp. 58 and 60.
[96] *GFBOs III*, VII.2, 7 and 14(iii).   [97] *GFBOs III*, V.4–7.

In Organisation No. 5, the leading ships of each two-ship subdivision turned simultaneously, the remaining ships following their leaders in succession.[98]

Battlecruisers   While VAC BCF was free to 'act as he considered necessary in carrying out his general instructions', the *GFBOs* clearly stated his priorities in action.

The primary function of battle-cruisers is the destruction of the battle-cruisers of the enemy . . .

If the enemy has no battle-cruisers present, or after his battle-cruisers have been destroyed, the function of our vessels of this class is to act as a fast division of the battlefleet and to attack the van of the enemy if it is possible to attain a sufficiently commanding position. The ideal would be an attack by torpedoes on the enemy's battle line, and such strong offensive action against all enemy cruisers, light-cruisers and torpedo craft at their van as to render such a position untenable by them.[99]

Armoured cruisers   Once the 1CS and 2CS had reached their positions F and P on deployment:

The primary function of cruisers in a Fleet action must be that of engaging the cruisers and light forces of the enemy . . . the more powerful cruisers may be able to act against the enemy's line of battle, but their first consideration must remain his auxiliary forces and the protection of the Battlefleet from their attack.[100]

Of the 3CS and 7CS, one would scout well ahead, the other guard against minelayers well astern.

Light cruisers   The functions of light-cruisers, not stated in order of importance, included:

The attack of the enemy's light-cruisers and torpedo vessels, whether these vessels be acting as torpedo craft or minelayers, and, as a consequence, the protection of our own battlefleet from such attack.

The support of our destroyers.

. . . if large numbers of enemy torpedo craft are attacking together, it will be necessary for the light-cruisers to engage them at close range, or even endeavour to run them down.

However, the *GFBOs* recognised that, since the majority of light cruisers were part of the BCF, no reliance could be placed on their falling back on the battlefleet prior to a general action. This would leave the 4LCS to act, to a certain extent, as the anti-torpedo boat armament of the battleships.

[98] *GFBOs III*, VII.8–9: and IX.1–2 and XXIX.3 and 6 (January 1916).
[99] *GFBOs III*, XXIV.6–7 (January 1916).   [100] *GFBOs III*, XXIV.8.

Its chief duty, like that of our destroyers, is to act against the enemy's destroyers. It is to support our flotillas against the enemy's and in their attacks on his battlefleet; it is not however tied to our flotillas and is to take the initiative. It is to attack the enemy's heavy ships with torpedoes if it is able to do so without prejudice to its primary duty.[101]

The *GFBOs* emphasised the need for initiative on the part of the captains of armoured cruisers and especially of light cruisers. While imprudence in light cruiser captains was neither suggested nor required, it was accepted that critical circumstances might arise in which the offensive must be taken regardless of circumstances.

The *GFBOs* 'Cruiser Instructions' that defined the duties of all cruisers ended with a subsection headed 'Reports of enemy during action'. This insisted:

Reports of [enemy] movements, *provided that they are made in good time*, may be of great value, and any ships in a position to see clearly what is occurring, when it is probable that the Commander-in-Chief could not, should not fail to report.[102]

These reports were to be signalled by searchlight if possible, otherwise by W/T.

Destroyers The 'Destroyer Instructions' of January 1916, which remained in force at Jutland, still insisted that their primary duty was to stop the German destroyers by gunfire and that torpedo attack on the German battle-fleet was secondary. Even so, the British flotillas were urged not to miss a favourable opportunity for a torpedo attack in low visibility: or when fleets were well engaged at medium ranges in ordinary visibility, provided they did not risk heavy losses. On the other hand, they were warned that such attacks might enable the enemy boats to elude them and then mount counter-attacks. Subsequent paragraphs expressed the hope that the British might have a sufficiently large superiority in cruisers to prevent, or at least to harass and impede, German torpedo attacks from their van; in such circumstances, the British van flotillas, with support from armoured and light cruisers, were authorised to move out to attack the enemy battlefleet with torpedoes.[103] Thus these destroyer instructions did envisage specific favourable circumstances in which the Grand Fleet destroyers were allowed to act offensively, despite the defensive priorities laid down so emphatically in the general instructions.

Submarines and minelayers Jellicoe hoped that submarines from the 11th Submarine Flotilla at Blyth would be able to join the Grand Fleet to take part in a fleet action but this aspiration was impracticable without boats of the new 'J'-class. Thus the only submarine order of possible relevance to the battle

---

[101] *GFBOs III*, XXIV.10–11. [102] *GFBOs III*, XXIV.17.
[103] *GFBOs III*, XXX.(1)–4 and 6–7. If bad weather made destroyer gunnery difficult, they would attack with torpedoes while the light cruisers would stop enemy torpedo attacks.

was that any groups that missed the enemy line should follow on the surface or push on towards Heligoland so as to threaten the German line of retreat.

Minelayers with the Grand Fleet were to take up position initially on the disengaged side out of danger from enemy fire. 'If required to lay mines on the enemy's route to his bases, instructions will be given to them by signal.'[104]

After action

After a decisive action, in the remaining hours of daylight cruisers of all classes and destroyers were to pursue the enemy, break up his large forces and inflict the utmost damage – though with the familiar proviso that large vessels must not overlook the possibility of being drawn over mines or submarines. The battleships would be guided by the movements and orders of the C-in-C by day and, it seems, also at night. Unlike the orders for action, there was no explicit provision for independent action by divisional commanders. After dark, the destroyers were required to attack and, having expended all their torpedoes, to engage the enemy destroyers with gunfire, while the cruisers were to continue the pursuit and destroy detached enemy ships.

However, if an action had not reached a decisive stage before darkness forced it to be broken off, the battlefleet would retire clear of the enemy so that it could move unobserved to a flank with the intention of renewing the attack at daybreak. Another reason for retiring would be that the enemy still possessed a great preponderance of torpedo craft. During the night:

Unless other forces are detailed, it will be the duty of the 1st and 2nd Light Cruiser Squadrons and the Harwich force to attack the enemy battlefleet with torpedoes if an opportunity offers, or to attack the enemy's destroyers and light cruisers, and if neither objective is practicable to endeavour to keep touch with the enemy's fleet.

The *GFBOs* defined after-action night cruising dispositions (signals 'LS9' and 'LS10') in which the battlecruisers (if present) and the armoured cruisers were astern of the battlefleet, although it was accepted that there might not be enough time to take up one of these positions. And, in any case, it was most probable that the battlecruisers and the 3LCS would be required to act independently under the orders of the VAC BCF.

The only provisions for reporting appeared in the section concerning an action that had been decisive. It ordered that ships should communicate only with the senior officers of their respective squadrons, thereby leaving the C-in-C free 'to make the large number of signals [relating] to the large questions that will require settlement'.[105]

---

[104] *GFBOs III*, XXIV.16 and XXVI.(1) and 5 (10 March 1916).   [105] *GFBOs III*, XIII.2–5.

German battle tactics

The translated German fleet orders (the 'O.X.O Papers') revealed to British commanders the tactical intentions of their opponents at the beginning of the War. No doubt, as with the *GFBOs*, these orders evolved to incorporate wartime experience but, for the British naval leaderships (and for us), they provided the best indications of how the Germans intended to fight a fleet action. The *Manoeuvring Instructions* were prefaced by the assertion that: 'Single line is the only useful formation for battleships'; this matched Jellicoe's assumptions and preferences, while the deployment signals gave details of how the Germans would deploy into line from their preparatory approach formations in columns.

The German 'Hints for Battle' declared that they were 'intended to show the aim and object for which everybody should strive, without attempting in any way to circumscribe the free decision and action, necessitated by a particular situation'. Also that:

The Leaders of Squadrons, &c., which have been ordered to act independently, or which have become so during the course of the action, are allowed full freedom of action within the experience gained by us.

But they then continued:

Against numerical superiority, an endeavour should be made to keep together, as far as possible, even as regards squadrons acting independently.

Furthermore, they anticipated that the C-in-C would remain in overall control.

It is to be hoped that, owing to our well organised action signals, we shall be able to carry out, even at an advanced state of the action, promptly and quickly, any ordered alteration of course or turn.

Even in visibility so limited that the C-in-C could not himself observe a massed torpedo attack, he still intended, after receiving a warning by wireless, to order the avoiding movement by the whole line. Thus, like the Royal Navy, the German Navy encouraged independent action – in principle. But, in practice, by insisting on the single battle line, on keeping together in the (probable) event of facing a numerically superior enemy, and on maintaining central control of the fleet in action, it gave its commanders, especially those of its battle squadrons, no greater scope for 'free decision and action'. Likewise, these translated documents suggest that German commanders received little guidance in tactical doctrine beyond the already quoted intention to close as quickly as possible to the infeasibly short range of 6,600–8,800 yards: and the desirability (except in stormy weather) of gaining the leeward position.[106]

---

[106] 'Tactical Order No. 1: Hints for Battle' in *German Tactical Orders* (see note 86), pp. 1, 3, 5, 7 and 8.

Again, as in the Royal Navy, the German battlecruisers and armoured cruisers were expected to act independently, without orders. As the 'fast division', the battlecruisers of the ISG were to attack the head of the enemy line with torpedoes and to engage his fast forces by gunfire in what was expected to develop into a local action. It was hoped that, after leading the scouting forces, the armoured cruisers of the IIISG could reach the head of the line on the disengaged side, from where their fire could assist in covering the destroyers from enemy attacks. However, two of the four ships mentioned were sunk in 1914 and 1915 and the two survivors in the IIISG were not present at Jutland. Before a battle, the more modern fast light cruisers would act as scouts and as a submarine screen. In action, their main duty was to support and protect the flotillas by their gun fire.[107]

Destroyers (with light cruisers) would form the guard under way against submarines and, due to the shortage of fast light cruisers, destroyers might have to augment the light cruisers as scouts. But, at the beginning of a fleet action, the eight destroyer flotillas (the number expected by Jellicoe) would take position on the disengaged side of the battle fleet. A pair of flotillas was stationed roughly abreast of the battlecruisers and three further pairs abreast of the van, centre and rear battle squadrons of the line. The two leading pairs were expected to attack from ahead, while those in the centre could, if the range fell sufficiently, attack through the line.

> The order to the flotillas to attack will be given by the two Leaders of Destroyers [in light cruisers], and as a rule on their own initiative . . .
>
> The main use of destroyers during a day battle must . . . be the massed attack on the van and line of the enemy and it should not commence till the two lines are closely engage.

Attack with torpedoes was the destroyers' primary duty, but opposition from enemy destroyers could be expected, in which case a gun engagement could not always be avoided, even though this might result in damage to torpedo equipment. Thus, compared with the *GFBOs*, the German orders gave priority to offensive action. But, in comparison with the destroyer tactics recommended by Beatty, German intentions were less aggressive, in that they intended neither to seize the initiative by early attack, nor to engage the more heavily gunned British boats unnecessarily.[108]

---

[107] *Ibid.*, pp. 1–4.

[108] *Ibid.*, pp. 4–5. *German Destroyer Tactics, January 1915*, pp. 21, 46 and 53 in 'German Fleet Orders' (see note 86).

4　Preliminaries

After the Battle of the Dogger Bank, for the remainder of 1915 the Grand Fleet continued to make regular sweeps into the North Sea, while the High Seas Fleet made only five fruitless sorties, none farther than 120 miles from Heligoland. Instead of surface operations, between February and August 1915, Germany conducted her first unrestricted U-boat campaign. A new phase began in January 1916 with the appointment of Vice-Admiral Reinhardt Scheer as Commander-in-Chief. He planned to exert a 'systematic and constant pressure' on the British, including sorties by the High Seas Fleet, in the hope that these would bring out some parts of the British fleet and create 'favourable opportunities for attack'.[1] Scheer's campaign began on 10 February 1916 with a destroyer sweep East of the Dogger Bank. This was followed on 5–6 March by a movement of his scouting forces, supported by the two dreadnought squadrons, to a position near the most westerly of the Frisian Islands, but this was too far south for a meeting with the British.[2] The British were next to take the offensive, in the form of a seaplane raid, launched from German waters, on the supposed airship base at Hoyer in Schleswig. By the early morning of 25 March, the carrier *Vindex* and the Harwich Force had advanced to a position just north of Sylt, with the BCF in support to the west of Horns Reef. The only result of the raid itself was the discovery that the base was actually at Tondern. Then, as the weather worsened, the destroyer *Medusa* was fatally damaged and after dark the light cruiser *Undaunted* was partly disabled, both in collisions. Beatty came south for a time in support as German light forces put to sea and, though much too late, the Admiralty ordered out the Grand Fleet early on the 26th. The German battlecruisers were then also at sea, with two supporting battle squadrons. Beatty and Tyrwhitt both turned back in the hope of meeting them as they advanced up the Schleswig coast, but by 6.30am the Germans had retired because of the atrocious weather. The British could draw several lessons from this rather chaotic operation. Ships damaged in German waters were, as

---

[1] *FDSF II*, pp. 132–4, 342–8, 412 and 420.　　[2] *FDSF II*, pp. 420–1. Tarrant, p. 45.

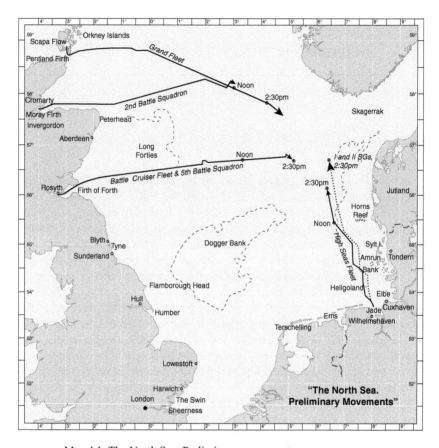

Map 4.1 The North Sea. Preliminary movements

Jellicoe feared, difficult to retrieve.[3] The Grand Fleet must sail in good time to be within supporting distance. And British advanced forces, even in terrible weather, had been able to operate in or close to German waters for about 30 hours without major losses.

After this operation, the First Sea Lord (Admiral Sir Henry Jackson) wrote to Jellicoe:

> It showed that the Germans are ready to come out when their coasts are threatened, and it looks as if your best chance of getting at them is to go for them, apparently on a minor scale, but really with the whole Fleet quite close by.

---

[3] *FDSF II*, p. 421. Corbett, pp. 290–6. Tarrant, pp. 45–6. *JP I*, p. 233.

Beatty too saw 'something more hopeful for the future, that they can under the new régime [Scheer's] be drawn'. But, in a private letter to Beatty, Jellicoe expressed his doubts about the Admiralty's wish for 'a more active policy [of] air raids, heavily supported'. The difficulty he saw was that, to avoid opposing aircraft, the raiding force must approach the coast at night and launch its seaplanes at daybreak. But then:

[T]he German heavy ships . . . won't be clear of the minefields & in a position where we could engage them before 4 p.m. This is no time to start a fight in those waters. It also involves our hanging about for a whole day in a bad locality . . . We can't wait for the following day as by then the T B Ds are out of fuel & the light cruisers very short.

Jellicoe believed the policy should be to avoid an engagement so close to enemy minefields and to submarine, destroyer and aircraft bases, even if 'we must wait until they give us a chance in a favourable position'. Beatty's reply, which showed no sign of his earlier hopefulness, accepted that, once the Germans discovered that they were not in superior force, they would be able to withdraw unharmed; that Jellicoe's arguments on the fuel question were 'unanswerable'; and that 'when the Great Day comes it will be when the enemy takes the initiative'. Both admirals were prepared to countenance further air raids as minor operations, but, as Beatty put it, the enemy 'will not come out in grand force when we set the tune'.[4]

Scheer was not long in taking the initiative. At midday on 24 April, he left the Jade for a raid on East Anglian ports. Rear-Admiral Bödicker commanded the ISG and, after *Seydlitz* struck a mine, he transferred his flag to the recently commissioned *Lützow*. At daybreak on the 26th, the three battle squadrons were positioned west of the Frisian Islands, while the battlecruisers had arrived off Lowestoft. Their bombardments of Lowestoft and Yarmouth were disrupted by the determined actions of the depleted Harwich Force, after which, rather than pressing home an attack on Tyrwhitt's ships, Bödicker withdrew while Scheer soon turned the battle squadrons for home. On the previous evening, having hastily refuelled after a previous operation, the BCF left Rosyth an hour or more before the Grand Fleet was ready to put to sea from Scapa. Both forces were then delayed by heavy seas, which also obliged them to part company with their screening destroyers. At 11.45am, when Beatty finally gave up hope of catching the retreating Germans, he was still 45 miles from the ISG, but he was also about 115 miles ahead of the 5BS, which was itself 80 miles in advance of the main battlefleet. Scheer had been informed by the German wireless station at Neumünster that strong enemy forces were at sea but, by retreating instead of uniting his forces, he missed the very opportunity that he

---

[4] *FDSF II*, p. 422. *JP I*, p. 231. *BP I*, pp. 301–3.

had been seeking, in full strength to meet portions of the British fleet as they came up piecemeal.[5]

Next, Jellicoe and Beatty mounted a new air raid. This would attack the base discovered at Tondern but it was also intended to bring out the High Seas Fleet. Thus one minefield was laid between Sylt and Horns Reef, another off Terschelling, with submarines positioned behind them. At dawn on 4 May, the seaplane carriers and escorts moved into position north of Sylt with the BCF to the west of Horns Reef; at 7am the battlefleet reached its cruising area south-west of the Skagerrak. Unfortunately, the sea conditions were such that only one seaplane succeeded in taking off and dropping its bombs. At about 9.30am, the light cruisers *Galatea* and *Phaeton* brought down the Zeppelin *L7* but at midday the Admiralty signalled that the Germans were apparently still unaware that the British fleet was at sea; at 2pm, Jellicoe ordered all his squadrons to return to their bases. An hour later, the High Seas Fleet headed northwards but it did not reach Sylt until 2.30am on the 5th. On his return, Beatty wrote to Jellicoe that he had been husbanding his destroyers' fuel and had believed that 'everything promised well toward fulfilling our final objective at daylight the next day'.

You can understand my disappointment when we were ordered to return to base. Why cannot the Admiralty leave the situation to those on the spot? . . . if we had been in the vicinity of Horn Reef at dawn we should have had a glorious time.[6]

Jellicoe seems to have left Beatty to assume that it was the Admiralty, not he, who had taken the decision to withdraw. Presumably on the basis of the intelligence he had received at noon, Jellicoe concluded that the Germans were not coming out. Beatty, after his experience of the Hoyer raid, may have been prepared to wait around in dangerous waters but, rightly or wrongly, such risks were too much for Jellicoe to entertain.

Meanwhile, in early March 1916, the 5BS reached full strength when *Valiant* joined the squadron at Scapa Flow. In the previous month, Beatty had opened a concerted campaign to get at least some of the fast battleships transferred to the BCF at Rosyth. But, given the present disposition of the British forces and the limited top speed of the *Queen Elizabeths* (not quite 24 knots), Jellicoe was opposed to the idea – not least because, as he wrote in a private letter to Jackson, 'the stronger I make Beatty the greater is the temptation for him to get involved in an independent action'. However, the question of where the 5BS should be based remained as part of a wider debate on the strategic positioning of the major British forces in the North Sea. Their separation between Scapa with Cromarty as an auxiliary base, Rosyth and Harwich

---

[5] *FDSF II*, pp. 424–7. Corbett, pp. 301–9. Tarrant, pp. 46–9.
[6] *BP* I, pp. 307–8. *FDSF II*, pp. 427–8. See also Corbett, pp. 309–11 and *GF*, pp. 182–5.

made it difficult to cover adequately the long, exposed English east coast against German raids. With adequate warning, forces from the first three could join up in the Long Forties – to the east of Aberdeen – before proceeding towards the Danish or German coasts.[7] But, as the Lowestoft Raid confirmed, against a German incursion into the southern North Sea, the departure of the BCF could not be delayed; then, as Jellicoe had anticipated since 1915, if Beatty met the German forces, he might be 100 miles or more ahead of the British battlefleet. If he encountered the whole High Seas Fleet, he might be able to retire, thereby drawing them into the arms of the Grand Fleet; but he also risked annihilation if the Germans succeeded in getting across his line of retreat.[8] As well as this danger, both the First Sea Lord and the Chief of the War Staff (acting Vice-Admiral Henry Oliver) had concluded that a decisive action with the German fleet was unlikely while the main British force remained so far north. They therefore urged Jellicoe to consider moving the Fleet to Rosyth and the Humber – though there was no question of such a move until the anchorages below the Forth Bridge had been made secure against submarine attack.[9] By mid-April, with the dreadnought strength of the main battlefleet squadrons at 24 and the Humber base ready, the Admiralty instructed Jellicoe to make a start by transferring there from the Forth the predread-noughts of the 3BS and the armoured cruisers of the 3CS. But after the Lowestoft Raid, Jellicoe proposed that the 3BS and 3CS, with *Dreadnought*, when refitted, as flagship, should be based in the Thames estuary; on 2 May, the squadrons arrived at Sheerness.[10]

Meanwhile Beatty's strength had been depleted by a collision on 22 April between *Australia* and *New Zealand*. Only *Australia* was seriously damaged and she did not rejoin the BCF until 6 June, after repairs at Devonport.[11] The continuing discussions on fleet redistribution were concluded by a conference held at Rosyth on 12 May. It was agreed that Rosyth would become the main base for both battleships and battlecruisers, with one battle squadron in the Humber. In reality, the move from Scapa Flow did not happen until April 1918.[12] But of more immediate significance, the conference also decided that Hood's 3BCS should go to Scapa to calibrate its guns and adjust the new Directors in *Inflexible* and *Indomitable*, and then carry out some much-needed target practice. To maintain Beatty's strength, the 5BS, commanded by Rear-Admiral Hugh Evan-Thomas in the *Barham*, would temporarily replace the battlecruisers. On 22 May, the five fast battleships arrived in the Forth – though *Queen Elizabeth* went directly into dock for refitting – and the 3BCS

[7] *GF*, pp. 172, 175, 180 and 186. Corbett, pp. 295 and 298.   [8] *JP I*, p. 152. *BP I*, p. 310.
[9] Gordon, p. 46. Black, pp. 149–51. *JP I*, pp. 22–30.
[10] Corbett, 315–7. *FDSF II*, p. 432. *GF*, pp. 181–2.
[11] Roberts, *Battlecruisers*, p. 123. Gordon, pp. 47–8.
[12] Black, pp. 151–4. *BP I*, pp. 299–301 and 309–12. Corbett, p. 317. *FDSF III*, p. 430–5.

sailed for Scapa Flow. At this time, Jellicoe was planning a new operation for 2 June to draw out the High Seas Fleet. A light cruiser force would make a bold incursion through the Skagerrak as far as The Sound and the Great Belt, with supporting battleships and battlecruisers in the Skagerrak and off the Norwegian coast. This operation was expected to provide an opportunity for the 5BS and the 3BCS to rejoin their usual fleets.[13] Thus Beatty could not expect to have Evan-Thomas under his command for long. Andrew Gordon concludes, though without citing his source, that in the eight days when the 5BS was at Rosyth: 'it seems that there was no meeting worth the name between the two admirals'. But, even if this was the case, Evan-Thomas evidently received at least some of the Battle Cruiser Orders, since at 8am on 31 May, he semaphored to the 5BS:

Attention is called to B.C. Orders No. 11, readiness for fighting, which are [sic] to be complied with.[14]

Thus it is likely that Evan-Thomas was aware of BCF action-doctrine, particularly the provisions of BCO4 that the absence of a signal from the Admiral usually denoted that he expected each ship (or, presumably, squadron) immediately to take whatever actions might be necessary.

Jellicoe's plans for 2 June were, of course, forestalled by the German operation that began on 31 May. While proceeding to the Lowestoft raid, Scheer had been informed that the current, partly unrestricted U-boat campaign was being called off. Certain that an attempt to continue the trade war under prize law regulations must result in heavy losses, Scheer recalled his submarine forces, with the intention of using them defensively in the Heligoland Bight but also offensively in coordination with the Fleet. He began planning a new operation, in which Hipper's scouting groups would bombard Sunderland at dawn, with the two dreadnought battle squadrons standing off in support some 50 miles east of Flamborough Head. U-boats would be ready off the enemy's bases to attack as the British ships came out in response. Initially, the IIBS of predreadnoughts was to be held back to defend the Bight but its commander, Rear-Admiral Franz Mauve, persuaded Scheer (who had commanded the squadron at the outbreak of the War) to allow his ships to accompany the dreadnoughts. The plan depended on extensive reconnaissance by Zeppelins to guard against the German squadrons being surprised by superior British forces. At first, the operation was scheduled for 17 May, the date by which the *Seydlitz* was expected to have been repaired. But on 9 May it was discovered that seven of the battleships of the IIIBS – the most modern in the fleet – had problems with their condensers, which would not be remedied until the 23rd. Then early

---

[13] Gordon, pp. 48–9 and 51. *BP I*, pp. 306 and 308. *CAWFS 1906–21*, p. 34. Corbett, pp. 320–1.
[14] Gordon, pp. 54–6. *OD*(M), p. 427.

on that day, *Seydlitz* failed the flooding tests on her repairs; she would not now be seaworthy until 29 May.[15]

After the first postponement, it was decided to send out the U-boats as they became ready. Between 17 and 22 May, ten boats took up initial positions in the central North Sea before, on 23 May, they moved into wedge-shaped sectors off the main British bases: two off the Pentland Firth to cover Scapa Flow and the Moray Firth; seven off the Forth; while *U47* was to reconnoitre Sunderland and then go to an area off Peterhead which also covered the exit from the Moray Firth. They were urged to avoid discovery and to wait until they received the wireless message: 'Take into account that enemy forces may be putting to sea'. This would actually indicate that the High Seas Fleet was putting to sea and that the U-boats should move close to the British bases. Three minelaying U-boats were also despatched; only *U75*, on the night of 28/29 May, was successful in laying a field, though, since it was to the west of the Orkneys, it was not a threat to ships leaving Scapa Flow for the North Sea. (The previous day, *U74* had been sunk near Peterhead by four armed trawlers.) *UB27* was ordered to force her way into the Firth of Forth but, after trouble with her engines and becoming entangled in a large net, she was forced to abandon her mission. *U46* and *U67* were positioned NW of Terschelling to cover any advance by the Harwich Force. (Two U-boats from the Flanders flotilla were also positioned off the Humber but they did not play any part in subsequent events.)[16]

The waiting U-boats had orders to return to their bases on the evening of 1 June, while, as May drew to a close, continuing unfavourable weather seemed set to rule out the use of airships for reconnaissance. On the 28th, Scheer issued an alternative plan that did not depend on the Zeppelins. Its object was still to draw out British forces. As Scheer himself described it:

Hipper . . . was . . . to leave the Jade at 2am and push on to the Skagerrak, keeping out of sight of Horns Reef and the Danish Coast, to show himself before dark off the Norwegian Coast, so that the British would receive news of the operation, and to carry out a commerce warfare during the late afternoon and the following night off and in the Skagerrak.

The main Fleet . . . was to follow at 2.30am to support the Scouting Forces . . . and to meet them on the [following] morning.[17]

The rendezvous was to be just off the entrance to the Skagerrak at 4am.[18] At 10.02pm on 28 May, Scheer ordered his forces to reach a state of readiness for an operation from 7am the next morning, though he had not yet given up the

---

[15] *FDSF II*, pp. 347–8. Scheer, pp. 129–34. Tarrant, pp. 44 and 49–50.

[16] Tarrant, pp. 50–3 and 241–3 (at the top of p. 242, *U24* should be *U22* and *U46* should not be in this group). On 5 June, the cruiser *Hampshire*, with Lord Kitchener aboard, was lost on *U75*'s minefield: *GF*, pp. 268–9.

[17] Tarrant, p. 54. Scheer's despatch, *OD*, p. 588.

[18] *OD*, 'German Plan I' shows the rendezvous at about 57°14' N, 7°13' E.

Sunderland plan. At 9.44am on the 30th, he ordered the Fleet to be assembled in the outer roads by 7pm at the latest, while at 10.04am, the Bruges wireless station broadcast the warning message to the waiting U-boats. With the unfavourable north-westerly wind still blowing, at 5.36pm, a coded message was broadcast which signified that the Skagerrak operation would be mounted on the 31st. At 1am the next morning, Hipper's scouting forces left their anchorages in the outer Jade Roads. At 2.30am, Scheer ordered the battle squadrons and their supporting vessels in the Jade to weigh anchor; the IIBS had already put to sea from the Elbe at 1.45am and at 4am they formed astern of the dreadnoughts. At about 7am, Hipper's battlecruisers reached the northern end of the swept channel through the British minefields west of the Amrun Bank; the battleships followed them some two hours later. As they reached the open sea, both forces turned NW to pass 35 miles to the west of the Horns Reef light vessel. At 11.53am, Scheer ordered the battlefleet onto course N towards the entrance to the Skagerrak, a turn that, it seems, had already been anticipated by Hipper.[19]

As the Germans put to sea, their wireless messages had already revealed many of their operational intentions to the Admiralty's signals intelligence organisation centred on Room 40, Old Building (40 O.B.). Following the capture of German naval codes in 1914, Room 40 and its outstations had become proficient at intercepting and decrypting the numerous German wireless messages and in deducing the structure of new code books as they replaced the old ones. Beginning early in 1915, at the instigation of the recently appointed Director of the Intelligence Division (DID) Captain Reginald Hall, a network of wireless direction-finding (DF) stations was created so that, if cross-bearings of a transmission could be taken by two or more stations, the position of the vessel responsible could be determined; the six stations covering the North Sea were under the DID's direct control. Hall selected one of his intelligence officers, Commander Herbert Hope, to provide the naval expertise needed for the analysis of these sources of signals intelligence; on 11 November 1914, Hope joined Room 40 where he kept the diary that was the basis of his running analysis of the naval situation. His position was pivotal in supplying intelligence to the Admiralty officers responsible for operations, the Director of the Operations Division (DOD), Captain Thomas Jackson, and his superior, the Chief of the War Staff (COS).[20] Both occupied offices in Admiralty House (the official residence of the First Lord adjoining the Admiralty in Whitehall) where they were assisted by three

---

[19] Frank Birch and William Clarke, 'A Contribution to the History of German Naval Warfare 1914–1918', Vol. I, table of German signals with Chapter X, 'Jutland', HW 7/1. Here, all times in German signals have been converted to Greenwich Mean Time (GMT); wherever possible, the time used is from the 'time group' in the message itself; thus it is equivalent to the British 'time-of-origin'. Also Tarrant, pp. 54–6, 65 and 272–4.

[20] Beesly, Chapters 1–4 and especially pp. 18–20 and 69–70. See also *FDSF III*, p. 176. 'Narrative of Capt. Hope' (before June 1926) appended to William Clarke, 'History of Room 40, O.B.', HW 3/3.

Duty Captains; the COS and DOD also had bedrooms in Admiralty House so they were immediately available day and night. Close by was a large map room and the War Registry through which passed all messages between the Admiralty and British naval bases and forces at sea.[21] In Room 40, each German message was decrypted and its translation was written out in full on a numbered 'flimsy' form from which carbon copies were made at the same time.[22] According to Hope (promoted to Captain by the time of Jutland), he retained one copy for reference while sending out one to the DOD and another to the DID. However, if the COS was present, he may have been shown the DOD's copy first although, since Oliver and Jackson worked so closely together, this made little difference. If Captain Hope thought it necessary, he also provided additional explanatory notes for the DOD.[23] Hope also sent hand-written notes to the DOD with the information obtained from direction finding; in addition to a position, these notes were usually able to identify the transmitting enemy ship from its call-sign. Admiralty orders for the C-in-C, Grand Fleet were sent through the War Registry: by secure land-telegraph when the Fleet was in harbour and for transmission from the Cleethorpes W/T station when he was at sea. The War Registry also distributed the typed forms that recorded British signals picked up by the 'Y-station' at Stockton. Copies of these 'Intercept' forms were sent to the DOD, the First Sea Lord and Sir Arthur Wilson; several are marked 'Seen by COS' and Oliver appears to have been shown them 'in rough' even before they were typed.[24]

Thus all the signals intelligence relating to a major operation like Jutland flowed to the COS and the DOD and their supporting staff in Admiralty House, where they could follow the developing situation on the maps in the map room and in Oliver's office. If anything in the intercepts needed clarifying, Hope could be consulted in person or by telephone.[25] When present, Oliver himself seems to have retained the decision on what intelligence should be passed on to commanders afloat – including the C-in-C, Grand Fleet – and how it should be

[21] Admiral of the Fleet Sir Henry Oliver, 'Recollections, Vol. II' (1946), pp. 103, 123, 125, 137–8, 180 and 189, OLV/12. Black, pp. 263–5 for Admiralty telephone directory for Feb. 1916.

[22] Carbon copies of the forms, each with a 5-digit serial number, are in 'Intercepts of German signals … Battle of Jutland', ADM 137/4710. Transcriptions of selected forms are in *NSA*, Appendix G and (though without serial numbers) in Birch and Clarke, table of German signals (see note 19) and in Hines, pp. 1150–3. A post-war log of German 'Jutland Signals' is in ADM 137/4067.

[23] 'Narrative of Capt. Hope' (see note 20) and Oliver, pp. 138 and 180 (see note 21). (Alistair Denniston's statement that one copy went to the COS rather than the DOD described the arrangements in the early days of Room 40: Beesly, pp. 17 and 44.)

[24] The DF notes (of 15, only two are explicitly addressed, both to DOD) and the British intercepts are in 'Jutland. Telegraphic Record (C.O.S.)', ADM 137/1642. Oliver, pp. 123, 125 and 180. E E Bradford, *Life of Admiral of the Fleet Sir Arthut Knyvet Wilson* (London: John Murray, 1923), p. 245.

[25] Black, p. 265 for Hope's telephone number and 40 OB location. Notice that the majority of the DOD's staff were in 37, 38 and 39b OB.

worded.[26] It was vital that Britain's ability to intercept and decrypt German signals be kept absolutely secret but, after the War, the *Naval Staff Appreciation* was very critical of the Admiralty's system as 'a policy of secrecy, amounting to an absolute obsession'. This view, which has been very influential, was probably inspired by Beatty who, after the Lowestoft Raid, had pronounced that: 'The Chief of the War Staff has priceless information . . . which he sits on until it is too late . . . the War Staff has developed into a One Man Show.'[27] If an exaggeration, the COS certainly had a pivotal role in the Admiralty's control of operations and we shall have to be alert for any vital information that was sat on as the Battle of Jutland unfolded.

From 16 May onwards, Room 40 had detected the despatch of some 16 U-boats to the North. 'As these boats were not heard of on the Trade Routes after the usual interval, the inference was that there was some possibility of North Sea activity.' Then for several days at the end of the month, German mine-clearing vessels had been busy 'particularly on the Northern Route out of the Heligoland Bight west of Amrun Bank up to Horn Reef'. A further pointer to Scheer's outward route was received on 30 May; a signal timed at 10.37am from Hipper requested, 'Tomorrow early aeroplanes are to search for enemy submarines, if possible . . . to the West of Amrun Bank and List.'[28] By then, Room 40 had already intercepted and decrypted Scheer's orders to the High Seas Fleet of 28 May (10.02pm) to assume a state of readiness and of 30 May (9.44am) to assemble in the outer roads no later than 7pm. The British had also picked up the warning to the waiting U-boats from the Bruges wireless station. But, because the codebook used was recent and still being built up by Room 40, the signal was sent out as 'Reckon on the proceeding out of our own [i.e. German rather than British] forces on May 31st and June 1st'. Thus what had been intended as a rather uninformative message actually served to raise British expectations. These were already high since German orders to lightships and for other measures, which were similar to those which had preceded earlier operations, were also being picked up.[29]

---

[26] Beesly (p. 41, see also p. 147) states that Oliver 'alone drafted almost every signal *in his own hand*' (my emphasis here and below). But this claim appears in the context of the handling of Room 40 intelligence and, as Halpern (p. 37) implies, it must only refer to signals based on the decrypts. Herbert Richmond, never slow to criticise Admiralty officers, had a great respect for Oliver, even though he recognised that the latter worked too hard and tried to do everything himself, *including his own typing* – Richmond, pp. 114, 142, 233, 244 and 256. The last point further undermines the notion that Oliver wrote out all Admiralty signals by hand.

[27] *NSA*, pp. 132–3. Beesly, pp. 149–50. Roskill, pp. 145–6. *FDSF III*, pp. 176–7.

[28] The Amrun Bank lay to the west of the island of Sylt, List being at the island's northern tip.

[29] Captain H W Hope, '31st May' and 'Notes of Action of May 31, June 1' in ADM 137/4168. Entry for Thursday 1 June in 'Captain Hope's Diary Feb 22nd-Dec 31st', ADM 137/4169. Birch and Clarke, table of German signals. Hipper's signal is not mentioned by Hope but is in Birch and Clarke's table.

At 3.01pm, the Admiral Commanding the German IIBS asked, 'Are prize crews to be left behind?' Since the IIBS normally provided the prize crews that brought in intercepted merchantmen, the affirmative reply suggested that the predreadnoughts would be taking part. Thus Scheer's coded order timed at 3.36pm on 30 May – sent out from Room 40 as 'On 31st May Most secret [?] 2490' – was recognised at once as the order for the operation to proceed. Further confirmation came with orders at 4.42pm to open the Wilhelmshaven barrier between midnight and 2.30am, and, at 6.41pm, for 'Flag to take over wireless in Deutsche Bucht at 9pm'. A further signal timed at 5.41pm was also received in Room 40, but it 'was made in an entirely new cipher, and was not deciphered until the afternoon of the 31st'.[30] The handling of this signal, which turned out to be about Scheer's W/T call-sign, has become notorious in Jutland historiography as evidence for a calamitous failure of communication between Room 40 and the DOD, Thomas Jackson (of which more later).

The decrypted German messages received from Room 40 enabled the Admiralty to signal Jellicoe (presumably in Oliver's own words) first that the Germans were preparing to go to sea and then that he should take the Grand Fleet eastwards beyond the Long Forties (east of Aberdeen) towards the Skagerrak (see Table 4.1).[31] The Admiralty gave Jellicoe all the information available on Scheer's outward route, while the order to rendezvous east of the Long Forties suggests that the COS and his staff had concluded that the Germans intended to continue northwards. (In view of the persistently unfavourable weather for airships, it is a mystery why the first signal supposed that the German object might be to meet returning Zeppelins.) Jellicoe himself chose the rendezvous for the battlefleet and the BCF for 2pm on the 31st. If the correct positions were reached, Beatty would then be 69 miles SbyE (magnetic) from the main fleet. This sort of distance had become routine during British sweeps made in response to German operations with unknown objectives.[32] But, if Beatty encountered a superior force while still scouting ahead, he would need more than 90 minutes to fall back on the support of the battlefleet.[33]

The decrypted signals sent out from Room 40 had established that both the ISG and the IIBS would be among the German fleet assembling in the outer

---

[30] Birch and Clarke, table of German signals (though it omits that for 5.41). Hope's 'Diary' and 'Notes of Action'. 'Intercepts' (see note 22) nos. 20293, 20310, 20311 and 20383.

[31] *JP I*, pp. 253–4 (it has been assumed that the first three signals, which are from this source, were sent by land telegraph). *OD*(M), pp. 398–9, 401, 403 and 405.

[32] Corbett, p. 324. *FDSF III*, pp. 51–3.

[33] This assumes an optimistic 20 knots for the battlefleet and, for the BCF with the 5BS in company, 24 knots.

Table 4.1. *Signals between Admiralty and C-in-C, 30 May*

Time of despatch	From	To	System	Message	Time of origin
pm, 30 May					
Noon, 2.20 (recd.)	Admiralty	C-in-C	[L/T]	Urgent . . . There are indications that German fleet are in outer roads by 7pm tonight and may go to sea early tomorrow. Object may be to have them ready to support returning Zeppelins. Sixteen German submarines are now at sea, most of which are believed to be in the North Sea, two are off Terschelling	
5.28	Admiralty	C-in-C	[L/T]	Urgent . . . Raise steam. Acknowledge	
5.55	Admiralty	C-in-C SO BCF	[L/T]	Germans intend some operation tomorrow and leave via eastern route and Horns Reef LV. Operation appears to extend over 31st May and 1st June. You should concentrate to the eastward of Long Forties ready for eventualities	1740
5.55	Admiralty	C-in-C	L/T	3BS, 3CS, 5LCS and Harwich destroyers will not be sent out until more is known	
7.30	C-in-C	SO 2BS	L/T	Leave as soon as ready, pass through 58°15′N, 2°0′ E, meet me 2pm tomorrow . . . 57°45′N, 4°15′E. Several Enemy Submarines known to be in North Sea	
8.15 (recd.)	C-in-C	SO BCF	L/T	Available vessels of BCF, 5BS and Destroyers, including Harwich destroyers, proceed to approximately . . . 56°40′N, 5°E. desirable to economise Destroyer fuel. Presume you will be there about 2pm tomorrow, Wednesday, 31st May. I shall be in about 57°45′N, 4°15′E by 2pm, unless delayed by fog. 3BCS, *Chester* and *Canterbury* will leave with me. I may send them on to your rendezvous. If no news by 2pm, stand towards me to get in visual communication. I will steer for Horn Reef from 57°45′N, 4°15′E	1937
9.00	C-in-C	Admiralty	L/T	Priority. Fleet leaving 9.30pm today, Tuesday	

roads, but this information was not passed on to Jellicoe. Presumably, he could be relied upon to assume that the ISG and the two German dreadnought squadrons would participate. But the presence of the IIBS was unusual and, had Jellicoe known of it, he might have realised that the Germans were mounting an exceptionally big operation. Not that this omission had any immediate consequences; all the available British forces were preparing to leave their anchorages. 30 May found *Iron Duke*, the 4BS, 1BS, 3BCS and 2CS at Scapa Flow; the 2BS and 1CS at Cromarty; and, at Rosyth, *Lion*, the 1BCS and 2BCS and the 5BS. The 3BCS was the first squadron to weigh anchor, at 8.50pm, the rest of Jellicoe's force following, *Iron Duke* at 9.57pm, in Organisation No. 2. From the Pentland Skerries, their course was 84° True (S83°E Magnetic)[34] until 1.30am on the 31st, then S77°E and, at 1.55am, S73°E, speed 17 knots; at 2.35am, Jellicoe ordered the first of the irregular two-point turns-together whereby the fleet zigzagged as an anti-submarine precaution. At 5am, he turned his ships to S50°E at 16 knots, a course designed to take him to his intended position at 2pm.[35] In the Cromarty Firth, the ships of the 2BS and 1CS weighed between 9.30pm and 9.40pm and, after steering N79°E, turned to S72°E at 11.20pm and to S87°E at 2.36am, speed 19 knots. At 8.36am, the 1CS sighted the battlefleet and by 9.17am were joining with the 2CS in the advanced cruiser line. It took longer for the 2BS to form up with the other battle squadrons, but, at 11.25, Jellicoe congratulated the 2BS on a 'Manoeuvre well executed'.[36] At Rosyth, Beatty's ships weighed anchor between 9.35 and 9.50pm, the 5BS at 10.03pm; he ordered an initial course of 66° True (N79°E), then S81°E from 1.15am, speed 18 knots. He commenced zigzagging at 2.30, increasing to 19½ knots at 2.45am – which gave a speed of advance of 18 knots. In response to a submarine alert from the light cruiser *Yarmouth*, at 8.22am his columns turned eight points in succession to port, before, at 8.40, reverting to course S81°E towards his two o'clock position.[37]

Of the vessels in Scapa Flow, the seaplane carrier *Campania* had been ordered at 6.37pm to leave last, astern of the light cruiser *Blanche*. But, somehow, *Campania's* watch seems to have missed the departure of the whole Grand Fleet, including *Blanche*, perhaps because the latter was not ordered by the C-in-C to show a stern light until about half an hour after she got underway. *Campania* herself did not weigh anchor until 12.40am and then proceeded alone at 20 knots. But Jellicoe thought that she did not have the speed to catch up and, at 4.37am, ordered her to return to base.[38] Thus the battlefleet would not be able to call on aerial reconnaissance until it joined forces with the BCF, which was accompanied by its own carrier, the *Engadine*.

---

[34] True courses have been converted to magnetic (normally rounded to a whole number of degrees) using a magnetic variation of 13°15′ W: Corbett, p. 327, n. 2. For the convention for expressing magnetic courses in degrees rather than as compass points, see *Grand Fleet Signal Orders*, January 1916, Section 8, ADM 137/266 and *GSB 1915*, p. 34.

[35] *OD*, p. 5 and *OD*(M), pp. 403–5, 408, 414–15 and 421–2. *Iron Duke's* track chart (*OD*, Plate 6a) differs in detail prior to 5am.

[36] *OD*(M), pp. 406–7, 409–11, 414–15, 429, 431 and 437.

[37] *OD*(M), pp. 408–9, 412–13, 415, 428, 430 and 434.

[38] William Schleihauf, 'What Happened to the *Campania*?', *Mariner's Mirror* (November 2004), 90.4, pp. 464–6. Additional signals in *OD*(M), pp. 410 and 414. *Campania* would have taken until about 4pm to close.

Orders of battle

Battleships and battlecruisers

Tables 4.2 and 4.3 show the organisations of the opposing battle lines by squadrons and, more importantly for manoeuvring, by divisions; in daylight, both sides opted for divisions of four ships. (At night, each British squadron constituted a division, with *Marlborough* leading the 3rd Division.)

Table 4.2. *British battle squadrons (except 5BS) in Organisation No. 5*

Squadron	Division (daytime)	Ship (admiral)	Class	Broadside (primary)
2BS	1st	*King George V* (Vice-Admiral Sir Thomas Martyn Jerram)	*King George V*	10–13.5in (1,400lb)
		Ajax		
		Centurion		
		Erin	n/a	
	2nd	*Orion* (Rear-Admiral Arthur Leveson)	*Orion*	10–13.5in (1,250lb)
		Monarch		
		Conqueror		
		Thunderer		
Fleet flagship	3rd	*Iron Duke* (Admiral Sir John Jellicoe)	*Iron Duke*	10–13.5in (1,400lb)
		Royal Oak	*Revenge*	8–15in
		Superb (Rear-Admiral Alexander Duff)	*Bellerophon*	8–12in
		Canada	n/a	10–14in
4BS	4th	*Benbow* (Vice-Admiral Sir Doveton Sturdee)	*Iron Duke*	10–13.5in (1,400lb)
		Bellerophon	*Bellerophon*	
		Temeraire		8–12in
		Vanguard	*St Vincent*	
1BS	5th	*Colossus* (Rear-Admiral Ernest Gaunt)	*Colossus*	10–12in
		Collingwood	*St Vincent*	8–12in
		Neptune	n/a	10–12in
		St Vincent	*St Vincent*	8–12in
	6th	*Marlborough* (Vice-Admiral Sir Cecil Burney)	*Iron Duke*	10–13.5in (1,400lb)
		Revenge	*Revenge*	8–15in
		Hercules	*Colossus*	10–12in
		Agincourt	n/a	14–12in

As well as *Queen Elizabeth*, on 30 May *Emperor of India* (*Iron Duke* class) was also in dockyard hands. The newest member of the *Revenge* class, *Royal Sovereign*, had joined the Grand Fleet on 25 May but she was not battle-ready and remained in harbour.[39] In the absence of the 5BS, Jellicoe led 24 dreadnought battleships in Organisation No. 5, which remained in force until nightfall. At 9.45am, Jellicoe had ordered Jerram by searchlight: 'Form divisions in line ahead disposed abeam to starboard. Columns eight cables apart'; that is, the divisions should be disposed in divisional number order from port to starboard. In close order, which was assumed unless ordered otherwise, ships in column were separated by 2½ cables, stem to stem; thus the columns were not yet at the manoeuvring distance of ten cables required for equal-speed manoeuvres.[40] Of the six divisions forming the British battleline, the most homogeneous were the 1st and 2nd, each (*Erin* excepted) of a single class of 'super-dreadnought'. The others were more various. The two stronger were the 3rd Division (though *Royal Oak* had only commissioned in May)[41] and the 6th; the weaker divisions were the 4th and especially the 5th, the latter's ships being armed only with 12in guns. Thus Jellicoe's disposition of the divisions to starboard implied a clear preference for a deployment led by the port column.[42] This had two advantages: three of the four strongest divisions would be leading; and the flagship would be about one-third of the way along the line, from which position the C-in-C could see more of what was happening in the van and give a direct lead to two-thirds of the line. Further, given the prevailing south-westerly winds in the North Sea and the probable approach courses of the two fleets from their bases, a port deployment gave a better chance of seizing the leeward position that was, normally, the better for gunnery. And, if the enemy was encountered to starboard, it might also be possible to get across the German line of retreat.

When the German battlefleet debouched from the swept channel through the minefields, it remained in single line-ahead in open order, with 700 metres (about 3½ cables) between ships and 3,500 metres (19 cables) between squadrons. This was the German Navy's preferred cruising formation; columns of divisions were regarded as a formation for the approach only.[43] Scheer lacked one modern dreadnought – *König Albert* of the *Kaiser* class was another recent victim of condenser trouble – while *Bayern* was not fully commissioned.[44]

---

[39] Campbell, p. 17. *OD*, p. 399.

[40] *OD*(M), p. 432. Manoeuvring distance was the distance apart of the ships in column multiplied by the number of ships in the longest column: *GSB 1915*, p. 292.

[41] *CAWFS 1906–21*, p. 36.   [42] McLaughlin, 'Equal Speed', pp. 128–9.

[43] Scheer, pp. 145–6. Tactical Order No. 24, 'Approach Formation', 1 March 1917 in *German Navy Tactical Orders*, April 1920, ADM 186/55.

[44] Scheer, p. 140. Campbell, p. 17.

Table 4.3. *German battle squadrons*

Squadron	Division	Ship (admiral)	Class	Broadside (primary)
IIIBS	Vth	*König* (Rear-Admiral Paul Behncke) *Grosser Kurfürst* *Markgraf* *Kronprinz*	*König*	10–12in
	VIth	*Kaiser* (Rear-Admiral H Nordmann) *Prinzregent Luitpold* *Kaiserin*	*Kaiser*	10–12in
Fleet flagship		*Friedrich der Grosse* (Vice-Admiral Reinhard Scheer)		
IBS	Ist	*Ostfriesland* (Vice-Admiral Ehrhard Schmidt) *Thüringen* *Helgoland* *Oldenburg*	*Helgoland*	8–12in
	IInd	*Posen* (Rear-Admiral W Engelhardt) *Rheinland* *Nassau* *Westfalen*	*Nassau*	8–11.1in
IIBS	IIIrd	*Deutschland* (Rear-Admiral Franz Mauve) *Pommern* *Schlesien*	*Deutschland*	4–11.1in
	IVth	*Schleswig-Holstein* *Hessen* *Hannover* (Rear-Admiral F von Dalwigk zu Lichtenfels)	*Deutschland* *Braunschweig* *Deutschland*	4–11.1in

The line was led by the Vth and VIth Divisions of, respectively, the *König* and *Kaiser* classes, followed by the flagship, *Friedrich der Grosse*. Then came the older dreadnoughts of the Ist and IInd Divisions; later, the flagship would remain with them when a gap opened in the line between the VIth and Ist Divisions.[45] The rear of the German line was formed, as two three-ship divisions, by six predreadnoughts of Mauve's IIBS.[46] Thus Jellicoe's battleline was superior both in numbers, heavy guns and, by three knots, in speed.

---

[45] Tarrant, p. 25 explicitly lists the flagship as part of the VIth Division but his *GOA*-based charts (e.g. pp. 95 and 160) show her ahead or astern of *Ostfriesland*. *GOA*, p. 267 does not assign her to a division. *AN*, p. 94 states explicitly that she was in the Ist Division.

[46] Tarrant, pp. 61 and 258. *Preussen* was in the Baltic and *Lothringen* unfit: Scheer, p. 140. *Hannover*'s position is that after 4pm on 31 May.

Table 4.4. *British battlecruisers and fast battleships*

Squadron	Ship (admiral)	Class	Broadside (primary)
Flagship	*Lion* (Vice-Admiral Sir David Beatty)		8–13.5in (1,250lb)
1BCS	*Princess Royal* (Rear-Admiral Osmond de B. Brock)	*Lion*	
	Queen Mary		8–13.5in
	Tiger	n/a	(1,400lb)
2BCS	*New Zealand* (Rear-Admiral H William Pakenham) *Indefatigable*	*Indefatigable*	8–12in
3BCS	*Invincible* (Rear-Admiral Hon. Horace Hood) *Inflexible* *Indomitable*	*Invincible*	6–12in
5BS	*Barham* (Rear-Admiral Hugh Evan-Thomas) *Valiant* *Warspite* *Malaya*	*Queen Elizabeth*	8–15in

Lion, as a fleet flagship, was not strictly part of the 1BCS, though she normally manoeuvred with that squadron. The 2BCS was reduced to two ships but the absence of *Australia* and the 3BCS was more than made up by the presence of the 5BS. At 2.50am on the 31st, Beatty ordered the 2BCS to take station three miles on the flagship's beam, while the 5BS followed astern. But, at 10.10am, he changed their positions, placing the 2BCS on a bearing NE at three miles, the 5BS NW at five miles. All three squadrons were in single line-ahead, in the order listed.[47]

Hipper flew his flag in the new battlecruiser *Lützow*; with *Seydlitz* repaired at last, he had all five of Germany's available battlecruisers at his disposal. After emerging from the minefields in the Heligoland Bight, Hipper's scouting forces led the German advance, with the ISG in line-ahead some 50 miles in advance of the High Seas Fleet.[48] Thus Beatty had, in numbers alone, a 2:1 superiority. If Jellicoe and Beatty had joined forces without incident later on the 31st, Beatty's BCF would still have enjoyed a numerical advantage of 9:5, although five of his nine ships would have been of the older types with 12in guns and inadequate armour protection. Jellicoe, on the other hand, would have regained

---

[47] *OD*, pp. 33, 45–6, 129–30, 147, 150, 160, 192, 416 and 434.   [48] Tarrant, pp. 62 and 259.

Table 4.5. *German battlecruisers*

Squadron	Ship (admiral)	Class	Broadside (primary)
ISG	*Lützow* (Vice-Admiral Franz Hipper) *Derfflinger*	*Derfflinger*	8–12in
	Seydlitz	n/a	10–11.1in
	Moltke	*Moltke*	
	Von der Tann	n/a	8–11.1in

the four ships of his fast division[49] and his numerical advantage would have increased to 28:22. With the 5BS in company, Beatty was limited to their top speed of just under 24 knots. With the BCF as normally constituted, its nominal top speed was set by the 25 knots of the 12in-gunned classes; this was little different from the 24.8 knot design speed of *Von der Tann*. However, while the British ships achieved speeds of over 26 knots on trial, the *Von der Tann* managed a maximum of 27.4 knots,[50] so Hipper had the advantage, coal permitting, if speed had to be forced.

The British advantage in offensive power was even greater. The right-hand columns of Tables 4.2–4.5 show the maximum broadside fire from the primary armaments; for both sides, only half the guns are counted in wing turrets and, due to their very limited cross-deck arcs, in the *en échelon* turrets of the *Invincibles*. Table 4.6 then compares the total broadside weights of fire before and after the junction of Jellicoe's and Beatty's forces.[51] If Jellicoe alone encountered Scheer's battle squadrons, the British advantage was almost 2:1; once the 5BS rejoined, the ratio increased to over 2.4:1. Beatty began the day with more than 3.5 times Hipper's weight of fire. And, even if the scouting forces did not meet until after the 3BCS and 5BS changed places, Beatty's advantage was still more than 2:1.

Of course, weight of primary broadside alone is only a crude measure of offensive potential. It takes no account of differences in gunnery efficiency or in the effectiveness of hits. Nonetheless, the ratios were large enough for there to be no doubt where the offensive advantage lay. On the other hand, German ships were, in general, stronger defensively in their protection against shellfire and underwater attack; the disparity was particularly stark in the comparison between all the German battlecruisers and Beatty's six older battlecruisers. But

---

[49] The 7th in Organisation No. 5: *GFBOs III*, I.
[50] Roberts, *Battlecruisers*, pp. 75–7. Gröner I, p. 63. Staff, *World War One*, pp. 15 and 24.
[51] Projectile weights from Campbell, p. 344.

Table 4.6. *Comparative battlefleet broadside weights of fire*

Admiral	Squadrons (including flagships)	Number of ships	Total weight primary broadside lb	British:German ratio primary broadside weight
Scheer	IBS, IIBS, IIIBS	22	137,312	
Jellicoe	1BS, 2BS, 4BS	24	272,780	1.99
	1BS, 2BS, 4BS, 5BS	28	334,220	2.43
Hipper	ISG	5	32,936	
Beatty	1BCS, 2BCS, 5BS	10	117,440	3.57
	1BCS, 2BCS, 3BCS	9	71,300	2.16

these differences in offensive and defensive potential only emphasised the tactical imperative facing Jellicoe and especially Beatty: that victory depended on bringing the full weight of their superior firepower to bear effectively on the German squadrons as quickly as possible once action commenced, preferably at the longer ranges that favoured the heavier British guns. Then, under a greater weight of fire distributed over fewer ships, German fire would be disrupted despite their ships' superior protection and the weaker protection of the British ships would not be put to the test.

Armoured cruisers

None of the three German armoured cruisers that survived in 1916 were fit to accompany the fleet.[52] In the Grand Fleet, the more modern examples of this obsolescent type were still expected to scout ahead of the battlefleet, sometimes with the BCF ahead and usually supported by the 5BS following astern. But on the morning of 31 May, only Hood's three battlecruisers were with the battlefleet. Initially, the 3BCS led the fleet though, with only two light cruisers and four destroyers in company, its usefulness as a scouting force was limited. Also on the previous evening, Jellicoe had already advised Beatty that he might send Hood's ships on to the battlecruiser rendezvous, in which case the battlefleet would have to rely entirely on the unsupported armoured cruisers as its advanced scouts. They are listed in Table 4.7 in their order in the scouting line from port (A) to starboard (G) in the lettered positions of the cruising dispositions.[53]

[52] Scheer, p. 135 (note).
[53] *OD*, pp. 6, 163 and *OD*(M), p. 403. *GFBOs III*, XXI, 'Cruising Dispositions' 'LS1' and (for position E) 'LS6' and 'LS8'. (Letter E was used in some diagrams for a flotilla position.)

Table 4.7. *British armoured cruisers*

Squadron	Ship (admiral)	Position	Class	Guns
2CS	*Cochrane*	A	*Warrior*	6-9.2in, 4-7.5in
	Shannon	B	*Minotaur*	4-9.2in, 10-7.5in
	Minotaur (Rear-Admiral Herbert Heath)	C		
	Hampshire	C (linking ship)	*Devonshire*	4-7.5in, 6-6in
1CS	*Defence* (Rear-Admiral Sir Robert Arbuthnot)	D	*Minotaur*	4-9.2in, 10-7.5in
	Warrior	D	*Warrior*	6-9.2in, 4-7.5in
	Duke of Edinburgh	F	*Duke of Edinburgh*	6-9.2in, 10-6in
	Black Prince	G		

On 30 May, with the 3CS already at Sheerness, *Achilles* refitting and *Donegal* detached off the Norwegian coast, the four armoured cruisers remaining at Scapa were reorganised by amalgamating the 7CS with the 2CS under the command of Rear-Admiral Heath. The 1CS, commanded by Rear-Admiral Sir Robert Arbuthnot, sailed with the 2BS from Cromarty. When the 1CS began joining the cruiser line at 9.17am on the 31st, Jellicoe had already ordered that the armoured cruisers should be 12 miles ahead of the battlefleet in the 'LS1' cruising disposition. Thus, in accordance with the *GFBOs*, the separation between the lettered positions on the disposition diagram was five miles.[54] *Hampshire* was probably about three miles astern of *Minotaur*,[55] while, further back, the light cruiser *Active* occupied the large hole in position J left by the absence of the 5BS. At 11.19am, Heath (now Senior Officer, Cruisers) informed Jellicoe that all eight cruisers were in their correct positions.[56]

With top speeds of 22–23 knots, they had only a small speed margin for keeping ahead of the battlefleet and for moving to their deployment positions in the van and rear of the battleline. Furthermore, in the absence of German ships of their own type, the first heavy ships they were likely to meet would be dreadnought battlecruisers or battleships; against such opponents, their

---

[54] *OD*(M), pp. 400, 402, 406, 426, 431 and 436. *GFBOs III*, XXI.2 and 'LS1'.
[55] At 5.44am, *Hampshire* was 7½ miles from *Iron Duke* when the screen was ten miles ahead: *OD* (M), pp. 417 and 424.
[56] *OD*, pp. 273, 302 and *OD*(M), pp. 414 and 437.

protection was quite insufficient,[57] though, it should be emphasised, little different from the battlecruisers of the 2BCS and 3BCS.

Light cruisers

In both fleets, the light cruisers were distributed between the scouting forces and the main battlefleets. Most were organised in squadrons, a few bore commodores or captains of destroyers, four in the Grand Fleet served as repeating ships, while two were temporarily attached to the 3BCS.

The 4LCS was positioned in line-abreast about four miles ahead of the battleship columns at ¾-mile intervals; Table 4.8 lists them in their order from port to starboard. With the divisions disposed to starboard, *Boadicea* and *Bellona* were, respectively, about nine miles on the port and starboard flanks of the 4LCS, while *Blanche* was astern of the two centre battleship columns. From these cruising positions, the three attached cruisers could deploy to the non-engaged side of the battle line to serve as repeating ships for their respective battle squadrons. *Active*, standing in for the refitting *Blonde*, would normally have acted as repeating ship between the flagship and the 5BS but, in their absence, she relayed signals to and from the armoured cruisers. *Castor* wore the broad pendant of the recently appointed Commodore (F) and she also led the 11DF.[58]

Scheer was accompanied by the five light cruisers of the IVSG and by the *Rostock* wearing the broad pendant of the First Leader of Torpedo-Boat Forces. The German battlefleet in single line was led by *Stettin*, probably about eight miles ahead, while *Stuttgart* brought up the rear. *Rostock* and *München* were, respectively, some five miles to port and starboard of the van squadron, the IIIBS, with *Hamburg* and *Frauenlob* similarly positioned on the IIBS at the rear. (The Leader of Submarines, Captain Hermann Bauer, was aboard *Hamburg*.) Each light cruiser was accompanied by a single destroyer. In contrast, light cruisers of Hipper's IISG were disposed in an arc of about eight miles radius centred on his flagship, *Lützow*. Table 4.10 lists them in order from port to starboard, and includes *Regensburg* on the starboard wing; she flew the broad pendant of the Second Leader of Torpedo-Boat Forces. Each light cruiser had its own small screen of from three to five destroyers (as detailed in the next section).[59]

Beatty positioned his three squadrons of light cruisers according to cruising disposition 'LS6'. This was actually a night cruising order but presumably he chose it because it left no doubt that the light cruisers should be in pairs separated by five miles and that their line should be eight miles ahead of the

---

[57] Parkes, pp. 441–9.
[58] *OD*, pp. 6, 297, 302, 378, 423 and Plate 12a. *GFBOs III*, IV, V.3 and 'LS1'. *GF*, p. 183.
[59] Tarrant, pp. 61–3 and 258. *GOA*, pp. 265 and 267. Scheer, p. 138.

Table 4.8. *British light cruisers with the battlefleet*

Squadron or command	Ship (commodore)	Class	Broadside
4LCS	*Calliope* (Commodore Charles le Mesurier)	*Calliope*	
	Constance	*Cambrian*	2-6in, 4-4in
	Comus	*Caroline*	
	Royalist	*Arethusa*	2-6in, 3-4in
	Caroline	*Caroline*	2-6in, 4-4in
Attached to: Fleet flagship and 5BS	*Active*	*Active*	
1BS	*Bellona*	*Boadicea*	5-4in
2BS	*Boadicea*		
4BS	*Blanche*	*Blonde*	
Commodore (F) and Captain 11DF	*Castor* (Commodore James Hawksley)	*Cambrian*	2-6in, 4-4in

Table 4.9. *German light cruisers with the battlefleet*

Squadron or command	Ship (commodore)	Class	Broadside
IVSG	*Stettin* (Commodore Ludwig von Reuter)	*Königsberg*	
	München	*Bremen*	5-4.1in
	Hamburg		
	Frauenlob	*Gazelle*	
	Stuttgart	*Königsberg*	
1st Leader, Torpedo-Boat Forces	*Rostock* (Commodore Andreas Michelson)	*Karlsruhe*	6-4.1in

battlecruisers. Table 4.11 lists the order of the pairs from port to starboard, leading ships first. *Yarmouth* as linking ship was placed four miles astern of *Falmouth*, the flagship of the senior light cruiser commander, Rear-Admiral Trevylyan Napier. The centre of the cruiser screen bore ahead (EbyS) from *Lion*, but its line of direction was NE-SW.[60] Beatty was also accompanied by two light cruisers acting as flotilla leaders. *Canterbury* and the recently

---

[60] *OD*, pp. 6, 172 and *OD*(M), p. 423.

Table 4.10. *German light cruisers with the battlecruisers*

Squadron or command	Ship (admiral or commodore)	Class	Broadside
IISG	*Elbing*	*Pillau*	4-5.9in
	Pillau		
	Frankfurt (Rear-Admiral Friedrich Bödicker)	*Wiesbaden*	5-5.9in
	Wiesbaden		
2nd Leader, Torpedo-Boat Forces	*Regensburg* (Commodore Paul Heinrich)	*Graudenz*	7-4.1in

Table 4.11. *British light cruisers with the battlecruisers*

Squadron or flotilla	Ship (admiral, commodore or captain)	Position	Class	Broadside
1LCS	*Galatea* (Commodore Edwyn Alexander-Sinclair)	A	*Arethusa*	2-6in, 3-4in
	Phaeton	A		
	Inconstant	B		
	Cordelia	B	*Caroline*	2-6in, 4-4in
3LCS	*Birkenhead*	C	*Birkenhead*	6-5.5in
	Gloucester	C	*Bristol*	2-6in, 5-4in
	Falmouth (Rear-Admiral Trevylyan Napier)	D	*Weymouth*	5-6in
	Yarmouth	D (linking ship)		
2LCS	*Nottingham*	F	*Birmingham*	5-6in
	Dublin	F	*Chatham*	
	Southampton (Commodore William Goodenough)	G	*Chatham*	
	Birmingham	G	*Birmingham*	
Leader, 1DF	*Fearless* (Captain (D) Charles Roper)		*Active*	5-4in
Leader, 13DF	*Champion* (Captain (D) James Farie)		*Calliope*	2-6in, 4-4in
Attached to 3BCS	*Chester*		*Birkenhead*	6–5.5in
	Canterbury		*Cambrian*	2-6in, 4-4in

Table 4.12. *Comparative total broadsides for light cruisers*

Admiral	Number of light cruisers	Total broadside guns	
		4in or 4.1in	5.5in to 6in
Scheer	6	31	
Jellicoe	10	43	12
Hood	2	4	8
Hipper	5	7	18
Beatty	14	27	48

commissioned *Chester* were attached to Hood's 3BCS; once the 3BCS rejoined the rest of the BCF, they would add further to Beatty's strength. No light cruiser was available to link Evan-Thomas first to Beatty and later to Jellicoe.[61]

Table 4.12 shows that the German admirals, Scheer in particular, were desperately short of light cruisers. At least the vessels of Hipper's IISG were modern designs; ship for ship they were, in terms of broadside weights of fire, comparable with the 'Town'-class light cruisers of the 2LCS and 3LCS. But none of the light cruisers with Scheer had guns bigger than 4.1in and, of the IVSG, only *Stettin* had turbine propulsion, while *Frauenlob* had been laid down in 1901.

Destroyers

On the eve of the Battle of Jutland, the British battlefleet flotillas under Commodore (F) James Hawksley were beginning to reorganise. Newly completed boats were also continually joining. An extreme case was *Ophelia* of the *M*-class. When she accompanied the 3BCS to sea on 30 May, she was under way for only the second time, the first having been on passage from her builders in Sunderland to Scapa Flow; thus she fought without having put in any gunnery or torpedo practice whatsoever.[62]

On 30 May, while two of the battlefleet's flotillas, the 4DF and 12DF, were at Scapa, the 11DF found itself divided between Scapa and Cromarty. Three destroyers were detached from the 4DF and one from the 12DF so that each could accompany an armoured cruiser of the 2CS. The 4DF also provided three more boats, plus the temporarily attached *Ophelia*, to screen Hood's 3BCS; these destroyers were led by Commander Loftus Jones in the *Shark*. When the 1BS and 4BS left Scapa Flow, they were screened by *Castor*, the flotilla leaders and the remaining destroyers of the 4DF and 12DF, and the four boats from the 11DF that were also present. At Cromarty, nine *M*-class destroyers of the 11DF

---

[61] *OD*, pp. 130, 163, 187–8 and 268. Campbell, p. 23.
[62] Corbett, pp. 318–19 and 427. *OD*, p. 316.

Table 4.13. *British flotillas with the battlefleet*

Destroyer flotilla	Boats	Number	Class	Screening
4DF	*Tipperary* (Captain (D) Charles Wintour), *Broke*	2	*Faulknor*	1BS and 4BS then battlefleet
	Achates, Ambuscade, Ardent, Contest, Fortune, Garland, Porpoise, Sparrowhawk, Spitfire, Unity	10		
	Hardy, Midge, Owl	3	*K (Acasta)*	2CS: *Hardy* with *Shannon*, *Midge* with *Hampshire*, *Owl* with *Minotaur*
	Shark (Commander Loftus Jones), *Acasta, Christopher*	3		3BCS
	Ophelia	1	*M*	
11DF	*Castor* (Commodore (F) James Hawksley)	Light cruiser		1BS and 4BS from Scapa, then battlefleet
	Manners, Marne, Michael, Mons	4	*M*	
	Kempenfelt	1	*Lightfoot*	2BS from Cromarty, then battlefleet
	Magic, Mandate, Martial, Milbrook, Minion, Moon,[1] *Morning Star, Mounsey, Mystic, Ossory*	10	*M*	
12DF	*Faulknor* (Captain (D) Anselan Stirling)	1	*Faulknor* *Lightfoot*	1BS and 4BS from Scapa, then battlefleet
	Marksman	1		
	Maenad, Marvel, Mary Rose, Menace, Mindful, Munster, Narwhal, Nessus, Noble, Nonsuch, Obedient, Onslaught, Opal	13	*M*	
	Mischief	1		2CS with *Cochrane*
	Oak	1	*I (Acheron)*	Attached to *Iron Duke*

[1] Joined flotilla 1.48pm on 31st (*OD*, p. 442).

were led by the flotilla leader *Kempenfelt*; they formed the screen for the 2BS. (*Moon* was on detached patrol on the 30th but was able to rejoin the rest of the 11DF at 1.48pm the next day.) Jerram later informed the C-in-C that, because he was so short of destroyers, none could be spared as a screen for the 1CS: and it appears that Arbuthnot's squadron remained without a screen thereafter. After the junction of the forces from Scapa and Cromarty, most of the destroyers combined to form the battlefleet screen; they extended across the heads of the battleship columns and along the outer flanks of the wing columns, with *Castor* and the 11DF on the bow of *King George V. Hardy, Midge, Owl* and *Mischief* continued with the 2CS, when necessary investigating any suspicious merchantmen encountered by the scouting line, while *Shark* and her three consorts remained with Hood.[63]

[63] *OD*, pp. 163, 169, 275–6, 279, 307, 313 and 315. *OD*(M), pp. 402, 426–7, 437, 439–40 and 442. Corbett, pp. 426–8. F&H, p. 202. *OD*(M), pp. and 442. *GFBOs III*, II(a).

Table 4.14. *British flotillas in the Southern North Sea*

Destroyer flotilla	Boats	Number	Class	With
Part of 1DF	*Beaver, Druid, Ferret, Hind, Hornet, Sandfly*	6	*I* (*Acheron*)	3BS
Part of 9DF	*Lightfoot*	1	*Lightfoot*	Harwich Force[1]
	Laforey, Lance, Lark, Lassoo, Laverock, Lawford, Leonidas, Lookout, Loyal, Lysander	10	*L* (*Laforey*)	
Part of 10DF	*Nimrod*	1	*Lightfoot*	
	Manly, Mentor, Milne, Miranda, Murray, Myngs	6	*M*	
	Matchless, Mastiff	2	*M*	3BS

[1] *Lennox* and *Meteor* detained with defects.

Table 4.15. *British flotillas with the BCF*

Destroyer flotilla	Boats	Number	Class	Screening
1DF	*Fearless* (Captain (D) Charles Roper)	Light cruiser		
	Acheron, Ariel, Attack, Badger, Defender, Goshawk, Hydra, Lapwing, Lizard	9	*I* (*Acheron*)	5BS
Part of 9DF	*Lydiard* (Commander Malcolm Goldsmith), *Landrail, Laurel, Liberty*	4	*L* (*Laforey*)	2BCS
	Moorsom, Morris (from 10DF)	2	*M*	
13DF	*Champion* (Captain (D) James Farie)	Light cruiser		
	Moresby,[1] *Narborough, Nerissa, Nestor, Nicator, Nomad, Obdurate, Onslow,*[1] *Petard, Pelican,*	10	*M*	*Lion* and 1BCS
	Termagant, Turbulent (from 10DF)	2	*Talisman*	

[1] Detached at 2.50pm to join *Engadine* (*OD*, pp. 224, 236 and 238).

While the 3BS had been based at Rosyth, the 1DF was expected to act as its destroyer screen but, following the transfer of the predreadoughts to the Thames Estuary, by 30 May, six boats of the flotilla had already proceeded southwards, though they would not join the 3BS in the Swin until the following day. The nine serviceable members of the 1DF remaining at Rosyth were assigned to screen the 5BS. The flotilla was formed from the 27-knot *I* (*Acheron*) class, while they were led by the small light cruiser *Fearless* which, at 25 knots, was even slower; thus the flotilla's speed was barely adequate for its task. The other flotilla based at

Rosyth was the 13th, of modern *M*-class destroyers, but it was still being formed and only ten boats were available on the 30th.[64] This was too few to form a screen even for two squadrons of battlecruisers; thus the Harwich force had been asked to make up the numbers from the 9DF and 10DF. When Beatty's force sailed from Rosyth, four *L* (*Laforey*)-class boats from the 9DF and two *M*-class from the 10DF screened the 2BCS, with *Lydiard* leading. The 13DF, with its Captain (D) in *Champion*, screened *Lion* and the 1BCS. This flotilla had been strengthened by two *Termagant*-class boats, though *Turbulent* had only been completed on 12 May. After losing boats to the BCF and two more to the 3BS, Tyrwhitt's Harwich Force was reduced to two leaders and sixteen destroyers (Table 4.14).[65]

A full-strength British flotilla consisted of a light cruiser and a flotilla leader, or two leaders, and between sixteen and twenty destroyers organised in four divisions.[66] The Germans continued to use the term 'torpedo-boat flotilla' – hence the use here of 'TF' in their abbreviated titles. At full-strength, a German flotilla comprised a leading boat and two half-flotillas, each of five boats. In the cruising formations taken up after the German forces reached open water on 31 May, there were three flotillas with the scouting forces and 3½ flotillas with the battlefleet. The IITF and VITF accompanied the light cruisers of the IISG that led the advance. The boats of the VITF were together in the centre of the arc of light cruisers with *Frankfurt* and *Wiesbaden*. But the large destroyers of the IITF were split between *Elbing* and *Pillau* on the port wing and *Regensburg* on the starboard wing. The IXTF screened the battlecruisers of the ISG, with five boats ahead on an arc centred on *Lützow* and three boats on each flank of Hipper's line.

The flotillas with the battlefleet were also fragmented. Of the IIITF, six boats were attached individually to light cruisers. But *G88* joined the IHF, the VTF and the VIITF in screening the battle squadrons, though the details are unclear. Of the twenty-six boats in the complete screen, two were ahead of the leading battleship, *König*, with twelve spread along one flank of the line of battleships, eleven along the other, the imbalance resulting from the enforced return of *V186* because of a leaky condenser.[67]

In destroyer numbers, Hipper had a modest superiority over Beatty – 30:27 – when they first met. Moreover, as a whole, the German boats were more modern and, at least nominally, faster; the six members of the *B97*-class were also bigger than anything on the British side. Hipper's destroyers had twice as

---

[64] *GFBOs III*, XXVII.10. *OD*, p. 341. Corbett, pp. 429–30.

[65] Corbett, p. 320. *OD*, pp. 224, 254, 341 and 405. *CAWFS 1906–21*, p. 78.

[66] *GFBOs III*, 'Attack Plans', p. 1 with 'Torpedo Attack by Destroyer Flotillas . . .', 1 May 1916. *War Vessels and Aircraft . . . Monthly Return, May 1916*, pp. 5–7, ADM 186/23.

[67] Scheer, pp. 138–9. Tarrant, pp. 61–3 and 258–60. Campbell, p. 25.

Table 4.16. *German flotillas with the scouting groups*

Torpedo boat flotilla	Leader/ half flotilla	Boats	Number	Class	Screen for squadron or light cruiser
	Leader	*B98*	1	*B97*	*Pillau*
IITF	IIIHF	*G101*,[1] *G102*	2	*G101*	*Regensburg*
		B97, B112	2	*B97*	*Pillau*
	IVHF	*B109, B110, B111*	3	*B97*	*Elbing*
		G103, G104	2	*G101*	*Regensburg*
	Leader	*G41*	1		*Wiesbaden*
VITF	XIHF	*V44, G86, G87*	3	*G37*	*Wiesbaden*
	XIIHF	*V69, G37, V45, V46, S50*	5		*Frankfurt*
	Leader	*V28*	1	*V25*	
IXTF	XVIIHF	*V27, V26, S36*	3	*V25*	ISG
		S51, S52	2	*G37*	
	XVIII HF	*V30, V29, S33, S34, S35*	5	*V25*	

[1] Half-flotilla leaders (Scheer, pp. 138–9) and leaders in bold.

Table 4.17. *German flotillas with the battlefleet*

Torpedo boat flotilla	Leader/ half flotilla	Boats	Number	Class	Screen for squadron or light cruiser
ITF	IHF	*G39*,[1] *G38, G40*	3	*G37*	IIIBS
		S32	1	*V25*	
	Leader	*S53*	1		Rostock
IIITF	VHF	*V71, V73, G88*	3	*G37*	V71 Stuttgart, V73 Hamburg, G88 IIIBS
	VIHF	*S54, V42, V48*	3		S24 München, G42 Frauenlob, V48 Stettin
	Leader	*G11*	1		
VTF	IXHF	*V2, V1, V3, V4, V6*	5	*V1*	IBS and IIIBS
	XHF	*G8, V5, G7, G9, G10*	5		
	Leader	*S24*	1		
VIITF	XIIIHF	*S15, S16, S17, S18, S20*	5	*S13*	IBS and IIBS
	XIV HF	*S19, S23*	2		
		(*V186*)[2] *V189*	2(1)	*V186*	

[1] Half-flotilla leaders (Scheer, pp. 138–9) and leaders in bold.
[2] *V186* sent back with a leaky condenser, 7.15am, 31 May.

Table 4.18. *Comparative total destroyer numbers and armaments*

Admiral	Number of destroyers	Total number of guns			Total number of torpedo tubes
		3in	3.5in	4in	
Scheer	32		75		150
Jellicoe	51		2	163	170
Hipper	30		110		180
Beatty	27	18		76	90

many torpedo tubes while, even in guns, the two sides were more or less evenly matched. Thus Hipper had a distinct advantage in destroyers which to some extent made up for his inferior strength in light cruisers. But Hipper's superiority was obtained at Scheer's expense. As the two battlefleets left harbour, Jellicoe enjoyed a numerical advantage of 50:32. Thus, although he did not know it, Jellicoe would not have to face the larger German destroyer force that had caused him so much apprehension since the beginning of the war. But his advantage was in more than numbers. The British flotillas mounted twice as many guns, all of heavier calibre, than their opponents; they even had a greater number of torpedo tubes; and the German scouting groups had been given priority in the allocation of the larger and more modern boats, that is those of the *V25* and later classes. With the battlefleet, only the IHF and IIITF, both under-strength, were so equipped. The VTF and VIITF, though at full strength, were formed mainly from the *V1* and *S13* classes, which were too small to be properly sea and battle worthy (the two exceptions were from the previous *V186* class). The only way that Scheer could have been given more destroyers would have been to send out more of the flotillas formed from earlier classes. But the rapid failure of *V186* may be an indication of their general state of repair; their reliance on mixed firing meant that their endurance depended on the stamina of their stokers; and, in any case, none of them were, individually, a match for the numerous British *M*-class boats now with the Grand Fleet. It appears that the German high command decided that more of these older destroyers would not add much, if anything, to the fighting strength of Scheer's flotillas.

Other British vessels

Contrary to Jellicoe's fears about minelaying by German ships, none carried mines into battle at Jutland. The only specialised minelayer present was the

British *Abdiel*, a converted flotilla leader of the *Lightfoot* class with stowage for eighty mines (in place of two of her 4in guns); she proceeded from Scapa in company with the 4LCS. The other British auxiliary vessel was the seaplane carrier *Engadine*; she accompanied the BCF from Rosyth in the line of light cruisers.[68]

On 30 May, the Admiralty ordered Vice-Admiral Sir Edward Bradford to have the 3BS ready to sail at daylight and to send his two *Hampshire*-class armoured cruisers of the 3CS to the Swin that day. But both Bradford's and Tyrwhitt's forces were held back until more was known of German intentions.[69] After the battle, the Admiralty justification for its caution was that:

On the 31st May 1916, it was not at all certain until some time after the engagement began that the *whole* German fleet had gone north by Horn Reef. The northern force might have been sent with the object of attracting all our forces towards the Skagerrak while another force accomplished another operation elsewhere [presumably to the south].[70]

Although the Lowestoft Raid was a worrying precedent and Room 40 had been unable to establish the exact nature of the German operation, none of the signals intelligence pointed to a division of their forces. But it seems that Jackson and Oliver preferred to hold the southern forces in reserve, anticipating that the Harwich Force might be needed later to relieve the BCF's light cruisers and destroyers. Eventually, as we shall see, Tyrwhitt in *Carysfort* was let off the leash early on 1 June; he sailed with the light cruisers *Cleopatra, Conquest, Aurora* and *Undaunted* and the destroyers of the 9DF and 10DF (Table 4.14).[71]

The British submarine flotillas based at Blyth (11SF) and at Harwich and Yarmouth (8SF) maintained regular patrols to the SE of the Dogger Bank and off Terschelling, respectively. In addition, on 30 May, three submarines left Harwich at 7pm with orders to spread on a line 270° from the Vyl light-vessel, which was anchored just south of Horns Reef. *E55, E26* and *D1* arrived on station around midnight on 31 May/1 June. Unfortunately, their orders had been prepared for the abandoned British operation intended for 2 June and so they spent most of their time until that date on the bottom, before returning late on 3 June.[72] At 11.20pm on 30 May, Jellicoe reported to the Admiralty that the 11SF was ready for sea, but added: 'Submit Admiralty may give it orders as situation develops'; evidently, with the rendezvous so far north, he saw no prospect of the Blyth submarines joining the fleet. At 10.20am the following day, the Admiralty ordered the Captain (S) at Blyth to send a destroyer and four

[68] *CAWFS 1906–21*, p. 77. *OD*, pp. 130 and 297.
[69] Corbett, p. 324. Campbell, p. 15. *OD*(M), pp. 398–9. *FDSF III*, Chart 1.
[70] Admiralty to Jellicoe, 17 July 1916 in *JP II*, pp. 25–6.   [71] *OD*(M), p. 454. *OD*, p. 341.
[72] Campbell, p. 15. *OD*, p. 343 and *OD*(M), p. 400. The destroyer *Lurcher* with *E31, E53* and *D6* also sailed from Harwich on the evening of the 30th for a position E of Southwold but they were not involved in subsequent events.

submarines to a position about SSE from the Dogger Bank, from which they might be ordered to new positions later; *Talisman, G2, G3, G4* and *G5* sailed at noon.[73]

*   *   *

Throughout the morning of 31 May 1916, a total of 250 warships – 151 British and 99 German[74] – continued on the courses that might intersect in the afternoon, somewhere close to the entrance to the Skagerrak. All the ships on both sides had been built since Tirpitz and his Kaiser had resolved to challenge British naval supremacy, and the great majority since Fisher had intensified the Anglo-German rivalry by the construction of the first all-big-gun battleships and armoured cruisers. The economies and industries of the two powers had created two fleets armed with guns and torpedoes that, in aggregate, could deliver destructive power at an intensity far greater than anything yet seen in the history of naval warfare. Soon that power was manifested in the naval Armageddon that both sides had anticipated for so many years.

---

[73] *OD*(M), pp. 411 and 434 (the position was in 54°30′N, 4° E). Campbell, p. 15.
[74] Neither *Campania* nor *V186* have been counted.

5   The Run to the South

Only *U32* and *U66*, both stationed off the Firth of Forth, picked up the warning message broadcast from Bruges that a German fleet operation was imminent. The commander of *U32* reasoned that, because of the recognised submarine threat, the BCF would leave under the cover of darkness; he therefore shifted to a position 80 miles east of the entrance to the Firth in the hope of making an interception at daybreak on 31 May. At 3.40am, *U32* sighted *Galatea* leading *Phaeton* at the port end of the BCF's cruiser line and fired a torpedo at the former. The U-boat's periscope then jammed in the fully up position, and she had to crash-dive to avoid being rammed by *Phaeton*. On resurfacing, *U32* observed what was probably the 2BCS and its destroyer escort, and, in a message timed at 5.50am, she reported '2 dreadnoughts, 2 cruisers, several torpedo boats ... steering south'.[1] To escape the patrols off the Forth, *U66* had moved NW'ward to an area some 60 miles east of Peterhead. At 5.00am, although unable to attack, she sighted first an armoured cruiser, then *Boadicea*, and finally Jerram's 2BS. The approach of their destroyer screen forced the U-boat to dive but at 6.48am, she was able to signal that she had seen '8 enemy dreadnoughts with light cruisers and torpedo boats ... steering north'. The two British courses are those listed in German signals appended to the *German Official Account* of Jutland. However, in both its text and in the British record of intercepted German signals, the course reported by *U32* was SE and by *U66*, NE. The Germans were also intercepting British wireless messages. At 6.40am, the Neumünster deciphering bureau reported that '2 large warships *or squadrons* [my emphasis] accompanied by destroyers have left Scapa Flow'. This was followed at 11.55am by a Firth of Forth weather report with the comment: 'This type of report occurs as rule only when the fleet is at sea.'[2] Early on 31 May, the weather still prevented air reconnaissance. It improved sufficiently to allow five Zeppelins to ascend belatedly between 11.25am and 12.46pm, but all

---

[1] Tarrant, pp. 58–9. GMS, pp. 272 and 274. *OD*(M), pp. 416–17 and 419.
[2] Tarrant, pp. 59–60. GMS, p. 274. 'Jutland Signals', Sheets 1 and 2 in 'Actions and Operations', ADM 137/4067.

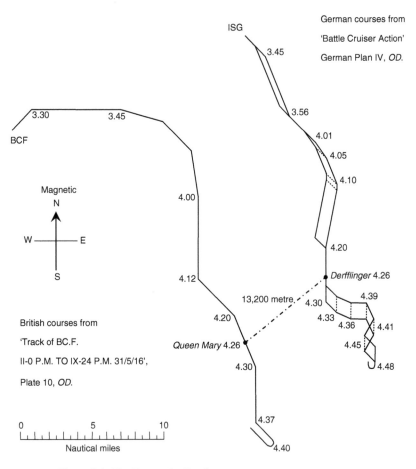

Figure 5.1 The Run to the South

encountered low cloud and hazy conditions and not one sighted a single British or German warship.[3] Even so, the Germans had received several quite strong indications that substantial British forces were already at sea. Yet the commanders of the High Seas Fleet seem to have been too committed to the operation to be deterred; they concluded:

[The] information ... gave no indication of the enemy's intentions. There was nothing to indicate either co-operation between the various forces sighted or an advance into the German Bight. Nor did these movements appear to be related in any way to the German undertaking. This intelligence, therefore, in no way affected the projected plan. On the

---

[3] Tarrant, pp. 62 and 76–7.

contrary, it only increased the hope that it would be possible to bring a part of the enemy's fleet to action.[4]

Once the High Seas Fleet left harbour, they observed almost total wireless silence. During the morning of 31 May, Room 40 received no signals that indicated that the enemy was at sea, though other messages showed that preparations were being made for airship reconnaissance.[5] Then Captain Hope received a directional 'fix' that he recorded on one of his handwritten sheets.

At 11.10 a.m. G.M.T. DK (call of Fleet Flagship) placed by Aberdeen York Lowestoft in its normal position in the Jade.
  Flag of A.C 1st C.S. [ISG] has not been heard this morning.

This was clearly the basis for the signal sent by the Admiralty to Jellicoe and Beatty at 12.30pm.

No definite news of enemy. They made all preparations for sailing this morning. It was thought the Fleet had sailed but directional wireless places flagship in Jade at 11.10GMT. Apparently they have been unable to carry out air reconnaissance which has delayed them.[6]

In fact, the transmission from the Jade was not what it seemed, but confirmation was still locked in the message in the new cipher that had been received in the previous evening. When Room 40 deciphered it, their translation, sent out to the Operations Division at 5.40pm on 31 May, read:

The head of the 3rd B. Squadron will pass [warlightship] at 3.30am. 2nd B. Squadron will take part in the undertaking [and will] join up with the 1st B. Squadron. Direction of the W/T in the German Bight will be carried out by Wilhelmshaven 3rd Entrance, which will have the W/T call [of the CinC. H.S. Fleet].
  (sd) CinC.
  Note from 40 O.B.
  Made last night in a new cipher, only now deciphered.[7]

Yet OD, and especially its Director Thomas Jackson, have been widely blamed for misleading Jellicoe and Beatty about the whereabouts of the German fleet.[8] In 1924, William Clarke, who had joined Room 40 in March 1916 and was

---

[4] *GOA*, p. 37. The conclusion that no move into the German Bight was indicated suggests that *U32* reported a course S rather than SE.
[5] 'Jutland Signals' (see note 2) Sheets 1 and 2.
[6] 'Jutland. Telegraphic Record (C.O.S.)', f. 22, ADM 137/1642. Corbett, Vol. III (2nd edn. 1940), p. 326b.
[7] Signal 20383, 'Intercepts of German Signals ... Battle of Jutland', ADM 137/4710; [ ] as in the original and the time sent out assumed to be in BST. It seems that not only the call-sign and frequency was transferred but also Scheer's usual wireless operator: Hines (citing Oliver's memoirs), p. 1130; Roskill, p. 388 n. 5.
[8] Some recent examples are Halpern, p. 316, Gordon, pp. 72–3 and S&H, pp. 57–8.

working there on 31 May, wrote 'An Admiralty Telegram', his account of how the Admiralty signal came to be sent. According to Clarke, Jackson hardly ever visited Room 40 and dismissed their decrypts as 'that damned stuff'. But on the morning of 31 May, the DOD strode in and asked where the British directional stations placed DK, the usual call-sign of Scheer's flagship. On being told that it was still in Wilhelmshaven, Jackson, without asking anything further, left immediately to inform the COS, Oliver, who is usually held to have drafted the signal sent at 12.30pm. Clarke continued:

Now DK was the Call Sign of the German C in C but it was only his Harbour Call Sign. Whenever the German fleet put to sea the C in C took a different Call Sign and transferred his normal one to the W/T station at Wilhelmshafen 3rd Entrance. This was of course to conceal the fact of the fleet being at sea and had been done on the occasion of the Scarborough raid, Lowestoft raid and at other times.

Clarke concluded that, since Jackson gave no one in Room 40 the opportunity to tell him of these precedents, the latter made the wrong deduction about the significance of the directional reports.[9]

Since Arthur Marder first drew attention to Clarke's account, Jackson has been repeatedly criticised both personally and professionally: Patrick Beesly called him 'insufferable' and Andrew Gordon a 'ridiculous, angry, blustering officer'. Yet Beesly himself acknowledged that the German signal concerning the call-sign switch had not been deciphered when Jackson visited Room 40,[10] while further questions are prompted by Hope's directional note, though its timing relative to Jackson's visit to Room 40 is not known. Whatever it may have been, the opprobrium heaped upon the DOD was only deserved if Clarke was correct both about Jackson's churlish behaviour towards Room 40 staff and in his assertion that there were precedents for the call-sign transfer. Recently, scholars have questioned both claims. Nicholas Black points out that, in his 1951 history of Room 40, Clarke himself wrote appreciatively of naval officers, including Thomas Jackson: 'We were treated with a consideration that was very creditable to them and encouraging to us.' However, in another chapter he complained: 'Our greatest handicap was complete ignorance of what use, if any was being made of our [deciphering] efforts ... There was never any camaraderie between us and those in O.D.' Black also notes that Clarke's description of Jackson's behaviour and attitude to signals intelligence is at odds with his previous career as a signals officer and in naval intelligence.[11] (It is therefore not surprising to find him enquiring about directional bearings and call signs.)

---

[9] William Clarke, 'An Admiralty Telegram', 1924, f. 7, BTY 9/9/11. For Oliver drafting the signal, see Beesly, p. 155.

[10] *FDSF III*, pp. 45–8. Beesly, pp. 152 and 155. Gordon, pp. 72 and also 415–16.

[11] Black, pp. 161–2 citing William Clarke, 'History of Room 40 O.B.' 1951, Ch. 2 p. 6 and 'Retrospect', pp. 2 and 7, HW 3/3.

In his reassessment of signals intelligence at Jutland, Commander Jason Hines USN has again drawn attention to the late decipherment of the signal of 5.41pm. Also, he was unable to find, in the logbook of German signals deciphered by Room 40 during the war, any confirmation of a call-sign switch just before the Scarborough Raid.[12] Neither are such precedents mentioned in Captain Hope's Jutland notes (though in his 'Narrative' he mentions different 'signs and portents' that had preceded earlier actions), nor in Clarke's Room 40 history, nor in the history of German naval warfare that Clarke co-authored after the War. This last history states that 'definite orders for the main fleet's departure were given at 5.41 pm. on [30 May]. To conceal the fact that the German ships were moving, a land station at Wilhelmshaven took over the call sign of the flagship late that evening.' Not only does this fail to make clear that the same signal ordered the call-sign switch, but nothing is said about the delay in deciphering it and it is omitted from the tabulation of important deciphered German signals.[13] Furthermore, Clarke did not mention the signal in 'An Admiralty Telegram'.

Since Clarke's writings are at once uncorroborated, inconsistent and mis-leadingly incomplete, they should not be accepted as historically accurate. In that case, the signal sent out at 12.30pm was an accurate summary of the information then available in the Admiralty. Nonetheless, it soon turned out to be spectacularly wrong. Later in the War, when Clarke met Beatty, then C-in-C, at Scapa, the latter asked: '[W]hat am I to think of O.D. when I get that telegram and in three hours time meet the whole German Fleet well out at sea?' Clarke repeated this story in his 1951 memoir, though embellished by Beatty declaring that he met the enemy fleet 'within an hour' of receiving the telegram.[14] In all his accounts, Clarke avoided mentioning the excusable delay in deciphering the German signal; perhaps it was somehow mishandled within Room 40. As for his attack on Jackson, Hines suggests that Clarke may have wished to minimise his own contribution to the answer given to Jackson's question, or just to dislike of the DOD.[15] Whatever Clarke's

---

[12] Hines, pp. 1128–9 and 1129 n. 72. A further search by the author and Mr David Ramsay for call-sign switches in 'Actions and Operations', ADM 137/4067 and the other Room 40 logs in ADM 137/3956–60 was also unsuccessful.

[13] 'Capt. Hope's Notes on Fleet Movements, 1914–1916', ADM 137/4168. 'Capt. Hope's Diary, Feb. 22nd–Dec. 31st 1916', ADM 137/4169. 'Narrative of Capt. Hope' in HW 3/3. Birch and Clarke, 'A Contribution to the History of German Naval Warfare 1914–1918', Vol. I, Ch. X, pp. 7–8 and table, HW 7/1.

[14] Clarke, 'Telegram' (see note 9), f. 6, 'History of 40 O.B.' (see note 11) and 'Retrospect' (see note 11), p. 7.

[15] Hines, p. 1130 n. 75. Jackson's personality did not, it seems, make him a likeable superior. While serving in the OD under Jackson in 1914–15, Herbert Richmond's criticisms of the DOD were untypically muted. But, by 1917, Richmond's diary called Jackson 'pigheaded' and 'universally execrated' and later repeated stories about him in the Middle East suggesting that he was over-bearing and incompetent: Marder, *Portrait of an Admiral*, pp. 152, 178, 236, 244, 247, 322 and 347.

motives,[16] without his testimony there is no justification for blaming either Jackson or Oliver for 'the Admiralty telegram'.

Contact

During the morning of 31 May, Beatty and Jellicoe maintained nominal courses of S81°E and S50°E respectively. At 9am, Jellicoe, reduced his speed of advance by a knot to 15 knots and at noon to 14 knots, making it easier for his destroyers to examine merchantmen in sight of the fleet and to regain station without consuming too much fuel.[17] Both Jellicoe and Beatty zigzagged as an anti-submarine precaution, routinely altering course by turns together every ten minutes. However, Beatty made large turns of four points alternatively to port and starboard, whereas the battlefleet's alterations were of only two points, first (say) to port and starboard, then to starboard and port, and so on. Hence the battlecruisers needed a speed through the water of 19½ knots to advance at 18 knots, whereas the difference for the battleships was only one knot.[18] As two o'clock approached, both forces had been equally delayed, being then about 16 miles NW of the planned turning-points; their relative positions were almost exactly as intended, with Beatty SbyE from Jellicoe at a distance of 71 rather than 69 miles.[19] When the Admiralty's signal was received by the two admirals at 12.41pm, it contained nothing demanding that wireless silence be broken to change the rendezvous. Until Jellicoe had definite information on Scheer's position, his main concern was to conserve his destroyers' fuel.[20]

The Admiralty signal reassured the British commanders that they would rendezvous as planned but they were already intent on that event well before the signal was received. At 10.05am, Beatty reformed his light cruisers on a line-of-bearing NE-SW, the centre of the line to bear five miles EbyS, that is, ahead. Then, at 10.10am, flag signals ordered the 2BCS to take station three miles to the NE of *Lion*, the 5BS five miles to the NW. This would place the 5BS beyond the range for flag signalling, but, at 4.28am, Beatty had already ordered *Tiger* to repeat all signals between him and *Barham*;[21] although the method was unspecified, it was evidently understood to be by searchlight. By

---

[16] Even though Beesly (p. 127) regarded Clarke as 'a most valuable witness', he admitted that 'during World War II, he [Clarke] seems to have become rather embittered, and some of his comments on his former colleagues need to be taken with a pinch of salt'.

[17] *OD*(M), 4.47, 5.0, 8.48, 9.05am and 12noon. *GF*, p. 203.

[18] For zigzags, see *OD*(M), 6.00–10.30am and 11.50am–1.35pm (Grand Fleet) and 2.40–8.10am and 8.50am–1.30pm (BCF): for speeds of advance, 8.45, 9.5 and 10.10am.

[19] Positions calculated from mean noon positions – *OD*(M), 12noon and 1.05pm – and speeds of advance of 14 and 18 knots.

[20] Godfrey, Ch. 1, p. 22. See also Gordon, pp. 73 and 415–16 for battleships oiling destroyers alongside – *OD*(M), 1.55pm.

[21] *OD*(M), 4.28, 10.5 and 10.10am. Godfrey, Ch. 1, p. 24.

presenting fronts inclined NE-SW, both the light cruisers and the battlecruisers were facing the probable direction from which the Germans might advance. In contrast, the 5BS were five miles in the wrong direction, either for supporting Beatty should he encounter a superior force, or for joining him in chasing a retreating enemy. They were, however, conveniently positioned for taking their place between the battlecruisers and the battlefleet in the combined fleets' cruising order. Thus Beatty seems already to have been thinking mainly about his meeting with Jellicoe.[22] The C-in-C, even before he received the Admiralty signal, was similarly preoccupied; at 12.20pm, he warned his cruisers: 'Battle Cruiser Fleet will probably be sighted later and is to be reported by visual.'

At 1.30, in preparation for turning towards and joining up with the battle-fleet, Beatty gave the orders (see Table 5.1)[23] that rotated his forces clockwise

Table 5.1. *BCF signals 1.30–2.27pm*

Time of despatch	From	To	System	Message	Time of origin
pm, 31 May					
1.30	SO BCF	SO 5BS	Flags	Take station on compass line of bearing NNW five miles	
1.30	SO BCF	Light cruisers	Flags	Take station according to lookout diagram No. 6, Centre of screen to bear SSE, line of direction ENE	
1.30	SO BCF	2BCS	Flags	Take station on compass line of bearing ENE three miles	
2.06	SO BCF	General	Flags	Resume original course together	
2.08	SO BCF	Destroyers	Flags	Take up position as s Submarine screen when course is altered to NbyE	
2.10	Galatea	SO BCF	SL	Two-funnelled ship has stopped steamer bearing ESE eight miles, am closing	1410
2.13	SO 2LCS	Nottingham	SL	Who is alter course signal for?	1408
				Reply: To light cruisers from Lion, stop was omitted by Nottingham in order to get subsidiary signal through as rapidly as possible	
2.15	SO BCF	General	SL	Alter course, leading ships together the rest in succession to NbyE	1351 [sic]
2.15	SO BCF	5BS	SL	When we turn to Northward, look out for advanced cruisers of Grand Fleet	1412
2.17	SO 5BS	5BS	Flags	Alter course in succession to NbyE	

---

[22] Gordon, pp. 67–9; see also pp. 98–9. The position of the 5BS would also have given them a head start if Beatty had been forced by a superior force to withdraw on the Grand Fleet: Black, pp. 157–8.
[23] From here onwards, important signals from *OD*(M) and GMS that are relevant to the narrative are listed in the tables. For the remainder of this chapter, all times are *post meridiem*, unless stated otherwise.

so that that they would be aligned on the anticipated course after the meeting, that is, SSE towards Horns Reef. *Tiger* must have repeated *Lion*'s flag signal by searchlight, since Evan-Thomas zigzagged twice by only two points to get into his new position five miles NNW from *Lion* just after two o'clock.[24] The light cruisers needed time to reach their new positions, especially *Galatea* and the rest of the 1LCS, which had to move further East relative to the flagship. The signal at 2.13 also suggests that one of *Lion*'s alter-course signals was not repeated properly within the 2LCS. Beatty waited until 2.06 before ordering all ships to resume the original course; two minutes later, he warned the escorting destroyers to reform in readiness for a turn to NbyE, which was made at 2.15. Beatty also instructed the 5BS, which was about to become his scouting force ahead, to look out for the advanced cruisers of the battlefleet. Evan-Thomas must have received both the 2.08 destroyer and 2.15 turn signals by searchlight, since he repeated the latter at 2.17 to turn the 5BS NbyE. Note that, in the *Official Despatches*, the 2.15 signal is listed as being sent only by searchlight. This cannot be right, since it was a general signal intended for the whole BCF; also, this particular record is suspect because of its early time-of-origin. However, it may be a garbled record that *Lion* had already taken back from *Tiger* the responsibility for searchlight repeats to *Barham*, though there is no actual signal record confirming this. After both forces had turned NbyE with the 5BS bearing NNW from the battlecruisers, *Lion* was closest to *Barham* and best placed for visual communication between the flagships.

Shortly before the turns NbyE, *Galatea*'s move Eastwards had brought into sight to the ESE a steamer, eight miles distant, that had been stopped by a two-funnelled ship; *Galatea* reported the sighting at 2.10 by searchlight and then, rather than turn with the remainder of the BCF, she and *Phaeton* closed to investigate at high speed.[25] Since there were no British vessels in that direction, the obvious inference was that the ship in question was German. But, assuming that *Galatea* had arrived at her correct position in the cruising order, she would have been about 15 miles right ahead of *Lion*;[26] thus her searchlight signal must have been relayed through the linking ship, *Yarmouth*, and possibly via other light cruisers as well. Thus this vital intelligence probably did not reach Beatty and his staff before the eight-point turns to port were initiated at 2.15. What had *Galatea* actually seen?

As Hipper continued to advance Northward, his cruising formation placed *Elbing*, on the port wing of the screen, almost abeam of *Lützow*. At 2.00, *Elbing* had sighted a Danish tramp steamer, the *N J Fjord*, to the westward and *B109* and *B110*, two of the destroyers accompanying the light cruiser, were sent to stop and

---

[24] *OD*(M), 1.38, 1.50, 1.55 and 2.04.   [25] *OD*, p. 172.
[26] The centre of the cruiser line was 12½ miles from *Galatea* and 8 miles SSE of *Lion*.

Table 5.2. *BCF signals 2.20–2.40pm*

Time of despatch	From	To	System	Message	Time of origin
pm, 31 May					
2.20	Galatea	General	Flags	Enemy in sight	
2.20	Galatea	SO BCF	W/T	Urgent. Two Cruisers, probably hostile, in sight bearing ESE, course unknown. My position 56°48 N, 5°21 E. (Received in Iron Duke 2.18pm)	1420
2.25	SO BCF	Destroyers	Flags	Take up position as Submarine screen when course is altered to SSE	
2.30	Galatea	SO BCF	W/T	Urgent. My 1420. Cruisers are stopped. (Received in Iron Duke 2.25pm)	1422
2.32	SO 5BS	5BS	Flags	Alter course two points together to port	
2.32	SO BCF	General	Flags	Alter course leading ships together the rest in succession to SSE	
2.33	SO BCF	General	Flags	… 22 knots	
2.33	SO BCF	General	Flags	Raise steam for full speed and report when ready to proceed	
2.35	SO 5BS	5BS	Sem.	Length of line is 12 cables instead of 9. Take up appointed station	
2.40	SO 5BS	5BS	Flags	Alter course in succession to SSE. Speed 22 knots	

examine the merchantman.[27] These destroyers actually had three funnels but *Galatea* also misidentified their type. At 2.20, she reported them by W/T as 'Two cruisers, probably hostile, bearing ESE'. As Beatty acknowledged in his despatch, this could have been 'merely an isolated unit of Light Cruisers'. Even so, 'The direction of advance was immediately altered to S.S.E., the course for Horn Reef, so as to place my force between the enemy and his base'.[28]

After the War, the events that followed Beatty's decision to turn SSE became the subject of bitter controversy.[29] Fortunately, at least the main sequence of signals (though not their repeats) was included in the *Record of Messages* bearing on Jutland that was compiled before the end of 1918 and published by the Communications Division of the Naval Staff in September 1919; this was before Beatty took office as First Sea Lord and began his efforts to influence the accounts of the battle that were then being written. (The *Record* was subsequently incorporated essentially unchanged as an appendix in the *Official Despatches*.[30]) As with

---

[27] Tarrant, pp. 64–5.   [28] *OD*, pp. 130–1.   [29] See Roskill, Ch. 15 and Gordon, Ch. 24.
[30] Naval Staff, Communications Division, *Battle of Jutland. Record of Messages Bearing on the Operation*, 23 September 1919, ADM 186/625. *OD*(M).

the previous turn to NbyE, the preparations for the new turn began with a signal to all destroyers (as before, this included those screening the 5BS) to be ready to take up the positions appropriate for a course SSE. Also as before, the 9 Pendant signal to turn SSE was hauled down seven minutes later at 2.32, while at 2.33 Beatty ordered his whole force to increase speed to 22 knots. All three signals are listed as having been made only by flags.

As they brought their fires forward, the battlecruisers began to emit dense clouds of coal smoke which were carried Eastwards by the westerly breeze; since their turn was to starboard, they were turning back into their own smoke.[31] The 5BS, however, did not conform. Also at 2.32, Evan-Thomas ordered the battleships to turn together two points to port, these being the initial turns that would re-establish the earlier routine four-point zigzag pattern about the new course NbyE.[32] With *Barham* now heading NbyW, *Lion* bore to starboard only one point from right astern; thus the 5BS's own smoke added to the difficulties caused by the battle-cruisers' smoke in both communicating visually between the two forces and making out *Lion*'s movements from *Barham*'s bridge. Then, after another three minutes, Evan-Thomas saw that his line was straggling and, at 2.35, ordered his ships to close up to three cables apart. Another 3–5 minutes went by before he ordered the 5BS to follow the battlecruisers SSE and to increase speed to 22 knots – the time of his signal was given at 2.40 but *Barham*'s Captain Arthur Craig reported that she turned at 2.38. This delay in turning increased the separation between *Lion* and *Barham* from five to about ten miles.[33]

The extent to which Evan-Thomas was responsible for this increase depends on what signals he received, and when. Determining the whole truth is probably now impossible, because the actual signal logs for the ships concerned were later destroyed.[34] But, in answer to a Parliamentary question on 14 March 1927, the then First Lord, William Bridgeman, stated that the 2.25 destroyer signal was recorded in *Barham*'s signal log as received by searchlight from *Lion* at 2.30: and as having been received by *Fearless* (the leader of the 5BS's destroyer screen) from *Barham* at 2.34.[35] However, Vice-Admiral Sir Geoffrey Barnard, a nephew to Evan-Thomas, insisted that his uncle always maintained that no destroyer signal 'giving any clue to the battle-cruisers' movements was ever reported to him on the bridge'.[36] These words, which appear to have been chosen with care, allow the signal addressed to all destroyer to have been received by *Barham* but suggest that her signalling staff failed to bring it to the Rear-Admiral's attention. This

---

[31] *BP II*, pp. 463 and 474. *JP II*, p. 448. Godfrey, Ch. 1, p. 27. *OD*, Pl. 10.

[32] For two earlier examples, see *OD*(M), 2.30 and 8.50am.

[33] *OD*, p. 198. Gordon, pp. 85–7 for the broad consensus on the new separation.

[34] Gordon, p. 558. See also *FDSF III*, p. 58 n. 1.

[35] Hansard, 14 March 1927, also Godfrey, Ch I, p. 26.

[36] Gordon, p. 687 and p. 657 n. 55 remarks on the 'potentially incriminating nuance' in this testimony. Barnard further states that his uncle also insisted that: 'NO executive signal [to turn SSE] was received by "Barham" at this time'.

conclusion is also consistent with his own signals at 2.32 and 2.35. The resumption of zigzagging[37] and his fussing about the length of his line both suggest that, even at 2.35, he still expected to continue generally NbyE while looking out for the battlefleet's cruisers. Bridgeman also told Parliament that the executive signal to turn was in *Barham*'s signal log as received by flags from *Lion* at 2.37, its wording being: 'Alter course, Leaders together, remainder in succession, to S.S.E, speed 22 knots.' It was therefore a combined repeat of Beatty's two flag signals of 2.32 and 2.33 and the same as *Barham*'s signal timed at 2.40. But, given the problems with smoke and the rapidly increasing separation of the flagships at the opposite ends of their lines, this repeat signal cannot have been sent by flags, while even a search-light signal from *Lion* would have been difficult to see. In fact, both Evan-Thomas and his flag-captain, Arthur Craig, maintained that the earlier flag signals were not repeated by searchlight until *Tiger* (in an unrecorded signal) asked *Lion* by wireless whether they should have been made to *Barham*. Thus, since after the turn SSE *Tiger* was better placed, it does seem more likely that she made the searchlight repeat.[38]

Evan-Thomas may not have realised until after 2.35 that the battlecruisers were turning. It would have been apparent once they were seen to be disappearing under cover of their own smoke, although 'to what course it was impossible to see'. As noted in the last chapter, Evan-Thomas was, after all, acquainted with the Battle Cruiser Orders, and he may have recalled their warning that Beatty might begin a manoeuvre before all ships had received and acknowledged the signal ordering it. But, in this case, he was unsure whether his force was required to follow the vice-admiral. He had not, as before previous turns, received a new course by search-light, while the order to look out northwards for Grand Fleet cruisers remained in force. Only a few small enemy vessels had been reported, against which the battlecruisers did not need the support of the 5BS. And there was the possibility that the vice-admiral might be 'going to signal another course to Fifth Battle Squadron – possibly to get the enemy light cruisers between us'.[39] Thus Evan-Thomas had several reasons for hesitating for a few minutes, even though Captain Craig may have been urging him to turn at once;[40] after five minutes at most, the searchlight repeat resolved Evan-Thomas's dilemma. But no significant delay would have occurred if *Lion*'s signallers, still commanded by Beatty's flag-

---

[37] Gordon, p. 82 suggests that *Barham* saw *Lion*'s 2.32 flag signal being hauled down and, being unable to read it, assumed that it was the expected order to resume zigzagging.

[38] Evan-Thomas letters in *BP II*, pp. 463 and 473–5. Vice-Admiral Arthur Craig Waller, 'The Fifth Battle Squadron at Jutland', *Journal of the Royal United Services Institution* (November 1935), LXXX, 520, pp. 792–3 quoted in Dreyer, p. 163. But Corbett, p. 331 n. 2 states: 'At 3.5 *Tiger* signalled that the 2.32 signal and signals made since had not been passed to *Barham*'.

[39] *BP II*, pp. 474–5. *BP I*, p. 257.

[40] Gordon, p. 82. *FDSF III*, pp. 58 n. 30 and 61; from Craig's *JRUSI* article (see note 38), Marder concludes, though without any obvious justification, that the flag-captain saw the 2.25 destroyer signal.

lieutenant, Lieutenant-Commander Ralph Seymour, had not neglected, in the full seven minutes between the destroyer signal and making executive the signal to turn SSE, to repeat the latter signal by searchlight and obtain an acknowledgement. Yet there was no good reason for these omissions while, if proper acknowledgements had not been received from the 5BS by 2.32, the tactical situation did not demand that the battlecruisers charge off regardless to cut off nothing bigger than an isolated force of cruisers. The *Grand Fleet Signal Orders* make clear that the responsibility for this signalling failure lay squarely with Beatty himself.

It is to be clearly understood that senior officers are responsible for informing ships under their immediate command of all messages that concern them.[41]

In any case, it should be emphasised that, while the distance between *Lion* and *Barham* had now increased to about ten miles, Beatty's own dispositions had already created an initial separation of five miles.

Meanwhile, at 2.34 the watch on *Galatea* realised that the two vessels they were chasing were not cruisers but destroyers; when they opened fire, *B109* and *B110* turned north. At the same time, *Galatea* also sighted *Elbing* bearing E on a course SSE, while *Elbing* reported what she thought was an armoured cruiser on an almost reciprocal bearing (WbyN).[42] The two cruisers then engaged each other and, despite the long range of 14,000–15,000 yards, *Elbing* made one hit; fortunately the shell, which fetched up just above a 4in magazine, did not burst.[43] *Inconstant* and *Cordelia* were then closing *Galatea* and so too, in accordance with Battle Cruiser Orders, was Rear-Admiral Trevelyan Napier in *Falmouth*.[44] Commodore William Goodenough regretted that the 2LCS

Table 5.3. *1/3LCS signals 2.31–2.34pm*

Time of despatch	From	To	System	Message	Time of origin
pm, 31 May					
2.31	SO 3LCS	Lion	SL	Am closing 1LCS	1425
2.34	Galatea	SO BCF	W/T	Urgent. Two ships reported in my 1420 are two destroyers. Am chasing	1430
				(Received in Iron Duke 2.34pm)	
2.34	Galatea	SO BCF	W/T	Urgent. One Cruiser, probably hostile, bearing E, steering SSE. My position 56° 50 N, 5°19E.	1430
				(Received in Iron Duke 2.30pm)	

[41] *Grand Fleet Signal Orders*, 15 January 1916, para. 4.5, ADM 137/266.
[42] *OD*(M), 2.34. *OD*, p. 172. GMS, p. 275.
[43] *OD*, p. 172. Tarrant, p. 66. F&H, p. 22. S&H, p. 62.   [44] *OD*, pp. 172 and 185.

'were badly placed when the enemy was first reported'; they were forced to shape courses to the south and east, *Nottingham* getting ahead on *Lion*'s port bow but *Southampton* remaining on her starboard quarter.[45]

On the German side, at 2.30 Rear-Admiral Friedrich Bödicker, commanding the IISG, ordered *Wiesbaden* and *Regensburg* to the east of him to close his flagship, the *Frankfurt*; he, with *Pillau* taking station astern, turned to port to support the *Elbing*. The IISG would end up strung out ahead of the battlecruisers of the ISG, on similar NW'ly courses. As soon as Hipper received the first reports of enemy vessels, he turned his battlecruisers together at 2.27 to WSW. He then seems to have headed SSW for a time in line-ahead. This move may have followed the misreading of a signal reporting that the British recognition signal was 'PL' – this was probably the challenge code flashed twice by *Galatea* as she bore down.[46] At first, this signal gave the impression that the ISG was about to encounter a force of twenty-four to twenty-six British battleships, while the shells falling about *Elbing* suggested inexplicably an enemy approach from the SSW. As the misread signal was retransmitted and reports came in from the IISG that only four British light (not armoured) cruisers were in sight, at 2.43 Hipper made a series of turns together to starboard that took him back towards the 1LCS; by 2.59 at the latest,

Table 5.4. *I/IISG signals 2.27–2.59pm*

Time of receipt	From	To	System	Message	Time of origin
pm, 31 May					
2.27	Elbing	C-in-C		Enemy armoured cruiser in sight bearing WbyN	1431
2.27	Lützow	ISG	Visual	Turn together to port to WSW	
2.30	Lützow	ISG	Visual	Follow in wake of SO's ship	
2.30	Frankfurt	Regensberg Wiesbaden	Visual	Close	
2.33	Elbing	C-in-C		I am under fire	1434
2.38	B109	Regensberg		Enemy's recognition signal is 'PL'	1435
2.43	Lützow	ISG	Visual	Turn together to starboard to WSW	
2.52	Lützow	ISG	Visual	Turn together to NNW	
2.55	Frankfurt	C-in-C		Not armoured cruisers but four cruisers of Calliope class, steering northwestwards	1450
2.59	Elbing	Lützow		Four enemy cruisers of Arethusa class in sight	1426
2.59	Lützow	ISG	Visual	Course NNW	

[45] Goodenough, p. 95. *OD*, p. 184. 'Etienne', p. 128.
[46] GMS, 3.27, 3.30 and 3.43. *GOA*, pp. 44–5. S&H, p. 61.

he was steaming NNW at 21 knots.[47] These sweeping course changes and the inconsistencies in the German sources suggest that the report of as many as twenty-six battleships may have shaken Hipper's nerve, though only briefly.

At 2.39, *Galatea* reported that she had sighted a 'large amount of smoke as though from a fleet bearing ENE' and then, at 2.51: 'Smoke seems to be seven vessels besides Destroyers and Cruisers. They have turned N.'[48] Now Beatty and his commanders, unlike their German opposite numbers, knew that enemy capital ships were close at hand. As other enemy light cruisers came up in support of *Elbing*, the 1LCS proceeded to the north-west in extended order,

Table 5.5. *LCS signals 2.39–3.25pm*

Time of despatch	From	To	System	Message	Time of origin
pm, 31 May					
2.39	Galatea	SO BCF	W/T	Urgent. Have sighted large amount of smoke as though from a fleet bearing ENE. My position 56°50 N, 5°19E. (Received in Iron Duke 2.35pm)	1435
2.43	Cordelia	Inconstant	Sem.	How many ships can you make out? I can make out one. Reply: One ship and two Destroyers	
2.45	Galatea	SO BCF	SL	Enemy apparently turned North	1445
2.51	Galatea	SO BCF	W/T	Urgent. My 1435. Smoke seems to be seven vessels besides Destroyers and Cruisers. They have turned North ... (Received in Iron Duke 2.51pm)	1445
2.55	SO 1LCS	Inconstant	SL	Where are our Battle Cruisers? Reply: Bearing WSW just hull down, apparently steering SE	
3.05	Galatea	SO BCF	SL	Several Cruisers and Destroyers bearing E, steering various courses ... Am keeping touch. Course N, 25 knots. Enemy cruisers have altered to NW	1505
3.05	Falmouth	SO BCF C-in-C	W/T	Urgent. Three cruisers, probably hostile, in sight bearing E, course N. My position 56°59 N, 5°31E. (Received in Iron Duke 3.8pm)	1500
3.08	Galatea	SO BCF	W/T	Urgent. Enemy ships reported have altered course NW, my course is NNW ...	1507
3.22	Galatea	SO BCF	SL and W/T	Urgent. Am leading Enemy NW, they appear to be following. My position 57°02 N, 5°23E. (Received in Iron Duke 3.29pm)	1520
3.25	Galatea	SO BCF	W/T	Urgent. Have sighted smoke on bearing ESE, apparently squadron astern of Cruisers steering WNW bearing ESE. (Received in Iron Duke 3.27pm)	1515

[47] *GOA*, pp. 44–5 and also p. 281 which lists a turn together W at 2.47 not in GMS, p. 276. These sources and the German charts (Tarrant, pp. 68 and 70) are not consistent about the turns made by the ISG.

[48] There are no indications that *Galatea*'s 2.39 report was received in *Barham* in time to have influenced Evan-Thomas's decision to turn SSE between 2.38 and 2.40.

keeping beyond gun range after being under fire again at 2.52. By 2.55, Beatty's battlecruisers were out of sight from *Galatea* and just hull down, bearing WSW, from *Inconstant*. By 3.05, enemy cruisers bore E from both *Galatea* and *Falmouth*, the latter reporting three of them. *Galatea*'s course was then N but, having observed the enemy altering to NW, she turned at 3.08 to NNW. In their despatches, both Alexander-Sinclair and Napier declared that their object was to draw the enemy towards the battlefleet, Napier stating:

Being far outranged, we endeavoured to keep touch without closing much, and to lead the enemy round to the direction of our Battlefleet (N.W.), whilst the Battle Cruisers were steering to the eastward to cut them off.[49]

At 3.12, *Elbing* could see four modern cruisers to westward at a range of 17,800 yards, with two more coming into view. At 3.15, *Lützow*, with only four British cruisers in sight, altered course to NW. At about 3.12, *Frankfurt* and *Pillau* opened fire, though without effect, at a range of 16,000 yards until their targets turned away slightly out of range.[50] At 3.22, *Galatea* signalled that she was still leading the enemy NW while, at about this time, she could again see the smoke of the ISG behind the IISG to the ESE.

Table 5.6. Engadine *signals 1.31–3.45pm*

Time of despatch	From	To	System	Message	Time of origin
pm, 31 May					
1.31	Falmouth	Engadine	SL	Close	
2.06	SO 3LCS	Engadine	SL	Your new cruising station 5½ miles S50°E from Falmouth	
2.31	Falmouth	Engadine	SL	Close Battle Cruisers	1430
2.37	SO 3LCS	Engadine	SL	Two enemy cruisers sighted about east. Take cover near Battle Cruisers	1435
2.47	SO BCF	Engadine	SL	Send up seaplanes to scout NNE. Am sending two destroyers to you	1445
3.05	SO BCF	Engadine	SL	Tell Seaplanes Enemy have turned N	1500
3.10	Engadine	Seaplane 8089	SL	Enemy has turned North	
3.31	Seaplane N82A	SO via Engadine	W/T	Cruisers three, Destroyers five. Enemy bearing and distance from me E 10 miles. Enemy course NW	1530
3.36	Seaplane N82A	SO via Engadine	W/T	Enemy's course is South	1530 [1533]*
3.45	Seaplane N82A	SO via Engadine	W/T	Three Cruisers, 10 Destroyers. Enemy's course is South	1545

* Correct time-of-origin of 1533 in *Engadine*'s reports, *OD*, pp. 264 and 267.

[49] *OD*, pp. 172 and 185.   [50] GMS, p. 276. *GOA*, p. 45.

Before returning to the movements of the battlecruisers, we must take note of an historic first, reconnaissance by seaplanes from a carrier accompanying a fleet. *Engadine* formed a part of the BCF's light cruiser screen under Napier's command. But when he engaged the German light cruisers, the 21½-knot *Engadine* would not have been able to keep up; at 2.31, he ordered her to close the battlecruisers, though this could take her into disturbed waters in which it would be more difficult to launch her seaplanes.[51] At 2.47, Beatty informed *Engadine* that he was sending two destroyers to escort her (*Onslow* and *Moresby* of the 13DF joined her at 3.30)[52] and he ordered the carrier to send up seaplanes to scout NNE. One of her two Short 184 reconnaissance seaplanes, piloted by Flight Lieutenant Frederick Rutland ('Rutland of Jutland') eventually took off at about 3.08, the delay being 'caused through the Ship having to keep clear of the Cruisers'. Rutland, having received information that the enemy was steering N, headed N10°E, low cloud and limited visibility forcing him to fly low. But, after about ten minutes, he and his observer, Assistant Paymaster George Trewin, sighted the leading light cruisers and destroyers of the IISG and, despite having to stand off about three miles due to anti-aircraft fire, they saw the German ships haul round from NW to S. They were able to send three reports by wireless to *Engadine* before at 3.45 being forced to descend by a broken petrol pipe. By that time, the main British and German were already in direct visual contact; thus it was of no consequence that *Engadine* failed to repeat the seaplane's reports by wireless immediately they were received, but instead attempted unsuccessfully to pass them by searchlight, first to *Lion* and then to *Barham*.[53] Beatty's despatch, without mentioning that he never received their reports, congratulated Rutland and Trewin on their achievement; he concluded 'that seaplanes under such circumstances are of distinct value'.[54] While *Engadine*'s seaplanes would not have another chance to demonstrate their capabilities, her own part in the battle was by no means over.

We left Hipper leading his five battlecruisers onto a course NNW at 2.59. He then increased speed to 23 knots and, with only four enemy light cruisers in sight, turned NW towards them, increasing speed again to 25 knots. But, at 3.20, two rapidly approaching columns of large vessels were sighted from the ISG, the tripod masts of the 2BCS being recognised two

---

[51] *OD*(M), 1.25am. Layman, pp. 176–7.
[52] *OD*, pp. 236 and 238. *Onslow* initially informed *Engadine* that she would be accompanied by *Nestor: OD*(M), 3.30.
[53] *OD*, pp. 263–7. S&H, pp. 65–7. F&H, pp. 25–6. Contrary to *OD*(M), the seaplane number in the *Engadine* reports is 8359.
[54] *OD*, pp. 131–2.

Table 5.7. *ISG signals 2.29–3.30pm*

Time of receipt	From	To	System	Message	Time of origin
pm, 31 May					
2.59	Lützow	ISG	Visual	Course NNW	
3.00	Lützow	ISG	Visual	Speed 23 knots	
3.13	Lützow	C-in-C		Only 4 enemy light cruisers in sight … Course NNW	1520 [*sic*]
3.15	Lützow	ISG	Visual	Course NW	
3.15	Lützow	ISG	Visual	Speed 25 knots	
3.24	Lützow	ISG	Visual	Speed 18 knots	
3.26	Lützow	ISG	Visual	Course NWbyN	
3.30	Lützow	General		IISG close on ISG. Large enemy ships in sight …	1529

minutes later. Hipper edged away one point to NWbyN before, at 3.30, ordering the IISG, spread out ahead in a north-westerly direction, to close his battlecruisers.[55]

On the British side, after *Galatea* had reported smoke from a fleet ENE that had turned N, Beatty, still using flag signals, ordered two turns to port, from SSE to SE and then to E by 3.01. No enemy ships had been sighted when, at 3.12, he increased speed to 23 knots; a minute later, he turned another four points to NE, increasing to 24 knots at 3.20. *Lion*'s flag signals could not have been seen from *Barham* and Evan-Thomas held his course SSE until 3.05; he then 'cut the corner' by turning ESE onto a converging course with *Lion*. However, at 3.21 Beatty broadcast a wireless message to senior officers giving his course as NE and speed 23 knots. At the same nominal time, Evan-Thomas turned the 5BS onto the same course and speed, which suggests that, on receiving Beatty's wireless signal, Evan-Thomas gave up any further attempt to close the gap by steering different, converging courses.

All the turns by the battlecruisers had been by 9 Pendant. Thus the 2BCS remained throughout about 3 miles from *Lion* on a bearing ENE, with *New Zealand* more likely to sight the enemy battlecruisers first. However, the time of 3.15 for the remark that she could make out five enemy ships may be too early; *Lion*'s 'Record of Events' notes that *New Zealand* reported 'enemy in

---

[55] Tarrant, p. 69. GMS, p. 277 has signals ordering the ISG to proceed at 18 knots at both 3.24 and 3.32 but *GOA*, p. 47 assumes that only the latter is correct.

Table 5.8. *BCF signals 2.40–3.25pm*

Time of despatch	From	To	System	Message	Time of origin
pm, 31 May					
2.40	SO 5BS	5BS	Flags	Alter course in succession to SSE. Speed 22 knots	
2.52	SO BCF	General	Flags	Alter course leading ships together the rest in succession to SE	
3.01	SO BCF	General	Flags	Alter course leading ships together the rest in succession to E	
3.03	SO 5BS	5BS	Flags	Ships in column to be 3½ cables apart	
3.05	SO 5BS	5BS	Flags	Alter course in succession to ESE	
3.12	SO BCF	General	Flags	Admiral intends to proceed at 23 knots	
3.13	SO BCF	General	Flags	Alter course leading ships together the rest in succession to NE	
3.14	SO 5BS	5BS	Flags	Alter course in succession to E, speed 22 knots	
3.15	New Zealand			Remarks: Sighted five enemy ships on starboard bow	
3.20	SO BCF	General	Flags	Admiral intends to proceed at 24 knots	
3.21	SO BCF	SOs of Squadrons	W/T	My position 56°48 N, 5°17E, course NE speed 23 knots	1515
3.21	SO 5BS	5BS	Flags	Alter course in succession to NE, speed 23 knots	
3.23	Princess Royal	SO BCF	Flags	Attention is called to EbyN	
3.24	Nottingham	C-in-C SO BCF	W/T	Urgent. Have sighted smoke bearing ENE five columns. My position 56°46 N, 5°14E	1522
3.25	Lion			Remarks: Enemy in sight on starboard bow	

sight' at 3.21 (though there is no corresponding signal), while *New Zealand*'s own report states that she observed 'five ships bearing starboard 40' at 3.24. *Princess Royal* drew attention to EbyN at 3.23 and the enemy was in sight from *Nottingham* at 3.22 and from *Lion* at 3.25. At 3.30, *Lion* obtained a first range of 23,000 yards.[56]

[56] REL. *OD*, p. 160.

Beatty's despatch described his approach after the turn SSE as follows.

'Galatea' reported at 2.35 p.m. that she had sighted a large amount of smoke as from a fleet, bearing E.N.E. This made it clear that the enemy was to the Northwards and Eastwards, and that it would be impossible for him to round the Horn Reef without being brought to action. Course was accordingly altered to the Eastward and North-Eastward, the enemy being sighted at 3.31 p.m. They appeared to be the 1st Scouting group of five Battle Cruisers.

After the first report of the enemy the 1st and 3rd Light Cruiser Squadrons changed their direction and without waiting for orders spread to the East, thereby forming a screen in advance of the Battle Cruiser Squadrons and 5th Battle Squadron by the time we had hauled up to the course of approach. They engaged the enemy Light Cruisers at long range ... the work of the Light Cruiser Squadrons was excellent and of great value.[57]

The sources used above tell a different story. Initially, the 1LCS and 3LCS had rushed eastward but they soon hauled round to the north and north-west. We do not know whether these light cruisers received Beatty's general order to turn SSE; *Inconstant*'s reply to SO1LCS's query at 2.55 suggests that they had not previously realised that the battlecruisers were heading south-eastward. Beatty's light cruiser commanders were aware that 'his general principle was to get between the enemy and his base'[58] but they had not received any direct orders from the vice-admiral. Now they had to decide how to respond to his new courses SE and E. Both concluded, apparently without consultation, that they should continue to draw the Germans NW'ward, while Beatty attempted to get across the German wake. This unnecessarily committed two-thirds of Beatty's light cruiser strength against the three German vessels of the same type that were in sight. The British ships did not even take advantage of their considerable superiority to press in both to attack and, more importantly, to obtain further information on the large vessels that they had sighted briefly between 2.35 and 2.45.

By the time the opposing battlecruisers sighted each other after 3.20, *Galatea* was about 14 miles NNE of *Lion*;[59] both the 1LCS and the 3LCS were thus too far away to play any part in the action that was now imminent. Fortunately, Hipper had also allowed three of his own light cruisers to forge ahead and Beatty did not lose his numerical superiority. A more serious outcome was that, because Beatty did nothing to prevent two of his three light cruiser squadrons from flocking away northwards, a large hole developed where his advanced cruiser screen should have been.[60] (Of the ships of his third squadron, the 2LCS, only *Nottingham* scrambled some way ahead of *Lion* but not far enough

[57] *OD*, pp. 130–1; also *BP I*, pp. 325–6.   [58] Goodenough, p. 95.
[59] Calculated from *Lion*'s reported position at 1515, *Galatea*'s at 1520.
[60] On the light cruisers leaving Beatty's front open, see both Ramsay, p. 48 and Godfrey, Ch. II, p. 2.

to give any advanced warning of enemy ships.) Thus his ill-judged large turn NE at 3.13 was made without any precise enemy reports – though, since he admitted in his despatch that he was already clear that the enemy was 'Northward and Eastward', he should not have turned directly towards them anyway. As a result, on sighting Hipper's force was not, as it should have been, well on *Lion*'s port bow but three points on her starboard bow. Thus Beatty was already too far north to block Hipper's retreat should he turn about towards Horns Reef.

Furthermore, since turning SSE at 2.32, Beatty had done nothing to concentrate his forces and dispose them for action. His series of general 9 Pendant signals shows that, despite the increased gap between him and the 5BS, he was content to leave them at a distance, while his two speed increases were no help to their catching up. As for the 2BCS, he left them bearing ENE, three miles from *Lion*. This alignment had been ordered initially because it was appropriate for meeting an enemy approaching from ahead when his own course was SSE. Yet he now expected to encounter the enemy somewhere north-easterly, and the actual sighting was to EbyN, only one point to starboard of *New Zealand*'s bearing from *Lion*. Thus the two weakly armoured battlecruisers were thrust forward three miles closer to the enemy and with no prospect of getting into line with *Lion* and the 1BCS without some violent manoeuvring. With the two sides on converging courses (the British NE, the German NWbyN) and the range already falling past 23,000 yards, Beatty now had little time to overcome the serious tactical problems that were entirely of his own making.

The first phase

With the ISG three points on his starboard bow, Beatty might have turned to port onto a similar NW'ly course. While still leaving the 2BCS closer to the enemy, he would have been able to close the 5BS and his errant light cruisers, and to continue leading Hipper towards the Grand Fleet. Hipper himself apparently anticipated such a move, since at 3.29 he ordered a distribution of fire from the right. But, since Beatty had been preoccupied with getting between the German ships and their bases, he probably hardly considered this possibility before at 3.28 *Lion* hoisted the flag signal to turn E and increase speed to 25 knots. This was followed a minute later by a further hoist addressed to the 2BCS for them to prolong the line ahead. However, at 3.30, with the range from *Lion* at 23,000 yards, only the general order to all squadrons to turn E by 9 Pendant (leading ships together, the rest in succession), speed 25 knots, was made executive.[61] Instead, at 3.34 the 2BCS was ordered to prolong the line astern; to do so, they had to make two tight turns of almost 16 points,

---

[61] VNE. *OD*(M), 3.30.

Table 5.9. *BCF signals 3.27–3.47pm*

Time of despatch	From	To	System	Message	Time of origin
pm, 31 May					
3.27	SO BCF	General	Flags	Assume complete readiness for action in every respect	
3.30	SO BCF	General	Flags	Alter course leading ships together the rest in succession to E, 25 knots	
3.32	SO BCF	General	Flags	Alter course leading ships together the rest in succession to East	
3.34	SO BCF	2BCS	Flags	Prolong the line by taking station astern	
3.35	SO BCF	SO 5BS	SL	Speed 25 knots. Assume complete readiness for action. Alter course leading ships together the rest in succession to E. Enemy in sight	
3.35	SO 5BS	5BS	Flags	Alter succession in course to E, speed 24 knots	
3.35	SO BCF	General	Flags	… 24 knots	
3.35	SO BCF	General	Flags	Enemy in sight bearing EbyN	
3.36	SO 2BCS	2BCS	Flags	Alter course in succession 16 points to starboard	
3.36	SO BCF	SOs of Squadrons	W/T	Present course and speed E, 25 knots. (Received in Iron Duke 3.32pm)	1530
3.40	SO BCF	C-in-C	W/T	Urgent. Enemy Battle Cruisers, five in number, bearing NE. Destroyers, large number, bearing NE, course unknown. Position of reporting ship 56°53′N, 5°28′ E	1535
3.40	SO 5BS	5BS	Flags	… 24½ knots	
3.45	SO BCF	Battle Cruisers	Flags	Form on a line of bearing NW	
3.45	SO BCF	C-in-C	W/T	Urgent. Course of enemy S55°E. My position 56°53′N, 5°33′E	1545
3.45	SO BCF	General	Flags	Alter course together to ESE	
3.46	SO BCF	Battle Cruisers	Flags	Lion and Princess Royal concentrate on enemy's leading ship	
3.47	Lion			Enemy opened fire	
3.47	SO BCF	General	Flags	Open fire and engage the enemy	

first to starboard and then to port, which enabled them to haul into line at 3.45.[62] At 3.35, Beatty reduced the speed of *Lion* and the 1BCS slightly to 24 knots.

[62] *OD*, p. 160 and Plates 9a and 31.

The 3.30 general signal, and a repeat of the 9 Pendant signal at 3.32, were made only by flags. Yet again, the signal record suggests that these orders were not received in *Barham* until a further signal, repeating several previous orders, was made by searchlight at 3.35. Thus, thanks to another oversight by *Lion's* signallers, the separation between *Lion* and *Barham*, which Evan-Thomas had reduced to about 6 miles, increased again by nearly 1½ miles.[63] This repeat signal, made, as it declared, with 'the enemy in sight', left Evan-Thomas – and leaves us – in no doubt that Beatty intended the 5BS to remain at a distance on parallel courses. Perhaps he had some notion of catching the ISG between two fires, though Hipper's next and obvious move quickly removed any such possibility. But it seems more likely, as Captain Roskill concluded uneasily, that Beatty feared, in the words of *Princess Royal's* fire-eating Captain Cowan, that the 'damned 5th Battle Squadron is going to take the bread out of our mouths'.[64]

As soon as the British battlecruisers turned E, Hipper responded to prevent Beatty cutting across his line of retreat. At 3.35, the ISG turned away 15 points in succession to SE, a move that, unknown to Beatty, would also draw him towards the advancing High Seas Fleet. As the ISG was completing its turn, at 3.40 Hipper ordered an easy speed of 18 knots (which would allow his outlying

Table 5.10. *ISG signals 3.29–3.48pm*

Time of receipt	From	To	System	Message	Time of origin
pm, 31 May					
3.29	Lützow	ISG	Visual	Distribution of fire from the right.	
3.32	Lützow	ISG	Visual	Speed 18 knots	
3.35	Lützow	ISG	Visual	Course SE	
3.35	Lützow	General		Enemy battle fleet in sight … Consists of 6 ships, steering N	1529
3.40	Lützow	ISG	Visual	Distribution of fire from the left	
3.40	Lützow	ISG	Visual	Speed 18 knots	
3.42	Lützow	ISG	Visual	Ships to be 500 metres apart	
3.45	Lützow	ISG	Visual	Turn together to SSE	
3.48	Lützow	ISG	Visual	Open fire	

---

[63] Corbett, Map 22. Corbett's maps were drawn by Lt-Cdr J F H Pollen, who had previously worked for Captain J E T Harper on the track charts for the *Official Record* (completed 1919, text only published 1927). These charts were passed to Corbett on 15 July 1921, who considered that they 'gave … an accurate interpretation of the existing records'. Corbett, p. viii. *JP II*, pp. 411, 464, 481 and 484. *BP II*, p. 454.

[64] Roskill, p. 155.

light cruisers to close more easily) and a distribution of fire from the left that would have omitted *Indefatigable*.[65] The range was now falling at a rate of about −550 yards/minute.[66] At 3.45, Hipper ordered a turn together to SSE 'to close the enemy more rapidly';[67] it would also have thrown out any rate previously obtained by the British ships. This turn together placed his battle-cruisers on a line of bearing NW from *Lützow*, that is, the line joining the ships was at an angle of two points to their course ESE (we shall encounter this type of formation again on the British side). At 3.48, *Lützow* opened fire, followed immediately by her consorts. These first salvos were timed at 3.47 in the British flagship and both *Lion* and *Princess Royal* fired back, concentrating on *Lützow*, within half a minute. Both *Tiger* and *New Zealand* opened fire at *Moltke* at 3.51, but *Queen Mary* did not commence until 3.53, at first only with her fore turrets. The ranges and targets of all the ships are tabulated below.[68] Since both *Lützow* and *Derfflinger* made several down corrections before straddling,[69] *Moltke*'s range was probably the most accurate, though *Princess Royal*'s

Table 5.11. *Ranges and targets*

British	Range in yards		German
Indefatigable	17,700	←	*Von der Tann*
	→ ?		
New Zealand	→ 18,100		
Tiger	→ 18,500		*Moltke*
	15,500	←	
Queen Mary	→ ~17,000		*Seydlitz*
	16,400	←	
Princess Royal	16,400	←	*Derfflinger*
	→ 16,000		
Lion	→ 18,500		*Lützow*
	16,800	←	

---

[65] GMS gives the time of this fire distribution signal as 3.30 but its position in the listing is consistent with the time of 3.40 in *GOA*, p. 57.

[66] This assumes that the enemy bearing from the British ships remained at R20 (20° to port), as recorded in *Lion* at 3.30 (REL) and in *Princess Royal* at 3.39.20 (*OD*, p. 387). *Lion*'s R32 at 3.35 is not consistent with her other recorded courses, bearings and signals. For rate calculations, see 'FCBD', App. XXVI.3.

[67] Tarrant, p. 78.

[68] *GOA*, p. 58. *OD*, pp. 143, 151, 155, 160, 387, 390 and 303. Up to 3.45, *New Zealand*'s times correspond well with her consorts'. All subsequent times are fast – no explanation has been found – and all have been corrected by a constant – 6 minutes. If applicable to *New Zealand* alone, these corrected times are in square brackets thus [3.51].

[69] Paschen, p. 33 (though his gunnery data often does not agree with other sources). von Hase, pp. 145–7.

was almost as good. But the other known British ranges were far too high, while the British fire distribution had also gone awry; the larger force had left out one enemy ship, *Derfflinger*, to fire unmolested at *Princess Royal*. The German distribution was not quite as Hipper had ordered, since *Von der Tann* was shooting at *Indefatigable* rather than *New Zealand*; perhaps *Von der Tann* had found it difficult to keep on her designated target as the 2BCS twice reversed course.

Could unfavourable visibility and wind have contributed to the British errors in range-finding and target selection? *Lion*'s officers recalled that, as the flagship turned E while recording an enemy range of 23,000 yards, the day had been 'glorious', 'perfect', with just the masts, funnels and part of the hull of their target being visible above the horizon from aloft.[70] *Lion*'s director layer confirmed: 'When action was sounded, the light was good', though he and others remarked that it deteriorated as the first phase of the action was ending. Beatty himself declared that, during the approach:

The visibility at this time was good, the sun behind us and the wind SE.[71]

However, all other sources describe the wind as a gentle westerly breeze, though they differ somewhat on the timing of a shift from NW to SW;[72] *Tiger*'s gunnery officer recollected that, at first

the weather was misty in patches, the visibility varying from 12 to 6 mile; wind west, force 3; sea calm.[73]

As the visibility became worse, it was more difficult looking eastward to make out the light grey hulls of the German ships in the mist, whereas, from the ISG, the British battlecruisers were silhouetted against a bright and clear western horizon.[74] But it seems that, during the approach, the visibility from the two sides did not differ greatly unless the mist intervened.

Once the ISG had turned SE, Beatty had no choice but to engage from the windward position. As he headed E, a westerly wind would pile up smoke in the wake of his ships, causing interference to those further back in the line. Then, as he turned to starboard onto a similar course to the enemy, the wind would carry the smoke onto the engaged side. If his ships remained in line astern, each (except *Lion*) would find its target obscured by the smoke from all those ships ahead. The solution was to form on a line-of-bearing inclined towards the

---

[70] REL. F&H, pp. 109 and 380: and see also Godfrey, Ch. II, p. 2.
[71] *BP I*, p. 356. F&H, pp. 30 and 398–9. *OD*, p. 132. 'The visibility was good but not abnormal': Midshipman N G Garnon-Williams, stationed in *Lion*'s conning tower. Garnon-Williams Papers, 85/26/1, IWM.
[72] F&H, p. 165. Pelly, p. 165. von Hase, pp. 153–4. *GOA*, p. 62. Scheer's despatch, *OD*, p. 592.
[73] F&H, p. 397. See also *OD*, pp. 155 and 162.
[74] *GOA*, p. 58. von Hase, p. 154. 'Etienne', p. 130. King-Hall, p. 451. Chalmers, pp. 230–1.

enemy; an angle of two points between the course and the line-of-bearing sufficed in a gentle breeze.[75] This formation ensured that each ship steamed in front of the smoke from all the ships ahead. At 3.43, *Lion* hoisted the signal to form on a line-of-bearing NW; its purpose, as Beatty declared in his despatch, was 'to clear the smoke'. At the same time, *Lion*'s 'Record of Events' noted a one-point turn to starboard, followed by a second starboard turn at 3.46; her track chart shows a turn from E to EbyS at 3.45.[76] Thus the inclination of the line-of-bearing was sufficient for a course of EbyS or ESE, though it left little margin for any turns further to starboard. There is agreement that the line-of-bearing signal was hauled down at 3.45; and that, literally at the last minute, it was followed at 3.46 by a fire distribution signal, ordering *Lion* and *Princess Royal* to concentrate on the leading German ship, with the remaining four ships to engage one-to-one with the four rear ships in the German line. This signal was not recorded in the logs of *Tiger* and *New Zealand*. *Lion* also made a third signal to alter course together to ESE. But while its time given in the *Official Despatches* was 3.45, in Beatty's own 'Narrative of Events', it was listed at 3.47, in the same hoist ordering his ships to open fire.[77]

If the line-of-bearing order was received on its own (meaning form the line-of-bearing on the present course E), the guide (usually, as in this case, the leading ship) held the course, while those astern fanned out to port so that they could arrive at the line-of-bearing at the right spacing; they would then turn together onto the original course. Since the ships astern had partially to over-haul those ahead, they had to increase speed relative to the guide. This was a complex unequal-speed manoeuvre which, even if the speed difference was as great as five knots, required about six minutes to complete. In fact, there is no evidence that *Lion* slowed down at all, while the 2BCS were struggling to regain the nominal fleet speed after their sweeping turns; thus the line-of-bearing could not have formed in this way until long after firing actually began. However, with *Lion* already turning to starboard, it may have been apparent, at least to those ships that could observe her movements clearly, that the leading ships should turn to starboard, though those further back would still have had to fan out to port.[78] Even so, another order after only two minutes to

---

[75] FCBD, App. XXVI.4 for method of calculation. Force 3 indicated a wind speed of 7–10 knots.

[76] VNE. *OD*, p. 132 and Plate 10. REL.

[77] *Cf. OD*(M) and VNE. Corbett, p. 344 n. 3, which in addition gives the time of the ESE signal as 3.47, as does a fair copy of *Lion*'s signal log in DRAX 4/3.

[78] Only later charts show the battlecruisers fanning out, though differently *cf.* Corbett, Map 23, *GOA*, Charts 4 and 5 (and, clearly derived from the latter, *FDSF III*, Chart 4; Campbell, Chart I; S&H, p. 69; and Tarrant, Figs. 16 and 18). *GOA*, Chart 5 also shows a turn together to S at about 3.52 preserving the line-of-bearing NW. But this turn could not have been made without a signal (none is recorded – see also Godfrey, Ch. II, p. 9); this line-of-bearing no longer avoided smoke interference; and it placed the rear British ships furthest from the ISG, contrary to the range records.

turn ESE would have been ambiguous; did it require an immediate turn (which would have resulted in a bent line and a continuing problem with smoke) or a turn delayed until the line-of-bearing had been formed? In contrast, if the turning signal had been made at the same time as that for the line-of-bearing, it could have been read as requiring all ships to turn to starboard; *Lion* would turn ESE immediately, the rest either fanning out to starboard by smaller angles, or simply delaying their turns ESE until they reached the correct bearing from the next ahead.[79] Any turn to port was better avoided since, with the enemy bearing EbyN, it would bring the enemy directly ahead, guaranteeing that only the fore turrets could bear. With these possibilities in mind, we can now examine how Beatty's ships fared during their approach.

Princess Royal identified five enemy battlecruisers just before 3.35, and, at 3.42.30, without orders, she selected the 'Right hand ship ("Lutzow" Class)' as her target. At 3.45 she noted that the 'Battle Cruisers were formed on a compass line of bearing N.W.' and that she received the signal confirming the concentration that she had correctly anticipated. While there is no explicit note of a turn ESE, her chart does show such a turn, also at 3.45. When she opened fire at 3.47.35, the target bearing was R42,[80] sufficient (though with little margin) for her after turrets to bear.[81] Her range was by far the most accurate of Beatty's ship, as was her rate of −400 yards/minute.

I think that at this time all the battle cruisers except 'P.R.' had underestimated the rate; we had [in *Tiger*].[82]

All this indicated that *Princess Royal* had enjoyed good views of the ISG and of *Lion* during the approach, uninterrupted by smoke from the flagship. As instructed by Battle Cruiser Orders, she had probably acted on her own initiative by '[h]auling out of the wake of the next ahead to avoid smoke'.[83] Thus she would already have been on a line-of-bearing from *Lion*, and would have had no difficulty in following the flagship's turn to ESE, whether or not she received an explicit signal to turn.

Queen Mary engaged *Seydlitz* rather than *Derfflinger*, contrary to Beatty's concentration signal. She was last to open fire and, despite her reputation as the BCF's crack gunnery ship, her initial range was about 17,000 yards, 1,000 yards in excess of *Princess Royal*'s. Also, she alone was reported as having

---

[79] The quickest method would have been to turn immediately in succession SE onto the line of bearing, and then together to ESE; however, the turn in succession was not signalled, nor do the charts show a turn SE until later.

[80] Red 42, i.e. 42° to port from right ahead. Green signified bearings to starboard.

[81] *OD*, pp. 147 and 387 and Plate 12. In the *Lion* class, the superstructure prevented Q and X turrets from training further forward than 30° on the bow (Roberts, *Battlecruisers, Queen Mary* deck plan. F&H, p. 110). However, some additional margin was necessary so that the trainers could aim continuously.

[82] F&H, p. 397 and also p. 29.   [83] *BP I*, p. 257 for BCO 4.

commenced with her fore turrets only.[84] This suggests that, having received the
signal for the line-of-bearing but not that for course ESE, she turned to port.
Next astern, *Tiger* did not even sight the enemy until 3.45, when only three
ships were visible initially from her control positions. She waited until about
3.51 before opening fire, but even so her initial range was equalled in inaccu-
racy only by *Lion*'s. *Tiger* did not take in the concentration signal nor do her
reports mention signals for a line-of-bearing or a turn ESE. Like *Queen Mary*,
she selected her opposite number in the German line rather than the next to the
right. Just after she opened fire:

The top reported that the funnel smoke of our battle cruisers ahead made their view
very bad.

(At the time, she was also experiencing 'Considerable interference from our T.
B.D's' smoke.)[85]

New Zealand's Captain was 'rather impressed by the little smoke interference there was'; hence, in taking station astern of *Tiger* at 3.45, she may have
reached the line-of-bearing NW. Even so, she missed Beatty's concentration
signal, although both *New Zealand* and *Indefatigable* chose the targets he
intended for them. However, their violent manoeuvres must have created
conditions of heel, vibration and rapidly changing bearings that made ranging
impossible; it was not until [3.45] that *New Zealand* '[c]ommenced ranging on
the 4th ship from the right'.[86] The 2BCS also had to recover the speed lost in the
turns. When *New Zealand* opened fire at [3.51], her engines were making over
300 revolutions per minute, more than she had managed at the Dogger Bank, so
the ranging of the 2BCS continued to be disrupted by vibration.[87] Thus *New
Zealand* – and doubtless *Indefatigable* too – had neither the time nor the
conditions necessary for accurate ranging and plotting. The 2BCS remained
longer on course E and then turned sharply to SSE at [3.54].[88]

The bad 'funnel smoke of our battle cruisers ahead' explains why *Tiger* did
not receive Beatty's concentration signal and why, when she did belatedly sight

[84] *OD*, p. 150 (times are BST) and Williams, p. 113 are reports from survivors. For *Queen Mary*'s
gunnery reputation, see Midshipman G M Eady, 'Account of Jutland' in 'Life in the Battle
Cruiser Fleet 1916', Eady Papers, 86/58/1, IWM.
[85] *OD*, pp. 389–90. F&H, p. 397. Captain Pelly's despatch (*OD*, p. 155) stated that, at 3.45, five
ships were sighted and that the 4th ship from the left [*sic*] was given as the target at 3.46: but,
since he also stated that they were 'bearing North and on the Port Beam', his account must be
suspect.
[86] *OD*, pp. 160, 162 and 393.
[87] Eady, 'With the Battle-Cruiser-Fleet at Jutland' in 'Life in the BCF' (see note 84). Eady claimed
327 rpm and 29.7 knots but these figures must be exaggerated. On trial, *New Zealand* managed
26.39 knots at 300 rpm: Roberts, *Battlecruisers*, p. 80. For the effects of vibration on gunnery,
see Chatfield, p. 109.
[88] *OD*, p. 160 and Plate 31. Plate 9a (also from *New Zealand*: see Gordon, pp. 608–9) shows the
turn SSE shortly before [3.54].

the enemy, only three ships were initially visible. *Queen Mary* seems to have had similar problems with signals and she too selected the wrong target. Both ships apparently ignored the provisions for fire distribution that had been part of fleet orders since 1913: that, when numbers permitted and subject to no enemy ship being unfired at, ships should concentrate on the enemy's leading ship or ships.[89] This was the distribution scheme assumed, without orders, by *Princess Royal* at 3.42 and by the 2BCS. However, they had clear views of the whole enemy line, whereas *Tiger*, and probably *Queen Mary*, did not. With the enemy fine on the port bow, the German flagship was especially likely to have been hidden by the smoke from ahead, so that either *Tiger* or *Queen Mary* could have mistaken the correct target on first sighting some of the enemy. However, once firing had begun, both ships knew that they were shooting at their opposite numbers, but were seemingly reluctant to change target. Alternatively, they may simply have overlooked the fire distribution orders, a mistake that would have been avoided if Beatty's concentration order had been sent in good time. In accordance with BCF orders, both ships could perhaps have done more on their own initiative to avoid the smoke from ahead. However, the orders stipulated that:

It is desirable that ships should not haul out more than one point [which may not have been enough] and that no movement should inconvenience others [difficult to avoid when the 2BCS were trying to haul into line on the port quarter].[90]

Without a lead from the flagship, both ships seem to have just followed in her wake.

Lion's rangetakers cannot have had any interference from the smoke of her consorts. Yet her surviving range records contain only three or four ranges taken during the whole course of the approach. They fell to 20,000 yards at 3.38/39 and to 18,500 yards by 3.46/47; this was the same as the opening sight range at 3.47½, when the target bearing was R42. Although *Lion*'s range-rate was −400 yards/minute at 3.39, her opening range-rate was only −150 yards/minute.[91] Because the ISG turned SSE while *Lion* was turning to ESE, the calculated rate, at least between the leading ships, was −570 yards/minute, only a slight increase on the previous value. Thus, compared with *Princess Royal*, *Lion*'s ranges were much too high, and she had failed to detect Hipper's final turn; it appears that, despite Beatty's reassurances to Jellicoe, the whole fire

---

[89] *GFBOs III*, XV.1 referred to Home Fleet General Order 15, 'Distribution of Gunfire', 8 December 1913 (and still in force on 1 October 1916) in ADM 137/260.

[90] *BP I*, p. 257 (BCO 4).

[91] *Lion*'s were never published but there are copies of REL in both the Beatty and Jellicoe papers and, also in Add 49014, a summary of data from *Lion*'s range plot. Jellicoe's copies were provided by Frederic Dreyer when DNO and DGD. Both documents show almost identical target bearings. The rangefinder ranges are few, differ in detail but show the same general trend. These records from *Lion* were made available to Captain Harper: *JP II*, pp. 472 and 474–5.

control organisation of his flagship was no more efficient than it had been during the practices of late 1915.

At 3.30, when she turned E, *Lion*'s range was 23,000 yards. This was close to the range of her guns when at maximum elevation, although the guns were then on the stops and could only have been fired as they rolled 'on'.[92] Except for *Von der Tann*, the equivalent figure for the German battlecruisers was 21,000 yards or less.[93] Thus in theory Beatty had an opportunity to open fire at ranges at which Hipper could barely reply. But, as we have seen, Beatty's ships were not ready to begin firing immediately after their turn. In any case, shooting at such distances was difficult and ineffective. A better indication of the maximum practicable range was the maximum range on the gun sights, which was typically 20,200 yards in *Lion* and 19,600 yards in *Derfflinger*.[94] These maxima were close to the range recorded in *Lion* at 3.38/9, when Beatty's line was still not ready. Thus the opportunity to fire unmolested was already past. After the Dogger Bank, Chatfield had warned that an accurate, rapid fire could be expected from the enemy at 18,000 yards, though Beatty wished to close without delay to as little as 12,000–14,000 yards. Thus it is unlikely that the latter intended to go beyond the recommendation for the battlefleet in the *GFBOs*.

it is not intended … to open fire at a greater range than 18,000 yards unless the enemy does so earlier … Ships must, however, be *ready* to open fire at extreme range.[95]

The last sentence is the nub of the matter. It was the duty of any commander to ensure that they made their approach on 'that steady course that is so important for gunnery',[96] that they were free from smoke interference and that each had a clearly designated target; only then could they commence ranging and plotting so as to be ready with an accurate range, range-rate and deflection whenever they were ordered to open fire. Beatty was no doubt misled by *Lion*'s high ranges and declining range-rates to think that he had time in hand before firing began. But that does not excuse the delays in getting ready to open fire.

Having left the 2BCS in their exposed position bearing ENE, Beatty's chosen course E left them little searoom and forced them to make two very tight turns. A course further to starboard (say the course ESE he ordered later) would have allowed the 2BCS to make easier turns; it would also have closed the range less rapidly, giving more time to prepare for action. But, having

---

[92] REL. Maximum range of 13.5in Mk. V was 23,800 yards at 20° elevation: Roberts, *Battlecruisers*, p. 89.

[93] German maxima 20,500 yards (*Lützow* and *Derfflinger*), 21,000 yards (*Seydlitz*), 19,500 yards (*Moltke*) and 22,500 yards (*Von der Tann*): GOA, p. 57.

[94] BP I, p. 210. von Hase, p. 152. The maximum sight range in *New Zealand* was 19,400 yards, more than the 18,300 yards attained at the Dogger Bank with the guns on the stops; ADM 137/305, f. 166.

[95] *GFBOs III*, XIV.1.   [96] Chatfield, p. 142; see also p. 134.

turned E, at 3.35 (the time-of-origin of his signal to the C-in-C), Beatty knew he was facing five enemy battlecruisers that were, at that time, turning about. He needed at once to form a line-of-bearing to prevent smoke interference; to alter course to ESE (or further) to reduce the rate, open the turret firing arcs and make it easier for the 2BCS to join the line; and to order his fire distribution.[97] Instead, he waited ten minutes or more, with severe consequences for his ships' gunnery. They lost vital signals in the smoke. As the Germans opened fire, they had not completed the formation of the line-of-bearing and *Queen Mary* had turned to port so that her after turrets could not bear.[98] She and *Tiger* had selected the wrong targets, while *Tiger*, and probably *Queen Mary* too, were still hampered by smoke from ahead. And the 2BCS were still struggling to maintain station. To make matters worse, the inconsistency between the two records of *Lion*'s signal to turn ESE, and the different ways in which it could have been interpreted by those ships that received it, suggest that, once again, *Lion*'s dysfunctional signalling organisation had added to the confusion in Beatty's line just as they went into action.

Beatty himself probably did not fully understand the serious gunnery implications of his delayed orders. William Goodenough, though an admirer, admitted that the pre-eminence of 'that ardent spirit Lord Beatty' did not derive from 'great professional knowledge, certainly not of gun or torpedo'. Unfortunately, at this critical moment, Beatty could not draw on the gunnery expertise of his flag-captain.[99] Chatfield recalled:

I was on the compass platform ... with my small staff. Beatty remained for a time on his own bridge below me with [his staff]. I wanted him to come on the compass platform and sent a message to Seymour, telling him to advise Beatty that the range was closing rapidly and that we ought almost at once to be opening fire ... But I could get no reply, the Vice-Admiral was engaged in an important message to the Commander-in-Chief. 18,000 [*sic*] yards. I told Longhurst [the gunnery commander] to be ready to open fire immediately.

Beatty did not join Chatfield until after *Lion* had opened fire.[100] The delay in doing so may have been due to Beatty (and Seymour) not paying attention to the rapidly developing tactical situation. But another (though unsubstantiated) possibility is that Beatty had indeed intended to press in to the range of 12,000–14,000 yards, which, after the Dogger Bank, he thought 'would suit us well'. Unfortunately, in either event, Chatfield was not on hand to warn that the Germans were likely to open an accurate, rapid fire at any moment.

Here, from his own despatch, is Beatty's description of the approach.

At 3.30 p.m. I increased speed to 25 knots and formed the Line of Battle, the 2nd Battle Cruiser Squadron forming astern of the 1st Battle Cruiser Squadron ... I turned to E.S.

---

[97] Beatty himself saw four ships on the port bow at 3.40, all five at 3.44: VNE.

[98] The reports from *Tiger* and *New Zealand* give no indication that they opened fire only with their fore turrets; however, their after turrets were probably on the very limits of forward bearing.

[99] Goodenough, p. 91. Roskill, p. 131.   [100] Chatfield, pp. 140–1.

E., slightly converging on the enemy, who were now at a range of 23,000 yards, and formed the ships on a line of bearing to clear the smoke ... Being between the enemy and his base, our situation was both tactically and strategically good.[101]

This is obviously at variance with all other sources, not least the 'Narrative' still to be found in Beatty's personal records. It implies that the turn ESE and the formation of the line-of-bearing happened much earlier than was the case and appears to be a deliberately calculated misrepresentation. Hipper understood very well what had gone wrong.

The fact that the English Battlecruisers, possibl[y] on account of bad light conditions or perhaps forming line of Battle too late, delayed opening fire, allowed us too to withhold our fire until the enemy was in effective gun range (15,000–16,000 yards). The possibility of obtaining a rapid gunnery superiority ... is principally to be attributed to this delay in opening fire which compelled the enemy to remain a longer time within effective gun range. An earlier opening of fire would have permitted the enemy to at once run out of range.[102]

Hipper's battlecruisers suffered no interference from their own smoke, which was carried by the wind onto the disengaged side. Furthermore, their stereoscopic range-finders could obtain ranges even from those targets that were enveloped in smoke. Even so, both *Lützow* and *Derfflinger* had to spot down some 1,600 metres (almost 1,750 yards) before straddling; von Hase, the gunnery officer of *Derfflinger*, believed that his rangetakers had been overwhelmed by the spectacle

Table 5.12. *ISG signals 3.53–4.05pm*

Time of receipt	From	To	System	Message	Time of origin
pm, 31 May					
3.53	Lützow	ISG	Visual	Increase speed	
3.54	Lützow	ISG	Visual	Follow in wake of the leading ship	
3.54	Lützow	General		6 enemy battle cruisers, also smaller vessels ... steering SE ... Course SSE, 18 knots. Am in action with 6 battle cruisers. Request position of own battle fleet	1546
4.00	Lützow	ISG	Visual	Turn together to SEbyS	
4.04	Lützow	ISG	Visual	Turn together to SbyE	
4.05	C-in-C	Fleet and AC Scouting Forces		Own battle fleet, 4 p.m. Position ... Course NW. Speed 15 knots	1609

[101]   *OD*, p. 132 and *BP I*, p. 326.
[102]   Hipper to Scheer, 'Lessons from the Skagerrak Battle' in DRYR 6/10 and ADM 137/1644.

of the approaching enemy dreadnoughts, since subsequently 'there was seldom a variation of more than 300 metres between any of the rangefinders, even at the longest ranges'.[103] By 3.52, both *Lion* and *Tiger* had been hit twice, whereas the British salvos were falling far over, endangering the light cruiser *Regensburg* and destroyers some 2,200 yards on the ISG's disengaged flank.[104] At 3.53–4, Hipper ordered his ships to increase speed (the amount is not known) and to follow in his wake; as they reformed in line-ahead, he led them onto course SE.[105] Even before she was hit, *Lion* began a series of small turns-away. Her director layer complained that '[w]ith [these] alterations of course, the ship was yawing considerably'. Nonetheless, she fired steadily, discharging nineteen salvos between 3.47½ and 4.00, an average of one salvo every 42 seconds. By 3.55, she had settled on a course SbyE, which she held until 4 o'clock.[106] As would be expected, the range between the leading ships reached a minimum of some 12,500 yards at around 3.54, before increasing again due to the diverging courses to about 16,800 at 4 o'clock.[107]

Table 5.13. *BCF signals 3.47–4.10pm*

Time of despatch	From	To	System	Message	Time of origin
pm, 31 May					
3.47	SO BCF	General	Flags	Open fire and engage the enemy	
3.55	SO BCF	C-in-C	W/T	Urgent. Am engaging Enemy. My position 56°53′N, 5°31′E	1550
3.55	SO BCF	General	Flags	Increase the rate of fire	1558
			W/T		
3.56	SO 5BS	Destroyers	Flags	Keep out of the way	
3.59	SO 5BS	Fearless	Flags	Fearless take station astern of Malaya	
4.00	SO 5BS	5BS	Flags	Open fire and engage the enemy	
4.10	Lion			Remarks: Indefatigable blew up	

[103] von Hase, pp. 145–8 and 153–4. Paschen, p. 30. British smoke would still have interfered with German aiming.

[104] VNE, though by 3.58, *Lion*'s salvos were short. Campbell, pp. 40, 67–9 and 73–4. *GOA*, p. 58.

[105] Line-ahead, course SE is shown on the chart with Scheer's despatch (*OD*, German Plan IV); see also von Hase, Sketch I. But *GOA*, Chart 5 (and Tarrant, p. 82) shows course SSE. Throughout the battle, Hipper used the 'follow in leader's wake' signal rather than 'alter course in succession' or similar.

[106] REL for salvos; it also notes four unquantified turns to starboard between 3.49 and 3.55 but the target bearings suggest *Lion* turned almost continuously until 3.53. The BCF's chart (*OD*, Plate 10) show just two untimed turns, to SE and then to SbyE, after 3.45. *BP I*, p. 356.

[107] Minima were *Derfflinger*, 12,300 yards at 3.53–4; *Princess Royal*, 12,800 yards at 3.53–5; *Lion*, 14,500 yards at 3.54. The ranges at about 4.00 are greater than would be expected from the calculated rates (FCBD, App. XXVI.12) but had Hipper's course remained SSE, the disparity would have been even greater. At the lower ranges, the German secondaries fired mainly against British destroyers – *GOA*, p. 60 – but do not seem to have been noticed by their targets.

Once engaged, Beatty made no further manoeuvring signals. Without signals from the flagship, Beatty's other battlecruisers were left, as required in Battle Cruiser Orders, to use their 'initiative and judgement' in following his movements and avoiding smoke interference.[108] Once he began turning southwards, there was no possibility of forming the line-of-bearing NW and in any case this was no longer appropriate. Like *Lion*, *Princess Royal* also 'gradually altered to southward'. Her first five salvos were fired at an average interval of 55 seconds. but she then only managed two more (the last at 3.55.15) in the next four minutes; this may have prompted Beatty's admonition at 3.55 to 'Increase the rate of fire'. As the rear ship in the concentration on *Lützow*, *Princess Royal* was expected to regulate her firing interval if there were difficulties with spotting. But, due to the unfavourable wind, she was also troubled by *Lion*'s smoke and from 3.59 by smoke from destroyers on her engaged side.[109] Thus she was unable to make anything of her accurate opening range and rate. Then at 3.56 her fire was badly disrupted by two hits that put her Argo Tower out of action; she was also hit again at about four o'clock. The revolving hood was repaired by 4.16 (though the rangefinder remained unserviceable); meanwhile control had to be transferred to B turret and her gunnery record practically ceases for this period.[110]

Queen Mary made the first British hits, on *Seydlitz*, at 3.55 and 3.57. The second holed (though did not penetrate) the barbette of the after superfiring C turret, igniting two fore and two main charges in the working chamber. Flash penetrated upwards to the gunhouse and downwards to the handing room where more charges were singed though none caught fire. Most of the turret crew were killed but the precautions introduced after the Dogger Bank had evidently proved effective. It seems that *Queen Mary* was no longer inconvenienced by smoke from ahead, which suggests that, compared with *Princess Royal*, she made a wider turn. Her survivors did not recall any hits on their ship until much later, while she made one more hit on the *Seydlitz*, probably between 4.00 and 4.10.[111]

Up to four o'clock, *Tiger* took another six hits from *Moltke*, even though the German ship (which remained undamaged) was the target of both *Tiger* and *New Zealand*. At 3.54, *Tiger*'s Q and X turrets were hit, with serious consequences for her gunnery. The director firing circuits to both turrets were cut. In Q, the gunsights were unusable so, while the guns could be laid and trained by director, they had to be fired by the turret on the sound of other guns firing; also the right-hand gun could be loaded only by hand and therefore fired only

---

[108] *BP I*, p. 256.   [109] *OD*, pp. 147–8, 151 and 387–8. *GFG&TOs*, 15. See also F&H, p. 30.

[110] *OD*, pp. 147–8, 151 and 388. Campbell, pp. 41 and 69–70. Brooks, 'Mast and Funnel', pp. 45–9.

[111] Campbell, pp. 41–2, 80–3 and 373–4. 'General Experience' (*Seydlitz*'s report after Jutland), ADM 137/1644, ff. 274–5. (The single most effective precaution was probably the removal of ready charges from the working chamber.) Williams, p. 122.

occasionally. In X turret, the guns were laid and fired individually but were mostly trained by director. Before these hits, *Tiger* had fired deliberately at one salvo per minute, while also reducing her range by no less than 2,500 yards between her second and fourth salvo. Afterwards, her gunnery officer 'increased her rate of fire as much as possible'; between 3.55 and 4.40, she averaged 1.8 salvos per minute and on nine occasions, fired three salvos in one minute. For the whole battle, her gunnery record contains 150 gun ranges while she expended a total of 303 rounds;[112] thus her salvos (if that is the appropriate term) contained barely more than two shots on average. Her system of firing and control remains obscure[113] but, whatever it was, it resulted in very few hits. However, during this first phase of the action, *Tiger* suffered repeatedly from smoke interference caused by destroyers trying to get ahead on the engaged side. At least she was lucky with the hit received at 3.55, since the base of the shell narrowly missed severing the main steam pipe in her port engine room. Subsequently, *Tiger*'s gun ranges continued downwards to reach a minimum of 10,500 yards just after 4 o'clock, while, at 4.04, *Moltke*'s range was 11,500 yards and still falling; each ship was probably hit once by the other at this time.[114] It seems that, perhaps while avoiding smoke interference, *Tiger*'s course took her considerably closer to the enemy line than the rest of the 1BCS.

At the rear of the British line, the 2BCS continued East at 25 knots until [3.54], when they altered course to SSE, a large turn that cannot have helped their shooting, except for opening the bearing arcs of their after turrets.[115] These courses kept them well clear of smoke from the 1BCS to starboard. *New Zealand*'s gun ranges reached a minimum at 3.56 (the 12,000 yards taken from her range plot is more likely than the 10,800 yards in her TS record in the *Official Despatches*) and then increased to about 13,500 yards at 4.00.[116] She was firing rapidly, a salvo every half minute, and she may even have crammed considerably more than four shots into each salvo. Her fire control cannot have

---

[112] Campbell, pp. 40–1 and 71–6. (NB ricochets, like hits nos. 7 and 12, have not been included in these and subsequent totals of hits.) *OD*, pp. 155 and 390–3. 'Report of Lt.Cmdr. Macnamara', *Tiger*, 4 June 1916 in BTY 6/6. F&H, pp. 86–8 and 397–401 (though Q not X fired 'only one gun except at long intervals').

[113] *Tiger*'s gunnery officer stated that he used 'double salvos separated by small corrections' (F&H, p. 397). The torpedo officer (*OD*, p. 157) claimed that the 'system of large down corrections and smaller up was used [but] it was frequently necessary to re-start the bracket, when the fall of two or three salvos had been missed' (S&H, p. 85). Neither method is apparent in *Tiger*'s actual range record (*OD*, pp. 389–93).

[114] *OD*, pp. 155 and 390. F&H, pp. 89–90. *GOA*, p. 62. Campbell, pp. 42–3, 73, 77 and 85.

[115] *OD*, p. 160. *OD*, Plate 31 shows a turn to SEbyS at [3.54] but Plate 9a (that accompanied RA2BCS's despatch) shows *New Zealand* only briefly on SSE around [3.54] before a turn S½W. For the large discrepancies between these charts, see Gordon, pp. 608–9.

[116] JMSS 49014 contains an uncensored version of *New Zealand*'s TS 'Record of Ranges' (*cf. OD*, pp. 393–5) and also 'New Zealand's Range Plot', a tabulation of correct times, individual rangefinder and gun ranges presumably taken from her range plot (probably now lost). Both show similar trends but differ considerably in detail.

been helped by the ranges from her Argo rangefinder mounting in the foretop averaging almost 2,300 yards higher than her other range-finders.[117] Also, whether knowingly or not, she was concentrating with *Tiger* on *Moltke*. With both British ships firing rapidly and without any apparent attempt at coordinating their fire, they could well have had great difficulty in distinguishing between their falls of shot, though neither mentions this problem. It is uncertain what system *New Zealand* used to control her furious barrage but it was wholly ineffective; despite the fact that she was not even under fire, she made not a single hit. *Indefatigable* was no more successful against *Von der Tann*.

At 4.00, Hipper ordered the ISG to turn together to SEbyS; from a course SE, this would have been a turn towards.[118] At the same nominal time, both flagships found each other's range. *Lützow* was hit twice on the forecastle, while a single shell struck *Lion*'s Q turret at the top edge of the armoured face plate. As well as firing four-gun salvos alternatively from her fore and aft turrets, *Lützow*'s gunnery officer Günther Paschen, to his later regret, elected to fire SAP rather than APC shell; of the eight definite hits made on *Lion* during the Run to the South, three failed to burst.[119] But the shell that struck Q turret did burst, just after it entered the gunhouse. It killed or wounded everyone there but the explosion also blew off the front roof plate and the centre facing plate. This seems to have dissipated its force so that, immediately after the hit, none of charges in the supply path from the handing room to the gunhouse were ignited; if all positions were full, there would have been eight full charges (32 bagged quarter-charges) in the turret.[120] Major Francis Harvey, RMLI, the officer of the turret, though severely burned, recognised the danger of fire spreading downwards and gave his dying order that the magazine doors be closed – he was awarded a posthumous VC. A further order to flood the magazines may have come from Harvey, or from Captain Chatfield immediately he saw that Q turret had been wrecked.[121] Though the contents of the magazine had been protected, the charges in the turret could not now be moved to safety. It appears that fire continued to smoulder in the upper compartments of the turret until the cordite charges, first in the working chamber and then in the handing room,

[117] Her 'Record of Ranges' contains 74 gun ranges; assuming that these are salvo ranges and that she expended a total of 420 rounds (Campbell, p. 347), she appears to have fired an incredible 5⅔ rounds per salvo. 'Range Plot' (see note 116).

[118] As shown on *OD*, 'German Plan IV'; however, *GOA*, p. 60 states that 'Hipper … bore away one point', as on Chart 5.

[119] Paschen, pp. 31 and 35. *BP I*, p. 356. Campbell, pp. 40, 67–9 and 345. von Hase, pp. 154–5.

[120] 'VNE'. *OD*, p. 143. F&H, pp. 93–8. Campbell, pp. 64–7 and 78–9. For the cordite supply path, see Campbell, pp. 371–2 and Brown, *The Grand Fleet*, p. 166.

[121] Private H Willows RMLI of Q turret, *BP I*, p. 354 (not Willons: www.dreadnoughtproject.org citing BTY 6/14/1). Chatfield, p. 141 stated that this had been forestalled by Francis. 'Autobiography of Chief Gunner Alexander Grant' in *The Naval Miscellany VII* (NRS, 2008), p. 398. Contrary to legend, Francis, though terribly burned, had not lost his legs: *FDSF III*, pp. xv and 62, n. 42.

ignited, killing nearly all the surviving turret crew members.[122] Despite the turret roof being missing and the handing room hatch being open, the pressure increase caused the magazine bulkheads to bulge, even against the pressure of the water in the magazines.[123] The time of this conflagration is uncertain. Beatty's personal narrative recorded 'Fire around Q turret of LION' at 4.28, but it may have started earlier.[124]

Lion's record of target bearings show that, immediately after the hit on Q turret, she turned away rapidly by almost three points so that, at least momentarily, A and B turrets were not bearing – though, by 4.04, despite three more hits, she had been brought back onto a new course S. *Princess Royal* held the course SbyE until 4.06, when she too turned S. An approximate estimate of *Lion*'s course suggests that she may, as least momentarily, have lost sight of *Lützow* behind *Princess Royal* and that, by 4.06, she was some 1,400 yards on *Princess Royal*'s bow.[125] This sudden swing to starboard was not on the BCF's track chart, which merely shows a small course alteration from SbyE to S at 4.00.[126] But it was twice confirmed by Captain Chatfield, though in somewhat different accounts. In 1923, in a letter to Roger Keyes, he wrote:

Lion actually made one considerable swing to Starboard about 2 Pts owing to Comd (N) saying Port 5 & then forgetting he had done so.[127]

But the version in his memoirs reads:

It was at this moment [after Q turret had been knocked out], seeing that the range was decreasing and not wishing to let it do so, I told Commander [N] Strutt to steer 5 degrees to starboard. Strutt gave the order. The Chief Quartermaster, however, misheard it as ordering him to give the ship 5 degrees of port helm. I suddenly saw the ship swinging off to starboard rapidly and had to bring her back and increase speed to resume our station. The ships astern, having seen the large flame shooting up, thought we were steering off because of the damage!

---

[122] For contradictory accounts of the effects of the hit in the gunhouse, *cf*. Campbell (p. 65), citing *GFG&TOs*, 15 and *Lion*'s gunnery officer (F&H, p. 97).

[123] *BP I*, p. 351. Campbell, p. 66. 'Grant' (see note 121, p. 398) was told that the supply cages were full. He said that there were no spare charges in the handing room but Willows (see note 121) suggests there may have been one or more broken charges there.

[124] 'VNE' for 4.28. At 4.29, *Princess Royal*'s officers saw 'A big fire raging in *Lion* amidships': F&H, p. 31. Willows gave the time of the hit as '4.20 or thereabouts' and of the cordite fire 'about ten minutes later'. *Lion*'s gunnery officer placed the cordite fire 'a few minutes' after the hit: F&H, p. 97. Chatfield's despatch (*OD*, p. 144) states that the fire flared up after the BCF turned N at 4.38. See also Grant, p. 399, though times are uncertain.

[125] REL. Campbell, pp. 41–2 and 67–9. F&H, p. 30 (though it is unclear why a starboard turn would 'avoid the smoke').

[126] *OD*, Plate 10. VNE for 4.02: 'A/c one point to Stbd'.

[127] Chatfield to Keyes, January 1923, p. 3A, Keyes Papers, BL. Port helm turned the ship to starboard.

> At 4.25, soon after we resumed our position ahead of the "Princess Royal" ... the "Queen Mary" ... blew up

In fact, at the time the ranges, including the few in *Lion*'s own records, were increasing.[128] Even so, given the imminent risk of a magazine explosion, there was nothing discreditable in 'steering off because of the damage'. Yet Chatfield preferred to dissemble rather than acknowledge the real reason for his initial order to turn away.

Meanwhile, at the rear the range from *Von der Tann* was falling to a minimum of 13,450 yards. Just before [4.02], she began hitting *Indefatigable*.

> two or three shots falling together hit "Indefatigable" about outer edge of upper deck in line with after turret. A small explosion followed, and she swung out of line, sinking by the stern. Hit again almost instantly near "A" turret by another salvo, she listed heavily to port, turned over and disappeared.

Curiously, this account by Rear-Admiral Pakenham did not mention that she disappeared under a towering cloud of smoke as she blew up; 1,071 officers and men were lost, all but two of her crew.[129] The often-reproduced photograph of *Indefatigable*'s final moments shows her sinking by the stern on *New Zealand*'s starboard quarter.[130] Until her magazines exploded, *Von der Tann* had fired 52 11in shells and 38 5.9in shells.[131] Assuming that the former were fired in salvos of four shells, her average salvo interval was a leisurely 70 seconds but, as Pakenham saw, she was evidently firing rapid salvos at the end.

As the two lines drew apart at the end of this first phase of the Run to the South:

> From the *Lützow* it appeared about this time [c.4.05] as if the British flagship hauled out of line, with a list of 10 degrees to starboard; she seemed to disappear at times behind the other vessels wrapped in a thick pall of smoke ... At times the enemy's fire ceased altogether and the tactical cohesion of the British line appeared to be seriously shaken.[132]

Beatty's line was in disarray; he had lost a battlecruiser to a numerically inferior opponent; and he had been decisively beaten in the gunnery duel, his ships making only six hits, whilst receiving at least 22.[133] He had quickly lost

---

[128] Chatfield, p. 143. REL and 'LION' (JMSS 49014), the latter containing more (probably sight) ranges.

[129] *GOA*, p. 61 (*Indefatigable* exploded 4.03). *OD*, pp. 158 and 160. Campbell, pp. 43, 60–2 and 338. F&H, p. 38. The two survivors were picked up by *S16* (Campbell) not *S68* (*GOA*).

[130] IWM Q.64302 in, for example, S&H and Gordon (Fig. 29). *New Zealand*'s navigating officer (F&H, p. 38) stated that his ship turned to port but that *Indefatigable* failed to follow round, but *New Zealand*'s gunnery record (*OD*, p. 394) noted a starboard turn at [4.00], nor do her charts show a port turn.

[131] *GOA*, p. 61.   [132] *GOA*, pp. 61–2: see also Paschen, p. 34 (in S&H, p. 92).

[133] Four hits have been credited to *Von der Tann* but the ricochets which struck *Lion* and *Tiger* – Campbell, pp. 67 and 75 – have not been included in the German total.

gunnery superiority and was unable to recover. Also, without tactical direction from the flagship, the vulnerable ships of the 2BCS, probably to avoid smoke from ahead, strayed dangerously close to the ISG. Once *Von der Tann* found the range, the deadly conjunction of her effective AP shell, *Indefatigable*'s weak armour and dangerous ammunition-handling in the British battlecruiser quickly led to her cataclysmic destruction.

The second phase

After the sinking of *Indefatigable*, Hipper turned his ships together at 4.04 to SbyE but his leading ships were soon obliged to cease firing as the range continued to increase; at 4.05, it reached 19,600 yards from *Derfflinger*. At 4.07 or a little later, the 1SG altered together to SbyW – slightly converging on the BCF – while at 4.12 Hipper ordered a speed of 23 knots.[134] Yet the *German*

Table 5.14. *ISG signals 4.04–4.51pm*

Time of receipt	From	To	System	Message	Time of origin
pm, 31 May					
4.04	Lützow	ISG	Visual	Turn together to SbyE	
4.07	Lützow	ISG	Visual	Turn together to SbyW	
4.12	Lützow	ISG	Visual	Speed 23 knots	
4.14	Lützow	ISG	Visual	Torpedo boats are to attack	
4.18	Lützow	ISG	Visual	Follow in wake of leading ship	
4.20	Frankfurt	Lützow		Enemy battle fleet in ... British 2BS, 5 ships. Enemy vessels are steering SE	1612
4.25	Lützow	ISG	Visual	Reduce seed	
4.26	Regensburg	IXTF	Visual	Lines are 10,900 yards apart. IXTF, advance to the attack	
4.27	Lützow	ISG	Visual	Turn together to SE	
4.34	Lützow	ISG	Visual	Turn together to ESE	
4.36	Lützow	ISG	Visual	Turn together to E	
4.38	Lützow	ISG	Visual	Turn together to SSE	
4.41	Lützow	ISG	Visual	Turn together to SSW	
4.44	Lützow	ISG	Visual	ISG: Open fire at battleships	
4.46	Lützow	ISG	Visual	Turn together to SE	
4.49	Lützow	ISG	Visual	Follow in wake of leading ship	
4.51	Lützow	ISG	Visual	Course N	

---

[134] *GOA*, pp. 63 and 65. von Hase, p. 152. *GOA*, p. 63 and Chart 6 and *OD*, German Plan IV time the SbyW turn at 4.10 or just after.

Official Account stated that the range from *Moltke* had continued to fall, to 10,400 yards at 4.08, when she decided the time was ripe to fire torpedoes, four of which were aimed at *Queen Mary*. While this range is surprisingly low, it still equalled the maximum running range of the G7** torpedo at medium speed, while *Moltke* was firing from a position well aft of *Queen Mary*'s beam.[135] Thus it is unlikely that these torpedoes, which would have run for 11 minutes at medium speed, reached the British line. They cannot have been among the torpedoes supposedly seen from the BCF at about 4.11 by *Lion, Princess Royal* and the destroyer *Landrail*. Since the last-named also reported a periscope to port and the light cruiser *Nottingham* a submarine to starboard, Beatty supposed that he had just passed through an enemy submarine screen.[136]

Hipper's turn to SbyW began to decrease the range to the BCF but it also soon brought his battlecruisers within the reach of the 15in guns of the 5BS. He may not then have been aware of this new danger; while the German account states that the battleships had been recognised by about 3.35,[137] they

Table 5.15. *5BS signals 3.35–4.30pm*

Time of despatch	From	To	System	Message	Time of origin
pm, 31 May					
3.35	SO 5BS	5BS	Flags	Alter succession in course to E, speed 24 knots	
3.40	SO 5BS	5BS	Flags	... 24½ knots	
3.42	Fearless			Sighted two Enemy Cruisers (six sighted at 3.50 p.m.)	
3.56	SO 5BS	Destroyers	Flags	Keep out of the way	
3.59	SO 5BS	Fearless	Flags	Fearless take station astern of Malaya	
4.00	SO 5BS	5BS	Flags	Open fire and engage the enemy	
4.17	C-in-C	SO 5BS	W/T	Are you in company with SO BCF?	1615
				Reply: Yes, I am engaging enemy	1630
4.27	SO 5BS	Destroyers	Flags	Take station ahead	
4.30	SO 5BS	5BS	Flags	Subdivisions separately alter course in succession two points away from Enemy preserving your formation	

[135] *GOA*, p. 62. *Tiger*'s range had been 12,000 yards at 4.06 but rose to 14,300 yards at 4.08: *OD*, p. 390. *Lion*'s target bearing at 4.08 was R127 (REL).

[136] *OD*, pp. 132, 148, 151 and 257 (though not in *Nottingham*'s despatch). VNE. F&H, p. 30. Godfrey, Ch. II, p. 12 mentions an unconfirmed rumour that the torpedo sighted 'may have been one that rolled accidentally out of the tube of one of our destroyers'.

[137] *GOA*, p. 48. Paschen (p. 33) made the improbable claim that that he could see the 5BS at 3.00 GMT astern of the battlecruisers when the latter were 26 kilometres (16 miles or 28,000 yards) distant.

were not mentioned in his two enemy reports originated at 3.29 and 3.46. After receiving *Lion*'s belated searchlight repeat signal, Evan-Thomas had continued E as ordered, *Barham* leading *Valiant, Warspite* and *Malaya*. At 3.40, he rather optimistically ordered a speed of 24½ knots. Although he probably could not yet see the German battlecruisers, he would soon have learned from Beatty's 3.45 signal to Jellicoe that five were present. Once Beatty had opened fire, Evan-Thomas began turning rather tentatively to starboard, heading ESE by 3.51.[138] A minute earlier, some of the light cruisers of the IISG, returning from their chase of the 1LCS and 3LCS, were glimpsed before the port beam. But *Fearless* and the 1DF were then still formed as a submarine screen so, until they were ordered to get out of the way by taking station on *Malaya*'s starboard quarter, their smoke prevented the battleships from opening fire. The three leading battleships fired a few salvos at *Frankfurt, Elbing* and *Pillau* but, after *Barham*'s third salvo appeared to straddle, the cruisers turned away under cover of 'smoke bombs' (canisters emitting artificial smoke) dropped astern. Once out of danger, they turned back SE'ward, followed by the British light cruisers on parallel courses. Having evaded the fire of the 5BS, *Frankfurt* reported their presence but mistook them for five battleships of the 2BS.[139]

At 4.04, *Barham* turned SE and, between 4.07 and 4.30, headed about SbyE.[140] Although the reports from the 5BS disagree, the three leaders probably commenced shooting before 4.11, with *Malaya* waiting until 4.15. The initial range was 19,000 yards while, except at the start, deteriorating light and visibility made target identification, range-finding and spotting difficult. Evan-Thomas ordered his ships to concentrate in pairs on the two rear German ships[141] and *Moltke* and *Von der Tann* were 'soon exposed to a regular hail of 15-inch projectiles'. Almost immediately, *Von der Tann* was hit near the stern but fortunately this did not permanently damage her steering gear. *Moltke* received two hits at about 4.16, one of which ignited ready-use ammunition at the No. 5 starboard 5.9in gun; flash passed down the hoist to the magazine, but no ammunition ignited there.[142]

---

[138] *OD*, p. 192 and Plate 10a (*Barham*'s track). There are only minor variations in courses and turning times between this chart and those from the rest of the 5BS (*OD*, Plates 17–19) but considerable differences in distances run: see Gordon, p. 607.

[139] *OD*, pp. 172, 185, 192–3, 198, 202, 242 and 245. F&H, p. 255. *GOA*, pp. 63–4. S&H, p. 93. Scheer, p. 150 note.

[140] *OD*, Plate 10a. From the 5BS, the distance of the BCF was estimated as 4–5 miles (*OD*, pp. 199 and 205) but is 7 miles on Corbett's Map 24.

[141] *OD*, pp. 193, 199, 202, 205, 213, 217 and 386; until about 4.30, *Valiant* and *Malaya* plotted ranges, the former enough to give a rate, though her opening range was estimated. F&H, pp. 117–18.

[142] *GOA*, pp. 64–5. Campbell, pp. 49 and 85–6.

Table. 5.16. *BCF signals 4.10–4.30pm*

Time of despatch	From	To	System	Message	Time of origin
pm, 31 May					
4.10	SO BCF	Princess Royal	W/T	Main W/T out of action	1605
4.11	Lion			Remarks: Nottingham reports Submarine on starboard side	
4.20	Lion			Remarks: Queen Mary blew up	
4.26	SO BCF	Princess Royal	W/T	Keep clear of smoke	1625
4.30	Southampton	C-in-C SO BCF	W/T	Urgent. One Enemy Cruiser bearing SE, steering NE. (My position 56°38 N, 6°07E)	1630

By 4.10, *Lion, Princess Royal* and, probably, *Queen Mary* were headed S,[143] with *Lion* (as Chatfield confirms) still out of line to starboard. The ranges of *Tiger* and *New Zealand* suggest that, having been nearer to the enemy, they were still hauling into line on more westerly courses. Despite smoke interference from destroyers, *Lion* and (as far as can be known) *Queen Mary* continued firing at their opposite numbers, while after the destruction of *Indefatigable*, *New Zealand* had switched her fire to *Von der Tann* at [4.03]. *Princess Royal*'s record contains only one range (19,100 yards at 4.06.50) between 3.55.15 and 4.15.28, and no indication either before or after this gap that she changed target.[144] Yet von Hase of *Derfflinger* implies that she had done so even before *Indefatigable* was destroyed, while the GFBOs forbad her from leaving her opposite number undisturbed after the British line was reduced to five ships. *Tiger* was attempting to keep her guns on the *Moltke*, but her control was distracted for a time by a German light cruiser at the head of the German line; they counted her as a battlecruiser and so fired at *Seydlitz* rather than *Moltke*. (This cruiser must have been the *Regensburg*, which had remained closer to the ISG and was struggling to get ahead.) To add to the problems with her damaged turrets, *Tiger*'s gunnery staff decided that her ragged salvos indicated that her director needed lining up. Thus, between 4.05½ and 4.10.5 (and also between 4.22 and 4.26.40, for the same reason), her turrets were aiming and firing individually; this presumably meant that Q turret was unable to fire at all. *Tiger* had not been provided with an Evershed target indicator system, so, with her director malfunctioning, she was not fully

---

[143] *OD*, Plate 10. F&H, p. 30. *Princess Royal*'s track (*OD*, Plate 12), showing her on ESE until 4.10 and the SSE until 4.38, conflicts with all other sources.
[144] *OD*, pp. 132, 388, 390 and 394. VNE.

equipped for keeping all her guns on the same target.[145] With the further confusion arising from the problem of identifying the correct target, it is not surprising that she made no further hits on *Moltke*.

At 4.12, *Lion* boldly altered course by four points to SE; thus the range to *Lützow* began to close rapidly, the estimated rate being about −700 yards/minute. Although without a signal from the flagship, Rear-Admiral Brock in *Princess Royal* responded appropriately by altering to SSE; by 4.19–20, *Lion* had evidently regained her position at the head of the line, since she too turned SSE.[146] During this new approach by the British ships, *Lützow* was hit twice at 4.15 and *Seydlitz* once by *Queen Mary* at 4.17; this last hit did serious damage to the aftermost starboard casemate but there was no ammunition fire and the anti-flash flaps sealed the ammunition hoist. Campbell reasonably concludes that the hits on the German flagship were made by *Princess Royal*, since her ranges at the time (five salvos at 18,500 yards) seem more accurate than *Lion*'s (21,275 yards at 4.15).[147] With his ships being hit by both the BCF and the 5BS, at 4.18 Hipper again ordered them to follow in his wake; in forming line-ahead on course S, the rear ships increased their distance from the 5BS. The turns by both sides reduced the rate to just over −250 yards/minute.[148] By 4.15–4.17, the range had fallen sufficiently for the ISG to reopen fire, though *Lion* was 'so enveloped in smoke and fumes as to be invisible at times from ships astern of the "Lützow" '.[149] von Hase confirms that *Lion* could not be seen from *Derfflinger*.

At [4].17 I again engaged the second battlecruiser from the left. I was under the impression that it was the same ship as I had engaged before, the *Princess Royal*. Actually, however, it was the *Queen Mary* ... this was due to the fact that, just as I was finding my target, Admiral Beatty's flagship, the *Lion*, was obliged to fall out of the enemy line for a time, and, owing to the heavy smoke covering the enemy line, could not be seen by us.

von Hase cannot be correct about the time at which *Lion* fell out of line but he verifies that she had still not regained the head of the line. Unfortunately, *Seydlitz* did not make the same mistake in identifying her target, so both she and *Derfflinger* concentrated on *Queen Mary*.[150] von Hase stated that *Queen Mary* was then firing at his ship. But he also claimed that she was firing full broadsides of eight guns (which was not one of the Royal Navy's recommended firing methods), and that his ship was hit twice at this time.[151] The latter

---

[145] *OD*, pp. 390–1. F&H, pp. 397–8. *GOA*, pp. 65 and 70. *DGBJ*, pp. 50, 170–1 and 244.

[146] *OD*, Plate 10. *DGBJ*, p. 28. F&H, p. 30.

[147] Campbell, pp. 48 and 79–82. *OD*, p. 388. REL.

[148] *OD*, German Plan IV shows the ISG turning S but *GOA*, p. 66 and Chart 6 as continuing SbyW; tactically, the former was more appropriate. *DGBJ*, p. 28.

[149] *GOA*, p. 66. Paschen (p. 34) says that he shifted to *Princess Royal* from 4.08 until after *Queen Mary* was sunk, but Beatty's narrative (VNE) recorded enemy salvos falling near *Lion* at 4.12, 4.17, 4.19 and 4.19½ and two hits at 4.24.

[150] von Hase, pp. 154 and 159.   [151] von Hase, p. 157. *MoG III 1915*, p. 10, AL.

assertion conflicts with Campbell's assessment that *Derfflinger* received no hits during the Run to the South. At first sight, there was no tactical reason for *Queen Mary* to change target. But one of *Queen Mary*'s survivors recalled that her TS reported the *Seydlitz* dropping out of line, that he saw her going down by the bows, and that his turret had shifted target, though to the fourth, not the second, enemy ship.[152] On balance, it seems that von Hase was probably wrong, and that *Queen Mary* continued to engage *Seydlitz*.

Beatty did nothing to form of the line-of-bearing N demanded by his course SSE, while his ships now had the worst of the visibility, though the Germans also found that observation of the fall of shot was becoming increasingly difficult. In the first version of his despatch, Beatty wrote:

The visibility to the North Eastward had become considerably reduced and the outline of the ships very indistinct. This, no doubt, was largely due to the constant use of smoke balls or charges by the enemy, under cover of which they were continually altering course or zig-zagging.

However, this excuse was omitted from his published despatch.[153] The only German battlecruisers that zigzagged were those under the hot fire from the 5BS. Nevertheless, there is no reason to doubt the deterioration in visibility. During her rapid approach on course SE, *Lion* recorded rangefinder ranges of 23,000 yards at 4.12 and 21,000 yards at 4.16, much higher than the ranges of her consorts. Even so, the downward trend was clear yet it was largely disregarded; the rates in use just before and after *Lion*'s turn to SSE were still only −200 and −150 yards/minute. Although the ranges themselves are lower, the surviving records from Beatty's other battlecruisers do not show any significant fall until 4.20 or later.[154] From *New Zealand*, it appeared that 'we were being led by the flagship on a snake-like course, to reduce the chances of being hit', which cannot have helped their ranging and aiming.[155]

The first hit by the 5BS on *Von der Tann* had temporarily damaged her steering gear; this, or her zigzagging to throw out the battleships' fire, may have taken her out of line to port, though she was also obscured by mist; by [4.16½], *New Zealand* had lost sight of her and shifted her fire to *Moltke*.[156] At about 4.18, *Von der Tann* engaged and even made one hit on *Barham*, but, at 4.20 and 4.23, the German battlecruiser also received two more hits. Campbell, though without explanation,

[152] F&H, p. 45; pp. 43–50 gives the complete account of PO Ernest Francis of X turret (excerpts in Williams and S&H).
[153] *OD*, p. 134. *GOA*, p. 65. *JP I*, p. 293.
[154] REL. *OD*, pp. 388, 390 and 394. *Tiger* and *New Zealand* may not have turned to port to follow the ships ahead until after *Lion*'s turn SSE.
[155] F&H, p. 39, which adds that, for 'the next half-hour the battle continued on a south-easterly course'. *OD*, Plate 9a shows *New Zealand* on SEbyS from 4.15, Plate 31 on S½E from 4.12; the latter accords better with her ranges.
[156] *GOA*, pp. 64–5. F&H, pp. 34, 118 and 141. *OD*, p. 394.

attributes these to *Tiger*.[157] But *Tiger*'s erratic fire was straying towards the head, not the rear, of the enemy line, while, if *Von der Tann* was obscured from *New Zealand*, she would have been even more difficult to see from *Tiger*. It is much more likely that these hits were due to the rapid and accurate fire of the 5BS. They holed, respectively, the fore and after barbettes but burst outside and no charges were ignited; however, the fore turret was jammed abaft the beam for the remainder of the battle, while the after turret was out of action until 8pm and then had to be worked almost entirely by hand. Though not due to enemy fire, at 4.35 both guns of her starboard wing turret failed to run out properly (they were not repaired until 7.30), while from 4.50 the right gun of the port wing turret had the same problem. *Moltke* also received another two 15in hits, at 4.23 and (the last British hit of the Run to the South proper) at 4.26.[158] If the hits on *Von der Tann* are credited to the 5BS, then Beatty's battlecruisers made no further hits in this second phase. After the three hits made early in their renewed approach, they again lost gunnery superiority. At 4.24, *Lion* received two hits from *Lützow*.[159] But, more seriously, and despite *Princess Royal* not even being under fire, the shooting of the British battlecruisers did nothing more to take the pressure off *Queen Mary*. She had probably already been hit twice by *Seydlitz*, on the quarter-deck and the after 4in battery before, at 4.20–1, the right gun of Q turret was put out of action.[160] von Hase spotted *Derfflinger*'s first straddle at 4.22.40, when his rate was −330 yards/ minute and range 15,200 yards. After spotting the fall of the next three salvos, he ordered rapid fire, which produced six salvos with an average interval of only 22 seconds. Even before his final salvo at 4.26.10, he had observed explosions beginning in *Queen Mary*.

First of all, a vivid red flame shot up from her forepart. Then came an explosion forward which was followed by a much heavier explosion amidships ... and immediately afterwards the whole ship blew up in a terrific explosion. A gigantic cloud of smoke rose [and] the masts collapsed inwards.

The big explosion forward broke the ship in half near the foremast.[161] It was probably caused by the second salvo seen to hit *Queen Mary*; just beforehand, the first salvo struck abreast of Q turret and may have started the fire that broke out in the working chamber.[162] The after part, as far forward as the after funnel,

---

[157] *GOA*, pp. 66 and 68. *OD*, pp. 193 and 205. Campbell, pp. 48 and 87.

[158] Campbell, pp. 90–4 and 86–7. *GOA*, p. 68.   [159] VNE. Campbell, pp. 67 and 69.

[160] *OD*, p. 150. F&H, pp. 45–6. Williams, p. 123. *Seydlitz*'s hit indicator (time-of-flight clock) broke down soon after the engagement began but *Derfflinger*'s, recently repaired, functioned properly (*Seydlitz*, 'General Experience', ADM 137/1644, f. 272. von Hase, pp. 134 and 159); thus, once they concentrated on *Queen Mary*, *Seydlitz* probably found spotting more difficult.

[161] von Hase, pp. 160–1. Admiral Brock also saw a bright flame shooting up just before a mass of cordite smoke: *OD*, p. 147. S&H, p. 103.

[162] *OD*, pp. 147, 150 and 155. F&H, pp. 40 and 42; from *Tiger*, there appeared to be 3 hits in the first salvo, 2 in the second. S&H, p. 103. Williams, p. 125.

was seen with the stern out of the water, the propellers still turning. It then rolled over to port and blew up;[163] the explosion was perhaps set off by the fire in Q turret's working chamber.[164] Eighteen officers and men were rescued by the British destroyers *Laurel* and *Petard* (one died after the battle) and two by the German *V28*; 1,270 were killed in the two catastrophic explosions.[165] *Queen Mary* probably received three hits up to 4.21 and between two and five just before the first explosions forward.

Shortly after 4.25, *Princess Royal* might have hit back, since her range at that time (14,900 yards) was close to the German ranges when *Queen Mary* blew up (14,400 yards for *Derfflinger*, 14,750 yards for *Seydlitz*). But then there was an unexplained gap of almost six minutes in her salvo record. Since Beatty originated a wireless signal at 4.25 ordering her to 'Keep clear of smoke', it appears that, once again, *Princess Royal* strayed into the flagship's smoke. She may have responded to the signal by turning to SE for a time. She now became the target for *Derfflinger*; Campbell mentions three more ill-documented and largely ineffective hits on the British ship, but only one has been added to the German total.[166] After the second and third hits on *Von der Tann* had disabled her fore and after turrets, she was forced to turn her midships turrets back to *New Zealand* and, at 4.26, made a hit on X barbette. It punched a hole in the armour but burst outside, without flame entering the turret structure; the turret was jammed for up to 20 minutes.[167] Hipper's two rear ships were still in danger from the fire of the 5BS, while his line was now also threatened with an attack from British destroyers. Only a minute or so after the destruction of *Queen Mary*, Hipper began a withdrawal – by turning away together, first to SE and then to ESE and E, eight points in all – that continued until 4.38.[168] After Beatty saw *Queen Mary* blow up, he famously remarked to Chatfield: 'There seems to be something wrong with our bloody ships today.' But *Lion* then turned two points not to port but to starboard, to S; this may have been immediately after the explosion or a few minutes later, when Q turret flared up and attacking German destroyers were launching torpedoes. As a result, *Lion*'s A and B turrets were unable to bear until she turned back to SSE, probably at 4.33.[169]

---

[163] F&H, pp. 35 and 40. S&H, pp. 107 and 108. Williams, pp. 125, 128 and 130.

[164] Although a survivor of Q turret stated that the explosion was in X turret (S&H, p. 107, Williams, p. 131), its supply trunk was already flooded as far as the working chamber (F&H, p. 46). Whereas the wreck of the after part is holed to expose Q turret's shell room and magazine (Burr, p. 43); many cartridge cases are visible around the hoist, so only some of the cordite can have ignited.

[165] Casualty list by Don Kindell at www.naval-history.net. *Petard* picked up only PO Francis of X turret: F&H, 48–9 and *OD*, p. 232.

[166] *GOA*, p. 67. *OD*, p. 388. F&H, pp. 30–1 though the turn SE is not shown on her chart (*OD*, Plate 12). von Hase, pp. 162–4. Campbell, p. 71.

[167] *GOA*, p. 68. Campbell, p. 76. S&H, p. 115.

[168] *GOA*, p. 71 and Charts 6 and 7 again agree on courses with *OD*, German Plan IV.

[169] Chatfield, p. 143. REL. VNE. *OD*, Plate 10. See F&H, p. 40 for the probable origin of the legend (repeated, for example, in Bennett, p. 76) that Beatty ordered a turn towards the enemy.

Having narrowly avoided the remains of *Queen Mary* by hauling out to port, *Tiger* changed target to *Seydlitz* but herself became the target for *Seydlitz* as well as *Moltke*. Her ranges fell to improbably low values (a minimum of 11,800 yards at 4.33.30) but it does appear that, once again, she got closest to the enemy and she received three further hits.[170] Against *Moltke, New Zealand*'s ranges did not begin to decrease decisively until after she had passed the wreck of *Queen Mary* on its starboard side. *New Zealand*'s ranges did not fall as far as those of her consorts, while there are several gaps in her salvo record;[171] apparently, she remained somewhere on their starboard quarter and their smoke interfered with her fire. As in the first phase, she made no hits on either of her targets.

In the second phase of the Run to the South, the 5BS scored at least 5, probably 7, hits on *Von der Tann* and *Moltke* at long range. The ISG must be allowed at least another 12 hits on the British battlecruisers, as well as the hit on *Barham*. Whereas, if the two hits on *Von der Tann* are discounted, the British battlecruiser tally was only three. These three were all made at the start, but these early successes were not sustained, though for different reasons. Although *Lion*'s range-finder ranges were too high, they showed a clear downward trend but the implied rate was ignored by her transmitting station. Shortly after 4.25, *Princess Royal* might have found the hitting range, had she not got into *Lion*'s smoke.[172] *Tiger*'s previous damage rendered her target selection uncertain and her fire ragged and ineffective. *New Zealand*'s own gunnery record establishes that she was slow in reducing the range and suggests that she suffered from smoke interference once she did so. As previously, *Lion*'s excessive ranges had serious tactical consequences. Her steep approach without signals pushed *Princess Royal* and the ships astern into closing the range too quickly. As they once more found themselves within the Germans' effective range, *Lion* was only just regaining her position at the head of the line, while there was no concerted attempt to form a line-of-bearing. Yet again, Beatty's impetuous tactics had failed to exploit the advantage of his heavier guns; they had left his ships still forming line under fire, while at least two of them would soon be hampered by smoke. Now the Germans also had the better visibility. Worst of all, with *Lion* still out of line, *Derfflinger* selected the wrong target; because the fire of the other British battlecruisers was too ineffective to punish this mistake, *Derfflinger* and *Seydlitz* were allowed to continue almost undisturbed with their fortuitous but fatal concentration on *Queen Mary*.

---

[170] OD, pp. 155 and 391. F&H, pp. 40 and 42. S&H, p. 112. Campbell, pp. 47–8 and 73–5; the probable ricochet at about 4.20 has not been counted.

[171] F&H, p. 40. *OD*, p. 394.

[172] Once again, *Princess Royal* did not live up to the ferocious reputation of her Captain, Walter Cowan: for which see Gordon, pp. 28–9.

As Hipper withdrew eastwards, the BCF began to check fire, first *Lion* at 4.33 and last *New Zealand* at 4.42. At least some of the 5BS were able to continue firing intermittently until 4.40, though at 4.30 they were twice obliged to turn away two points in subdivisions by the threat of German destroyer attacks.[173] Meanwhile, the 2LCS had been scouting ahead and at 4.30 *Southampton* reported sighting an enemy cruiser to the SE. This was the first indication that the High Seas Fleet was at sea; their appearance would shortly force Beatty to retire on the Grand Fleet. But, before moving to this new phase of the battle, we must go back in time to follow the development of the destroyer action that was now raging between the battlecruiser lines.

The destroyer action

After Beatty turned East at 3.30 and then hauled round towards the southward, the light cruiser *Nottingham* seems to have maintained her position ahead of *Lion*. Soon after 4 o'clock, *Dublin* was about half a mile on the flagship's disengaged bow, while *Southampton* and *Birmingham* were already forward of *Lion*'s beam, drawing further ahead.[174] At 3.30, the destroyers of the BCF were still in their screening positions with most of them along the flanks of the battlecruiser columns.[175] At 3.34, Beatty ordered Pakenham to prolong the battlecruiser line astern and his own screen, the 13DF, to take station ahead. Pakenham seems to have relied on this signal to warn his six screening destroyers from the 9DF and 10DF that he was about to swing sharply to starboard, thereby cutting across the bows of *Laurel, Moorsom* and *Morris* on his starboard flank; the port screen consisted of *Lydiard, Liberty* and *Landrail*. Further signals from Pakenham and Beatty then ordered these boats to take station ahead of *Lion*, whereas the 13DF, all *M*-class boats, were instructed to take station two miles before the starboard beam – even though the four *L*-class boats were slower than the rest, and they were starting from further back. After the turns by the 2BCS, its screening destroyers found themselves on the battlecruiser's engaged beam and quarter. To prevent her smoke interfering with their fire, *Laurel* passed under *Indefatigable*'s stern and proceeded on the disengaged side. *Moorsom* and *Morris* (10DF) steamed up the engaged side to get ahead. So too did *Lydiard, Liberty* and *Landrail* (in that order) though they soon lagged behind; at 3.55, *Tiger*'s gunnery report complained of 'Interference from T.B.D. smoke'.[176]

Lion and the 1BCS had been screened by the 13DF led by the light cruiser *Champion*, although *Moresby* and *Onslow* were still detached as an escort for *Engadine*; they would be released to rejoin the flotilla at 4.12. When the

---

[173] REL. *OD*, pp. 193, 388, 391 and 394. *OD*(M), 4.30pm.
[174] *OD*, pp. 180, 184 and Plate 14. F&H, pp. 77–8. 'Etienne', p. 128.
[175] *OD*, p. 245 (1DF) for a typical screening organisation.
[176] *OD*, pp. 254, 256–60 and 390 and Plate 21.

Table 5.17. *BCF light forces' signals 3.34–5.08pm*

Time of despatch	From	To	System	Message	Time of origin
pm, 31 May					
3.34	SO BCF	2BCS	Flags	Prolong the line by taking station astern	
3.34	SO BCF	13DF	Flags	Take station ahead	
3.36	SO 2BCS	2BCS	Flags	Alter course in succession 16 points to starboard	
3.37	SO 2BCS	9DF	Flags	9DF take station ahead of Lion	
3.38	SO 2BCS	Destroyers	Flags	Take station ahead 5 cables	
3.42	SO BCF	13DF	Flags	Take station 2 points before the starboard beam 2 miles	
3.42	SO BCF	9DF	–	Take station ahead	
3.55	SO BCF	Captain D13	W/T	Opportunity appears favourable for attacking	
3.55	SO 2LCS	2LCS	SL	Spread for lookout duties on a line of bearing NW in sequence in which ships now are from Lion	
3.56	SO BCF	Captain D1 and D13	Flags	Proceed at your utmost speed	1548
4.09	SO BCF	Champion via Princess Royal	W/T	Attack enemy with torpedoes. (Not logged as having been received by Champion until 5.16pm [*sic*]. This signal was passed to Champion by Princess Royal at that time, presumably owing to Lion's W/T being out of action)	1602
4.10	SO BCF	Princess Royal	W/T	Main W/T out of action	
4.11	SO BCF	Destroyers	SL	Clear range	
4.12	Onslow	Engadine	Sem.	Can you dispense with my services? Reply: Yes, certainly	
4.15	SO 2LCS	Nottingham	SL	Support destroyers	
4.17	Birmingham	SO 2lCS	Sem.	I am porting a little to give Nottingham and destroyers room	
4.25	Nottingham	SO 2LCS	SL	Am edging to starboard to keep smoke clear of Lion	
4.38	Champion	SO BCF	W/T	Course of Enemy's battlefleet is ENE, single line ahead. Van Dreadnoughts. My position 56°51 N, 5°56E	1630
4.43	SO BCF	Destroyers	Flags	Recall	
5.08	Nestor	Captain D1	W/T	All torpedoes fired, speed reduced to 17 knots	1705

battlecruisers opened fire, *Champion*, despite Beatty's 3.42 signal, took station on *Lion*'s starboard bow; thus Captain (D) James Farie anticipated Beatty's urging at 3.55 that 'Opportunity appears favourable for attacking'. *Champion* then moved further ahead, followed by all but one of her destroyers in three divisions in line-ahead, disposed abeam, with the 2nd Division – in order *Nestor* (Commander the Hon. Barry Bingham), *Nomad* and *Nicator* – on the port wing. *Obdurate*, however, had become separated and remained about 1,000 yards on *Lion*'s engaged side.[177] Meanwhile, *Lydiard*'s division struggled onwards on the engaged side 'rather than lose all chance of making a torpedo attack'; it was probably their smoke that made spotting difficult from *Princess Royal* at 3.59. In his despatch, Beatty singled out *Lydiard* and *Landrail* as 'causing considerable interference from smoke' at about 4.05. At 4.11, he ordered all destroyers to clear the range, at which *Lydiard* and her two consorts turned 16 points to starboard and passed down the engaged side to join *Laurel* astern.[178]

At 4.00, Beatty ordered a destroyer torpedo attack. But, at 4.05, *Lion*'s main wireless had been put out of action, and it is uncertain when the wireless repeat of his order sent via *Princess Royal* was received in *Champion*. However, at least two destroyers saw the flag signal for the attack flying in *Lion*, and, at 4.15, *Champion* ordered the attack, to be led by Bingham and the 2nd Division.[179] The reports from the 3rd Division – *Narborough* and *Pelican, Petard* and *Turbulent* – are contradictory, but it appears that they were next, followed by *Nerissa* and *Termagant* of the 1st Division.[180] *Obdurate* attacked on her own from the engaged side, while *Moorsom*, with *Morris* as much as a mile astern, tagged onto *Nestor*'s division. Initially, *Nestor* and the rest steamed hard on a course diverging from their battlecruisers by two or three points in order to reach a favourable position to attack the ISG from ahead.[181]

Hipper had allowed at least three of his five light cruisers (the position of *Wiesbaden* is uncertain) to race off to the north-west, taking their screening

Table 5.18. *ISG flotillas signals 4.14–4.26pm*

Time of receipt	From	To	System	Message	Time of origin
pm, 31 May					
4.14	Lützow	ISG	Visual	Torpedo boats are to attack	
4.26	Regensburg	IXTF	Visual	Lines are 10,900 yards apart. IXTF, advance to the attack	
4.26	V29	IXTF	Visual	Torpedo boats are to attack	

[177] *OD*, pp. 229, 231, 233, 259 and 349. F&H, pp. 56, 59, 61 and 65. S&H, p. 85. In *OD*(M), the 3.56 signal was addressed to Captains D13 and D1, but the latter was screening the 5BS.

[178] *OD*, pp. 132, 148, 254 and 257–8.

[179] VNE. *OD*, pp. 224, 240 and 349. F&H, pp. 59, 62 and 65. The time of receipt of the wireless repeat should probably be 4.16pm.

[180] *OD*, pp. 229, 233, 235 and 262. F&H, p. 57.

[181] *OD*, pp. 231, 240, 259–60 and 344–5. F&H, p. 60. S&H, p. 119.

destroyers with them. Thus only the flotilla leader *Regensburg* (Commander Paul Heinrich), the four large *G101*-class destroyers accompanying her and the eleven destroyers of the IXTF remained close to the ISG.[182] At 4.14, Hipper ordered these destroyers to attack; thus at about the same time as the British destroyers moved out, the German IXTF began to close unobtrusively. When the range had fallen to some 11,000 yards, they turned inwards in four groups led respectively by *V28, V27, V29* and *V30*. *Regensburg* then moved across in a south-westerly direction to support the IXTF, followed by *G101-104*.[183]

As the British attack began, at 4.15 Commodore Goodenough ordered *Nottingham* to support the destroyers. In her despatch, *Dublin* stated that she received a similar order but that she was too close to *Lion* to cross her bows without causing excessive smoke interference. As *Lion* was gradually opening the range, *Nottingham* altered to starboard to avoid getting in her way, but she then cut through the destroyers of the 3rd Division, forcing *Petard* and *Turbulent* to reduce speed and then proceed independently. *Nottingham* claimed to have fired on the enemy destroyers for a time before joining *Southampton*, but in his memoirs Goodenough did not mention any orders to his light cruisers to support the destroyers, implying that, instead, he had kept in a favourable position for observing ahead.[184] None of the British destroyers mentioned supporting fire from the 2LCS, whereas many commented ruefully on the effective support given by *Regensburg*.[185] As for *Champion*, she was sufficiently far advanced to sight the High Seas Fleet at the same time as *Southampton*: and one report mentioned her leading destroyers back from the attack.[186] However, Farie did not claim any active part in the action and there are no reports from either side of *Champion* making her presence felt.

As *Nestor*'s division advanced, *Nomad*'s propeller bearing began to make alarming noises. She slowed down and gave permission for *Nicator* to pass her, but after tightening up leaking joints *Nomad* was again able to keep up. Having reached a favourable position on *Lützow*'s starboard bow, *Nestor* turned 12–14 points to port preparatory to running down to launch torpedoes; *Nicator, Nomad* and probably others followed in succession. Fire, already being exchanged with the German destroyers of the IXTF and *Regensburg*, intensified as the range closed rapidly. *Nestor* and *Nicator* claimed to have sunk the leading German boat, and, certainly, *V27* leading the second German group was crippled by gunfire.

---

[182] The boats of the XIHF that screened *Wiesbaden* were unable to reach the head of the line until 4.48: Tarrant, p. 102.

[183] *GOA*, pp. 69–70. Tarrant, p. 102. F&H, pp. 397–8. The time of 4.26 for the German signal ordering the advance seems rather late; *Nicator*'s report (*OD*, p. 240) stated that she opened fire on the enemy at 4.20 at a range of 7,000 yards.

[184] *OD*, pp. 180, 229 and 231. F&H, p. 57. Goodenough, p. 95.

[185] *OD*, pp. 235, 240, 262 and 346. F&H, pp. 58, 64 and 66. S&H, pp. 122–5.

[186] F&H, p. 55 (though *Badger* of the 1DF actually screened the 5BS). *OD*, Plate 21 shows *Champion* W and astern of the attacking 13DF.

Unfortunately, most of the return German fire fell over on *Nomad*; before she could fire any torpedoes, she was hit repeatedly, most seriously in the engine room and was soon brought to a halt. *Nestor* and *Nicator* pressed on; each fired two torpedoes at the German battlecruisers at ranges of 5,000–6,000 yards – though one of *Nicator*'s officers recalled that her second torpedo stuck in its tube, endangering the ship for a time. As they successfully evaded the British torpedoes, the ISG was seen to turn four points away. Although Bingham's despatch states that they turned in succession, he probably saw some of their turns-away together between 4.27 and 4.36.[187]

As this British attack was delivered, the German destroyers were already withdrawing on their battlecruisers, one group towards the rear and the other towards the van. Between 4.27 and 4.36 they had fired ten torpedoes at the British battlecruisers at ranges of 8,000–9,000 yards, though without effect. *Nestor* and *Nicator* swung to starboard to ENE and went after the second (van) group, though they then came under heavy fire from the secondary armament of the ISG at ranges which came down to only 3,000 yards. Each boat fired one more torpedo before turning back. But *Nestor* soon received two hits in her boilers, bringing her to a standstill; Bingham attributed this damage to heavy fire from the *Regensburg*. As *Nestor* was hit, she veered to starboard, thereby preventing *Nicator* from firing her last torpedo. *Nicator* (Lieutenant Jack Mocatta) then escaped without damage, passing the stopped *Nomad* before rejoining *Champion*. However, Bingham's sketch chart implies that their joint attack was made on the ISG before they turned almost 16 points, whereas Mocatta claimed that it came after this turn and his sighting the High Seas Fleet, and that his target was the second German battleship. Since Mocatta reported even shorter ranges than Bingham and *Nestor* had an agonising wait before the High Seas Fleet came up, it seems more likely that the ISG had been their target.[188]

The position reached by *Petard* and *Turbulent* after *Nottingham* cut across their bows is uncertain. Since *Turbulent* was lost with all hands during the night, we only have *Petard*'s despatch to go on. This declared that they attacked immediately after *Nestor*'s division and that *Petard* engaged the approaching German flotilla with gunfire. She then fired a torpedo (set for high speed to run at a depth of 6 feet) at a group of German boats. Their leader *V29* was hit and seen a few minutes later with her decks awash and obviously sinking; the German account declared that she fired four torpedoes at the British battle-cruisers before she foundered (though none of them hit). Her crew and that of

---

[187] *OD*, pp. 240, 345–6 (Bingham's despatch of 14 May 1918, written when a PoW) and 349–50. F&H, pp. 62–3, 65–6 and 70 (extracts from Bingham's book, pp. 138–47). In both despatch and book, Bingham's times are usually later than would be expected. For the difficulty of recalling times after being in action, see S&H, p. 121. Tarrant, p. 93 states that *V27* was hit while returning from launching torpedoes.

[188] Tarrant, p. 93. *OD*, pp. 240–1 and 346–7. F&H, pp. 64 and 66–7.

V27 were rescued under fire by *V26* and *V35, V27* being sunk by German gunfire.[189] After a further exchange with the German destroyers, *Petard* went on to fire her three remaining torpedoes at the ISG between 4.27 and 4.40 at ranges of 6,500–7,000 yards; *Turbulent* may also have fired one or more torpedoes at about this time. The BCF having by then turned northwards, *Petard* proceeded to rejoin *Champion*. She cannot have been far from *Nestor*, since she drew alongside and offered a tow as Bingham's boat was steaming slowly in the same direction. However, since *Nestor* was then still making headway, Bingham refused. *Petard* then went ahead and, in passing the wreck of *Queen Mary*, picked up one of the few survivors, P.O. Ernest Francis.[190]

Moorsom also reported that she attacked with *Nestor*'s division, and she too turned to port, though by only 6–8 points, to run down on the bow of the enemy. But she became embroiled in the gun action with the IXTF and had to give up this torpedo attack. Once the German destroyers were driven off, *Moorsom* went off on her own. After the ISG turned northwards, she sighted the High Seas Fleet and fired two torpedoes at the van. Shortly afterwards, a shell holed her after oil tanks, but she still made a second attack with the remaining two torpedoes; unfortunately, she made no hits. On her way back, she passed *Nomad* lying stopped, but *Moorsom*'s officers decided that, with the enemy battlefleet approaching, it would be suicidal to stand by the crippled destroyer.[191] *Morris* seems to have taken an independent part in the gun action with the enemy boats; after they were driven off, she came within torpedo range of the ISG but was unable to fire due to other British destroyers fouling the range. She then rejoined *Moorsom* in company with *Lydiard* and *Champion*.[192]

After *Nottingham* cut through their division, *Narborough* and *Pelican* continued their approach, but both complained that they were prevented from opening fire or launching torpedoes by *Moorsom* and *Morris* coming up in the opposite direction. When *Narborough* sighted the High Seas Fleet, her commander decided to retain all his torpedoes for a fleet action rather than fire them at long range. *Nerissa* and *Termagant* commenced their attack on the ISG on a northerly course but 'owing to the enemy turning 16 points, this attack had eventually to be carried out on a Southerly course', just after they passed the stopped *Nomad*. Both destroyers exchanged fire with enemy destroyers (perhaps some of the *G101*-class) and with *Regensburg*. Only *Nerissa* was able to fire two torpedoes, at a range of 7,000 yards, and she claimed that one of them appeared to

---

[189] *OD*, pp. 231–2. F&H, pp. 57–9 (though these notes by an officer of *Petard* state that she attacked after *Nerissa* and *Termagant*). Tarrant, p. 93. *GOA*, p. 70.

[190] *ATFJ*, p. 8. Campbell, p. 56. *OD*, pp. 232 and 347. F&H, pp. 58–9 and 67.

[191] *OD*, pp. 260. F&H, pp. 60–1. The latter account from *Moorsom* describes her as 'messing about between the lines for one and a half to two hours' while the *ATFJ* times for her firing torpedoes were 5.10 and 5.30 (p. 9). But her encounter with *Nomad* suggests these times are too late.

[192] *OD*, pp. 260–1.

hit the rear battlecruiser. *Obdurate*, on moving out, soon became engaged with the approaching enemy destroyers and with *Regensburg* at ranges falling from 6,000 to 3,000 yards; she was hit twice, though had no casualties. *Obdurate* was then too far astern to deliver a torpedo attack and rejoined *Champion*.[193]

Of the eleven British torpedoes fired at the ISG,[194] just one scored a belated hit, though not on the rear ship. Soon after Hipper turned his ships northwards at about 4.50, *Seydlitz* sighted first one and then more tracks of approaching torpedoes. She tried to avoid them by sharp turns, so much so that, when her luck ran out at 4.57, she was hit on the starboard side, forward of the fore barbette, close to where she had struck a mine on 24 April. The damage was extensive but the torpedo bulkhead held, even though it and the armoured deck were strained and leaking; she developed only a slight list and was able to maintain full speed.[195] The torpedoes seen from *Seydlitz* were probably those fired by *Petard* and *Nerissa* and perhaps by *Turbulent* as well, but it is not known which made the hit.

As the BCF and the ISG steamed away northwards, *Nestor* and *Nomad*, the latter some two miles to the eastward, could do little but await their destruction by the advancing High Seas Fleet. Even so, *Nestor* drove off a German destroyer with gunfire and fired her remaining torpedo at the German battleships. As *Nomad* listed to port, she managed to launch her four torpedoes at what were thought to be *Kaiser*-class battleships, though her last torpedo may have damaged its tail – neither these torpedoes nor *Nestor*'s scored a hit. Almost immediately, the IBS appeared out of the haze with *Nomad* almost directly in their path. She identified *Thüringen* and *Posen* as she was deluged with rapid salvos at ranges falling to 500 yards. She received hits in a boiler and in the fore magazine, which blew up. Commander Paul Whitehead only then ordered his crew to abandon ship just before she foundered; they were picked up by three German boats of the VTF. Then it was *Nestor*'s turn. As the men waited, her first lieutenant, Maurice Bethell, kept them occupied by laying out cables, ostensibly in hope of a friendly tow. As their ship began to sink under the storm of German shells, Bingham ordered 'Abandon ship', but Bethell turned aside to help a mortally wounded signalman and was not seen again. Bingham – who would be awarded the Victoria Cross – and almost all the survivors were picked up by the Germans, Bingham himself by *S16*. Despite the intense bombardment that had descended on *Nestor* and *Nomad*, their total casualties were just 14 killed and 12 wounded, the latter and the 152 uninjured crew becoming prisoners of war.[196]

[193] *OD*, pp. 229–31, 233–5 and 262. *ATFJ*, p. 8.

[194] This total includes the two torpedoes fired by *Nestor* and *Nicator* during their second attack. *ATFJ*, p. 9, assumes the attack was on the High Seas Fleet, but Bingham's despatch (of May 1918) was not available to its compilers.

[195] S&H, pp. 127–8. Tarrant, p. 102.

[196] *OD*, pp. 347–8 and 350–1. *F&H*, pp. 67–71. Letter from Lt. Cmdr. Paul Whitfield, 8 June 1916 in ADM 137/4808. Liddle, p. 111. Campbell, pp. 101 and 338.

Movements of the battle fleets

When *Galatea*'s first wireless reports of enemy light forces were received in *Iron Duke* from 2.18, the battlefleet was still steaming about SE½E at 15 knots. Between 2.35 and 3.00, Jellicoe's ships began raising steam for full speed; the columns ceased zigzagging, forming in line-ahead and adjusting their relative bearings in preparation for turning to the pre-planned course towards Horns Reef. They increased speed to 17 and then 18 knots and at three o'clock, Jellicoe turned the Grand Fleet by 9 Pendant to SEbyS. He then commanded the cruiser screen to move ahead so that the centre would lie on the line of advance 16 miles ahead of the battleships. He increased speed again to 19 knots at 3.18 and at 3.27 broke radio silence to inform Beatty of his position, course and speed. At 3.59, after Beatty announced that he was engaging the enemy, Jellicoe asked for 20 knots. The fleet had never previously attained this speed and a consequence was that the armoured cruisers never drew more than 12 miles ahead. At 4.25, Jellicoe permitted the battleships to '[k]eep just clear of wake of next ahead if it helps ships to keep up'.[197]

As the Grand Fleet approached the rendezvous, Hood's 3BCS had been 20 miles ahead of the battleships. By 3.15, he was heading ESE at 22 knots, apparently with the object the blocking the line of retreat to the Skagerrak of the German light cruisers then being chased to the N by the 1LCS and 3LCS. Once Jellicoe knew that the BCF was in action, at 4.05 he ordered Hood to proceed immediately to support them. Hood had already anticipated the order, since he had increased speed to 24 knots at 4.00 and turned SSE at 4.02; by 4.06, he was making 25 knots towards Horns Reef. From his own position and *Lion*'s position and course as given him by Jellicoe, he could have reckoned on *Lion* being some 46 miles SbyW, heading about SEbyE.[198] Thus his course was probably determined more by the general tactical situation than by any hope of catching Beatty in the near future. Jellicoe had heard nothing about the 5BS and, after Beatty's signal at 3.55, nothing more on the progress of the battlecruiser action. In response to a direct enquiry from Jellicoe, Evan-Thomas confirmed that he too was engaging the enemy. But this reassurance was quickly overshadowed by *Southampton*'s report at 4.30 of an enemy light cruiser to the SE, the first indication of a new enemy force coming into play.

After midday, the High Seas Fleet had continued N at 14 knots in open order, that is, in single line with 700 metres between the battleships and 3.5 kilometres

---

[197] *OD*, pp. 6 and 272. *GF*, p. 206. In accordance with *GFBOs III*, XXI.2, on being ordered ahead by 16 miles, the cruisers also opened out to 8 miles apart (*OD*, p. 285).

[198] *OD*, pp. 6, 13 and 14. *GF*, pp. 203 and 211; Jellicoe here gave the later 3BCS course as SbyE and *Indomitable*'s despatch (*OD*, p. 163) as 137° (SEbyS = 133°). Beatty reported the *enemy* course as S55°E. F&H, p. 226.

Table 5.19. *Grand Fleet signals 2.35–4.35pm*

Time of despatch	From	To	System	Message	Time of origin
pm, 31 May					
2.35	C-in-C	General	Flags	Raise steam for full speed and report when ready to proceed	
2.43	C-in-C	General	Flags	Alter course together two points to port. Speed 17 knots. Guides to bear NEbyE from Guide of fleet	
2.55	C-in-C	General	Flags	… 18 knots	
2.57	C-in-C	General	Flags	Raise steam for full speed with all despatch	
3.00	C-in-C	General	Flags	Assume complete readiness for action in every respect	
3.00	C-in-C	General	Flags	Alter course leading ships together the rest in succession to SEbyS	
3.10	C-in-C	Cruisers	SL	Take up cruising disposition No. 1. Centre of screen 16 miles from B.F. Speed of advance 18 knots. Assume complete readiness for action	
3.15	SO 3BCS	C-in-C	SL	Priority. My course ESE, 22 knots	1510
3.16	C-in-C	General	Flags	Columns to be one mile apart	
3.18	C-in-C	General	Flags	… 19 knots	
3.27	C-in-C	SO BCF	W/T	My position at 1515, 57°50 N, 4°15E, course SEbyS, speed 19 knots	1526
3.31	C-in-C	SO 2CS	SL	Centre of screen should bear SEbyS	1530
3.55	SO BCF	C-in-C	W/T	Urgent. Am engaging Enemy. My position 56°53 N, 5°31E	1550
3.59	C-in-C	General	Flags	… 20 knots	
4.00	SO 3BCS	3BCS	Flags	… 24 knots	
4.02	SO 3BCS	General	Flags	Alter course in succession to SSE	
4.05	C-in-C	SO 3BCS	W/T	Proceed immediately to support B.C.F. position 56°53 N, 5°31E, course S55°E at 3.50	1604
4.05	C-in-C	General	Sem.	Battle Cruiser Fleet are engaging Enemy's Battle Cruisers	1605
4.15	SO 3BCS	C-in-C	W/T	My position, course and speed: 57°39 N, 5°35E, SSE, 25 knots	1606
4.17	C-in-C	SO 5BS	W/T	Are you in company with SO BCF?	1615
				Reply: Yes, I am engaging enemy	1630
4.25	C-in-C	Battlefleet	Sem.	Keep just clear of wake of next ahead if it helps ships to keep up	1620
4.30	Southampton	C-in-C SO BCF	W/T	Urgent. One Enemy Cruiser bearing SE, steering NE. (My position 56°38 N, 6°07E)	1630
4.30	Nottingham	SO 2LCS	Sem.	Two Cruisers SSE	
4.32	Birmingham	SO 2LCS	Sem.	One four-funnelled Cruiser	1604 [sic]
4.35	Southampton			Remarks: Challenged four-funnelled Cruiser bearing SE. No reply	

Table 5.20. *High Seas Fleet signals 11.35am–4.36pm*

Time of receipt	From	To	System	Message	Time of origin
am, 31 May					
11.53	C-in-C	General	Visual	Course N	
pm, 31 May					
2.35	Lützow	C-in-C		Several smoke clouds from enemy vessels in sight	1427
3.10	C-in-C	General	Visual	General Quarters. Full speed. Course N	[1506]
3.13	Lützow	C-in-C		Only 4 enemy light cruisers in sight. Position of ISG … Course NW	1520
3.25	F. der Grosse	Fleet	Visual	Ships to be 700 metres (766 yards) apart	
3.35	Lützow	General		Enemy battle fleet in sight in … consists of 6 ships, steering N	1529
3.40	F. der Grosse	Fleet	Visual	Full speed	
3.54	Lützow	General		6 enemy battle cruisers, also smaller vessels in …, steering SE. ISG in … Course SSE, 18 knots. Am in action with 6 battle cruisers. Request position of own battle fleet	1546
4.05	C-in-C	General	Visual	Course NW	
4.05	C-in-C	Fleet AC SGs		Own battle fleet 4pm position … Course NW. Speed 15 knots	1609
4.11	F. der Grosse	General	Visual	Ships to be 500 metres (547 yards) apart	
4.20	C-in-C	General	Visual	Course W	
4.20	Frankfurt	Lützow		Enemy battle fleet in … British 2BS, 5 ships. Enemy vessels are steering SE	1612
4.21	C-in-C	Rostock		Leader of Torpedo Boats. Assemble torpedo boats belonging to battle fleet	1621
4.21	F. der Grosse	General	Visual	Course N	
4.28	Stettin	Fleet	Visual	Firing observed NNW½W, distant about 4 miles	
4.30	C-in-C	Lützow		To AC Scouting Forces. Own battle fleet …, steering N. Speed, 15 knots	1631
4.35	F. der Grosse	All Flotillas	Visual	To starboard	
4.36	F. der Grosse	General	Visual	Increase speed	
4.36	Stettin	F. der Grosse	Visual	IISG in sight, bearing NNW¼W	

between squadrons. At 3.10, following Hipper's first unspecific report of enemy vessels, Scheer ordered 'General Quarters' (action stations) and 'full speed', an increase to 15 knots.[199] When Hipper signalled at 3.35 that six heavy enemy

---

[199] Scheer, pp. 145–6. 'Full speed' meant 'the maximum speed which the slowest ship can maintain with all boilers without forcing [allowing] for an increase of 2 knots during half-an-hour without forcing': *Manoeuvring Instructions for the Fleet, 1914*, p. 6 in 'German Fleet Orders', ADM 186/17.

ships were in sight steering N, he was about 50 miles from the main fleet. Then at 3.54 he announced that he was in action with six enemy battlecruisers that were now headed SE. At 4.05 Scheer turned NW; he also closed up his line to 500 metres between ships and 1,000 metres between squadrons but he continued in single line rather than reforming into the usual 'preparatory formation' of columns disposed abeam. At about this time, he also ordered *Hannover* to move to the end of the line; thus Rear-Admiral von Dalwigk zu Lichtenfels would be able to lead the battlefleet should it be necessary to reverse course. Then at 4.20 Scheer turned W in the hope of catching the BCF between two fires. However, just as his ships were altering course, he received the report from Bödicker in *Frankfurt* that he had sighted what he identified as five ships of the 2BS. With the ISG apparently facing eleven heavy ships (and with the possibility of more battleships coming up in support) Scheer at once ordered his forces back to the course N that would gain touch with Hipper as quickly as possible.[200] With action imminent, he ordered his destroyers to assemble on their flotilla leaders and the leader of flotillas, the light cruiser *Rostock*, and to move to starboard onto what would soon be his disengaged flank. The light cruiser *Stettin*, flying the broad pendant of Commodore Reuter commanding the IVSG, led the battle line and by 4.28 she could make out firing ahead some four miles on her port bow. At 4.36, she reported sighting the IISG bearing NNW¼W, though this was probably Hipper's flotilla leader, the *Regensburg*, then engaged with British destroyers. From the British side, from 4.30 to 4.35, one or two German light cruisers could be made out from the 2LCS, one of which had four funnels;[201] this must have been *Rostock* (the only four-funnelled cruiser with the High Seas Fleet) while *Stettin* had probably been sighted as well. With the cruiser forces in contact, the next stage of the battle was about to begin.

---

[200] Scheer, pp. 146–7. *GOA*, pp. 54–6.
[201] Tarrant, pp. 61 and 75–6. *Southampton* challenged the four-funnelled cruiser bearing SE but received no reply.

6　The Run to the North

At 4.33, when the 2LCS was two miles in advance of *Lion* in line-ahead, *Southampton* announced by searchlight that she could see battleships to the SE in the same direction as the enemy cruiser that she had already reported.[1] Undaunted, Goodenough pressed on to obtain more information and in the hope of making a torpedo attack. At 4.38, he broadcast the first of three more detailed reports addressed to Jellicoe and Beatty (of which more later). After two more minutes, *Nottingham* fired a single torpedo set for extreme range at the seventh German battleship (*Kaiserin* of the IIIBS), though without success; the other three light cruisers concluded that they could not reach a position for an effective attack, presumably because their torpedoes had been set for long range. The 2LCS continued to advance bows-on to the enemy while the Germans, uncertain of whether they were hostile, still held their fire. At 4.45, Goodenough hauled down the turn signal that had been flying for the last five minutes.[2] As soon as his ships veered away revealing their four-funnelled profiles, some half a dozen German battleships opened fire as the 2LCS retired in line-abreast with *Southampton* nearest the enemy. Even at 5.00, the enemy battleships were still bearing E, so it is not surprising that the 2LCS remained under a hot fire for most of the next hour. They were obliged to zigzag continually to dodge the enemy salvos, *Southampton*'s navigator steering the ship away from where he thought the next salvo would fall; they were so successful that the 2LCS survived without a single direct hit, though they were regularly deluged by shell slashes and showered with splinters from near misses.[3]

---

[1] *OD*, p. 180. F&H, p. 78. *Champion* apparently sighted the enemy battle fleet even before *Southampton* but did not send a report until 4.38.

[2] Goodenough, p. 95. *OD*, pp. 176 and 184. 'Etienne', pp. 133–4 (excerpts also in F&H, pp. 80–4). F&H, pp. 75–6 and 79. Goodenough's despatch states that, after closing, the 2LCS turned N'ward at 5.00 but all other reports state that the turn-away was at 4.45. The charts of *Nottingham* and *Falmouth* indicate that their initial course was W'ward but that they turned N'ward later: *OD*, Pls. 14 and 15.

[3] 'Etienne', pp. 134 and 137–8. F&H, pp. 77 and 79. Goodenough, p. 95. *OD*, pp. 178–9. *OD*(M), 5.00pm.

Table 6.1. *2LCS signals 4.33–5.00pm*

Time of despatch	From	To	System	Message	Time of origin
pm, 31 May					
4.33	Southampton	SO BCF	SL	Battleships SE	
4.45	SO 2LCS	Birmingham	SL	Turn	
5.00	SO 2LCS	2LCS	Flags	Alter course in succession to NNW	

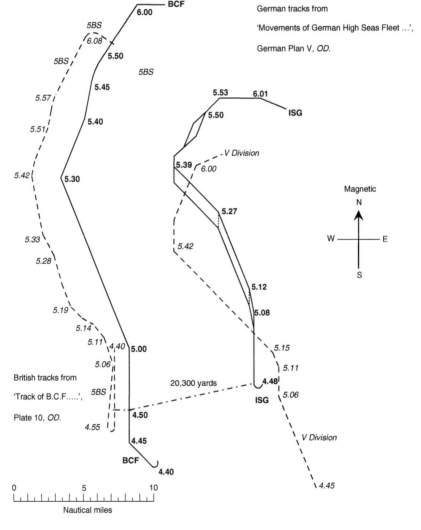

Figure 6.1 The Run to the North

It appears that, as he withdrew Eastwards, Hipper did not sight the approaching High Seas Fleet until 4.38, when he turned the ISG first to SSE and then even further to SSW. These turns brought him once more within range of the 5BS. At 4.40 Evan-Thomas ordered a renewed concentration in pairs on the

Table 6.2. *ISG signals 4.38–4.51pm*

Time of receipt	From	To	System	Message	Time of origin
pm, 31 May					
4.38	Lützow	ISG	Visual	Turn together to SSE	
4.41	Lützow	ISG	Visual	Turn together to SSW	
4.44	Lützow	ISG	Visual	ISG: Open fire at battleships	
4.46	Lützow	ISG	Visual	Turn together to SE	
4.49	Lützow	ISG	Visual	Follow in wake of leading ship	
4.51	Lützow	ISG	Visual	Course N	

Table 6.3. *5BS signals 4.18–4.50pm*

Time of despatch	From	To	System	Message	Time of origin
pm, 31 May					
4.18	SO 5BS	5BS	Flags	Ships in column to be 3 cables apart. Speed 24 knots	
4.30	SO 5BS	5BS	Flags	Subdivisions separately alter course in succession two points away from the Enemy preserving their formation	
4.30	SO 5BS	5BS	Flags	Alter course together four points to port	
4.31	SO 5BS	5BS	Flags	Negative alter course together four points to port	
4.40	SO 5BS	5BS	Flags	Subdivisions separately alter course in succession two points away from the Enemy preserving their formation	
4.40	SO 5BS	5BS	Flags	Concentrate in pairs from the rear	
4.45	SO 5BS	5BS	Flags	Form single line ahead	
4.45	SO BCF	General	Flags	Have sighted Enemy battlefleet bearing SE	
4.48	SO BCF	5BS	Flags	Alter course in succession 16 points to starboard	
4.50	Lion			Remarks: Passed 5th Battle Squadron steering on opposite course	

rear of the ISG. At the same time, he was forced for the second time to hoist the single Preparative Flag, seemingly in response to the approach of the German XIHF; two of their seven torpedoes were reported (though only in Evan-Thomas's despatch) to have crossed his line-ahead and astern of *Valiant*. However, the timing of this attack is uncertain, since the German accounts state that it only began at 4.48 and that it was made after the BCF turned about and passed the 5BS. Hipper returned the fire of the 5BS at 4.44; a short but fierce engagement followed in which *Seydlitz* (the third in line) was hit at 4.50 and *Barham* was probably also hit.[4] At 4.45, Evan-Thomas ordered his ships to form single line and a minute later Hipper turned away together to SE.

Notwithstanding Beatty's later outrage at the Admiralty's 12.30 signal:

> In the Battle Cruiser Fleet it had been constantly assumed that the German battle cruisers would never be found far from adequate support, and thus no surprise was felt when their battle fleet was sighted.

At 4.37, Beatty turned briefly SE towards the enemy before at 4.40 ordering a 16-point turn in succession to starboard, that is to NW. Although the wording of three despatches implies that this turn was made just after the High Seas Fleet had been sighted, Beatty's own narrative declares that he himself did not see them until 4.43. Beatty's 4.40 flag signal was the first recorded manoeuvring signal since 3.47. It

Table 6.4. *BCF signals 4.40–4.50pm*

Time of despatch	From	To	System	Message	Time of origin
pm, 31 May					
4.40	SO BCF	General	Flags	Alter course in succession 16 points to starboard	
4.42	Lion			Remarks: Sighted Enemy battlefleet ahead	
4.43	SO BCF	Destroyers	Flags	Recall	
4.45	SO BCF	Princess Royal	Sem.	Report Enemy's battlefleet to C-in-C, bearing SE	
4.45	SO BCF	General	Flags	Have sighted Enemy battlefleet bearing SE	
4.47	SO BCF	Fearless	Flags	Pick up men in water round us	
4.48	SO BCF	5BS	Flags	Alter course in succession 16 points to starboard	
4.50	Lion			Remarks: Passed 5th Battle Squadron steering on opposite course	

---

[4] *OD*, pp. 193 and 199. Tarrant, p. 102. Campbell, pp. 55, 76 and 80.

was listed by the *Official Despatches* as a general signal, that is as applying to all the ships under Beatty's command; furthermore, the message description is the same as that for the subsequent signal to the 5BS at 4.48, which Rear-Admiral Brock stated explicitly was made using the Compass Pendant.[5] When addressed to multiple columns, this signal required that bearings relative to *Lion*'s course and distances be preserved. But, with the 5BS still some eight miles astern and his light cruisers both ahead and astern, this was impossible. So, if the signal was made as listed, it appears to have been yet another mistake by *Lion*'s signallers. However, it was probably not even seen by the 5BS while, according to Stephen King-Hall's memoir, although it was read by *Southampton*, she delayed her turn for five minutes.[6] Beatty would presumably have approved of this display of initiative, even if he had intended the 2LCS to turn with the battlecruisers. At about 4.45, Beatty, reverting to manoeuvring without signals, led the battlecruisers to starboard onto a course N. One object of this turn was to prevent the range to the ISG from increasing too rapidly.[7] The second was to put the BCF on an almost opposite course to the 5BS, thereby making clear Beatty's declared intention that 'The Fifth Battle Squadron must pass on our disengaged side'.[8] In 1923, Evan-Thomas recalled that, when they passed, their distance apart 'was in my opinion about one mile – If anything, a little less', though an officer in *Warspite* thought it was 'about half a mile'.[9]

Table 6.5. *High Seas Fleet signals 4.36–4.54pm*

Time of receipt	From	To	System	Message	Time of origin
pm, 31 May					
4.36	F. der Grosse	General	Visual	Increase speed	
4.36	Stettin	F. der Grosse	Visual	2SG in sight, bearing NNW¼W	
4.42	F. der Grosse	General	Visual	Alter course. Leading ships of divisions together; the rest in succession 2 points to port [to NNW]	
4.45	F. der Grosse	General	Visual	Distribution of fire from the right, ship against ship	
4.46	F. der Grosse	General	Visual	Open fire	
4.54	C-in-C	General		Increase speed	

---

[5] *OD*, pp. 144, 148, 155, 158 (quote from Pakenham's despatch) and 160 and Pl. 10. VNE. *Lion*'s time of sighting in *OD*(M) of 4.42 must be late since the enemy are described as 'ahead'.

[6] Corbett, p. 340 and Map 27. 'Etienne', p. 133.

[7] *OD*, Pl. 10 and p. 144. F&H, p. 113; *Lion*'s gunnery officer mistook the ISG's turn as outward (to port).

[8] Chalmers, p. 283 (though the author wrongly claims that Beatty was then engaging Hipper).

[9] *BP II*, p. 464; Evan-Thomas described the distance of two miles (Corbett, p. 340 and Map 26) as 'considerably overstated'. F&H, p. 141.

To the South, Scheer had first sighted ships in action at 4.32, when the High Seas Fleet was still in single line. At about 4.36, he increased speed to 17 knots and, at 4.42, turned his divisions, leading ships together, the rest in succession, to NNW. At 4.45, he ordered 'Distribution of fire from the right, ship against ship' and, a minute later, 'Open fire'.[10] However, at the time, the 2LCS were revealing their identity to the Eastward, while the BCF and the 5BS to the North-west were approaching each other on opposite courses; thus the intention behind Scheer's fire distribution order cannot have been easily divined. Among his van ships, *Kronprinz* (perhaps) and *Kaiser* opened fire on the 2LCS, as did *Friedrich der Grosse* and the IBS; ranges were from 14,200 to 20,800 yards. However, the fall of shot soon became confused and only *Ostfriesland* and *Nassau* continued after 5 o'clock; King-Hall believed that, later in the Run to the North, his squadron was mainly the target of the German predreadnoughts. Of the other van ships, *Grosser Kurfürst, Markgraf* and *Prinzregent Luitpold* opened fire on the BCF; *König* may have done likewise, though she appears to have identified her target group as battleships. While the British battlecruisers were then nearer than the 5BS, the former's smoke may have carried towards the German ships. This may explain why *Kronprinz* (whether or not she fired briefly at the 2LCS) and *Kaiserin* soon engaged the British battleships at a range of 21,000 yards.[11] Having turned away from the 5BS's fire at 4.46, Hipper may have noticed that they and the BCF would soon pass and that the battleships' fire would then be obstructed. At 4.49, he seized his moment to turn his own battlecruisers together to form line on a course S before leading them through 16 points in succession to N,[12] though this did not prevent the hit on *Seydlitz* at 4.50.

Around the time that Beatty turned N at 4.45, *Lion*'s unsteady signalling organisation was dealing with a rush of signals.[13] At 4.43, the destroyers were recalled. At 4.45, a flag hoist, presumably intended mainly for the information of Evan-Thomas, announced the sighting of the enemy battlefleet bearing SE. At the same time, *Lion*'s semaphore instructed *Princess Royal* to report the sighting, though unfortunately, as we shall see, the resultant wireless signal reached *Iron Duke* in a garbled form. *Lion*'s next signal, at 4.47, ordered *Fearless* to pick up men in the water (this must have referred to survivors of *Queen Mary*); but it is not mentioned in any of the despatches from the 1DF and may well not have been seen by them. SO BCF's next signal ordered the 5BS to turn 16 points in succession to starboard, that is away from the BCF and the enemy further to the East. As already noted, this signal was made with the Compass Pendant, but in this case the meaning was clear since it was addressed

---

[10] Scheer's despatch, *OD*, pp. 591–2. Tarrant, p. 106. *GOA*, Chart 7 and p. 74.

[11] Tarrant, pp. 99–101. Gordon, pp. 617–18 provides a valuable analysis of the *Kriegstagebücher* of the ships of the IIIBS. 'Etienne', p. 136.

[12] *OD*, German Plans IV and V for the ISG's turns.   [13] Gordon, pp. 137–8.

to a single column. In the *Official Despatches*, it was listed with a time-of-despatch of 4.48. For flag signals, this was normally the time when the signal was hauled down, that is made executive. But, in this instance, as *Lion*'s assistant navigator at Jutland (later Rear-Admiral W S Chalmers, Beatty's biographer) recalled, this was the time at which it was hoisted. Evan-Thomas recorded in his despatch:

At 4.50 p.m., 'Lion' approached the Fifth Battle Squadron steering to the Northward with the signal flying to the Fifth Battle Squadron – 'Turn 16 points in succession to starboard'; this turn was made after our battle-cruisers had passed at 4.53, and the Fifth Battle Squadron altered course a little further to starboard to follow and support the battle-cruisers.

New Zealand's gunnery officer confirmed that the '5th B.S. held on longer than the battle cruisers and finally turned up on our starboard quarter'; hence the turn was of 17 rather than 16 points. By 1923, this signal and its timing had become part of the Jutland controversy and Evan-Thomas insisted:

Fifth Battle Squadron was definitely ordered to turn to Starboard. The signal was 'Compass 16' which was not hauled down [until] some time after *Lion* had passed; so it should be stated.[14]

Thus, in accordance with signalling protocol, Evan-Thomas did not execute the turn until the signal was hauled down, so that the 5BS was left trailing astern of the battlecruisers. In his despatch, *Barham*'s Captain Craig stated that the gap between them was 'about two miles', as did King-Hall in his memoirs; he was well placed to judge from *Southampton*, then a further mile astern of the 5BS. However, an officer in *Malaya* reckoned that 'our battlecruisers ... were already quite 7,000 or 8,000 yards [3½-4nm – nautical miles] ahead of us', though this may have included the nine cables (0.9nm) between *Barham* and *Malaya*.[15] Corbett gave the separation as 'some three miles'; this became the accepted figure and it was later cited without comment by Craig (by then Vice-Admiral Craig Waller) in a 1935 article, in which he insisted:

The 'Lion' had the [turn] signal ... easily visible to the naked eye as we passed close to her. Shortly afterwards, the signal was hauled down, and the 'Barham's' helm put over. The alleged delay by the 5th B.S. in making this turn is imaginary; the time taken to turn and the great loss of speed during such a turn is quite sufficient to account for the 5th B. S. being 3 miles astern of the battle cruisers when steadied on the Northerly course.[16]

[14] Chalmers, p. 239. *OD*, p. 193 and Pl. 10a. F&H, p. 36. *BP II*, p. 464 (but see Gordon, p. 406 for an accurate reproduction of Evan-Thomas's sketch of *Barham* hauling across the wake of the BCF).
[15] *OD*, p. 199. 'Etienne', pp. 134–6. F&H, p. 120. *OD*(M), 4.18.
[16] Corbett, p. 343 (though Maps 26 and 27 show a gap of 4 miles). *Journal of the Royal United Services Institution*, LXXX (Nov. 1935) No. 520, p. 794.

Assessing this claim is difficult not least because of the variations in the times reported by the 5BS. *Lion* approached on their port bows at 4.50 and they were forced to cease firing at the ISG at 4.53–54 as their targets were blanked by the passing battlecruisers.[17] The times of turning are between 4.53 and 4.57; however, some, not all, of this spread can be explained because, with the ships spaced at three cables (600 yards) and steaming at 23 knots, each should have arrived at the turning point some ¾ minute after the next ahead. Until the Compass Pendant signal was hauled down, the BCF and 5BS continued on opposite courses at a combined speed of 48 knots; each minute's delay after *Lion* and *Barham* passed increased the subsequent gap between them by 0.8nm. *Barham* then advanced by about 500 yards (0.25nm) before completing the turn of 17 points onto course NbyE in two minutes,[18] after which her speed was probably about 10 knots.[19] During this turn, the BCF at 25 knots (the speed ordered at 4.52) steamed ahead by 0.85nm. Thus if, as suggested by Andrew Gordon,[20] the delay was as much as three minutes, the resultant gap would already have been 3.5 miles as the turn was completed. However, the gap would then have increased further while the battleships strove to regain their previous speed. To arrive at a better estimate of the actual delay requires a knowledge of both the speed lost in the turn and the rate at which it could be regained afterwards. Unfortunately, precise values for the *Queen Elizabeth* class as they were at Jutland have not been found. But estimates based on figures for older dreadnoughts indicate that, assuming that the eventual gap between the two flagships was between two and three miles, *Lion*'s signal was hauled down and *Barham* put her helm over between one and two minutes after they passed.[21] To have enabled *Barham* to haul into line three cables astern of *New Zealand*, the turn sign would have had to be made executive about 55 seconds before the flagships would have passed. Thus the delay in making the turn was not, as Craig-Waller declared, imaginary.

The flag-captain stated that some of the IIIBS were seen astern of the ISG before *Barham*'s turn, while *Malaya* in the rear observed the German fleet in three or four columns before she put her helm over. Whereas Evan-Thomas reported that the enemy battle fleet was not sighted from *Barham* bearing approximately SSE until a few minutes after she steadied on her northerly

---

[17] *OD*, pp. 193 and 206. *Lion*'s times are earlier: 4.50 both for passing – *OD*(M) – and for the 5BS turning – VNE.

[18] *OD*, pp. 193, 199, 202, 206, 217 and Pls. 10a and 17–19.

[19] *MoG 1915* (p. 173) indicates that speed could be as much as halved after turns exceeding 4 points. *Remarks on Handling Ships 1934* (reference courtesy John Roberts) states that speed of the *Queen Elizabeth* class (by then bulged) dropped from 23 to 9.7 knots in a 16 point turn taking 1min 48secs.

[20] Gordon, p. 140.

[21] *Remarks on Handling Ships* (London: HMSO, 1911) pp. 14, 16, 20, 38 and Diagrams 1 and 9, ADM 186/632. E C Tupper and K J Rawson, *Basic Ship Theory* (Oxford: Butterworth Heinemann, 2001) p. 538 for tactical diameter.

course.[22] Even if this were so, *Lion* had already signalled at 4.45 that the enemy battlefleet was in sight. So although, by hoisting the Compass Pendant signal, *Lion* had assumed direct control of the 5BS's turn, Evan-Thomas should have been aware of the consequences if he delayed his turn until the signal was made executive;[23] we shall return in the penultimate chapter to the question of whether the separation between the battlecruisers and battleships was due only to a delay by *Lion*'s signallers in making the signal executive and to Evan-Thomas's over-punctilious adherence to signal convention.

As the 5BS turned in succession, they were vulnerable to a concentration of fire on the turning point: or, to be exact, on the same fixed arc around which each ship normally steamed one after the other. As each ship turned, it became the aiming point but, because the arc remained in the same place, no allowance was needed for the movement of the target along the line of fire.[24] However, determining deflection was more difficult because the target's speed fell throughout the turn and the target course was changing continuously. Probably, a suitable value, determined mainly by spotting, could only have been arrived at after a few ships had made their turns. Notwithstanding the difficulties, British officers expected a concentration on the turn and those in *Malaya* were in no doubt that they had been subjected to one.

I did not like [the turn] being done in succession. When it was time for *Malaya* to turn, the turning point was a very 'hot corner' and the enemy had, of course, concentrated on that point . . . it is doubtful whether we, the last ship of the line, would have got through without a severe hammering if the Captain had not used his initiative and turned the ship early.

Captain Boyle confirmed that: 'Enemy's battle Fleet opened fire on the turn so "Malaya" turned short'.[25] Yet the German accounts stated that, while *Kronprinz* and *Kaiserin* were already firing at the 5BS, the IIIBS did not concentrate on the turn. Campbell goes further by denying that any of the German battleships were then firing at the 5BS, though, as Gordon points out, this statement is contradicted by their *Kriegstagebücher*.[26] For all that, none of the British battleships were hit during the turn itself, while *Malaya* remained undamaged for the time being. But *Barham*, as soon as she steadied on her Northerly course, received a damaging hit at 4.56–58 that, among much else, wrecked her auxiliary wireless office, started a cordite fire in her S2 (Starboard No. 2) 6in casemate and perforated the roof of the forward 6in magazine, though without igniting any charges. A second hit at 5.01 then put her main wireless out of action as well.[27]

[22] *OD*, pp. 193, 199 and 217. *Warspite* (p. 202) stated that the enemy battleships were sighted as the 5BS turned.
[23] Gordon, p. 149.
[24] Thus the enemy bar of the Dumaresq or *EU-Anzeiger* could be set at right angles to the line of fire.
[25] F&H, p. 120. *OD*, p. 217.   [26] Tarrant, p. 101. Campbell, p. 98. Gordon, pp. 141–6.
[27] *OD*, p. 200. Campbell, pp. 126–9.

Table 6.6. *BCF signals 4.52–5.30pm*

Time of despatch	From	To	System	Message	Time of origin
pm, 31 May					
4.52	SO BCF	General	Flags	… 25 knots	
4.55	SO 5BS	5BS	Flags	Observe attentively the Admiral's motions	
5.1	SO BCF	5BS	Flags	Prolong the line by taking station astern	
5.2	SO 3LCS	SO 1LCS	SL	I am keeping up to keep clear of Battle Cruisers	1700
5.5	SO 5BS	5BS	Flags	Engage the Enemy's right from 1 to 4	
5.10	SO BCF	General	Flags	… 24 knots	
5.10	SO 5BS	5BS	Flags	… 25 knots	
5.14	Warspite			Remarks: Hit	
5.20	Warspite			Remarks: Sighted Enemy's battlefleet	
5.22	Tiger	SO 1BCS	Sem.	After 6in magazine flooded, two guns out of action	1725
5.30	SO 5BS	5BS	Flags	Proceed at your utmost speed	

The BCF's chart shows that, meanwhile, Beatty headed N until at 5.00 he turned NNW, the course held until 5.30. However, the turn directions and target bearings in the record from *Lion*'s transmitting station suggest that, as soon as the 5BS had passed on her port side, she made two turns to port totalling just over four points, before returning to about her original course before the turn NNW.[28] If they were made, these turns would certainly have made it easier for the 5BS to haul into line or, as Evan-Thomas intended, to get on *New Zealand*'s starboard quarter; but they are not mentioned in any of the Jutland despatches nor shown on any of the accompanying charts.[29] Between 4.59 and 5.02, *Lion* received three hits, which can only have encouraged Beatty to turn away. NNW was the 'Bearing of Grand Fleet' noted in Beatty's narrative at 4.52 while the same reckoning – based on *Lion*'s position at 4.45 and extrapolating from *Iron Duke*'s last reported position, course and speed at 3.15 – would have given a distance of 67 miles.[30] Thus Beatty's new course took him directly towards Jellicoe's present position. However, Beatty's immediate priority was to lead Hipper and Scheer to Jellicoe without suffering any more major losses; with the Grand Fleet apparently almost 70 miles off, Beatty could assume that he had plenty of time to alter later onto an intercepting course.

The 5BS were the last of the capital ships to reverse course. As *Barham* completed her 17-point turn, Evan-Thomas hoisted 'Observe attentively the Admiral's motions', which enabled him to turn the 5BS in succession without

---

[28] *OD*, Pl. 10. REL gives the turning times as: 16 points as 4.36 (4 min fast on the BCF chart); to port at 4.50–1 and 4.53–4; to starboard at 4.56–7 and to port again at 4.58½.

[29] However, these turns are shown (but without comment in the text) on Corbett's Maps 26–7 and on the later charts with the *GOA* (Tarrant, p. 104). It appears that Harper had seen *Lion*'s TS record.

[30] Campbell, pp. 124–5. VNE. *NSA*, Ch. V, sect. 40 has almost the same figures: bearing N22°W and 66 miles.

signalling delays. At 5.01, Beatty ordered the battleships, as usual by flags alone, to 'Prolong the line by taking station astern', but *Barham* did not respond until 5.06 when she made the first of three two-point turns-away. As *Valiant*'s despatch confirmed:

At 5.12 p.m. 'Valiant' straddled forward and aft, and the whole Fifth Battle Squadron was under heavy fire from the greatly superior forces of the enemy ... At 5.13 p.m., 'Valiant' altered course to port and took up a position on the port quarter of the 'Barham', as the Fifth Battle Squadron was altering course slowly to port to get astern of our Battle Cruisers

At 5.16, *Barham* turned back to starboard; the 5BS then proceeded, with minor course alterations, generally to the NNW.[31] Even though his flagship was being hit when Beatty ordered him to prolong the line, Evan-Thomas had delayed for five minutes before turning to follow the battlecruisers. Hence he missed an opportunity to close the gap to the BCF and to prevent the High Seas Fleet from reducing the range further.

In his despatch, Evan-Thomas stated that, after the turns Northward by the 5BS and the ISG:

'Barham' and 'Valiant' continued to engage the enemy battle-cruisers, while 'Warspite' and 'Malaya' fired at the head of the enemy's battle fleet at a guessed range of 17,000 yards which proved to be about 19,000 yards.[32]

Barham opened fire at 5.02 at a range of 20,400 yards falling to 18,300 yards at 5.10. At 5.05, about the time he eventually turned away, he ordered his ships to 'Engage the Enemy's right from 1 to 4'; this seems to refer to the leading enemy battleships. Yet *Valiant* reopened on the enemy battlecruisers at 5.06, mainly 'at the second from the right, but due to mist and smoke this ship was occasionally obscured and the plainest target had to be fired at'. After her turn N, the visibility from *Warspite* made the ISG 'very bad targets', so she engaged the leading enemy battleship at a range of 17,000 yards. But, after only a few salvos, her target had drawn right aft (probably as she followed *Barham*'s turn-away), and for 'the next half hour fire was intermittent and ineffective on the enemy battle cruisers'. She seems to have sighted the enemy battle fleet again at 5.20; perhaps, as implied by Evan-Thomas's despatch but not confirmed by her own, she then re-engaged the leading battleships. At 5.00, *Malaya*, probably then still on *Warspite*'s port quarter, opened fire on a *König*-class battleship at the guessed range of 17,000 yards. At 5.05, 'Enemy has our range exactly, so hauled out a little [further?] to port' but, from 5.12, 'we were under a very heavy constant fire from at least four ships of the enemy High Seas Fleet'.[33]

---

[31] *OD*, Pl. 10a and p. 206. *Valiant's* despatch noted 'that a very accurate fire was being concentrated on the turning point'.

[32] *OD*, p. 194; Pl. 16 shows ranges of 19,000 yards to both the ISG and the IIIBS.

[33] Gunnery reports for *Barham* and *Valiant* in JMSS 49014, ff. 158 and 160. *OD*, pp. 202, 206–7, 218 and Pl. 18.

Table 6.7. *Grand Fleet signals 4.54–5.15pm*

Time of despatch	From	To	System	Message	Time of origin
pm, 31 May					
4.54	C-in-C	General		Increase speed	
4.58	C-in-C	General		Alter course, leading ships of divisions together, the rest in succession, two points to port. Course NW, utmost speed	
5.05	C-in-C	General		Alter course, leading ships of divisions together, the rest in succession, two points to starboard. Course NNW	
5.15	C-in-C	General		Alter course, leading ships of divisions together, the rest in succession, two points to port [to NW]	

Table 6.8. *ISG signals 4.55–5.13pm*

Time of receipt	From	To	System	Message	Time of origin
pm, 31 May					
4.55	Lützow	ISG	Visual	Course N	
4.57	Lützow	ISG	Visual	Distribution of fire from the right, ship against ship	
5.02	Lützow	ISG	Visual	All battle cruisers, reduce speed	
5.06	Lützow	ISG	Visual	All battle cruisers, increase speed	
5.10	Lützow	ISG	Visual	All battle cruisers, turn together to NbyW	
5.10	AC Scouting Forces	2nd Leader of Torpedo Boats	Visual	Please direct torpedo boats to close to a position on the starboard bow	
5.13	Lützow	ISG	Visual	All battle cruisers, turn together to NNW	

At 4.58, Scheer ordered a turn by divisions to NW and demanded 'Utmost speed'. But on this course only the fore turrets could bear and he turned back to NNW at 5.05. Perhaps to keep all their guns bearing, the four *Königs* of the leading Vth Division continued NNW until they turned briefly away to N at 5.06 (as we shall see, this was about the time that *Onslow* and *Moresby* were attempting a torpedo attack) and then back to NNW at 5.11. At 5.15, Scheer once again ordered a turn to NW but the German chart shows the VIth and Ist Divisions, the latter led by the flagship, turning only

one point to port. After their turn N, the ISG were about seven miles ahead of their battle fleet. They held their course until 5.10 and, after two one-point turns together, also headed NNW.[34]

For the first half-hour or so of the Run to the North, the visibility was considerably worse for the British, as attested by many despatches and accounts from ships large and small. While the sun remained behind clouds, there was no glare but the British ships were silhouetted against the clear Western horizon – though, as von Hase noted, this was not enough to keep the BCF in sight. To the Eastward, the German ships were constantly obscured by smoke and mist, while their outlines and the splashes of falling salvos were difficult to make out against dark cloud – a 'vile background' according to Goldsmith of *Lydiard*. *Barham*'s captain reported that 'any enemy which showed up for long enough to lay on was selected' – which probably explains why hits were received by ships not named as targets.[35] However, the Germans had their own difficulties. Due to powder fumes and smoke, the ISG, some seven miles ahead, could be seen only occasionally from their battle fleet. From the start of this phase, von Hase found that ranges were 'scarcely ever less than 18,000 m [19,600 yards]. I only fired to make quite sure that the enemy were still out of range, and ... contented myself with isolated shots from one turret.'[36]

After their turn N at 4.45, Beatty's three leading battlecruisers began firing somewhat irregularly and without success at the ISG, mostly on beam bearings. *Lion*'s TS record contains a sketch of her target with a profile similar to any of the ISG's three rear ships, although Chatfield described the target as 'the enemy leading ship ("Von Der Tann"?)'; *Lion* fired four salvos at her in 4½ minutes. The hit on *Lion* at 4.59 ignited ready-use cordite at the 4in guns, and the fire could not be extinguished for some time because the fire mains had been punctured. Another hit shortly afterwards wrecked the sick bay and smoke penetrating below gave the impression of a fire in X magazine, which was partly flooded before the mistake was rectified. *Tiger* took a hit in her after funnel, perhaps from a ricochet, and, at this time, she also suffered a fracture in the run-out control valve of A turret's right gun The four hits on the BCF were probably the work of the ISG but some might have been made by the IIIBS.[37]

Just before turning NNW, *Lion* reopened, apparently without changing target, firing seven more salvos in 6½ minutes, the last at 5.04; at 5.08, the TS record noted 'Enemy went away in the mist and smoke'.[38] After 4.46, *Princess Royal* expended three salvos at a three-funnelled light cruiser

---

[34] Tarrant, p. 104 quoting *GOA*, p. 80. Courses from *OD*, German Plan V are similar to those from *GOA*; see Tarrant, pp. 104 and 106. von Hase, p. 166.

[35] *OD*, pp. 134, 194, 199, 202, 206, 216 and 254. F&H, 79, 114, 122 and 285. JMSS 49014, f. 158.

[36] Scheer's despatch, *OD*, p. 592. von Hase, p. 171.

[37] *OD*, p. 144. Campbell, pp. 124–5, who attributes them specifically to *Lützow* and *Seydlitz*.

[38] REL. *OD*, p. 144.

(probably *Regensburg*) and, from 4.51, three more at the 'Right hand, Battle Cruiser steering to the left'. At 4.56, she shifted to the leading battlecruiser and fired four more salvos before ceasing fire at 5.02.40. *Tiger* engaged the third battlecruiser from the left but, as previously, identified her as a *Derfflinger*; eleven salvos were fired between 4.55 and 5.07. After her target appeared to drop out burning, *Tiger* switched to the second battlecruiser from the left for three salvos, the last at 5.09.45. The ranges from these three British battlecruisers had been from 17,000 to 21,000 yards. From *New Zealand*, the range mostly exceeded the maximum of 18,000 yards on her gunsights and she managed to fire only three salvos at the right-hand enemy battlecruiser, the last at 5.00. Thus, by 5.04, three of Beatty's battlecruisers had ceased firing while, before 5.10, all were out of action and had lost sight of the enemy. *Lion*'s turret crews were given permission to get out on the roofs while, at 5.15, *Princess Royal*'s officers noted: 'Lull in the action. People going out to stretch their legs and get a little fresh air'; she was the first to re-engage but not until 5.34.[39] From *Derfflinger*, 'it was not long before they [the BCF] vanished from our view in mist and smoke' and, in confirmation, on the German chart the BCF track ends at 5.15.[40] Thus the 5BS was left unsupported to bear the fire of the ISG and of all the battleships of the High Seas Fleet that could reach them. At 5.10, when out of range, Beatty reduced his speed to 24 knots while Evan-Thomas, perhaps more in hope than expectation, called for 25 knots.

Once the 5BS and BCF had passed each other at 4.53–54, and especially after the 5BS had taken up position on *Lion*'s starboard quarter, the fast battleships became a nearer and more visible target for the German battlefleet as it closed on converging courses. Yet *Markgraf* and *Prinzregent Luitpold* continued to engage the BCF. But at 4.58, *Grosser Kurfürst* transferred her fire to *Valiant* and, by 5.10 if not earlier, *König* was also shooting at the 5BS.[41] When all the ships of the ISG had completed their turns, at 4.57 Hipper engaged the BCF, ordering a distribution of fire from the right. But by five o'clock, *Von der Tann* was supposedly firing at *Malaya* although, not least because after turning short she had hauled out onto *Warspite*'s port quarter, she seems the least likely choice.[42]

Despite their advantage in visibility, the Germans did not escape unharmed for long. The 5BS succeeded in making some early hits on the IIIBS. That on

[39] *OD*, pp. 388, 391–2 and 394. F&H, p. 32. Account of F C Woodhouse (Liddle Collection) transcription at www.dreadnoughtproject.org/tfs/index.php/. Chatfield, p. 145 mentions nothing except 'an occasional exchange of salvos' between 4.50 and meeting the Grand Fleet.

[40] von Hase, p. 172. *OD*, German Plan V.

[41] *GOA*, p. 80 and Gordon, pp. 617–18. The latter rightly concludes that *Markgraf* is unlikely to have continued firing at *Tiger* until 5.25. By 5.15, *König*'s target was probably *Valiant* or *Malaya*.

[42] *GOA*, p. 81. Gordon, pp. 144–5. Campbell (p. 126) credits *Derfflinger* with four hits on *Barham* but von Hase's account (pp. 166 and 172) states that the German battleships engaged the 5BS. However, von Hase also states (p. 167) that he fired eight salvos at *Princess Royal* between 4.45 and 4.50, when other sources indicate that the ISG engaged the 5BS.

Grosser Kurfürst at 5.09 was a short but *Markgraf* was hit on the waterline at 5.10, which caused some flooding, while two more hits, causing only slight damage, may have been made at about this time.[43] The first hits on the ISG were two forward on *Seydlitz* at 5.06 and 5.08; they were followed at 5.10 by a hit on her starboard wing turret, after which the right gun could be elevated only by coupling it to the left.[44] All three hits were probably also made by the 5BS, though it is just possible that *Tiger* scored the second hit. *Lützow* was struck once on the waterline at 5.13, while at 5.25 two hits destroyed both her main and auxiliary wireless installations. She took a further hit at 5.30 between the P4 and P5 casemates but this did little damage. *Derfflinger* was hit at 5.19; fires were started and holes opened up which admitted water to the fore part of the ship. *Moltke* suffered no hits during the Run to the North. Neither did *Von der Tann* but at 5.15 the guns of her port wing turret – the only one still working – jammed and would not run out; since the 'steady course requisite for good shooting was no longer necessary', Captain Zehnker was able to zigzag at will.[45]

The two hits on *Barham* at 4.58 and 5.01 have already been described. She was hit again at 5.08 and 5.10, resulting in more serious destruction of light structures. Thereafter, she escaped further damage, as did *Valiant* throughout the Run to the North. Campbell attributes all four of *Barham*'s hits to *Derfflinger* but, in view of von Hase's rueful comments, this seems unlikely.[46] After Evan-Thomas turned away, the German battleships directed their fire at *Warspite* and especially at *Malaya*; the latter reported:

we were under a very heavy constant fire from at least four ships of the High Seas Fleet. Only flashes were visible, and six salvos were falling around the ship each minute, and at one time, counting some that were probably meant for 'Warspite' *nine* salvos fell in rapid succession.

A turret officer recalled:

I had counted soon after the turn the number of enemy ships firing at us, and the 9th ship was the rearmost that I thought I saw open fire. I believe this was at times increased by the German battle cruisers joining in against us, although I cannot say that I noticed them myself.[47]

Despite, or perhaps even because of, being the target for so many German ships, *Malaya* did not receive her first hit until 5.20 while five minutes later a

---

[43] Campbell, pp. 144–5. *GOA*, p. 82.

[44] Campbell, pp. 138–9. Staff, *World War One*, pp. 175–8 (hits 1, 2 and 11). *GOA*, p. 82, mainly based on Captain Egidy's despatch (Staff, *World War One*, pp. 184–6), describes these three hits but also four subsequent hits in this phase that Campbell (pp. 232–4 and 265) and the German damage report (hits 4, 16, 21 and 23) place later in the battle (see Chapter 8).

[45] Campbell, pp. 134–43. *GOA*, p. 82, though it is unlikely that the 5.13 waterline hit on *Lützow* put her wireless out of action.

[46] *OD*, p. 200. Campbell, pp. 126 and 129–30.   [47] *OD*, p. 218. F&H, p. 120.

splinter cutting the steam pipe to the starboard siren made communication to the top impossible for several minutes. At 5.27, a shell struck the roof of X turret; it burst outside and, although the roof was dished inwards and the rangefinder broken, the turret remained in action. Shortly thereafter, the desperate expedient would have been adopted of firing the starboard 6in guns short to throw up a screen of splashes, had not the whole battery been put out of action at 5.30. One of two shells hitting close together struck near the S3 gun. Cordite in ready-use and carrying cases was ignited by fragments, the fire spreading rapidly through the battery with terrible consequences for the gun crews. Flash passed down the ammunition hoists to the 6in shell room. But for prompt action preventing the ignition of more cordite charges, fire would have spread through open scuttles to the 6in magazine; the ship might then have been lost as this and then the adjacent forward 15in magazine exploded. Up to 5.37, *Malaya* probably received three more hits, those striking under water caused flooding and a leakage of fuel oil; the ship took on a list to starboard of 4° but fortunately contamination of oil fuel by sea water did not slow her down until it caused a temporary reduction of boiler output at about six o'clock.[48]

Warspite received fewer hits though the exact number is debatable. Campbell allows only two for the Run to the North but, as Gordon points out, this is strongly belied by the vivid account of the damage she received by the ship's Executive Officer, Commander Humphrey Walwyn.[49] Unfortunately, although he describes his experiences in what seems to be chronological order, he gives no times and the events of the Run to the North are followed without a break by those that came later, as the Grand Fleet was deploying. Of Campbell's two hits, the first does not seem to correspond with any described by Walwyn; the second, in the fore funnel, might have been the same as the one that put Walwyn in 'a deuce of a funk', though he remembered it as going through the after funnel. Walwyn then mentions an earlier hit on the waterline abreast the capstan engine; while this does not match anything in Campbell, it seems to be the same as that recorded by Surgeon Gordon Ellis as *Warspite*'s first hit. Of Walwyn's next two hits, the first, on the boy's mess deck, is also described by Ellis as causing the first casualty during the Run to the North.[50] Since Walwyn's next three hits came from the port side, it appears that they can only have been made later. Thus it seems that his ship received at least five hits during the Run to the North. Even though *Warspite* and *Malaya* had survived with their main armament, buoyancy and machinery largely intact, they had

---

[48] *OD*, pp. 217–18. Liddle, pp. 109–10 with facsimile of notes by Asst. Paymaster Lawder. Campbell, pp. 130–3. F&H, pp. 120–1 for temporary jam of B turret's loading cage. S&H, pp. 154–61 for eyewitness accounts, including of the rapidly fatal effects of cordite burns.

[49] Campbell, p. 130. Gordon, p. 413. F&H, pp. 142–8.

[50] S&H, pp. 154 and 160. Campbell, pp. 173 and 178; the last two match Campbell's later hits three and thirteen in effect.

been in great danger; no wonder that, at 5.30, Evan-Thomas gave the order permitting each of his battleships to 'Proceed at your utmost speed'.

Light cruisers and destroyers

Before we follow the battleships and battlecruisers in the second part of the Run to the North, we should first locate the opposing light forces as they reformed around their capital ships. At 4.12, the 3LCS and the 1LCS had turned SE on a

Table 6.9. *1/3LCS signals 4.12–5.30pm*

Time of despatch	From	To	System	Message	Time of origin
pm, 31 May					
4.12	SO 3LCS	SO 1LCS	SL	What are you going to steer? Reply: I am steering SE. Am altering to SSE to go between the Enemy's fleet	
4.19	SO 1LCS	SO3LCS	SL	Am I in your way? My course SSE. Will you steer the same?	
4.25	SO 3LCS	3LCS	Flags	Alter course in succession to SSE	
4.30	SO 3LCS	Galatea	SL	It seems they are going through Horns Reef and not Skager-rack. If all Light Cruisers got together I think we could deal with Northern Squadron. I make them 16000	1630
4.34	SO 3LCS	3LCS	Flags	Form single line-ahead in sequence of fleet numbers. Ships in column open order	
4.40	SO 3LCS	SO 1LCS	SL	When your squadron have [*sic*] passed me, I will edge over	1647
4.41	SO 3LCS	3LCS	Flags	Admiral intends to proceed at 22 knots	
4.52	SO 3LCS	SO 1LCS	SL	Look out for Enemy battlefleet steering N	1630
4.56	SO 3BCS	SO BCF	W/T	What is your position, course and speed?	1655
5.00	Lion			Remarks: Sighted 1 and 3LCS on starboard bow	
5.02	SO 3LCS	SO 1LCS	SL	I am keeping up to keep clear of Battle Cruisers	1700
5.12	SO 3LCS	SO 1LCS	SL	Can you see what Enemy's Cruiser are doing astern of us? Reply: No. I can see nothing of them	
5.12	SO 3LCS	3LCS	Flags	Alter course in succession to NWbyN	
5.20	SO 3LCS	3LCS	Flags	Alter course in succession to NNW	
5.21	SO 3LCS	Gloucester	SL	Can you see Enemy Cruisers right astern?	1720
				Reply: Yes, I think they are firing at us, but are 1,000 yards short	
5.30	SO 1LCS	1LCS	Flags	Ships to be in open order	

parallel course to the IISG. After some hesitant discussion by searchlight between the two commanders,[51] they steered SSE with the apparent intention of cutting between the IISG and Hipper's battlecruisers. At 4.30, when the enemy light cruisers were still some 16,000 yards off, Napier suggested, as well he might have, that the two British squadrons – eight light cruisers – could deal with the isolated IISG. He claimed in his despatch that: 'we then endeavoured (at 4.30 p.m.) with the First Light Cruiser Squadron to engage the four enemy light cruisers which appeared to be detached to the northward of the enemy's main body'. But their endeavour appears to have been abandoned shortly after *Southampton*'s wireless report of the enemy fleet had been received.[52] Napier's 4.56 signal suggests that, even then, he could not see Beatty's battlecruisers. But at 5.00, the two light cruiser squadrons were sighted on *Lion*'s starboard bow, when they hauled round to starboard from SSE to NW. Although they took station on Beatty's starboard (engaged) bow, Napier's signal at 5.02 indicates that they were not sufficiently far ahead to act as an effective scouting force. They probably did not sight the ISG – from *Galatea* on the starboard beam at 16,000 yards – until after they had turned Northwards at about 5.30.[53] This was not a good position for a torpedo attack, so, even if Beatty did order such an attack at some time during the Run to the North, none was made.[54]

Table 6.10. *BCF destroyer signals 4.12–5.20pm*

Time of despatch	From	To	System	Message	Time of origin
pm, 31 May					
4.12	Onslow	Engadine	Sem.	Can you dispense with my services? If so, I will join 5th B.S. Reply: Yes, certainly	
4.43	SO BCF	Destroyers	Flags	Recall	
4.50	SO BCF	Destroyers	Flags	Close and take station ahead	
4.55	SO BCF	Captains 1 and 13DF via Princess Royal	W/T	Destroyers close nearer Admiral (Received by Champion 5.18)	1650
5.20	SO BCF	Destroyers	Flags	Form a submarine screen	

[51] For Napier's lack of initiative, see Andrew Lambert, 'Sir Trevylyan Napier', *ODNB* and *FDSF III*, p. 44.

[52] *OD*, p. 185. F&H, p. 106. Evidently, *Wiesbaden* had joined up with *Frankfurt, Pillau* and *Elbing*.

[53] *OD*, Pl. 15 and pp. 134 and 173. The 'enemy cruisers' seen right astern of the 3LCS at 5.12 were, if not British, perhaps a unit of the HSF.

[54] An anonymous report from *Galatea* (F&H, p. 107) mentions an order from *Lion* (not in *OD*(M)) for a torpedo attack 'shortly after 5.0 p.m.' but this is probably a confusion with the later order made at 5.47, which could not be carried through (*OD*, p. 173).

Once released by *Engadine* from their escort duties, *Onslow* (Lieutenant-Commander Jack Tovey, the future Admiral of the Fleet) and *Moresby* of the 13DF proceeded at 30 knots to close the 5BS. But, having sighted both battle-cruiser forces steering approximately NNE, Tovey turned about from SSE onto the same course, initially taking station about three miles on *Lion*'s engaged bow. He soon found that his distance from the BCF was opening rapidly and that he was closing the ISG. Shortly after reaching a promising position for beginning a torpedo attack, about five points on the engaged bow at a range of 18,000 yards, four enemy light cruisers appeared and opened a heavy and accurate fire; they must have been the IISG moving ahead on Hipper's disengaged side. Their good shooting forced the two British destroyers at 5.05 to separate, lest they present a double target, and to retire. *Onslow* did not get within torpedo range and returned to a station astern of the 1LCS on *Lion*'s engaged bow. *Moresby*, under the probably wrong impression that she was attacking enemy dreadnoughts, pressed on. She got within 6,000–8,000 yards of the leading ship before firing a single long-range torpedo at the third in line; eight minutes later, her commanding officer 'observed an upheaval due to a Torpedo', but it was not a hit. *Moresby* too then withdrew before rejoining *Champion*.[55] She and *Onslow* were probably the two destroyers seen from *Galatea* 'zigzagging like a couple of snipe . . . a tornado of shells falling all round them'.[56]

The charts with Scheer's despatch show that all the German light forces, led by the IISG, remained on the disengaged sides of his battlecruisers and battleships throughout the Run to the North. Positioned between the IISG and ISG, the IITF was followed by *Regensburg* with the VI and IX TFs. *Rostock*, the IIITF and the IHF were to the East of the Vth Division of battleships, while the VTF and VIITF were similarly positioned relative to the IIIrd Division of predreadnoughts. In the wake of the rear IVth Division, the elderly cruisers of the IVSG, *Frauenlob* especially, must have been steaming flat out to keep station.[57]

Except for *Onslow*, the British destroyers also took up positions on the disengaged side of their capital ships. As soon as the BCF had turned 16 points, *Lion* made the destroyer recall signal, though few can have seen the flag hoist.[58] It was soon followed by flag and wireless signals ordering the destroyers to close and take station ahead, though the W/T order was not received in *Champion* until 5.18. At 4.42, *Fearless* and the 1DF were still in line-ahead astern of the 5BS. On sighting the battlecruisers coming North, they turned 16 points together – thus leaving *Fearless* in the rear – perhaps taking station on *Lion*'s disengaged bow before dropping back onto beam bearings. At 5.20,

---

[55] *OD*, pp. 135 and 236–9 and German Plans V and VI. Tarrant, p. 103.
[56] F&H, pp. 106–7 though the report assumes the two destroyers had attacked with Bingham in *Nestor*.
[57] *OD*, German Chart VI, diagram 2.
[58] It was mentioned in only four destroyer despatches: *OD*, pp. 241, 257, 259 and 262.

Beatty ordered all his destroyers to form a submarine screen but *Fearless*, though steaming at full speed, continued to fall astern, while most of the 1DF destroyers (of the 27-knot *Acheron* class) were 'unable to get into position as "Lion" was steaming 24 knots'.[59] After their attacks on the ISG, the surviving destroyers of the 13DF and 9DF rejoined *Champion*, though their leader had herself to return from the forward position in which she had sighted the High Seas Fleet at 4.30; thus she may not have taken in Beatty's flag signals made at 4.43 and 4.50. Some of the despatches from her destroyers give their position as in line astern some two to four miles on the port quarter of the battlecruisers and the port beam of the 5BS. However, none mention either the flag signal at 5.20 to form a submarine screen or any forward movement to that effect. On the contrary, the three *L*-class boats that had already rejoined were unable to keep up. The fourth boat, *Laurel*, picked up survivors from *Queen Mary* and then steered to rejoin the 9DF. *En route*, she observed a light cruiser, probably of the 2LCS, under fire and endeavoured to lay a covering smoke screen but her effort went unacknowledged in the light cruisers' despatches.[60]

Table 6.11. *Tyrwhitt's signals 4.50am–5.35pm*

Time of despatch	From	To	System	Message	Time of origin
am, 31 May					
4.50	Commodore T	Admiralty	L/T	Urgent. No orders have been received for Harwich force yet. Reply: Orders are to remain at one hour's notice ...	0450
pm, 31 May					
4.45	Commodore T	Admiralty	L/T	314. Have you any instructions?	1645
5.00	SO 3BS	Admiralty	W/T	Urgent. I am proceeding to Black Deep light vessel	1700
5.15	Admiralty	Commodore T	L/T	Your 314. Complete with fuel. You may have to relieve Light Cruisers and Destroyers in B. C.F. later	1715
5.15	Commodore T	Admiralty	L/T	315. Priority. Urgent. I am proceeding to sea	1710
5.35	Admiralty	Commodore T	W/T	Your 315. Return at once and await orders	1725

---

[59] *OD*, pp. 242, 246–7 and 249–52. F&H, p. 256.
[60] *OD*, pp. 234, 235, 241, 254–7 and 259–61.

As the BCF ran North, Commodore (T) Reginald Tyrwhitt of the Harwich Force was still in harbour. At 4.50am, after Tyrwhitt's reminder that he was still waiting for further instructions, the Admiralty had confirmed their previous order that his ships should remain at an hour's notice; at that time, despite the signals intelligence indicating that the Germans intended to leave towards Horns Reef, nothing definite had been received to alleviate Oliver's fears of a simultaneous movement towards the Dover Straits. Almost 12 hours later, the Harwich Force had begun to intercept W/T signals indicating that an action had commenced; at 4.45pm, Tyrwhitt again telegraphed the Admiralty pleading for instructions. Then, at 5.00, Admiral Bradford informed the Admiralty by wireless that he was moving the 3BS and its destroyers to an anchorage closer to Harwich. At 5.10, having received no reply from the Admiralty, Tyrwhitt originated a final signal announcing that he was proceeding to sea; presumably this was transmitted before the land-telegraph link to *Carysfort* (wearing his Broad Pendant) had been disconnected, thereby allowing him to turn a telegraphic blind eye to the unwelcome instructions from the Admiralty timed at 5.15. But Horns Reef was some 330 miles from Harwich; at an economical speed of 20 knots, it could not have been reached until about ten o'clock the next morning. Thus the Harwich Force had already been held back too long to intervene that day.[61] At 5.35, Tyrwhitt was peremptorily ordered to 'Return at once and await orders'; having done so by 6.30, he would have to wait until early the following morning before he was permitted to leave harbour again.

The Grand Fleet

After increasing speed to 20 knots at 3.59, the Grand Fleet continued SEbyS while the armoured cruiser line attempted to increase their distance ahead to 16 miles.[62] After Beatty's signal at 3.55, Jellicoe heard nothing more apart from Evan-Thomas's brief confirmation that he was engaging the enemy. The C-in-C only became better informed once Goodenough in *Southampton* had sighted the High Seas Fleet. At 4.38, 4.48 and 5.00, he sent detailed wireless reports each giving his estimated position, enemy course (N in all three reports) and bearing and, in the last signal, the enemy's distance from him. Beatty's own report was relayed through *Princess Royal* at 4.45. According to the *Official Despatches*, this signal as transmitted gave his position and the enemy bearing SSE: but it was received in *Iron Duke* without the position, with a wrong enemy course of SE and an exaggerated number of enemy battleships. Jellicoe confirmed this in 1922, though not, it seems, in his earlier

---

[61] *OD*, p. 341. James, p. 154. Corbett, Map 16 and pp. 349 and 447. *Monthly Return, May 1916*, p. 5, ADM 186/23. *JP II*, p. 26.
[62] *OD*, p. 272.

Table 6.12. *British signals 3.10–5.04pm*

Time of despatch	From	To	System	Message	Time of origin
pm, 31 May					
3.10	C-in-C	Cruisers	SL	Take up cruising disposition No. 1. Centre of screen 16 miles from B.F. Speed of advance 18 knots. Assume complete readiness for action	
4.17	C-in-C	SO 5BS	W/T	Are you in company with SO BCF?	1615
				Reply: Yes, I am engaging enemy	1630
4.30	Southampton	C-in-C SO BCF	W/T	Urgent. One Enemy Cruiser bearing SE, steering NE. (My position 56°38 N, 6°07E)	1630
4.38	Southampton	C-in-C SO BCF	W/T	Urgent. Priority. Have sighted Enemy battlefleet bearing approximately SE, course of Enemy N. My position 56°34 N, 6°20E	1638
4.40	SO 1CS	1CS	SL	Am steering SE to close Minotaur	1635
4.43	Duke of Edinburgh	Black Prince	SL	Am steering SE to close Defence	1640
4.45	SO BCF	C-in-C via Princess Royal	W/T	Urgent. Priority. Have sighted Enemy's battlefleet bearing SE. My position 56° 36 N, 6°4E.	1645
				(Received by C-in-C as 26–30 battleships, probably hostile bearing SSE, steering SE)	
4.47	C-in-C	General	Sem.	Enemy's battlefleet is coming North	1645
4.48	Southampton	SO BCF C-in-C	W/T	Urgent. Priority. Course of Enemy's battlefleet N, single line ahead. Composition of van Kaiser class. Bearing of centre E. Destroyers on both wings and ahead. Enemy's Battle Cruisers joining battlefleet from Northward. My position 56°29 N, 6°14E	1646
4.51	C-in-C	Admiralty	W/T	Urgent. Fleet action is imminent	1650
5.00	Admiralty	C-in-C	W/T	At 4.9 Enemy battlefleet 56°27 N, 6° 18E, course NW, 15 knots	1700
5.00	Southampton	C-in-C	W/T	Enemy's battlefleet is steering N, bearing from me E, 10–11 miles distant. Position 56°33 N, 6°00E	1700
5.04	C-in-C	Attached cruisers	Flags	Take up station for the approach	

accounts. However, when writing the *Naval Staff Appreciation*, the Dewar brothers were able to examine individual ships' signal logs. They declared that *Iron Duke* did receive *Lion*'s position but also the enemy's bearing (SSE), course (SE) and number (26–30), and the signal was also recorded in this form by *Shannon*.[63] Whatever version of this signal eventually reached Jellicoe, it did not change his appreciation of the situation; probably before he read it, he had signalled that the enemy was coming North and to the Admiralty that a fleet action was imminent.

How soon did Jellicoe expect to meet Scheer? In his unpublished appendix for *The Grand Fleet*, he noted that *Southampton*'s reports between 4.30 and 5.00 implied that she had been steaming at speeds between 35 and more than 60 knots. Nonetheless, the last of these signals contained the important additional information that the enemy fleet bore E from *Southampton* at a distance of 10–11 miles. This was supplemented by the Admiralty's signal, also timed at 5.00, which gave a speed for the German battlefleet, until then unknown, of 15 knots. This report also gave an enemy position and course at 4.09 but, since the position was only seven miles from that of *Southampton* at 4.38, this additional information was disregarded.[64] Nonetheless using a mean of *Southampton*'s individually suspect positions and the enemy speed of 15 knots and course N, *Iron Duke*'s navigators predicted that by six o'clock the High Seas Fleet would be 30 miles right ahead, and at 6.14, 19½ miles on practically the same bearing.[65] Jellicoe's despatch indicates that, just after 5 o'clock, he supposed that his scouting line of armoured cruisers were 16 miles ahead and spread 8 miles apart. Their line was formed as in Table 4.7, with *Warrior* 5 cables (1,000 yards) astern of *Defence* and *Hampshire* as linking ship about 9,000 yards astern of the two flagships. Jellicoe also remarked on the poor visibility to the Eastward, while the cruisers' reports give visibilities of three to six miles at about 5.30.[66] Thus he probably expected that his scouting line would sight the enemy ahead at 6.14 or a little earlier. As he wrote in *The Grand Fleet*:

The 'plot' ... showed that we of the Battle Fleet, might meet the High Seas Fleet approximately ahead and that the cruiser line ahead of the Battle Fleet would sight the enemy nearly ahead of the centre.[67]

The enemy would have been too distant for an immediate deployment but, if they held their supposed course N, Jellicoe could wheel his columns to port using the Compass Pendant; this would keep the High Seas Fleet ahead as the range closed and permit a later rapid deployment by 9 Pendant. But for the time

---

[63] *JP II*, p. 422. *NSA*, Ch. VI, par. 40. *AN*, p. 104. '*Shannon* ... record of W/T traffic' in 'Second Cruiser Squadron War Records 1915–1918, Vol. I', ADM 137/2142.

[64] *JP II*, pp. 422–3. Calculation confirms that the High Seas Fleet's reported position at 4.09 was 7 miles from *Southampton*'s at 4.38 (though bearing SW) and even closer – 3 miles SEbyS – to *Southampton*'s at 4.46.

[65] *JP II*, p. 423. Jellicoe's 'General Remarks', *AN*, pp. 108–9. Similar distances and bearing are obtained by plotting the supposed movement of the High Seas Fleet on *Iron Duke*'s track chart (*OD*, Pl. 6a).

[66] *OD*, pp. 12, 15, 270, 274, 280 and 286–7.   [67] *GF*, p. 217.

being Jellicoe preferred to wait on events while holding his course SEbyS and pressing on at 20 knots.

Lion's report of 4.45 placed her about nine miles NNW of *Southampton*'s position at 4.46. Thus, if it was received correctly in *Iron Duke*, it could have warned that the High Seas Fleet might be further to the North and West than was suggested solely by *Southampton*'s reports. Goodenough, busy dodging enemy salvos, did not report again until 5.40, while Beatty, even though under no pressure after 5.12, did not see fit to keep Jellicoe informed. Thus the C-in-C did not know that, after 5 o'clock, both the British and German forces were steering NNW or even NW, nor that both the BCF and 5BS were making 24 knots with at least the van of the German battlefleet keeping pace. Furthermore Jellicoe may well have assumed that the 2LCS was in its usual position in the cruiser screen ahead of the battlecruisers, whereas it was actually bringing up the rear. All these factors meant that contact would actually be made earlier than could have been predicted in *Iron Duke*. Only one factor, also unknown to Jellicoe, might have delayed contact. His armoured cruisers never increased their distance ahead beyond 12 miles and as the fleets approached each other, it was probably no more than 10 miles.[68] In accordance with *GFBOs*, they did initially open out to a separation of eight miles. But, in the deteriorating visibility, visual contact became more difficult; at 4.40, Arbuthnot in *Defence* altered course inwards by one point to SE to close Heath in *Minotaur* and, within a few minutes, *Duke of Edinburgh* and (probably) *Black Prince* made similar turns. An hour later, the separation between the cruisers in the starboard half of the screen had been reduced to about six miles, the limit of visibility between them.[69] Thus these ships remained on the same bearings from *Iron Duke* that were implicit in Jellicoe's cruising disposition order, but they were closer than expected; for example, *Black Prince* bore SSW but at 18 rather than 26 miles from the flagship.

Completing the Run North

At a quarter past five, Beatty's battlecruisers were steering NNW, out of action, while the 5BS, soon to turn onto similar courses, was about to be subjected to the undivided fire of the ISG and the *Königs* of the Vth Division. At 5.16, Jellicoe informed Beatty by wireless of *Iron Duke*'s position, course and speed. The position was actually that for 5.00[70] but, since this was not indicated in the

[68] *OD*, p. 272 and Pl. 26a (though Pl. 11a places the cruisers 16 miles ahead). F&H, p. 162.
[69] *OD*, pp. 285–6 and Pl. 11a. To close *Defence*, *Duke of Edinburgh* would have needed to turn inwards by two points (rather than the one point signalled), and *Black Prince* by three points.
[70] *OD*, p. 12 and Pl. 6a; see also *GF*, p. 213. Unlike *OD*(M), both accounts give Lat. 57°24′ E.

Table 6.13. *British signals 5.16–5.40pm*

Time of despatch	From	To	System	Message	Time of origin
pm, 31 May					
5.16	C-in-C	SO BCF	W/T	My position 57°25 N, 5°12E, steering SEbyS, speed 20 knots	1713
5.22	Tiger	SO 1BCS	Sem.	After 6-inch magazine flooded, two guns out of action	1725
5.25	SO BCF	General	Flags	Prepare to renew the action	
5.30	SO 5BS	5BS	Flags	Proceed at your utmost speed	
5.30	Falmouth			Remarks: Sighted Cruisers port bow	
5.35	SO BCF	General	SL	Alter course in succession to NNE	
5.40	SO BCF	General	Flags	Open fire and engage the Enemy	

signal, Beatty's navigators had to assume that it was for 5.13, the signal's time-of-origin; thus *Iron Duke* was actually 4.3nm further SEbyS than they thought.[71] Their plot would have shown that, at 5.13, *Iron Duke* was 44nm about NNW from *Lion*,[72] a bearing between the flagships that had hardly changed since 4.52. At 5.25, Beatty made a general signal by flags to 'Prepare to renew the action', further confirmation that the battlecruisers were not then engaging the enemy. The 5BS, under particularly heavy fire, hardly needed such urging and Beatty knew that they were hotly engaged since his own narrative noted, again for 5.25: '5BS still firing hard'. The actual turn in succession to NNE was signalled by searchlight, presumably so that the light cruisers and flotillas could conform. The turn itself was made some time between 5.27 and 5.35, it being shown on the BCF chart at 5.30.[73]

Both Beatty's despatch and narrative noted for 5.35: 'C-in-C. N.16 W',[74] as would have been predicted by *Lion*'s putative plot. This also reveals a second reason for the turn NNE. If, using the information available to Beatty just after the turn, the courses of the two flagships are projected further ahead, they show *Lion* at 6.00 cutting across *Iron Duke*'s bows 14 miles directly ahead. If the battlefleet was then still in its cruising disposition, this point would have been close to the centre of the line of armoured cruisers, so Beatty could also have

---

[71] From her reported positions at 3.15 and (supposedly) 5.13, *Iron Duke* appeared to have advanced at an average speed of 20 knots, so *Lion*'s staff would have had no reason to suspect the latter time. *Iron Duke*'s track chart (*OD*, Pl. 6a) indicates that her reported 3.15 position was out by about 6 miles in a direction NWbyW and that her speed up to 4.00 was no more than 19 knots.

[72] This assumes that *Lion*'s courses since 4.45 were as shown on *OD*, Pl. 10.

[73] VNE. *OD*, Pl. 10 and pp. 135 and 148.   [74] *OD*, p. 135. VNE.

anticipated that they would have already sighted him, perhaps as early as 5.40. We can only speculate about what he would have done next. But, with the Grand Fleet 14 miles to port and the High Seas Fleet probably over seven miles to starboard (see gun ranges below), he would have had space and time to continue across the heads of the British columns; this would have allowed him to reach a position from which he could haul in ahead of the 2BS when, as Jellicoe wished to do, the fleet deployed on the port column. At the same time, Beatty would also be leading the enemy ships, without their sighting the Grand Fleet, into a favourable position for a British deployment to port in a NE'ly direction.

Table 6.14. *German signals 5.13–6.00pm*

Time of receipt	From	To	System	Message	Time of origin
pm, 31 May					
5.13	Lützow	ISG	Visual	All battle cruisers, turn together to NNW	
5.15	C-in-C	General		Alter course, leading ships of divisions together, the rest in succession, 2 points to port [to NW]	
5.17	Lützow	ISG	Visual	All battle cruisers, reduce speed	
5.19	C-in-C	Lützow		AC, Scouting Forces: Take up the chase	1721
5.23	Lützow	ISG	Visual	All battle cruisers, increase speed	
5.25	C-in-C	General		Increase speed	
5.26	Lützow	ISG	Visual	All battle cruisers, turn together to NW	
5.30	F. der Grosse	General	Visual	Alter course, leading ships of divisions together, the rest in succession, 2 points to starboard [to NNW]	
5.39	Lützow	ISG	Visual	All battle cruisers, follow in the wake of the leading ship	
5.40	Lützow	Moltke	Visual	Transfer fire of heavy guns to battleships	
5.44	Lützow	ISG	Visual	All battle cruisers, turn together to NNE	
5.44	C-in-C	General		Follow leading ship. Alter course. Leading ships of divisions together; the rest in succession to N	
5.50	Lützow	ISG	Visual	All battle cruisers, turn together to N	
5.51	C-in-C	General		Reduce speed	
5.53	Lützow	ISG	Visual	All battle cruisers, follow in the wake of the leading ship	
5.55	Lützow	ISG	Visual	All battle cruisers, turn together to E	
5.55	C-in-C	General		Increase speed	
6.00	Frankfurt	AC Scouting Forces		Am under fire from enemy battleships	

By 5.17, both the ISG and German battleships had turned further to port in order to keep the 5BS within range, though Hipper then reduced speed, perhaps to lessen his separation from the battlefleet. This may have added to the concerns expressed in Scheer's despatch.

As at [5.20] the fire of the I Scouting Group and of the ships of the V Division seemed to slacken, I was under the impression that the enemy was succeeding in escaping, and therefore issued an order to the Senior Officer of Scouting Forces, and therefore the permission to all vessels, for the 'general chase'.[75]

However, his signal was addressed only to Hipper and ordered him to 'Take up the chase', which Hipper could well have read as a public rebuke; Scheer's later claim that his order applied to all ships may have been an attempt to withdraw the criticism. As ordered, at 5.23 Hipper increased speed and at 5.26 he turned together NW, at about the same time that *Lützow* lost all her W/T communications. With Beatty turning NNE then or shortly afterwards, the opposing battlecruisers were soon on quite sharply converging courses, though this was probably not immediately apparent to either side. By this time, the visibility was becoming as bad for the Germans as it had been for the British. As an officer in *Nottingham* remarked:

At times the sun would come out for a few minutes and light up the Hun out of the mist, and also dazzle him.

By 5.40, the visibility from the ISG made it difficult to distinguish the enemy ships while, for all the German ships, 'the setting sun [was] making it more and more difficult and finally practically impossible to range, and to spot'.[76] The German chart also suggests that, on their NW'ly course, the after turrets of the battleships could not bear, a disadvantage that would be made worse by British turns to starboard across their bows. At 5.30, Scheer turned away two points to NNW, though the ISG held its course until 5.39 before the battlecruisers turned together into line-ahead steering N.[77] By then, Hipper was coming under fire from the BCF but, without wireless, he was unable to inform Scheer.

At 5.33, enemy ships were glimpsed from *Lion* but, shortly after 5.34, *Princess Royal* was first to reopen fire, though she fired only two more salvos (at 14,000 and 15,300 yards) in the next ten minutes. *Lion*'s first salvo at 5.39½ was at 10,000 yards on a bearing of G107, though only her target's wake could be made out; five more salvos followed by 5.44, during which some salvos, thought to be from *Princess Royal*, were seen falling right and short. When *Lion*'s seventh salvo at 14,500 yards was spotted as a straddle, five more rapid

---

[75] Scheer's despatch, *OD*, p. 592.
[76] F&H, p. 77. von Hase, p. 177. Scheer, despatch, *OD*, p. 593.
[77] *OD*, German Plan V; Hipper's 5.39 signal ordering the ISG to follow in his wake did not specify a course, but the turn N by *Lützow* led them into line-ahead.

salvos were fired at half-minute intervals.[78] Both Captain Chatfield and the gunnery control officer claimed that their target was a *König*-class battleship but *Lützow* was hit at 5.45, probably by their rapid fire.[79] *Tiger* selected a target bearing G105 described as '3rd ship from the left, apparently "Seydlitz" '; her gunnery record contains seventeen ranges averaging 14,700 yards between 5.46 and 6.05. *New Zealand* fired intermittently at the battlecruiser second from the left between 5.46 and 5.58; initially her estimated range was 18,000 yards and bearing G76 but, by the time her target was nearly lost in the smoke and mist, the range had fallen to 14,300 yards.[80] Although only *Lützow* was hit, the volume of fire from Beatty's battlecruisers probably helped to push the ISG, who could not reply, further to the Eastward. While the sources are contradictory, German charts show them steering NE in line-ahead by about 5.50.[81]

Evan-Thomas claimed that, after he called for 'Utmost speed', 'course was altered a little to starboard to support the battlecruisers'. However, *Barham*'s chart shows no significant change of course until 5.41, by which time *Malaya* was no longer being hit. *Barham* then led the 5BS, with some small course alterations, generally NNE'ward, while the BCF turned a point to port to NbyE at 5.40 and then two points to starboard to NEbyN at 5.50.[82] Throughout, the 5BS continued in action, most effectively with the ISG. At 5.35, *Valiant* observed them 'in port quarter line bearing 135° Green'. At 5.40, she was 'engaging about fourth ship from the right, being the only ship that was sufficiently visible to fire at' but by 5.53 the light was much improved. Thus it is likely that *Valiant* contributed to the hits made at 5.55. *Derfflinger* was hit once, probably twice, near the bows; by the end of the battle, over 2,000 tons of water had entered through the holes that had been opened up forward.[83] Campbell identifies two further hits on *Seydlitz* at about 5.55 and an additional hit made at an unknown time during the Run to the North.[84] At 5.57, she had a fire under her forecastle and by 6.08 she was slowly taking up a list to starboard. Meanwhile, the German Vth Division, especially the leading *König* and *Grosser Kurfürst*, had drawn ahead. By 5.49, the intense fire from *Warspite* and *Malaya* (which could no longer be seen) forced Rear-Admiral Behncke in *König*, then some three miles ahead of *Friedrich der Grosse*, to turn away NNE

---

[78] REL. *OD*, p. 388. F&H, p. 115.

[79] *OD*, p. 144. F&H, p. 144. Campbell, p. 135 (though his crediting of the hit to *Princess Royal* is unlikely). *König* had a midships turret, smaller funnels and differently-sited boat derricks but these differences from *Lützow* could have been overlooked in bad visibility: *cf.* Gröner I, pp. 27 and 56.

[80] *OD*, pp. 156, 160, 392 and 394–5.

[81] *OD*, German Plans V and VI Dia. 3 and Tarrant, p. 108. Hipper's 5.53 signal probably formed the ISG into line astern of *Lützow* when she turned NE.

[82] *OD*, p. 194 and Pls. 10 and 10a.   [83] *OD*, p. 207. Campbell, pp. 135–7.

[84] Campbell, pp. 139–42. However, no times are given for these hits (3, 5 and 9) in the German damage report (Staff, *World War One*, pp. 176–8). This report lists a total of twenty-three heavy hits on *Seydlitz* so a total of six during the Run to the North is a reasonable estimate.

and reduce speed to 18 knots. Scheer had already ordered a turn N at 5.44 and that the fleet should follow in *König*'s wake; at 5.51 he also reduced speed, to 15 knots, to enable his divisions to close up as they formed single line-ahead.[85] *König* was hit near the bows at 6.03, apparently by a large fragment from a short.[86]

At 5.30 or 5.33, *Falmouth* sighted 'two or three cruisers approaching from the NW'. They must have been *Black Prince* and *Duke of Edinburgh*, though the latter did not sight the light cruisers (which she identified as the 2LCS) until 5.40. At 5.36, *Falmouth* informed *Black Prince* by searchlight of 'Battle Cruisers engaged to the SSW of me'; since the light cruiser had probably just turned NNE, the signal probably referred to the BCF. While Napier ought to have reported his sighting to Beatty as well, there is no record of such a signal. Indeed, Beatty's turn to NbyE at 5.40, towards the Grand Fleet, suggests that he was then not aware of their close proximity. His despatch states only that:

At 5.50 p.m. British Cruisers were sighted on the Port Bow, and at 5.56 p.m. the leading Battleships of the Grand Fleet bearing North 5 miles.[87]

5.50 was also the time of his turn back to NEbyN. Meanwhile, Jellicoe first learned that gunfire was already audible to the Southward in reports received at 5.40 from *Minotaur* and also from *Hampshire* and *Comus* (4LCS). Since *Black Prince*'s report to the C-in-C at 5.42 was only 'received by me considerably later',[88] the first actual sighting reported to him seems to have been Arbuthnot's at 5.46 describing unspecified 'Ships in action bearing SSW, steering NE'.[89] Hence, though probably not much before 5.50, both Jellicoe and Beatty were aware that their forces were coming into contact on their respective starboard and port bows and, in Jellicoe's case particularly, much earlier than expected. Jellicoe's increasingly pressing dilemma on how and when to deploy his battleships into line will form a major part of the next chapter, but we should first complete this account of the Run to the North by Beatty's forces.

These were being led by the light cruisers of the 1LCS and 3LCS. At 5.40, *Galatea* (1LCS) reported that, to starboard, the enemy battle cruisers were turning away (in the German signals, the time of their turn NNE was 5.44).

---

[85] *OD*, German Plan V shows turns N at 5.42 and then NE at '5.40' instead of 5.50.

[86] Scheer's despatch, *OD*, p. 593. Tarrant, p. 109. Campbell, p. 143.

[87] *OD*, p. 135: also pp. 185 and 286.

[88] *OD*, p. 16. *GF*, pp. 217–18. *NSA*, Ch. VII, par. 47 and App. F. *Shannon*'s W/T record (see note 63).

[89] *Duke of Edinburgh*'s despatch (*OD*, p. 286) describes a 5.40 searchlight signal from *Black Prince*:
    ' "Light Cruisers, 3, bearing S.S.E., steering N.E." ... which signal was passed to "Defence" '. At the same moment, *Duke of Edinburgh* sighted what she thought was the 2LCS; probably, both she and *Black Prince* had sighted the 3LCS, also of the *Town* class. A plot of bearings, position and gun ranges suggests that Arbuthnot reported the bearing of the ISG.

Table 6.15. *British signals 5.30–6.00pm*

Time of despatch	From	To	System	Message	Time of origin
pm, 31 May					
5.30	Falmouth			Remarks: Sighted Cruisers port bow	
5.36	Falmouth	Black Prince	SL	Battle Cruisers engaged to the SSW of me	1735
5.40	Minotaur	C-in-C	SL	Report of guns heard South. (Reports also received from Hampshire and Comus)	
5.40	Galatea	SO BCF	W/T	Enemy Battle Cruisers altering course to starboard.	1740
				(Time of receipt not shown in Lion's log)	
5.40	Southampton	C-in-C SO BCF	W/T	Urgent. Priority. The Enemy's battlefleet have altered course NNW. My position 56°46 N, 5°40E	1740
5.42	Black Prince	C-in-C and SO 2CS	W/T	Enemy Battle Cruisers bearing South five miles. My position 56° 59 N, 5°24E	1740
5.45	SO 2LCS	Warspite and Barham	SL	Enemy torpedo craft are approaching from ESE	
5.46	SO 1CS	SO 2CS C-in-C	W/T and SL	Ships in action bearing SSW, steering NE. My position 57°07 N, 5°38E	1745
5.47	SO BCF	Light Cruisers	Flags	Attack the Enemy with torpedoes	
5.48	Falmouth	SO Cruisers	SL	Two heavy Enemy ships bearing SSE, steering NE. My position 57° 07 N, 5°45E	1745
5.50	Southampton	C-in-C SO BCF	W/T	Urgent. Priority. Enemy's battlefleet has altered course to N. Enemy Battle Cruisers bear SW from Enemy battlefleet. My position 56° 50 N, 5°44E	1750
5.55	Inconstant			Remarks: Battlefleet sighted	
5.55	SO BCF	General	Flags	. . . 25 knots	
5.55	C-in-C	Marlborough	SL	What can you see? Reply: our battle Cruisers bearing SSW, steering E, Lion leading ship	1800 1805
				Further reply from Marlborough: 5BS bearing SW	
5.56	SO BCF	General	Flags	Alter course in succession to NEbyE. Speed 25 knots	
6.00	SO 5BS	5BS	Flags	Enemy in sight. SSE. Battlefleet	
6.00	SO BCF	General	Flags	Alter course in succession to E	

However, by 5.45, *Falmouth* could also see two heavy enemy ships bearing SSE, so it appears that the two light cruiser squadrons were not widely spread. At 5.47, Beatty ordered all his light cruisers to attack with torpedoes but it was already too late, even for the two squadrons ahead. As they increased speed to get into position, they met up with the advanced cruisers of the Grand Fleet and were forced to avoid them as they turned first to port and then to starboard; Alexander-Sinclair in *Galatea* thought they were preparing for a deployment to starboard.[90] In the 2LCS astern of the 5BS, *Southampton*'s wireless had once more crackled into life at 5.40 after a 40-minute silence; she reported, correctly, that the enemy battlefleet was steering NNW at 5.40 and N at 5.50. The first signal did not reach *Iron Duke* until 5.48 but it placed *Southampton* 17 miles NNW½W from her position at 5.00, indicating that both sides had been steaming in that direction for most of the intervening time.[91]

Between 5.53 and 5.55, the ISG, which previously had appeared from the BCF to be hauling gradually away, made their large turn to course E.[92] Hipper had several pressing reasons for altering course decisively. First, his battlecruisers were under a hot fire from the BCF and the 5BS, to which they could not reply effectively because of the deteriorating visibility – though, as we have seen, the turn did not save them from several hits that struck soon afterwards. Second, they were experiencing difficulties in maintaining the high speed that they needed to keep their opponents, especially the 5BS, at long range; clinker from stony coal was clogging their furnaces, the stokers and coal trimmers were becoming exhausted and, in some ships, the supplementary oil firing had been choked by sediment from the fuel tanks.[93] And, third, from 5.36 Hipper's light cruisers of the IISG on his starboard side had been in action with *Chester*, one of the two light cruisers in company with the 3BCS. An account of this engagement will be given in the following chapter; for now it suffices to know that Admiral Hood's battlecruisers themselves engaged the IISG from 5.50 to 6.00.[94] Rear-Admiral Bödicker in *Frankfurt* did not report his predicament until 6.00 (he then described his new opponents as enemy battleships) but, since Hipper turned E soon after the 3BCS opened fire, his turn was probably hastened by the sound and flashes of heavy guns in that direction and his realisation that his light cruisers needed immediate support.

Just three minutes after the ISG turned away, at 5.56 Beatty sighted *Marlborough* heading the 6th Division of the Grand Fleet bearing either N at

---

[90] *OD*, p. 173.

[91] *AN*, pp. 104–5. *Southampton*'s positions at 5.40 and 5.50 implied her course was NE and speed 27.4 knots.

[92] *OD*, p. 135. German Plan V has a turn in succession at 5.53 but GSM as together at 5.55. von Hase, p. 177 and Sketch I, the latter showing *Derfflinger* completing her turn E at 5.55.

[93] Tarrant, pp. 109–10. See also von Hase, p. 172.

[94] *OD*, pp. 164 and 268. F&H, p. 239. *Inflexible* and *Indomitable* gunnery reports in BTY 6/6.

five miles (Beatty's despatch) or NbyE at six miles (the BCF's chart). This was much closer than he had previously expected. At the same moment, he may have turned two points to NEbyE,[95] but it was now certain that something more decisive was required. He no longer had the searoom to continue NE'wards in order to shepherd the enemy across the heads of Jellicoe's columns in preparation for a port deployment in that direction. In any case, this had ceased to be a possibility because, although the German battle line was still steering NNE, Hipper was now leading the head of their line Eastwards. Furthermore, as stipulated by the *GFBOs*, Beatty's primary function was the destruction of the enemy battlecruisers; thus, with the ISG rapidly disappearing into the smoke and mist on their new course, he too had to respond by turning E, which he did at 6.00.[96] This course had other attractions. Without changing course too sharply, it turned *Lion* away from the rapidly approaching *Marlborough*. And it could still take the BCF across the heads of the battleship columns to a position ahead of the port division.[97] In his despatch, Beatty wrote that, having sighted the 1BS, 'I thereupon altered course to East and proceeded at utmost speed'.[98] Neither then nor later did he elaborate on what he expected would happen next. But, if Hipper drew Scheer Eastwards, the BCF would have been well placed to lead a deployment onto the same course E. However, if this was Beatty's plan, it would quickly be overtaken by events.

Astern of the battlecruisers, the 5BS continued NNE'ly, even after 5.56 when *Valiant* observed the BCF 'turning Eastward with the apparent idea of heading off the enemy and crossing his "T" '. At 6.00, *Valiant* fired a single torpedo at the enemy battlefleet, then on a parallel course; her target, which she did not hit, bore G140, range 14,000 yards. *Malaya* was also unsuccessful when at 6.05 she fired a torpedo at the third German battleship, bearing G135, range 12,900 yards.[99] After *Barham*'s wireless had been completely wrecked around 5 o'clock, it seems that no attempt was made to arrange alternative communications with the C-in-C, for example through the undamaged *Valiant*. Thus Evan-Thomas had no warning of the meeting with the Grand Fleet until *Marlborough* and some of the 6th Division were sighted at 6.06–07; only then did the 5BS turn E to follow the battlecruisers.[100]

The turns Eastward by the ISG, the BCF and the 5BS mark the end of the Run to the North. However, it is convenient to include in the gunnery analysis of this phase of the battle the hit made on *Lion* at 6.05, which Campbell attributes to *Lützow*.[101]

---

[95] *OD*, p. 135 and Pl. 10 respectively; the latter shows a steady course NEbyN until 6.00.

[96] *GFBOs III*, XXIV.7. REL. *OD*, Pl. 10. VNE times for the turns are later: to NEbyE at 6.00 and E at 6.04.

[97] It is not possible to be more precise because of the discrepancies in course, bearing and distance between 5.56 and 6.04.

[98] *OD*, p. 135.   [99] *OD*, pp. 207, 215, 219 and 221.

[100] *OD*, pp. 194, 207 and 219. *Warspite*'s sighting of 'the Grand Fleet' at 6.00 (p. 202) may have been of the armoured cruisers.

[101] Campbell, pp. 124–5.

During the Run to the North, Beatty's battlecruisers received five hits, all but one at the start before they went out of action; most were probably made by the ISG. If *Warspite* was hit five times, the total number on the 5BS was sixteen. In total, the ISG received up to fourteen hits, the IIIBS, five.[102] Thus, in this phase of the battle, the numbers of hits scored by the two sides was similar. But, of the nineteen British hits, only one can be attributed with reasonable confidence to the BCF (though another one is just possible). It was fortunate for the reputation of British gunnery that the 5BS shot to such good effect in difficult circumstances.

As we come to the end of the Run to the North, we should examine Beatty's account as given in his despatch.

The weather conditions now [at 5.00] became unfavourable, our ships being silhouetted against a clear horizon to the Westward, while the enemy was for the most part obscured by mist, only showing up clearly at intervals. These conditions prevailed until we had turned their van at about 6 p.m. Between 5 and 6 p.m. the action continued on a Northerly course, the range being about 14,000 yards. During this time the enemy received very severe punishment, and undoubtedly one of their Battle Cruisers quitted the line in a considerably damaged condition. This came under my personal observation, and was corroborated by 'Princess Royal' and 'Tiger'. Other enemy ships also showed signs of increasing injury.

Here, there is not the slightest hint that the battlecruisers were out of action between 5.10 and 5.35. During that interval, ranges were much longer than 14,000 yards. The range of *Tiger*'s final salvo at 5.09.45 was 17,800 yards and it then increased so that the enemy remained out of sight. Later, during the spell of rapid fire when *Lion* probably scored her only hit, she recorded a range of 14,500 yards at 5.44½, so 14,000 yards was about right towards the end of the Run to the North. None of the despatches from *Princess Royal* or *Tiger* provide any corroboration that an enemy battlecruiser fell out of line in a damaged condition and none did so. If Beatty observed any such thing, it must have been after the BCF renewed the action and what he saw was *Derfflinger* having 'to leave the line for a short time when we saw that the enemy had our range'.[103] Finally, while Beatty pushed the enemy van gradually NE'wards by re-engaging, he did not 'turn' it at about 6 o'clock. At 5.53–55, Hipper was first to alter course sharply to the East towards the action between the IISG and the 3BCS; Beatty's own turn was no more than a response, albeit with the praise-worthy objective of keeping the ISG under fire. Once again, these claims conflict with other reports from the BCF, even from *Lion* herself, and so appear to have been intended to mislead.

---

[102] The splinter damage to *Malaya* at 5.25 is not included in the 5BS total.

[103] von Hase, p. 177; he assumed that this had been 'imperceptible to the enemy'.

Hood's expectations for meeting Beatty had been transformed by *Southampton*'s 4.48 report that the whole German fleet was heading North; at 4.50, Hood turned in succession to SbyE. *Invincible*'s reckoning from the positions at 4.46 would have indicated to Hood that the 2LCS then bore almost due S; thus his course seems to have been calculated to intercept the German forces to the E of *Southampton*. But, unknown to Hood, the German forces soon turned Northwesterly, while the difference in reckoning between the Grand Fleet and the BCF meant that the 2LCS was further to the West than he realised. Consequently, his chosen course had taken him to the E of the advancing German battlefleet. But, about five miles NE of Hipper's battlecruisers, the IISG (*Frankfurt* leading *Pillau, Elbing* and *Wiesbaden*) was proceeding ahead of the Scouting Group flotillas (the II, VI and IX TFs) and *Regensburg*;[1] thus this group of vessels was closer to Hood's line of advance.

As *Invincible* led *Inflexible* and *Indomitable* in that order SbyE, the four accompanying destroyers of *Shark*'s division formed a submarine screen. The light cruiser *Canterbury* was stationed five miles ahead while the recently commissioned *Chester* was now positioned about WNW from the 3BCS at a distance of six miles. In the variable visibility – 16,000 yards in some directions, only 2,000 in others – *Chester* could not be seen from the battlecruisers.[2] At around 5.30, she heard gunfire and saw flashes to the SW, probably from the ISG; she reported to *Invincible* by searchlight and turned to investigate. At 5.36, she sighted a three-funnelled cruiser and one or two destroyers on her starboard bow. Uncertain of their identity (the ships of the 1LCS also had three funnels), she challenged them but received no reply before, as she turned W and then Northwards onto an approximately parallel course, she sighted two more German light cruisers. Having allowed her to close to only 6,000 yards, *Frankfurt* opened fire, followed by her three consorts, though *Elbing* and *Wiesbaden* were soon ordered to cease fire to make spotting easier.[3] *Chester*, still under helm, fired her first and only full salvo after *Frankfurt*'s second but

---

[1] Tarrant, pp. 115 and 117.   [2] *OD*, pp. 163, 165, 170 and 188. F&H, 226.
[3] *OD*, p. 188. F&H, p. 231. Tarrant, p. 115.

Table 7.1. *3BCS signals 4.00–6.26pm*

Time of despatch	From	To	System	Message	Time of origin
pm, 31 May					
4.00	SO 3BCS	3BCS	Flags	. . . 24 knots	
4.02	SO 3BCS	General	Flags	Alter course in succession to SSE	
4.15	SO 3BCS	C-in-C	W/T	My position, course and speed: 57° 39 N, 5°35E, SSE, 25 knots	1606
4.50	SO 3BCS	3BCS	Flags	Alter course in succession to SbyE	
5.32	Canterbury	SO 3BCS	SL	Can see flashes ahead	
5.38	SO 3BCS	Destroyers	Flags	Close	
5.40	Indomitable			Remarks: 3BCS altered course towards Enemy without signal	
5.40	Inflexible			Remarks: Enemy Light Cruisers port bow	
5.45	Canterbury			Remarks: Cruiser Kolberg class and Destroyers starboard bow	
5.52	Canterbury			Remarks: opened fire	
5.55	SO 3BCS	3BCS	Flags	Open fire and engage the Enemy	
5.56	Indomitable			Remarks: Inflexible and Indomitable opened fire	
6.00	Indomitable			Remarks: Enemy three-funnelled Cruiser out of action	
6.05	SO 3BCS	3BCS	Flags	Disregard the Admiral's motions	
6.06	SO BCF	SO 3BCS	W/T	My position is 55°58 N, 5°37E, course E, speed 25 knots	1805
6.10	Indomitable			Remarks: Sighted battlefleet starboard side	
6.12	SO 3BCS	SO 3LCS	SL	Where is Lion?	
6.15	Indomitable	Indomitable and Inflexible	Flags	Form single line-ahead in the sequence in which ships now are	
6.15	Indomitable			Remarks: Invincible resumed Guide of Fleet	
6.15	Inflexible			Remarks: Altered course to avoid torpedo	
6.26	SO 3BCS	3BCS	Flags	. . . 20 knots	

the British cruiser was then badly hit by the third or fourth German salvo and by several more as the Germans concentrated. Portside, *Chester*'s No. 1 gun was disabled and its crew and many of the crews of the Nos. 2 and 3 guns were killed or wounded. More injuries were caused by a shell bursting on the starboard sounding machine. Centralised fire control was disabled after fragments from a hit on the side armour severed the voice-pipes from the

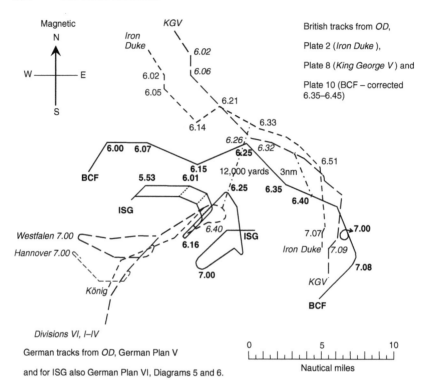

Figure 7.1 Windy Corner to the BCF's 32-point turn

transmitting station, and the after control position was knocked out.[4] Of the young and inexperienced gun crews, forty-seven out of one hundred were killed or injured, many succumbing to shock; because the shallow gun shields did not extend down to the deck, three quarters of the wounds were below the knee. Among the fatally injured was Boy First Class Jack Cornwell, the sightsetter of the forecastle gun, who was awarded a posthumous VC for remaining at his post.[5] Outnumbered and with only her quarterdeck gun in local control able to bear continuously, *Chester* turned away NE'wards at emergency full speed; by zigzagging towards the fall of the last salvo, she avoided further serious damage. At 5.42, the IISG turned together to NNE in pursuit.[6] Hood may not have received *Chester*'s earlier searchlight report since he did not lead round onto a

---

[4] *OD*, p. 189. Capt. Lawson's further report, 13 June 1916, ADM 137/1946, ff. 534–48. F&H, pp. 232 and 234. S&H, pp. 179 and 181–2.

[5] S&H, 180 and 183. Dreyer, p. 131. *CAWFS 1906–21* p. 59.

[6] *OD*, pp. 189–91 and German Plans V and VI (Diagram 3). F&H, p. 232. Lawson (see note 4) ff. 534–5.

Northwesterly course until 5.40, when gun flashes were seen to the SW. This left
his destroyers on his port quarter; *Canterbury* also closed at full speed. The turn
was just in time; a few minutes later, *Chester* emerged from the mist on the port
bow surrounded by shell splashes, followed a minute later by what were noted as
three German light cruisers. The hard-pressed *Chester* hauled across *Invincible*'s
bows to safety on her starboard bow.[7]

Now Bödicker had to face a more powerful foe. At 5.50, *Invincible* opened
fire, followed at 5.55 by *Inflexible* and *Indomitable*. By the time *Inflexible*
engaged the second light cruiser from the right at an opening range of 8,000
yards, the IISG had altered 16 points to port, *Frankfurt* and *Elbing* each firing a
torpedo as they turned at the 3BCS, though to no effect. *Inflexible*'s range-rate
changed rapidly from 800 closing to 900 opening; but, nonetheless, just as the
IISG was dropping smoke boxes to cover its withdrawal to the Southward,
Pillau received a hit, probably from *Inflexible*, that put four of her eight boilers
out of action so that she could make no more than 24 knots. In *Wiesbaden*, the
rear ship, a 12in shell exploded in her engine room, wrecking both her engines
and bringing her to a complete stop to become the almost helpless target of

Table 7.2. *IISG signals 5.58–6.15pm*

Time of receipt	From	To	System	Message	Time of origin
pm, 31 May					
5.58	Wiesbaden	XIIHF	Visual	Turn away; proceed at utmost speed	
6.00	Frankfurt	AC Scouting Forces		Am under fire from enemy battleships	
6.01	Wiesbaden	SO IISG		Both engines are disabled; am incapable of manoeuvring	
6.02	2nd Leader of Torpedo Boats	II, VI and IX TFs		Directly ahead of the leading ship	
6.02	Frankfurt	Derfflinger		To AC Scouting Forces and C-in-C: Am under fire from enemy battleships.–SO IISG	1801
6.10	Frankfurt	C-in-C		Enemy battleships in ... SO IISG	
6.10	Frankfurt	C-in-C		Wiesbaden disabled ... SO IISG	1821
6.14	SO IISG	Regensburg		Send a torpedo boat to Wiesbaden to take her in tow	
6.15	SO IISG	AC Scouting Forces		Wiesbaden is disabled; she is on the starboard quarter	

---

[7] *OD*, pp. 163, 189–90 and 268. F&H, pp. 227 and 233.

many passing British ships. Bödicker could make out only the dim outlines of the ships firing at him and at 6.00 and later he reported them as enemy battleships, giving the impression that elements of the British battlefleet were well to the East of their actual position.[8] He also informed Scheer and Hipper that *Wiesbaden* had been disabled and, at 6.14, he ordered Commodore Heinrich in *Regensburg* to send a destroyer to take her in tow – but the situation was developing much too rapidly for this to be possible.

As Hood opened fire at the IISG, he ordered Commander Loftus Jones, leading the four destroyers in *Shark*, to proceed independently and they soon made out German light cruisers and destroyers apparently commencing a torpedo attack on the 3BCS. To the commanding officer of *Acasta*, the Germans 'appeared to become undecided as to what our force consisted of . . . and turned from their torpedo attack to engage us with gunfire'. Their first wave (*V69*, *V46* and *S50* of the XIIHF) fired four torpedoes but a second group (*G37* and *V45*) only two before they became involved with *Shark*'s division. The advance of the IXTF was hampered by the withdrawing XIIHF and only *V28, S52* and *S34* were able to launch one torpedo each; the remainder joined the destroyer *mêlée*, during which *S36* fired one and *V28* a second torpedo (one of their targets may have been the four-funnelled *Chester*). A third attack by four of the large destroyers of the IITF was also disrupted by the boats retiring from the earlier waves and only *G104* fired a single torpedo at 6.08. Commodore Heinrich then directed the remainder of the flotilla to join the XIHF in a further attack on the outnumbered British destroyers, though by then they were being supported by *Canterbury*.[9]

As they moved out to attack, *Shark*'s division could see the IISG, a destroyer flotilla and a flotilla cruiser; *Shark*'s crew thought that the torpedo that they then fired was at a four-funnelled cruiser. But *Rostock* was then out of sight on the starboard beam of the IIIBS so the target was probably *Regensburg*.[10] *Shark* led *Acasta, Ophelia* and *Christopher* into action, *Shark* herself being the target for *Regensburg, G41* and *B97*. By about 6.10, *Shark* had been forced to turn away 16 points to port and was soon brought to a stop, much damaged and with only the midship gun in action. Still under heavy fire, she drove off one German destroyer but then *G41* fired a torpedo from 1,500 to 1,800 yards which struck abreast the after funnel; *Shark* sank almost immediately. Already slightly wounded, Loftus Jones had been spotting for the midship gun but, about five minutes before the torpedo hit, his leg was shot away. He was able to order his crew to save themselves but cannot have survived for long after *Shark* went down; he too was awarded the VC. The water was very cold and only seven

[8] F&H, p. 239. *OD*, p. 164. *Indomitable* and *Inflexible* gunnery reports in BTY 6/6. Tarrant, pp. 117–18 and 120. *GOA*, p. 91.
[9] F&H, p. 235. *OD*, pp. 268 and 307. Tarrant, pp. 117–18. *GOA*, pp. 92–3.
[10] For conflicting identifications, see *OD*, pp. 164, 268, 307, 313–14 and 317 and F&H, p. 239. German Plan VI, Diagram 3.

men lived to be picked up by the Danish steamer *Vidar* at about 10pm (one died afterwards).[11]

On seeing *Shark* stopped, *Acasta* turned to close, as she did so firing a torpedo at the leading enemy battlecruiser at a range of about 4,500 yards, but the explosion she then saw was not a hit.[12] She passed quite close to *Shark* to offer assistance, but *Acasta* herself then took two hits in the engine room; these were perhaps from *Frankfurt*, which had sighted her alongside *Shark*. Due to burst steam pipes and damaged steering gear, *Acasta* was unable to stop or steer.

At about 6.30, having barged through our own destroyer flotillas ahead of the battle fleet ... we at last got the ship stopped, and lying there only about 200 yards from the battle line, held a very fine review of the Grand Fleet coming into action.[13]

Despite the heavy enemy fire, some of it coming later from the ISG, *Ophelia* and *Christopher* were not hit. They were able to retire towards British light cruisers (probably the 3LCS) and take up positions ahead of the BCF. At 6.29, *Ophelia* fired a torpedo at an enemy battlecruiser but the upheaval of water that she saw a few minutes later was not a hit; *Christopher* also aimed a torpedo at the leading enemy battlecruiser but was then masked by light cruisers. *Canterbury* engaged the German light cruisers that were punishing *Shark* and *Acasta* but her subsequent movements are unrecorded until she joined up with the 3LCS at 7.15. After *Chester* withdrew to a position on *Invincible's* starboard bow, she soon lost touch with the 3BCS; somehow she became mixed up with the Grand Fleet destroyers before, at 6.50, attaching herself to the 2CS.[14]

As the IISG were disappearing Southward, a good deal of firing coming from to Westward could be heard in the 3BCS and they altered course to port in that direction. Soon, torpedo tracks were sighted from all three battlecruisers. *Invincible* turned to starboard but her helm jammed and she appeared to stop briefly, letting off steam. Three or four tracks were seen from *Inflexible* and, according to *Indomitable*, she turned to port; one torpedo ran slowly down the port side only about 20 feet distant. *Indomitable* turned away from at least three torpedoes, outrunning one moving alongside some 20 yards away. The tracks seemed to come from the German light cruisers but, given that the avoiding turns were made at 6.13–6.15, the torpedoes were probably fired by the flotillas. *Invincible* hoisted the 'Disregard' but quickly hauled it down; then, flying the

---

[11] *OD,* pp. 316–20. S&H, p. 186. Tarrant, p. 118 quoting *GOA*, pp. 93–4; *B98* was hit on her after twin torpedo tube and her mast went overboard.

[12] The ISG probably came into sight as they were reversing course to fall back on the High Seas Fleet – see further below.

[13] F&H, p. 236 (*Acasta's* CO also said he crossed *Lion*'s bows). *OD*, pp. 307–8 and 319. Tarrant, p. 118.

[14] *OD*, pp. 190, 268, 314 and 316. F&H, p. 233.

signal to form single line-ahead, she led *Inflexible* and *Indomitable* Westwards towards the intensifying sound of firing.[15]

The battlecruisers turn Eastwards

Hipper turned E between 5.53 and 5.55, but enemy cruisers and destroyers then appeared to the North and seemed to be assembling for a torpedo attack. They were probably the advanced forces of the Grand Fleet and the BCF meeting up amidst enough confusion to preclude any concerted action. But to Hipper they appeared a real danger when his own flotillas had been drawn Eastwards to attack the 3BCS. According to the German signal list, at 5.59, a minute before *Frankfurt* reported that she was under fire from enemy battleships, Hipper ordered the ISG to turn away to starboard together onto an opposite course, though other sources give later times. Even if Bödicker's report did not prompt

Table 7.3. *ISG signals 5.53–6.10pm*

Time of receipt	From	To	System	Message	Time of origin
pm, 31 May					
5.53	Lützow	ISG	Visual	All battle cruisers, follow in the wake of the leading ship	
5.55	Lützow	ISG	Visual	All battle cruisers, turn together to E	
5.58	Wiesbaden	XIIHF	Visual	Turn away; proceed at utmost speed	
5.59	Lützow	ISG	Visual	Torpedo boats to attack	
5.59	Lützow	ISG	Visual	Turn together to starboard until ships are in single line ahead in the opposite direction	
6.00	Lützow	ISG	Visual	Reduce speed	
6.00	Frankfurt	AC Scouting Forces		Am under fire from enemy battleships	
6.01	Wiesbaden	SO IISG		Both engines are disabled; am incapable of manoeuvring	
6.02	Frankfurt	Derfflinger		To AC Scouting Forces and C-in-C: Am under fire from enemy battleships.–SO IISG	1801
6.10	Frankfurt	C-in-C		Enemy battleships ... SO IISG	
6.10	Lützow	ISG	Visual	Turn together to starboard until ships are in single line ahead in the opposite direction	

[15] F&H, pp. 227 and 239–40. *OD*, pp. 164, 167 and 170. This narrative attempts to navigate between the inconsistencies in these source and the signals.

Hipper's decision to turn away, it surely convinced him that his position was untenable and that he must at once fall back on the High Seas Fleet, some seven miles astern.[16] Unfortunately, the conflicting accounts of this manoeuvre cannot be reconciled, but it appears to have involved two large turns to starboard, the second of which, timed at 6.10 in the signals, was a turn together onto an opposite course; it enabled the ISG to haul into single line-ahead in advance of the IIIBS with both squadrons on a course NE.[17] The only British ship that may have observed these two big turns was *Duke of Edinburgh*.[18]

After Scheer turned N at 5.44 and handed over the lead to Behncke in *König*, by about 6.15 the IIIBS and IBS were steering Northeasterly but the IIBS was only just turning from a Northerly course. Even as *Wiesbaden* was being disabled, Scheer and his staff, still unaware of the presence of the British battlefleet, were occupied in debating how long they should continue the pursuit of the BCF. But by 6.10 at the latest, they had been informed by *Frankfurt* that the IISG to the NE were in action with 'enemy battleships' and by 6.15 firing between the two battle lines had commenced. At 6.17, *König* initiated a two-point turn together to port by the dreadnought squadrons that was intended to bring assistance to the stopped *Wiesbaden* but the German battleships soon had to turn away again from the British fire.[19] But the full extent of their predicament may not have been clear until 6.25 when a report from the VTF,

Table 7.4. *High Seas Fleet signals 6.17–6.25pm*

Time of receipt	From	To	System	Message	Time of origin
pm, 31 May					
6.17	König	IIIBS		Turn together 2 points to port	
6.18	C-in-C	General		Turn together 2 points to port	
6.21	C-in-C	General		Follow in wake of leading ship	
6.25	SO VTF	C-in-C		According to statements from destroyer Nomad, there are 60 large ships in the vicinity, including 20 modern battleships and 6 battle cruisers	1630 [*sic*]

---

[16] *OD*, German Plan V. von Hase, p. 177. Tarrant, p. 114. *GOA*, p. 83.

[17] The least problematic sequence of turns by the ISG seems to be: 5.53, NE in succession into line; 5.55, together to E; 5.59 or later, together to starboard into line-ahead, course SW with *Von der Tann* leading (i.e. not a turn onto an opposite course); 6.10, together to starboard into single line on the opposite course NE, *Lützow* again leading. These courses are consistent with *Derfflinger*'s in von Hase, Sketch I (though this shows the third turn as not being completed until 6.07 and the fourth until 6.15) and with *OD*, German Plan VI, Diagrams 3 and 4. For the SW'ly course, see Scheer's despatch, *OD*, p. 593 and Tarrant, p. 114.

[18] F&H, p. 175 but her chart (*OD*, Plate 11a) is wrong.

[19] Scheer, pp. 149–51. *OD*, German Plan VI, Diagram 4.

based on statements by prisoners from the *Nomad*, revealed that they were facing pretty much the whole of the British dreadnought fleet. However, even when the first report of enemy battleships came in, Scheer had little option but to allow the battlefleet to continue in an unwieldy line some nine miles long, taking its lead from the ISG and the IIIBS as they were pushed further Eastwards.[20] It was already far too late to adopt a more flexible formation.

touch between the two opposing lines [i.e. between the BCF and the ISG] had not been severed sufficiently, for the German fleet to have found time to reform into a wide preparatory formation [in columns] with the cruisers extended ahead in a scouting line, so as the guard against surprise.[21]

Even as Beatty's battlecruisers turned E at 6.00, their targets were disappearing in the mist. At 6.03, *Lion* and *Princess Royal* had to shift to a light cruiser on forward bearings, though each battlecruiser was able to fire only one salvo before she retired into the mist.[22] Between 6.07 and 6.12, *Tiger* turned her 6in guns on a disabled light cruiser on her starboard bow; this vessel eventually drifted down between the lines, so she was probably the *Wiesbaden*. At about 6.06, *New Zealand* also ceased fire after three salvos at what she identified as the leading enemy battleship (bearing G71).[23] At 6.06, Beatty informed Jellicoe by searchlight that the enemy battlecruisers bore SE. In his despatch, he claimed that three battlecruisers and some *König*-class battleships were then visible, though the gunnery records suggest that

Table 7.5. *BCF signals 5.55–6.08pm*

Time of despatch	From	To	System	Message	Time of origin
pm, 31 May					
5.55	SO BCF	General	Flags	… 25 knots	
5.56	SO BCF	General	Flags	Alter course in succession to NEbyE. Speed 25 knots	
6.00	SO 5BS	5BS	Flags	Enemy in sight. SSE. Battlefleet	
6.00	SO BCF	General	Flags	Alter course in succession to E	
6.01	C-in-C	SO BCF	SL	Where is Enemy's B.F.? (Repeated at 6.10) Reply: Have sighted Enemy's battlefleet bearing SSW. (Received in Iron Duke 6.14 p.m.)	
6.06	Lion	C-in-C	SL	Enemy's B.Cs. bearing SE	
6.08	New Zealand			Remarks: sighted Grand Fleet on port bow	

[20] Tarrant, pp. 137–8.   [21] *GOA*, p. 83 also p. 112.
[22] REL. *OD*, p. 388. Target bearings were G35 and G40, respectively.
[23] *OD*, pp. 392 and 395. *New Zealand*'s remarks at 6.08 suggest her times were still fast but her timetable states (*OD*, p. 160) that she sighted the Grand Fleet NbyE at 5.56.

they had already vanished; without a visible target for his heavy guns, at 6.07 he turned to starboard to ESE.[24] The disappearance of the ISG is explained by Hipper's turn about together onto a SW course at around this time.

Having positioned *Onslow* on *Lion*'s engaged starboard bow, Tovey decided to stay where he was 'in a most advantageous position for repelling enemy's Destroyer attack, or delivering an attack myself'. At about 6.05, he saw the ISG making turns E and then about SE, and Beatty's battlecruisers following shortly afterwards. But he then sighted a broken-down enemy light cruiser with three funnels only some 6,000 yards from the BCF in a position from which she could fire torpedoes. *Onslow* moved in at once to attack *Wiesbaden* with gunfire; fifty-eight rounds were fired at ranges from 2,000 to 4,000 yards, many of them hitting. While closing, Tovey saw the ISG turning again (this was probably Hipper's second large course reversal) thereby placing *Onslow* on their port bow at about 11,000 yards. Having ordered all four torpedo tubes to be readied for firing, Tovey turned to port to bring the enemy onto his starboard beam at 8,000 yards. Unfortunately only one torpedo could be fired before a hit amidships on her engaged side enveloped the destroyer in steam. Thinking that all his torpedoes had been fired, Tovey turned away at a reduced speed of ten knots. His sub-lieutenant, who had been sent to investigate, then seized the opportunity to fire a second torpedo at the *Wiesbaden* at a range of about 3,500 yards; several of *Onslow*'s crew were certain that it exploded below the conning tower, though *Wiesbaden*'s only survivor recalled that it opened up the stern. Then the German battlefleet could be seen emerging from the mist, with *Onslow* some 8,000 yards on their port bows; she fired her remaining two torpedoes, which appeared to run satisfactorily but did not make any hits. During her action, she had received two hits in her No. 2 boiler room and at 7.00 was forced to stop after using all her feed water. Without electric power, she was unable to reply to an offer of assistance from *Champion*, her flotilla leader, as she (and the rest of the British forces) raced away SE'wards. At 7.15, *Defender* of the 1DF closed to enquire if she could assist – at 6.30, she had been hit in her forward engine room by a 12in ricochet that had not exploded. Tovey, having learned that she could make only ten knots, asked to be taken in tow. After many difficulties, they eventually reached Aberdeen at 1pm on 2 June.[25]

At 6.06, first *Marlborough* and then others of the 6th Division were sighted from *Barham*, apparently heading ESE. At 6.07, *Valiant* recorded *Marlborough*'s distance as about three miles and her bearing, relative to a course NE, as R10, that is about NEbyN; this is only one point different from the reciprocal bearing of the 5BS at 6.05 as reported from *Marlborough*. Evan-Thomas 'concluded that this

---

[24] *OD*, p. 135 and Plate 10 but VNE gives course alterations to E at 6.04 and to SSE at 6.15.

[25] *OD*, pp. 237–8 and 250. F&H, pp. 249–58. Leading Stoker Zenne's ghosted memoir, ff. 30 and 33, ADM 137/1644. *Acasta* (pendant number 59) not *Onslow* was sighted from the 3LCS: *cf.* *OD*, pp. 136 and 186.

Table 7.6. *5BS signals 5.55–6.18pm*

Time of despatch	From	To	System	Message	Time of origin
pm, 31 May					
5.55	C-in-C	Marlborough	SL	What can you see? Reply: Our Battle Cruisers bearing SSW, steering E, Lion leading ship	1800 1805
				Further reply from Marlborough: 5BS bearing SW	
6.00	SO 5BS	5BS	Flags	Enemy in sight. SSE. Battlefleet	6.00
6.10	Barham	C-in-C	Flags W/T	Enemy's battlefleet SSE	
6.18	SO 5BS	5BS	Flags	Alter course in succession 16 pints to port	

was the head of the battle-line, and that the Fifth Battle Squadron would be able to form ahead of the battle fleet' and he led his battleships to starboard to E and, by 6.17, to EbyS or ESE. Even before sighting *Marlborough, Valiant* and *Barham* had lost sight of the enemy in the mist, though they reopened fire at 6.14–6.15. At 6.17, the visibility was good enough for *Valiant*'s range to be 19,000 yards. Her target bearing SSE was the same as the bearing of the enemy battlefleet reported by Evan-Thomas at 6.10.[26]

Windy Corner

After 6 o'clock, Jellicoe's advanced forces on his starboard flank were encountering Beatty's leading ships at the narrow end of the shrinking wedge-shaped area between the two fleets that became known as Windy Corner. Its edges were defined by the courses of the battlecruiser squadrons and the 5BS as they steered E and then ESE, and by the line-of-bearing NEbyE between the guides of the battleship columns. With the BCF in sight and in action, it was clear that the battle fleet must soon deploy from columns into line. By continuing Eastwards, Beatty was already giving the impression that he expected a port deployment, while the congestion ahead of the 6th Division militated against a starboard deployment. Jellicoe's final deployment will be examined below. For now it suffices to know that at 6.02 he turned the battlefleet by 9 Pendant from SEbyS to S; this caused the 'wedge' to narrow even faster until he turned back to SE at 6.06. Then at 6.15 he deployed to port, course SEbyE with the 1st Division leading; all the other columns turned in succession NEbyE before following in the wake of *King George V.* Later, at 6.55, the battlefleet turned S by 9 Pendant.

[26] *OD*, pp. 194, 207 and Plates 10a and 16–19.

Table 7.7. *British signals 5.55–6.35pm*

Time of despatch	From	To	System	Message	Time of origin
pm, 31 May					
5.55	Inconstant			Remarks: Battlefleet sighted	
6.02	C-in-C	General	Flags	Alter course leading ships together, rest in succession to South. Speed 18 knots	
6.02	Captain D1	1DF	Flags	Close	
6.02	SO 1LCS	SO 3LCS	Sem.	I was told to keep touch with Battle Cruisers. It seems to be getting a bit thick this end. What had we better do?	
6.02	Southampton	C-in-C and SO BCS	W/T	Urgent. Have lost sight of Enemy's battlefleet. Am engaging the Enemy's Battle Cruisers. My position is 56°57 N, 5°43E, course NNE, speed 26 knots	1800
6.06	C-in-C	General	Flags	Alter course leading ships together the rest in succession to SE	
6.27	SO 1LCS	Inconstant	SL	My speed has been reduced to 18 knots. Go on with 1LCS and try and get ahead of battlefleet	
6.30	SO 1LCS	1LCS	Flags	1LCS join Inconstant	
6.35	Inconstant	Phaeton and Cordelia	Flags	Take station astern of Inconstant	

Until Beatty turned E at 6.00, the 1LCS and 3LCS had been ahead of the battlecruisers, with the 1LCS somewhat closer to the enemy.[27] But his flotillas were strung out on his disengaged flank. They were led by the 1DF (apart from *Acheron* and *Ariel*, at 27 knots the slowest British destroyers present)[28] though their leader *Fearless* had not kept up. The remainder were further back, while the 2LCS brought up the rear, remaining under a heavy fire until about 6.05. To the North, the battleship columns were still steering SEbyS, either 1 or 1.1 miles apart,[29] with the advanced line of six armoured cruisers about ten miles ahead of the battle fleet. The battlefleet's light cruiser squadron, the 4LCS, was also in line-abreast, spread ¾–1 mile apart, 4–5 miles ahead of the battleships;

[27] *Onslow* mentioned only the 1LCS as being ahead of her: *OD*, p. 237.

[28] *Acheron* and *Ariel* were 29-knot Thorneycroft specials, *Attack* a 28-knot Yarrow special: *CAWFS 1906–21*, p. 75.

[29] For a 10 cable separation: *OD*, pp. 72 and 176; *OD*(M), 3.16pm; von Schoultz, p. 127 and *GSB 1915*, p. 292. For 11 cables, Jellicoe's despatch (*OD*, p. 16) and *GFBOs III*, II(a).

Calliope, flying the broad pendant of Commodore Charles Le Mesurier, was on the port wing with the fast minelayer *Abdiel*. *Active* was further ahead as linking ship to *Hampshire*, while *Boadicea, Blanche* and *Bellona* were at the rear of the fleet.[30]

The first contact between Jellicoe's and Beatty's forces was that between *Falmouth* and *Black Prince*. By 5.40, assuming that the latter's signal referred to the British battlecruisers, she was five miles North of the BCF while *Duke of Edinburgh* had sighted what were probably the 3LCS.[31] With some of the 1CS already in view, *Falmouth* led the 3LCS gradually to starboard to join in with the battlefleet screen steering about SE at 6.06. Here they were much restricted for room, the 1CS, 4LCS and the battlefleet's destroyer screen all moving in the same direction, but Napier noted that: 'The First Light Cruiser Squadron managed to turn away and get clear and thus ease the crowding'. The 1LCS had also met the armoured cruisers and observed them close by, swinging first to port and then through 12 points to starboard (see below). At 6.02, Alexander-Sinclair signalled by semaphore from *Galatea* to Napier: 'It seems to be getting a bit thick this end. What had we better do?' Whether or not Alexander-Sinclair received a reply, he soon turned Westwards to avoid *Defence* as she cut across his bows, and then Northwards before taking his squadron between the 4th and 5th Divisions of the battle fleet.[32] The time of his Westward turn may have been rather later than the 6.07 given in his despatch, since officers of *Colossus* remarked approvingly on 'the masterly way in which some light cruisers … cut through the lines at full speed, one of them passing only a few yards across our bows as we turned to port into battle line'.[33] Unfortunately, their dash took the 1LCS into the danger zone from German shells that were now falling around the rear battleships. Just as *Galatea* turned up onto a similar course, a piece of shell (probably a splinter from an 'over') damaged one of her forced-draught fans, reducing her speed to 18 knots. At 6.27, *Inconstant* was ordered to go on with *Phaeton* and *Cordelia*; they passed round the far side of the repeating light cruisers and did not reach the head of the line until 7.25. *Galatea* followed and would later offer assistance to the stricken *Acasta*.[34] By turning E early, the 3LCS kept a position ahead of the battlecruisers, though *Falmouth* and *Yarmouth* were separated from *Birkenhead* and *Gloucester* when the 1CS cut through their squadron. At 6.07, *Falmouth* and *Yarmouth* joined in the fire at the *Wiesbaden*; *Falmouth* also fired a torpedo at her at a range of

---

[30] *OD*, pp. 297–8, 302, 368, 378 and 380. F&H, pp. 259 and 268.

[31] *OD*, p. 286. They were thought to be the 2LCS but the 3LCS cruisers were also four-funnelled.

[32] *OD*, pp. 173, 185–6 and Pl. 15. F&H, p. 137.

[33] F&H, p. 184. The light cruisers concerned were thought to be '*Calliope*'s squadron' which had similar profiles, except that *Calliope* and *Constance* had two rather than three funnels.

[34] *OD*, pp. 172–4. Temporary repairs would, by about 2.30am the following morning, enable *Galatea* to reach 24 knots. F&H, p. 237.

5,000 yards but without seeing a hit. *Falmouth* then shifted her fire to two other enemy light cruisers, probably from the IISG, that were firing at British destroyers.[35] She and *Yarmouth* would soon be in a position to engage the approaching ISG.

The 1DF was able to hold its position on the port beam of the 1BCS as Beatty turned Eastwards. In addition to six of the flotilla being limited to 27 knots, they also had difficulties avoiding the Grand Fleet flotillas and cruisers, though they held their course while the other vessels went under their stern. It was not easy even for *Attack* to keep *Acheron*, the divisional leader, in sight; the latter's captain, Commander Charles Ramsey, seems to have been pressing forward to give a lead. *Defender* may also have been in front until she was hit at about 6.30; she turned out to pass down between the fleets before going to the aid of *Onslow*. At that time, the rest of the 1DF were on the port beam and quarter of the 1BCS and 2BCS but by 7.00 they had drawn ahead and were able to form a submarine screen for the BCF.[36] *Fearless*, already astern of her flotilla, had been unable to keep pace and, after finding herself at 6.08 streaming smoke across the front of the battlefleet, she turned about to join other light cruisers and destroyers gathering in the rear.[37] *Champion* and the other BCF flotillas, despite their superior speed, did not follow the 1DF. Perhaps *Fearless* had demonstrated that, if they did so, their smoke would obscure the range for the battle fleet. Also, Windy Corner was becoming ever more congested. An officer of *Nicator* (13DF) remembered:

The contrast between the calm manoeuvring of the battle fleet followed by the battle cruisers and 5th Battle Squadron, as compared with the seeming confusion of the small craft was extraordinary. It seemed like Piccadilly Circus with the policemen on strike, and the motor 'buses pushing their way through all the smaller vehicles.[38]

The despatches from these flotillas, including that of Captain (D) James Farie, are singularly uninformative for this period; all we know is that these vessels, mostly modern *M*-class destroyers, ended up, like *Fearless*, on the battle fleet's disengaged quarter, a position from which they could play no part in the rest of the daylight action. By 6.00, *Southampton* had lost sight of the enemy battle-fleet and was engaging their battlecruisers. Goodenough's 2LCS had no pro-spect of reaching the van but, by taking up deployment position N at the rear on the engaged quarter,[39] he would later be able to move out to report once more on the movements of the enemy fleet.

---

[35] *OD*, p. 186. F&H, pp. 159 and 274. *Falmouth*'s torpedo was not listed in the *ATFJ*.

[36] *OD*, pp. 247, 250–1. F&H, p. 256. See *OD*, p. 245 and *OD*(M), p. 400 for *Defender*'s leading position.

[37] *OD*, p. 242. When she crossed the battle fleet's front, they were perhaps headed S.

[38] F&H, p. 355.

[39] *OD*, pp. 176 and 262 and Pl. 1. *GF*, pp. 224–5 and 232–3. Goodenough, p. 96.

As the armoured cruisers led the advance of the battlefleet, their last-minute reorganisation would soon require Rear-Admirals Heath and Arbuthnot to make critical decisions without the aid of up-to-date battle orders. They had distributed their ships along the scouting line in the six positions A–G prescribed in the *GFBOs*, but there were no longer separate wing squadrons to take positions after deployment well ahead and astern of the fleet, from which they could scout ahead and prevent enemy submarines and minelayers from operating astern. However, as deployment became imminent, neither admiral seems to have issued any orders instructing his cruisers how they should distribute themselves between these flank positions and positions F and P on the deployment diagram. The reports from Heath's 2CS are somewhat contradictory but, since they saw little of the enemy while trying to take up position F in the van, only an outline of their movements is needed. Heath admitted, with considerable understatement, that a 'somewhat wide sweep was made'. Echoing the *GFBOs*, Jellicoe excused the delay by asserting that the 2CS 'made a sweep to the Eastward to ensure that no enemy minelayers were at work in that direction'; he added that the 'conditions were exceedingly difficult for making out ships'.[40] Soon after the sounds of firing were heard to the South, *Minotaur* sighted two large ships and altered course to NE to bring her starboard guns to bear. Having received no reply to her challenge, she was about to open fire when the ships were recognised as *Invincibles* of the 3BCS. They were also seen from *Shannon* (next in line) shortly after 6 o'clock. *Hampshire* turned NE with *Minotaur* but then briefly engaged a three-funnelled cruiser apparently of the *Kolberg* class, perhaps one of the IISG. *Hampshire* then sighted a battlecruiser that replied correctly when challenged; *Inflexible* made contact briefly with British armoured cruisers at this time. Having lost sight of the Grand Fleet, at about 6.10 Heath informed *Shannon*: 'I am going round to take up position in the van for Easterly deployment'. As *Cochrane* joined his line in a position between the flagship and *Shannon*, the 2CS altered course gradually to port until they had turned through 32 points onto SE'ly courses after 6.25. *Shannon* received Jellicoe's 6.15 deployment order by wireless signal and she observed the battlefleet deploying at 6.28. *Hampshire* was ordered to close at 6.25 but did not take station astern of *Shannon* until after 6.40. Subsequently, the 2CS continued ESE 4–5 miles on the disengaged side of the leading battleship, *King George V*, though drawing ahead only very slowly.[41]

At 5.42, as the BCF's light cruisers were approaching, Arbuthnot ordered the 1CS to close his flagship *Defence*. *Duke of Edinburgh* turned to port and she

[40] *OD*, pp. 15 and 270.
[41] *OD*, pp. 272–6, 279–80 and Pl. 24. F&H, p. 227. '*Shannon* . . . record of W/T Traffic' in 'Second Cruiser Squadron War Records 1915–918 Vol. I', ADM 137/2142. Heath was 'SO Cruisers' and his course signals were addressed to 'Cruisers' but nothing else suggests that he intended Arbuthnot's 1CS to conform.

Table 7.8. *2CS signals 5.40–6.43pm*

Time of despatch	From	To	System	Message	Time of origin
pm, 31 May					
5.40	SO 2CS	Shannon	SL	I think you had better keep your Destroyer within half a mile and give her a position	
6.00	SO Cruisers	Cruisers	Flags	Alter course in succession to NE. Proceed at your utmost speed	
6.00	SO Cruisers	Cruisers	SL	Form single line ahead in the sequence in which ships now are. Open fire South	
6.07	SO Cruisers	Cruisers	SL	Cease fire	
6.10	SO Cruisers	Cochrane	SL	2CS form single line ahead in sequence of fleet numbers . . . 21 knots. Cease fire	
6.10	SO 2CS	Shannon	Sem.	I am going round to take up position in the van for Easterly deployment	1810
6.13	SO 2CS	Hampshire	SL	Can you see our battlefleet, and which way are they steering?	1812
6.15	SO 2CS	2CS	Flags SL	Form single line-ahead in sequence of fleet numbers. Ships in column to be in open order	
6.17	SO 2CS	Destroyers	Flags	Form submarine screen	
6.22	Hampshire	SO 2CS	SL	Our battlefleet appears to be standing to the Southward bearing SWbyW	1810
6.25	SO 2CS	Hampshire	SL	Close Minotaur	
6.27	SO 2CS	Destroyers	Flags	Form single line-ahead in sequence of fleet numbers. Take station on the port beam of Minotaur, one mile	
6.35	SO 2CS	2CS	Sem.	Keep me informed of movements of our own battlefleet	1830
6.38	SO Cruisers	Cruisers	Flags	Alter course in succession to SSE	
6.40	Hampshire	SO 2CS	SL	Shall I take station in the line? Reply: Yes, take station astern of Shannon	
6.42	SO 2CS	Hampshire	Flags	Take station 2½ cables astern of Shannon	
6.43	SO 2CS	2CS	Flags	Form single line-ahead in the sequence in which ships now are	

Table 7.9. *1CS signals 5.42–8.51pm*

Time of despatch	From	To	System	Message	Time of origin
pm, 31 May					
5.42	SO 1CS	1CS	Flags	Close	
5.50	Duke of Edinburgh			Remarks: Defence opened fire at Enemy	
5.53	SO 1CS	Warrior	Flags	Open fire and engage the Enemy	
6.09	Duke of Edinburgh			Remarks: Duke of Edinburgh opened fire	
6.10	Duke of Edinburgh			Remarks: Enemy Cruiser appeared to be hit and on fire	
8.51	Black Prince	C-in-C	W/T	Urgent. Submarine on port hand, 56°55 N, 6°11E	2045

also saw *Black Prince* do likewise, seemingly by as much as 12 points. But shortly afterwards, an officer aloft in *Duke of Edinburgh* saw the *Black Prince* turn away. He assumed that she had realised that she was too distant to join the rest of the squadron and had decided, in accordance with the *GFBOs*, to take station astern of the battlefleet. At about 5.50, she was seen from *Warrior* 'moving to her station on deployment'.[42] However, since the direction of deployment had not then been decided, she was probably taking up a preparatory position well out on the fleet's starboard flank.

Near the centre of the cruiser line, *Defence*, with *Warrior* 5 cables astern, continued SEbyS. Arbuthnot evidently had no immediate intention of moving wider on the starboard flank in readiness for occupying one of the deployment positions in the line; rather, he was more concerned to gain touch with the enemy. This he did at about 5.47, when three, possibly four, enemy light cruisers were sighted from *Warrior* about four points on the starboard bow, that is bearing about SbyW. *Defence* altered course three points to port to bring the nearest cruiser (the second or third) onto a beam bearing of G80; this move would have taken him across the heads of the starboard battleship columns. The target had three funnels and was identified as one of the *Pillau* class (which made up half of the IISG). *Warrior* increased speed to close up and, beginning at 5.53, she and *Defence* fired three salvos each at extreme range with a ship interval of 12 seconds 'under the concentrated pair ship fire organisation which the squadron had worked up', but all fell short.[43] The 1CS had sighted the IISG but, having just encountered the 3BCS, the latter probably did not notice the shorts from the 1CS. After checking fire, *Defence* led round to starboard in two turns that brought the same target ahead and

---

[42] *OD*, pp. 286 and 293 and Pl. 11a. F&H, pp. 174–5.
[43] *OD*, pp. 290–1 and Pls. 26a and b. F&H, pp. 162–3.

then on a port bearing of R40. At this time, *Warrior* encountered British light cruisers that passed under her stern fairly close, while *Galatea* observed *Defence*'s turns to port and starboard from close by. At 6.05, *Defence* and *Warrior* opened fire on the same enemy ship as before, *Warrior* claiming that their hits brought her almost to a stop. She must have been the *Wiesbaden* though, of course, by that time she had already been crippled by the 3BCS. As *Duke of Edinburgh* closed her consorts, she had observed both phases of their fire; at first, she had been masked by British light cruisers but at 6.08 she too turned to starboard and opened fire at their common target (though her control officer identified her as one of the *Augsburg* class). The 1CS were now coming under fire by heavy shells from the German battlecruisers and battleships, though they could not see their assailants through the smoke and mist. But, though immobilised, *Wiesbaden* was still in a position to fire torpedoes at the approaching BCF, so Arbuthnot's three cruisers continued to close their quarry on a course that was taking them into great danger.[44]

Until 5.58, the 4LCS continued in line-abreast between the armoured cruisers and the battleship columns. The squadron's reports and chart are notably inconsistent, but they seem to have closed up their line by moving towards *Calliope* on the port wing. After racing through the line of the 3LCS before turning up ahead of them, at 6.10 the 4LCS formed single line-ahead on an Easterly course. They were then two miles North of the BCF and SEbyE three miles on the starboard bow of *King George V.* As the signals indicate, the light cruisers may have turned SEbyE together at 6.22, but their chart shows them maintaining a general heading ESE until 6.45. At 6.40, *Calliope* was still three miles from *King George V* bearing EbyS.[45] *Abdiel* remained close to *Calliope* until the fleet deployed, after which she

Table 7.10. *4LCS signals 5.58–6.22pm*

Time of despatch	From	To	System	Message	Time of origin
5.58	SO 4LCS	4LCS	Flags	Close	
6.00	SO 4LCS	4LCS	Flags	From single line abreast to starboard, ships to be five cables apart	
6.10	SO 4LCS	4LCS	Flags	Form single line ahead in sequence of fleet numbers	
6.11	SO 4LCS	4LCS	Flags	Alter course 16 points to starboard	
6.22	SO 4LCS	4LCS	Flags	Alter course together to SEbyE	
6.22	SO 4LCS	4LCS	Flags	Form single line ahead in sequence of fleet numbers. Speed 25 knots	

---

[44] *OD*, pp. 173, 286–8 and 291 and Pl. 11a. F&H, pp. 162–3 and 175–6.

[45] *OD*, pp. 185–6 and 296 and Pl. 12a. F&H, pp. 270–1 and 274. Le Mesurier to C-in-C, 6 August 1916 in ADM 137/1946, f. 626.

'legged it' around the head of the line to her action station on *Iron Duke*'s disengaged beam.[46] The light cruiser *Active* apparently did not realise that the 5BS was present in the rear and she lacked the speed to keep up with the 4LCS; thus she took station on the disengaged beam of the 1st Division as an additional repeating cruiser. On deployment, *Boadicea, Blanche* and *Bellona* moved up to similar positions abeam of *Orion, Iron Duke*'s 3rd Division and *Colossus*, respectively.[47]

In their cruising dispositions, the destroyers with the Grand Fleet formed a submarine screen ahead and on both flanks of the battleship columns. The information in the despatches from these flotillas is also sparse, but *Castor* was on the bow of *King George V*; it seems that the 11DF and the rather depleted 4DF formed the port half of the screen, the 12DF, led by Captain (D) Stirling in *Faulknor*, the starboard half.[48] As would be expected, the boats of the 12DF became mixed up with the BCF destroyers. Some had to turn under the sterns of the 1DF; *Faulknor* had to stop her engines and others to go astern, while *Obedient* also had to stop to avoid colliding with *Lion*. Overs were also falling among them and *Marvel* was hit in the eyes of the ship by a heavy shell which fortunately did not burst.[49] At 6.08, Jellicoe ordered his destroyers to take up the preparatory positions for a deployment to port. This required the two port flotillas to move to positions 2–3 miles on and before the beam of the 1st Division, and the 12DF to go in the opposite direction to three miles before the beam of the 6th Division. But, as Jellicoe recognised, there was insufficient time to reach these positions before the actual deployment at 6.15.[50] Nonetheless, despite the congestion at Windy Corner, the 12DF was able to drop back gradually to positions abeam of the 1BS and eventually of the 5BS; however, *Maenad* got 'a bit of a shock when the *Revenge* fired a salvo of 15-inch bang over our heads at quite a short distance'.[51] After deployment, the 12DF having taken the rear position, the 11DF and the 4DF were supposed to form up three miles ahead of *King George V* at the head of the line. In *The Grand Fleet*, Jellicoe stated that, because of the short notice of the deployment and the subsequent series of course alterations by the fleet to starboard, these two flotillas did not get into position until 7.10, and this appears to agree with the narrative of one of *Castor*'s officers.[52] Other sources suggest that Hawksley may have been able to stay ahead of the 2BS rather than on their disengaged beam,[53]

---

[46] *OD*, p. 298. F&H, pp. 259–60.

[47] *OD*, pp. 87, 302, 368, 370 and 378 and Plate 1. The absent *Blonde* was designated as linking ship between SO 5BS and the C-in-C: *GFBOs III*, V.3.

[48] *OD*, Pl. 15. F&H, 133, 202, 352 and 417. Dreyer, p. 158.   [49] F&H, pp. 133–4 and 256.

[50] *GF*, p. 219. *GFBOs III*, 'Destroyer Diagram', p. 50 and Memorandum, 7 April 1916.

[51] *GFBOs III*, Memorandum 16 April 1916. F&H, pp. 134–5 and 417.

[52] *GFBOs III*, Memorandum 16 April 1916. *GF*, pp. 219 and 222. F&H, p. 203.

[53] *Cf. OD*, Pl. 1 (Battle Plan, 6.40) and *GF*, pp. 224–5 and 232–3 (approximate positions, 6.45 and 7.15). Plotting *Castor*'s movements from her signals between 6.29 and 7.00 – in *OD*(M) – indicates that she and the 11DF stayed ahead of the battleships.

but, either way, neither the 11DF (which was closer to the enemy) nor the 4DF were in action with the enemy until after 7 o'clock.

Jellicoe's deployment

At 5.40, Jellicoe received the first reports from ships of the Grand Fleet indicating that the running fight between the BCF and the German fleet was approaching, though not from the expected direction. The visibility was already deteriorating and would soon become 'extremely baffling, partly due to misty clouds appearing and dissolving and partly to the layers of smoke from funnels and Ships firing'. Though variable, the limits of visibility were generally estimated at between 4½ and 6 miles. The sea remained calm with a light wind from the SW.[54] Also at 5.40, after a gap of 40 minutes, *Southampton* reported her position and that the enemy was then steering NNW, though her signal was not recorded in *Iron Duke* until 5.48. At 5.50, Goodenough announced that the German battlefleet had altered course to N but, to Jellicoe's mystification, the signal placed the enemy battlecruisers SW from their battleships. However, the bearing was received in *Shannon* as W; since both bearings were coded as single letters,[55] the error may have been caused by radio interference, though perhaps *Southampton* sent the reciprocal bearing by mistake. She did not give the enemy battlefleet's bearing or distance from herself in either signal. But, by assuming that at 5.40 the distance was still 10–11 miles to the East, *Iron Duke*'s track chart could have predicted that, at 6.00, the High Seas Fleet would have been located not 30 miles ahead but 20 miles one point on the starboard bow, that is SSE. This was another indication that the enemy would be encountered sooner than had been expected. At 5.45, the Admiralty despatched a new report based on an intercepted signal giving the German position, course and speed at 4.30; it was received in *Iron Duke* at 5.53 but it probably did not reach the bridge until about 6 o'clock. By that time it was obvious that the enemy was very close and Jellicoe had more immediate concerns. As he wrote in 1922, 'as it gave the enemy's position at 4.30 p.m., it was obviously of little use for fixing it 1½ hours later'.[56]

Even though her reports were incomplete, *Southampton* had again distinguished herself as the only BCF ship providing information to the C-in-C. All reports should have stated the identity and course of the vessels sighted and provided enough information to enable their bearing and distance from the C-in-C to be determined.[57] By these criteria, Jellicoe was no better served by the ships of the Grand Fleet. At 5.42, *Black Prince* reported battlecruisers five

---

[54] Dreyer, p. 145. *OD*, pp. 77 (quote), 78, 93, 124 and 357. von Schoultz, p. 127.
[55] *GF*, p. 219. *Shannon* W/T Record (see note 41), f. 110. *GSB 1915*, p. 33.
[56] *JP II*, pp. 423–4.   [57] *GFBOs III*, XII, pp. 19 and 20. Dreyer, p. 156.

Table 7.11. *Reports to Jellicoe 5.40–6.15pm*

Time of despatch	From	To	System	Message	Time of origin
pm, 31 May					
5.40	Minotaur	C-in-C	SL	Report of guns heard South. (Reports also received from Hampshire and Comus)	
5.40 [5.48][1]	Southampton	C-in-C SO BCF	W/T	Urgent. Priority. The Enemy's battlefleet have altered course NNW. My position 56°46 N, 5°40E	1740
5.42	Black Prince	C-in-C and SO 2CS	W/T	[Enemy][2] Battle Cruisers bearing South 5 miles. My position 56°59 N, 5°24E	1740
5.45 [5.53][1]	Admiralty	C-in-C	W/T	Enemy main force at 4.30 56°31 N, 6°5E, steering N, 15 knots. (Received in Iron Duke 5.53)	1745
5.46	SO 1CS	SO 2CS C-in-C	W/T and SL	Ships in action bearing SSW, steering NE. My position 57° 07 N, 5°38E	1745
5.48	Falmouth	SO Cruisers	SL	Two heavy Enemy Ships bearing SSE, steering NE. My position 57°07 N, 5°38E	1745
5.50	Calliope	C-in-C	SL	Have observed what appears to be flashes of guns SSW	
5.50	SO 1BS	C-in-C	Sem.	Gunflashes and heavy gun firing on starboard bow	
5.50 [5.52][3]	Southampton	C-in-C SO BCF	W/T	Urgent. Priority. Enemy battlefleet has altered course to N. Enemy Battle Cruisers bear SW from Enemy battlefleet. My position 56°50 N, 5°44E	1750
5.53	Benbow			Remarks: firing reported off starboard bow	
5.55 [5.55][1]	C-in-C	Marlborough	SL	What can you see? Reply: Our Battle Cruisers bearing SSW, [3–4 miles][4] steering E, Lion leading ship	1800
[6.07][1]				Further reply from Marlborough: 5BS bearing SW	1805
5.56	Colossus			Remarks: Battle Cruisers (British) sighted starboard bow	
6.01 [6.14][1]	C-in-C	SO BCF	SL	Where is Enemy's B.F.? (Repeated at 6.10) Reply: Have sighted Enemy's battlefleet bearing SSW.	

Table 7.11. (*cont.*)

Time of despatch	From	To	System	Message	Time of origin
6.02	C-in-C	General	Flags	(Received in Iron Duke 6.14 p.m.) Alter course leading ships together, rest in succession to South. Speed 18 knots	
6.02 [6.03][1]	Southampton	C-in-C and SO BCF	W/T	Urgent. Have lost sight of Enemy's battlefleet. Am engaging the Enemy's Battle Cruisers. My position is 56°57 N, 5°43E, course NNE, speed 26 knots	1800
6.06	C-in-C	General	Flags	Alter course leading ships together the rest in succession to SE	
6.06	Lion	C-in-C	SL	Enemy's B.Cs. bearing SE	
6.08	C-in-C	Destroyers	Flags	Take up destroyer disposition No. 1	
6.10 [6.12][1]	Barham	C-in-C	Flags W/T	Enemy's battlefleet SSE	[1810][4]
6.15	C-in-C	General	Flags W/T	The column nearest SEbyE is to alter course in succession to that point of the compass, the remaining columns altering course leading ships together the rest in succession so as to form astern of that column, maintaining the speed of the Fleet [Equal Speed, CL]	

[1]   Time received in *Iron Duke*: *AN*, pp. 104–5.
[2]   Received in *Iron Duke, Marlborough* and *Shannon* as 'Battle cruisers': *AN*, pp. 104–5 and *Shannon* W/T Record (see note 41) f. 109.
[3]   Time received but ship not specified: *AN*, p. 104.
[4]   *NSA*, p. 163. *AN*, p. 105. *OD*, p. 64.

miles S but, despite the wording in the *Official Despatches*, she probably did not give their nationality; for unexplained reasons, this report did not reach Jellicoe until 'considerably later' but he then assumed, probably correctly, that they were 'our own vessels'. At 5.46, Arbuthnot signalled that unspecified ships were in action SSW, steering NE. Jellicoe thought these might be the enemy battlecruisers but, in the unpublished appendix which he drew up in 1922 for a new edition of *The Grand Fleet*, he said that he had been suspicious of Arbuthnot's reported position because it placed her too close to *Iron Duke*.[58] In fact, the armoured cruisers had been unable to move ahead by the ordered 16 miles; their positions, if plotted on *Iron Duke*'s track chart, locate them 8–9 miles ahead, which is probably only a mile or two too close to the flagship.

At 5.50, *Calliope* (on the port wing of the 4LCS) informed the C-in-C by searchlight that she could see flashes of guns SSW while, even less precisely, Burney reported flashes and heavy firing 'on the starboard bow'. At 5.55, Jellicoe asked him: 'What can you see' and *Marlborough* replied at 6.00 that Beatty's battlecruisers were in sight 3–4 miles to the SSW, steering E.[59] At 6.01, *Iron Duke* herself sighted *Lion* bearing G64-5. In *The Grand Fleet*, Jellicoe included a plan of the Jutland deployment which gives quite a good general impression of the movements of the battlefleet and the BCF; this shows *Lion* at 6.00, 6.4 miles from *Iron Duke* bearing G75.[60] With visual contact established, Jellicoe demanded of Beatty: 'Where is Enemy's B.F.?' – but he would have to wait for another five minutes before receiving any sort of reply.

By 6 o'clock, 'flashes of gunfire were visible from ahead round to the starboard beam, and the noise was heavy and continuous'. It was evident to Jellicoe that the enemy's heavy ships were close and that he would soon have to deploy his battleship columns into single line. But to judge which wing column should lead the deployment, and on what course, he needed to know the bearing, distance and course of his enemy. *Southampton*'s reports indicated that Scheer was still ahead bearing SSE and steering N – though Jellicoe found the supposed position of the ISG 'almost incredible'. But the 1CS could be seen in action ahead yet they were not falling back on the battlefleet and Jellicoe concluded (correctly for the time being) that their opponents were not battleships.[61] (The brief action further ahead between the 3BCS and the IISG does not seem to have been observed from the battlefleet.) Likewise, all the reports from the Grand Fleet had indicated that the German battleships were not ahead but further on *Iron Duke*'s beam, bearing S or even W of S. As for their course, *Defence* had reported an action headed NE. Yet Beatty could now be seen steering E, which may have suggested that at least the ISG had already turned away in a more Easterly direction.[62]

---

[58] *AN*, pp. 41 and 104 and *Shannon's* W/T record for omission of 'enemy'. *GF*, pp. 217–18. *JP II*, p. 424.

[59] *NSA*, p. 163. *AN*, p. 105, *OD*, p. 64 and *GF*, p. 218 all give the distance (omitted from *OD*(M)), as 3–4 miles.

[60] *OD*, pp. 55 and 57. *GF*, p. 218 and 'Plan of … Deployment', pp. 250–1. Although the plan shows *Lion* 3½ miles SSW from *Marlborough*, *Lion* should perhaps be shown 1.2 miles further E, which corrects disparities with *Iron Duke*'s reported bearings of *Lion* and *Lion*'s of *Marlborough*.

[61] *GF*, pp. 218–19. However, other observers in the Grand Fleet thought the cruisers were coming in: *OD*, pp. 357, 361, 363 and 365.

[62] Neither Beatty nor Jellicoe was aware of the turns through 32 points by the ISG that enabled them to fall back on their battlefleet.

Before considering Jellicoe's subsequent moves, we need to examine his options for deployment. Four general determinants were already apparent. First, at about 5.40, Jellicoe had ordered his Flag Captain, Frederic Dreyer, to have ranges taken all round in order to establish the most favourable direction for gunnery; Dreyer (who saw this precaution as 'typical of Jellicoe's clear mind') reported that the best direction for visibility was then to the Southward and that it would draw Westwards as the sun sank.[63] Second, the optimum enemy bearing was to windward which, given the wind direction, was SW'ward. Third, Jellicoe had disposed his battleship divisions to favour a port deployment led by the 2BS. Fourth, Jellicoe would if possible choose a course after deployment with the object of 'bringing the enemy to action before he can gain his own waters'.[64] An ideal deployment formed the fleet by 9 Pendant into a single straight line with the bearing of the enemy at right angles to the course after deployment. This could be completed in only four minutes but required that, before deployment, the guides of the columns were already on a line-of-bearing at right angle to the enemy's bearing. At six o'clock, Jellicoe's columns were steering SEbyS with the column guides on a line-of-bearing NEbyE from *Marlborough* at the head of the starboard column. This disposition would have favoured a 9 Pendant deployment but only in the increasingly unlikely event that *Southampton*'s earlier reports were correct.[65] With the enemy further to the South, then in less urgent circumstances the possibility of a 9 Pendant deployment might have been preserved by adjusting the line-of-bearing appropriately; but this required a complex unequal-speed manoeuvre that would have taken over 20 minutes to complete.[66] The alternative was to deploy by Oblique Pendant but this too was an unequal-speed manoeuvre and took about 30 minutes to complete. Furthermore, these unequal-speed manoeuvres required close control of speeds and relative positions and, while in progress, ships were out of line and, to varying extents, masked each other's fire; these presented serious risks when the enemy was close and might open fire at any moment. Thus it must already have been apparent to Jellicoe that he would have to deploy rapidly by some form of equal-speed manoeuvre, if not by 9 Pendant then by the Equal Speed Pendant. However, the latter method had never been practised by the Grand Fleet. If an enemy was not sighted on the correct bearing for deployment by 9 Pendant, the preferred method was to deploy by Oblique Pendant. The latter had been

---

[63] Dreyer, pp. 129 and 145.
[64] *GFBOs III*, VII.5. See also McLaughlin, 'Equal Speed' for detailed analysis of deployment options.
[65] Because of the uncertain position of the enemy battlecruisers and the omission of an enemy course, Goodenough's signal at 6.02 cannot have been of any assistance. His reported position at 6.00 was five miles S of *Iron Duke*'s.
[66] *GFBOs*, III.5. *AN*, p. 42 n. 2.

continually practised so as to be ready for this eventuality, even though it 'takes a little time for the divisions to get clear of each other in order to avoid the blanketing of their guns by other ships of their own Fleet'.[67] In contrast, an Equal Speed Pendant deployment did not result in any masking, but for a time there was a distinct bend in the line upon which the enemy might concentrate; it seems that this was regarded as distinctly more objectionable. However, another reason for not practising deployment by Equal Speed Pendant may have been that it was hardly more complicated than successive turns by 9 Pendant and Compass Pendant, which were used all the time for manoeuvring the Fleet; in contrast, the Oblique Pendant deployment was a difficult man-oeuvre requiring special instructions.

At 6.02, Jellicoe turned the battlefleet by 9 Pendant to S; he also reduced speed from 20 to 18 knots 'to admit of ships closing up'. At the time, his information on the enemy battlefleet was still vague – somewhere on the starboard bow on a course between N and E. Jellicoe gave three rather different explanations for his turn. In his despatch, he stated simply that it was 'to take ground to starboard'. But, in *The Grand Fleet*, he added that it was 'with a view to clearing up the situation without altering the formation of the Battle Fleet'. Finally, his unpublished 1922 appendix stated that the turn was made with 'a view to clearing up the situation and bringing the enemy with greater certainty ahead'.[68] Taking ground to starboard had several possible objects. First, it closed the range to enemy forces that were somewhere on the starboard bow. Second, provided the enemy was not too wide on the starboard bow before the turn S, maintaining that course for a few minutes before turning back SE'ly would bring the enemy 'with greater certainty ahead'; thus Jellicoe may have hoped that, with the enemy ahead, he would still be able to deploy rapidly by 9 Pendant NEbyE (the line of bearing of the guides was unchanged), close to the enemy course NE reported by Arbuthnot.[69] Third, a deployment to port, either by 9 or Equal Speed Pendant, must result in a *loss* of ground to starboard; thus Jellicoe may already have decided that, whichever equal-speed deployment he might use, it would be on the port wing column.

Immediately after the turn S, it became apparent from the sounds of firing that the heavy enemy ships were even closer, though their bearing remained uncertain. At 6.06, 'the fleet was turned back by 9 Pendant to S.E. *preparatory*

---

[67] Dreyer, pp. 160–1. 'Tables for use when deploying by Oblique Pendant' 24 February 1916, JMSS 49011; a plot based on Table 2 shows that, had Jellicoe deployed to port by Oblique Pendant, the fire of the rear ships of divisions 2 to 5 would have been blanketed by the leading ships of the divisions next to starboard – in divisions 4 and 5, for about 15 minutes.

[68] *OD*, p. 16. *GF*, pp. 218–19. *JP II*, pp. 420 and 424. In these accounts, it is unclear in places whether enemy bearings are relative to the courses S or SE'ly, though probably the latter was meant.

[69] For the turn S, see also *NSA*, pp. 79–80 and *AN*, p. 42.

to deployment to port'.[70] Also at 6.06, Beatty at last reported by searchlight though he did not answer Jellicoe's question directly, stating only that the enemy battlecruisers bore SE. A minute later, *Lion* turned to starboard from E to ESE ahead of *Marlborough*, with only two points between their courses. For Jellicoe, the evidence was accumulating 'that the enemy's Battle Fleet was on our starboard side, but on a bearing well before the beam'.[71] The words from his despatch italicised above are further evidence that he may already have decided to deploy to port but, if not, he had made up his mind by 6.08 when he ordered his destroyers to take up the preparatory positions for a port deployment.[72] But the question remained of whether to deploy by 9 Pendant NEbyE or by Equal Speed Pendant, which was suitable for any course between NEbyE and SE.

Yet Jellicoe still did not know the bearing of the enemy's battlefleet or, with any certainty, its course. At 6.07, he received a report from *Marlborough* that the 5BS had been sighted bearing SW, though as usual without any indication of distance. But, as we have seen, the fast battleships, like the battlecruisers, had lost sight of the enemy in the mist and neither reported further for the moment. At 6.10, Jellicoe again asked Beatty: 'Where is the enemy's B.F.?' At last, at 6.14, *Lion*'s searchlight flashed: 'Have sighted Enemy's battlefleet bearing SSW'. With *Iron Duke*'s Yeoman of Signals calling each word of Beatty's reply, Jellicoe could make his decision (which was his alone) as soon as the whole message had been received. *Barham* also reported by wireless that she had sighted the enemy battlefleet bearing SSE at about the same time; while the signal records indicate that her message was received in *Iron Duke*'s wireless office at 6.12, Jellicoe insisted that he did not get it until 6.15.[73] In any case, he could only guess the distances from *Barham* to *Marlborough* and to the German ships; whereas *Lion* was in sight from *Iron Duke* on a SE'ly bearing and Jellicoe now 'assumed that the course of the enemy was approximately the same as that of our battle cruisers'.

There was no time to lose, as there was evident danger of the starboard wing column of the Battle Fleet being engaged by the whole German Battle Fleet before deployment could be effected.[74]

A 9 Pendant deployment was no longer appropriate since it would have led to a course diverging from that of the enemy. This left only a deployment on the port column by Equal Speed Pendant, with the port column taking a course that

---

[70] *OD*, p. 16 with my emphasis. Also *GF*, pp. 218–19.

[71] *GF*, 'Plan of Deployment' (see note 60) and p. 220.

[72] *GF*, p. 219. Signal 'CJ1' positioned the destroyer for a port deployment: *GFBOs III*, 'Destroyer Diagrams' (p. 50) and Memorandum, 7 April 1916, ff. 333–4.

[73] Dreyer, pp. 144, 146, 147 note and Plate 11. *GF*, pp. 219–20.

[74] *OD*, p. 53. *GF*, pp. 220 and 'Plan of Deployment'.

would close the enemy and, if possible, threaten his line of retreat to his bases in the Heligoland Bight.

Jellicoe waited until he had heard the whole of Beatty's signal before:

> He stepped quickly on to the platform around the compasses and looked in silence at the magnetic compass card for about twenty seconds ... Then he looked up and broke the silence with the order in his crisp, clear-cut voice to Commander A.R.W.Woods, the Fleet Signal Officer ... '*Hoist equal-speed pendant S.E.*'

Now, since they had never previously deployed in this way, this was not an order familiar to anyone on *Iron Duke*'s bridge; Jellicoe's chief of staff Charles Madden later remembered being astonished by this deployment 'by the rectangular method'. This unfamiliarity probably explains why, as given, Jellicoe's order was ambiguous; because there was no change in compass course, it did not indicate which wing should lead the deployment. Woods asked if he could make it a point to port so that the fleet would know that it was to deploy on the port wing column. Jellicoe agreed at once and at 6.15 Woods ordered 'Equal Speed, Charlie London' to be hoisted; the order was broadcast by wireless at the same time.[75] As it happens, Woods need not have requested the change in course, since the signal could have been made in the alternative form in which the course change was expressed as a number of points relative to the previous course; the Equal Speed Pendant hoisted inferior to a Zero numerical flag would have expressed Jellicoe's intention exactly.[76] Perhaps Woods forgot the alternative form, though he may well have preferred to make as small a change as possible to his admiral's instruction.

Jellicoe did not wait for all ships to reply to his signal before ordering Dreyer to begin the deployment; *Iron Duke*'s siren sounded two short blasts and she turned seven points to port onto a course NEbyE, the line-of-bearing of the guides. The flagships of adjacent columns immediately did likewise, the other ships following their flagships in succession. *King George V* noted the deployment signal as received at 6.13 but her track chart shows her not turning to SEbyE but holding on SE until 6.26 before turning EbyS.[77] Jellicoe had deployed just in time. As most of his battleships turned NEbyE, a few enemy shells, some ricochets, fell around *Iron Duke*, *Vanguard* and *Revenge*. But, after the enemy emerged from the mist opposite *Colossus*, one full salvo fell only 200 yards short of her, while another salvo straddled *Hercules*'s forecastle. And, just after she turned, *Marlborough* was able to fire seven salvos at a *Kaiser*-class battleship bearing G110, range 13,000 yards (though she seems to have opened fire with an estimated range of only 10,000 yards).[78] In four minutes, the British battlefleet was in a single line, albeit with a bend of six

---

[75] Dreyer, pp. 146, 147 note and 169.   [76] *GSB 1915*, pp. 17–18 and 33.
[77] Dreyer, pp. 146–7. *OD*, p. 116 and Pl. 8.   [78] *OD*, pp. 53, 65, 70, 72, 76, 78, 84 and 357.

(or perhaps seven) points through which the 2nd to 6th Divisions would pass in turn to form astern of *King George V.* As Dreyer emphasised with his habitual italics: '*We had not yet sighted any German vessels from the* Iron Duke',[79] yet Jellicoe had attained nearly all of the objectives of deployment. The British divisions were led by the powerful 2BS. They enjoyed both the light-gage and wind-gage for gunnery. They were beginning to interpose themselves between the German fleet and its bases and they were even crossing the German 'T'. And from both segments of the British line their potential targets in the German van were on beam bearings. Jellicoe had accepted the risk of an enemy concentration on the bend in the line but in the knowledge that the enemy would be contending with unfavourable visibility; in fact, all British ships went through the bend without coming under fire. However, despite his brief turn to the S, he could not avoid losing ground to starboard. Thus the enemy was and would remain at or beyond the limits of visibility and the British ships would be unable to make the most of their advantages.

In *The Grand Fleet* (published in 1919) Jellicoe declared:

My first and natural instinct was to form on the starboard wing column in order to bring the Fleet into action at the earliest possible moment, but it became increasingly apparent, both from the sounds of gunfire and the reports from the *Lion* and *Barham*, that the High Sea Fleet was in such close proximity and on such a bearing as to create obvious disadvantages in such a movement.

This implies that, even though he had ordered his destroyers at 6.08 to prepare for a port deployment, he was still considering a starboard deployment as late as 6.14, when *Lion*'s report put the enemy battlefleet about SbyE from *Marlborough*.[80] From course SE, a starboard deployment by Equal Speed Pendant had to be straight ahead or with a turn to starboard. But, even on SE, the enemy would be only some three points on the starboard bows of the 6th Division and Burney would soon have to turn away in succession to port to bring his targets, now thought to be on an Easterly heading, onto beam bearings. The leading divisions would obstruct the fire of the remainder as the latter headed SWbyS before making their two turns to starboard; thus the weaker divisions would receive the enemy's concentrated fire while the stronger divisions hauled into line. The enemy would also have the opportunity to concentrate on the two turning points, while the two large turns would disrupt the fire of the British battleships as they came into action. Jellicoe also made the reasonable, though wrong, assumption that the German destroyers were ahead of their battlefleet and so would be close enough to mount an attack as the British began their deployment, when his own destroyers were still moving to

---

[79] Dreyer, pp. 146 and 147.
[80] Bearing to nearest compass point *cf. GF*, p. 250, 'Plan of Deployment' and p. 290, diagram of starboard deployment.

positions on the flanks. The Germans might even be close enough to fire torpedoes from their own line.[81] That Jellicoe felt obliged to catalogue in his book the many objections to a starboard deployment suggests that he was already aware of the criticisms of his port deployment that would surface in 1922 in the *Naval Staff Appreciation*.[82] Indeed, his counterarguments are so persuasive that it seems probable that he never felt any real impulse to form on the starboard wing column[83] and that his declaration to that effect was no more than a sop to his critics. His judgement was vindicated in 1925, when the *German Official Account* of Jutland declared that, if Jellicoe had deployed to starboard, 'he would ... have led his ships into a position which would have been only too welcome to the German fleet'.[84]

Carnage between the lines

As Jellicoe turned back to SE from S, *Defence*, followed by *Warrior* and *Duke of Edinburgh*, continued to close *Wiesbaden* on a course almost at right angles to that of Beatty's battlecruisers. However intent Arbuthnot may have been on destroying his quarry, he can hardly have failed to notice that, from 6.07, his ships were being straddled by heavy German shells,[85] or to realise that, with deployment therefore now imminent, he should have been not ahead of the battleship columns but already on their starboard flank. Unfortunately, the safer route to this position was blocked by the congestion at Windy Corner. Thus, short of abandoning his attack on *Wiesbaden* and deploying towards the 'wrong' flank – which Arbuthnot would almost certainly have considered a dereliction of duty[86] – he was obliged to press on and then attempt to reach the flank on the engaged sides of the battlecruisers and the 5BS. He continued to close the *Wiesbaden* to a range of only 5,500–6,000 yards until, at 6.15, *Defence* and *Warrior* cut across *Lion*'s bows, forcing her to veer sharply to port from ESE to ENE. *Warrior* had passed so close that *Duke of Edinburgh* was unable to follow; she turned away onto a course parallel with *Lion*'s, some 600–800 yards on Beatty's port beam. However, she soon fell astern and was also passed by light cruisers and destroyers, presumably the 3LCS and 1DF keeping pace with the battlecruisers.[87]

Once across *Lion*'s bows, at 6.17 *Defence* turned sharply to starboard so that she might pass down between the lines. *Warrior* closed to three cables astern

[81] *GF*, pp. 220–1 and 290. Jellicoe himself did not mention the masking (blanketing) of the rear divisions but this was one of principal objections listed in Dreyer, pp. 161–2.
[82] *NSA*, Chapter VIII. See also McLaughlin, 'Equal Speed', pp. 134–5.
[83] On heading S between 6.02 and 6.06 with the starboard columns thrust forward, Jellicoe might have briefly contemplated a starboard deployment but he never mentioned this possibility.
[84] *GOA*, p. 99.   [85] *OD*, pp. 286 and 291 and Pl. 11a.
[86] For his unbending character, see Paul Halpern, 'Arbuthnot, Sir Robert Keith', *ODNB*.
[87] *OD*, pp. 136, 144, 286, 291 and Pl. 10. F&H, pp. 163 and 176.

and made her own turn at 6.19. As the battlecruisers moved away, the two armoured cruisers were in clear view 1–1½ miles from the British battlefleet (which had just begun to deploy) abeam of *Neptune* in the 5th Division.[88] The 12DF, which was dropping back gradually to its position in the rear, was even closer, with *Defence* and *Warrior* as little as 600 yards on the flotilla's starboard bow and beam. From *Neptune*, Arbuthnot's ships 'were almost continuously hidden by splashes, they were being repeatedly hit by heavy shell, and must have been going through hell on earth'. At 6.19–6.20, according to *Warrior*'s despatch, *Defence* was hit by two salvos in quick succession, after which she blew up completely.[89] The majority of accounts agree that the first of these salvos set off the after magazine and that she disappeared under an enormous column of flames and smoke after the second salvo struck near the fore turret. There were no survivors from her crew of 903.[90] It is uncertain which German ships began the cannonade at the 1CS. When one of these four-funnelled cruisers was sighted from *Derfflinger*, her control officers were concerned that she might have been the *Rostock*. While they hesitated, Paschen of *Lützow* had no doubts; commencing at 6.16 at a range of 8,300 yard on a forward bearing of R30, he ordered five salvos, three of which straddled, before his target blew up. However, four battleships of the IIIBS – *Grosser Kurfürst, Markgraf, Kronprinz* and *Kaiser* – joined in at the same time, so the last two fatal salvos to strike *Defence* could have come from any of these five ships. Immediately after the explosion, *Lützow* and *Derfflinger* were obliged to give all their attention to the British capital ships[91] but *Warrior* reported that she remained under fire from about four enemy battleships. She began to withdraw so that her smoke would not obstruct the fire from the British line but, despite her zigzagging, she received many hits; one wrecked her bridge shortly after 6.17, others struck the quarterdeck, the upper deck and below and above the waterline. By 6.26, all electric instruments and hydraulic power in her turrets had failed and, as she turned away, her speed fell as her engine rooms began to fill with water.[92] But, just as it seemed that she must soon go the same way as *Defence*, German attention was diverted towards a considerably more valuable target.

---

[88] *OD*, pp. 286, 291 and 363. F&H, pp. 161 and 193.

[89] *OD*, pp. 291 and 331–2. F&H, pp. 135–6, 163 and 192 (also 160–1).

[90] *OD*, pp. 201, 291, 300 and 363 and F&H, pp. 135, 136 and 419: but *OD*, pp. 73, 159, 208 and 361 differ. An observer in *Colossus* saw flames from the after magazine spreading along the ammunition passages serving the 7.5in turrets to the forward magazine: Campbell, p. 181 and *Technical History and Index, TH25, Storage and Handling of Explosives in Warships*, p. 2, AL. This is consistent with the condition of the wreck – Innes McCartney, 'The Armoured Cruiser *Defence* ...', *International Journal of Nautical Archaeology* (2012), 41.1, pp. 56–66.

[91] von Hase, pp. 179–80. Paschen, p. 36. Tarrant, p. 127.

[92] *OD*, pp. 65, 207, 289 and 291–2. F&H, p. 164.

At 6.06, *Marlborough* could be seen from *Barham* on the port bow and, some minutes later, others of the 6th Division could also be made out. But no other battleships were visible and Evan-Thomas concluded that this was the head of the battle line and that he would be able to form up ahead; thus he altered to about ESE, converging on the SE course recently resumed by the main battlefleet.[93] Two minutes before the deployment, the 5BS was on the starboard beam of *Colossus* and after the deployment they were astern and on her starboard quarter. The 5BS were seen to be under fire but *Barham* and *Valiant* were replying by 6.15.[94] It was 6.19 when Evan-Thomas saw more divisions of the Grand Fleet as they were deploying to port. Recognising his mistake and that, if he attempted to follow Beatty's battlecruisers towards the van, he would mask the fire of the battlefleet, he decided to make a large turn to port (a second turn to starboard would then have been necessary) to haul into line astern of the 6th Division. As he described it:

This was done without signal, and all ships were exceedingly well handled by their Captains, and came into line by turning with 'Barham' in the quickest possible time.[95]

The reality was much less satisfactory, though many details remain obscure. Evan-Thomas implied that his four battleships turned together, yet his 6.18 signal ordered a 16-point turn in succession. Further, Captain Craig reported that the turn was about eight points, that speed was also reduced, and that the leading German battleships (which he identified as *Königs*) seized the opportunity to concentrate on the turning point[96] – which only existed if the turns were in succession. A turn together without signal while also reducing speed seems like a recipe for confusion. Even if the turn was in succession, it may have been compromised if, as one report seems to suggest, *Malaya* was not in line but on *Warspite*'s port quarter.[97] However her situation arose, *Warspite*, after altering course to port, found herself apparently approaching *Malaya*. *Warspite*'s Captain Phillpotts gave the helm order 'Port 20°', thus initiating a quite rapid turn to starboard. The helm was put over too quickly and, perhaps in part due to damage to the steering engine caused by a hit or near miss, jammed at 'Port 15°' when 'Amidships' was ordered. *Warspite* then shaved close under *Valiant*'s stern onto the latter's starboard quarter before continuing round towards the enemy line. Attempts to use the engines to stop her turning only reduced the speed at which

---

[93] *OD*, pp. 64 and 194. *Barham*'s and *Malaya*'s charts show ESE, *Valiant*'s and *Warspite*'s EbyS – *OD*, Plates 10a, 19, 17 and 18 respectively.

[94] *OD*, pp. 78 and 207 (*Colossus*'s time for deployment was 6.12).

[95] *OD*, p. 194 and also p. 200.

[96] *OD*(M), 6.18 and *OD*, p. 200. Evan-Thomas's diagrams XI and XII (*OD*, Pl. 16) also show turns together.

[97] F&H, p. 150; this account and its illustrative diagram are suspect due to inconsistencies both internal and with other despatches, including that of *Warspite*'s captain – though he was supposed to have checked it.

she was closing the enemy, so her captain decided to go full speed ahead and the ship turned almost two complete circles before, by going astern with the port engines, she managed to check her swing and stagger away to the Northward.[98] As she circled, she was the first reasonably visible target for the German battleships and, between 6.20 and 6.24, *König, Friedrich der Grosse* and the leading ships of the IBS – *Ostfriesland, Thüringen* and *Helgoland* – all opened fire at her at ranges between 9,600 and 15,300 yards. *König* at the head of the battle line was then turning from NE to ENE and soon lost sight of her target; in view of her position, she may actually have fired at one of the other ships of the 5BS. But *Ostfriesland* kept up a protracted cannonade at *Warspite* (though probably not until as late as her claimed 6.45) while the other three battleships fired about 20 rounds each before losing sight of their target. *Oldenburg* and *Nassau* (also of the IBS) fired only a few rounds at 15,300 yards.[99] For the reasons given in the previous chapter, *Warspite* probably received 11 hits during this intense concentration; seven were on the port side that she presented to her assailants as she came closest to them. During her gyrations, centralised fire control was impossible; fire was maintained by her turrets in local control but she probably did not make any hits.[100]

As *Warrior* approached the circling *Warspite*, the latter was considerably closer to the enemy than the rest of the 5BS; they continued through the turns that would take them into line astern of *Agincourt*, which Walwyn of *Warspite* saw 'a long way off firing like blazes'. It appears that *Warspite* was making her first circle when *Warrior* attempted to pass astern but, as the battleship continued to turn to starboard, she passed under *Warrior*'s stern, screening the armoured cruiser from enemy fire and, in her captain's opinion, saving her from being sunk. *Warrior* was then able to withdraw around the rear of the British battle line. Here she observed an armoured cruiser, which can only have been the *Black Prince* taking her designated deployment position well in the rear;[101] if so, this was the last time she was sighted in daylight.[102] *Warrior* herself was in a serious condition. It was estimated that she had been hit by at least fifteen heavy shells as well as about six of lesser calibre and her casualties would eventually reach seventy-one killed and thirty-six injured. The engine rooms continued to fill with water but they could not be reached due to fires raging aft. Although the engines could not be stopped, they continued to turn while there

---

[98] *OD*, pp. 202–3 and 208. F&H, p. 149.   [99] Tarrant, p. 129.

[100] Campbell, pp. 173–8 (hits 3 and 13 are assumed here to have occurred earlier), 187–8, 193 and 195. *OD*, p. 203.

[101] *OD*, p. 292; *Warrior* is not even mentioned in *Warspite*'s despatch and her 'particularly gallant act' was quite unintentional. F&H, pp. 150 and 164. *AN*, p. 41. A few reports – *OD*, pp. 84, 200–1 and 208, F&H, pp. 136 and 159–60 – confuse *Black Prince* with either *Defence* or *Warrior* or even have her accompanying the other two.

[102] At 8.45, she made a W/T report of a submarine from a position which placed her 20 miles NEbyE from *Iron Duke* at that time (as plotted on *OD*, Plate 6a).

was steam available, enabling *Warrior* to set a course to the NNW at 10–11 knots. Just before 7 o'clock, she encountered the *Engadine* and asked the seaplane carrier to stand by. The Engineer Commander having predicted that the engines must stop before long, fires were drawn and steam cut off at the boilers and at 8.00, *Warrior* was taken in tow by *Engadine*. 'Taking in tow was an exercise that Sir Robt. Arbuthnot made the ships of his squadron practice, and from this we now profited.' Course was then shaped for Cromarty at a speed of about seven knots. Unfortunately, during the night the weather deteriorated and the water in *Warrior* continued to rise. By 7.15 a.m. it was clear that her stability was fast disappearing and *Engadine* was called alongside to take off her crew. At 8.25 a.m. *Warrior* was abandoned, down by the stern and with her upper deck only a few feet above water, and *Engadine* proceeded to Rosyth, arriving at 1.35am on 2 June.[103]

Warspite had been badly damaged by shellfire but she was not disabled and her casualties – ultimately fourteen killed and thirty-two wounded – were comparatively light. After her withdrawal, she attempted to take station astern of *Malaya*; *Dublin* and *Valiant* reported that she was in the line by 6.45 and 6.58 respectively, while the destroyer *Maenad* also saw her take up her station. But before *Warspite* had closed to 5 cables' distance, she was found to be still unmanageable, so she again withdrew Northwards to shift over to her alternative steering engine, while the opportunity was also taken to survey her damage. Captain Phillpotts concluded that for the time being only a moderate speed was safe but it was 8.50 before he reported that, although she had two big holes abreast the engine room, she could steam 16 knots; he also requested the position of the battlefleet, though he did not give his own position.[104] With darkness falling, Evan-Thomas must have decided that an unescorted *Warspite* would have been too at risk from enemy destroyers or submarines if she attempted to rejoin the 5BS; at 9.07, he ordered her to return to Rosyth, though, as she would find next morning, she was still vulnerable to U-boat attack.[105]

The BCF chart shows that, after veering to port at 6.15 to avoid *Defence* and *Warrior*, the battlecruisers continued ENE for ten minutes.[106] Chatfield's despatch claimed that the passage of the armoured cruisers 'caused "Lion" to cease fire and lose touch with the enemy'; however, this is not borne out by her transmitting station record, which shows her firing nine or ten salvos at the left-hand enemy battlecruiser, mostly bearing G96, that is, about SbyE, at a range falling from

---

[103] *OD*, pp. 264 and 292–3. Campbell, p. 338. *OD*(M) *passim* but especially 31 May, 6.55–8.00pm and 1 June, 6.30–8.25am. F&H, pp. 165–73 and 406–16 for detailed accounts of the attempt to save *Warrior*.

[104] *OD*, pp. 181, 203 and 209. Campbell, p. 340. F&H, pp. 153–6. *OD*(M), 8.50pm.

[105] *OD*(M), 9.07pm. *OD*, p. 203.

[106] *OD*, Pl. 10. Other sources also have this course at similar times: VNE (6.19–27); *OD*, Pl. 12 (*Princess Royal*, 6.18–24) and Pls. 9a and 31(*New Zealand*, both 6.20–30).

10,250 to 8,250 yards. Near the end of this series, rapid fire was ordered at 6.19 and Campbell credits *Lion* with two hits on *Lützow*.[107] Unlike *Lion, Princess Royal* was engaging an enemy battlecruiser at about the time of the turn to port but her gunnery record contains only three ranges, the last at 6.19 being 12,000 yards when the bearing was G98. The 1CS may have briefly attracted the enemy's fire away from her but she was soon under heavy fire from what were thought to be *König*-class battleships. A little before 6.22, *Princess Royal* was hit by two shells from the same salvo. One permanently jammed the training of X turret by displacing and distorting the barbette. The other damaged condenser casings in the after engine rooms, inflicted many casualties among the after 4in gun crews and ignited some cordite, though the fire was soon brought under control.[108] After her turn to port, *Tiger* once more engaged her earlier target, the third battlecruiser from the left, now bearing G85 but her ranges plummeted from 15,000 to as little as 6,200 yards; assuming that her target was *Seydlitz*, she did not make any hits. *New Zealand* continued firing as she turned to port, though she seems to have changed from the first to the second battleship from the left, bearing G90; the ranges of her five salvos at this ship were from 10,350 to 9,500 yards.[109] Thus, although the actual ranges from Beatty's battlecruisers differ substantially, their reported bearings all indicate that the ISG and the Vth Division were pretty well abeam.

Beatty's course ENE diverged by only one point from that of the rear divisions of the Grand Fleet as they approached the turning point, while the van divisions were already heading across his bows; even Beatty's own revised chart of the battle indicated that, had he held on, he would have collided with the 1st Division at about 6.30. His course should have been considerably further to starboard: both to extricate his ships from the area bounded by the two arms of the still-deploying Grand Fleet and to take him well ahead of *King George V* to his own deployment position – this, according to the *GFBOs*, was supposed to be some seven or eight miles on the leading battleship's starboard bow.[110] Perhaps he delayed turning back towards the enemy because he was reluctant to expose his four surviving battlecruisers to more of the damage that was being inflicted on *Princess Royal*.

However, the situation was soon transformed by the appearance of Hood and the 3BCS. They had been heading West towards the sound of gunfire but, on seeing flashes on the port bow, turned Southwards. At about 6.20, enemy battlecruisers were sighted ahead and Hood turned again to port onto a course about SE before promptly engaging the ISG.[111] According to Beatty:

---

[107] *OD*, p. 144. REL. Campbell, p. 183.
[108] *OD*, pp. 148–9, 151 and 388. Campbell, pp. 170–2: who attributes the hits to *Markgraf*.
[109] *OD*, pp. 156, 392 and 395. Campbell, p. 187.
[110] *OD*, Pl. 8a. *GFBOs III*, XXIII, deployment diagram, p. 41.
[111] F&H, p. 227. *OD*, pp. 164–5 and 170. *Indomitable*'s chart (*OD*, Pl. 13) shows her turning directly from WbyS to SE½E but her despatch gives the later course as 153° (about SbyE). *Inflexible*'s course was described as 'easterly'.

At 6.20 p.m. the 3rd Battle Cruiser Squadron ... appeared ahead, steaming South towards the enemy van. I ordered them to take station ahead, which was carried out magnificently ... At 6.25 p.m. I altered course to the E.S.E. in support.

However, there is no other record of this order, while a bearing and station 'ahead' makes no sense while Beatty's course was still ENE. Almost certainly, Hood turned to engage on his own initiative, while Beatty just followed in his wake – though the BCF chart shows a large turn from ENE to SE at 6.25 followed by a turn to ESE at 6.35.[112] After her turn SE, *Lion* fired seven salvos, the last at 6.31½, at an unidentified target bearing G84–G87 at an opening range of 8,300 yards, while *Tiger* and *New Zealand* checked fire at 6.29 and 6.27½ respectively.[113] When *Inflexible* opened fire at 6.20 only one enemy ship was visible at first, which was thought to be a *König*-class battleship; she bore G80 at a range of 8,000 yards. By 6.28, the next ship astern, which was apparently firing from five turrets, could be made out and, since she was not under fire, *Inflexible* shifted to her. At 6.20 or a little later, *Indomitable* opened fire at a range of 9,500 yards on 'the centre enemy Battle Cruiser' bearing G90. Another British ship was also firing salvos at the same target – *Indomitable* was laying and firing by 'Individual', which, she claimed, enabled her to distinguish the fall of her own shots. She also 'considered that the third enemy Battle Cruiser was engaged by "Lion" '. During this action, *Lützow* received eight hits, *Derfflinger* three and *Seydlitz* one. It appears that *Indomitable* engaged *Derfflinger* throughout and that *Inflexible* fired initially at *Derfflinger* – mistaking her quite similar profile for that of a *König* – before shifting to *Seydlitz* with her five turrets.[114] That being so, all eight hits on *Lützow* can be attributed to *Invincible*; these included the four hits in the vicinity of the bow and broadside torpedo flats (the latter also forward) which were the principal causes of her later foundering.[115]

At the start of the engagement, the 3BCS were scarcely visible from the ISG in the mist and little troubled by enemy fire. But, a few minutes before she was lost, *Invincible* received several hits; *Indomitable*, which was also straddled, saw one of these hits strike the flagship aft.[116] In the words of *Invincible*'s gunnery control officer, Commander Hubert Dannreuther:

[112] *OD*, p. 136 and Pl. 10.

[113] REL. *OD*, pp. 388, 393 and 395, *Princess Royal* firing a single salvo at 6.30 at what might have been a battleship.

[114] Gunnery reports by *Indomitable* and *Inflexible* (both 10 June 1916) in BTY 6/6 (no other copies of these have been found). See also F&H, p. 227, which suggests that later the first three German battlecruisers were visible from *Inflexible*.

[115] Campbell, pp. 183–7 for hits on the ISG. See also Paschen, pp. 36–7, though some of the hits described as having been made at this time probably happened later at 7.15–18: Campbell, pp. 218–20.

[116] von Hase, p. 181. *Indomitable* gunnery report (see note 114). *OD*, pp. 164–5 and 168.

A few moments before the 'Invincible' blew up, Admiral Hood hailed the Control Officer in the Control Top from the fore bridge: 'Your firing is very good, keep at it as quickly as you can, every shot is telling.'

Thus *Invincible* had broken into the rapid fire that accounts for her many hits. But then:

at 6.34 p.m. a heavy shell stuck 'Q' turret and, bursting inside, blew the roof off. This was observed from the control top. Almost immediately following there was a tremendous explosion amidships indicating that 'Q' magazine had blown up. The ship broke in half and sank in 10 or 15 seconds.[117]

It is likely that the adjacent P magazine also blew up and that the explosions then smashed through the machinery spaces fore and aft to ignite cordite in A and X magazines; the ship then broke in two due to the structural damage amidships.[118] 1,026 officers and men were killed; there were six survivors, three, including Dannreuther, from the fore top. They saw the bow and stern pieces of their ship standing vertically clear of the water before they were picked up by the destroyer *Badger* of the 1DF shortly after seven o'clock.[119]

Beginning at 6.22, Hipper had led the ISG in a large turn to starboard from NE to about SSE.[120] This was probably prompted mainly by the two hits just made by *Lion* on *Lützow*, since as yet the 3BCS were scarcely visible. One of these hits had started a serious fire in the vicinity of B turret – it was also noticed from *Derfflinger* – so that control had to be transferred to *Lützow's* after position. From 6.24, *Derfflinger* engaged what she thought were enemy battleships to the NE at ranges of 6,500–7,600 yards; her targets often disappeared from sight, spotting was difficult (only salvos falling well short could be clearly distinguished) and von Hase had to rely for ranges largely on his range-taker's measurements. Both the leading German battlecruisers were being hit, *Lützow* severely, without being able to reply effectively. von Hase recalled:

This went on until [6.29]. At this moment, the veil of mist in front of us split across like the curtain of a theatre. Clear and sharply silhouetted against the uncovered part of the horizon we saw a powerful battleship [*sic*] with two funnels between the masts and a third close against the tripod mast. She was steering an almost parallel course with ours at top speed.[121]

Meanwhile, *Lützow* had already turned away to the South from the British fire but now she too found a British battlecruiser clearly in sight, four

---

[117] *OD*, p. 168. *Indomitable* also timed the explosion at 6.34 but *Inflexible* at 6.30; *OD*, pp. 165 and 170.

[118] Brown, '*Invincible*'. Innes McCartney, 'Jutland 1916 . . . The Wreck of the Battle Cruiser HMS INVINCIBLE', *Skyliss* (2012), 2, pp. 168–76.

[119] Campbell, p. 338. *OD*, pp. 168–9.   [120] *OD*, German Plans V and VI, Diagrams 4 and 5.

[121] von Hase, pp. 181–3.

points on her quarter. With fire controlled from the after position, *Lützow* straddled with her second salvo (fired with a DOWN correction of 400 metres). As her fall-of-shot indicator sounded for her third salvo, the control officer (Lieutenant-Commander Bode) saw the red flames of hits among the splashes and, a few seconds later, his target blew up. Paschen, the gunnery officer, acknowledged that *Derfflinger* was also firing at *Invincible* but insisted that Bode should be credited with her destruction.[122] von Hase declared that the ship that he had just sighted had been firing at his ship, but he made a similar claim, probably also wrong, about *Queen Mary*. His description of his target may also have benefited from hindsight since, after the battle, *Derfflinger* claimed to have sunk a ship of the *Queen Elizabeth* class. Despite these reservations, it is likely that he was indeed shooting at *Invincible*. He fired his first salvo at the range-finder range of 9,000 metres (9,600 yards) and spotted the fall as 'Over. Two hits'. He then ordered '100 down. Good, Rapid', that is, with a salvo interval of 20 seconds. At 6.31, he fired his last salvo and 'for the third time we witnessed the terrible spectacle that we had already seen in the case of the *Queen Mary* and the *Defence*'. *Derfflinger* then trained her guns onto the next British battlecruiser from the right but ceased fire at 6.33.[123]

While engaging the 3BCS, the ISG also had to contend with *Falmouth* and *Yarmouth* of the 3LCS. From their position on *Lion*'s starboard bow, they had seen the 3BCS arriving from the Northward and the British and German battlecruisers turning onto parallel courses. The two light cruisers with the 3BCS were now about 2,000 yards on their port beam and the two leading German battlecruisers some 6,000 yards before their starboard beam. *Falmouth* and *Yarmouth* engaged the leading enemy ship with gunfire and *Lützow* responded with her 5.9in; each light cruiser also fired a torpedo, *Falmouth* claiming, though incorrectly, that she made a hit. *Invincible* was seen to blow up at about 6.30 (Napier believed the explosion 'was the result of a shot into her magazine') and 'Soon after, the enemy Battle Cruisers turned away to westward'[124] – but, as we shall see, Napier did not report this important observation until later, and only then in response to a query from Beatty.

---

[122] Paschen, pp. 37–8.

[123] von Hase, pp. 183–5 and 189; he claimed implausibly that the silhouettes of the *Invincibles* and *Queen Elizabeths* had 'a perplexing similarity'.

[124] *OD*, pp. 137 and 186 for Napier's despatch. For other, though inconsistent, reports, see F&H, pp. 274 and 276. *Falmouth*'s torpedo was probably fired at 6.25 rather than 6.55 and *Yarmouth*'s at 6.30: *cf. GFG&TMs*, p. 51 and *ATFJ*, p. 9.

The battlefleets engage

Having arrived at the turning point, the 2nd to 6th Divisions altered course in succession at three- to four-minute intervals onto the deployment course. *Iron Duke*'s time for her turn SEbyE was 6.21 (though one of her charts has 6.23) and *Marlborough* put her helm over at 6.34.[125] The 5BS (less *Warspite*) formed up astern of *Agincourt* at 6.30 and followed her round after she turned at about 6.36. By about 6.38, the deployment of the British battlefleet into line was complete.[126]

As Beatty's battlecruisers headed ENE, they crossed the lines of fire of some of the battleships that had not yet reached the turning point. When *Marlborough* opened fire at 6.17, the battlecruisers had already drawn ahead and their smoke had cleared. Some two miles nearer the enemy, they then came up on the 4th Division's quarter, from which the German ships could be seen as 'grey misty outlines through the intervals in the Battle cruisers and their smoke'.[127] Beatty's slightly diverging course seems to have been enough to clear *Iron Duke*'s front just as she turned SEbyE, thus revealing first the

Table 7.12. *Grand Fleet signals 6.19–6.33pm*

Time of despatch	From	To	System	Message	Time of origin
pm, 31 May					
6.19	C-in-C	SOs in company. (Call sign of SO 3BCS apparently used)	W/T	Priority. Present course of fleet SEbyE	1815
6.23	C-in-C	11DF	Flags	Present course of fleet is SEbyE	1815
6.24	Southampton	C-in-C SO BCF	W/T	Enemy battlefleet bear 10–11 miles SSE. Course of Enemy battlefleet NE. My position 56°58 N, 5°51E	1820
6.24	SO 4BS	4th Division	Flags	Open fire and engage the Enemy	
6.26	C-in-C	Dreadnought Battlefleet and attached Cruisers	W/T and Flags	. . . 14 knots	
6.33	C-in-C	General	Flags	. . . 17 knots	

---

[125] Dreyer, p. 149. *OD*, pp. 65 and Pls. 2, 1a, 6a (for *Iron Duke*'s turn at 6.23), 7a and also 29.

[126] *OD*, pp. 17, 92, 194 and 219. F&H, p. 128. *GF*, p. 223. Dreyer, p. 148.

[127] *OD*, pp. 65, 361, 363 and 366.

disabled *Wiesbaden* and, at 6.26, the leading German battleship, the *König*. After Beatty turned to follow the 3BCS, at about 6.30 his battlecruisers passed between *Erin* and the enemy fleet, while by 6.33 he had cleared the ranges of all the British battleships.[128] *Erin* complained that the 2BS's view had been obscured by the dense smoke from the *Duke of Edinburgh* on *Lion*'s disengaged side. The 1st Division continued to be hampered by the lingering smoke and cordite fumes from Beatty's battlecruisers, light cruisers and destroyers; thus the four leading battleships caught only momentary glimpses of the enemy and were unable to open fire.[129] Their problem persisted until *Duke of Edinburgh*, which had taken up a position on the starboard bow of *King George V*, crossed ahead; at 7.17, she joined up with the armoured cruisers of the 2CS.[130]

After the 6.15 deployment, Jellicoe ordered a speed of 14 knots but the time and reason for this reduction remain uncertain. His despatch states that it was made 'on deployment to allow the battle-cruisers, which were before the starboard beam, to pass ahead'; in *The Grand Fleet*, he added that 'the reduction ... caused some "bunching" at the rear of the line as the signal did not get through quickly. The reduction, however, had to be maintained until all the battle cruisers had formed ahead'. In the 1BS, *Marlborough* and others had to reduce further to eight knots; *St Vincent* even had to stop, although shortly after 6.32 (about the time when these ships were turning to SEbyE) she nonetheless came up on *Neptune*'s beam, masking her line of fire until 6.40.[131] Also the 5BS, when hauling into line, found that they were going too fast; at 6.42, *Valiant* came very close to *Barham* before hauling out on the latter's port quarter and reducing to slow speed.[132] It is unclear when Jellicoe's signal for 14 knots was made executive. The despatches of *King George V*, *Bellerophon* and *Marlborough* make it 6.20; *Iron Duke* and *Agincourt*, 6.25; *Revenge* 6.30[133] and the Jutland messages have a time-of-despatch of 6.26. As for an explanation, to Captain Gustav von Schoultz, the Russian naval attaché aboard *Hercules*, it appeared that:

Admiral Jerram is holding back his squadron as he has to wait for the battle cruisers to take station ahead of the Battle Fleet.

von Schoultz also recalled that *Hercules*, *Revenge* and *Marlborough* were all too close to the ship ahead.[134] Perhaps Jerram contributed to the bunching by reducing speed without orders, while station-keeping would have been harder if, before deployment, the battleship columns had been spaced at 10 rather than 11 cables. Whether or not Jellicoe was anticipated by Jerram, the speed reduction, with its attendant disruption to the line, was only necessary because Beatty

---

[128] *OD*, pp. 53 and 58. Dreyer, p. 149. *GF*, p. 222. See Chapter 4 for the orders of the battlefleets.
[129] *OD*, pp. 108 and 110.   [130] *OD*, pp. 270, 275, 280 and 286–7.
[131] *OD*, 16, 65 and 89. *GF*, p. 222.   [132] *OD*, pp. 208–9. F&H, p. 128.
[133] *OD*, pp. 53 (though Dreyer's speed was 15 knots), 65, 84, 116 and 361.
[134] von Schoultz, p. 131.

held so long to his converging course with the 1st Division. Even after Beatty turned SE'wards at 6.25, Jellicoe waited until the battlecruisers had drawn clear of the leading divisions before, at 6.33, he increased speed to 17 knots.

As they steamed NEbyE towards the turning point, several ships of the 2nd to 5th Divisions glimpsed the stopped *Wiesbaden* but, although none were able to open fire, most made out her three funnels. But while *Orion* thought she was a *Kolberg*, in the bad visibility *Thunderer* identified her at the time as an old armoured cruiser of the *Prinz Adelbert* class and *Benbow* as a *Helgoland*. *Orion*'s range was 12,000 yards but at 6.28 *Collingwood*'s was 9,000 yards. Of these four divisions, only *Bellerophon* at 6.15 could make out some misty outlines of German battleships beyond Beatty's battlecruisers.[135]

As *Marlborough* began the deployment of the 6th Division, four *Kaisers* and four *Helgolands* (presumably the German VIth and Ist Divisions) could be dimly seen. At 6.17, *Marlborough* opened fire on one of the *Kaisers* bearing G110 (i.e. about SbyE) at an estimated range of 10,000 yards, though later increasing to 13,000 yards; seven salvos were fired in four minutes, with hits claimed for the fifth and seventh. *Marlborough* ceased fire when her target was hidden by an enemy cruiser bearing G98 at a range-finder range of 10,500 yards. At this ship, identified either as a *Roon*-class armoured cruiser with one funnel gone or as a predreadnought of the *Braunschweig* class, five heavy salvos were fired from 6.25 but hits could not be distinguished since two or three other ships were also firing at her. *Marlborough*'s 6in guns joined in at 6.27 until fire was checked at 6.29. During this firing, the right hand gun of A turret was put permanently out of action by cracks in the barrel. From *Revenge*'s disjointed despatch, it appears that, after deployment, she fired intermittently at the leading predreadnoughts of the German IIBS but they were so indistinct that no ranges were obtained and some salvos were fired unspotted. At 6.20, *Hercules* fired her first salvo at a disabled enemy ship, apparently with four funnels and of the *Roon* class; then, at about 6.30, *Hercules* fired seven or eight salvos at the least indistinct of three *Kaiser*-class battleships, though with continual checks due to the haze.[136] At 6.24, though the target could only just be made out, *Agincourt* opened fire at 10,000 yards at what was believed to be an enemy battlecruiser. One hit was spotted before this ship was obscured by a British armoured cruiser, most likely the *Warrior*. At 6.32, *Agincourt* briefly re-engaged the same target until blanked by some British destroyers (probably the 12DF); she then switched to an enemy cruiser, yet again supposedly a *Roon*, before losing sight of the enemy at 6.34,

---

[135] *OD*, pp. 79, 95, 109, 127, 361, 371 and 375. F&H, p. 181. Once it was realised that *Prinz Adelbert* and *Friedrich Carl* had already been sunk, *Orion*'s identification for *Thunderer*'s target was adopted in Jerram's despatch. Beginning at the Heligoland Bight action, light cruisers were misidentified by both sides as armoured cruisers: Goldrick, *Before Jutland*, pp. 95, 123 and 126.

[136] *OD*, pp. 65, 70–1, 73 and 84–5 and Pl. 7a. von Schoultz, p. 130.

just before she turned SEbyE. After forming astern of *Agincourt*, *Barham* (though not, it seems, *Valiant* or *Malaya*) opened fire again, first at the *Wiesbaden* (correctly described as a three-funnelled cruiser) and then at a *König*-class battleship, although Captain Craig declared that several hits were also made on a ship of the *Kaiser* class. However, Campbell was unable to confirm either these hits or those claimed by the 6th Division.[137]

After the British battleships made their turns in succession to SEbyE, only a few had better than fleeting opportunities to fire at the enemy battlefleet, while the *Wiesbaden* continued to be a distraction. Of all the Grand Fleet, Jellicoe's flagship did most to inflict damage on the enemy. Just after she made her turn, she sighted 'a [stopped] 3-funnelled cruiser somewhat like the "Kolberg" class' bearing G80; beginning at 6.23, 'to clear bores of Guns' *Iron Duke* fired four salvos at a range of 11,000 yards. Then, having sighted the ships of the leading German Vth Division at 6.26, she switched target to the *König* bearing G70, that is, about SbyW. Jellicoe did not permit fire to be opened until he was certain that his own battlecruisers were clear.[138] When firing commenced at 6.30, the Dreyer Table Mark IV had been set to a target inclination of 100 to the left, equating to a target course just S of E; the gunnery commander noted:

Error reported by Rangefinder Plot was 500 yards. Range 11,000. Bracket used 800.

Using the Director throughout, *Iron Duke* fired four salvos at intervals of 35, 40 and 50 seconds, the third and fourth without correction, the fourth definitely straddling. Rapid fire was then ordered; the next three intervals were 30, 25 and 23 seconds, though the firing rate then slowed for the final four salvos as *König* was seen turning away into the smoke and mist, altering course by 12–14 points.[139] Though *Iron Duke* was not under fire, this was, as Campbell declared, 'a fine display of speedy and accurate shooting'; he identified seven direct hits plus an apparent ricochet on *König* at this time. Rear-Admiral Behncke was slightly injured as a result of a hit on the conning tower roof. Three of these hits caused propellant fires. The most dangerous struck the lower edge of the armour belt and penetrated a 5.9in magazine but the fire was extinguished by seawater rushing in; most of the 1,630 tons of water that were in the ship by midnight were due to this hole, and the order to flood the port forward magazine group.[140]

At the head of the 2nd Division, *Orion* sighted a ship of the *Kaiser* class bearing G105 on a slightly diverging course at a range-finder range of 11,100 yards. From 6.33, *Orion* fired four salvos, the last spotted as a hit with 13,300

[137] *OD*, pp. 91–2, 194 and 201. Campbell, pp. 187–8 and 196.
[138] *OD*, pp. 53, 58, 60 and 62. *GF*, p. 223.
[139] *Iron Duke*'s complete gunnery reports are in ADM 137/302 ff. 29–35, the somewhat censored versions in *OD*, pp. 55–61. For salvo times (10th salvo at 6.35.55), see *OD*, p. 58 but p. 55 times the 10th salvo at 6.37.10. 43 rounds were fired in the first 9 salvos (*OD*, p. 53).
[140] *OD*, p. 53. Campbell, pp. 156 and 187–93.

yards on the sights, but by 6.37 the enemy was lost in the spray and mist thrown up by a short salvo from another ship. At 6.30, *Monarch* saw a light cruiser (also judged to be a *Kolberg*) apparently stopped, bearing G75 and fired three salvos, the third straddling, at 10,400 yards. Then, at 6.33, she sighted three *Königs* and two *Kaisers* bearing G95 at 12,000 yards, but she could only fire two salvos at the leading *König* and one at a *Kaiser* before all the enemy battleships disappeared. Apart from *König*, only *Markgraf* received a direct hit during this first engagement between the battlefleets, though the latter also had a near-miss that may have bent her port propeller shaft. Campbell suggests that *Orion* scored the hit on *Markgraf* and that *Monarch* made one of the hits on *König*.[141] It seems better to attribute all the hits on *König* to *Iron Duke* and to allow that the damage to *Markgraf* could have been caused by either or even both of the other two.

Astern of *Iron Duke*'s 3rd Division, only two ships, *Benbow* and *Colossus* – both divisional flagships – were able to fire more than a couple of salvos at the German line. At 6.30, though with difficulty, *Benbow* succeeded in getting her director onto a 'Ship of "Lützow" or "Kaiser" class' (more likely the latter), bearing G73. With just two initial ranges from X turret averaging 16,000 yards, she fired four slow salvos between 6.30 and 6.38 before her target was obscured by smoke from a burning enemy cruiser drifting down between the lines. At 6.40, two more salvos were fired at the same target until it was hidden by smoke and mist. Unusually, all these were two-gun salvos fired only from A and B turrets. *Colossus*, apparently just after her turn into line, at 6.30 fired three deliberate salvos at the enemy battlefleet (though she did not describe her target), followed at 6.32 by four salvos at a supposedly four-funnelled cruiser stopped on her starboard beam.[142]

Of the other British battleships that fired during this phase of the battle, at 6.31 *Conqueror* opened on a *König* class at a rough range of 12,000 yards but this battleship quickly disappeared in the haze, so fire was briefly shifted to a cruiser; by suggesting that she was probably of the *Pillau* class, *Conqueror* came closest to identifying *Wiesbaden* correctly. At 6.28, *Thunderer* also fired at this same cruiser; as did *Royal Oak* between 6.29 and 6.33 with 15in and 6in salvos; *Superb* between 6.26 and 6.50; and *Canada* at 6.38.[143] *Bellerophon* joined in but one of her officers explained why *Wiesbaden* still remained afloat.

at 6.33, though we were rather doubtful as the whether the cruiser [sighted earlier] was one of our own or a German, we opened fire on her, as all other ships were firing at her, at a range of 14,700 yards. This was . . . the first concentration firing on a large scale which had ever taken place, so the results naturally were rather disappointing. The German

---

[141] *OD*, pp. 110–11, 371 and 373. Campbell, pp. 193–5.

[142] *OD*, pp. 79, 127–8 (also pp. 353–5) and 383.

[143] *OD*, pp. 98, 110–11, 355, 366, 375 and 377. *Thunderer*'s despatch and the 2BS summary imply that she was then masked by *Conqueror* and *Iron Duke* and that she fired between *Iron Duke* and *Royal Oak* but this most probably happened later.

cruiser was quickly hidden by a solid wall of water ... but she didn't seem to suffer much, and as none of us had the faintest idea as to which salvos were whose, fire control was rather hopeless.[144]

Thus it was not possible to correct by spotting the considerable variation in the ranges obtained for this one target. Between 6.32 and 6.45, *Temeraire* (with a range of only 8,000 yards) and *Vanguard* added to the confusion while identifying their target as *Roon* and the even older *Freya* respectively. In the 1BS at the rear, after *St Vincent* dropped astern at 6.40, *Neptune* fired at an indistinct battleship at a range of 11,000 yards but both her salvos appeared to fall short.[145] At 6.39, *Marlborough* sighted a *Kaiser*-class battleship at a range of 13,000 yards but, after one salvo, the target turned away and disappeared. *Revenge* perhaps continued firing at battleships and the *Wiesbaden* but, without range-finder ranges, she was almost certainly wasting her ammunition.[146]

Due to the smoke and mist, Jellicoe himself had been able to make out only three or four enemy ships from *Iron Duke* and he had no idea of the enemy's formation.[147] Now, at about 6.40, just after his own ships had formed into single line-ahead, firing died out as the last of the visible German battleships vanished into the murk. Once again Jellicoe urgently needed reports of the enemy's movements so that contact might be regained.

Scheer's first *Gefechtskehrtwendung*

Despite the destruction of *Invincible* shortly after 6.30, the German forces were in an increasingly difficult situation. Scheer knew that he was facing practically the whole of the Grand Fleet but he could make out little more than the flashes of their guns in an arc of fire extending from NNW round to E.[148] As the British deployment continued, the German van was caught in the open jaws formed by the two segments of the line; then, as more and more British battleships turned onto the final deployment course SEbyE, they crossed the German 'T', forcing the ships at the head of the German line to veer away to starboard. At 6.22, the ISG had turned approximately SSE but, under *Invincible*'s rapid and effective fire, *Lützow* was forced to alter course to S. At 6.30, when *König* was engaged by *Iron Duke*, Behncke's flagship was heading E but, before she vanished, she appeared to turn away by 12–14 points. The German battlecruisers were not in sight from *Friedrich der Grosse* but Scheer could see that *König* was under a heavy fire and that the head of his line was giving way. By 6.36, *König* too was heading S, the rest of the Vth Division was turning SE and the VIth Division

---

[144] F&H, p. 181 and also 198.   [145] *OD*, pp. 89, 357–8 and 363.
[146] *OD*, pp. 65, 73 and 84. Burney's chart (*OD*, pl. 7a) but not his despatch claimed *Marlborough*'s target was hit repeatedly and appeared very low aft.
[147] *GF*, p. 223.   [148] Scheer, p. 152 and despatch, *OD*, pp. 593–4.

Table 7.13. *High Seas Fleet signals 6.21–6.55pm*

Time of receipt	From	To	System	Message	Time of origin
pm, 31 May					
6.21	C-in-C	General		Follow in wake of leading ship	
6.27	2nd Leader of Torpedo boats	IITF	Visual	Follow in the wake of the Senior Officer's ship	
6.27	SO IISG	IITF	Visual	Make room	
6.27	2nd Leader of Torpedo boats	IITF	Visual	Follow in the wake of the Senior Officer's ship	
6.28	F. der Grosse	General	Visual	Manoeuvre with small turns	
6.32	Rostock	IIITF	Visual	Assemble for an attack on the requisite line of bearing	
6.36	C-in-C	General		Turn together 16 points to starboard	
6.37	Rostock	IIITF	Visual	Proceed ahead to the attack–(At the enemy!) By semaphore: Proceed ahead on the port bow	
	SO IIITF	IIITF	Visual	Turn off to starboard; fire 3 torpedoes	
6.39 or 6.42	Rostock	IIITF and IHF	Visual	Torpedo boats are not to attack	
6.39	C-in-C	General		Course, W	
6.40	Rostock	IHF		Torpedo boats are not to attack	
6.55	Rostock	IHF and XIIHF		Boats to go to Lützow and fetch AC Scouting Forces	

was steering E; the IBS was still steaming NE and the IIBS about NNE. Scheer was now concerned that, as his battleships passed through the curve at the head of his line, the British line would have an opportunity to concentrate as it steamed past. Scheer also anticipated that Jellicoe would soon follow a turn S, thereby trapping the ISG between the lines and initiating a running fight on this heading. Furthermore, the German forces would both stand out against a light horizon and the setting sun while their opponents would remain hidden in mist and smoke; and, the wind having backed towards the SW, they would be also hampered by their own smoke. To Scheer, there was only one way out – to withdraw by ordering an action-turn-together by 16 points.[149]

The preferred German method for simultaneous turns together in action was the *Gefechtswendung* or action-turn-together: the most drastic variant being the *Gefechtskehrtwendung* or action-turn-about through 16 points. These turns

---

[149] *OD*, German Plan V and Plan VI, Diagram 5 and Scheer's despatch, p. 594. Scheer, p. 153. *GOA*, pp. 113–14. Tarrant, p. 138.

could be ordered even when a line was curved; if carried out correctly, no ship could turn too early while, as each ship turned a little later than the ship that would become her next ahead, the distance between them increased somewhat, minimising the risk of collision. Scheer declared:

At our peace manoeuvres great importance was always attached to [these turns] being carried out on a curved line and every means employed to ensure the working of the signals. The trouble spent was now well repaid.[150]

Whether or not the lines in these practices were curved as acutely as was now the case, at 6.36 (or perhaps 6.33) he ordered an action-turn-about to starboard.[151] If the line had been continuous, the turn would have been initiated by *Hannover*.[152] But due to the high speed and frequent course changes, the predreadnoughts of the IIBS had been unable to close up. Captain Redlich in *Westfalen*, the rearmost dreadnought, seized the initiative by turning through 16 points immediately; then, on Scheer signalling 'Course W' at 6.39, Redlich took over as guide of the fleet. The charts with Scheer's despatch indicate that the rest of the IBS also first turned onto an opposite course of about SW before turning in succession to W in *Westfalen*'s wake. Most of the IIIBS turned successively onto similar Southwesterly courses, which brought them onto the starboard quarter of the IBS; from this position, they should have had little difficulty in following the IBS onto the course W. However, *König*'s wireless was by then out of action and she did not receive the action-turn-about signal; she did not turn until 6.41 when the 'Course W' signal was hoisted by those astern of her. (This delay, perhaps by as much as eight minutes, emphasises that, although the progress of an action-turn-together along the line was controlled by flags, its prompt execution depended on the broadcast of the order from the flagship to all ships by wireless.) In *Markgraf*, the bearings of her propeller shaft were now overheating; she was forced to stop her port engine and she had considerable difficulty in maintaining her position in the line. The turns-away finally stopped any ships that were still shooting at *Warspite*, except for two final salvos fired by *Ostfriesland* as the range increased rapidly from 13,700 to 17,000 yards. *Prinzregent Luitpold*, which claimed to have been engaging a member of the *King George V* class since 6.15 (though without hitting anything), also ceased fire.

To begin the action-turn-about by the IIBS, *Hannover* probably turned 16 points simultaneously with *Westfalen*. The predreadnoughts then remained on the disengaged side of the dreadnoughts. Rear-Admiral Mauve in *Deutschland*,

---

[150] Scheer, p. 153 and also *Manoeuvring Instructions for the Fleet 1914*, p. 36 in 'German Fleet Orders', ADM 186/17.

[151] Both GSM (time 6.36) and *GOA*, p. 114 (time 6.33) translate the signal as a 'Turn together 16 points to starboard'.

[152] For the order of the German battle line, I have accepted that shown in the charts accompanying the *GOA* as reproduced by Tarrant, especially Figs. 24, 33 and 43 (though note that Fig. 8, 'Cruising formation', is different).

now the squadron's rear ship, briefly considered dropping back astern of the IIIBS but, having realised that his ships would hamper the ISG and its flotillas, he decided that he should try to reach his correct position ahead of the IBS.[153] As for the battlecruisers, they had observed the 16-point turns by the battleships earlier than had *König* but it is uncertain whether any part of the ISG executed an action-turn-about. By 6.37, *Lützow* could only steam slowly so, unable to conform to the others' movements, she turned SW in an effort to withdraw. Command of the battlecruisers now devolved upon Captain Johannes Hartog of *Derfflinger* but her signal halliards had been shot away, the wireless aerials were so damaged that signals could only be received, and the searchlights 'were not ready for use'; thus he had no alternative but to attempt to lead from the front. The German history states that *Derfflinger, Seydlitz* and *Moltke* turned to starboard – though not whether this was together or in succession – but that *Von der Tann* turned to port.[154] Although von Hase's and Scheer's charts differ in detail and timing, both suggest that the four battlecruisers reached a position on the port beam of those battleships that were still steaming to the SW and on a similar course. Shortly after turning, *Derfflinger* had to stop her engines for a few minutes to secure the after torpedo net that was in danger of becoming entangled with the port propeller, though fortunately no enemy ships were in sight at the time. Just beforehand, *Seydlitz, Moltke* and *Von der Tann* were not in close touch but they now came up quickly and took their prescribed place in the battlecruiser line.[155] However they made their turns, it is probable that these three were once again in line astern of *Derfflinger* and that thereafter they followed her lead by turns in succession.

Despite some minor delays and confusion in what had been the van, Scheer's action-turn-about had successfully pulled his main forces out of action. The German history declared that by 6.45 'this difficult and dangerous manoeuvre had been practically completed without incident'.[156]

Scheer did not issue any explicit orders to his flotillas but some attempted to cover his withdrawal. After their engagement with the 3BCS and *Shark*, the IITF, though attached to the ISG, seem to have taken station on the disengaged side of the German battle line. Thus, when the leading battleships were forced to turn away, this flotilla, comprising the most capable destroyers on the German side, was confined by the curving line and prevented from taking any part in the subsequent attack.[157] Commodore Michelsen in *Rostock* and

---

[153] *GOA*, pp. 114–15. *OD*, German Plan V and Plan VI, Diagram 5. The IVSG were initially astern of the IIBS and seem then to have followed the motions of the predreadnoughts.

[154] *GOA*, p. 116, which states that 'the "Von der Tann" at [6].38 p.m. turned to port . . . through East to North in order to place herself astern of the "König" ' yet on p. 115 that *König* turned from her Southerly course no earlier than 6.41. See also von Hase, p. 190 and Tarrant, pp. 141 and 143.

[155] von Hase, Sketch I and pp. 190–1. *OD*, German Plan V.   [156] *GOA*, p. 115.

[157] *GOA*, p. 113. Scheer, p. 153.

boats of the IHF and IIITF were better placed on the starboard bow of the IIIBS. At 6.32, when *König* was being punished by *Iron Duke*, Michelsen ordered the IIITF to assemble for an attack, though its commander, who could see little of the enemy, asked for a direction in which to proceed. The IIITF then moved out but, having sighted the indistinct outlines of hostile dreadnoughts, was still closing when Michelsen, on seeing his battlefleet's action-turn-about, cancelled the attack. His order was not received in time to prevent *G88*, *V73* and (probably) *V48* each firing a torpedo, though he later criticised the IIITF's commander for then withdrawing. Times are uncertain but this attack was probably seen from *Collingwood* and *Barham*, the latter also reporting four torpedoes that passed through the line; both ships opened fire with their secondary armaments, *Barham* claiming a hit. The German history stated that, as they withdrew, *V48* and *S54* attacked a disabled British destroyer (though this went unnoticed in *Onslow* and *Acasta*) and that *V48* received a hit that seriously reduced her speed. *G42* attempted to take her in tow but, under heavy fire, was finally forced to abandon her. *G42* then laid a smoke screen to cover what had become the rear of the German line.[158]

Meanwhile, Michelsen in *Rostock* with the IHF had passed between *Von der Tann* and *König* to a position on the disengaged side of the Vth Division. Seeing that *Lützow* was in a bad way, he then despatched boats of the IHF and XIIHF to her assistance. *G39* at once went alongside to take off Hipper and his staff, while *G38* and *G40* joined *G37* and *V45* in laying a smoke screen[159] – though this would prove insufficient to protect *Lützow* from further damage. It is possible that *Lützow* was sighted at 6.44 from *Benbow* bearing SW, bows-on and apparently stopped with destroyers around her; however, *Benbow* identified a '3-funnelled enemy ship ("Helgoland" class?)' and, in any case, did not open fire.[160]

A lull in the firing

Iron Duke's fire control staff saw their target turn away into the mist at 6.37, as did Captain Dreyer. From *Marlborough*, the *Kaiser*-class battleship briefly engaged at 6.39 was also seen to do the same. These observations of single ships were not reported to Jellicoe and Burney[161] but, even if they had been, it

[158] *GOA*, pp. 109–10 and 116–17. *OD*, 96 and 201. However, at the other end of the line *Duke of Edinburgh* (at 6.47) and *King George V* each sighted a torpedo, though these were attributed to a submarine: *OD*, pp. 108, 287 and 288.

[159] *GOA*, pp. 116–17. Tarrant, p. 143.

[160] *OD*, pp. 382–3 (the typed original in ADM 116/1487 reads 'bows on'). At 6.45, *Benbow* sighted: 'Four 2-funnelled ships and one 4 funnelled ship bearing Green 100°–120° when they turned away ("Benbow's" course S.E.)'.

[161] Dreyer, pp. 149 and 168–9. *OD*, p. 71. Both Dreyer and Jellicoe (*JP II*, p. 450) claimed that Burney saw but did not report Scheer's course reversal but this is not the impression given by Burney's despatch; only *Marlborough*'s gunnery report mentions her target's turn-away.

Table 7.14. *Grand Fleet signals 6.29–7.00pm*

Time of despatch	From	To	System	Message	Time of origin
pm, 31 May					
6.29	C-in-C	Dreadnought Battlefleet and attached Cruisers	W/T and Flags	Subdivisions separately alter course in succession to SSE, preserving their formation.	
				(Negatived)	
6.33	C-in-C	General	Flags	. . . 17 knots	
6.40	SO 1BS	Colossus	Sem.	Why are you hauling out of line?	
				(Note.–Made three times, no reply.)	
6.44	C-in-C	Dreadnought Battlefleet and attached Cruisers	W/T and Flags	Divisions separately alter course in succession to SE preserving their formation	
6.50	Marlborough			Remarks: Marlborough struck starboard side	
6.54	C-in-C	SO BCF SO 3BCS SO 2CS	W/T	Present course of fleet is South	1854
6.54	SO BCF	C-in-C	W/T	Submarine in sight in position 57°02 N, 6°24E	1845
6.55	C-in-C	Dreadnought Battlefleet and attached Cruisers	W/T and Flags	Alter course leading ships together the rest in succession to South	
6.55	C-in-C	SO 1BS	SL	Can you see any Enemy Battleships? Reply: No	1850
6.57	Marlborough	C-in-C	W/T	Urgent. Have been struck by a mine or torpedo, but not certain which	1855
6.58	Marlborough	C-in-C	W/T	Urgent. Have been struck by a torpedo	1857
7.00	K.G.V	C-in-C	SL	There is a Submarine ahead of you	1859
7.00 (rec'ved)	SO BCF	C-in-C	SL	Enemy are to Westward	1755 [sic]

is very unlikely that they would have been taken as definite signs of a concerted turn-about by the whole High Seas Fleet. *Erin*'s report observed that, at about 6.30: 'Enemy's battle fleet must then have turned 16 points' but, since she did not fire her heavy guns once during the battle,[162] this was almost certainly a later deduction rather than a direct observation. Thus *Falmouth* remained the only British ship to have seen the Germans turn Westwards.

By 6.40, the British battle line had been largely straightened out, though the 5th Division were probably then temporarily out of position after they turned away two points by Preparative to avoid the torpedo attack by the IIITF.[163] By 6.45, there was a lull in the firing all along the line though, until about 6.54, there were further brief sightings of the enemy, albeit nothing that revealed their actual movements.[164] Thus neither Jellicoe nor any of his divisional commanders had any notion that Scheer had executed an action-turn-about and that the leading German divisions were then steering W; Jellicoe's first Plan of the Battle (dated 18 June 1916) shows the High Seas Fleet hauling round gradually on a single curving course from NE to SW.[165] Dreyer confirms that Jellicoe neither saw nor was informed of *König*'s turn-away. But, whatever Scheer's course might have been, the C-in-C had directly observed *Iron Duke*'s fire,[166] which was aimed about SbyW, so it must have been clear to him that, to regain touch, a turn to starboard would be needed. According to the British signal record, at 6.29 *Iron Duke* had hoisted the signal 'Subdivisions separately alter course in succession to SSE preserving their formation' though this cannot have been made executive since it was subsequently negatived – in *Shannon*'s record, at 6.40.[167] Instead, at 6.44 Jellicoe employed the same signal format to order his divisions to alter course to SE, a more tentative turn by only one rather than three points. Jellicoe does not seem to have explained these orders although, in *The Grand Fleet*, he declared that 'the van had hauled in to south-east without signal shortly after deployment'. Yet *King George V*'s chart shows her heading SE until 6.26 but then turning away to EbyS and ESE before turning back, though only to SEbyE, at 6.43;[168] however, six other battleship charts, from *Orion* to *Marlborough*, do show turns to SE between 6.44 and 6.50.[169] Jellicoe probably intended the 6.29 hoist as a warning that, once all his ships had turned SEbyE, he would turn his subdivisions by three points to close the enemy. But it is uncertain how this turn would have differed from a simple – and protracted – alteration of course in succession by the whole fleet, though the times of the individual turns to SE after 6.44 suggest that leading ships did

---

[162] *OD*, p. 110. Campbell, p. 346.
[163] *OD*, p. 96. From 6.40, Burney demanded three times of *Colossus* 'Why are you hauling out of line?' but received no reply.
[164] *OD*, pp. 79, 219 and 355 for the lull and pp. 94, 99 and 383 for sightings.
[165] The later chart submitted on 29 August noted that 'At this period enemy made two 16 point turns. This is confirmed by German accounts of the battle.' *OD*, Plates 1a and 4a.
[166] Dreyer, p. 168. *GF*, p. 223.   [167] *Shannon*'s W/T record, f. 110.
[168] *GF*, p. 266. *OD*, Pl. 8.   [169] *OD*, Pls. 2, 4, 7, 29, 30 and 7a.

not have to wait before commencing the turn.[170] Even so, a one-point turn to SE, however executed, was not enough and in 1932 Jellicoe acknowledged that:

[I] might have altered course gradually to south to close the enemy at say 6.45 p.m. instead of waiting until 6.55 . . . The reason I delayed was because I thought the enemy disappearance was due to thickening of the mist.[171]

At 6.55, still with no enemy battleships in sight, he at last ordered a decisive turn to South by 9 Pendant.

The alteration was made 'by divisions' instead of 'in succession' in order that the enemy could be closed more rapidly . . . This large turn (of four points) . . . involved some small amount of 'blanketing' of the rear ships of one division by the leading ships of that next astern [but this] was unavoidable and the loss of fire was inappreciable.[172]

Notes made aboard *King George V* claimed that she turned South at 6.56 'just previous to a signal being made' and Jellicoe accepted that Jerram had 'just anticipated this signal'.[173] Even if, despite the nominal times, Jerram did turn slightly early, he had not taken useful advantage of the discretion granted to the van squadron by the *GFBOs* to close the range. It happened that *King George V* had been forced to alter course sharply to starboard at 6.51 to avoid colliding with the 4LCS but, rather than continuing to close, she had quickly turned away again, continuing SEbyE until 6.56.[174] As for the cause of this brief deviation,

Table 7.15. *4LCS signals 6.43–6.52pm*

Time of despatch	From	To	System	Message	Time of origin
pm, 31 May					
6.43	SO 4LCS	4LCS	Flags	Alter course together 12 points to starboard	
6.48	SO 4LCS	4LCS	Flags	Alter course together 12 points to port	
6.51	SO 4LCS	4LCS	Flags	Alter course in succession to SSE	
6.52	SO 4LCS	Champion	SL	Am going round starboard bow of King George V	

---

[170] The wording of the signals at 6.29 and 6.44 is similar to the definition of a turn by Compass Pendant which emphasises 'preserving . . . the Formation of the Columns'. While the Compass Pendant was probably used in making these signals, no instructions have been found for turning a fleet in line-ahead by this pendant.

[171] 'Errors made in Jutland Battle', 1932 in *JP II*, p. 450.

[172] *GF*, p. 226. This seems to confirm that the 9 Pendant turn at 6.55 could close more rapidly than the probable Compass Pendant turn at 6.45.

[173] *OD*, p. 117. *GF*, p. 226.   [174] *OD*, pp. 111 and 117 and Pl. 8.

at 6.40 *Calliope* bore EbyS from Jerram's flagship, that is a little on her disengaged bow. It seems that, when the battleship turned SEbyE at 6.43, the 4LCS altered course to starboard by 12 points in order to get into position on her engaged bow. But, having misjudged the manoeuvre, the light cruisers had to haul away to port by either 8 or 12 points before reaching their objective soon after seven o'clock.[175]

Towards the rear of the British line, at 6.45 *Marlborough* saw clearly the track of an approaching torpedo; she was able to haul briefly out of line to port so that it passed harmlessly astern. But at 6.54, without any warning, a second torpedo hit her on the starboard side under the fore bridge. The diesel engine and hydraulic rooms flooded immediately but the torpedo bulkhead protecting the B-turret and 6in magazines limited the damage. Water entering the forward boiler room made it necessary to draw the fires but by 7.30 the pumps had the water level under control. *Marlborough* developed a starboard list of no more than 8° but was still able to develop revolutions for 17 knots though, due to the hull damage, her speed over the ground was only about 15.8 knots. At 7.00, shortly after turning S, *Marlborough* sighted three more torpedoes to starboard and altered course first to starboard and then to port; one passed astern with two more passing ahead shortly afterwards. As she veered to starboard, she passed the stopped *Acasta* only one cable on her port beam;[176] *Acasta*'s captain thought that she had a fortunate escape since previously *Marlborough* had been heading straight for her.[177] Where these five torpedoes came from is uncertain. The first three may have been fired during the attack by the IIITF or by *V48* after she was disabled, while *Wiesbaden* could also have been responsible. *Marlborough*'s chart shows the last two coming from the position which had been occupied by the supposed *Braunschweig*-class battleship that she had engaged earlier. From 7.03, she again fired at this same position, only the target was now identified as an 'Armoured Cruiser. ?Prinz Adelbert'. Four salvos were fired in two minutes, the third and fourth appearing to open up the side; the guns then ceased fire as the target seemed to be completely disabled and sinking fast. Even so, at 7.10 *Marlborough* fired a torpedo at what may have been the same ship (this target also had three funnels).[178] There seems little doubt that, on all these occasions, *Marlborough*'s target was the *Wiesbaden*. She still lay where she had been disabled by the 3BCS, at the approximate centre of the irregular arc that had been traversed by the Grand Fleet as it headed NEbyE, SEbyE, SE and then S. She may have been sighted

[175] Commodore le Mesurier to C-in-C, 6 August 1916 in ADM 137/1946, f. 626. *OD*, p. 296 and Pl. 12a.

[176] *OD*, pp. 65–7, 71, 100, 103–5 and Pl. 7a. F&H, p. 217.

[177] F&H, p. 237. Other battleships, from *King George V* to *Hercules*, reported passing *Acasta*: *OD*, pp. 58, 71, 73, 79, 85, 89, 117 and 361.

[178] *OD*, Pl. 7a and pp. 71 and 101.

again by *Hercules* at 6.47 but she became visible once more to other ships of the 1BS only after they turned S. As usual, she was variously identified. In the 5th Division, *Colossus* fired three salvos at her at 7.00 but *Neptune* fired only one since so many other ships were shooting at her.[179] Of the 6th Division, *Marlborough* engaged her with the main armament while *Revenge* (and possibly *Agincourt*) opened on her with the 6in guns. *Revenge* remarked that, although *Wiesbaden* was apparently reduced to a wreck, she still refused to sink.[180] It seems that, left alone as a floating shambles after the fleets had passed, she did not finally founder until early the following morning; her single survivor was picked up by a Norwegian steamer late on 2 June.[181]

The BCF's 32-point turn

After the sinking of *Invincible*, all six surviving British battlecruisers lost touch with the enemy; they sighted no more German capital ships until 7.13.[182] The BCF's chart shows *Lion* turning away to ESE at 6.35, two minutes after the time in Beatty's despatch for *Invincible*'s blowing up, and then turning back to SSE at 6.45; at 6.53, Beatty ordered a speed of 18 knots.[183] Between 6.37 and 6.40, one torpedo missed *Princess Royal* and three passed *Tiger*; the latter opened fire with her 6in guns on German destroyers attacking the British battlefleet and claimed to have sunk at least one (perhaps she hit *V48*).[184] Beatty declared that, by 6.40, his four battlecruisers were clear of the 1BS, which then bore NNW, three miles from *Lion*; this is not greatly different from the bearing of about NWbyW, 4.9 miles that can be calculated from *Calliope*'s observations of the two flagships made at the same time.[185] Also at 6.40, Beatty asked *Falmouth* by searchlight for the position of the German battlecruisers; the reply, probably sent at 6.45, was: 'Last seen 1820. Altered course to W, engaged by 3BCS'. This perhaps encouraged Beatty to turn SSE, just after Jellicoe ordered the battlefleet to alter course to SE. However, Beatty kept this important observation of the enemy course (though the time is too early) to himself until 6.55 (the time-of-origin of his searchlight signal is clearly a misprint) and, even then, he reported only that the 'Enemy are to Westward'. By the time this signal reached

---

[179] von Schoultz, p. 132. *OD*, pp. 73, 79 and 89.

[180] *OD*, pp. 67, 84 and 92. On seeing *Marlborough* hit, *Revenge* had hauled out to port about one cable. A number of her officers then felt a shock; her captain believed she struck and sank the imagined submarine that supposedly torpedoed *Marlborough*.

[181] Zenne's memoir (see note 25) ff. 26–38. Campbell, pp. 294–5 and 395. F&H, p. 195.

[182] REL. *OD*, pp. 388, 393 and 395. *Indomitable* and *Inflexible* gunnery reports (see note 114).

[183] *OD*, Pl. 10. The turning times in both VNE and Chatfield's despatch (*OD*, p. 145) are slightly later: 6.36 for the loss of *Invincible*; 6.37 for the turn ESE; an intermediate turn to SE at 6.44; 6.48 for the turn SSE; but 6.53 for the reduction to 18 knots.

[184] *OD*, pp. 149, 151 (the latter's torpedo direction is probably wrong), 156 and 393.

[185] Beatty to C-in-C, 8 July 1916 and le Mesurier to C-in-C, 6 August 1916 in '15. Track of Battle Cruiser Fleet' in *Jutland Miscellaneous Papers*, ADM 137/1946, ff. 612 and 626. *OD*, p. 137.

Table 7.16. *BCF signals 6.21–7.00pm*

Time of despatch	From	To	System	Message	Time of origin
pm, 31May					
6.21	SO BCF	BCF	Flags	... 26 knots	6.21
6.35	Indomitable	SO BCF	SL	What speed are you doing? Reply: 15 knots	
6.37	Princess Royal	SO BCF	SL	Following received: present course of fleet is SEbyE	
6.40	SO BCF	Badger	SL	Pick up men from ship on starboard hand	
6.40	SO BCF	SO 3LCS	SL	What is bearing of Enemy's Battle Cruisers? Reply: Last seen 1820. Altered course to W, engaged by 3BCS	1845
6.42	SO BCF	Destroyers		Destroyers take station ahead	
6.46	New Zealand			Remarks: Sighted 3BCS one point on starboard bow	
6.50	SO BCF	General	Flags and SL	3BCS prolong line astern	
6.53	SO BCF	General	Flags	... 18 knots	
6.54	SO BCF	C-in-C	W/T	Submarine in sight in position 57°02 N, 6°24E	1845
7.00 (received)	SO BCF	C-in-C	SL	Enemy are to Westward	1755 [*sic*]

Jellicoe at 7.00, the battlefleet had already turned S and the information had ceased to have any tactical relevance.

When *Invincible* blew up, *Indomitable* was about three cables astern of *Inflexible* with the other battlecruisers coming up astern. Just as the ISG was disappearing, one of the *Derfflinger* class was seen from *Indomitable* to fall out of line very low in the water; she must have been the *Lützow*, though the Director Gunner cannot, as he claimed, have seen her sink. *Inflexible* led *Indomitable* to port to pass the wreck of *Invincible*. *Indomitable* (her Captain Kennedy was now the Senior Officer) eased her speed in case she needed to lead a turn to starboard in order to continue the action. This precaution proved unnecessary since at 6.35 *Inflexible*'s Captain Heaton-Ellis quickly altered course by two points to starboard and, at 6.45, with *Lion* coming up on her starboard side, by a further four points, probably to a course about S. But then at 6.50 Beatty ordered the 3BCS to prolong his line astern. In his despatch, Kennedy wrote:

I desire to emphasise the fact that, when ... Captain ... Heaton-Ellis ... found himself leading the squadron ... he at once followed the highest traditions of the Service by closing the enemy.[186]

This deserved praise can also be read as a criticism of Beatty for stopping their pursuit of the enemy ships that had destroyed their flagship. In fact, *Indomitable*'s chart may indicate that she and *Inflexible* continued Southwards until 6.56; probably, the other battlecruisers crossed their wakes before they turned about together and, by 7.00, formed astern with *Indomitable* leading.[187] Whatever their precise movements, their navigation must have been considerably complicated by *Lion*'s gyrations after her turn SSE at 6.45.

Despite Beatty's life-long refusal to admit it, there is little doubt that, between 6.50 and 7.05 approximately, *Lion* led the 1/2BCS in a complete circle by turning 32 points to starboard. The BCF's own chart, which was submitted to the C-in-C before Beatty's despatch of 12 June 1916, shows a 32-point turn, though rather imprecisely with only one time, 7.00, at about one third of the way round the circle.[188] Both charts submitted by *New Zealand* also show complete circles, one lasting from 6.55 to 7.05, the other with a single time (6.35) which must be a misprint for 6.55.[189] *Falmouth*, maintaining her position on *Lion*'s bow, made turns through 32 points, though her plotted times were earlier, between 6.47 and 7.00. *Tiger* did not submit a chart. Only the chart of *Princess Royal* has no sign of a circle, just a brief turn from SE to S at 6.50 followed by a turn back to SEbyS at 7.00.[190] A week after the battle, Commanders (N) Strutt of *Lion* and Creighton of *New Zealand* met and agreed that they had both turned through 32 points; Strutt's assistant navigator, W S Chalmers, concurred but Beatty would not allow it and made Chalmers change *Lion*'s track chart. And, although Chalmers did not mention it in his 1951 biography of Beatty, he later assured both Marder and Roskill that *Lion* had indeed turned a complete circle.[191] Beatty's influence is apparent even in the first plan of the battle, signed by Jellicoe on 18 June 1916; although the other courses for the BCF correspond with those on their own track chart, there is no sign of the circle at 7.00.[192]

Neither Beatty's despatch nor his narrative mention any large turns at around 7 o'clock. The despatch of *Lion*'s Captain Chatfield was written on 4 June but,

---

[186] *OD*, p. 166: also pp. 165 and 170 and *Indomitable*'s gunnery report.

[187] *OD*, Pl. 13 shows *Indomitable* turning S, though not until 6.51, then an apparently instantaneous turn of 15 points to port at 6.56 and a turn to EbyS at 7.05.

[188] *OD*, Pl. 10 and p. 143. What appear to be the original tracings for this chart, showing the circle at 7.00, are in DRAX 1/57.

[189] *OD*, Pls. 31 and 9a respectively.

[190] *OD*, Pls. 12 and 15 and pp. 137 and 186. For Harper's summary (19 December 1919) of the chart evidence, see *BP II*, pp. 433–7.

[191] Creighton to Harper, 12 November 1919 in *BP II*, p. 431. *FDSF III*, pp. 149–50. Roskill, pp. 176, 326–7 and 389 n. 26.

[192] *OD*, Pl. 1a.

by the time it was submitted to the C-in-C as an enclosure to Beatty's despatch of 12 June, the top of the relevant page had been cut off (as Jellicoe would soon confirm). What remains now reads:

14. Course continued to be altered to starboard to close the enemy ... at ... 6.48 p.m. to S.S.E.

...

15. The ship continued to circle to starboard but was unable
[End of page. Top of next page cut off.]
At 7.3 p.m. course was altered to S.S.E. and at 7.6 p.m. to South; at 7.9 p.m. to S.S.W. and at 7.11 p.m. to S.W. by S.[193]

In his memoirs, Chatfield was careful to remove himself from the bridge as soon as the large turn to starboard had commenced.

The battle cruisers being now some distance ahead of the Battle Fleet and the visibility too low to justify the Admiral in closing in on the enemy battle Fleet unsupported, Beatty told me to alter course 180 degrees to starboard. There was nothing for me to do at the moment [this confirms that no enemy ships were in sight] and I was anxious to go below to see how the ship had fared, and the lot of the wounded. I asked Captain Bentinck, Chief of Staff, if he would take command on the bridge for me for ten minutes. This he was delighted to do.[194]

On 25 June, Jellicoe's chief of staff, Rear-Admiral Madden, asked Bentinck to revise the BCF track chart and to explain why the distance run between 6.35 and 7.05 was so short. The next day, Bentinck, who, as we have just seen, was conning *Lion* at the critical time, explained in a telegram that:

Between 6.55 and 7.5 P.M. 'LION' turned through 32 points so that the 6.55 and 7.5 positions are identical. The run between 6.45 and 7.5 is correct. Run from 6.35 to 6.45 is shown 1.8 miles too little on tracing.[195]

The first sentence in particular was not the version of events allowed by Beatty, who doubtless insisted on the partial recantation that Bentinck sent to Madden on 3 July; this repeated that the course between 6.35 and 6.45 was too short but now declared:

Between 6 45 and 7.0 two large turns were made and also course was irregular owing to failure of gyro compass.[196]

---

[193] The tops of the page in question have been cut off in both copies of Chatfield's typed despatch in TNA: ADM 137/302, f. 297 and ADM 137/1945 ('Secret Packs of the C-in-C') f. 297. See *OD*, p. 143 for dates but the printed despatch (p. 145) makes no mention of the mutilated page and the words 'but was unable' were replaced by a full stop.

[194] Chatfield, pp. 146–7.

[195] Telegram 26 June 1916, 'Track of BCF' (see note 185) f. 610. The lengthened run increased *Lion*'s apparent speed from 13 to 23 knots but her actual speed is uncertain: *cf.* her signals at 6.21 and 6.35.

[196] Telegram and memo, 3 July 1916, 'Track of BCF', ff. 612 and 610–11.

Beatty himself now took over the correspondence, writing direct to the C-in-C on 8 and 12 July. These and later letters contain many discrepancies and only those statements that help in establishing on what actually happened will be cited here. Beatty now alleged that the run ESE had only lasted from 6.35 to 6.41, which allowed him to claim that previous plots had placed the BCF 1.8 miles too far to the East. As for his movements after 6.50:

Altered course 8 points to Starboard on losing sight of the enemy and for purpose of observing our own Battle Fleet. During this time due to gyro failure the ship swung to the Northward of West. On observing the Battle Fleet course was altered to the Southward and at 7.5 p.m. ship was steadied on SSW.[197]

(Beatty never made the point himself but, after his turn SSE, *King George V* was directly astern, so it is possible that the initial object of his turn to starboard was to obtain a clearer line of sight for his searchlight signal that the enemy was to Westward.) His next communication was on 17 July when Beatty sent the C-in-C his own plan of the battle.[198] This showed a longer run of four miles between 6.35 and 6.45 but also that, after 6.50, *Lion* turned some 16 points to starboard, then 16 points to port and finally eight points to starboard to SW; why, especially if he was trying to avoid straying too far East, he did not follow the first 16-point turn by a direct eight-point turn to SSW, remained unexplained. Jellicoe and his staff were unconvinced. On 28 July, the C-in-C reminded Beatty that the BCF's chief-of-staff had described a turn of 32 points; Jellicoe also noted that 'What appears to have been a reference to [the turns between 6.45 and 7.05] has evidently been cut out from "LION'S" report . . . of 4 June 1916', and that on the latest BCF chart the battlecruisers were too close to the battlefleet (they were shown bearing S, two miles).[199] In his reply of 4 August, Beatty insisted on his version of events, though he did supply the new information that an 'Entry in Commander N's notebook shows that "LION" commenced her big turn at 6.50'. He denigrated Bentinck's statement by declaring that 'the Officers concerned with the ships' reckoning were not on board', yet he must have known that his navigators actually agreed with Bentinck about the 32-point turn. Beatty continued:

A 32 point turn did not in fact take place. The portion cut out of 'LION'S' report was a reference to the fact that the Battle Fleet did not appear to be steering a course in support of the Battle Cruisers. I considered this undesirable to include.[200]

---

[197] Beatty to C-in-C, 8 and 12 July 1916, 'Track of BCF', ff. 612 and 617.
[198] *OD*, Pl. 8a and p. 143 and 'Track of BCF', f. 618 for covering memo. Harper concluded that Beatty signed this plan only in 1920 so that it could be included in the *Official Despatches* (Plate 8a) and that his signature was not the one he used in 1916: see *JP II*, pp. 478–9 note. However, some published charts were neither signed nor dated *e.g. OD*, Pls. 12 (*Princess Royal*'s) and 31 (*New Zealand*'s).
[199] C-in-C to Beatty, 28 July 1916, 'Track of BCF', ff. 620–2.
[200] Beatty to C-in-C, 4 August, 'Track of BCF', ff. 624–5.

Yet, a little earlier in Chatfield's despatch, in a passage that was not cut out, he had already implicitly criticised the battlefeet for not supporting the battlecruisers.

At 6.53 p.m. speed was reduced to 18 knots to keep station on the Battlefleet, who were leading away to port owing to a Destroyer attack.[201]

This false impression may have been formed in *Lion* in the few minutes after the BCF turned SSE but the battlefleet continued SE. But even then the BCF were not in touch with the enemy while, after the battleships turned S at 6.55, there was no question of their 'steering a course in support of the Battle Cruisers'. Thus it is much more likely that the excised passage gave an honest account of *Lion*'s turn as she 'continued to circle to starboard'. And Beatty's allegation that his flag-captain's despatch had criticised the C-in-C's leadership probably explains why Chatfield felt no obligation to back up his admiral's denial that the BCF turned through 32 points.

After receiving this letter, Jellicoe, short of accusing Beatty of lying, had no option but to drop the matter. But the C-in-C did ask Commodore Le Mesurier of the 4LCS for any observations of the BCF and of *King George V* that they had taken during the daylight action. As we have seen, these give some credence to Beatty's reported position relative to *King George V* at 6.40, though *Calliope* did not sight the BCF again until after it took station ahead of the battlefleet.[202] The closest we can now get to Beatty's true movements after 6.35 is the BCF's original chart submitted with his despatch but with corrections based on Bentinck's telegram. Thus, after running about 3.9 miles ESE from 6.35 to 6.45, *Lion* turned SSE before, at some time between 6.50 and 7.05, she led the 1/2BCS for some ten minutes through a complete circle. As they turned, at about 7.00, *Indomitable* and *Inflexible* hauled in astern of them. With the whole BCF now in line, *Lion* steadied briefly once more on a SSE'ly course before turning gradually Southwesterly. Starting from Beatty's position for the 1BS at 6.40 and plotting the battlecruisers' track on *King George V*'s chart, it turns out that at 7.05 *Lion* was about 1.4 miles SEbyS from the leading battleship. Yet Beatty's later chart of the whole battle shows *Lion* as two miles S of *King George V*, directly ahead of the battleships.[203] Instead, the battlecruisers were three points on the disengaged bow of *King George V*. Hence they were more distant from the enemy fleet that, as Jellicoe was about to discover, was now bent on renewing the action.

---

[201] *OD*, p. 145.   [202] Telegrams and letter, 6 August 1916, 'Track of BCF', ff. 625–7.
[203] The reasons for preferring the BCF's chart to the courses and speeds in Beatty's narrative and Chatfield's despatch are explained in the next chapter. *OD*, Pl. 8a.

8   The remains of the day

To begin by summarising the disposition of Jellicoe's forces after his order to turn South by 9 Pendant at 6.55: it appears that the 1st, 2nd, 4th and 5th Divisions altered course almost together while *Iron Duke* may have led round a few minutes earlier.[1] When the turns had been completed, the divisions were disposed quarterly with their guides on a line of bearing extending NW from *King George V.* However, a minute before the signal was hauled down, *Marlborough* had been hit by a torpedo so that the turns by the 6th Division were delayed until 6.58–7.00, and even then *Marlborough* had to take further avoiding action when more torpedoes were seen.[2] Evan-Thomas's despatch stated that a torpedo was sighted from the 5BS at this time and *Valiant*'s report that he turned his squadron away two points by the Preparative flag at 6.56; they did not turn back onto the course South until 7.06–7.10.[3] At 17 knots, the leader of a following division took about 3½ minutes to reach the turning point of a four-ship division ahead. Thus the later turns by *Marlborough*'s division and the 5BS meant that, at least approximately, they followed in the wake of the 5th Division; consequently, the whole 1BS and the 5BS more or less in line astern.

We have seen that, after the battlecruisers had completed their 32-point turn, at 7.05 they bore SEbyS 1.4 miles from *King George V.* Of the light cruiser squadrons that had put to sea with Beatty, only the 3LCS had kept its position ahead of the BCF. *Birkenhead* and *Gloucester* rejoined *Falmouth* and *Yarmouth* at 7.05. At about this time, *Canterbury* also joined Napier's squadron while the 1DF (except for *Badger*) formed a submarine screen ahead of *Lion.* After *Christopher* and *Ophelia* of the 4DF rejoined the 3BCS, presumably they too became part of the screen.[4]

The battle squadrons turning to starboard made it difficult for the 2CS on their disengaged port side to draw ahead. Steaming in the order *Minotaur,*

---

[1] *OD*, pp. 54, 79, 117 and 128 and Pls. 2, 4, 8, 29 and 6a.
[2] *OD*, pp. 85, 92 and 100 and Pl. 7a.
[3] *OD*, pp. 195 and 205 and Pl. 7a. Evan-Thomas stated that the 5BS turned 'Northwards' just after *Marlborough*'s torpedo hit but he gives the time as 'about 7.18'.
[4] F&H, p. 277. *OD*, pp. 186, 268, 314 and 316. In this and the next two paragraphs, sources for ships' movements already cited in Chapter 7 are not repeated.

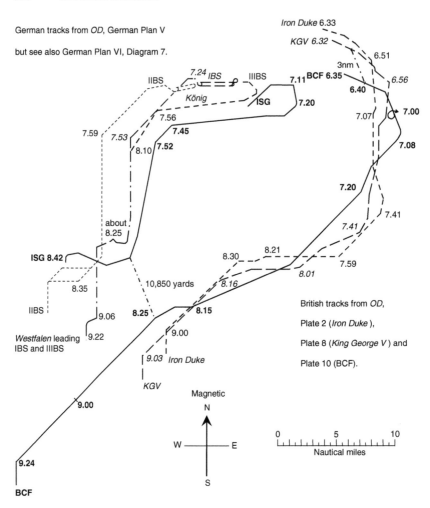

Figure 8.1 The remains of the day

Cochrane, Shannon and *Hampshire*, they were joined at 6.50 by the damaged *Chester*, which formed astern of *Hampshire*. By 7.10, the armoured cruisers were three to four miles on *King George V*'s port side with many light craft in between, while the battle cruisers were about four miles on *Minotaur*'s starboard bow. At about 7.15, *Duke of Edinburgh* also joined Heath's flag, though the reports disagree on whether she took station ahead or astern of *Hampshire*.[5] Of the light craft near the van of the battlefleet, the 4LCS, making its second

[5] *OD*, pp. 270, 272, 275–6, 283 and 288. *OD*(M), 7.20.

attempt between 7.00 and 7.15, reached its action station two miles SSW on the starboard engaged bow of *King George V.*[6] As for *Castor* and the destroyers of the 11DF and 4DF, some may have been able to keep ahead of the 2BS, though there had been 'considerable congestion of ships – light cruisers and destroyers – abreast the leading squadron'. By 7.10, they were in position ahead of the 2BS with the 4DF on the 11DF's disengaged beam.

The minelayer *Abdiel* and the four attached cruisers held their positions on the disengaged beam of the battlefleet; the destroyer *Oak* (tender to the flagship) was on *Iron Duke*'s beam near *Abdiel* and *Blanche.*[7] Outside them, *Inconstant, Phaeton* and *Cordelia* of the 1LCS pressed on towards the head of the battle line; *Galatea* followed and by 6.45 she could make 22 knots.[8] Goodenough's 2LCS had taken station on the engaged quarter of the 5BS while *Faulknor* and the 12DF had initially dropped back abeam of the 5BS; thus, roughly as shown on Jellicoe's 'Battle Plan' for 6.40, they were probably then ahead of the light cruisers. The same plan located *Fearless, Champion* and the boats of the 13DF, 9DF and 10DF on the disengaged quarter of the 6th Division. This position – from which an attack on the enemy could have been made only if the 2LCS and 12DF attacked first – was confirmed by *Fearless* and by the then Sub-Lieutenant Oram of *Obdurate*. But it was not mentioned in any of the reports from *Champion* or the destroyers, although that from *Morris* (10DF) confirmed that: 'We took no further part in the engagement'.[9]

Scheer's second *Gefechtskehrtwendung*

At 6.45, just after Jellicoe turned his divisions by one point to SE, *Moltke* reported that: 'The Enemy's van bears EbyS'. By that time, the German IBS and IIIBS were mainly heading W, though there may have been some curvature in the line, with the IIBS on the IBS's port bow and the ISG on the IIIBS's port quarter. At 6.48, Scheer ordered all his ships to alter course, leading ships together, the rest in succession, by two points to starboard; then, at 6.55, he signalled them to execute a second action-turn-about. Perhaps, as claimed by the German official history, the initial two-point turns were intended to close the still invisible enemy. But they also disposed the four dreadnought divisions quarterly, the formation for which German tactical orders gave express instructions on making an action-turn-about. These stipulated that the rear ship of each division, about to become its leader, should turn not through 16 points but onto

[6] *OD*, pp. 296 and 385. It is assumed that *Calliope* took until 7.15 to get two miles ahead of *King George V.*
[7] F&H, p. 203. *OD*, Pl. 1 'Battle Plan ... 6.40 p.m.'   [8] *OD*, pp. 173–4. *OD*(M), 6.45.
[9] *OD*, pp. 176, 242, 261–2 and 331 and Pl. 1. Oram, p. 164. See also *GF*, pp. 224–5 and 232–3.

Table 8.1. *German signals 6.45–7.05pm*

Time of receipt	From	To	System	Message	Time of origin
pm, 31 May					
6.45	Moltke	C-in-C		Enemy's van bears EbyS	
6.48	C-in-C	General		Alter course. Leading ships together, the rest in succession. 2 points to starboard	
6.50	Deutschland	IIBS	Visual	Alter course in succession; 2 points to starboard	6.50
6.55	C-in-C	General		Turn together 16 points to starboard	
7.00	Lützow	Moltke	Visual	Lützow can only proceed at half speed … (passed on to C-in-C by W/T)	
7.00	Lützow	Moltke	Visual	To Seydlitz: AC Scouting Forces is coming later on to Seydlitz	
7.02	C-in-C	General		Reduce speed	
7.05	Derfflinger	ISG	Visual	All battle cruisers. Follow in wake of the Senior officer's ship	
7.05	Rostock	F. der Grosse		Markgraf's port engine disabled. Can no longer maintain my position in the line – Markgraf	

a course corresponding to their initial line-of bearing, in this instance through 14 points to E; the remaining ships turned initially through a full 16 points but then turned back to follow in the wake of the new leader. The advantage of this variant of the *Gefechtskehrtwendung* was that the initial quarterly disposition gave each division a better view of the turns by its neighbours in the line; thus the main purpose of the two-point turns at 6.45 may have been to assume this favourable formation in readiness for the subsequent turn-about. Since the predreadnoughts and battlecruisers were not in line, they made wider turns so that the ISG could again lead the line and the IIBS bring up the rear. The reduction of speed at 7.02 appears to have been intended to allow the line to close up.[10]

Though neither Commander-in-Chief knew of the other's move, just as Scheer ordered this second action-turn-about to E, Jellicoe turned his battle squadrons S. The British battleships were now heading at right angle across the German line of advance and would soon, for the second time, cross Scheer's T. Scheer's

---

[10] *OD*, German Plan V and Plan VI, Dia. 5. *GOA*, p. 125 (which states that only the IIIBS reduced speed). *JP I*, p. 253. 'Tactical Order No. 5', 17 April 1914 in ADM 137/4326.

explanation to the Kaiser for placing his fleet in this potentially disastrous situation read:

It was as yet too early to assume 'night cruising order'. The enemy could have compelled us to fight before dark, he could have prevented us exercising our initiative, and finally he could have cut off our return to the German Bight.

There was only one way of avoiding this: to deal the enemy a second blow by again advancing regardless of consequences, and to bring all the destroyers to attack.

This manoeuvre would necessarily have the effect of surprising the enemy, upsetting his plans for the rest of the day, and, if the attack was powerful enough, of facilitating our extricating ourselves for the night. In addition this afforded us the opportunity of making a final effort to succour the hard-pressed WIESBADEN, or at least to rescue her crew.[11]

The notion of 'surprising the enemy' echoes Nelson's remark about his tactics at Trafalgar, and the German official historian accepted that Scheer 'knew that this movement would very soon expose him to a second "crossing of the T" ' and that the 'arguments in favour of this decision were almost the same as those employed by Nelson'. But, confusingly, Captain Groos then added that 'this similarity was ... purely accidental' and that 'under the altered battle conditions of a modern naval action the circumstances were completely different'. Indeed, it is hard to credit that any admiral of the dreadnought era would have chosen deliberately to cross his own T; Nelson's plan for Trafalgar, which even at the time was a finely judged gamble, was appropriate only when gun ranges were short and the opponent's gunnery was inferior.[12] Even so, Scheer himself added to the impression of faulty tactical judgement by admitting to the Kaiser that: 'In peace time ... one would deny that I had any ability to lead a fleet, had I executed such a manoeuvre as I did at the Skagerrak'. After a good dinner, he admitted: 'My idea? I had no idea ... The thing just happened'. In the opinion of his own Chief-of-Staff, 'if an admiral had brought about such a situation in manoeuvres, or at a war game, he would never be entrusted with another command'.[13]

Yet Scheer may simply have believed that, once the British pressure had ceased and with his own fleet intact, it was his duty to seek contact once more with the enemy.[14] Furthermore, he may not have anticipated the worst possible tactical outcome. During the first fleet encounter, he could see little of the enemy battleships but at about 6.35 their gun flashes extended in an arc from NNW round to E, giving a broad impression that they were heading approximately SE. Scheer also overestimated the British losses; in addition to *Invincible*, *Defence* and *Warrior*, he believed that a *Queen Elizabeth*-class battleship, another

---

[11] Scheer's despatch, *OD*, p. 594.   [12] Mackay and Duffy, pp. 209–10 and 212.
[13] *GOA*, p. 124. *FDSF III*, p. 128 and n. 50 citing von Weizsäcker (Scheer's flag-lieutenant) and von Trotha (COS) to the Austrian Naval Attaché. Halpern, p. 322.
[14] *FDSF III*, p. 127 and n. 48.

armoured cruiser, a light cruiser and two destroyers had also been lost.[15] Thus he could have assumed that Jellicoe was more inclined to turn away somewhat than to renew the attack; in that case, a course due East would lead to an inclined approach with an angle between courses of about four points. Even so, the British van already bore EbyS at 6.45, so Scheer should have realised that his own van would probably encounter the centre rather than the head of the British line and risk being encircled; also his destroyers would be in a poor position for attacking. Yet these disadvantages may have seemed acceptable if they avoided leaving *Wiesbaden* beyond succour too far to port.[16] But in reality Jellicoe did not even know that the High Seas Fleet had retreated Westwards for a time, while Scheer did not anticipate the British turn S. As Marder concluded:

Whatever Scheer's thinking may have been, his manoeuvre did not 'surprise' Jellicoe or 'upset his plans'. Rather it was Scheer who was surprised when he found his way barred and his van being crushed.[17]

Scheer's signals suggest that, after the second action-turn-about, his attention remained focussed on the *Wiesbaden*. At 7.00 he ordered Michelsen, the 1st Leader of Torpedo Boats, to rescue her crew. Probably because *Wiesbaden* was

Table 8.2. *German destroyer signals 6.52–7.05pm*

Time of receipt	From	To	System	Message	Time of origin
pm, 31 May					
6.52	2nd Leader of Torpedo boats	VITF	Visual	Torpedo boats to attack!	
6.54	2nd Leader of Torpedo boats	IXTF	Visual	Torpedo boats to attack!	
6.55	Rostock	IHF and XIIHF		Boats to go to Lützow and fetch AC Scouting Forces	
7.00	C-in-C	Leader of Torpedo Boats	Visual	Rescue Wiesbaden's crew	
7.00	Rostock	IIITF	Visual	Go to Wiesbaden and rescue crew	
7.03	Rostock	IIITF	Visual	3 boats to go to Wiesbaden to rescue crew. Direction NE	
7.03	S53	V71	Visual	To Group-Leader. Go to Wiesbaden with your 3 boats and rescue crew. Direction NE	
	Rostock	IIITF	Visual	IIITF, faster	
7.05	C-in-C	Rostock	Visual	Send assistance to Wiesbaden	

---

[15] *OD*, pp. 593–4.   [16] Rahn, pp. 172 and 270.   [17] *FDSF III*, p. 129.

still under fire, Michelsen committed only three boats from the VHF; *V71* led out *V73* and *G88* between the Vth and VIth battleship divisions, urged on by Michelsen and Scheer. From the British line, a solitary German destroyer was seen approaching *Colossus* at 7.03 and soon more were sighted. By 7.11, they were under fire from *Iron Duke, Royal Oak, Benbow, Bellerophon* and *Colossus* and from *Neptune*, which made out 'about six or eight German destroyers' attacking at 7.10. The German history suggests plausibly that the boats under fire were actually the VHF and perhaps also the previously damaged *V48*. Under this intense bombardment, the senior flotilla officer decided that the rescue attempt was hopeless and ordered his boats to turn back, though in doing so *V73* fired one torpedo at the British line and *G88* fired three, all at a range of 6,600 yards.[18] *Neptune* saw her attackers fire torpedoes before they were driven off; subsequently, three torpedo tracks were observed from her foretop, of which one, despite her use of the helm, passed very close.[19] *Neptune*'s claim to have sighted more destroyers than the three from the VHF may have been a simple mistake. But the German signal record contain two signals from Heinrich, the 2nd Leader of Torpedo Boats, timed at 6.52 and 6.54, ordering attacks by the VITF and IXTF. The IXTF and XIHF did not attack until 7.15 but, of the XIIHF, *V69, V46* and *S50* are mentioned by the German history only as having stayed with the IITF;[20] perhaps these three, while returning from their earlier attack on the 3BCS, obeyed Heinrich's order and attacked with the VHF.

From their position in the British rear:

At 6.47 p.m. the Second Light Cruiser Squadron turned in towards the German line partly to finish off a disabled battleship [*sic*], but more to observe the enemy's rear, their course being in doubt.

Southampton attempted to deliver the *coup de grace* with 6in salvos at 6,000 yards, *Wiesbaden* replying gamely with a single gun. Then German battleships were sighted beyond the target, which were thought to be 'our old friends the pre-Dreadnoughts'. But the 'absolute rain of shells' that then descended on the British light cruisers were fired, according to the German history, from the van, first by *Markgraf* (commencing at 7.05), then by *Derfflinger, König* and *Grosser Kurfürst* (7.07) and, a little later, by *Kaiser* and *Prinzregent Luitpold*. The range, initially 9,800, increased to 18,000 yards as the 2LCS beat a hasty retreat to the NNE, 'zig-zagging like snipe' to avoid hits. Goodenough, mindful as ever of a cruiser's principal duty, at 7.04 reported his position and the enemy's bearing (SSW) and estimated course (ESE).[21]

---

[18] *GOA*, pp. 125 and 128. *OD*, pp. 54, 63, 79, 90, 99, 120 and 128. F&H, p. 184. S&H, p. 251.
[19] *OD*, p. 90. A torpedo was seen from *Agincourt*'s foretop just missing astern but it was thought to have come from a submarine: *OD*, p. 92.
[20] *GOA*, p. 135.
[21] *OD*, p. 176. Goodenough, p. 46. F&H, pp. 266–7. 'Etienne', pp. 142–3. *GOA*, p. 125.

Table 8.3. *Grand fleet signals 6.54–7.15pm*

Time of despatch	From	To	System	Message	Time of origin
pm, 31 May					
6.54	C-in-C	SO BCF, SO 3BCS, SO 2CS	W/T	Present course of fleet is South	1854
6.55	C-in-C	Dreadnought Battlefleet and attached Cruisers	W/T and Flags	Alter course leading ships together the rest in succession to South	
6.55	C-in-C	SO 1BS	SL	Can you see any Enemy Battleships? Reply: No	1850
7.00	K.G.V	C-in-C	SL	There is a Submarine ahead of you	1859
7.00 (rec'ved)	SO BCF	C-in-C	SL	Enemy are to Westward	1755 [sic]
7.04	Colossus			Remarks: Marlborough hauled out of line to starboard	
7.04	Southampton	SO BCF	W/T	Urgent. Priority. Enemy battlefleet steering ESE. Enemy bears from me SSW. Number unknown. My position 57°02E, 6°07E (Received in *Iron Duke* 7.00)	1900
7.05	C-in-C	Dreadnought Battlefleet and attached Cruisers	W/T Flags	Alter course together three points to starboard	
7.09	C-in-C	Dreadnought Battlefleet and attached Cruisers	W/T Flags	Alter course together three points to port	
7.09	Benbow	C-in-C	Sem.	Enemy Destroyers SW (Received in Iron Duke 7.16)	1908
7.09	C-in-C	Dreadnought Battlefleet and attached Cruisers	W/T Flags	Alter course together to South	
7.10	SO 1BS	Collingwood	Flags	Follow in the wake of your next ahead	
7.12	C-in-C	1BS	SL	Take station astern of 4BS	
7.13	SO 4BS	4th Division	Flags	Subdivisions separately alter course in succession two points away from the Enemy preserving their formation	
7.15	SO 4BS	4th Division	Flags	Speed 13 knots. Alter course together two points to starboard. (Negatived)	

At 7.00, Jellicoe had received Beatty's signal 'Enemy are to Westward' but, since the BCF were not then in touch, this can only have been a delayed and incomplete version of *Falmouth's* report of 6.45. However, the enemy line was not completely invisible; at 6.55, as they turned S, *St Vincent* and *Revenge* had sighted German capital ships and both probably opened fire soon afterwards; *Neptune* did likewise at about 7.04.[22] None of these ships sent a report to the C-in-C, but the sound of salvos from the 1BS can only have confirmed the impression given by Goodenough's signal that the enemy was again closing in. At 7.06, 'the whole battle line was turned together three more points to starboard to close the range further'. These turns by Blue Pendant to SWbyS formed the ships of each division on a line-of-bearing N, a disposition in which station keeping was more difficult than in line astern.[23] Even as *Iron Duke* turned, she had a target in view and her turrets then trained to pick up the left-hand ship on a forward bearing of G28. Thus there must already have been more than one ship visible from the flagship and at 7.09, Jellicoe turned his divisions back into line-ahead on a course S by a Blue Pendant turn to port.[24] The 1BS and 5BS were now once more, at least approximately, in a single line and closest to the advancing enemy. The leaders of the 5th to the 1st Divisions were again disposed on a line-of-bearing extending NW-SE, with *King George V* and the 1st Division furthest ahead but also furthest away from the enemy. This quarterly disposition was a consequence of his bold four point turn S by 9 Pendant to seek out the enemy. But the obstruction to the fire, of the rear ships in each division especially, was not at all 'inappreciable', their starboard firing being restricted to an arc from right ahead to about one point before the beam – unless a rear ship was prepared, like *Thunderer*, to fire over the bows of the leader to starboard; Jellicoe recalled this caused 'some slight inconvenience on the bridge' of *Iron Duke*.[25] To enable all his divisions to develop their full weight of fire, the C-in-C needed to reform his battleships into a single line. At 7.12 he ordered the 1BS to take station astern of the 4BS; as well as freeing up the firing arcs of the 4BS, this would reduce the exposure of the 1BS (and the 5BS following astern) to enemy attacks. However, at 7.09 Sturdee in *Benbow* had warned Jellicoe of enemy destroyers to the SW and at 7.13 Sturdee took the prescribed action for evading torpedoes by turning the 4th Division away two points to port by the Preparative flag. These turns were also in the general direction necessary to haul into line astern of the 3rd Division. Although, according to the signal record, Sturdee negatived the speed and course orders timed at 7.16, his despatch confirms that he did form astern of the 3rd Division, so the orders were probably carried out

---

[22] *OD*, pp. 85, 89, 94 and Pl. 6.   [23] *GF*, pp. 41, 228 (time of turn 7.05) and 235.
[24] *OD*, pp. 56 and 58. *GF*, p. 228 where Jellicoe stated that the second Blue Pendant turn was made towards a submarine reported just after the first such turn; however, *King George V's* signal was at 7.00.
[25] Quotations from *GF*, p. 226. The 7pt. firing arc has been calculated assuming ships in column at 2½ cables and columns at 1.0 and 1.1 miles, leaders bearing SEbyE.

a little later, once *Benbow* had fallen astern of *Canada*.[26] These moves by the 4th Division can only have complicated the efforts of the 1BS to form astern and, as we shall see later, the 1BS may not have obeyed Jellicoe's 7.12 order immediately. It is sufficient for now to record that, of the 1BS, by 7.15 only *Collingwood* was not yet engaging German capital ships. Astern of them, *Valiant* and *Malaya* of the 5BS opened fire at 7.10 and 7.20 respectively. Ahead, in the 4BS all except *Vanguard* began engaging targets, mostly identified as battlecruisers, between 7.13 and 7.20. But, in the British van, only *Orion* and *Monarch* of the 2nd Division were able from 7.14 to fire for any length of time; they were probably engaging *Lützow* at long range.[27] Thus by 7.20 the ships at the head of the German line were under fire by most of the ships of the British 4BS, 1BS and 5BS. It is necessary to emphasise that, even for the British, the visibility remained bad, ships firing at whatever they could see with, at best, a quick range-finder reading.[28] Nonetheless, even by 7.15, the leading German ships, which were still closing the range with their T well and truly crossed, were beginning to suffer severely. Only desperate measures could now extract them from an untenable tactical position.

Scheer's third *Gefechtskehrtwendung*

From 7.12 onwards, the leading German ships, mainly in the ISG and Vth Division, were under a steadily increasing fire from the British line, of which they could see nothing but the flashes of the guns.[29] At 7.13, Scheer ordered his four remaining battlecruisers to turn together at their utmost speed directly towards the enemy.[30] However, within a minute or two, he seems to have realised that a head-on approach towards the British centre was asking too much, since he then ordered the ISG to operate against the enemy van.[31] His signal (as usual by flags and W/T) may not have been received in *Derfflinger* until 7.17 but, as soon as it was read, Captain Hartog turned, probably with the ISG following in succession, to SbyE onto a course parallel with the enemy, thereby bringing his full broadsides to bear. The ISG came as close as 7,700 yards to the British line; at 7.16–7.17,

---

[26] *OD*, pp. 122 (where the time of the Preparative signal is 7.10) and 358. JMSS 49029, f. 3.
[27] Details with references can be found later in this chapter.   [28] *OD*, pp. 18 and 376.
[29] *GOA*, p. 130. Scheer's despatch, *OD*, p. 595.
[30] Scheer's signal has been variously translated: *GOA*, p. 131; GSM, p. 283; von Hase, p. 196; *FDSF III*, p. 130, though it is inconceivable that the order was sent using different code groups. In fact, the single 'R' flag was used: *OD*, German Plan VI, Dia. 7. Its meaning was:
　　'TURN TOGETHER UPON THE ENEMY. RAM. All ships of the Line or of the Division indicated turn together and at their utmost speed steer for the enemy's line on a course as near as possible perpendicular to his own.' (*Manoeuvring Instructions for the Fleet, 1914*, p. 38 in ADM 186/17.) See also Rahn, pp. 172 and 270.
[31] *OD*, German Plan VI, Dia. 7 indicates that 'Signal R' was followed by 'Signal T', though it seems that by 1916 it had a different meaning from that in *Manoeuvring Instructions … 1914*, pp. 44 and 51 (manoeuvre in sections).

Table 8.4. *German signals 7.10–7.25pm*

Time of receipt	From	To	System	Message	Time of origin
pm, 31 May					
7.10	Derfflinger	ISG	Visual	Increase speed	
7.13	C-in-C	ISG		Battle cruisers, turn towards the enemy. Attack!	
7.14	Derfflinger	ISG	Visual	Turn towards the enemy	
7.14	C-in-C	ISG		Battle cruisers to operate against the enemy van	
7.15	Derfflinger	ISG	Visual	Operate against the enemy van	
7.15	Derfflinger	ISG	Visual	Speed 23 knots	
7.18	C-in-C	General		Turn together 16 points to starboard	
7.20	Deutschland	IIBS	Visual	Course NW	
7.20	C-in-C	General		Increase speed	
7.21	C-in-C	General		Torpedo boats to attack	
7.21	Rostock	All Flotillas	Visual	Assemble for an attack on the requisite line of bearing	
7.22	C-in-C	General		Course W	
7.23	Rostock	All Flotillas	Visual	Proceed ahead to the attack. (At the enemy!)	
7.25	Deutschland	IIBS	Visual	Course W	

Colossus was twice hit by *Seydlitz*, the only German hits during this phase of the battle.[32]

With the ISG providing cover, at 7.18 Scheer ordered his third *Gefechtskehrtwendung*, again to starboard. 'But on this occasion the execution of this manoeuvre, so close to the enemy and under the full weight of his broadsides, was much more difficult than before'. Since 7.10, *König* had been under a heavy fire. She and the others ships of the Vth Division were being punished severely 'because the battle cruisers, drawing across the head of the line, forced them to reduce speed, and finally ... some of the ships of this division, as well as some of the [VIth] had to stop engines and even go astern ... "König" had to turn to S.E. again in order to bring her broadside to bear on a course parallel to the enemy'.[33] Thus, even before the action-turn-about, the German van had crumpled up and turned away to starboard. In doing so, the *Kaiserin* had closed up so far on her next ahead that *Prinzregent Luitpold* had been forced to sheer out of line even further to starboard. At the German rear, the action-turn-about was probably executed

---

[32] *GOA*, p. 133, which states that the flagship's signal was not made out until 7.17. *OD*, pp. 79–80 and 82–1. F&H, pp. 186–7. Campbell, p. 218.

[33] *GOA*, p. 131.

without much difficulty, though Mauve initially ordered the predreadnoughts of the IIBS onto a course NW and the IBS also briefly followed this course. The new leaders of both squadrons – *Hannover* and *Westfalen* – turned W once Scheer confirmed at 7.22 that this was his intended course.[34] In the Ist Division, *Helgoland* was hit at 7.15. Whether for this reason or, as the German historian claimed, 'to hasten matters', Vice-Admiral Schmidt in *Ostfriesland* commenced the turn at once. Before the turn, *Friedrich der Grosse* had been next ahead of the *Ostfriesland* and astern of the *Kaiserin*, though the latter was already out of line to starboard. After the turn, *Kaiserin* attempted to increase her distance from *Ostfriesland* in order to leave room for *Friedrich der Grosse*; but then *Prinzregent Luitpold* came up at high speed. 'This forced the "Kaiserin" to remain outside the line for a considerable time before she could haul in astern of "Prinzregent Luitpold" '; thus these two ships eventually exchanged places in the line.[35] All the German battleships executed the action-turn-about by turning to starboard, except for *Friedrich der Grosse*, which turned out to port. In his memoirs, Scheer acknowledged that: 'This might have led the ships following behind to think that there was a mistake in the signalling', but he explained that his intention had been to 'save the ships in front of the *Friedrich der Grosse* from a difficult situation' – the ships in question being, presumably, *Kaiserin* and *Prinzregent Luitpold*. Scheer also praised Schmidt for preventing confusion astern by turning early in order to force the rest of the IBS round to starboard.[36] However, if the German historian is correct, Schmidt's turn was part of the problem rather than its solution, and, in any case, the early turn by the *Ostfriesland* can only have added to the congestion on the starboard side of *Friedrich der Grosse*. Scheer was right that his lone turn to port could have caused serious confusion in his line and it is unlikely that he would have risked it unless his flagship's starboard turn was completely blocked.

The Vth Division also had problems in turning about. *Markgraf*, with her port engine stopped, could no longer develop her full speed; in order to get away from the area under fire and to gain ground in the probable new direction of the fleet, her captain also turned early, before his next astern, *Kronprinz*. *Markgraf* then pushed *Grosser Kurfürst*, her next ahead before the turn-about, to the SW for a time but eventually the division hauled into line astern of *Kaiser* with *Markgraf* leading *Kronprinz* (thus they too swapped places) and *Grosser Kurfürst* and *König* bringing up the rear.[37]

For several exceedingly perilous minutes the fleet flagship and the ships of the [Vth] and [VIth] Divisions were consequently proceeding at slow speed very close to one another

---

[34] *GOA*, p. 132. *OD*, German Plan V.

[35] *GOA*, pp. 131–2. For the order of the German battleline before and after the action-turns-about, see Tarrant, pp. 116 and 184 (based on *GOA* charts); however, the charts on pp. 164 and 172 show *Kaiserin* astern of *Friedrich der Grosse* after the turn-about.

[36] *GOA*, p. 132. Scheer, pp. 157–8.

[37] *GOA*, p. 132. If the 'and' beginning the last line of the first paragraph is omitted, the text can be read as conforming to the chart (Tarrant, p. 184).

and almost in line abreast ... Recognising the danger of the situation, Captain Brüninghaus hauled out about 450 yards to windward [ESE] with the 'König' and laid a smoke screen between the enemy and his own line, whilst still straddled by the enemy's salvoes ... At [7].25 p.m. the 'Kaiser' fired her last salvo at 17,500 yards, the target bearing aft ... At [7].28 p.m. the captain ... gave orders for as much smoke as possible to be made as the enemy still appeared to be able to find targets along the German line [including *Kaiser* herself].

At 7.27, Scheer made a general signal to alter course to SW, speed 17 knots. The ISG had meanwhile conformed to the movements of the battlefleet, turning to WSW at 7.20 and then to W, but they held this course in order to catch up with the battle squadrons. The battlecruisers remained for a time under a heavy concentration but the IISG and destroyers had laid smoke screens to the SW'ward and these now took effect. *Seydlitz* received her final hit at 7.30.[38] At 7.20, smoke from the burning *Lützow* also carried between the ISG and the enemy; she was last seen from the fleet flagship abeam at about 7.20, apparently still able to steam at moderate speed.[39]

With her destroyer escort, *Lützow* was attempting to withdraw to the SW but she was still in sight at long range (19,000 yards or more) from some ships of the 2BS. Campbell identifies five hits on the German battlecruiser between 7.15 and 7.18. One completely disabled the right-hand gun of A turret while a second between C and D turrets caused heavy casualties in the after dressing station and, by cutting the power cables to D, reduced the turret to hand working. *Lützow* then turned away to starboard.[40] A hit on the starboard side somewhere below B barbette flooded the forward 5.9in magazine and other spaces, adding yet more water in the fore part of the ship. She was also hit on the side of B turret; fragments of armour were driven in, wrecking the right gun and igniting a fore charge in the hoist. 'Then we must have been lost to sight by the enemy, and, although the whole English line passed us by, we were not fired at and were able to devote all our energy to repairs. And there was plenty to do.'[41]

Derfflinger paid dearly for her gallant leadership of the depleted ISG. Between 7.14 and shortly after 7.20, she received no less than 14 hits. Either of the first two, by 15in shell, could have led to her destruction. The first struck the edge of the roof of D turret and burst inside. Two main and two fore charges were ignited, one pair in the right cartridge loading tray, the second pair in the right cartridge hoist, which was down in the working chamber. Flash then spread to the magazine handing room, igniting a further five main and eleven

---

[38] *GOA*, p. 132. *OD*, German Plan V. Staff, *World War One*, pp. 181–2 (hit 21).

[39] von Hase, p. 207. Scheer's despatch, *OD*, p. 596. *GOA*, p. 142.

[40] At 7.15, *Calliope* observed an enemy battlecruiser surrounded by destroyers steering slowly NW: *OD*, p. 296.

[41] Paschen, pp. 36–8. Campbell, pp. 218–20. Paschen confirms the hit between C and D turrets but states that the damage to A and B turrets was caused by a single shell and that it occurred before the sinking of *Invincible*.

fore charges – though no charges in unopened magazine cases caught fire. All but one of the turret's crew of seventy-five were killed by flames and gas but, although there may have been some delay in flooding the magazines and shell rooms, there was no explosion. Through voice pipes, the gases reached the gunnery communication station, which had to be abandoned for ten critical minutes. Two or three minutes later, a second 15in shell struck the barbette of C turret; it pierced the 10¼in armour and burst between the two guns. Five main and five fore charges were ignited in the turret and working chamber but only two main and two fore charges in the handing room. Five or six of the crew were able to escape. Propellant gases penetrated all four engine rooms and other compartments but gas-masks enabled most crews to remain at their posts. Of the other hits, one wrecked the No. 3 Port casemate; one exploded under the bridge, blowing away the chart house; and the last, by a 12in APC, struck the fore conning tower without holing the armour. von Hase attempted to engage the enemy at ranges from 12,000 to 8,000 metres (13,000 to 8,700 yards) though he could see scarcely anything of them. Soon, his ship was reduced to two turrets and, with the failure of the director training indicator in B turret, he could only control A turret from the fore control position. *Derfflinger* fired a torpedo at a range of 8,000 metres but, as the ISG turned away, its targets now drew astern before disappearing behind the smoke screen laid by the IISG and the destroyers.[42]

Seydlitz, having closed to as little as 7,700 yards, also attracted a weight of British fire and received five hits. The fourth at 7.27 struck the right gun of her port wing turret; the gun itself was wrecked, the director pointer gear was disabled so that the turret could no longer fire with the others, and splinters put the No. 5 Port 5.9in gun out of action. The fifth hit the lower edge at the rear of the already disabled superfiring turret. Most of the burst was inside the gunhouse, igniting two fore and two main charges that had survived the earlier conflagration. von Hase observed that, just as in his own ship, 'flames as high as houses' leapt up from this turret, and that *Seydlitz* was badly down by the bows. *Moltke* again escaped unscathed but, in *Von der Tann*, a shell from the port quarter hit the after conning tower. While the armour was only scarred, splinters entered the slits, killing four and injuring everyone else inside.[43]

Of the German battleships that had been leading, *König* escaped with just one hit below the port aftermost casemate; it burst inboard and caused extensive damage to light structures.[44] Her next astern, *Grosser Kurfürst*, received

---

[42] Campbell, pp. 220–32. *GOA*, p. 134. von Hase, pp. 196–206; von Hase alone puts the hit on C turret first.

[43] Staff, *World War One*, pp. 178–82 (hits 12, 13, 16, 19 and 21). von Hase, p. 207 confirming that the second hit on and propellant fire in C turret occurred at this time. Campbell, pp. 234–5. *GOA*, p. 134.

[44] Campbell, p. 236. *GOA*, p. 131; pp. 143–4 refers to ten hits on *König* but some are described earlier (pp. 109 and 111) as having occurred at about 6.35 and Campbell assigns the remainder to the earlier action.

seven hits. Of these, the structural damage from two hits forward resulted in most of the fore-part gradually flooding until eventually there was over 3,000 tons of water in the ship. A hit on the main belt just abaft the fore-funnel caused further flooding but two more near A and B barbettes did not affect the turrets themselves. *Markgraf* was hit once at 7.14 and *Kaiser* twice at 7.23 and 7.26; Campbell states that these three were all made by TNT-filled CPC fired by *Agincourt* and that, in one case, the TNT burnt quietly rather than exploding. In the centre, at 7.15 *Helgoland* was struck by a heavy shell that made a large hole in the forward side armour, through which about 80 tons of water entered.[45]

German destroyer attacks

By about seven o'clock, Heinrich in *Regensburg* had closed on the ISG with the IXTF (now reduced to nine boats) and the four boats of the VITF (the leader *G41* and the XIHF) in company.[46] However, the IITF, his fastest and most powerful flotilla, was far astern; due to their large turning circles, they had had difficulty in following his movements during the attack on the 3BCS and in avoiding the IISG while returning.[47] Of the battlefleet flotillas under the command of Michelsen in *Rostock*, only four boats of the IIITF – the leader *S53* and the three boats of the VHF that rejoined him after abandoning the attempt to rescue *Wiesbaden*'s crew – were in an attacking position, on the starboard bow of *König*. As soon as the British battleships opened up, *Regensburg* and her accompanying flotillas came under fire, so, even though they were still assembling, they must have been among the German destroyers sighted early on from the British line. Both Michelsen and Heinrich concluded that the critical tactical situation demanded an immediate torpedo attack, though apparently only just before Scheer issued his own general order to this effect. However, the timings are uncertain. Whereas the German history states that the VITF and IXTF moved out at 7.15, followed by the IIITF at 7.23, the signals record gives times of 7.21 for Scheer's order, and 7.21 and 7.23 for *Rostock*'s orders to assemble and to proceed. Probably, being already under fire, Heinrich initiated his attack at the earlier time. But it is surprising that Scheer waited until three minutes after his action-turn-about signal before ordering a covering destroyer attack; perhaps he found an explicit order necessary because Michelsen had failed to act on his own initiative.

Regensburg accompanied her two flotillas until she was abreast of *Derfflinger*, after which Heinrich turned back to bring up the lagging IITF. The destroyers advanced through the smoke laid by *Lützow*'s escort to behold the whole British battlefleet in a great curve on courses that appeared to be from ESE to SSE. *G41*

---

[45] Campbell, pp. 237–46. *GOA*, p. 131; p. 143 allots eight hits to *Grosser Kurfürst* and five to *Markgraf*.

[46] This section is based on *GOA*, pp. 135–9.

[47] *GOA*, p. 138 claims that they had barely changed position for almost three-quarters of an hour.

led the VITF in the first attack, closing to within 7,700 yards of the enemy before she and *G86* were hit as they turned off to fire their torpedoes. *G41* managed to fire two, the other three boats three each 'under favourable conditions'. Although the speeds of *G41* and *G86* were reduced, all four returned safely after laying a screen of smoke and artificial fog.[48] This covered the IXTF for a time as it attacked further to the North. Then, under a withering fire, they too closed to 7,700 yards as their leader *V28* was hit. Despite shells falling all around them, they all fired torpedoes: *V28, S36* and *S51* one each; *V26* two; and the other five boats three each at ranges down to 6,600 yards.[49] Then, chased by cruisers and destroyers advancing from the British line, the IXTF withdrew, although their smoke and fog screen did not prevent *S35* from being hit amidships by a heavy shell which broke her in two; her casualties included her own crew and also survivors from *V29*. At 7.30, *S51* was also hit, so she and *V28* followed at reduced speed putting up clouds of black smoke. The flotilla reformed on *Rostock*, its leadership being transferred first to *V27* and then to *V30*. Between them, these two flotillas had fired as many as thirty-one torpedoes at the British line.[50]

When the IIITF commenced its attack, the German battlefleet was already making its 16-point turn so the boats had to break through a gap in the centre of the Vth Division. They advanced to the Northern edge of the smoke screens laid by the VITF and IXTF but, when they cleared the wall of smoke, there were no large ships in sight, only a few destroyers to the Southward, towards which they steered. *S54*, which had returned in time to follow about 650 yards astern, kept on Eastwards when the rest of the flotilla turned S; she was just able to make out a line of battleships but could get no closer than 10,000 yards before firing a single torpedo at 7.45.[51] British destroyers were then heading Northwards on an opposite course towards the IIITF and engaged them at about 6,000 yards before turning about onto a parallel course. *G88* fired a torpedo at what she had mistaken for a light cruiser but, when more light cruisers and destroyers were sighted further away, the IIITF laid a smoke and fog screen to cover the ISG and headed SW towards their own battlefleet.

The VTF and the VIITF had been stationed at the rear of the German line and had not fired any of their torpedoes. They had already turned about with the squadrons near them before they received Scheer's general order for the destroyers to attack. Although the situation in the van could not be made out, the commander of the VIITF decided that an attack would be hopeless and he

---

[48] For the German fog apparatus see Campbell, p. 204.

[49] Each torpedo was probably set to run more or less perpendicularly to its target's course, in which case these ranges represent the distances run to reach the British line should it not take avoiding action. This left the 25% range margin prescribed in the German tactical orders to allow for a British turn-away (Chapter 2).

[50] This total assumes that *S35* fired three torpedoes before she was sunk.

[51] By that time the British battleships was steering SW (see below).

remained on the disengaged side of the IIBS 'so as not to divest the new van of the fleet entirely of torpedo boats'. In contrast, the VTF at once turned about towards the *Rostock*. Michelsen ordered them to head ESE without delay but they did not emerge from the smoke and fog clouds until 7.50. They sighted only a few enemy cruisers and numerous destroyers, which engaged the VTF at very long range. At 7.52, without support, the flotilla turned back SW to follow the IIITF towards the main German fleet. Earlier, when the IITF eventually came up, its first attempt at an attack was completely obscured by one of the German smoke screens, supposedly that laid to protect *Lützow*. But, at that moment Heinrich, noticing that the enemy fire was dying away, hoisted the signal 'Follow in the wake of the Senior officer's ship', at which the IITF broke off its attack and took station on the *Regensburg*, just as she was having to manoeuvre to make room for the ISG as they turned away.

In the end, only the boats of the VITF and IXTF, and one boat of the IIITF, succeeded in firing torpedoes at the British battle line. This was hardly the 'massed attack' proclaimed by the German historian; out of the total German strength of six and a half flotillas, it was in effect mounted by no more than a single flotilla and two half-flotillas, none at full strength. Nonetheless, a total of thirty-two torpedoes had been fired and they would have a decisive effect on Jellicoe's tactics just as Scheer turned his battle fleet away in considerable confusion.

From the British battlefleet, the harbinger of the German torpedo attacks was the solitary destroyer sighted from *Colossus* coming down on the starboard bow at a range of only 4,000 yards; at 7.05, the battleship fired with both 12in and 4in guns but, despite her claim of a sinking, there were no German losses at this time.[52] As the British battlefleet turned back into line heading S at 7.09, more German destroyers were coming into view at ranges from 8,000 to 10,000 yards. Four minutes previously, *Bellerophon* had sighted a destroyer on a forward bearing of about G35. Then, after the three-point turn, *Iron Duke* sighted her first destroyer bearing G63,[53] while *Benbow* was firing at destroyers bearing G56 shortly before her turn-away by Preparative.[54] *Royal Oak* reported a similar target bearing of G65, though, from *Conqueror* and *Neptune*, which also opened fire on destroyers between 7.09 and 7.12, their targets were further abeam.[55] Since the most favourable position for launching a daylight torpedo attack was from a position bearing about 60° on the target's bow, at least a few of the German destroyers were threatening an effective attack and there was some justification for Sturdee's two-point turn-away by Preparative. Jellicoe, both in his despatch and in *The Grand Fleet*, made a point of emphasising that the first attackers approached from a bearing of G60; however, he did not mention that, after *Iron Duke* apparently

---

[52] *OD*, p. 79. The destroyer may have been the *V48* receiving further damage (*GOA*, p. 136) though she was not sunk until later.
[53] *OD*, pp. 54, 63 and 120. F&H, pp. 181–2.   [54] *OD*, pp. 122 and 128. JMSS 49029, f. 3.
[55] *OD*, pp. 90, 99 and 377.

sank her first target, she shifted to a boat in a less favourable position almost abeam (G84) at 9,000 yards.[56] This attack was probably that improvised by the boats of the IIITF after their attempt to rescue *Wiesbaden's* crew.

The British cannonade

As these German destroyers were driven off, the action between the opposing heavy ships intensified. In the difficult visibility, target identification by the British ships was often uncertain and, once they began manoeuvring to reform the line, their reported relative target bearings are of limited value; furthermore, once the Germans commenced their action-turn-about, they were, as *Monarch* remarked of the ISG, 'very much scattered and appeared to have no formation'.[57] The similarities between the silhouettes of the *Kaiser, König* and *Derfflinger* classes did not help identification,[58] while there was a marked disposition – eight battleships did so – to claim the target, either definitively or tentatively, as *Derfflinger* or *Lützow*.[59] The isolated *Lützow* with her escort of destroyers should have been a distinctive target, except that, because the VITF and IXTF advanced from the van of the ISG, she was not the only German battlecruiser with destroyers close by.

Nonetheless, it is likely that the final hits on the crippled *Lützow* were made by *Monarch* and/or *Orion*. At 7.15 and 7.14 respectively, both opened fire, at long ranges (17,300–19,800 yards) and on bearings before the beam, at a *Derfflinger*-class battlecruiser escorted by destroyers.[60] *Orion* fired six salvos, *Monarch* five, and both claimed straddles by their last two salvos. At 7.19, *Monarch* also sighted the rest of the ISG in some disorder bearing G110 at 16,000 while, at 7.21, *Orion* saw an enemy battleship leading a column bearing G98 at a range of 14,800 yards, but neither were able to fire again.[61] Of the other ships of the 2BS, *Ajax* fired briefly at about 7.10 and *Centurion* at 7.25. At 7.17, *King George V* fired nine rounds short at 12,800 yards at a leading battleship or battlecruiser with three destroyers laying a smoke screen; the shorter range suggests that the target was perhaps *Derfflinger* or *König*.[62] Until 7.14, *Conqueror* enjoyed a lull in the action and even allowed her gun crews to fall out on top of their turrets, from which they cheered the sunken *Invincible*, thinking she was German; subsequently, they fired only at destroyers. The squadron's rear ship, *Thunderer*, fired at two overlapping *Kaisers* through a gap between *Iron Duke* and *Royal Oak* but she did not report a time.[63]

---

[56] *OD*, pp. 19 and 63. *GF*, pp. 228 ad 259.   [57] *OD*, p. 373.

[58] Gröner I, pp. 25, 27 and 54–6.

[59] They were *Orion, Monarch, Royal Oak, Superb, Benbow, Bellerophon, Colossus* and *Neptune*.

[60] *Orion* sighted her target at 7.09 bearing G60 and observed that others of the 2nd Division were firing at the same ship; *Monarch's* opening bearing was G76.

[61] *OD*, pp. 372–3 and Pl. 9.

[62] *OD*, pp. 112, 116, 377 and 383. JMSS 49029, f. 6. Respectively, *King George V, Ajax* and *Centurion* fired only 9, 6 and 19 rounds during the whole battle: Campbell, p. 346.

[63] S&H, p. 250. F&H, pp. 199–200. *OD*, pp. 375 and 377.

Table 8.5. *BCF signals 6.53–7.40pm*

Time of despatch	From	To	System	Message	Time of origin
pm, 31 May					
6.53	SO BCF	General	Flags	... 18 knots	
7.15	SO BCF	General	Flags	... 22 knots	
7.22	SO BCF	General	Flags	... 24 knots	
7.40	SO BCF	General	Flags	... 18 knots	

In the weeks after the battle, Beatty, as well as denying that his battle-cruisers had gone round in a circle, also attempted to establish that, between 7.20 and 7.45, they had been some two miles further to the Westward (closer to the enemy) than Jellicoe would accept.[64] As described at the end of the previous chapter, a chart of the movements of the BCF relative to the 2BS can be made by plotting *Lion*'s corrected track on the track chart submitted by the 2BS. If this is continued further, it shows *Lion* at 7.12 hauling across the bows of *King George V* at a distance of 1.4 miles and, as we shall see in a moment, she was able to open fire again at 7.13½.[65] Even so, this plot probably underestimates the distance from the battlefleet van to the BCF which, at 7.15, it shows as 1.8 miles; this compares with a distance of 2.6 miles from *King George V* to the rear battlecruiser that can be deduced from observations of the two ships made by *Calliope* at 7.15.[66] (When compared with two later reports, by *Calliope* at about 7.28 and by *Minotaur* at 8.00,[67] this same plot corresponds quite well as to relative distances from *King George V* to the BCF but the relative bearings are about two points to starboard; thus, if it errs, it does so in Beatty's favour.)

At 6.54, Jellicoe had informed the senior officers of the BCF, 3BCS and 2CS by wireless that the course of the fleet was South but in his despatch Beatty stated that he did not receive the signal until 7.06. Whether or not as a

---

[64] Jellicoe to Beatty, 28 July 1916 in '15. Track of Battle Cruiser Fleet' in ADM 137/1946, f. 622.

[65] *Lion*'s track from *OD*, Pl. 10 as corrected plotted on *OD*, Pl. 8. An alternative plot based on the similar courses and speed from Beatty's narrative and Chatfield's despatch (VNE and *OD*, p. 145) takes the BCF further South and East to cross ahead of *King George V* too late, at 7.25.

[66] Distances and bearings from *Calliope* in letters of 6 August ('Track of BCF' – see note 64 – f. 626) and 15 October 1916 (*OD*, p. 385) but 7.15 time taken from Le Mesurier's despatch (*OD*, p. 296) when *Calliope* took station ahead of *King George V* and sighted an enemy battlecruiser.

[67] *OD*, p. 385 and Pl. 24.

direct response, at 7.08 he led round from SEbyE to SW before crossing ahead of *King George V.* At 7.15, he turned SSW but after five minutes back to SW, a course he then held until 7.45. He kept his speed at only 18 knots until he increased to 22 and then 24 knots, at 7.15 and 7.22 at the earliest. According to *Calliope*'s observations, by about 7.28 the BCF had drawn further ahead, with *Indomitable* 3½ miles from *King George V* bearing SW½S.[68] Between 7.13½ and 7.16, *Lion* fired four salvos opening at 16,100 yards on a bearing of G73; the target, presumably one of the two battlecruisers and two battleships (apparently *Königs*) mentioned in Beatty's despatch, soon turned away into a destroyer smoke screen. At 7.23, three battlecruisers were sighted briefly on a bearing of G90 but they too were soon lost in smoke.[69] At 7.14, *Princess Royal* fired a single salvo at a battlecruiser, range 18,000 yards. At 7.16 or 7.17, *Tiger* sighted four enemy ships, of which two were thought to be battlecruisers; she opened fire at the third from the left at 19,800 yards bearing G70 but fired only three salvos before her target turned away into a dense smoke screen at 7.20.[70] *Indomitable* may have briefly engaged a battlecruiser but the time is uncertain, while the reported range (14,000 yards) seems too short and the bearing (G46) too far forward.[71] Neither *New Zealand* nor *Inflexible* were in action with German heavy ships at this time.

At the other end of the British line, *Valiant* reopened at 7.10 and continued until 7.23 when the enemy 'altered course together away from us, and broke off the action'. At 7.20, *Malaya* re-engaged briefly at a range of 10,400 yards but from *Barham* the enemy remained lost to view.[72] In the 1BS ahead, *St Vincent* and *Revenge* had opened fire on the German line at about 6.55. They continued until 7.26 and 7.22 respectively when, in both cases, their targets were seen to turn away by at least eight points as they disappeared behind destroyer smoke screens. *St Vincent*'s target, which she considered to be a *Kaiser*, lay near the starboard beam and was twice obscured as the range fell slowly from 10,000 to 9,500 yards.[73] According to Captain Kiddle's despatch, *Revenge* fired initially at the leading German battlecruiser; but, since other ships were firing at her, *Revenge* then shifted to the fourth battlecruiser, *Von der Tann*, at which she also fired a torpedo at a range of about 9,000 yards at about 7.15. Thus perhaps *Revenge* should be credited with the hit on *Von der Tann*'s after conning tower, except that Kiddle wrote later that both his targets (at ranges from 11,000 to 9,900 yards) were *Kaisers*.[74]

[68] 'Track of BCF', f. 626 and *OD*, p. 385, with observation times of 7.30 and 7.28 respectively.
[69] *OD*, p. 137. VNE, 7.06. REL.   [70] *OD*, pp. 152, 156, 388 and 393. F&H, p. 403.
[71] *OD*, p. 165 (time 7.26). *Indomitable* gunnery report, BTY 6/6 (time 7.15).
[72] *OD*, pp. 201, 209 and 219.   [73] *OD*, p. 94. JMSS 49029, f. 88.
[74] *OD*, pp. 85 and 382 and Pl. 6. The plate incorrectly identified the first target as *Seydlitz*. A burst of flame aft was noticed on the second target.

Neptune was next of the 1BS to open fire, at about 7.04, on what she described as the leader of two *Lützow*-class battlecruisers. But at 7.10 she seems to have broken off as she turned away from enemy destroyers and then dropped astern to be blanketed by *St Vincent*. At 7.06, *Agincourt* sighted what she thought was the German Vth Division and, having opened fire at 11,000 yards, claimed at least four hitting straddles; these must have secured the hits on *Markgraf* and *Kaiser*.[75] *Marlborough* and *Hercules* both opened fire at 7.12. *Marlborough* identified her target as the left-hand of three *König*-class battleships, bearing one point before the starboard beam, initially at 10,200 yards. Between 7.12 and 7.18, she fired fourteen salvos, claiming hits by the 6th (near the foremast), 12th (under the bridge), 13th and 14th. She was the only British capital ship to develop such a sustained burst of firing during this phase of the battle. On the assumption that she could not see *König*, she probably made most of the seven hits on *Grosser Kurfürst*, since some of the actual hits were close to the positions claimed by *Marlborough*. Under her intense fire, her target hauled out of line and then, as observed by Admiral Burney, 'the enemy battlefleet in sight were [*sic*] observed to turn at least eight points until their sterns were towards our line. They ... disappeared into the mist'.[76] *Hercules* convincingly identified her target as the second ship of the ISG, *Seydlitz*. Fired at ranges of about 9,000 yards, shells from the fifth and sixth salvos were observed striking abaft the fore-funnel and abreast the main-mast.[77] *Colossus* saw *Derfflinger* suddenly emerge from the mist bearing about G105 and at 7.15 opened fire at an estimated range of 9,000 yards. She claimed hits with her 4th and 5th salvos and that her target burst into flames; this was probably one of the turret fires in *Derfflinger*. As *Colossus* was firing, at 7.16 she was hit twice by *Seydlitz*. One shell glanced off without exploding but the other burst in the superstructure just abaft the fore-funnel, igniting cordite at the 4in guns though the fire was soon put out. One or two minutes later, she was showered by splinters from two more heavy shells bursting short, which wrecked a searchlight and severely injured two men.[78] *Collingwood* saw *Colossus* being hit before, at about 7.20, firing at a battlecruiser of uncertain type; the range was about 8,000 yards and *Collingwood* claimed immediate hits in the short time before the target disappeared in dense smoke from attacking destroyers.[79]

[75] *OD*, pp. 89 and 92. F&H, 195. Campbell, p. 245.

[76] *OD*, pp. 66, 71 and 101; however, Campbell, pp. 237–43 attributes 4 of the hits on *Grosser Kürfurst* to 15in shells. At 7.25, *Marlborough* fired an ER torpedo at a *Kaiser*-class, range 12,000 yards (see also *ATFJ*, p. 9).

[77] *OD*, pp. 73–4; the left-hand ship was identified as *Derfflinger* or *Lützow*, the second as *Seydlitz* or *Moltke*.

[78] *OD*, pp. 79–80 and 82–3. F&H, pp. 185–9.   [79] *OD*, pp. 96–7.

Of the 4BS, only the rear and leading ships made early sightings of large enemy ships. At 7.00, *Vanguard* observed an enemy battlecruiser (possibly *Lützow*) badly on fire aft but subsequently she was blanketed by *Colossus* and fired only at destroyers and a light cruiser.[80] *Iron Duke* opened fire at 7.13, her target, thought to be a battleship, 'apparently had a number of Destroyers around her'; initially, the range was 15,400 yards, bearing G74. *Iron Duke* fired four salvos but, having initially misjudged the inclination, did not claim any hits. At 7.18, the target 'was hidden by a very good Smoke Screen made by his Destroyers' and Captain Dreyer recalled the 'Enemy steaming directly away'.[81] At 7.15, the visibility from *Royal Oak* became much clearer for a few moments. She was able to make out three battlecruisers to Westward on her starboard beam and opened fire at the leader at 14,000 yards; several hits were observed aft before this battlecruiser turned away into the mist. Fire was shifted briefly to the next ship before she too was lost in mist. Both the target identifications and the observed locations of the hits suggest that the targets were *Derfflinger* and *Seydlitz*. From *Superb*'s inconsistent reports, it seems that at around 7.20 she fired seven salvos at about 12,000 yards, her target turning away heavily on fire aft. *Superb*'s description of one ship astern of the target as resembling a *Helgoland* is the only reported British sighting of the German Ist Division. Also at 7.20, *Canada* fired four salvos at about 14,000 yards at what she took to be a *Kaiser*-class on her starboard beam, but all were spotted as well short.[82]

In the British 4th Division, *Benbow* and *Bellerophon* both opened fire at 7.17 at *Derfflinger*, while *Bellerophon* also noted *Seydlitz* astern. As would be expected after Sturdee's turn-away by Preparative, their target bearings were abaft the beam – G132 for *Benbow* and, for *Bellerophon*, G120 at a range of 11,000 yards. Both ships observed hits near the target's after turrets but then there were too many splashes to spot the fall of shot; *Bellerophon* saw the target turn away behind a 'most effective' destroyer smoke screen before both battleships ceased fire, at 7.28 and 7.30 respectively. *Temeraire* opened fire at about 7.15, also at the leading German battlecruiser, though the line-of-fire was only just clear of the bows of *Colossus*. *Temeraire* fired seven salvos commencing at about 12,500 yards but she did not see any hits. At first the target was beam-on but it 'then turned away until stern on, continuing round to starboard, and disappeared in the mist'.[83] In *The Grand Fleet*, Jellicoe declared:

Although [the enemy's] retirement was not visible from *Iron Duke* owing to the smoke and mist, and was, therefore, not known to me until after the action, it was clearly seen

[80] *OD*, pp. 358–9.   [81] *OD*, pp. 54, 56, 58–61. ADM 137/302, ff. 29 and 34.
[82] *OD*, pp. 99, 124 and 355. JMSS 49029, ff. 86 and 88.
[83] *OD*, pp. 128, 362, 364 and 383. ADM 137/302, f. 140. F&H, p. 182.

from the rear of our line . . . No report of this movement . . . reached me, and at first it was thought that his disappearance was due to the thickening mist.[84]

But, as we have just seen, the enemy turns-away were seen from the 4BS, not only by *Bellerophon* and *Temeraire* but by *Royal Oak* and *Superb* directly astern of *Iron Duke*. Furthermore, the flagship's Captain Dreyer reported her target as last seen 'steaming nearly directly away'. It is hard to believe had Jellicoe had no inkling that the High Seas Fleet had turned away and was retiring.

Jellicoe turns away

Only nine of the British battleships reported when they stopped firing at the retreating German big ships, at times from 7.18 (*Iron Duke*) to 7.28 (*Benbow*).[85] But, all along the British line, firing, by both primary and secondary armaments, had to be redirected at the German flotillas covering Scheer's withdrawal. Between 7.15 and 7.22, *Royal Oak, Canada, Vanguard, Colossus, Marlborough, Revenge* and *Agincourt* opened fire at attacking destroyers, while *Benbow* may have fired at destroyers more or less continually from 7.09 to 7.28.[86] By 7.25, *Conqueror, Iron Duke* (from 7.24) and *Malaya* were also engaging destroyers, as were *Indomitable* and *Inflexible*.[87] As some ships lost touch, others joined in – by 7.32, *Bellerophon, Temeraire, Hercules* and *Valiant*.[88] Ranges varied from 6,000 to 7,000 yards (*Colossus* and *Hercules*) to about 11,000 yards (*Conqueror* and *Marlborough*). Twelve battleships – all the 2BS except *Conqueror, Superb*, all but *Colossus* of the 5th Division and *Barham* – and the four leading battlecruisers did not take any part in repelling the German attacks, though *Lion* warned the BCF of enemy destroyers approaching at 7.23.

The reported bearings of the German flotillas from British battleships were few and sometimes difficult to interpret because their times are close to those of the turns-away that Jellicoe would soon order. Of the 2BS in the van, at 7.25 *Conqueror* observed a torpedo attack 'from the starboard quarter . . . rough range 11,000 yards' that cannot have seemed any kind of threat.[89] From the divisions in the centre, all but one of the relevant reports are reasonably consistent with *Conqueror*'s. Dreyer's despatch, augmented by several of *Iron Duke*'s gunnery reports, provide quite a detailed picture of the attacks.

---

[84] *GF*, pp. 230–1.
[85] *OD*, pp. 54, 59, 71, 80, 128, 372 and Pl. 6. JMSS, Add 49029, ff. 86 and 88.
[86] *OD*, pp. 82, 85, 92, 99, 101, 120, 128, 355 and 358. F&H, p. 219.
[87] *OD*, pp. 54, 63, 113, 170 and 219. BTY 6/6.
[88] *OD*, pp. 74, 121, 209 and 364. F&H, p. 182.
[89] *OD*, p. 377: also p. 373 for *Monarch*'s ambiguous report of destroyers bearing 'about 95 green'.

At 7.18, German destroyers were observed laying a smoke screen. By 7.24, a minute after the flagship turned from S to S19°E, six destroyers were in range at 10,000 yards, initially bearing G135; the 6in guns engaged them, a subsequent bearing of G115 being due to fire being divided between two destroyers. Then at 7.27 the turret guns fired one salvo at a destroyer bearing G110 (range 9,000 or 9,600 yards).[90] Thus it appears that, just before the turn-away at 7.23, the enemy destroyers bore abaft the beam by at least 6° and perhaps as much as 26°, and that, at 7.27, the turrets' target was still 20° abaft the beam. Astern of *Iron Duke*, at 7.16 or soon after, *Royal Oak*'s 6-in guns fired 'on the enemy Destroyers on starboard beam, who were zigzagging frequently'. *Canada* recorded that: 'At 7.25 engaged destroyers attacking abaft starboard beam with our 6-inch', though it is unclear whether this was before or after a turn-away of two points; at 7.30, she also fired three 14in salvos at the leading destroyer 'abaft starboard beam'. Between 7.26 and 7.30, *Bellerophon* fired at four destroyers that were probably abaft the beam. But this was not the situation described by *Temeraire*. At some time between 7.15 and 7.30, she sighted an enemy flotilla 'a little before the starboard beam ... The 4-in. guns were manned and opened fire and, as the position of the enemy seemed so favourable to an attack, the main armament was also put on to them ... range ... about 9,000'.[91]

Of the 1BS, *Collingwood* stated that at about 7.20 she sighted destroyers attacking 'from about 2 points before the beam', range about 9,000 yards. *Marlborough* was less precise, describing an enemy flotilla as 'attacking on the starboard bow ... range 11,000 yards' at 7.19. Assuming that these were gun ranges; that the ranges of 6,600–7,700 yards in the German reports were their perpendicular distances from the British lines; and that the flotilla seen from *Marlborough* was no more than four points before the beam; then both flotillas threatened an effective attack. Their torpedoes could be evaded by turning away immediately by almost four points from an attack at the shorter range, by almost three points at the longer range – though only if the new course was maintained for the whole torpedo running time.[92] In contrast, the reports of *Conqueror, Iron Duke, Canada* and *Bellerophon* indicate that the enemy flotillas were abaft the beam in positions from which their torpedoes did not pose a significant threat. *Royal Oak* placed them on the beam, which required a turn-away of only one point to evade their torpedoes entirely. And, if the destroyers reported by *Temeraire* were only 'a little before the starboard beam', they were not in a position 'so favourable to an attack'.

---

[90] *OD*, pp. 54, 56, 59 and 61–3.   [91] *OD*, pp. 99, 355 and 364. F&H, p. 182.
[92] See discussion of turns-away in Chapter 2. More precisely, the calculated maximum turn-away for a perpendicular distance of 6,600 yards is 42°, for 7,700 yards, 30°.

Table 8.6. *Grand Fleet signals 7.12–7.43pm*

Time of despatch	From	To	System	Message	Time of origin
pm, 31 May					
7.12	C-in-C	1BS	SL	Take station astern of 4BS	
7.13	SO 4BS	4th Division	Flags	Subdivisions separately alter course in succession two points away from the Enemy preserving their formation	
7.15	SO 4BS	4th Division	Flags	Speed 13 knots. Alter course together two points to starboard. (Negatived)	
7.16	C-in-C	SO 2BS	SL Flags	2BS take station ahead	
7.18	C-in-C	2BS	SL	Increase speed of engines	
7.18	C-in-C	2BS	Flags	Proceed at your utmost speed	
7.20	RA 1BS	5th Division	Flags	Follow in the wake of your next ahead	
7.20	C-in-C	Dreadnought Battlefleet and attached Cruisers	W/T Flags	… 15 knots	
7.21	C-in-C	2BS	Flags	Alter course together four points to port	
7.22	C-in-C	Dreadnought Battlefleet and attached Cruisers	W/T Flags	Subdivisions separately alter course in succession two points away from the Enemy preserving their formation	
7.23	SO BCF	General	Sem. SL	Enemy's destroyers are approaching to attack.	
7.25	C-in-C	Dreadnought Battlefleet and attached Cruisers	Flags	Subdivisions separately alter course in succession two points away from the Enemy preserving their formation	
7.28	SO 2BS	2BS	Flags	… 15 knots	
7.35	C-in-C	Dreadnought Battlefleet and attached Cruisers	W/T Flags	Alter course leading ships together rest in succession to SbyW	
7.36	C-in-C	Dreadnought Battlefleet	W/T	Form single line-ahead in sequence of fleet numbers	1936
7.40	SO 2BS	2BS	Flags	… 18 knots	
7.40	C-in-C	SO 2BS	SL	My course SW	
7.42	C-in-C	3rd and 4th Divisions	Flags	Form single line-ahead in sequence of fleet numbers. Course SW	
7.43	C-in-C	SO BCF	W/T	Present course of fleet SW	1940

At 7.12, Jellicoe had ordered the 1BS to 'take station astern of the 4BS'. But there may then have been a delay because, in the following six minutes, *Marlborough*'s fourteen rapid and effective salvos at *Grosser Kurfürst* would have required a steady course. Shortly after this, Burney's flagship sighted destroyers attacking under cover of a smoke screen. He reported:

I immediately hoisted the signal 'NM' informing our flotillas astern that the enemy flotillas were making an attack. At the same time the preparative was hoisted, and I turned my division away.[93]

This was in the right direction for forming astern of the 4BS. But, at the time, the 4th Division was probably not yet in line with the 3rd Division and *Colossus* was heavily engaged with *Derfflinger*; also, Rear-Admiral Gaunt's 7.20 signal suggests that the 5th Division was in some disorder. Thus both divisions of the 1BS were no longer in line astern and they were probably also closer to the enemy than the centre and van battle squadrons. Beginning at 7.16, in a series of increasingly urgent signals, Jellicoe ordered the Jerram's 2BS to take station ahead of *Iron Duke* and to increase to their utmost speed. This move was needed to give all these powerful ships unobstructed lines of fire. But it could only be completed by the two divisions of the 2BS, which were still on a line of bearing NW-SE, edging towards and ahead of *Iron Duke* until they were clear to haul into line. At 7.18, the first destroyers of a new German wave were sighted from the flagship but, according to Jellicoe's post-war accounts, at 7.20 the rear ships of the 2nd Division were still close to *Iron Duke*'s port bow. The C-in-C then ordered a reduction in speed to 15 knots but only a minute later commanded the 2BS to alter course together four points to port so that he would be clear to turn away.[94] At 7.22, *Iron Duke* hoisted the Preparative flag signifying that all subdivisions should turn away by two points in succession. (Both the 7.20 and 7.22 signals were addressed to the whole battlefleet but presumably Jerram was expected to deduce that they did not apply to his squadron.) However, within a few minutes Jellicoe was informed by one of his staff officers that the first Preparative 'turn was insufficient to clear the torpedoes [and] a further turn of two points was made for a short time'.[95]

Although many ships recorded turns-away at around the times of the two Preparative signals, in some cases course alterations were less than would be expected. Of the flagships, *King George V*'s chart shows only a one-point turn

[93] *OD*, p. 66. These signals are not in *OD*(M).
[94] 1922 appendix, JMSS 49040, f. 118 (not in *JP II*, p. 432). *GF*, p. 259. *JP II*, p. 450.
[95] *GF*, p. 229; the editor's footnote suggests that Commander Roger Bellairs was using the Bunbury Calculator.

(from SbyW to S) at 7.28; yet her 'Notes' state that she altered a full four points to port, though at the early time of 7.20, but then added that, at 7.27:

'King George V' had to alter course to starboard to avert collision with light craft in the van. 'Duke of Edinburgh' much in the way and making a lot of smoke.

Orion's chart has a single three-point turn-away. One of *Iron Duke*'s charts shows a single two-point turn at 7.23, though her captain's despatch states that it was by only 19°. *Benbow* may have turned by a total of four points from SbyW.[96] *Colossus*'s chart shows a single two-point turn. *Marlborough*'s chart and her captain's despatch describe a two-point turn at 7.18 to SSE (this was probably in response to Burney's order) and a further turn-away of one or two points at 7.22, the time of Jellicoe's first Preparative signal; however, the despatches of *Revenge* and *Hercules* mention only single Preparative turns.[97] This was, however, a period of intense action during which navigational records were probably not maintained meticulously. Furthermore, by the time that Jellicoe decided that he needed to turn away from the enemy destroyer attacks, the fleet was in some disarray, so each ship doubtless had to find its own individual compromise between the C-in-C's general intentions and the demands of station-keeping. Overall, the result was to increase somewhat the distance between the two fleets but, as Jellicoe later insisted:

The turn of the British battle Fleet opened the range some 1,750 yards, but *it was not this turn which led to the difficulty of keeping touch with the enemy*. That difficulty was due to the fact that the German Fleet made a very large turn to the westward under cover of a smoke screen.[98]

After the turns together by the 2BS and in subdivisions in succession by the other battle squadrons, the nominal course was SE but the fleet was undoubtedly in 'a ragged and irregular disposition'. Probably to ensure that the turns-away would evade the torpedoes, Jellicoe waited until 7.35 before ordering a 9 Pendant turn back to SbyW and at 7.36 he ordered the battlefleet to form single line-ahead. At 7.40, Jellicoe informed Jerram that the flagship's course was SW. At 7.42, the 3rd and 4th Divisions were ordered to form single line-ahead on that course and the 2BS began to form ahead of *Iron Duke*; however, *King George V* only turned from WSW to SW into line at 7.53.[99]

At 7.22, the time of the first Preparative turn-away, Jellicoe also ordered the 4LCS to move out from its action station on *King George V*'s starboard bow to attack the approaching enemy destroyers. Only a minute later, he was warning

[96] *OD*, pp. 54 and 117 and Pls. 2, 8 and 29 though Pl. 6a (*Iron Duke*) shows no significant change from course S between 7.10 and 7.32. For *Benbow*, JMSS 49029, f. 3.
[97] *OD*, pp. 74, 85 and 101 and Pls. 4 and 7a.
[98] *GF*, p. 260 with original emphasis. *Iron Duke*'s track chart (*OD*, Pl. 2) shows the range opening by 1,900 yards.
[99] *AN*, p. 59. *OD*, pp. 74, 117 and Pl. 8.

Table 8.7. *British light forces' signals 7.22–7.45pm*

Time of despatch	From	To	System	Message	Time of origin
pm, 31 May.					
7.22	C-in-C	SO 4LCS	Flags	4LCS prepare to attack the torpedo vessels of Enemy. Proceed at your utmost speed	
7.22	SO 4LCS	4LCS	Flags	Alter course eight points to port	
7.22	SO 4LCS	4LCS	Flags	. . . 20 knots	
7.23	C-in-C	SO 4LCS	SL	Do not get in the way of firing of Battle Cruisers	
7.26	Commodore F	1st Half-Flotilla	Flags	Attack Enemy destroyers bearing WNW	
7.27	SO 4LCS	4LCS	Flags	. . . 25 knots	
7.32	C-in-C	SO 4LCS	SL	Do not go too near Enemy's battlefleet	1931
7.36	Commodore F	11DF	Flags	Cruising order No. 2. Course SSW	
7.36	SO 4LCS	4LCS	SL	Alter course eight points to port	
7.39	Constance	General	Flags	Torpedo passed from starboard to port	
7.39	SO 4LCS	4LCS	Flags	Submarine port side three points from right ahead	
7.40	C-in-C	Destroyers	SL	Recall	
7.40	SO 4LCS	4LCS	Flags	Am taking station on battlefleet	
7.45	C-in-C	Destroyers	SL	Tell Castor to come back. Destroyers recalled	

them not to get in the way of the firing of the BCF (so it seems that both forces were still visible from the flagship). The 4LCS soon sighted a German half-flotilla bearing NWbyN, steering towards and apparently threatening the 2BS, and engaged what was probably the IXTF at ranges of 8,000–9,000 yards; Le Mesurier's despatch claimed that the German leader disappeared and that another boat was disabled (they were probably *V28* and *S35*). He also reported that, between 7.25 and 7.35, at least six torpedoes passed ahead or through the track of the 4LCS; evidently the squadron had intervened too late to prevent the German boats from firing.[100] At 7.26, Commodore (F) Hawksley in *Castor* moved out with half of the 11DF to drive off a German flotilla. This was probably again the IXTF but the British boats only got within range of one straggler, which may be one reason why the attack was not mentioned in Hawksley's despatch. He then wished to go on to attack the disorganised German line, but the destroyers

---

[100] *OD*, pp. 296 and 385.

were recalled by Jellicoe at 7.40.[101] Even then, it seems that Hawksley did not give up until peremptorily ordered to come back by the C-in-C. Meanwhile, the 4LCS, having been cautioned by Jellicoe not to get too near the enemy battlefleet, had returned to their station on the engaged bow of *King George V.*

At the rear of the British line at about 7.30, the 2LCS observed a few German destroyers laying a smoke screen and another lying, apparently stationary, on the wrong side of the smoke. The light cruisers fired a few salvos at her before she came under fire from *Faulknor* and the 1st Division of the 12DF (*Obedient, Mindful, Marvel* and *Onslaught*). Captain Stirling then ordered this division to attack, *Obedient* reporting on their return that they had sunk a *V*-class destroyer (her number had been shot away) flying a commodore's pendant; this may have been the damaged *V48* (though she was not even a half-flotilla leader). The 1st Division was also straddled by enemy destroyers further West; they were probably the IIITF.[102]

The six torpedoes that were sighted from the 4LCS were no more than a fraction of those that had been fired at the British line. Of those that came close to hitting their targets, almost all were sighted between 7.33 and 7.35 from the battleships of the 1BS, especially from the rear 6th Division. At their LR setting of 28–28.5 knots, the German torpedoes ran to their maximum range of 10,950 yards in between 11 and 12 minutes, so they must have been fired from 7.21 onwards when the VITF and IXTF were attacking. According to *St Vincent*: 'To avoid enemy torpedoes crossing the track of the First Battle Squadron, all ships were frequently under helm', though neither she nor her next ahead, *Neptune*, reported any near misses. But *Colossus* turned to port at 7.35 to avoid a torpedo, perhaps two, coming from to starboard; she hoisted the warning Black Pendant and may have

Table 8.8. *British destroyer signals 7.38–7.50pm*

Time of despatch	From	To	System	Message	Time of origin
pm, 31 May					
7.38	Captain D12	12DF	Flags	Open fire, South-West	
7.40	Captain D12	12DF	Flags	Attack the torpedo vessels of the Enemy bearing SW	
7.45	Faulknor	SO 2LCS	SL	Am sending a division of Destroyers to attack Destroyers on my starboard beam	
7.50	Captain D12	12DF	Flags	Alter course together four points to starboard	

---

[101] *OD*, pp. 303 and 305; during the night actions, *Castor*'s bridge was extensively damaged, so records of earlier actions were probably then lost. F&H, p. 203.

[102] *OD*, pp. 176, 332 and 339. F&H, pp. 208–9, 267 and 419. 'Etienne', pp. 143–4.

seen another three tracks as well. *Collingwood* took in the warning signal and was already turning away when she saw a torpedo heading straight for her. 'Large helm was put on and the torpedo passed very close astern. At the same time another was observed to pass about 30 yards ahead'.[103] From *Marlborough*, approaching torpedoes could be seen from aloft nearly a mile away and she was able narrowly to escape being hit a second time.

At 7.33 three torpedoes were observed on starboard beam and bow, course was immediately altered to starboard and then to port, one passed ahead, one astern and the other very close or under the ship.[104]

At 7.35, *Revenge* avoided two torpedoes by turning to port, one passing about 10 yards ahead and the other about 20 yards astern; at 7.43 she had to haul out to port again so that two more torpedoes could pass astern. Shortly after *Hercules* altered course to SbyW at 7.35, she was forced to turn away again by six points when two tracks were seen to starboard from aloft; one torpedo ran along the starboard side to cross the bows 40 yards ahead, the second went close under the stern. Lastly, at 7.35 *Agincourt* spotted the tracks of two approaching torpedoes but they passed ahead after she altered course.[105]

In marked contrast, no torpedoes were sighted from the leading 2BS or from the 4BS in the centre. However, at about 7.35 a single torpedo was seen by the destroyer *Oak* travelling slowly SE'wards to cross some 200 yards ahead of *Iron Duke*; it then sank about 2,000 yards on the port side of the line, evidently at the end of its run. From even further forward, the rear battlecruiser *Inflexible* logged a torpedo as passing 150 yards astern but not until 7.45.[106] It is unclear which German flotilla fired these torpedoes or the two sighted by *Revenge* at 7.43 – if, that is, they were real.

The many torpedoes avoided by the 1BS (14 at least, 11 by the 6th Division) leave no doubt that the squadron was a principal focus of the German attacks, and that their turns-away had been insufficient to take these battleships beyond the reach of the torpedoes fired by the VITF and IXTF. The limited information on the bearings of these flotillas indicated that a turn-way of three or four points was needed but it was made only in some cases. Also, Burney's turn-away by Preparative at 7.18 may have been made before the German torpedoes were fired; if it was seen by the attackers, they may have adjusted their aim accordingly. Whereas, apart from *Oak*'s single torpedo, none threatened either the 2BS or the 4BS. Clearly their turns-away were sufficient to evade any torpedoes that might have been fired at them. But the sparse information on their attackers, though not entirely consistent, suggests that they did not need to turn away so far, or even at all. By 1932, in his notes on 'Errors made in Jutland Battle', Jellicoe accepted that the 2BS had not been in danger.

---

[103] *OD*, pp. 80, 94 and 97. F&H, p. 187.   [104] *OD*, p. 101. F&H, p. 219.
[105] *OD*, pp. 74, 85–6 and 92.   [106] *OD*, pp. 92 and 300. *AN*, p. 59 n. 2.

In view of the fact that the van squadron of battleships was not nearly as much exposed to the destroyer attack at 7.22 as was the rest of the Battle Fleet, Jerram might, I think, have independently altered course back to close the enemy before I signalled a general alteration of course. Possibly he may have been influenced not to do so by the fact that I had at 7.21 ordered his squadron to alter course 4 points to port. I did this because his rear ships were in the way of the leading ships of the centre squadron altering to port.

But he did not go any further in admitting that the turns-away themselves were an error, though he did acknowledge that, as Jerram did not turn back, 'I might have ordered him to close'.[107] For now, we shall leave the final word to Jellicoe's second-in-command of the 3rd Division, Rear-Admiral Duff, whose view of the battle from *Superb* can have differed little from that of the C-in-C. Yet Duff did not see the German attacks as particularly threatening and his despatch was less that wholehearted in its support for turning away.

The attack was neither made with dash nor was it pressed home, whether on account of the fire from the 6-in. guns of our ships or the threat of a counter-attack by our Light Cruisers, I do not know. The Destroyers, however, before they retired, were well within long-range distance, and possibly the attack might have proved effective, had the Fleet not been turned away by the 'Preparative'.[108]

Hunting for Scheer

Scheer's third action-turn-about reversed the order of steaming of the IIBS and IBS. At 7.25 the IIBS altered course to W in conformance with Scheer's signal

Table 8.9. *High Seas Fleet signals 7.18–7.52pm*

Time of receipt	From	To	System	Message	Time of origin
pm, 31 May					
7.18	C-in-C	General		Turn together 16 points to starboard	
7.20	Deutschland	IIBS	Visual	Course NW	
7.20	C-in-C	General		Increase speed	
7.22	C-in-C	General		Course W	
7.25	Deutschland	IIBS	Visual	Course W	
7.27	C-in-C	General		Course SW. Speed 17 knots	
7.45	F. der Grosse	General	Visual	Course S	
7.52	C-in-C	General		Course S	

[107] *JP II*, p. 450 and also Dreyer, p. 166. As we have seen, Jerram may not have turned away as far as ordered.
[108] *OD*, pp. 124–5.

of 7.22. The IBS, now led by *Westfalen* with *Friedrich der Grosse* bringing up the rear, also headed W and then SW at 17 knots as signalled by the C-in-C at 7.27; the squadron then continued SW until 7.45, or perhaps as late as 7.53, before turning S. The IIBS turned SW and then, a little later than the IBS, altered course to S at 7.59. The modern dreadnoughts of the IIIBS made their action-turn-about under fire and for a time were heading Westerly more in line-abreast than line-ahead. But they somehow managed to manoeuvre into line in something like reverse order, with *Prinzregent Luitpold* leading *Kaiserin, Kaiser, Markgraf, Kronprinz, Grosser Kurfürst* and *König*. They headed W½S until 7.56, then SWbyW. At 8.10, the IIIBS turned in the wake of IBS, so that all the German dreadnoughts were in single line-ahead, steaming due South. After turning away from the British fleet at 7.20, the ISG also headed W½S before turning SW at 7.45 and, at 7.52, to S½W, a course that converged gradually on that of the battle squadrons with the object of taking station ahead. At 8.10 – three minutes after sunset at 8.07[109] – the IIBS were some two miles West of the column of dreadnoughts with *Hannover* leading and *Deutschland*, the rear predreadnought, on the starboard beam of *Westfalen*. The battlecruisers were in an exposed position two or three miles on *Westfalen*'s port beam. Meanwhile the striken *Lützow* with her escort of four destroyers passed astern of the battle squadrons to seek cover on the disengaged flank. The four modern light cruisers of the IISG were about 4½ miles ahead of the IBS and the five older ships of the IVSG a further three miles ahead. Of the German flotillas, the IIITF, after a final unsuccessful attempt to reach the *Wiesbaden*, was the last to rejoin the torpedo boat leaders in *Rostock* and *Regensburg*, except for the VTF that was still returning to the fleet from the NE.[110]

Ahead of the British battlefleet, Beatty's ships continued SW until 7.45 or perhaps 7.50 before altering course two points to WSW.[111] The 3LCS, now joined by *Canterbury*, kept their position ahead of the battlecruisers. Of the 1LCS, *Inconstant* leading *Phaeton* and *Cordelia* reached the congested head of the battle line at about 7.25 to find the BCF about four miles further ahead; the light cruisers pressed on to position themselves on the battlecruisers' engaged quarter. (*Galatea* did not reach the van of the battlefleet until 8 o'clock, where she remained.) The armoured cruisers of the 2CS (now accompanied by *Duke of Edinburgh* and *Chester*) were also attempting to draw ahead of the 2BS. *Minotaur* and *Cochrane* may have crossed the bows of *King George V* as early as 7.20, although *Duke of Edinburgh* were still in the way of *King George V* at 7.27. Before the battlefleet altered course to SW at 7.40, the whole of Heath's force was in station ahead and then drew gradually further forward towards a position on the BCF's port quarter.[112] After their part in driving off the German

---

[109] *AN*, p. 60 n. 1.   [110] *OD*, German Plan V and Scheer's despatch, p. 596. *GOA*, p. 150.
[111] *Cf. OD*, Pl. 10 with *OD*, p. 145 and VNE.   [112] *OD*, pp. 173–4, 186, 275 and 280.

Table 8.10. *British signals 7.40–8.21pm*

Time of despatch	From	To	System	Message	Time of origin
pm, 31 May					
7.40	Lion	C-in-C	W/T	Enemy bears from me NWbyW distant 10–11 miles. My position 56°56 N, 6°16E. Course SW. Speed 18 knots	1930
7.40	BCF	General	Flags	... 18 knots	
7.43	C-in-C	SO BCF	W/T	Present course of fleet SW	1940
7.45	Southampton	C-in-C	W/T	Urgent. Enemy has detached unknown number of ships, type unknown, which are steering NW at 7.15. My position 56°50 N, 6°27E	1945
7.45	SO BCF	SO 2CS	SL	Pass to leading British battleship. Leading enemy Battleships bear NWbyW, course about SW.	1945
				(Note K.G.V passed to C-in-C. Received in Iron Duke via K.G. V. 7.59)	
7.47	SO BCF	C-in-C	W/T	Urgent. Submit van of battleships follow Battle Cruisers. We can cut off whole of enemy's battlefleet.	1950
				(Received in Iron Duke 7.54)	
7.50	SO BCF	Minotaur	SL	What ship are you? Reply: Minotaur	
7.52	C-in-C	General	Flags	Admiral has resumed Guide of fleet	
8.00	SO BCF	Light Cruisers	SL	Sweep to the Westward and locate the head of the Enemy's line before dark.	2000
				(Passed to 3LCS by SO 3LCS at 8.14)	
8.00	SO 3LCS	3LCS	Flags	Light Cruisers form on a compass line of bearing South, course W	
8.00	C-in-C	General	Flags W/T	Divisions separately alter course in succession to West preserving their formation. Speed 17 knots	
8.00	C-in-C	SO BCF	W/T	Present course of fleet is West	2000
8.07	Shannon	SO Cruisers	SL	Battlefleet altering to WbyN¾N. 17 knots	2000
8.09	SO 3LCS	SO BCF	Flags	Ships bearing NbyW	2010
8.14	C-in-C	SO 2BS	SL	2BS follow our Battle Cruisers	2010
				(Logged as having been received in K.G.V. at 8.07)	
8.15	SO BCF	Minotaur	SL	What is bearing of our leading battleships? Reply: NNE five miles King George V	2010

Table 8.10. (*cont.*)

Time of despatch	From	To	System	Message	Time of origin
8.17	SO BCF	Battle Cruisers	Flags	Alter course in succession to W … 17 knots	
8.18	SO 2BS	RA 2BS	SL	Follow me	
8.21	SO BCF	General	Flags	Alter course in succession to WSW	
8.21	C-in-C	Dreadnought Battlefleet and attached Cruisers	W/T	Alter course leading ships together the rest in succession to WSW	
8.21	C-in-C	SO BCF	W/T	Present course of fleet is WSW	2020

destroyer attacks, the 4LCS and the 11DF returned to their positions on the bow of *King George V.* At the rear of the British line, the 1st Division of the 12DF, after sinking *V48*, rejoined *Faulknor* at about 8 o'clock.[113] It may have taken until 7.52, when Jellicoe resumed Guide of the Fleet, for all the battlefleet squadrons to form in single line-ahead steering SW.

Southampton's signal despatched at 7.45 suggests that, despite a five-minute time disparity, she may have seen the brief turns NW by the German battle squadrons at 7.20. In this and subsequent signals, *Southampton* continued to report her position but unfortunately her dead-reckoning remained seriously in error. If these positions are plotted on *Iron Duke*'s track chart, Goodenough's light cruiser apparently bore about EbyS from the fleet flagship at a distance increasing from 11 miles at 7.45 to 13½ miles at 8.53. Whether or not Jellicoe knew that the 2LCS was now at the rear of the line, it must have been clear that these positions were certainly wrong and of no help in establishing the enemy's position. Thus Jellicoe, who had lost sight of the German battlefleet soon after their action-turn-about, had to rely largely on Beatty for reports of the enemy. In his despatch, the Vice-Admiral gave the impression that he had remained in action for some 15 minutes.

we re-engaged at 7.17 p.m. and increased speed to 22 knots. At 7.32 p.m. my course was S.W., speed 18 knots, the leading enemy Battleships bearing N.W. by W. Again after a very short time the enemy showed signs of punishment, one ship being on fire and another appeared to drop astern … and at 7.45 p.m. we lost sight of them.

Not unreasonably, Jellicoe concluded in his own despatch that: 'At 7.32 p.m. [the] battle-cruiser fleet were inflicting considerable punishment on the enemy'.[114] In fact, as we have seen, of those battlecruisers that fired a few

[113] 'Track of BCF', f. 626. *OD*, pp. 296, 332, 339, 385 and Pl. 12a.
[114] *OD*, pp. 20 and 137–8.

salvos at about 7.17, all had ceased firing by 7.20. But at least the enemy remained intermittently in sight so that, at 7.40, Beatty was able to report that, at 7.30 when his course was SW and speed 18 knots, the enemy bore 10–11 miles NWbyW. He also gave a position but this placed *Lion* not ahead but about five miles E of *Iron Duke*. *Lion*'s subsequently reported positions continued to locate her to the East of the flagship and so, like those of *Southampton*, must have been discounted. At 7.43, Jellicoe informed Beatty that the battlefleet's course was SW but Beatty did not report that, soon afterwards, he turned WSW.[115] The Vice-Admiral's next signal was despatched at 7.47 or a few minutes later.

Urgent. Submit van of battleships follow Battle Cruisers. We can cut off whole of enemy's battlefleet.

It was received in *Iron Duke*'s wireless office at 7.54 but it required decrypting and Jellicoe later insisted that it 'could not possibly . . . have reached the bridge before 8 p.m. and it was actually some minutes later than this'.[116] Thus it is uncertain whether Jellicoe read it before or after Beatty's next signal, which contained the important new information that the enemy, still at 7.45 bearing NWbyW, was steering about SW. For unexplained reasons, this signal was sent by searchlight first to *Minotaur* and then through *King George V* to be received in *Iron Duke* at 7.59 (at least, as we have seen, searchlight signals could be read to the C-in-C as they were being received). Jellicoe now believed that Scheer's course was similar to his own; it can be no coincidence that, to close the enemy, at 8.00 he ordered all divisions to turn separately in succession to W, speed 17 knots. As a general signal, this would appear to have applied to the BCF as well as to the battlefleet but, despite being informed by the C-in-C (also at 8.00) that 'Present course of fleet is West', Beatty continued WSW. However, he did order his light cruisers, probably at 8.00, to sweep to the Westward; the 3LCS turned W in line-abreast at 24 knots, the three light cruisers of the 1LCS then replacing them in the BCF's van by moving up on the port side of the battlecruisers.[117]

Jellicoe's turn West at 8.00 was bolder than he knew since Scheer had already turned South, a course that might cross the British Ts. While the British course closed the range rapidly, the divisions were disposed quarterly on a line-of-bearing NE from *King George V* with the 5BS furthest from the enemy on the starboard wing.[118] Thus, as had happened earlier, there was a risk that firing arcs would be blanketed by ships in adjacent columns. However, the

---

[115] At 7.45 on *OD*, Pl. 10 but at 7.50 in *OD*, p. 145 and VNE.
[116] *JP II*, p. 432. Signal timed at 8.07 in '*Shannon* . . . record of W/T Traffic' in 'Second Cruiser Squadron War Records 1915–918 Vol. I', ADM 137/2142.
[117] *OD*, pp. 174–5 and 186; Napier's time for *Falmouth*'s turn W was 7.50.
[118] *OD*, pp. 195 and 201.

visibility and light after sunset still favoured the British forces; Jellicoe could reasonably expect that, on sighting the enemy, he would be able to turn back by 9 Pendant into line-ahead SW before the enemy found his range – from the information available to him, this would have been on a course about parallel to that of the enemy. Beatty's urgent submission that the van battleships should follow him became a part of the Jutland Controversy; in Jellicoe's words, 'the insinuation has been made that Sir David Beatty was imploring a reluctant Commander-in-Chief to follow him'. But, whether or not the 'follow me' signal arrived before or after the signal that the enemy's course was SW, it provided no useful guidance to Jellicoe. If before, it merely urged him to do what he believed he was doing already, following the battlecruisers SW. If after, when Jellicoe had already turned W, to the C-in-C 'it seemed obvious that the battleships were steering the better course to intercept the enemy'.[119] Since the BCF were not in sight from *Iron Duke*, Jellicoe could only guess at their actual position. He did not know it, but until 8.10 both *Lion* and *King George V* remained in sight from *Minotaur*; the bearings and distances from Heath's flagship, which did not change much, establish that *Lion* was some 8.3 miles from *King George V* bearing SWbyW. By 8.15, this was known to Beatty following his query to *Minotaur*, but not to Jerram, whose appreciation of the situation was further obscured after visual touch between the 2CS and *King George V* was lost at 8.18.[120]

At 8.09, Napier in *Falmouth* reported by flags to Beatty that he had sighted unidentified ships bearing NbyW but they were probably not the same as the five enemy light cruisers that were engaged by the 3LCS from 8.18 bearing WbyN.[121] Only at the later time did Beatty at last turn W, though not for long; *Lion* turned back to WSW at 8.20–1, just after she briefly sighted, and fired one salvo at, a German ship with two masts and three funnels bearing G67 at 10,500 yards. However, it appears that, before ships of the BCF began to re-engage the enemy, Jellicoe had decided to act on Beatty's earlier submission. At 8.14 or even earlier (note the times of origin and receipt), the 2BS was ordered to 'follow our Battle Cruisers', though without any indication of how this might be done; perhaps Jellicoe hoped that the BCF had remained in sight from *King George V*. According to her chart, she altered course at 8.16 to WSW,[122] which was one point to starboard of *Lion*'s actual bearing. However, the remaining battle squadrons soon altered course to the same heading, turning WSW by 9 Pendant at 8.21, Beatty being informed at once by wireless. Thus not only the van but the whole battlefleet was following his battlecruisers.

---

[119] *JP II*, pp. 432–3.
[120] *OD*, Pl. 24 and *Minotaur*'s reply to Beatty. VNE. ADM 137/2142, f. 112.
[121] *OD*, pp. 186 and 277.   [122] REL. *OD*, Pls. 8 and 10.

Table 8.11. *3LCS signals 8.09–8.46pm*

Time of despatch	From	To	System	Message	Time of origin
pm, 31 May					
8.09	SO 3LCS	SO BCF	Flags	Ships bearing NbyW	2010
8.15	SO 3LCS	3LCS	Flags	… 20 knots	
8.17	Falmouth			Remarks: Opened fire	
8.19	Falmouth			Remarks: Zeppelin in sight port beam (uncertain)	
8.20	SO 3LCS	Light Cruisers	Flags	Open fire and engage the Enemy	
8.25	SO 3LCS	3LCS	Flags	… 25 knots	
8.28	Falmouth	C-in-C SO BCF	W/T	Urgent. Am engaging Enemy's Cruisers. My position 56°47 N, 5°46E	2022
8.30	SO 3LCS	Birkenhead and Yarmouth	Sem.	Form astern	
8.46	Falmouth	C-in-C SO BCF	W/T	Battle Cruisers unknown. Bearimg of Enemy N. Course of Enemy WSW. Position of reporting ship 56°42 N, 5°37E	2045

Table 8.12. Stettin *signals 8.21–8.25pm*

Time of receipt	From	To	System	Message	Time of origin
pm, 31 May					
8.21	Stettin	C-in-C		4 enemy light cruisers in 007ε – SO IVSG	2021
8.25	Stettin	C-in-C		IVSG requested by SO IIBS to take station ahead of the battle fleet	

The five light cruisers of the 3LCS, after sighting what were probably enemy ships NbyW at 8.09, continued their Westward sweep in line-abreast at one-mile intervals. At 8.18, they saw the five light cruisers of the IVSG bearing WbyN at 9,600 yards. Napier at once turned his squadron into line-ahead; presumably they also began to close up as they headed first S and by 8.25 SW. They were sighted from the IVSG at 8.17, both squadrons promptly opening fire. The IVSG also turned towards their opponents so that, with the courses converging, the range fell to a minimum of 6,000 yards. Visibility was bad for both sides – from *Yarmouth*, 'it was impossible to spot ... under the hopeless light conditions' – but it was worse for the Germans, only the two leaders *Stettin* and *München* being able to return fire to any extent (the latter fired sixty-three rounds). They made no hits but *München* was struck by two 6in shells, one wrecking the casings around the after boilers so that subsequently steam could be maintained only with difficulty. This can only have added to the British speed advantage, which enabled them to haul across the enemy's bows. At 8.32, when the course of the 3LCS was WSW, the German squadron altered course eight points away to evade the fire of the British ships but also to draw them towards the IIBS. Napier followed, turning W and then WNW, but by 8.38, when the range had increased to 10,200 yards, the enemy was lost in the mist and growing darkness. As the Rear-Admiral reported:

We then found ourselves drawing across the bows of the enemy Battle Cruisers, who I think were being engaged by our Battle Cruisers, and we turned to about W.S.W., and then S.S.W. to regain our position ahead of our Battle Cruisers.

When they did so, *Inconstant* and her two consorts formed astern of the 3LCS.[123] During their action, both *Falmouth* and *Stettin*, as light cruisers should, made enemy reports, although the positions given by *Falmouth* appeared to place her about four miles WbyN from *Iron Duke*.

At 8.19, *Frankfurt*, flagship of the IISG, reported that she had sighted two *Chatham*-class light cruisers (the 3LCS had very similar profiles) and, more importantly, the British battlecruisers steering SW. But the warning was already too late, since *Lion* and *Princess Royal* opened fire as it was being transmitted. According to the German history: 'Beatty's sudden appearance so far to the southward came as a great surprise to the German battle cruisers' and presumably also to Scheer. Since 7.42, the only wireless signals reporting the enemy had suggested that the British fleet bore somewhere between NE and SSE, steering ESE. But it appears that *Lützow's* report did not reach Scheer and 'the impression ... became rife that the last thrust at the centre of the British line had apparently robbed it of all desire to press on after the German fleet'.[124] Indeed, at 8.00 the situation had seemed quiet enough for Hipper to warn *Moltke* that he would board her later; but, just as he was about to order the ISG to stop engines, the BCF engaged them once more and *G39* was forced to retire. The ISG, now reduced to four ships, was in no state to renew the action. *Derfflinger* had 3,400 tons of water in the ship and only A turret was fully working, though B turret could still fire in local control. *Seydlitz* was badly down by the bows and listing to starboard; the superfiring turret was burned out, the aftermost turret was without power training and, in the port wing turret,

---

[123] *OD*, pp. 175, 186–7 and 397. *GOA*, pp. 151–2.

[124] *GOA*, pp. 146 and 153. Five Zeppelins were airborne by 11.30am but persistent haze and low cloud prevented them from seeing anything of the battle: *GOA*, pp. 39 and 149–50.

Table 8.13. *German signals 7.32–8.19pm*

Time of receipt	From	To	System	Message	Time of origin
pm, 31 May					
7.32	V30	2nd Leader of Torpedo Boats	Visual	Large enemy vessels to the SE	7.32
7.42	Frankfurt	C-in-C		Lützow under fire from strong hostile forces; bearing NE – SO IISG	1922
7.48	SO IXTF	2nd Leader of Torpedo Boats		To C-in-C and AC Scouting Forces – Reported enemy vessels are steering ESE. There are more than 20 of them	1940
8.00	G39	Moltke	Visual	AC Scouting Forces is coming later on to Moltke	8.00
8.01	Lützow	Seydlitz		Enemy bears SSE is drawing past to port of Lützow, and consists of 6 armoured cruisers	
	2nd Leader of Torpedo Boats	IITF		Enemy bears SSE is drawing past to port of Lützow, and consists of 6 armoured cruisers	
8.08	2nd Leader of Torpedo Boats	IITF		IITF will be detached for a night attack on the enemy's battle fleet at 8.45. Enemy is believed to be in sector E to NE . . .	
8.10	2nd Leader of Torpedo Boats	IITF		The sector ordered is to be changed to read ENE to ESE	8.10
8.15	2nd Leader of Torpedo Boats	VITF XIIHF		Proceed towards the enemy in sector ESE to SE at 8.45 . . .	8.15
8.19	Frankfurt	C-in-C		162γ right, centre, two Chatham class 008ε. Enemy armoured cruisers steering SW – SO IISG	2019

Note: The complete orders to the German flotillas are in a later table.

only one gun remained in action and the director gear was disabled. *Von der Tann*'s forward turret was disabled, her after turret could only be hand-trained while, although the run-out gear in the midships turrets had been partly repaired, the trouble was expected to recur.[125] Only *Moltke* remained fully

---

[125] *GOA*, pp. 91, 144–5 and 153. von Hase, pp. 202, 207–8 and 214. Campbell, pp. 142 and 234.

effective. Beatty still had six battlecruisers, but *Lion, Princess Royal* and *Tiger* all reported that they each had two guns out of action, though in the flagship one gun in A turret could only be hand-loaded and one in X turret was temporarily disabled. Beneath *Tiger*'s Q turret, the smaller of the magazines was flooded. *Inflexible* had one gun out of action[126] but the armaments of *New Zealand* and *Indomitable* were intact.

When the BCF opened fire, little more than the flashes of their guns to the SE could be seen from the ISG.[127] At 8.19, *Lion* fired one salvo with a range of 10,500 yards at a ship with two masts and three funnels bearing G67. Having altered course from W to WSW at 8.20–8.21, at 8.22 *Lion* reopened at the left-hand battlecruiser, range 10,800 yards, bearing G113; Chatfield described her as 'either "Lützow" or "König" class'. After her first salvo at *Derfflinger, Lion* broke immediately into rapid fire, which Chatfield described as 'rapid salvoes'. In all she fired fourteen of these salvos, three in the first minute and the rest at half-minute intervals; her target turned away at 8.25½ and she ceased fire at 8.28 when the enemy retired into the mist. *Lion*'s spotting corrections appear random,[128] but visibility was bad and five salvos were not spotted at all. Only one hit was seen, at 8.24,[129] and this may have been the single actual hit made on *Derfflinger*; this struck A barbette and, while it did not penetrate, it tem-

Table 8.14. *BCF signals 8.09–8.25pm*

Time of despatch	From	To	System	Message	Time of origin
pm, 31 May					
8.09	SO 3LCS	SO BCF	Flags	Ships bearing NbyW	2010
8.10	SO BCF	General	Flags	Ships open fire	
8.17	SO BCF	Battle Cruisers	Flags	Alter course in succession to W ... 17 knots	
8.17	New Zealand			Remarks: Enemy opened fire	
8.20	Inflexible			Remarks: Opened fire	
8.21	SO BCF	General	Flags	Alter course in succession to WSW	
8.25	SO BCF	General	Flags	Alter course in succession to SW	

---

[126] *OD*(M), 7:50, 7:55 and 8:10. Campbell, p. 74.

[127] Scheer, p. 159 and despatch, *OD*, p. 596.

[128] The first seven corrections were: D800, Rapid; D800; U400, L5; R10; D800; Hit, U200, R5; U400, R10 – REL.

[129] REL; the notes of 'ammunition remaining' (see also *OD*(M), 1 June, 9.35am) suggest that after 7.13 *Lion*'s 'salvoes' were fired largely by B and X turrets.

porarily jammed the training of A turret.[130] Probably just after she ceased firing, *Lion* led the BCF away to SW.[131]

Of the other British battlecruisers, *Princess Royal* opened fire at the leading enemy battlecruiser at 8.18 bearing G60 and by 8.25 she had fired another six salvos, the range falling from 12,000 yards to 9,350 yards. At 8.30, she fired a torpedo, perhaps set for extended range (ER), at a three-funnelled battleship, the centre of three, the range 10,000 yards, bearing G105; a minute or two later she fired two salvos at what was perhaps the same ship at 9,500 and 9,850 yards.[132] At 8.21, *Tiger* began shooting at a three-funnelled battleship described as 'Apparently "Helgoland" class' and as both the 'Right-hand of two' and '3rd from left'. *Tiger* fired a total of nineteen salvoes until 8.36; for the third salvo, the target bearing was G76; her ranges fluctuated widely, particularly the 3,000 yards jump between 8.28 and the next salvo at 8.30, though at 8.29 the target was seen to alter away. Three straddles were claimed on a target that scarcely replied and appeared to be burning fiercely. When the enemy was lost to sight at 8.40, it was getting dark.[133] *New Zealand* recorded that, after she altered course W, she sighted five [*sic*] enemy battlecruisers bearing G60 and that, either at 8.21 or 8.24, she opened fire at an estimated range of 11,500 yards on the '3rd Ship from right' which 'appeared to be a "Seydlitz" class'. As six more salvoes were fired, the range fell to a minimum of 9,100 yards. By 8.30: 'Enemy on fire forward and hauling out of line listing heavily', apparently sinking. *New Zealand* fired one more salvo at 8.36, possibly at the fourth enemy ship but it then became impossible to spot.[134] From *Indomitable*, it seemed that the enemy battlecruisers opened fire first, at 8.20. She replied at 8.21 or later, engaging what appeared to be the *Seydlitz* though she was described as both the second ship and the second from the rear. Initially the range was 8,800 yards and bearing G45; like her consorts, it appears that *Indomitable* opened fire while she was still heading W. As the light faded rapidly, *Indomitable* shifted to the third enemy battlecruiser and fired a few salvoes. 'At 8.42 p.m. we ceased fire the enemy bearing 307° [about NW½N], but we could not see to spot'. At the rear of the BCF, *Inflexible* was in action between 8.20 and 8.30 with what was thought to be a *Kaiser*-class battleship. Even before she disappeared in the mist, 'Spotting was very difficult on account of the light and the funnel and cordite smoke of the Battle Cruiser Fleet which was rolling down the engaged side.'[135] The BCF did not escape damage entirely; *Lion* was struck by a 5.9in shell while *Princess Royal* was hit by a heavy shell that did not explode but passed through both struts of the foremast and the fore-funnel between them.[136] In his short report telegraphed to the Admiralty on 3 June, Beatty stated that,

---

[130] von Hase, p. 214. Campbell, p. 264.   [131] *Cf. OD*, Pl. 10, VNE and REL (target bearings).

[132] *OD*, pp. 149, 152 and 388–9. For ER, *cf. GFG&TMs*, p. 50 and *ATFJ*, p. 9.

[133] *OD*, pp. 157 and 393. F&H, pp. 403–4.   [134] *OD*, pp. 161–2 and 395.

[135] *OD*, pp. 165–6 and 170. Gunnery reports in BTY 6/6.   [136] Campbell, p. 264.

after the battlecruisers had disappeared, 'Enemy Battleships were then sighted and opened fire on us, necessitating our hauling out to port'. But he did not repeat this excuse for his turn-away SW in his full despatch.[137]

There are two mysteries associated with the conclusion of what would prove to be the BCF's last encounter with enemy ships. First, at about 8.40 all the battlecruisers felt a heavy shock, severe enough to knock *Indomitable*'s Captain Kennedy off the compass platform. Many thought they had been torpedoed or mined, *Indomitable* hauling briefly out of line, though none found damage subsequently. On their starboard beams, *New Zealand* observed a burst of air underwater and *Inflexible* a large swirl of oil. Second, Beatty's narrative of events records that, half a minute *before* the shock, *Lion*'s course was N35°W (NWbyN), though in Chatfield's despatch this was the course at 8.30.[138] Yet none of the BCF charts show what would have been a sharp turn towards the enemy. As for the heavy shock,[139] the observations of *New Zealand* and *Indomitable* suggest either an explosion or the sudden implosion of a large compartment in a vessel sunk earlier. But the BCF's chart puts them at the time eight miles from the wreck of *Queen Mary* and further still from the position of lost destroyers. Both mysteries, which do not seem to be related, remain open questions.

As the ISG came under attack, *Seydlitz* and *Moltke* opened fire at 8.20, *Derfflinger* and *Von der Tann* a little later. But they could only rarely see their targets distinctly, spotting was impossible and their shooting was frequently interrupted; *Von der Tann* was unable to fire more than eight 11in rounds and fifteen 5.9in rounds. Although *Princess Royal* also fired on *Derfflinger* initially, the hit on the leading German battlecruiser was probably made by *Lion*.[140] Despite the ambiguities in their target descriptions, it seems that both *New Zealand* and *Indomitable* engaged *Seydlitz* before shifting their

Table 8.15. *Scheer's signals 8.26–8.52pm*

Time of receipt	From	To	System	Message	Time of origin
pm, 31 May					
8.36	C-in-C	Fleet		Course S	
8.52	C-in-C	General		Course S	

---

[137] *Cf. OD*(M), 3 June, 0.16am and *OD*, p. 138.

[138] *OD*, pp. 138, 145, 149, 157, 161, 166 and 170. VNE. F&H, p. 403.

[139] Coincidentally or not, at 8.40 *Shannon* felt considerable shock from something bumping along her bottom: *OD*, pp. 281 and 284.

[140] *GOA*, p. 153. Campbell, p. 264 times the hit as 8.28.

fire briefly to *Moltke*. Between 8.24 and about 8.30, *Seydlitz* received five more hits. The first wrecked the Port No. 4 casemate and ignited a cordite charge. The second burst above the fore bridge, splinters killing four and wounding five, including three in the conning tower. The third hit on the roof of the aftermost turret put both upper hoists out of action. The final two hits, though neither went through the 12in armour, holed it so that water entered two outer coal bunkers and then spread further.[141] We must hope that *New Zealand* made some, if not the majority, of these hits since otherwise she cannot be credited with a single hit during the whole battle. Several of the BCF's salvos fell near the two leading German dreadnoughts although *Westfalen* and *Nassau*, being masked by the ISG, were at first unable to reply. At 8.25 or slightly later, the ISG, under a fire that they could not return, turned sharply away by about eight points, cutting close across the bows of the IBS; *Derfflinger* fired her last shot at 8.31. *Westfalen* was forced to reduce speed and also to turn away Westwards with the rest of the IBS following in succession. *Posen* (now fourth in the reverse order) was able to open fire as she turned at 8.28 and she continued until 8.35 but her efforts went unnoticed in the British ships. The IIIBS seems to have followed the lead of the IBS.[142]

The German charts show that, after the ISG and the dreadnought squadrons turned Westwards, they cut across the wake of the IIBS, which held its course S. Even before the other battleships turned away, the predreadnoughts had been under fire from *Tiger*, though she identified her target as a *Helgoland*, also three-funnelled. *Princess Royal* also fired two salvoes at the IIBS after 8.31. At about that time, *Hannover* led the squadron onto a course SW that would bring all their guns to bear but the enemy could still not be seen clearly. Of the six ships, *Hannover, Hessen* and *Schlesien* were able to fire, respectively, eight, five and nine rounds, *Deutschland* just one. At 8.34, *Schlesien* was hit by splinters; at 8.35 one of *Schleswig-Holstein*'s casemates was put out of action by a heavy shell, while *Pommern* too may have been hit since she briefly hauled out of line. Seeing his ships ahead under a heavy fire, Rear-Admiral Mauve ordered them to turn away together to Westward onto a similar course to that of the battlecruisers and dreadnoughts.

But, much to everyone's surprise, the enemy did not follow, and as far as could be estimated from his gunflashes, seemed to draw past the van of the German fleet on a south-westerly course. Soon after that his guns also became silent.[143]

It is probable that, with *Westfalen* leading, the German dreadnoughts turned back in succession to S in response to Scheer's signal (listed as addressed to

---

[141] Campbell, pp. 252–3 and 265–9 except that *Princess Royal*'s reports do not state that she fired at *Seydlitz*. Staff, *World War One*, pp. 178–82 (hits 8, 14, 15, 17 and 23).

[142] *GOA*, pp. 153–4. von Hase, p. 216. *OD*, German Plans V and VI, Dia. 8.

[143] *GOA*, pp. 154–5.

'Fleet') at 8.36. But the IIBS may not have resumed the Southerly course, by means of a second turn together, until the C-in-C's order of 8.52. The ISG continued WNW until 8.42 before turning through 16 points and then gradually back to S by 9.02.[144]

We now return to the British battlefleet after it turned W at 8 o'clock, the battleships preceded by the 4LCS, 11DF and 4DF. At about 8.05, smoke was sighted to the WNW from *Calliope*. What soon appeared as a German half-flotilla advancing SSW towards the rear of the BCF was actually the VTF (of 11 boats) still trying to rejoin the High Seas Fleet. At 8.11, Hawksley in *Castor* ordered half of the 11DF to attack the destroyers bearing NW from him but he instructed *Kempenfelt* and the remainder of the flotilla to hold back unless the enemy was in force. *Castor* also reported her sighting by flags to Jerram but the information did not reach the C-in-C until 8.26. Le Mesurier promptly led out

Table 8.16. *British light forces' signals 7.58–8.38pm*

Time of despatch	From	To	System	Message	Time of origin
pm, 31 May					
7.58	Commodore F	11DF	Flags	Alter course in succession to West	
8.11	Commodore F	1st Half Flotilla	Flags	Attack Destroyers NW	
8.12	Commodore F	Kempenfelt	FL	Do not follow unless Enemy are in force	
8.14	Commodore F	SO 2BS	Flags	Enemy's Destroyers bearing NW	
				(Passed to C-in-C 8.26)	
8.15	Commodore F	SO 4LCS Kempenfelt	FL	12 enemy Destroyers NW	
8.15	Kempenfelt	3rd Division of Destroyers	FL	Take station astern	
8.16	SO 4LCS	1st Division, 4LCS	Flags	Support Castor	
8.18	SO 4LCS	4LCS	Flags	Proceed at your utmost speed	
8.22	Commodore F	1st Half Flotilla	Flags	Reform	
8.25	SO 4LCS	Constance and Comus	Sem.	Get out on quarter and open fire on Destroyers ahead	
8.38	C-in-C	Comus	FL	Who are you firing at? Reply: Enemy's B.F. bearing West	
8.38	Commodore F	11DF	Flags	Take up cruising order No. 2. Speed 22 knots	

[144] *OD*, German Plan V. von Hase, Sketch I.

his first division (*Calliope, Constance* and *Comus*) to support the 11DF, following them NW and opening fire at 8.18. But the VTF made smoke and turned away 'and, following the "Rostock" and the other flotillas in company with her, finally broke through the line to the westward between the ships of the 3rd Squadron'. Since the VTF did not develop an attack, Hawksley turned back, *Castor* resuming her position with the rest of the 11DF at the head of the battlefleet. But Le Mesurier pushed on to sight the enemy battlefleet to the NW, steering S at a distance of 8,000 yards. He identified the ships as belonging to the *Deutschland* and *Kaiser* classes but the leading ships were probably *Helgolands* of the German Ist Division. *Calliope* swung to port and at 8.30 fired a torpedo at a range of 6,500 yards bearing 257° (W). But even before her submerged tube had been flooded, she was straddled by fire from the German line and had to turn away, zigzagging two points on either side of an Easterly course. Le Mesurier reported that there had been an explosion on a *Kaiser* at 8.38 but his torpedo did not in fact find a mark. From the German line *Prinzregent Luitpold* fired one heavy salvo and *Kaiser* two but the *Markgraf* used her secondary armament to deadly effect, making five 5.9in hits that disabled two 4in guns and hit *Calliope*'s after dressing station; the casualties totalled ten killed and twenty-nine wounded. *Constance* and *Comus* did not fire torpedoes and withdrew without damage.[145] Although the reported times vary considerably (from 8.18 to 8.40), several British battleships observed the three light cruisers on their starboard bows returning under fire, *Bellerophon* noting at 8.25 that the gun flashes came from big ships in the same direction. All three broke through the British line onto the disengaged side, after which *Constance* and *Comus* went ahead of the damaged *Calliope*. At 8.38, *Comus* was close enough to the flagship on the starboard side to inform the C-in-C by flashlight that the enemy battlefleet was bearing W.[146]

Thus, between 8.18 and 8.21, firing broke out at three points across the British front: the 3LCS at the IVSG bearing WbyN; the BCF at the ISG and the IIBS bearing about NNW; and the 4LCS at the VTF bearing NW. But Jellicoe received no reports of the enemy's heavy ships nor was he informed even of the presence of enemy light forces until 8.26 (by *Castor* through *King George V*) and 8.28 (*Falmouth*). Before this he had to rely on what could be heard and seen from *Iron Duke*. When at 8.21 he turned his divisions by 9 Pendant 'towards the sound of gunfire', his course WSW probably left Beatty's battlecruisers on the port bow and the German ships engaging the BCF on the starboard bow. Next, at 8.25 Jellicoe turn backed to W by 9 Pendant at 8.25, his probable object being to make ground more rapidly to the Westward so as to regain contact before the light failed completely. But his columns were then once again in the

---

[145] *OD*, pp. 297 and 303 and Pl. 12a. *GOA*, pp. 150–1. F&H, pp. 269–70.
[146] Dreyer, p. 151. *OD*, pp. 99, 113, 297 and 376 and Pl. 12a. F&H, pp. 182–3.

Table 8.17. *Grand Fleet signals 8.14–8.38pm*

Time of despatch	From	To	System	Message	Time of origin
pm, 31 May					
8.14	Commodore F	SO 2BS	Flags	Enemy's Destroyers bearing NW	
8.15	Marlborough			(Passed to C-in-C 8.26) Remarks: Marlborough sighted Submarine starboard bow	
8.21	C-in-C	Dreadnought Battlefleet and attached Cruisers	W/T	Alter course leading ships together the rest in succession to WSW	
8.21	C-in-C	SO BCF	W/T	Present course of fleet is WSW	2020
8.25	C-in-C	Dreadnought Battlefleet and attached Cruisers	W/T Flags	Alter course leading ships together the rest in succession to West	
8.28	C-in-C	Dreadnought Battlefleet	W/T Flags	Alter course leading ships together the rest in succession to SW	
8.28	Falmouth	C-in-C SO BCF	W/T	Urgent. Am engaging Enemy's Cruisers. My position 56°47 N, 5°46E	2022
8.30	C-in-C	SO BCF	W/T	Present course of fleet is SW	2024
8.31	Benbow			Remarks: Torpedo passed the ship from port to starboard	
8.38	C-in-C	Comus	FL	Who are you firing at? Reply: Enemy's B.F. bearing West	

unfavourable quarterly disposition and 'at 8.28 p.m. [the battlefleet] was turned by divisions to south-west into line ahead, heading for the sound of the guns of the battle-cruisers'. It is possible that this turn was hastened because, about this time, a few enemy capital ships were glimpsed from the British line. Writing in 1922, Jellicoe himself drew attention to 'a note made in B turret of the *Iron Duke* at 8.25 p.m. "Nine heavy ships ahead" and this report was probably an additional reason for the turn into line ahead'.[147] *Bellerophon* too observed the flashes from the German battleships that fired at the fleeing *Calliope* but,

---

[147] *JP II*, pp. 433–4 (the wording suggests that he could not recall whether this observation was reported to him). *OD*, pp. 56 and 60; at 8.29–8.32, *Iron Duke*'s turrets trained to either G60 or G80 and then to G70.

whether or not Jellicoe himself saw signs of ships of the High Seas Fleet, he did not know that they were still heading S. Nonetheless, although his turn SW was away from the enemy, the new course was still closing the range. But only for a couple of minutes, until all the German columns – except, for another five minutes, the IIBS – turned sharply away onto Westerly courses. This rapid withdrawal as the light was failing ensured that there would be no final engagement between the battlefleets. But because the German dreadnoughts soon turned back in succession to the converging course S while the BCF and Grand Fleet continued SW, there would be one more contact between the battleships before darkness fell completely.

To what extent had the 2BS been able to obey Jellicoe's order to follow the BCF? At 8.18, Jerram ordered Rear-Admiral Leveson in *Orion* to follow the 1st Division. *King George V*'s chart shows her altering to SW at 8.26 though this was not because the BCF were in sight. Even so, by 8.29 at the latest, all the British capital ships were on the same course, which they would hold until after nine o'clock. At 8.21, Jerram originated a signal to Beatty confirming that the

Table 8.18. *British signals 8.14–9.05pm*

Time of despatch	From	To	System	Message	Time of origin
pm, 31 May					
8.14	C-in-C	SO 2BS	SL	2BS follow our Battle Cruisers	2010
				(Logged as having been received in K.G. V. at 8.07)	
8.18	SO 2BS	RA 2BS	SL	Follow me	
8.21	C-in-C	SO BCF	W/T	Present course of fleet is WSW	2020
8.25	SO BCF	General	Flags	Alter course in succession to SW	
8.30	C-in-C	SO BCF	W/T	Present course of fleet is SW	2024
8.40	SO 2BS	SO BCF	W/T	Priority. What is your position, course and speed? Am following you	2021
8.45	SO 2BS	C-in-C	W/T	Urgent. Our Battle Cruisers are not in sight	2044
8.46	C-in-C	SO BCF	W/T	Indicate the bearing of Enemy	2046
				(Logged by SO BCF as having been received from Galatea. Vide 2100 SO BCF to Galatea)	
8.55	SO BCF	SO 2CS	SL	Please give me position of 2BS. Reply: Not in sight. When last seen bearing NNE five miles at 8.10	
9.01	SO BCF	SO 2BS	W/T	My position now 56°40 N, 5°50E, course S50°W, speed 17 knots	2040
9.05	SO BCF	Galatea	W/T	Your 2046. NbyW	2100

2BS were following the BCF but asking for the latter's position, course and speed; however, perhaps because, while the battlecruisers were in action, their gun flashes gave a good indication of their bearing, the signal was not transmitted until 8.40. Five minutes later, Jerram informed the C-in-C that the BCF were not in sight and Jellicoe quickly ordered Beatty to indicate the bearing of the enemy, though this would not by itself have been much assistance to Jerram. However, although this signal was received correctly by *Shannon* at 8.51, it was logged in *Lion* as having been received from *Galatea*; *Lion*'s answer, which was not made until 9.05, seems to have been ignored by *Iron Duke*. Although there was no direct visual contact between the 2BS and the BCF, by 8.45 both formations were in sight from *Shannon* and her observations establish that the battlecruisers were almost ahead of *King George V*, bearing SW½W at a distance of 9.6 miles.[148] Thus, unknowingly, Jerram was still obeying the order to follow the battlecruisers. But, by the time Beatty got round to informing Jerram of his position at 9.01 – though the BCF's dead-reckoning errors rendered the information of little use – SO 2BS had a more immediate concern, the identity of the heavy ships that could be made out to the WNW. But, before considering his dilemma, we should examine the movements of the German flotillas during the preceding hour.

The intent behind Scheer's order at 8.00 for flotilla attacks remains uncertain but his further signal at 8.15 made clear that he wanted Michelsen to mount attacks after nightfall. At the time, the VTF and IIITF were still rejoining the fleet while some of the flotillas that had taken part in the earlier attacks were now no longer capable of mounting effective attacks. Of the eight survivors of the IXTF, none had more than one torpedo left, while *V28* and *S51* were also slowed by damage. These two and *S52* took station on the IBS, presumably to act as a screen ahead of the dreadnought line. The remaining five,[149] together with the VIITF and *G42* of the IIITF, joined *Rostock* as she began making her way towards the head of the line. It seems that this group was initially on the engaged side of the battle line but they were soon joined by the VTF as it was driven back by the 4LCS; Michelsen then led them all to Westward through the IIIBS at the rear of the line. Subsequently, his attempt to draw ahead was hampered and delayed by the battle squadrons turning away after 8.30. *G41*, the leader of the VITF, had also fired all her torpedoes, while the three boats of the XIHF each had only one left;[150] the 2nd Leader, Heinrich, who wanted to use only boats with two or more torpedoes for the night attacks, despatched this half-flotilla (and, it may be assumed, *G41*) to the head of the line. In company

---

[148] *OD*, Pl. 8 and pp. 113 and 281. *Shannon*'s W/T Record (see note 116); she informed *Minotaur* that, at 9.00, *King George V* bore NNE about eight miles. At 8.55, the 2BS was not in sight from *Minotaur*, probably because of the dense smoke from the whole 2CS.
[149] *V26* and *V36* (XVIIHF), *V30*, *S33* and *S34* (XVIIIHF).   [150] *V44*, *G86* and *G87*.

Table 8.19. *German signals 8.00–8.57pm*

Time of receipt	From	To	System	Message	Time of origin
pm, 31 May					
8.00	C-in-C	Leader and 2nd Leader of Torpedo Boats		Direct all flotillas to attack	
	2nd Leader of Torpedo Boats	IITF		Enemy bears SSE is drawing past to port of Lützow, and consists of 6 armoured cruisers	
8.08	2nd Leader of Torpedo Boats	IITF		IITF will be detached for a night attack on the enemy's battle fleet at 8.45. Enemy is believed to be in sector E to NE. Square from which to start will be signalled later. Flotilla is to return to Kiel round the Skaw, should return journey to German Bight appear inadvisable. Further flotillas are being directed to attack in sectors to the southward of you. I will make my 0.00 a.m. position by W/T	
8.10	2nd Leader of Torpedo Boats	IITF		The sector ordered is to be changed to read ENE to ESE	
8.15	C-in-C	Leader and 2nd Leader of Torpedo Boats		All torpedo boats are to attack during the night. 1st Leader of Torpedo Boats is to conduct the attack.	2012
8.15	2nd Leader of Torpedo Boats	IITF XIIHF		IITF and XIIHF detached	
8.15	2nd Leader of Torpedo Boats	VITF XIIHF		Proceed towards the enemy in sector ESE to SE at 8.45. 8.30 position 161γ	
8.30	Regensburg	C-in-C Leader of Torpedo Boats		IITF is advancing to attack in sector ENE to ESE and XIIHF, ESE to SE, starting from 161γ at 8.30. Flotillas were directed to attack before 2012 – 2nd Leader of Torpedo Boats	2026

Table 8.19. (*cont.*)

Time of receipt	From	To	System	Message	Time of origin
8.35	Rostock	C-in-C		2nd Leader of Torpedo Boats will direct attacks of flotillas allotted to him independently – Leader of Torpedo Boats	2031
8.45	S53, SO IIITF	Regensburg		5 boats of IIITF present. Request orders and position	
8.45	Regensburg	IIITF		Stay where you are	
8.57	Rostock	C-in-C [*sic*]		IIITF report position – Leader of Torpedo Boats	2050

with *Regensburg*, Heinrich kept three boats of the XIIHF[151] and all ten large destroyers of the IITF, the latter not having been in action. The return of the IIITF had been delayed by their attempt to reach the *Wiesbaden* and the signal at 8.45 from their leader *S53* suggests that she and the four boats with her[152] were unsure of their position relative to the fleet.

Even before Scheer's second order, Heinrich had taken the initiative by ordering the IITF to prepare for a night attack at 8.45, though he quickly changed the sector for their advance to be between ENE and ESE.[153] (During the night, the option granted to the IITF of returning round The Skaw would prove to have an unfortunate outcome.) This order was quickly followed by another for the XIIHF to proceed in sector ESE to SE. Scheer's 8.15 signal may have temporarily raised doubts about Heinrich's authority to direct these attacks but this was explicitly confirmed by Michelsen in his 8.35 signal. Already, at 8.15, Heinrich had detached the IITF and XIIHF and led them Northwards preparatory to starting their attacks from square 161γ at 8.30 (though the signals leave uncertain the intended times of the actual attacks). This square was just West of the position of the German flagship at 8.00, so he was pulling back to a position astern of the German rear 'in order to obtain a better view unobstructed by haze and smoke' and 'so as to avoid obstructing the Leader of Torpedo Boats'; as the German official historian regretted, he thereby 'confined his flotillas to the tactically less favourable northern sectors'. Even so, when they advanced at 8.30, 'they . . . encountered hostile forces earlier than intended and before it was quite dark'. Although the IITF sighted numerous

---

[151] *V69, V46* and *S50* together expended only four torpedoes against the 3BCS.

[152] *V71, V73, G88* and *S54. GOA*, pp. 145–6 and 165. *S32* (also IHF) is unaccounted for.

[153] A sector was a segment of a circle bounded by two specified compass lines of bearing. The lines spread out from the centre of a starting square, each square being referred to by codes like 161γ.

destroyers – probably the gaggle of flotillas bringing up the British rear – both German attacks, which were dismissed as 'rather feeble', were driven off by the 2LCS. Only a few of the attackers were sighted from Goodenough's light cruisers and one hit was seen. This was probably on *S50* of the XIIIHF, which was struck by a 6in shell which did not explode but reduced her speed to 25 knots. The times in the British and German accounts differ somewhat, but the latter state that at 8.50 the IITF was forced to turn away Southwards and then eventually Westwards, and that, after 8.52, the XIIIHF came under a sustained fire at ranges as short as 3,300–5,500 yards. It was considered still too light for an effective attack so the three boats turned off about WNW; *S50* then joined up with the battlefleet while *V69* and *V46* resumed their ordered course at 9.10.[154]

After turning back rather than supporting Le Mesurier's attack, *Castor* and the 11DF had returned to their position ahead of the 2BS but astern of the 4LCS's 2nd Division of *Caroline* and *Royalist*. With the British forces steering SW, once the German line turned back to their course S, it was only a matter of time before, at about 8.50, the two light cruisers sighted three German battle-ships closing slowly from the NW or NNW at a distance of 8,000 yards. Because they could make out boat cranes, the light cruisers supposed that they had predreadnoughts in view but they had actually sighted the leading ships of the IBS, which were similarly fitted. While not needing to deviate from his course SW, Captain Ralph Crooke of *Caroline* ordered a torpedo attack; at 9.00 she fired two torpedoes and *Royalist* one.[155] At the same time, *Caroline* reported the German ships by flashlight to *King George V* but the signal was neither logged as received nor passed on. Thus Jellicoe was unaware of the attack by his leading light cruisers when, at 9.01 with darkness setting in, he ordered the battleship division to alter course separately in succession to S, preparatory to taking up the night cruising order. *King George V* herself turned S at 9.03 and she seems to have sighted the ships already attacked by the 4LCS at 9.05.[156] It appears that, at the same moment, Crooke was urging *Castor* and the 11DF to follow up his attack. But this was quickly negatived by Jerram because 'Those ships are our Battle Cruisers'. The sub-lieutenant in charge of *King George V*'s A turret reported to the Control Officer aloft that he could see their cranes and that therefore they must be German, though whether this opinion reached Jerram is uncertain; in any event, the Vice-Admiral 'was certain that the vessels seen on our starboard beam were our own battle-cruisers. The Navigating Officer of my Flagship, who had just come from the

---

[154] *GOA*, pp. 146 and 155–6. *OD*, German Plan VII and pp. 176 and 181. F&H, p. 267. 'Etienne', p. 144. Only *Southampton* and *Dublin* reported firing at the German attackers.

[155] *OD*, p. 297 and Pl. 12a. F&H, pp. 271–2. The *Nassau* class had a searchlight tower just ahead of the main mast that, in the fading light, could have been mistaken for a third funnel: Gröner I, pp. 20 and 25.

[156] von Schoultz, p. 137. *OD*, p. 117 and Pl. 8. *OD*(M), 9.07 (TOO 2105).

Table 8.20. *British light forces' signals 8.35–9.20pm*

Time of despatch	From	To	System	Message	Time of origin
pm, 31 May					
8.35	Caroline	2nd Division, 4LCS	Flags	… 18 knots	
8.38	Commodore F	11DF	Flags	Take up cruising order No. 2. Speed 22 knots	
8.50	Comus	Boadicea	FL	What is speed of fleet?	
8.50	Caroline	Royalist	FL	Attack with torpedoes	
9.00	Caroline	SO 2BS	FL	Three ships bearing NW 8,000 yards. May be attacking with torpedoes. Apparently old Battleships. (Not logged in K.G.V. signal log)	2055
9.01	C-in-C	Dreadnought Battlefleet	W/T Flags	Divisions separately alter course in succession to South preserving their formation	
9.05	Caroline	Royalist	FL	Did you fire any torpedoes? Reply: yes, one	
9.05	King George V			Remarks: Caroline apparently made signals to Destroyers to attack	
9.06	SO 2BS	Caroline	SL	Negative. Those ships are our Battle Cruisers	
	Caroline	SO 2BS	SL	Those are evidently Enemy ships. (Also made by Commodore F at 9.15)	
	SO 2BS	Caroline	SL	If you are quite sure attack	
9.07	SO 2BS	C-in-C	W/T	Urgent. Our Battle Cruisers in sight bearing WNW, steering SW	2105
9.20	Constance	Caroline	FL	Calliope on starboard bow of Iron Duke. I think she is damaged	
9.20	Caroline	4LCS	FL	1st Division take station astern of 2nd Division	

battle-cruiser fleet, was also certain.'[157] But Crooke insisted that: 'Those are evidently Enemy ships'; Jerram then responded: 'If you are quite sure attack',

---

[157] *FDSF III*, p. 147, n. 83. *OD*, p. 108. Even if the enemy ships appeared to have three funnels, the silhouettes of *Nassau*-class ships had many detailed differences from those of British battlecruisers.

though the light cruisers were then returning after firing their torpedoes. At 9.15, Commodore Hawksley in *Castor* signalled his agreement with Crooke.

British light forces were not sighted from the leading German battleship *Westfalen* until shortly after 9.00, probably just as *Caroline* and *Royalist* were discharging their torpedoes. At first, because the position of the IVSG was not known, the identity of the ships in sight, apparently a light cruiser leading seven destroyers, was uncertain. But, when they did not respond to a search-light challenge, at 9.08 *Westfalen* and *Nassau* opened fire at a range of 8,100 yards and, after *Westfalen*'s fifth salvo, *Caroline* and *Royalist* turned away, to S at 9.10 and SEbyS at 9.15; though straddled, they were not hit. As the German ships opened fire, they altered course in succession six points to starboard to WSW to avoid any torpedoes but even so two tracks were seen from *Nassau*, one passing close to the bow, the other under the ship. At 9.10, they resumed their course S, parallel to the British battle squadrons; the German official history remarked that 'the destroyers astern of "Caroline" ... made no attempt to take advantage of this exceptional opportunity to employ their torpedoes'.[158]

In his despatch, Jerram accepted that: 'If they [the IBS] were enemy ships and no attack was made, the fault is mine and not that of the "Caroline" '. In fact, when he initially negatived the attack by the 4LCS, it was already too late. But he withdrew his objection while *Castor* and the 11DF were still in a good attacking position; after the turn S, they remained on the starboard bow of the 2BS with the enemy closing on their starboard quarter. At first, Hawksley thought the approaching ships were enemy battlecruisers, until Jerram sowed doubts by insisting that they were British. In his despatch, the Commodore continued to describe the ships as battlecruisers though, after he saw them firing at the light cruisers, he can have been in no doubt that they were hostile. Yet:

> I turned the Flotilla away from the Battle Cruisers [*sic*], and expected the Fleet to open fire on them
>   The leading Battle Cruiser then fired a star shell, which appeared to justify the opinion that they were enemy ships; but as the Fleet still held their fire I could not attack, as it was not dark enough to make an attack unsupported by fire from the Fleet.[159]

There was nothing in the *Grand Fleet Battle Orders* to justify holding back until the fleet provided supporting fire; especially in poor visibility, destroyers were expected to attack at once.

> It ... must be understood that our flotillas are not to miss a favourable opportunity for successful torpedo attack on the enemy's battlefleet, particularly on ships of the

---

[158] *GOA*, pp. 156–7. F&H, p. 271. S&H, pp. 279–80. *Comus* may have come up in support as the 2nd Division withdrew: *OD*, p. 297.

[159] *OD*, pp. 109 and 303.

'Dreadnought' type. Such opportunities are likely to present themselves in low visibility, and should be seized immediately.[160] (Emphasis in original)

The star shell fired by the leading *Westfalen* was observed by many British ships at about 9.15, some nine minutes after Jerram had given his consent to an attack. However, while he should not bear much responsibility for Hawksley's failure to act, Jerram must be criticised, if not for his urgent report to Jellicoe at 9.05 that the BCF bore WNW, then for not correcting it as soon as he had been persuaded that they were actually enemy ships. It is also regrettable that Jerram did not then open fire. As it was, Jellicoe was both unaware that the enemy battlefleet had been in sight from the van and the C-in-C was given a false impression of Beatty's position as the BCF continued SW.

If only Jellicoe had continued SW in line-ahead on a converging course for a few more minutes after 9.01, Jerram's doubts would have been dispelled and the battle squadrons following the 2BS might also have sighted the IBS. The IBS would almost certainly have turned away sharply Westwards and, with the light failing, only a brief action would have been possible. But, even so, significant damage could have been done to the leading German dreadnoughts, while there would have been no doubt about the position of the enemy as night fell. Could Jellicoe have anticipated that the two battlefleets were about to meet just after nine o'clock? To answer, we must look at the scant information on the position of the High Seas Fleet that reached him prior to his turn S. At 8.38, *Comus* informed him that the enemy (actually the IIIBS in the rear) was to the West.[161] At 8.46, *Falmouth* reported from a position that placed her at 8.45, five miles WNW from *Iron Duke*; the signal stated that the enemy bore N and was heading WSW, though no distance was given. If the position had been correct, the enemy bearing from the flagship would have been roughly NW. Next, at 8.57, *Southampton* announced that at 8.55 she had engaged enemy destroyers bearing W. The last report to reach Jellicoe before the turn S was from Beatty; it stated that at 8.40 enemy battlecruisers and predreadnoughts bore N34°W (NWbyN) 10–11 miles, steering SW. But, like *Lion*'s previously reported positions, this one was clearly wrong. Jellicoe knew that the battlecruisers were well ahead; he had previously turned SW towards the sound of the BCF's guns and he now had confirmation that like him they too were steering SW. He could only guess at their distance; in 1922, he assumed that they were five or six miles ahead of *King George V* and this is the best indication of his estimate at the time. If a position for *Lion* six miles SW from *Iron Duke* is plotted on the flagship's chart, together with the relative position of the enemy as reported by Beatty, then the enemy's position from the flagship at 8.40 becomes WNW

---

[160] *GFBO*, XXX.3 (January 1916) and 'Destroyer Addendum', II.6 (1 October 1915).

[161] Jellicoe insisted that he had asked *Comus*: 'What ships are firing at you?': *JP II*, pp. 434 and JMSS 49040.

Table 8.21. *British signals 8.38–9.15pm*

Time of despatch	From	To	System	Message	Time of origin
pm, 31 May					
8.38	C-in-C	Comus	FL	Who are you firing at? Reply: Enemy's B.F. bearing West	
8.46	Falmouth	C-in-C SO BCF	W/T	Battle Cruisers [probably hostile in sight number][1] unknown. Bearimg of Enemy N. Course of Enemy WSW. Position of reporting ship 56°42 N, 5°37E	2045
8.57	Southampton	C-in-C	W/T	Urgent. Am engaging Enemy Destroyers. Enemy ships bearing W from me, number unknown. My position 56°38 N, 6°09E	2055
8.59	Lion	C-in-C	W/T	Urgent. Enemy Battle Cruisers and pre-Dreadnought Battleships bear from me N34° W, distant 10 to 11 miles, steering SW. My position 56° 40 N, 5°50E, course SW, 17 knots	2040
9.01	C-in-C	Dreadnought Battlefleet	W/T Flags	Divisions separately alter course in succession to South preserving their formation	
9.05	SO 1BS	C-in-C	W/T	Urgent. Enemy Destroyers are attacking Light Cruisers from Westward	2101
9.07	SO 2BS	C-in-C	W/T	Urgent. Our Battle Cruisers [*sic*] in sight bearing WNW, steering SW	2105
9.10	Southampton	C-in-C	W/T	Enemy reported in my 2055 has been driven to the NW. My position 56°35 N, 6°09E	2112
9.10	C-in-C	SOs of Squadrons and all Captains D	W/T	Present course of fleet is South	2104
9.15	Minotaur			Remarks: White rocket starboard quarter	
9.15	Benbow			Remarks: Rocket showing stars starboard bow	
9.15	Shannon	SO 2CS	SL	King George V bears NNE about eight miles	2100

[1] Missing words from *Shannon*'s W/T record, ADM 137/2142, f. 113.

about 11 miles; in 1922, Jellicoe reached almost the same conclusion – WNW, 12 miles.[162] Furthermore, since the 3LCS was a part of the BCF, a similar three-point correction, to about WbyN, would have been justified in the enemy bearing deduced from *Falmouth*'s report.

Thus the four reports pointed to the High Seas Fleet bearing between W and WNW from the Grand Fleet. However, none of them indicated that Scheer was heading S on a converging course; instead, the two reported courses, WSW and SW, suggested that the range, about 11 miles at 8.40, was either constant or increasing slowly. Hence, as Jellicoe ordered the fleet to turn S at 9.01, he had no reason to anticipate that, almost immediately, the enemy van would be sighted from *King George V*. However, when in 1932 Jellicoe was contemplating the 'Errors made in Jutland Battle', he accepted that 'it would have been wise if I had closed the enemy battle fleet when *Comus* reported that she was firing at it at 8.38 p.m. Had I done so I might have been able to fire a few rounds at them before they turned away'.[163]

Even after the turn S, the only actual reports he received consisted of further signals about Goodenough's action in the rear with the German destroyers, and Jerram's thoroughly misleading report of 9.07. However, there were clear audible and visual signs of the enemy being approximately Westward. In *Iron Duke* herself, at 9.09, 'Heavy firing on starboard beam' was noted in the TS and all turrets trained to G90; then, at 9.14, B turret saw a 'Star Shell burst on starboard beam'. From *Colossus*, firing was heard and seen on the starboard bow at 9.05 and the star shell was logged at 9.20. At 9.15, *Thunderer*, next ahead from *Iron Duke*, also recorded heavy firing, though on the starboard quarter. Although times vary, the spectacle of the star shell was also seen from other ships:
– *King George V* at 9.20 bearing G110
– *Monarch* at 'about 9.30' on the starboard bow
– *Benbow* at 9.14 on the starboard bow
– *Bellerophon* at 'about 9.0 p.m . . . some way away on our starboard beam'
– *Vanguard* at about the time her division altered course S, the star shell bearing West.[164]

The differences between the times and bearings of this single, conspicuous event are typical of the discrepancies that are found between individual despatches. Even so, there is sufficient agreement to support the broad conclusions that, around 9.15 to the Westward, first heavy firing was heard and then a star shell soared aloft: and that these portents could hardly have been missed by Jellicoe.

---

[162] *JP II*, p. 434. *OD*, Pl. 6a.   [163] *JP II*, p. 451.
[164] *OD*, pp. 56, 60, 80, 114, 129, 358, 374 and 376. F&H, p. 183. *Royal Oak* implied that she saw the star shell just after observing the 2LCS in action at 8.55; *Vanguard* also saw the 2LCS opening fire at 8.56: *OD*, pp. 99 and 210.

Thus as night fell, both battlefleets were briefly beam-to-beam, steaming S on parallel courses. But at 9.14, Scheer originated a signal that declared his intentions for the remainder of the operation. It was picked up and translated in Room 40 as:

CinC to HS Fleet: Our own main body is to proceed in maintain course SSE¼E speed 16 knots.[165]

From then on, if Jellicoe held his course S, the two fleets would be on converging courses with the distinct possibility of a night encounter at the point of intersection. In the meantime, the two Commanders-in-Chief had still to redispose their forces for the night.

---

[165] Signal 20410 in 'Intercepts of German Signals ... Battle of Jutland', ADM 137/4710 and see Hines, p. 1151.

9   Night and morning

Having turned South at 9.01pm, Jellicoe did not deviate from his course and speed of 17 knots until about 2.30am the following morning, when he turned N. While it was plain that Scheer had no stomach for a battlefleet action and would now attempt to regain his ports in the Jade estuary, Jellicoe lacked precise information on the enemy's position and course. At the time of his own turn S, the reports suggested a bearing of about WNW and a course about SW, whereas by 9.15pm, there were visible and audible signs that at least a part of the German force lay to the Westward, a position that they could have reached only if Scheer had turned S even earlier than Jellicoe. But, whichever was the case, Jellicoe could still conclude correctly that the 'British Fleet was between the enemy and his base'.[1] It is uncertain whether he also realised that, if he needed it, he enjoyed an advantage in fleet speed of up to three knots. The Admiralty had not informed Jellicoe that Scheer was accompanied by the IIBS, so the first report of the presence of the German predreadnoughts was that from Beatty at 8.59; however, there are no definite indications that its significance was recognised in the flagship either then or later.

Although the Grand Fleet was well positioned to obstruct the direct routes to the Jade, one return route remained open to Scheer – ENE towards the Skagerrak, then round The Skaw before proceeding through the Kattegat and the Kiel Canal. But The Skaw was about 190 miles distant,[2] almost 12 hours steaming at 16 knots. It would have been apparent to Scheer that, if his retreat was detected quickly, he would be caught by the faster British fleet either at The Skaw or in the broader reaches of the Kattegat. Jellicoe, on the other hand, would have realised that, as actually happened, by 9am on 1 June his older destroyers would be running short of oil;[3] he would not have relished the prospect of a chase into more confined waters with only half his flotillas to screen the fleet. The disadvantages apparent to both sides probably explain why neither Commander-in-Chief even mentions the possibility that the High Seas Fleet might have taken the Kattegat route.

[1] *OD*, p. 20.   [2] *OD*, German Plans I and VII.   [3] *OD*, pp. 255, 258, 259, 309 and 313.

To return directly to the Jade, Scheer would have to use one of the swept channels through the British minefields in the Heligoland Bight.[4] These minefields were mainly South of 55°N (the latitude of the island of Sylt just off the Jutland coast) and east of 7°E (the longitude of the Ems estuary). By regular mine-sweeping, which was known to the British, the Germans kept clear two channels that were suitable for both leaving and returning to the Jade.[5] The outer end of one channel was 14 miles South of the Horns Reef Light Vessel; the channel then ran SE'wards towards Sylt before turning Southwards between Sylt and the Amrun Bank towards the Jade. From *Iron Duke*'s position at 9.00,[6] the channel entrance bore SSE at a distance of 97 miles. Thus at 17 knots it could be reached in 5.7 hours, that is, by 2.45am next morning, well after first light at about 2.00 but before sunrise at 3.09.[7] The second channel began just north of the Ems estuary and then extended Eastwards outside the chain of the Frisian Islands towards the Jade. The Ems entrance was 176 miles South of Jellicoe's 9.00pm position; even at 17 knots, Scheer could not have reached the channel entrance until after 7.30am. There was one other possible return route, through the gap in the British minefields that left a channel running WNW from Heligoland. Its outer end was also South of *Iron Duke*'s 9.00pm position but, at 140 miles, rather closer than the Ems. Although the gap itself appeared on German charts, it was not, according to British charts of the German swept channels, kept clear. Also, even if the Germans had been using it previously, they became suspicious of the area once mines were found on its Northern edge – as reported in a German signal decoded by Room 40 on 28 May. The Admiralty had informed Jellicoe of the general directions of all three routes, but they did not tell him that the Germans were now unlikely to risk going through the gap to Heligoland.[8]

Jellicoe sent a preliminary short despatch to the Admiralty by land-telegraph from Scapa Flow late on 2 June. In this first and, we may suppose, unvarnished account of the battle, he wrote:

At 9 p.m. light being very bad, mist increasing, fleet was turned to a course South to pass between Mine Area 1 and Horn Reef in order to intercept the Enemy should he return by either Sylt or Ems channels.[9]

Although the exact extent of this mine area is uncertain, it was close to the SE edge of the Dogger Bank. The course South would take the battlefleet at about 1am through the middle of the gap between Horns Reef to the East and the

[4] Corbett, p. 390 and Map 44. *AN*, pp. 69–70 and Dia. 40.
[5] The High Seas Fleet had put to sea through another swept channel that ran from Heligoland close to several British minefields to seaward of the Amrun Bank. But it was not known to Jellicoe and was only used outward bound: *FDSF III*, p. 156.
[6] From *OD*, Pl. 6a, 56°38N, 5°43E.   [7] *GOA*, p. 197. *OD*, p. 148. Oram, p. 171. Harper, p. 2.
[8] *OD*, German Plans I and VII. Corbett, Map 44. *NSA*, p. 120 and Dia. 47.   [9] *OD*(M), p. 574.

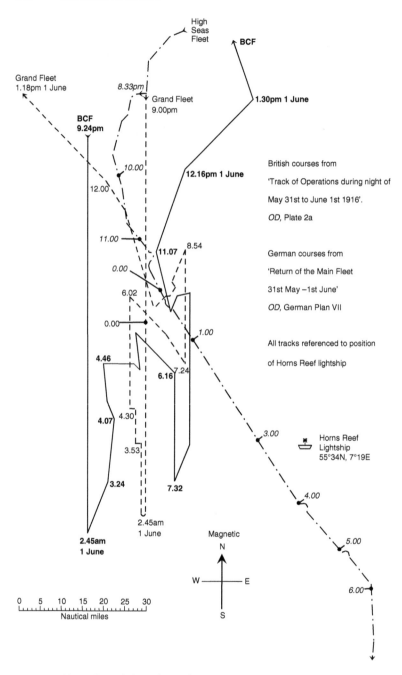

High
Seas
Fleet

BCF

Grand Fleet
1.18pm 1 June

8.33pm

Grand Fleet
9.00pm

1.30pm 1 June

BCF
9.24pm

British courses from

'Track of Operations during night of

May 31st to June 1st 1916'.

OD, Plate 2a

10.00

12.16pm 1 June

12.00

11.00

8.54

11.07

German courses from

'Return of the Main Fleet

31st May –1st June'

OD, German Plan VII

0.00

6.02

0.00

1.00

All tracks referenced to position

of Horns Reef lightship

4.46

6.16

7.24

4.30

4.07

3.00

3.53

Horns Reef
Lightship
55°34N, 7°19E

3.24

7.32

4.00

2.45am
1 June

2.45am
1 June

5.00

Magnetic

N

W — E

S

6.00

0   5   10   15   20   25   30
Nautical miles

Figure 9.1 Night and morning

Dogger Bank to the West.[10] It was also the direct course towards the entrances to both the Ems and Heligoland channels – although Jellicoe made no mention of the latter in this first despatch. But in the extended narrative that accompanied his full and secret despatch of 18 June, the emphasis is different.

> I was loth to forego the advantage of position, which would have resulted from an easterly or westerly course, and I therefore decided to steer to the southward, where I should be in a position to renew the engagement at daylight, and should be favourably placed to intercept the enemy should he make for his base by steering for Heligoland or towards the Ems and thence along the north German coast.[11]

By the date of this narrative, there was no doubt that the High Seas Fleet had in fact returned through the Sylt channel and Jellicoe had some explaining to do. Perhaps, by not mentioning the route past Horns Reef, he was trying to suggest that he did not even consider it, but this had already been contradicted by his initial despatch; probably, Jellicoe still had all three return routes in mind. But, if Scheer remained somewhere to the West, perhaps even on a SW'ly course that would take him some way towards the Dogger Bank, then, by continuing S, the Grand Fleet would draw ahead and be well placed to intercept the German ships at daylight as they turned towards their chosen route home. However, should Scheer fall astern, he would then be able to haul across the British wakes towards Horns Reef. Jellicoe's course S did nothing to block such a move directly. But at least the option remained, provided it was taken soon enough, of turning later towards Horns Reef in order to arrive at dawn, at about the same time that Scheer might also get there. The German escape was not yet inevitable.

The oncoming night was not only misty but dark with no moon and an overcast sky[12] – promising conditions for surprise destroyer attacks. Despite the experience of the earlier daylight actions, Jellicoe remained pessimistic about relative strengths in torpedo vessels.

> Each side possessed a considerable number of destroyers, it being most probable that the enemy was largely superior in this respect . . . as it was logical to expect that every available torpedo-boat destroyer and torpedo-boat had been ordered out . . . I rejected at once the idea of a night action between the heavy ships, as leading to possible disaster owing, first, to the presence of torpedo craft in such large numbers, and, secondly, to the impossibility of distinguishing between our own and enemy vessels. Further, the result of a night action under modern conditions must always be very largely a matter of pure chance.[13]

Evidently, Jellicoe would do nothing to bring on a night action between the battle fleets; this was one 'advantage of position' that followed from keeping ahead of a slower enemy. Such a night engagement would have been even more

---

[10] *Talisman* and four submarines at 54°30N, 4°E were S of Area 1: *OD*(M) pp. 440 and 486. For the Dogger-Bank – Horns Reef passage, combine Corbett's Maps 16 and 44.

[11] *OD*, p. 21.   [12] von Hase, p. 217. Harper, p. 2. *OD*, p. 74. von Schoultz, p. 148.

[13] *OD*, pp. 20–1.

chancy if destroyers were also involved and Jellicoe was surely right that such an affair, necessarily at short ranges, would be chaotic and its result at best uncertain; he might also have added that, at such ranges, the German capital ships, with their thicker armour and, in many cases, heavier secondary batteries, would have had a distinct advantage.

Having altered course in succession from SW in line-ahead to S, the British battlefleet was briefly in four-ship columns disposed quarterly. But at 9.17pm, Jellicoe ordered it to reform in Organisation 2, in which each battle squadron constituted a division. The columns were disposed abeam one mile apart, 'the object of the formation being that the divisions should remain clearly in sight of each other during the night, in order to prevent ships mistaking each other for enemy vessels'.[14] From Jellicoe's twice-stated concern about the problems of distinguishing friend from foe, it seems that he had little confidence in the effectiveness of British recognition signals. His chosen column spacing was only about half the length of each column; thus changes of course could be made only by unequal-speed manoeuvres that took time and would have been difficult to execute in the dark. The formation also left little room for turning away from torpedo attacks whether from ahead or on the beam. It appears that

Table 9.1. *Grand Fleet signals 7.49–10.08pm*

Time of despatch	From	To	System	Message	Time of origin
pm, 31May					
7.49	C-in-C	Marlborough	SL	Are you alright? Reply: Can only steam 17 knots	1945
9.01	C-in-C	Dreadnought Battlefleet	W/T Flags	Divisions separately alter course in succession to South preserving their formation	
9.10	C-in-C	SOs of Squadrons and all Captains D	W/T	Present course of fleet is South	2104
9.17	C-in-C	General	Flags W/T	Assume 2nd organisation. Form divisions in line ahead disposed abeam to port. Columns to be one mile apart	
10.03	SO 5BS	5BS	FL	Alter course in succession 16 points to starboard	
10.07	SO 5BS	5BS	FL	Alter course in succession 16 points to port	
10.08	SO 5BS	5BS	FL	... 18 knots	

[14] *OD*, pp. 21 and 33. *GFBOs III*, I.

the column separation was unusually close – the *GFBOs* assumed a default separation at night of five miles unless a different distance was specified[15] – but that Jellicoe was prepared to accept its disadvantages in order to preserve visual contact between his battleship columns. The *German Official Account*, with justification, criticised this inflexible British disposition.

Should one of the wing divisions become engaged or be forced, by a torpedo attack, to turn towards the next division, the whole fleet might easily be thrown into the most awful confusion, a further reason for avoiding all engagements in this formation.[16]

Since the fleet was disposed to port, the 2BS (now the 1st Division) led by *King George V* formed the starboard (westerly) column with, on its port beam, the 4BS (2nd Division) with *Iron Duke* at its head. But the positions of the battleships of the 3rd and 4th Divisions – that is, of the 1BS and the three remaining members of the 5BS – are less certain. In Organisation No. 2, the third column should have been led by *Marlborough* and the three other ships of what had been the 6th Division and were now the 5th Subdivision; they should have been ahead of what was now the 6th Subdivision led by *Colossus*. But *Marlborough*'s earlier torpedo hit had reduced her speed over the ground to about 15.8 knots;[17] thus, given the fleet speed of 17 knots, she and her (sub)division were falling astern by at least one mile in each hour, as would the 5BS at the rear while the fleet remained in single line-ahead. After the fleet reformed for the night, it appears that *Colossus* and her subdivision remained ahead and took the lead of the third column; her despatch states that, at 2.28am, *King George V*'s division was in sight on the starboard beam. As for the 5BS, by 10.00pm they had drawn a long way ahead of *Marlborough* and, to regain station, they turned about twice, first to starboard at 10.03 and then to port at 10.08. *Valiant*'s report states that, at 10.08, the 'First Division of First Battle Squadron now bearing 1 mile on port beam'; thus the 5BS had already moved Westwards and were approximately astern of the 4BS. The same report is the only source for a second pair of 16-point turns between 10.42 and 10.50. Whether or not the 5BS made a second attempt to remain astern of *Marlborough*, Evan-Thomas had seen that she was going 'very slowly' and he soon increased speed so that he would not find himself too far astern of the main battlefleet in the morning. By early dawn, the 5BS had again edged Westwards since they sighted the 2BS ahead about three to five miles. After the whole battlefleet turned N shortly after 2.30am, at 2.38 *Colossus* observed the three ships of the 5BS in company.[18]

[15] *GFBOs III*, II(b).   [16] *GOA*, p. 168. Tarrant, p. 189.   [17] *OD*, pp. 67, 74 and 105.
[18] *OD*, pp. 81, 195–6, 210–11 and Pl. 18.

Table 9.2. *1BS signals 1.56–10.31am*

Time of despatch	From	To	System	Message	Time of origin
am, 1 June					
1.56	SO 1BS	Revenge	FL	I must ease down and will haul out of line to starboard, you continue on	0155
1.56	SO 1BS	C-in-C	W/T	Obliged to ease to 12 knots. Remainder of Division continuing at 17 knots	0155
2.17	SO 1BS	Revenge	FL	I am going to transfer to you in Fearless	0215
2.21	SO 1BS	Fearless	FL	Come alongside on my port side. I am going to transfer to Revenge in you	
2.30	RA 1BS	C-in-C	FL	Marlborough's division is not in visual touch	0230
2.50	Hercules	Revenge	Sem.	How does your reckoning compare with mine, as reference position made at 9.45 p.m. last night? I make it we are now 12 miles NW of Iron Duke	0235 0300
				Reply: Working from Iron Duke's reference position for last night, I make our position NbyE seven to eight miles	
3.00	SO 1BS	Revenge	Sem.	Haul out of line to starboard and stop engines	0300
3.15	SO 1BS	C-in-C	W/T	I am now transferring to Revenge. What is your position, course and speed?	0314
3.20	C-in-C	Revenge	W/T	My course at 2.30 a.m., North, 16 knots. Close me	0307
4.00	SO 1BS	Marlborough	W/T	Proceed to Tyne or Rosyth by M Channel. Destroyers will be sent when available. You should ask for local destroyers to convoy you. There are four of our Submarines S of Area 1	
7.33	SO 2CS	C-in-C	SL	1BS in sight N	0731
7.45	SO 5BS	C-in-C	SL	1BS in sight bearing N	0730
10.31	Blanche	C-in-C	SL	Three ships accompanied by TBDs bearing SbyE, steering N, apparently Revenge's division	1025

At 1.55am, *Marlborough*'s subdivision had probably fallen astern of the leading battleships by seven miles or more. By that time, her officers feared that, in her partly flooded A boiler-room, the shored-up bulkheads could not stand the strain of the present speed for much longer. At 1.56, Burney signalled

that that his flagship would have to haul out of line and reduce to 12 knots, though he ordered his other three ships to press on at 17 knots. He then instructed *Fearless*, which had taken station astern of *Agincourt* for the night, to transfer him and his staff to *Revenge*. The transfer was completed between 3.00 and 3.15, after *Revenge* and her two companions had turned N at 2.55. But, despite some contacts with other ships, Burney's three ships would wander about in the mist and rain until they eventually rejoined Jellicoe's flag in the evening of 1 June.[19] As we shall also see later, *Marlborough*, to which *Fearless* returned as escort, made her own way to safety on 2 June.

Table 9.3. *British Signals 9.20pm–2.01am*

Time of despatch	From	To	System	Message	Time of origin
pm, 31 May					
9.20	Constance	Caroline	FL	Calliope on starboard bow of Iron Duke. I think she is damaged	
9.27	C-in-C	SOs of Squadrons, Commanders of Divisions of Battlefleet and Captain D11	W/T	Destroyers take station astern of battlefleet five miles	2115
9.31	Caroline	4LCS	FL	... 18 knots. Form single line-ahead in sequence of fleet numbers	
9.32	C-in-C	Abdiel	W/T	If there is time before daylight lay mines in position given for operation M and then proceed to Rosyth via S. side of Area 1. (Received by Abdiel 10.05)	2132
9.30	Captain D12	12DF	FL	Alter course in succession to South ... 18 knots	
9.38	Captain D12	12DF	FL	... 12 knots	
am, 1 June					
2.01	SO 4LCS	4LCS	FL	Prepare to form in single line abreast to starboard. Take station ahead. Ships in column to be five cables apart	

---

[19] *OD*, pp. 68, 101 and 105. von Schoultz, pp. 152–3.

As the battle squadrons reorganised themselves, the light cruisers and destroyers also took up their night positions. The 4LCS reassembled at the head of the battlefleet and at about 9.35pm formed astern of *Calliope*; they probably then took station ahead of *Iron Duke*, with *Galatea* in company.[20] At the other end of the line the 2LCS, after driving off the IITF and XIIHF, moved to a position W or NW of the battlefleet. At 9.27, Jellicoe ordered his destroyers to 'take station astern of battlefleet five miles'. Of the flotillas with the battleships, only the 11DF and the 4DF had been ahead of the fleet, with the 11DF to starboard. To reach their new position, at 9.50 the 4DF turned 16 points and was able to pass through the lines; the 11DF must also have turned about and probably steamed up the starboard side of the battlefleet before turning again close to the 2LCS. Of the flotillas in the rear, the 12DF, which had been two cables astern of *Agincourt*, dropped back by reducing speed from 17 to 12 knots for an hour;[21] the 13DF and the boats of the 9DF and 10DF probably did likewise. As subsequent events will show, once in position their order from West to East was: the 11DF with *Castor*; the 4DF; the 13DF with *Champion*; the 9/10DF; and the 12DF.

Jellicoe's narrative explained that:

[My] course enabled me to drop my destroyer flotillas astern, thus at one and the same time providing the battlefleet with a screen against attack by torpedo craft at night, and also giving our flotillas an opportunity for attacking the enemy's heavy ships should they also be proceeding to the southward with the object of regaining their bases.

This differs somewhat from the passages quoted earlier by implying that Jellicoe expected the enemy battlefleet to follow quite closely, creating opportunities for his own destroyers to attack the enemy van but also for their flotillas to attack his rear. But again he does not mention what now seems obvious: that once Scheer had drawn astern, he would be able to head SSEs towards Horns Reef and the shortest return route. Even so, Jellicoe did take one specific step to obstruct a return via the Sylt channel.

At 9.32 p.m., 'Abdiel' was directed to lay mines in wide zig-zags from a position 215° [about SW] from the Vyl light-vessel in a mean direction 180°, ten mines to the mile. This operation was successfully accomplished.[22]

On 4 May 1916, *Abdiel* had already laid a line of mines S of the Vyl lightship across the Sylt channel close to its outer end. The new line, which (probably coincidentally) was close to the swept exit route that ran outside the Amrun Bank, certainly added another hazard for a retiring fleet attempting to follow the Sylt channel itself. But, as Jellicoe's signal to *Abdiel* makes clear, her

---

[20] *OD*, pp. 22, 173, 297 and Pl. 12a; but see F&H, p. 270 for a position on the fleet's port beam.
[21] Goodenough, p. 96. 'Etienne', pp. 146–7. *OD*, pp. 322 and 332. F&H, p. 289.
[22] *OD*, p. 21.

mission had already been planned as part of the 'Operation M' that had now been overtaken by events. In accordance with the same plan, three submarines were already spread on a line WbyN from the Vyl light-vessel at distances of 4 (*E55*), 12 (*E26*) and 20 (*D1*) miles. But they were unaware that the High Seas Fleet was at sea and remained on the bottom.[23] In despatching *Abdiel*, Jellicoe was sending her to the entrance of the only return route that could be mined before daylight, and by making use of a pre-existing plan he avoided any need for detailed instructions. Thus her mission may have been no more than a convenient expedient. It does not necessarily indicate a serious concern that Scheer might head for Horns Reef and the Sylt channel, not least since two lines of mines and three submarines spread over 16 miles could do no more than hinder the passage of an entire fleet.

At 9.16pm, Beatty received Jellicoe's advisory signal that the battlefleet was now steering S but, for the moment, the BCF continued SW. At 8.52, the ISG bore N and were steaming SSW and by 9.00 'the enemy' was NbyW heading WSW. Beatty's despatch repeated the bearing NbyW (though it also referred to this as 'North-Westward'), gave a course SWbyS, 'which as near as could be judged was correct', and concluded that 'we had established ourselves well between [the enemy] and his base'. His appreciation was thus close to Jellicoe's.

In view of the gathering darkness and for other reasons, viz.: (*a*) Our distance from the Battle Fleet; (*b*) The damaged condition of the Battle Cruisers; (*c*) The enemy being concentrated; (*d*) The enemy being accompanied by numerous Destroyers; (*e*) Our strategic situation being such as to make it appear certain that we should locate them at daylight under favourable circumstances, I did not consider it desirable or proper to close the enemy Battle Fleet during the dark hours. I therefore concluded that I should carry out the Commander-in-Chief's wishes by turning to the course of the Fleet . . . My duty in this situation was to ensure that the enemy Fleet could not regain its base by passing round the Southern flank of our forces.[24]

The BCF turned S at either 9.24 or 9.30,[25] after which Beatty reported his position, course and his speed of 17 knots as at 9.35. He gave no explanation of how the enemy fleet, which he knew was limited to a fleet speed of 16–17 knots by the presence of the predreadnoughts of the IIBS, might move up from a position that was now almost astern so that it could pass to the South of the British columns.

Just before dark, the 1LCS (less *Galatea*) had taken station astern of the 3LCS. The signal record suggests that these squadrons may then have lost touch with the battlecruisers for a time and that they did not turn S until 9.41. At some time after ten o'clock, *Inconstant* obeyed Beatty's delayed order for the

[23] Corbett, pp. 320–1, 390 and Map 44. *OD*, Pl. 3a and p. 343. *OD*(M), pp. 400 and 440.
[24] *OD*, pp. 138–9: also VNE.   [25] Cf. *OD*, p. 139 and Pls. 10 and 11 with VNE and *OD*(M).

Table 9.4. *BCF signals 9.15–10.05pm*

Time of despatch	From	To	System	Message	Time of origin
pm, 31 May					
9.15	Shannon	SO 2CS	SL	King George V bears NNE about eight miles	2100
9.17	Duke of Edinburgh	Shannon	FL	Your masthead light is burning	
9.30	SO BCF	General	Flags	Alter course in succession to South	
9.32	SO BCF	Princess Royal	FL	Please give me challenge and reply now in force as they have been lost. (Challenge and reply passed as requested)	
9.38	SO BCF	C-in-C	W/T	My position now 56°35 N, 5°41E, course SW, speed 17 knots. Enemy's bearing NbyW, steering WSW. (Received in Iron Duke 9.41)	2100
9.41	SO BCF	SO 1LCS	W/T	1LCS take station WbyS four miles. Keep a good look-out for movements of Enemy bearing NbyW (Received by Iron Duke as 'Take station NW')	2107
9.41	SO 3LCS	3LCS	SL	Alter course in succession to South	
9.43	SO BCF	C-in-C, SO 2BS, SOs 1,2,3 LCS, Captain D13	W/T	My position 56°28 N, 5°38E. course S, speed 17 knots	2135
9.57	Badger	SO BCF	FL	Have ordered 1DF to screen BCF	2250 [*sic*]
10.00	Inconstant	SO 3LCS	FL	Inconstant with 1LCS, less Galatea, are astern of you	2200
10.05	Princess Royal			Remarks: Opened fire on Cruisers on starboard beam. 10.20 p.m. ceased firing	

1LCS to take station WbyS, one point before *Lion*'s starboard beam (he also warned them to look out for enemy ships bearing NbyW). *Princess Royal*'s remarks are the only indication that she may have fired on the 1LCS as they dropped back into position abeam. For the night, the 3LCS remained on *Lion*'s starboard bow. *Badger*, with the few survivors from *Invincible*, had rejoined the 1DF at 8.30; the eight boats of the flotilla, with *Christopher* and *Ophelia*, would continue to form the BCF's submarine screen.[26] At 8.45 the 2CS (with *Duke of Edinburgh* and *Chester*) was on the port quarter of the BCF, 6 miles to the East. They turned S at 9.03 with the battlefleet but at 9.10 veered away to about WSW towards the battlecruisers. At 9.37 they too turned S at 17 knots, when they were perhaps one mile astern of *Inflexible*, but by 2.45am the following morning, the gap had opened to six miles.[27]

At 9.32pm, *Lion* breached signals security by asking *Princess Royal* for the challenge and reply then in force; these were recognition codes in the form of short letter sequences exchanged by searchlight or flashlight using Morse code. *Lion*'s request was seen from *Castor* and *Princess Royal*'s reply from *Manners* (11DF); Hawksley thought that the request might have been made by an enemy ship and that it could explain why at 10.05 his ship was challenged 'by the first two signs of the challenge of the day [though t]hey then made T, followed by R'.[28] However, the recognition system was inherently insecure; as soon as a British ship made the challenge, it was known to the enemy and could be used to give the appearance of a British ship (and perhaps to obtain the response). As soon as the battlecruiser forces made contact in the afternoon, both the IVHF and *Seydlitz* thought they had learned the recognition code, though the battlecruiser's reading – 'JO' – did not agree with the destroyers'. After dark, *Elbing* reported (improbably) that the British recognition signal after 10pm was 'Ü' (• • – –): though *Frankfurt* corrected this to 'UA' (• • – • –). As we shall see, during the night actions, even when German ships flashed the wrong codes, they were enough to cause doubt and delay. Jellicoe included *Lion*'s indiscretion among his 'Errors made in Jutland Battle', but Marder thought that too much had been made of it.[29]

Table 9.5. *German reports of British recognition codes*

Time of receipt	From	To	System	Message	Time of origin
pm, 31 May					
2.38	B109	Regensburg		Enemy's recognition signal is 'PL' – 4th Half Flotilla	1435
10.22	Elbing	C-in-C		To Fleet: Enemy recognition signal from 10pm onwards is 'Ü'	
10.45	Frankfurt	C-in-C		To Fleet: Enemy's challenge is 'UA' (not 'Ü') – SO IISG	2233

[26] *OD*, pp. 139, 175, 187 and 248.   [27] *OD*, pp. 275, 281 and Pls. 24 and 25.
[28] *OD*, pp. 303–5.
[29] *FDSF III*, pp. 154–5 and note 8. https://en.wikipedia.org/wiki/Morse_code. *JP II*, p. 451. *Elbing*'s mistake points up another problem with short recognition codes; they were too easily misread, especially in the heat of action.

Durchhalten

Scheer did not even consider either of the Southerly return routes that Jellicoe and Beatty were trying to cover. At 9.10pm, his War Diary declared that 'by dawn we must be at Horns Reef in order not to be cut off from the Bight by strong pursuing enemy forces coming up from the south . . . from bases in the south of England'. His despatch read that:

It might be taken for granted that the enemy would endeavour to force us to the Westward by attacks with strong forces during the hours of dusk, and by destroyer attacks during the night, in order to force us to give battle at daybreak . . . The Main Fleet . . . had to make for Horns Reef, in close order, by the shortest route, and to maintain this course in defiance of all attacks of the enemy.

As a first step, at 9.06 Scheer initiated a request for airship reconnaissance off Horns Reef at dawn (of which more later).[30] Then, at 9.14, Scheer ordered the turn towards Horns Reef, course SSE¼E, speed 16 knots.[31] His insistence that the course must be maintained was expressed by the word *Durchhalten*, an exhortation to 'stick to it through thick and thin'.[32]

The German sources do not give a clear description of the movements of the battle squadrons in response to Scheer's order. On one of the charts that accompanied Scheer's despatch, the last marked position of the IIBS at about 9.05 was on the starboard beam of the IBS.[33] At 9.17, the leading predreadnought *Hannover* sighted four enemy ships to the Southward, one with a high masthead light. The time, which corresponds exactly to that of the warning signal to *Shannon* that her masthead light was burning, records the moment when the 2CS, heading WSW to follow the BCF, hauled across the bows of the IIBS. Thus, when Beatty himself turned S, the enemy fleet already bore E of N and he was in no position to obstruct Scheer's intended course to Horns Reef. While the ISG and the leading ships of the IIIBS had suffered severely, Scheer believed that, with the exception of *Lützow*, his big ships would be able to keep station 'at the high speed of 16 knots'. He anticipated that the van of his battle line in particular would have to repulse enemy torpedo attacks during the night: but that the predreadnoughts of the IIBS would be unsuited for this task because of their weaker resistance to torpedo hits. Thus his signal originated at 9.29 ordered the IIBS and the ISG to take station astern of the IIIBS; this left the

---

[30] *FDSF III*, pp. 160–1. Scheer's despatch, *OD*, p. 596. *GOA*, pp. 212–13.

[31] Hines, p. 1151 and signal 20410 in 'Intercepts of German Signals . . . Battle of Jutland', ADM 137/4710. The orders to the IIIBS and the battlecruisers that appear twice in GSM were, in the Room 40 log, only in a second signal timed at 9.29: see signal 20411.

[32] Tarrant, pp. 183 and 285. *Cassell's German and English Dictionary* (London: Cassell, 1953 edn.).

[33] *OD*, German Plan V.

Table 9.6. *Scheer's signals 8.52–9.50pm*

Time of receipt	From	To	System	Message	Time of origin
pm, 31 May					
8.52	C-in-C	Fleet		Course S	
9.00	C-in-C	Von der Tann		(Passed down the line.) Armoured cruisers. Take station astern	
	C-in-C	Naval Airship Division		Morning reconnaissance off Horns Reef urgently required	2106
9.10	C-in-C	General		Battle fleet course SSE¼E; this course is to be maintained. Speed 16 knots. IIBS take station at rear of the line. Battle cruisers are to prolong the line astern	2114
	C-in-C	General		IIBS take station astern IIIBS. Battle cruisers take station at the rear of the line. IISG take station ahead and IVSG to starboard	2129
9.30	Hannover	C-in-C		Enemy in sight ahead, 4 ships in 166γ – 2nd Admiral, IIBS	2117
9.45	C-in-C	Fleet		Battle fleet's course is SSE¾E	2146
9.50				Noted: By a 16-point turn together to port and a 16-point turn in succession to port, the IIBS took station astern of König	

dreadnought squadrons in reverse order with the almost undamaged IBS in the van, *Westfalen* leading the line.[34] It was probably in response to this order that the IBS and IIIBS turned to SWbyW in order to get ahead of the IIBS. Scheer's 9.29 signal also ordered the IISG to form ahead of the battlefleet and the IVSG to starboard. At 9.45, by which time the dreadnought squadrons were probably in line, Scheer adjusted his course to SSE¾E. Then, beginning at 9.50, the IIBS took station astern of *König* by means of two 16-point turns to port, the first together, the second in succession; this reversed their order so that the flagship, *Deutschland*, was once again leading the squadron. Apparently, by 9.50 the ISG was on the port beam of the dreadnoughts.[35]

---

[34] Scheer's despatch, *OD*, pp. 596–7. He seems to have had anticipated the order to the ISG with a signal to *Von der Tann* at 9.00.

[35] *GOA*, pp. 166–7 (see also Tarrant, pp. 184–6) but with the assumption that Scheer's signal repositioning his forces was made once at 9.29.

Table 9.7. *German signals 7.15–10.12pm*

Time of receipt	From	To	System	Message	Time of origin
pm, 31 May					
7.15	Elbing	SO IISG		One condenser leaking; can no longer proceed at high speed	
9.00	G39	Moltke	Visual	Report state of armament AC Scouting Forces	
9.00	Moltke	G39	Visual	Heavy armament serviceable. Secondary armament, greater part serviceable . . . There are 300 tons of water in the ship	
9.15	König	C-in-C		Lost sight of Lützow in 007ε; she was steering S at slow speed – SO, IIIBS	2105
9.30	G39	Moltke	Visual	Please sheer out to port and stop – AC Scouting Forces	
9.50	G39	Moltke	Visual	AC Scouting Forces will board Moltke	
9.55	Moltke	G39	Visual	Moltke has stopped	
10.12	G40	Rostock		To Fleet and König; Lützow at 10.30 [*sic*] with 4 boats in 018ε, centre. Course SSW. Speed 13 knots	2150

At nine o'clock, Hipper, then still aboard the destroyer *G39*, had been informed that *Moltke* was largely undamaged; subsequent signal times indicate that he hoisted his flag in her soon after 9.55. Either unaware of the intended position for the ISG or perhaps unwilling to go to the rear, he ordered the battlecruisers, then on the port beam of the IBS, to the head of the line at 20 knots. But only *Moltke* and (for a time) *Seydlitz* could comply; neither the badly damaged *Derfflinger* nor *Von der Tann*, whose dirty fires required prompt cleaning, could make more than 18 knots. Once the C-in-C repeated the order to fall back, the last two formed astern of the IIBS shortly after ten o'clock.[36] *Lützow* was last seen from the battlefleet by *König* (then the rear ship) at 9.15 steaming slowly S; at 9.50, *G40*, one of her escort of four destroyers,[37] reported that she was heading SSW at 13 knots.

When the IISG was ordered to take station ahead at 9.29, it was proceeding up the line to port of the battle squadrons. *Frankfurt* and *Pillau* pushed on but *Elbing* had developed condenser problems and could not keep up; she therefore took station with the IVSG. Earlier, soon after nine o'clock, the IVSG had been joined by Michelsen in *Rostock* who had kept in hand five boats of the IXTF, *G42* (VIHF) and probably also *S32* (IHF).[38] When *Hannover* sighted the British armoured

---

[36] *GOA*, pp. 167–8 and 170. Tarrant, p. 187. Both state that Hipper boarded *Moltke* at 9.15.

[37] The escort comprised *G37* and *V45* (XIIHF) and *G38* and *G40* of the IHF. *G39* (also IHF) remained with *Moltke*.

[38] *GOA*, p. 166. *V26* and *S36* (XVIIHF), *V30*, *S33* and *S34* (XVIIIHF); later, *S32* would be close to *Rostock*.

cruisers ahead, the IVSG was on the starboard beam of the rear ship of the IIBS; Rear-Admiral von Dalwigk zu Lichtenfels then ordered them to move ahead again (though they were not ordered to attack). Scheer had ordered the IVSG to screen the fleet to starboard. But, despite the belief of Commodore von Reuter in *Stettin* that, as ordered, the IVSG were to the SW of the battlefleet,[39] their subsequent encounters with British ships show that in the darkness they strayed onto the port bow of the line.

Table 9.8. *German destroyer signals 8.45pm–0.18am*

Time of receipt	From	To	System	Message	Time of origin
pm, 31 May					
8.45	S53, SO IIITF	Regensburg		5 boats of IIITF present. Request orders and position	
8.45	Regensburg	IIITF		Stay where you are	
8.57	Rostock	C-in-C [*sic*]		IIITF report position – Leader of Torpedo Boats	2050
9.02	Rostock	C-in-C		To V and VII TFs. VIITF is to advance from 165γ in Sector SE to SbyE; VTF in Sector SbyE to SSW – Leader of Torpedo Boats	2056
9.08	Regensburg	C-in-C		To II and VI TFs. At 9.00 rear ship of own battle fleet was in 165γ bottom. Course S	2103
9.09	Rostock	C-in-C		To Leader of Torpedo Boats *re* 2050: 5 boats in 165γ with 2nd Leader of Torpedo Boats. IIITF	2058
9.30	Hannover	C-in-C		Enemy in sight ahead, 4 ships in 166γ – 2nd Admiral, IIBS	2117
9.40	Rostock	C-in-C		To XVIIIHF: Reference 2117 (from Hannover) Attack the Enemy – Leader of Torpedo Boats	2139
9.48	B98	Rostock		General. 5 enemy light cruisers and many destroyers in 020ε; am being driven off. I am steering NW – IITF	2150
9.55	Rostock	C-in-C		To XVIII HF: Reference 2139 (with regard to attacking the enemy) Sector SSW to SW – Leader of Torpedo Boats	2148
10.36	Rostock	C-in-C		To all flotillas: By [2] a.m.[1] all flotillas are to be reformed and in company with battle fleet off Horns Reef, or on the way round the Skaw – Leader of Torpedo Boats	2232
am, 1 June					
0.18	G101	C-in-C, 1st and 2nd Leaders of Torpedo Boats		Am proceeding around the Skaw	2352

[1] Corrected from *GOA*, p. 166.

[39] *GOA*, pp. 166–7. Tarrant, p. 191.

By 8.58 five boats of the IIITF had joined Heinrich in *Regensburg*, after which he remained at the very rear of the line, astern of *Derfflinger* and *Von der Tann*. The damaged *S50* (XIIHF) joined them at 10.27. The commander of the IIITF then sought permission to launch an attack but 'Heinrich considered it advisable to keep them back as a reserve for unforeseen eventualities'.[40] The two undamaged boats from the XIIHF (*V69* and *V46*) had returned to their allotted sector ESE-SE at 9.10; at 10.42, they observed fighting a long way off to starboard but they did not encounter any enemy forces. The other boats with the battlefleet were those that had already run short of torpedoes. The three of the IXTF that had taken station on the IBS seem to have remained in place while the four of the VITF occupied positions in the gaps between the battleships of the IIIBS.[41]

After the IITF and the XIIHF had been despatched prematurely by Heinrich into the sectors ENE-ESE and ESE-SE, at 9.02, Michelsen tried again, ordering the VIITF and VTF to advance from positions near the rear of the line – the VIITF (nine boats) into sector SE-SbyE, the VTF (eleven boats) into sector SbyE-SSW.

In selecting these sectors he had in mind that the enemy, who was to eastward when the action was broken off, would during the night probably make to the southward [*sic*] under the coast of Jutland, so as to bring the German battle fleet to action again at dawn off Horns Reef.

Their fires were already very dirty from the hard steaming that had been necessary during the day; even at 15 knots, sparks and clouds of smoke from their funnels made them visible from a long way off. Also the VTF's sector coincided with the then course of the High Seas Fleet, while that of the VIITF corresponded with the new course towards Horns Reef; proximity to the battlefleet, with the real risk of misidentification, would be unavoidable. The VTF advanced S½W and was twice forced to pass through the battle line; it was unable to split up into four groups to widen its search until 11 o'clock and even then was limited by the condition of its fires to 18 knots. Half an hour later, two of the groups – which included *V2*, *V4* and *V6* – turned SE but, although some boats of this flotilla came close to the later actions between the British 4DF and the IBS, they did not become involved. (At 0.20am, the group led by *G11* were fired at briefly by a German cruiser.) The VIITF, proceeding together at 17 knots, passed under the stern of the IIIBS at 9.30pm but the XIVHF was mistaken for the enemy; a salvo fired at 2,000 yards fell just 50 yards astern of *S23*. Commodore von Koch in *S24* altered course to SE to get further away

[40] *GOA*, p. 166. *S53, V71, V73, G88* and *S54* of the IIITF.
[41] *GOA*, pp. 156 and 195. V28, *S51* and *S52* (IXTF). *G41* and the XIHF (*V44, G86* and *G87*).

from his own battlefleet, which led to his making the first contact with the 4DF.[42]

At 9.40, acting on *Hannover*'s sighting of the 2CS, Michelsen initiated an attack by the boats that he had held back in reserve (five of the IXTF and *G42*); then, at 9.55, he assigned them to the sector SSW-SW. They advanced SWbyS but at midnight, having seen nothing of the enemy, they turned towards Horns Reef. At 0.40am, they met up with the group of the VTF led by *G11*.[43] From 9.40pm, the large, modern destroyers of the IITF resumed their search of sector ENE-ESE for a time but drew a complete blank.[44] When Heinrich first despatched them, he had given them permission to return round The Skaw. Then, at 10.30, Michelsen ordered all the flotillas to be reformed and in company with the battle fleet off Horns Reef by 2am, or to be on the way round The Skaw – though, contrary to the text of *German Official Account*, there was nothing in the signal about using the second route 'only in the event of their being driven off'. With explicit permission from both torpedo boat leaders, at 0.18am *G101* informed them and the C-in-C that the IITF was withdrawing; they took with them all but one of the torpedoes with which they had begun the battle. Michelsen's order to regroup at dawn had been prompted by his concern that, having spread many of his flotillas in the sectors extending from ENE to SW, they might be dispersed further by encounters with enemy light forces and would not be able to regain their stations in time for the expected fleet action.[45] But it hardly encouraged them to persist in their searches for the enemy and both the IITF and IXTF gave up at around midnight, two hours before first light.

The first night actions

Soon after ten o'clock, the German battle line was proceeding SSE¾E at 16 knots while the British columns continued S at 17 knots. Thus, if the Germans had been visible from a British ship their *relative* movement would have appeared to be ENE at 8.9 knots: that is, while getting closer to the British line of advance, they were also falling astern. If, when the German van turned towards Horns Reef, the two battlefleets had still been beam-to-beam, it might well have converged on the British rear. Instead, seemingly due to the delays in forming the German line, it fell back abaft the British beam, so that the vessels

---

[42] *GOA*, pp. 156, 165 (for quotation, which would make better sense if 'southward' read SSE'ward), 170 and 195–6.

[43] *GOA*, pp. 167 and 195–6. The orders were addressed only to the XVIIIHF (three boats) but were also obeyed by two more from the XVIIHF and *G42*.

[44] *GOA*, pp. 156 and 195. The signal from *B98* at 9.48 appears to relate to their earlier encounter with the 2LCS; Scheer's chart (*OD*, German Plan VII) times the sighting of enemy vessels in 020ε at 8.45.

[45] *GOA*, pp. 165–6 (quotation) and 195.

Table 9.9. *British destroyer signals 9.45–10.55pm*

Time of despatch	From	To	System	Message	Time of origin
pm, 31 May					
9.45	Commodore F	11DF	FL	Alter course in succession to ENE. Take up cruising order No. 4	
9.50	Commodore F	11DF	FL	Alter course 16 points outward	
9.55	Commodore F	11DF	FL	Alter course in succession to NE, speed 22 knots	
9.58	Garland	Captain D4	W/T	German Destroyers steering SE	
10.00	Contest	Captain D4	FL	German Destroyers steering SE	2200
10.03	Garland	Captain D4	W/T	German Submarines astern	2200
10.25	Captain D4	C-in-C	W/T	Submarine five miles North of Dragonfly (?) at 10 p.m.	2220
10.27	Contest	Captain D4	FL	Contest fired one round at three German destroyers astern steering SE	2225
10.30	Canada	C-in-C	FL	Contest to Captain D. Urgent. German T.B.D. steering NE	
10.30	Garland	Commodore F	FL	Garland firing at Enemy's Destroyers astern	2225
10.42	Captain D12	12DF	FL	. . . 17 knots	
10.43	Fortune	Captain D4	W/T	Fortune fired one round at 9.55 in direction torpedo came from	2235
10.48	Contest	Captain D4	W/T	Destroyers off starboard quarter steering E	
10.55	Porpoise	Captain D4	W/T	German destroyer astern steering East	2250

Table 9.10. *German light forces' signals 9.55–10.46pm*

Time of receipt	From	To	System	Message	Time of origin
pm, 31 May					
9.55	Frankfurt	C-in-C		5 enemy cruisers steering ENE in 017ε – SO IISG	2158
10.45	S24 [VIITF]	Rostock		To Fleet: destroyers steering S and steaming at high speed in 054α – VIITF	2220
10.46	Frankfurt	C-in-C		Am in action with enemy light cruiser – SO IISG	2202

at the head of the German line soon came into contact with the British light forces as they moved into position five miles astern of their fleet. The series of night encounters that now began involved many small vessels in sudden, violent actions; the closer they were to important engagements, the less the time available for their few officers on open bridges to keep a record of events. Thus, inevitably, their reports are often sketchy, with times either omitted or varying from one to another. The accounts which follow attempt to put events in their correct order using what are the most likely reported times, although most remain approximate at best.

At 9.45pm *Castor* and the 11DF turned about to take station astern, though the sequence of turns in Hawksley's signals seems incomplete. As the 2LCS headed S somewhere on the battlefleet's starboard quarter, the 11DF passed them to starboard on an opposite course, the rear destroyer firing a single shot that, fortunately, whistled overhead. The flotilla was then seen to turn up onto a parallel course and disappeared ahead. *Frankfurt* and *Pillau* of the IISG, ahead of the German fleet, must also have been in the same vicinity. At 9.58, they sighted what they thought were five enemy light cruisers steering ENE; the course suggests that they actually sighted *Castor* and some the *M*-class destroyers with her. Just as the German light cruisers fired torpedoes at only 1,200 yards, their targets turned about and were not hit. Without opening fire or switching on their searchlights, the German light cruisers also turned away, so as not to draw the British ships towards their fleet. Neither the 2LCS nor the IISG are mentioned in Hawksley's despatch, so they were probably not sighted from *Castor*.[46]

At much the same time (about 9.50) but probably further Eastward, the 4DF, having passed through the battleship lines, was steering N and NE to its position in the rear. As the VIITF proceeded SE in its allotted sector, they sighted the 4DF but at first mistook it for their own IITF. Once the VIITF had approached to within 500 yards without receiving a response to the German recognition signal, they decided to attack, *S24, S15, S16* and *S18* firing one torpedo each; they then continued to advance SSE½E. However, once again the British destroyers turned about to S so the German torpedoes passed harmlessly astern. von Koch turned in the same direction without disclosing his presence by gunfire or searchlight.[47] *Garland* of the 4DF saw the German recognition lights and that the VIITF had fired torpedoes and she also fired at them.[48] Both she and *Contest* reported German destroyers steering SE to Captain (D) Charles Wintour in *Tipperary* but only *Garland* used wireless. Subsequent signals and also notes taken in *Sparrowhawk*[49] suggest that the 4DF and VIITF may have

[46] *OD*, p. 303. 'Etienne', pp. 146–7. F&H, p. 289. Tarrant, p. 192.
[47] Tarrant, p. 192. *GOA*, pp. 170–1 and 195. *OD*, pp. 311–12.
[48] The time of 9.02 in *Garland*'s despatch (*OD*, p. 314) should probably be 10.02.
[49] F&H, p. 329. *Sparrowhawk* sighted 9–10 destroyers that were thought to be British until she heard the reports to *Tipperary*.

continued in intermittent contact until 10.50 but the latter saw no further action. By W/T, both *Contest* and *Porpoise* reported enemy destroyers steering SE and then E, while *Canada* apparently passed an earlier report from *Contest* to the C-in-C, though with a course of NE. It is not known whether any of these wireless reports were taken in by *Iron Duke*.

Around 10.15, the IVSG, on the port bow of their battlefleet, fought two actions in close succession, first with *Castor* and the eight destroyers of the 11DF: and then with the 2LCS. At about 10.05, *Castor, Marne* and others of the 11DF, then on the starboard quarter of the fleet, sighted three or more German light cruisers on the starboard bow or beam. From *Castor* (though not from *Marne*), the Germans were seen to make a partly correct challenge, which seems to have caused enough uncertainty so that the two leading German ships were first to switch on searchlights and open fire, at a range of about 2,500 yards. *Castor* received more than six hits, some setting fire to her motor boat and extensively damaging her fore bridge; her W/T was put temporarily out of action, but she was able to inform the C-in-C through *Kempenfelt* at 10.50 that she had been in action with enemy cruisers. *Marne* was hit by a single 4.1in shell but it failed to explode. Only *Castor, Marne* and *Magic* fired torpedoes though, contrary to claims from some boats, none hit;

Table 9.11. *British light forces' signals 10.46–11.38pm*

Time of despatch	From	To	System	Message	Time of origin
pm, 31 May					
10.46	C-in-C	Commodore F	W/T	Urgent. Are you engaging Enemy's Destroyers?	2243
					2300
				Reply: No (Reply via Kempenfelt)	
10.50	Commodore F via Kempenfelt	C-in-C	W/T	My position, course and speed South 17 knots, have been engaged by Enemy Cruisers. (This signal crossed 2243 from C-in-C)	2240
11.26	Captain D4	Garland	W/T	11DF is on your starboard beam	2315
11.30	SO 2LCS	Nottingham	FL	My wireless is shot away, answer calls for me and report the action	
11.38	SO 2LCS via Nottingham	C-in-C SO BCF	W/T	Urgent. Have engaged Enemy's Cruisers 10.15 p.m., bearing WSW (Received in Iron Duke 11.38 p.m.)	2240

the 'remainder which were near "Castor" . . . say they were so blinded by "Castor's" guns they could not see anything, and the others were so certain . . . that we were being fire on by our own ships that they decided not to fire their torpedoes'. Since *Castor* was drawing nearly all the enemy fire (one of her executive officers thought the Germans could not see the black-painted British destroyers), Hawksley regretted that a good opportunity for firing torpedoes was lost. Despite being under fire forward, *Castor* made good practice with her two after 6in guns until both sides turned away and lost touch.[50] She had been engaged with *Hamburg* and *Elbing*, which were at the rear of the IVSG. Among the hits made by *Castor* on *Hamburg*, one holed the after engine room and another struck a gun; three stokers and the whole gun crew were seriously injured. One British torpedo passed harmlessly underneath *Elbing*. In turning, *Castor* missed one of the boats of the second half-flotilla (led by *Kempenfelt*) by inches;[51] thus they must have been in close company even though they had no part in the action.

The Flotilla then proceeded South after the Battle Fleet, my [Hawksley's] object being to be within reach of the Fleet at daybreak should the Fleet have found the enemy and a Fleet action take place.[52]

Apart from one minor encounter with a few enemy destroyers soon after midnight, *Castor*, *Kempenfelt* and their fourteen *M*-class destroyers saw no more of the enemy.

While *Hamburg* and *Elbing* were still engaged with *Castor* and the 11DF, *Moltke* and *Seydlitz* cut close across the bows of the IVSG. The leading light cruiser, *Stettin*, was forced to reduce speed and, astern of her, *München*, *Frauenlob* and *Stuttgart* hauled out to port; these turns, apparently also followed by *Stettin*, brought them into contact with the 2LCS. Uncertain of the identity of the vessels they had sighted, the Germans flashed their challenge signals, which in this case were promptly answered by a heavy fire.[53] As the 2LCS had proceeded S, with *Southampton* leading *Dublin*, *Nottingham* and *Birmingham*, at about ten o'clock they may have heard and seen to starboard something of *Castor*'s action. Then, at 10.15, they sighted ships on their starboard beam heading SSE on a converging course at 1,500 yards. *Southampton* and *Dublin* both made out five vessels (*Southampton* thought they were a cruiser and four light cruisers) whereas *Nottingham* initially saw only one but identified her as one of the three-funnelled *Stettin* (*Königsberg*) class. *Southampton*'s officers were less certain but orders were given to flood

---

[50] *OD*, pp. 303–5. F&H, p. 351. *GFG&TMs*, pp. 51–2 and *ATFJ*, p. 11 both state that *Castor* and *Marne* fired one torpedo each and *Magic* two torpedoes but the times differ and for *Magic* are inconsistent with *Castor*'s despatch.
[51] Tarrant, pp. 192–3. F&H, p. 351.   [52] *OD*, p. 304.   [53] Tarrant, p. 193.

the starboard torpedo tube as a precaution. Both squadrons challenged almost simultaneously using their respective systems. According to the reports from the 2LCS, the Germans briefly flashed coloured lights; other reports,[54] while less than consistent, state that they showed strings of red and green lights, probably vertical. Almost together, the two sides decided that the other was hostile, switched on searchlights and opened fire at what was point-blank range, from 800 to 2,000 yards. To the British, it seemed that all their opponents turned on searchlights, but only *Southampton* and *Dublin* did the same; they then received the concentrated fire of the enemy, but *Nottingham* and *Birmingham* were able to make good practice largely undisturbed – though their bridge personnel were almost blinded each time the forecastle guns fired. The ships under fire, especially *Southampton* and *Dublin*, were hit at once and soon suffered severe casualties. In *Southampton*, many of the gun crews, poorly protected by their open-backed gun shields, were mown down by splinters. A small cordite fire aft was soon extinguished but flames as high as the fore-top erupted abaft the main-mast and between the second and third funnels. Those from between the funnels came from the central ammunition-hoist and *Southampton*'s officers feared that she might blow up at any moment. But prompt action both to prevent the flames spreading along the ammunition-passage and to close the hatches stopped flash reaching the magazines. Nonetheless, the effects of the burning cordite were terrible, though Stephen King-Hall could not bring himself to describe them.

The most dreadful cases were the 'burns' – but this subject cannot be written about.

Dublin too had a large fire between decks but this was also quickly extinguished.[55] *Southampton* received about twenty hits with twenty-nine killed and sixty wounded; *Dublin* had eighteen hits resulting in three killed (including the Navigating Officer) and twenty-seven wounded.[56]

The numbers of hits and casualties from gunfire were less serious in the IVSG. *Stettin* was hit twice; a splinter severing the steam-pipe to the siren put an end to her attempt to fire a torpedo and she turned away in the hope of drawing the British cruisers towards *Moltke* and *Seydlitz*. The ships at the rear also joined in the action, *Hamburg* being hit only once but the splinters killed ten men and wounded the captain and others on and near the fore-bridge, while *Elbing*'s single hit killed four and wounded fourteen. The intense

---

[54] *Cf. OD*, pp. 230, 232, 234, 303, 310, 320, 323, 365 and 380. F&H, pp. 131, 309 and 318. S&H, p. 316.

[55] *Southampton: OD*, pp. 176–8; Goodenough, p. 96; F&H, pp. 290–2; 'Etienne', pp. 148–55 (quotation p. 155). *Dublin: OD*, p. 181; F&H, p. 299. *Nottingham: OD*, Pl. 14; F&H, pp. 286–7. *Birmingham: OD*, p. 179.

[56] Campbell, pp. 340 and 390–2. *OD*, pp. 181–2.

gunnery exchange probably lasted for some five to ten minutes before both sides turned away and extinguished their searchlights.[57] At 10.21, *Southampton* fired the torpedo, set for high speed, that had been readied in her starboard tube, her target 'a group of hostile searchlights, which were the only things visible'.[58] Just as the two sides were separating, the 21in torpedo found the old *Frauenlob*. She quickly heeled over and then capsized, with the loss of her captain, eleven officers and 308 men. *Stuttgart*, her next astern, only just managed to avoid her by hauling out to starboard and, having lost touch with the IVSG, joined up with the IBS. *Hamburg* was also forced off station when *Moltke* crossed her bows in the middle of the engagement, yet the battlecruiser gave no assistance to the IVSG. After turning away, *Stettin* and *München* took no further part in the fighting but the next encounter shows that *Hamburg, Elbing* and also *Rostock* fell back, like *Stuttgart*, to positions near the IBS in the German van.[59]

The 2LCS turned away by altering course together to port, after which *Southampton* resumed the course S and 'remained astern and on the starboard quarter of the centre of the battle fleet during the night, as it was not known what protection they had against torpedo attack'. Because her wireless had been shot away, Goodenough's report of the action did not reach the C-in-C *via Nottingham* until 11.38. According to *Nottingham*'s navigating officer, *Dublin* turned further away than the others, by eight points; either then or at 11.00, she lost touch with the rest of the squadron. Without a navigating officer and hampered by a suspect compass and badly damaged charts, dead-reckoning was impossible; eventually she met up by chance with the battlefleet at 8.05am the next morning. *Nottingham* was able to close up and follow *Southampton*. But *Birmingham*, having turned away Eastwards, found herself approaching the 5BS and was obliged to turn Northwards, thereby losing touch with her consorts. She then took station on the starboard quarter of the 5BS until, at daybreak, she sighted *Southampton* and *Nottingham* on her starboard bow and rejoined.[60]

The 4DF dismembered

The 4DF, having turned to follow the British battle squadrons Southwards, did not encounter the main enemy force until almost 11.30, about an hour after the 11DF and 2LCS had broken off their engagements with the IVSG. The delay was probably due to three factors, though their relative importance remains unclear: the 4DF turned S later than the 11DF and also took a position further to

---

[57] Tarrant, p. 194. *OD*, pp. 176–7. Goodenough, p. 96. F&H, pp. 287, 291, 297 and 299.
[58] F&H, p. 290. Also *OD*, p. 178; *GFG&TMs*, p. 51; *ATFJ*, p. 12.
[59] Tarrant, p. 194. S&H, p. 303.   [60] *OD*, pp. 177, 179 and 181–3. F&H, pp. 287–8 and 301.

Table 9.12. *4DF signals 11.01pm–2.00am*

Time of despatch	From	To	System	Message	Time of origin
pm, 31 May					
11.01	Captain D4	Broke	FL	Give me manoeuvring room. You have lights on fore bridge and forecastle	2252
11.22	Unity	Fortune	W/T	Switch off stern light	
11.26	Captain D4	Garland	W/T	11DF is on your starboard beam	2315
11.47	Ambuscade	Captain D4	W/T	Have fired two torpedoes and heard one explosion (Via Indomitable to SO BCF)	2342
am, 1 June					
0.10	Achates	Commodore F		2nd Division of 4DF still steering South, is this correct? Reply: Yes	0007 0031
0.30	Contest	Achates	W/T	Have lost 1st Division, can only steam 20 knots. Request instructions	0016
0.33	Achates	Commodore F	W/T	Am being chased to the eastward	0031
0.42	Garland	Commodore F	W/T	I am at present steering S. What shall I steer?	0030
0.56	Commodore F	4DF and 12DF	W/T	My course and speed are S, 18 knots	0045
2.00	Ambuscade	Commodore F	W/T	Have expended all torpedoes. I am alone. Position 0200, 56°0 N, 6°08E doubtful, request instructions	0155

the Eastward; and the IVSG had been well ahead of their battlefleet. As the 4DF's course converged on that of the German battlefleet, the 1st Half Flotilla was led by Wintour in *Tipperary* followed by *Spitfire, Sparrowhawk, Garland* and *Contest*; astern, the 2nd Half Flotilla was in the order *Broke, Achates, Ambuscade, Ardent, Fortune, Porpoise* and *Unity*.[61] The majority of their despatches agree that unknown vessels were first seen on the starboard beam or quarter at or just before 11.30.[62] They were thought to be light cruisers, mainly with three funnels, but, as one of her officers recalled 'we had absolutely no idea of where the enemy were, and only a very vague idea of the position of our own ships'; other despatches make the same point. The vessels were in fact the four German light cruisers that had rejoined their battle line and

---

[61] *OD*, pp. 308, 309 and 328.
[62] Earlier times were reported by *Spitfire* and *Broke*, but both would soon be heavily damaged.

Table 9.13. *German signals 10.34pm–1.30am*

Time of receipt	From	To	System	Message	Time of origin
pm, 31 May					
10.34	C-in-C	Fleet		Battle fleet's course SEbyS	2232
	C-in-C	Westfalen		Course SE¾S for Horns Reef light ship	2302
11.52	S32	C-in-C Leader of Torpedo Boats		070α. Am disabled	2340
am, 1 June					
0.09	König	C-in-C		Rostock disabled – SO IIIBS	
	Leader of Torpedo Boats	IIITF		Send one boat to Rostock	
	Elbing	IIITF	Visual	This is Elbing; am helpless. Please come alongside	
0.32	Rostock	C-in-C		Hit by torpedo in 055α. Main W/T installation disabled; can steam 17 knots	0032
0.47	S54 [IIITF]	C-in-C		Rostock hit by a torpedo. Speed 15 knots. Position at 2.00 [*sic*] 077α – Leader of Torpedo Boats	0037
1.05	SO IIITF	Regensburg		Elbing is just able to keep afloat. Captain requests decision – IIITF	0105
	Nassau	C-in-C		One cruiser with 4 funnels destroyed by gunfire, one destroyer sunk by ramming. Have taken station astern of IIBS. Maximum speed 15 knots	0130

were now on its port side. Wintour's 11.26 signal suggests that the German vessels may have been mistaken in *Tipperary* for the 11DF (though, according to an unsubstantiated report from *Sparrowhawk*, Wintour thought they were the 1LCS). The 4DF's despatches disagree on whether *Tipperary* made the challenge, but they accept that the German ships were first to turn on their searchlights and to open fire. The leading British boats must have been visible from the start from the IBS; *Westfalen* illuminated *Tipperary* and poured in no less than ninety-two rounds of 5.9in and forty-five rounds of 3.5in at 1,500–2,000 yards, though probably not all these were aimed at the British leader; to *Tipperary*'s crew, it seemed that she was hit by only four salvos before she was given up as done for. Wintour was probably killed by the first salvo, which struck near the bridge. A serious fire blazed up in the forward coal bunker but exploding ready-use ammunition frustrated all attempts to control it. There were very heavy casualties amidships, and hits in the engine room ruptured a main steam pipe and brought her to a halt; despite everything, the after gun kept firing until enveloped in escaping steam. *Tipperary*'s only surviving executive officer, who was in charge aft, stated that she fired both starboard torpedoes but the range was so short that they ran under the target.[63]

Nassau and *Rheinland* joined *Westfalen* in firing at *Tipperary*, while *Spitfire* and *Sparrowhawk* were also illuminated and *Spitfire* was hit several times. But this left most of the 4DF free to direct their fire at the battleships' searchlights, putting many out of action; men were killed and wounded in all three battleships, *Westfalen*'s Captain Redlich being among the wounded, though he remained in command. Astern of the blazing *Tipperary*, the remaining boats of the 1st Half Flotilla and *Broke* turned away, firing torpedoes as they did so at ranges of about 1,000 yards. *Spitfire*'s first of two torpedoes was aimed at a cruiser with four very tall funnels, which she claimed to have hit. *Sparrowhawk, Garland, Contest* and *Broke* fired one torpedo each, the last three at cruisers. Even after *Tipperary* had been set alight, the Captain and navigating officer of *Broke* remained convinced that her assailants were British; the starboard after torpedo was fired only when a stray searchlight beam allowed them to identify the ships as German.[64]

The German light cruisers on the port side of the van battleships were *Elbing, Stuttgart* and *Hamburg* of the IVSG, and *Rostock* with the destroyer *S32* astern of her. They also fired at the 4DF but they were in a dangerous position from which they could not easily turn away. The torpedoes and gunfire from the British line also threatened the battleships and *Westfalen* turned away eight points to starboard. This gave the light cruisers the opportunity, though a perilous one, to follow and escape between the battleships. *Elbing*, in trying to pass ahead of *Posen*, was hindered by *Stuttgart* and, in the confusion, the battleship, the fourth in line, struck *Elbing* on the starboard quarter. Holed below the waterline, both *Elbing*'s engine rooms flooded; unable to manoeuvre and with an 18° list, she drifted helplessly down the German line on the disengaged (starboard) side. *S32* was also stopped after one of two shell hits cut her main steam pipe. *Rostock* was struck by two shells but she was then crippled by a torpedo that exploded against her port side.

---

[63] *CAWFS 1906–21*, pp. 77–8 for *Tipperary*'s mixed coal/oil firing but her reports imply that she had two single torpedo tubes per side, not two twin tubes.

[64] *Tipperary: OD*, p. 327; F&H, pp. 339–41. *Spitfire: OD*, pp. 306–7 and 329; F&H, 320–1. *Sparrowhawk: OD*, pp. 320–1; F&H, 329–30. *Garland: OD*, p. 314; F&H, pp. 316–17. *Contest: OD*, p. 308. *Broke: OD*, p. 323; F&H, pp. 307–8; S&H, pp. 311–12. *GOA*, pp. 177–8. Rahn, p. 184 for Redlich's criticisms of the British attacks.

Two boiler rooms and five bunkers were flooded and, even after some compartments had been pumped out, 930 tons of water remained; she could only follow the fleet slowly and with frequent stops. Although several of the 4DF claimed torpedo hits, *Rostock*'s profile matched only *Spitfire*'s target description, so the latter probably made what would prove to be the only torpedo hit by the 4DF.[65]

With *Tipperary* out of action, leadership of the 4DF devolved on Commander Walter Allen of *Broke*. She had turned away SE as she fired her torpedo but then resumed the course S, probably sooner than the others since she could see none of them ahead. *Sparrowhawk* lost sight of *Spitfire* but then found *Broke* and took station astern, while *Garland, Contest* and *Achates* were not far behind. Perhaps, as claimed by *Broke*'s navigating officer, Allen intended to collect the flotilla for another attack, but contact with the enemy was renewed too soon for anything to be organised. About five minutes after turning S, *Broke* sighted a large ship well before her starboard beam steaming about SSW, which suggests that this was before the German van had resumed its SE'ly course. Still hesitant, Allen ordered the challenge to be made; in response, the *Westfalen* switched on in quick succession her recognition lights (green, or green and red) and her searchlights and at once opened fire. From 11.40 she fired thirteen rounds each of 6in and 3.5in, while *Rheinland* joined in before engaging *Sparrowhawk*; both battleships also turned away briefly to Westward. The two British boats began to turn away preparatory to firing torpedoes: but *Broke*'s sights had not come on when she received a hit in the lower bridge that killed the quartermaster and telegraph man, shattered the wheel- and engine-room telegraphs and jammed the helm hard-a-starboard. *Broke* swung rapidly to port and drove straight into *Sparrowhawk*, cutting half-way into the ship just before the bridge. The impact hurled her sub-lieutenant and several of her ratings onto *Broke*'s forecastle, where, later, twenty-three of *Sparrowhawk*'s crew were found, though the officer scrambled back aboard his own ship. Fortunately, the enemy had ceased firing, perhaps because both vessels were enveloped in escaping steam. *Garland*, which had already had one very close encounter with *Sparrowhawk*, narrowly missed the two destroyers while they were locked together. But *Contest* sliced off some five feet of *Sparrowhawk*'s stern and, in doing so, jammed the rudder hard-a-port. After *Broke*'s engines had been stopped and her after steering position connected up, she pulled clear. Neither boat was in a sinking condition but, although *Sparrowhawk*'s casualties were modest (in all, six killed) she was in a bad way; the bridge, mast and foremost

---

[65] Scheer's despatch, *OD*, p. 597 and German Plan VII. *GOA*, pp. 171–81 and Tarrant, pp. 198–201, though both imply that *Rostock* passed twice through the German line (improbable) and that she was not torpedoed until the second British attack.

funnel had gone over the side and the whole forward part of the hull was barely attached (trapped within it, the two ship's dogs could be heard howling but it was impossible to get them out). Her wireless was altogether out of action and an improvised installation refused to work. The jammed rudder was immovable and, despite attempts to steer with the engines while going astern, she could make no headway. However, *Broke* had suffered severe casualties (forty-seven killed, including the surgeon, and thirty-six wounded) but, although the forward part was flooded, the foremost engine-room bulkhead held and she could still make 10 knots. Her wireless too was out of action, so neither boat can be criticised for not reporting their experiences. The same cannot be said for the still undamaged boats of the flotilla, whose wireless signals failed to report that the 4DF was in action with battleships.[66]

After her first attack, *Spitfire* intended to reload one tube with the spare torpedo that was kept on deck.[67] She also continued firing at the German searchlights to distract their fire away from the fiercely burning *Tipperary*. *Spitfire*'s course took her close to the next British flotilla to the Eastward (as we shall see, probably still the 13DF led by *Champion*) and, apparently to reveal herself as friendly, she switched on her lights for a few seconds before turning South again. Both her gunfire and her lights attracted German salvos; injuries to her torpedo ratings and the wrecking of her torpedo davit ended her attempts to reload. Even so, she turned back to fire her guns at an enemy ship that still had a searchlight on *Tipperary*. As *Spitfire* closed, she sighted two more of the enemy steering SE'wards before the nearer turned towards her with the clear intention of ramming; despite *Spitfire*'s avoiding efforts, at about 11.40 the two ships collided port-bow to port-bow. *Spitfire* described all three enemy ships as cruisers and presumed that the ship that had rammed her, which appeared to have three funnels and two boat cranes, belonged to the elderly *Freya* class. In fact, she had crashed into the *Nassau*. As *Spitfire* scraped down her port side, *Nassau* could not depress her guns sufficiently to hit but the blast demolished the destroyer's bridge, searchlight platform, mast and foremost funnel. *Nassau* left 20 feet of her side plating on *Spitfire*'s forecastle; until it could be stopped, the resulting hole above the waterline reduced the battleship's speed to 15 knots and she began to drop astern down the port side of the German line. Sixty feet of *Spitfire*'s plating was torn away from the stem aft but there was little flooding at lower levels and the third bulkhead held. Three of her four boilers remained serviceable and she could

---

[66] *Broke: OD*, pp. 323–4; F&H, pp. 308–12. *Sparrowhawk: OD*, p. 321; F&H, 330–5. Also *OD*, pp. 308–9 and 314; F&H, pp. 317; Tarrant, pp. 200–1 and *GOA*, p. 180.

[67] The despatches of *Ambuscade*, *Porpoise* and *Spitfire* (*OD*, pp. 309–10, 312 and 329) state clearly that each had only one spare torpedo *cf. CAWFS 1906–21*, p. 75 which lists the *Acasta* class with two spares.

still make six knots. But her lights and other electric circuits were short-circuited, so fire-fighting in the dark was hazardous and, with the mast down, it proved impossible to rig up a temporary wireless installation. She managed to get clear of the fighting and, despite the extensive damage, her total casualties were not heavy – six killed and twenty wounded.[68] It is probable that *Spitfire*'s encounter with *Nassau* occurred after *Broke* and *Sparrowhawk* collided; one of *Garland*'s officers recalled that his ship, after avoiding the two boats while they were still interlocked, followed *Spitfire* back towards *Tipperary* before *Garland* was driven off by enemy fire.[69] In addition, the enemy courses reported by *Broke* and *Spitfire* suggest that the latter's encounter was the later one.

It appears that, for a time, *Garland* made off Eastwards and Southwards, as did *Ambuscade* (she probably fired two torpedoes as she turned away). After about ten minutes, *Garland* found the remnant of the 2nd Half Flotilla and took station between *Fortune* and *Porpoise*, with *Ambuscade* and *Ardent* ahead of them. *Ambuscade* was perhaps still following *Achates*. But *Achates*, after forming the impression that British cruisers were in action between her and the German line, cancelled a torpedo firing order and she did not participate in the next attack. Just on midnight, *Westfalen* turned away once more to allow *Stuttgart* and *Hamburg* to pass ahead of her. Then, as the 4DF's course S converged once again on the IBS, the flotilla sighted four large enemy ships to starboard. As before, the German ships switched on green and red recognition lights, which were followed at once by a blaze of searchlights and intense fire. *Fortune*'s recognition number 30 painted on her bows could be clearly seen from *Westfalen*; in 28 seconds, the battleship fired seven rounds of 5.9in and eight of 3.5in, enough to leave *Fortune* burning fiercely and apparently sinking, though she was seen from *Ardent* still gallantly firing her guns. Her actual foundering seems to have gone unrecorded and, while some of her crew were rescued later, sixty-seven of her crew were lost. *Rheinland, Posen, Oldenburg* and *Helgoland* also fired at the 4DF at ranges from 1,700 to 900 yards, while torpedoes were seen from the first two. *Porpoise* had to haul out to clear the crippled *Fortune* but the smoke and steam pouring from the latter provided some screening from the enemy searchlights. Even so, *Porpoise* received a hit that burst the air chamber of her spare torpedo, the explosion severing her main steam pipe. Hits also destroyed her forebridge wheel and telegraphs but, steering from her after position, she was able to withdraw NbyW. As the flotilla turned away, *Ambuscade, Ardent* and *Garland* each fired a torpedo but their torpedoes

---

[68] *OD*, pp. 306–7 and 329–30. F&H, pp. 322–5. Tarrant, pp. 198–200 and 203, though it is unlikely that *Spitfire* alone was responsible for the damage to the three leading German battleships.
[69] F&H, pp. 317–18.

were seen and avoided. British gunnery was more successful; a shell exploding in *Oldenburg*'s fore upper searchlight caused many casualties in the vicinity of the bridge and she was heading for a collision until her wounded Captain seized the wheel.

Achates and *Ambuscade* got away to the Eastward, although they lost touch at about 0.30am; both worked their way round the enemy rear to resume a course S but only *Ambuscade* found *Castor*, at 3am. *Garland* withdrew under fire and, after searching for about half an hour, she encountered *Contest* proceeding at 20 knots, throwing up an immense sheet of spray from her damaged bows; *Contest* then formed astern of *Garland* for the remainder of the night. *Ardent* made the fateful decision to turn S yet again in the hope of picking up *Ambuscade*. Instead, she found herself approaching the battleships of the German van as they crossed her bows from starboard to port. It was too late to get away but she fired a torpedo at *Westfalen*, though without result. She had already been seen from the battleship, her number 78 showing up clearly in the searchlight beams. In 4 minutes, 20 seconds, *Westfalen* fired twenty-two rounds of 5.9in and eighteen rounds of 3.5in, reducing *Ardent* to an utter wreck. Her leading telegraphist suggested making a report but shortly afterwards, the enemy opened fire again at point-blank range and Lieutenant-Commander Arthur Marsden ordered the survivors to save themselves. Although about forty men jumped overboard, only Marsden and two others survived the five hours in the water before rescue came, though one of the men died later.[70]

With *Ardent* and *Fortune* sunk and the rest scattered, the dismemberment of the 4DF was complete, though some would see further action. *Tipperary* continued to burn fiercely and both she and *Sparrowhawk* close by were immobilised. *Spitfire*, despite her battered state, and *Achates* returned to harbour on their own while *Porpoise* would later meet *Garland* and *Contest* (*Ambuscade* remained with the 11DF). *Unity*, the rear boat, had a couple of ineffectual encounters with the enemy but by midnight she had lost sight of the 4DF and found herself following another British flotilla; only at daylight did she find that they were a group led by *Lydiard* and the 9DF.[71]

The three concerted attacks by the 4DF (without *Unity*) were all made on similar converging courses at short ranges, so they were easy targets for the secondary armaments of the IBS. However, in the first attack, because the German ships had concentrated mainly on *Tipperary*, many of the other destroyers were able to fire torpedoes with little hindrance. Although no

[70] *OD*, pp. 309–12 and 314–15. F&H, pp. 317–19 and 344–7. Campbell, p. 289. *GFG&TMs*, p. 51 and *ATFJ*, p. 12. *GOA*, pp. 182–5. Tarrant, pp. 201–5. Corbett, p. 422.
[71] *OD*, pp. 309, 312–13 and 330. F&H, pp. 326–8.

battleships were hit, *Rostock* was seriously damaged and, in the resultant confusion in the German line, *Elbing* was rammed. But, forewarned, the Germans were ready for the next attacks. The second was quickly disrupted as *Broke* was badly hit and she and *Contest* careered into *Sparrowhawk*. With both leaders already out of action, the third attack seems to have been more a collective than a coordinated effort, in which *Fortune* was sunk and *Porpoise* damaged. Thus neither attack resulted in any further torpedo hits, though, in both the first and third attacks, gunfire from the 4DF caused significant German casualties.

The end of *Black Prince*

After her brush with *Spitfire*, *Nassau* had been dropping astern down the port side of the German line. Shortly after midnight, both she and *Thüringen* (now sixth in the line) sighted a ship with four funnels, 1,100 yards on the port bow. The stranger did not reply to the challenge and turned sharply away, but the German searchlights had already revealed her as a British armoured cruiser. She was the *Black Prince*, which, after taking up her deployment position protecting the British rear, now blundered into the centre of the High Seas Fleet. *Thüringen* opened at once with her secondary armament, firing twenty-seven 5.9in and twenty 3.5in shells that raked the target from the stern forward. As flames roared upwards to the height of the masts, between 0.07 and 0.15am *Ostfriesland*, *Nassau* and *Friedrich der Grosse* joined in until *Black Prince* was reduced to a mass of glowing wreckage, drifting down the German line until she vanished in a tremendous explosion. *Nassau* had to turn inwards to avoid her and only narrowly avoided a collision with *Kaiserin* by going full astern; *Nassau* then rejoined the line in a position between *Hessen* and the rear ship, *Hannover*.[72]

As *Black Prince* came under fire, she may have been sighted from *Achates*. After the destruction of *Spitfire*'s forebridge, a good part of the ship's company had assembled aft. Suddenly, they sighted on their starboard quarter a large ship on fire steering straight for the stern. This ship missed them by a few feet but was so close that:

the very crackling and heat of the flames could be heard and felt. She was a mass of fire from foremast to mainmast, on deck and between decks . . . She appeared to us to be a battle cruiser as her funnels were so far apart, but afterwards it transpired that quite possibly she was the unfortunate *Black Prince* with her two centre funnels shot away.

Soon afterwards, about midnight, there came an explosion from the direction in which she had gone.[73]

---

[72] *GOA*, pp. 183–4. Tarrant, p. 203.

[73] F&H, p. 326, also *OD*, pp. 306–7 and 330. In her despatches, *Spitfire* described the burning ship as a battlecruiser of the *Moltke* type with two widely spaced funnels.

The loss of *Turbulent*

As *Tipperary* led the 4DF into action, three more British flotillas – the 13DF, 9DF and 12DF – were some two miles to the Eastward, steering South in columns disposed as little as one cable apart.[74] Thus they were well positioned to mount further attacks on the High Seas Fleet as it pressed on towards Horns Reef. Closest to the enemy was the newly formed 13DF led by Captain (D) James Farie in *Champion*, now reduced to seven of its own boats plus *Termagant* and *Turbulent*. Next to port came *Lydiard* (Commander Malcolm Goldsmith) leading the 9DF – three more *L*-class boats and *Morris* (at about 10pm, Goldsmith had ordered *Moorsom*, which was short of oil due to earlier damage to her tanks, to return to base).[75] The most Easterly flotilla was the 12DF, a strong and undamaged formation comprising two leaders, *Faulknor* (Captain (D) Anselan Stirling) and *Marksman*, and thirteen *M*-class destroyers. At 0.04am, Stirling informed Commodore (F) that the 1BS was five miles to the South – though the actual distance to *Marlborough*'s subdivision was probably less. Both the 13DF and the 12DF, but not, apparently, the 9DF, had seen something of the actions of the 11DF and the 2LCS, though certain reported times and details are problematic; the light cruiser reported by *Faulknor* as crashing through the 12DF was perhaps *Dublin*.[76]

Table 9.14. *British destroyer signals 0.04–0.56am*

Time of despatch	From	To	System	Message	Time of origin
am, 1 June					
0.04	Captain D12	Commodore F	FL	1BS is South five miles. Am I to follow you or steer South after fleet?	2350 0015
				Reply: Keep in touch with fleet	
0.05	Captain D12	12DF	FL	Alter course in succession to ESE	
0.16	Captain D12	12DF	FL	Admiral intends to proceed at 17 knots	
				Remarks: 0.16. Enemy Cruiser on either bow opened fire. Flotilla spread	
0.30	Captain D12	Commodore F	W/T	My course and speed at 0.15, S, 17 knots	0017
0.56	Commodore F	4DF and 12DF	W/T	My course and speed are S, 18 knots	0045

[74] *OD*, Pl. 22 and pp. 259 and 256 (*Liberty* misidentified the flotilla to port as the 11DF). Oram, p. 170.
[75] *OD*, pp. 255 and 260.
[76] *OD*, pp. 230, 234, 241, 263 and 339. F&H, pp. 355 and (for *Faulknor*) 362–3.

The heavy firing at the 4DF that began at 11.30pm was seen from all three flotillas, from the 13DF and 9DF on or abaft their starboard beam. The 12DF's 1st Division observed (but failed to report) 'one of our flotillas attack enemy Battle fleet on our starboard bow'. According to Farie:

About 11.30 p.m. heavy firing was opened on our starboard beam, apparently at some of our Destroyers between the 13th Flotilla and the enemy. I hauled out to eastward as I was unable to attack with any of our own Flotilla, our own forces being between me and the Enemy. I then resumed course South ... Destroyers of the 13th Flotilla, with the exception of H.M.S. 'Obdurate' and H.M.S. 'Moresby', lost touch with me.

From *Lydiard*, it seemed to Goldsmith that:

Fire was opened on us by a line of large ships which we took to be our own ... 'Champion' suddenly increased to high speed and disappeared to starboard [*sic*]. I continued S.

However, his diagram for 11.30 shows *Champion* veering away to port to SE at 25 knots and this is borne out by Stirling's despatch.

At 11.30 p.m. – Being forced off course, to port, by one of our own Flotillas led by a cruiser (believed to be 'Champion'), increased to 20 knots, course S.S.E. Cruiser kept pressing us to port and eventually our course was N.E. Reduced to 15 knots to let cruiser and destroyers pass ahead ...
   At 12.15 a.m. – Strange Flotilla having passed ahead, altered course to South, speed 17 knots. These alterations of course were estimated to have put us 5 [miles] to east of our original position and to have dropped us 10 [miles] astern of Fleet.

At 11.40pm, *Nerissa* of the 13DF:

Observed firing and searchlights abaft starboard beam, a ship apparently attacked by destroyers, many salvoes fell between 'Nerissa' and 'Moresby', who was next ahead.
   11.45. Lost touch with 'Moresby' and remained in company with 'Lydiard'.[77]

Goldsmith, who also thought he was under fire, albeit from his own fleet, had continued S. Whereas Farie had run far to the Eastward while pushing the 12DF well away from the enemy fleet. Thus he had broken up the concentration of flotillas that were already in sight of the German battlefleet – though only *Champion* and *Nerissa* seem to have recognised them as such. And Farie had left those destroyers still in touch with the enemy without direction from a senior officer.

In his despatch, Goldsmith described himself as 'in nominal command' of the destroyers detached from the Harwich Force. Now he was responsible for not only the five boats of the 9DF but the seven members of the 13DF left behind by *Champion*, though it is uncertain how closely the latter were following him. Further, according to Goldsmith's despatch, he was not even

---

[77] Quotations respectively from *OD*, pp. 339, 224–5, 255, 332 and 235. Also *OD*, Pl. 22.

aware of the line of stragglers astern until 6am the following morning, since they were hidden from him until the haze cleared; also *Nicator* apparently did not realise until daylight that *Champion* was no longer in company. The exact order of the destroyers following *Lydiard* is uncertain, though *Laurel* was astern of *Morris* at the rear of the 9DF, while subsequent events suggest that they were followed by *Nerissa, Termagant, Nicator, Narborough, Pelican, Petard* and *Turbulent* in that order.

After *Champion* disappeared, *Lydiard* 'continued S. and eventually turned S. W. and W. to get on other side of the big ships – who still spasmodically opened fire towards us'.[78] The 9DF reached its objective without incident. If Goldsmith or any of its other commanders realised that they had crossed ahead of the enemy van, and had therefore been in an ideal position to mount a torpedo attack from ahead, they did not say so in their despatches. In the 13DF, *Narborough* had been unable to make out whether the vessels firing heavily on the starboard beam were hostile. But *Nicator* assumed that they were enemy battleships or cruisers being attacked by destroyers and, by about 0.15am, they were only ¾ mile from her. At about 0.30, the 13DF also altered course to SW. As they did so, it appeared from *Narborough* that a large vessel had crossed the rear of the flotilla from starboard to port. During the First Watch (8pm to midnight) there had been a British armoured cruiser, apparently of the *Warrior* class, on her starboard quarter; this can only have been *Black Prince*. Now *Narborough* assumed that they had sighted either this same vessel or a British light cruiser. But, when about 1,000 yards on the starboard quarter, the stranger showed red and green recognition lights for a few seconds before switching on searchlights and opening a heavy fire at the rear of the flotilla. *Pelican* saw two ships on her starboard quarter and took them to be British light cruisers; when the red and green recognition lights were followed by the glare of searchlights, a beam lighted briefly on *Pelican*'s stern before swinging aft towards *Petard* and *Turbulent*. Though *Pelican* was no longer illuminated and she still had a full complement of four torpedoes, her commanding officer decided that his position was unfavourable for attack, held his course and soon lost sight of what were now clearly enemy vessels. *Nicator* had only one torpedo remaining but *Narborough* had fired none of hers; yet, despite the fire at the two rear destroyers, both pushed on and soon lost sight of the enemy.[79]

Petard's Lieutenant-Commander Evelyn Thomson was in no doubt that he was in the presence of the enemy.

At 12.15 a.m. course was altered to S.W. by W., and about ten minutes later the line crossed ahead of a division of German Battleships. I sighted the leading Battleship about

[78] *OD*, pp. 254–5 (*Lydiard*), 256 (*Laurel* under *Champion*'s orders), 235 (*Nerissa*) and 241 (*Nicator*).

[79] *OD*, pp. 230 (*Narborough*), 234 (*Pelican*) and 241 (*Nicator*) and also, for 13DF course, pp. 232, 234–5 and 263.

six points on my starboard bow, steering S.E. at about 400 to 500 yards. This ship switched on recognition lights, consisting of two red over one white [*sic*] light ... As 'Petard' had no torpedoes left, I could not attack ... I passed about 200 yards ahead ... As soon as we were clear of her stem, she illuminated us with searchlights, and we came under a heavy fire from her and the next ship in the line.

Petard's casualties were nine killed and six wounded but would have been fewer had her surgeon-probationer not been killed by a hit on her after gun. Despite a considerable oil fire fed from a burst pipe, she was able to get away to rejoin Goldsmith at daylight.[80]

From the German line, at 0.45am the second battleship *Rheinland* sighted a destroyer to starboard and turned away to port; she must have been one of the British boats that had already crossed ahead (this and subsequent German times for this encounter are somewhat later than those in the British reports). Twenty minutes later, *Westfalen* saw two large destroyers on her port bow; fearing that they would attack from both sides, Captain Redlich steered straight for them. His starboard battery fired three salvos (in all thirteen rounds of 5.9in and six of 3.5in) at the leading destroyer, which appeared to bear the number '606' – *Petard*'s pendant number was 'G66'. But the boat to port, apparently to avoid being rammed, turned away onto a parallel course. By altering course one point to starboard, *Westfalen* brought all her port guns to bear; after she had fired twenty-nine 5.9in and sixteen 3.5in, one of *Turbulent*'s boilers was seen to explode. Still afloat, she was overtaken by the German line and received a second cannonade from *Thüringen* before capsizing. She finally sank after *V71*, at the German rear with *Regensburg*, fired two torpedoes at her (the first ran too deep); *V71* and *V73* picked up thirteen survivors but ninety-six of *Turbulent*'s crew were killed.[81]

The opportunity missed by the British destroyers, whether knowingly or not, is captured in the rueful comment of *Petard*'s Thomson.

If only 'Petard' had had some torpedoes left, I am certain a successful torpedo attack could easily have been made.

However, the full consequences were apparently not recognised even in those boats that realised that they had crossed ahead of the German battlefleet; an officer of *Nicator* recalled:

We saw three or four big ships, obviously German [but] we hardly realised what was taking place, and it somehow did not strike us that this was the German fleet breaking through the line.[82]

[80] *OD*, pp. 232–3 (quotation). F&H, pp. 354–6. Campbell, p. 340.
[81] *GOA*, p. 191. Tarrant, pp. 211 and 213. Campbell, pp. 293 and 338. Unusually, *Westfalen* misrecorded the second destroyer's number as '27'. 'H27' was the pendant number of *Porpoise* (damaged earlier) though, like her sister *Spitfire* (see F&H, p. 328), the prefix letter was probably omitted. *Turbulent*'s pendant number was 'G42': www.dreadnoughtproject.org/.
[82] *OD*, p. 233 (*Petard*) and F&H, p. 356 (*Nicator*).

Yet none of the destroyers saw fit to make a report. Many of the 13DF may have assumed, like *Nicator*, that *Champion* was still in the lead and responsible for reporting: but Goldsmith's silence seems inexcusable. Even if he believed initially that the big ships in sight were British, he must at least have suspected that they were hostile as they continued firing at the British destroyers, especially those in the rear, and he should have reported accordingly.

The general situation was now that no British ships lay close to the course SEbyS of the High Seas Fleet for Horns Reef. Apart from the 12DF and *Champion*'s small group to the NE'ward, all other British forces were SW'ward of the German advance, mostly heading S. But, before following the two fleets as they moved further apart on these divergent courses, we must look back to review what little information reached Jellicoe about the enemy's movements and his encounters with British light forces.

Enemy sightings and reports

We should begin by asking what had actually been seen from the British battlefleet of the actions astern. The 2BS, forming the most Westerly column, saw least of the night fighting. *Monarch* (sixth in line) seems to have observed the 11DF in action on her starboard quarter, though not, as she supposed, against a division of battleships. Later, *Conqueror* saw a ship on her port quarter illuminated by four others and burning end-to-end before flaring up;[83] she probably witnessed the last moments of *Black Prince*. At about 10.30pm, a large enemy cruiser was sighted from the two rear ships of the squadron, *Thunderer* and, 2½ cables further astern, *Boadicea*; from the light cruiser, the enemy bore about two points abaft the starboard beam. After *Moltke* and *Seydlitz* had barged across the bows of the IVSG, *Seydlitz* could no longer maintain *Moltke*'s 22 knots and lost sight of the latter's shaded stern light; the two then proceeded independently. In seeking a way past the British fleet, *Moltke* approached the 2BS from to starboard and was seen to challenge three times with red and green lights before turning off. She was only in sight from *Boadicea* for about 30 seconds, insufficient time to execute the order to fire the starboard torpedo. In *Thunderer*, Captain James Ferguson had other concerns.

Fire was not opened as it was considered inadvisable to show up battlefleet unless obvious attack was intended.[84]

At 10.50, *Boadicea* probably saw the burning *Southampton* and her attackers about two miles astern. The light cruiser *Active* had also taken station for the night at the rear of the 2BS but she did not see *Moltke*. She reported two actions: at about 10.15

---

[83] *OD*, p. 374. F&H, p. 201.
[84] Ferguson made the unsubstantiated claim that the enemy cruiser was then attacked hotly by British destroyers.

Table 9.15. *British enemy reports 9.52pm–1.00am*

Time of despatch	From	To	System	Message	Time of origin
pm, 31 May					
9.52	Active	Boadicea	FL	I propose to take station astern of you. Reply: Right	
10.12	Benbow			Remarks: Firing commenced starboard beam	
10.40	Boadicea	Thunderer	FL	Enemy's ships on starboard beam	
10.40	Boadicea			Remarks: Sighted Enemy's Cruisers showing four red and four green lights horizontal. Shown three times	
10.45	Benbow			Remarks: Heavy firing on starboard quarter	
11.30	Minotaur			Remarks: Observed flashes port quarter, apparently gun fire	
11.30	Birmingham	C-in-C SO BCF	W/T	Urgent. Priority. Battle Cruisers, unknown number, probably hostile, in sight NE, course S. My position 56°26 N, 5°42E	2330
11.34	Benbow			Remarks: Firing reported astern and on port quarter	
11.39	Benbow			Remarks: Firing port quarter	
11.45	Benbow			Remarks: Firing port quarter (long distance)	
am, 1 June					
0.05	Superb			Remarks: Observed firing astern from 0.05 to 0.15, also 0.30 large flare astern and firing	
1.00	Fearless			Remarks: Vessel blown up on starboard quarter	

just abaft the starboard beam some three miles distant; and at 'about 11.0 p.m.' with a four-funnelled enemy cruiser that seemed to sink, which could have been either *Southampton* or *Rostock. Active*'s Captain Percy Withers reported:

Fire was not opened, as there were doubts as to which were hostile ships, in addition to which I did not feel justified in indicating the position of the Battle Fleet.[85]

After her first meeting with the 2BS, *Moltke* seems to have found them blocking her way on two or three further occasions, though they did not see her again. She was forced to turn S for a time but, after her final encounter at 0.30am, she was able to close the German battlefleet.[86]

[85] *OD*, pp. 114 and 380 (*Boadicea*), 302 (*Active*) and 376 (*Thunderer*).
[86] *GOA*, pp. 173–5 but *cf.* Tarrant, pp. 193–5 for *Moltke*'s passing ahead of the Grand Fleet. GMS, 1.27am.

Iron Duke led the 4BS which formed the centre column. The despatch of Captain Dreyer noted only 'the proximity of Heavy Enemy's Ships' but other reports from the flagship are somewhat more informative; that from the Gun Control Tower stated: 'We appeared [after dark] to get well ahead of the High Sea Fleet, which had been firing at intervals right aft on the Starboard Quarter' while, from the Director Tower, 'at various intervals firing was heard astern'. From the destroyer *Oak*, stationed just two cables before *Iron Duke*'s port beam, the actions astern between 9.30pm and midnight bore between NW and NbyE.[87] Next in line, *Royal Oak* reported firing breaking out on the starboard quarter at 10.12 and 10.45. *Superb* noted much firing at 10.13 on her starboard quarter, 'apparently a destroyer action'; at 11.30 and 11.43: 'Firing observed right astern, but no direct flashes seen, only the glare of gun flashes'; then at 0.25am, the same on the port quarter. *Benbow* noted firing commencing at 10.15pm on her starboard beam but heavy firing on her starboard quarter at 10.45; from 11.34 to 11.45, firing was astern and on the port quarter. Similarly, *Bellerophon* saw the firing move from the starboard quarter to astern at 11.40 and, after midnight, onto the port quarter. Between 10.10 and 10.35, *Vanguard* at the rear thought she could see a torpedo attack on the 2BS to starboard with torpedo craft clearly visible in the searchlight beams. But Captain James Dick:

Considered it better not to take any action revealing presence of 4th Battle Squadron, of which enemy T.B.Ds. appeared to be ignorant.

This was probably a good thing since the 'enemy Flotilla leader ... observed to be struck several times by shell' could have been *Castor* or *Southampton*.[88]

By 11 o'clock, the 5BS was probably roughly astern of the 4BS. The 1BS was to port, *Colossus*'s subdivision in the lead and *Marlborough*'s subdivision on the port beam of the fast battleships. Despite their more forward position, both *Colossus* and *Neptune* apparently saw on their starboard quarter the 2LCS in action and the fire in *Southampton*, and, about an hour later, firing and gun flashes right astern. Both the 5BS and *Marlborough*'s subdivision had better views of the fighting to the Northward, though there are still many detailed differences between their reports. Nonetheless, all describe much the same sequence of engagements, 'the first on the starboard beam, the others taking place in succession towards the stern' (Burney).[89] All three battleships of the 5BS saw an action on the starboard beam at 10.15 or just after, while *Barham* and *Valiant* described a second phase of heavy firing from 10.39. Ten minutes later, *Valiant* sighted a *Southampton*-class cruiser to Westward, which must have been the *Birmingham*. Next, at 11.35–11.40, another heavy action began,

[87] *OD*, pp. 54, 61, 62 and 300.
[88] *OD*, pp. 100 (*Royal Oak*), 121 and 358–9 (*Vanguard*) and 367. F&H, p. 183 (*Bellerophon*).
[89] *OD*, p. 67, also pp. 80–1 and 90.

about on the squadron's starboard quarter, between British light forces and heavy German ships. *Valiant* made out two large German ships steering Eastwards with 'at least two funnels and a crane amidships', but perversely identified them as cruisers.[90] *Malaya* knew better: 'The leading ship ... had two masts, two funnels and a conspicuous crane (apparently "Westfalen" class).' Yet *Malaya* kept this vital information to herself. Furthermore, she made out the leader of the British light forces only about two miles astern, near enough to identify her as a flotilla leader (though of the *Talisman* rather than the *Faulknor* class). Yet neither *Malaya* nor *Valiant* made any attempt to support *Tipperary* when she was illuminated, even though the searchlights would have provided excellent aiming points. At about 11.30, *Birmingham* could also see the leading German ships from her position nearby but her captain, Arthur Duff, 'was convinced from their appearance and speed that they were enemy battlecruisers' and he promptly made a report to both Jellicoe and Beatty. *Birmingham* had sighted the IBS as they turned away briefly from the attack by the 4DF; thus the reported course S was different from the SEbyS that Scheer had been steering since 10.34 and to which the High Seas Fleet would soon return. The 5BS last glimpsed the enemy between 0.12 and 0.45am, when they noted more heavy firing and one or more explosions astern.[91]

Table 9.16. *German signals 10.34pm–1.27am*

Time of receipt	From	To	System	Message	Time of origin
pm, 31 May					
10.34	C-in-C	Fleet		Battle fleet's course SEbyS	2232
	C-in-C	Westfalen		Course SE¾S for Horns Reef light ship	2302
	C-in-C	General		Position of own battle fleet at 11.00 012ε. Course SE¾S	2306
am, 1 June					
0.08	Seydlitz	C-in-C		4 enemy armoured cruisers in 093α, steering S	
	C-in-C	Lützow through G40		Position of own fleet at 0.30, 073α. Course SEbyS	0044
1.27	G39	C-in-C		Moltke at 0.30 in 59α. Course S. Speed 24 knots. Am being driven off by 4 large enemy vessels. Shall endeavour to close on battle fleet at dawn – AC Scouting Forces	0104

---

[90] By May 1916, the only surviving German armoured cruisers in the fleet were *Prinz Heinrich* and *Roon* (2 and 4 funnels respectively), whereas 19 battleships in the I, II and IV BSs fitted the description. *Monthly Return*, May 1916 in ADM 186/23. Gröner I, pp. 16–24.
[91] *OD*, pp. 179–80 (*Birmingham*), 195–6 and 201 (*Barham*), 210–11 (*Valiant*) and 219–20 (*Malaya*).

Burney's despatch stated that four night attacks were observed from *Marlborough*. They were distinct enough to be plotted on her chart with times of 10.05pm (bearing abeam), 10.40, 11.25 and 0.10am, the last, seven points abaft the beam, being accompanied by a heavy explosion. The plotted points give a clear impression of enemy forces heading about SSE on a course that crossed *Marlborough*'s wake at around 0.30. At that time, *Hercules* (next but one astern) saw the final action, in which *Turbulent* was sunk, bearing NbyE. Meanwhile, *Seydlitz* had been trying to find a way through towards Horns Reef, though her speed was limited now that, due to flooding forward, water was coming over the forecastle. At about midnight, her aft lookout reported: 'Several large ships, darkened, approaching from astern' – though, as they overtook her, their guns remained fore-and-aft. *Marlborough* saw smoke ahead crossing the bows before what appeared to be a large ship passed down the starboard side. The next ship, *Revenge*, made the challenge but received the wrong reply ('PL') before the stranger, which 'had the appearance of a Battle Cruiser and resembled our own', disappeared rapidly astern. *Seydlitz* had turned away making as much smoke as possible. She was not mentioned in *Hercules*'s despatch but that from *Agincourt* (Captain Henry Doughty) stated, though without a time:

A ship or Destroyer closed 'Agincourt' at high speed during the night ... I did not challenge her, so as not to give our Division's position away.

The light cruiser *Fearless*, which after falling behind had taken station astern of *Agincourt* after dusk, also saw what she thought was a *Kaiser*- or *König*-class battleship pass down the starboard side but:

As she was not engaged by the ships ahead no action was taken, it being too late to fire a torpedo when she could be identified as she was then well abaft the beam.

Agincourt's description does not seem to fit the struggling *Seydlitz* but the battlecruiser reported sighting four enemy armoured cruisers at 0.08am; four minutes later she was able to shape a course for Horns Reef.[92]

Thus, in summary: three British battleships and two light cruisers sighted what they realised or suspected were enemy ships but then did nothing that would have indicated the position of the British columns; the same was also true of *Valiant* and *Malaya*. *Active*'s 4in guns could have achieved little beyond revealing herself and the battleships ahead, while both she and *Vanguard* might have fired on British ships. The encounters of *Thunderer, Agincourt* and *Fearless* were only fleeting, while *Valiant* and *Malaya* would probably have

---

[92] *OD*, Pl. 3 and pp. 67–8, 101 and F&H, p. 220 (*Marlborough*), *OD*, pp. 74, 86, 93, 243 and 253. For *Seydlitz* and *Moltke, GOA*, pp. 174–5 and Staff, *World War One*, p. 186; see also S&H, pp. 333–4 and 336 and Looks, pp. 311–12.

lost sight of *Westfalen* and *Rheinland* as soon as they switched off their search-lights. Thus it is unlikely that any of these British battleships would have been able to fire more than a few salvos. Nonetheless, if *Agincourt* did sight *Seydlitz*, even one or two additional hits might well have been enough to prevent the wallowing battlecruiser from getting back to harbour. And the sudden descent of 15in shells on the van of the IBS would certainly have disrupted their fire at the 4DF and might have thrown the German line into confusion. On the other hand, it is surely no coincidence that all these British ships were at the rear of their columns, where they were particularly vulnerable to attack by the searching German flotillas, which, as we now know, failed to find any major targets during the night.

Despite all that was seen from the battlefleet, not a single ship reported its observations to Jellicoe. Most were well aware that the actions astern had moved from the starboard beam and quarter soon after 10pm to the port quarter by about 0.30am. Six supposed they had sighted large enemy cruisers, three, German battleships. The most egregious reporting failures must be by *Malaya* and by Vice-Admiral Burney in *Marlborough*, whose plot of the successive actions astern had given a very good indication of the course of the High Seas Fleet towards Horns Reef. The shining exception was *Birmingham* of the 2LCS, though unfortunately (as we shall see) Jellicoe would draw the wrong conclusions from her report. Although the *GFBOs* said nothing about the need for enemy reporting during the night after an indecisive action late in the day, the orders applicable to the aftermath of a decisive daytime action would have worked just as well at night;[93] if Jellicoe had felt the need for more information on the enemy's movements without too much message traffic, a brief order to his flag officers was all that was needed. In its absence, it is unlikely that, even if *Malaya* had reported her sighting of *Westfalen* to *Barham*, the vital information would have got any further; writing in 1936, *Barham*'s captain (by then Vice-Admiral Arthur Craig Waller), insisted:

It is certainly doubtful whether the various observations of enemy ships made by ships of our battle fleet ought to have been reported to the C.-in-C. I was on the bridge all night with my Admiral, and we came to the conclusion that the situation was known to the C.-in-C. and that the attacks were according to plan. A stream of wireless reports from ships in company with the C.-in-C. seemed superfluous and uncalled for. The unnecessary use of wireless was severely discouraged as being likely to disclose the position of our fleet to the enemy.[94]

---

[93] *GFBOs III*, XIII.3(iv).
[94] Vice-Admiral A Craig Waller, 'The Fifth Battle Squadron at Jutland', *JRUSI*, Vol. LXXX, November 1935, p. 799.

This deference to the C-in-C was probably typical of nearly all Jellicoe's senior officers; he received no enemy reports because they regarded him as omniscient. However, Craig Waller's excuses for withholding wireless reports are spurious; the *GFBO* just mentioned described how reports from individual ships did not need to be transmitted directly to the C-in-C, while any danger of wireless direction finding disclosing the fleet's position arose mainly before, not after, contact had been made.

Jellicoe stands on

Jellicoe's narrative of the battle says little of his decision to continue S.

No enemy ship was seen by the battlefleet during the night, except by 'Active' astern of the Second Battle Squadron. Firing was heard astern, searchlights were seen in use, and a fair number of star shells were fired by the enemy, which gave a brilliant illumination, and it was evident that our destroyers and light-cruiser squadrons were in action.

From reports received subsequently, it is fairly certain that the German battlefleet and battle-cruisers crossed astern of the British battlefleet and made for the Horn Reef channel.

In assessing these claims, we need to ask: what could be seen from *Iron Duke* of the actions in the rear; what information about the enemy reached Jellicoe before contact was lost at about 0.30am; and what despatches were available to him before he signed his narrative on 19 June 1916.[95]

The reports from *Iron Duke* herself state that, after dark, it appeared that the British battlefleet had got well ahead of the High Seas Fleet and that the enemy fire had been right aft or slightly to starboard. However, firing on the port quarter was seen from *Oak*, close on the flagship's beam and from *Superb*, next but one in line; thus, while not certain, it is likely that Jellicoe and his staff saw some signs that the German ships in action had crossed astern of the British columns. However, even if this was not the case, the main change in relative bearing was clear enough. At about 9.15pm, enemy firing had been to the West; by 11.30, it was astern, that is, to the North. This eight-point change could only have come about if, for most of the intervening time, the High Seas Fleet had been steering a course well to the East of South. This had evidently brought them into contact with the British flotillas that Jellicoe had ordered astern, and it was also the course that would take them towards Horns Reef.

This straightforward view of the situation was muddied by the reports sent to Jellicoe by Beatty and Jerram and, to some extent, by the Admiralty. As

---

[95] *OD*, pp. 22 and 32.

Table 9.17. *Reports to Jellicoe 8.59–11.38pm*

Time of despatch	From	To	System	Message	Time of origin
pm, 31 May					
8.59	Lion	C-in-C	W/T	Urgent. Enemy Battle Cruisers and pre-Dreadnought Battleships bear from me N34°W, distant 10–11 miles, steering SW. My position 56°40 N, 5°50E, course SW, 17 knots	2040
9.07	SO 2BS	C-in-C	W/T	Urgent. Our Battle Cruisers in sight bearing WNW, steering SW	2105
9.38	SO BCF	C-in-C	W/T	My position now 56°35 N, 5°41E, course SW, speed 17 knots. Enemy's bearing NbyW, steering WSW. (Received in Iron Duke 9.41 p.m.)	2100
9.43	SO BCF	C-in-C, SO 2BS, SO 1,2,3 LCS, Captain D13	W/T	My position 56°28 N, 5°38E. course S, speed 17 knots	2135
9.48	C-in-C	SO BCF, SOs of Squadrons, Commanders of Divisions and all Captains D	W/T	Reference position 9.45 56°26 N, 5°47E, course S, speed 17 knots	2145
9.55	Admiralty	C-in-C	W/T	Three Destroyer flotillas have been ordered to attack you during the night	2105
9.58	Admiralty	C-in-C	W/T	At 9.00, rear ships of Enemy B.F. in 56° 33 N, 5°30E on southerly course. (Received in Iron Duke 10.23 p.m.)	2158
10.41	Admiralty	C-in-C	W/T	At 10.41 the Admiralty informed the C-in-C that the enemy was believed to be returning to its base as its course was SSE¾E and speed 16 knots	2241
10.50	Commodore F via Kempenfelt	C-in-C	W/T	My position, course and speed South 17 knots, have been engaged by Enemy Cruisers. (This signal crossed 2243 from C-in-C)	2240
11.30	Birmingham	C-in-C SO BCF	W/T	Urgent. Priority. Battle Cruisers, unknown number, probably hostile, in sight NE, course S. My position 56°26 N, 5°42E	2330
11.38	SO 2LCS via Nottingham	C-in-C SO BCF	W/T	Urgent. Have engaged Enemy's Cruisers 10.15 p.m., bearing WSW (Received in Iron Duke 11.38 p.m.)	2240

discussed in the last chapter, Jellicoe deduced from *Lion*'s 8.59 signal that at 8.40 enemy vessels were 11–12 miles from *Iron Duke* bearing WNW. At 9.38, *Lion* transmitted a new report giving her position, course and speed at 9.00 and a new enemy bearing (NbyW) and course (WSW). As before, her reported position wrongly placed her within sight of *Iron Duke* – as Jellicoe declared in

1924, 'in the position which I knew the *King George V.* was in'.[96] But, assuming that the errors in *Lion*'s two positions were the same, they indicated that, between 8.40 and 9.00, the BCF had proceeded SWbyW at 21 knots and, therefore, that *Lion* was still some five miles ahead of *King George V.* However, if that was the case, *Lion*'s reported enemy bearings and courses were inconsistent; the two-point change in bearing implied (as we know, correctly) that the enemy course between 8.40 and 9.00 had been close to S, not SW, let alone WSW. There are no indications that this disparity was recognised in either British flagship. But, even if it was not, doubts about *Lion*'s position had already been raised by Jerram's signal – which he failed to correct – that, at 9.05, the BCF had been in sight from *King George V* bearing WNW. Given the persistent errors in *Lion*'s reports of her positions, it is understandable that Jellicoe preferred to rely on Jerram's report. From it, the C-in-C deduced an enemy position at 9.00 of 56°47′N, 5°24′E, which was NWbyN from *Iron Duke* at a distance of about 13 miles.[97]

At 9.55, the Admiralty transmitted the first of three signals that were based on German messages that had been deciphered by Room 40 (as described in the next chapter, other vital intelligence was withheld). The first signal can only have added to Jellicoe's apprehensions about night-time torpedo attacks. The second was despatched at 9.58 but was not received in *Iron Duke* until 10.23. It gave the position of the rear ships of the enemy battlefleet and their approximate course – 'Southerly' – at 9.00 (Jellicoe was not told that it was based on a report from *Regensburg*).[98] The course did not agree with those reported by Beatty but it did conform with one of Jellicoe's scenarios – that Scheer would follow him Southwards. The course also matched what might have been inferred from *Lion*'s enemy bearings. But the position located the rear of the High Seas Fleet at 9.00 some nine miles WSW from *Iron Duke* and closer still to *King George V* and to either of *Lion*'s possible positions.[99] Jellicoe concluded that the 'Admiralty position was obviously incorrect' and that, since the enemy 'would obviously have been in action with some of our ships, the information was disregarded as inaccurate'.[100] Yet very soon some ships had indeed 'obviously ... been in action', since from *Iron Duke* herself

[96] 'General Remarks (by Lord Jellicoe)', Appendix G, *AN*, p. 112, published 1924.

[97] 'Remarks' (see note 96) pp. 111–12. Also 1922 unpublished appendix to *The Grand Fleet*; see JMSS 49040, ff. 128–9 for text omitted from *JP II*, p. 435. Enemy distances and bearings both calculated and plotted on *Iron Duke*'s track chart, *OD*, Pl. 6a. (To obtain the enemy position, Jellicoe apparently assumed that *Lion* was some 3 nm WNW from *King George V* and the enemy 12 nm NbyW from *Lion*.)

[98] Hines, p. 1151. *OD*, 'German Plan VII' suggests that the position reported by *Regensburg* was closer to the van than the rear.

[99] Distance and bearing as calculated and as plotted on *OD*, Pl. 6a. In both his appendices, Jellicoe stated or implied that the Admiralty's position for the enemy was 10 miles SW from *Iron Duke* at 9.00.

[100] 'Remarks', p. 112. Appendix 1922, JMSS 49040, f. 128.

heavy firing was heard at 9.09 and a star shell was seen at 9.14, both on the starboard beam, that is, W after the flagship turned S. Thus the enemy bearing implied by the Admiralty's second signal – WSW at 9.00 – was about *three points South* of what Jellicoe and his staff heard and saw for themselves. Whereas, having dismissed this signal as 'obviously incorrect', Jellicoe was left with his earlier conclusion, based on Jerram's report, that at 9.00 the enemy bore *five points North* of the firing observed from *Iron Duke* soon afterwards.[101]

The third Admiralty signal was timed at 10.41, and it gave a clear indication of Scheer's general intentions and a precise course and speed. Unlike the text given in the *Official Despatches*, the message actually sent was definitive.

German Battle Fleet ordered home at 9.14 p.m. Battle Cruisers in rear. Course S.S.E. ¾ E. Speed 16 knots.[102]

But, in his published 'Remarks' of 1924, Jellicoe insisted: 'The deduction to be drawn from the Admiralty message depended largely on the time . . . that the course S.S.E. ¾ E. was adopted.' He also referred to 'evident signs of destroyer fighting in rear, at a long distance astern'. But Jellicoe could not have forgotten, either during the battle or when writing after the War, that he had positioned his flotillas five miles astern, hardly 'a long distance'. However, if the German battlefleet had been, as he preferred to believe, 13 miles to the NWbyN at 9.00, it would already have been on the starboard quarter after the Grand Fleet turned S – a bearing that would have been maintained if the German fleet had also continued S. Unfortunately for this idea, it required the German fleet to close from 13 to 5 miles in an hour and a quarter, a clear impossibility. But there was a better explanation of the fighting astern. German forces had been in action to the Westward at about 9.15. If, as suggested by the Admiralty signal, they had turned shortly afterwards to SSE¾E at 16 knots, their movement ENE *relative to the British battlefleet* would have brought them into contact with the British light forces following five miles astern. This interpretation also gave some credibility to the Admiralty's position for the enemy at 9.00, since a bearing WSW, even if three points too far South, was more consistent with a relative movement ENE than the position favoured by Jellicoe bearing NWbyN. But Jellicoe never mentioned this explanation nor, significantly, the firing to the Westward around 9.15, which did not fit with his own version of events. Instead, in his published 'Remarks', he insisted that the effect of the fighting astern

---

[101] Jellicoe implied ('Remarks', p. 112) that, since '*Lion* was reporting Battle Cruisers, which were presumably in the van', the enemy centre would have been even further to the North; in fact *Lion* had also reported enemy predreadnoughts, which would have been expected to bring up the German rear.

[102] Hines, p. 1151: also Corbett, 2nd edition (1940) p. 436.

'would be to turn the enemy to the northward and westward, even if he had originally intended to take the passage to the Horn Reef'; and that 'other reports received at about the same time made it appear that the enemy would make for a more westerly approach to his base'. In fact, three further reports received between 10.50 and 11.38 do not support this interpretation. That from *Castor* stated only that at 10.40 her course was S; it said nothing about the course of the enemy cruisers that she had engaged. Next, *Birmingham* reported that at 11.30 she had sighted a number of enemy battcecruisers steering S and bearing NE; this, he claimed in 1924, indicated that the battlecruisers were 'following us, and . . . that a S.S.E. ¾ E. course was not being followed'.[103] In this published appendix, Jellicoe went no further. But in his earlier unpublished appendix of 1922, he noted correctly that *Birmingham*'s reported position placed her 'some 30 miles nearly right astern of the *Iron Duke*, but slightly on her starboard quarter'. This distance was improbably great but, even so, the bearing of the enemy from *Birmingham* implied that the battlecruisers had already crossed *Iron Duke*'s wake. Last, at 11.38, Goodenough's delayed report stated that at 10.15 he had been engaged with enemy cruisers (type unspecified) bearing WSW. Not least due to the large errors in *Southampton*'s dead-reckoning, Jellicoe did not know her position relative to the battlefleet. Nonetheless, the two reports from the 2LCS gave a broad impression of enemy cruisers moving from a 10.15 position bearing WSW from the British light forces in the rear to one at 11.30 bearing NE.

In his published remarks, Jellicoe insisted that:

It should be realised that implicit reliance could not be placed on 'Intercepts'. I could not assume, for instance, that because the High Seas Fleet had steered a course S.S.E. ¾ E. at some time between 9 and 10 p.m., that this course would be maintained.[104]

And he seized on *Birmingham*'s enemy course to conclude:

The position therefore at 11.30 p.m. seemed to be that the High Sea Fleet was following astern of me and on the same course; it seemed therefore clear that the certain way to intercept the enemy on the morrow was to stand on.[105]

Yet, in deciding that the course SSE¾E was no more than a brief deviation from a course S, Jellicoe was prepared to reject so much information that pointed to the precise opposite. The Admiralty's signal originated at 2158 read as a *verbatim* report of an intercepted signal that unambiguously ordered the enemy fleet to return home in the direction of Horns Reef. The report of the enemy position at 9.00 agreed better with what could be seen of the enemy from

---

[103] Quotations from 'Remarks', p. 112.   [104] 'Remarks', p. 113.
[105] Appendix 1922, *JP II*, p. 436.

the flagship shortly after that time than with the position preferred by Jellicoe, which was based on inconsistent reports from Beatty and Jerram. The few enemy reports that reached Jellicoe after nine o'clock either provided no new information or were more in accord with what could be seen of the enemy from the battlefleet at about 9.15, 10.15 and 11.30, these observations being consistent with the Admiralty's information that Scheer turned SSE¾E after 9.14. And Jellicoe seems to have ignored the obvious advantages for Scheer of the route past Horns Reef.

We shall return to the question of why Jellicoe was so determined to hold on Southwards in the final chapters, after we have examined his actions for the rest of the night and the following morning. But we can consider here two other factors that may have influenced his decisions up to midnight. The first was the close spacing he had chosen for his columns, which meant that a three- or four-point turn to port could only have been made by the unequal-speed manoeuvre signalled by Compass Pendant. While there were comprehensive instructions for such turns in the *General Signal Book 1915*,[106] executing them in the dark without lights was not without risk; even one ship making a mistake might throw the whole battlefleet into confusion, so Jellicoe may have been very reluctant to alter course. Second, by the time the signals from the Admiralty and from *Birmingham* reached him, he may have been too tired to choose correctly between their contradictory courses. His flag-captain recalled that, probably after midnight:

During the night Jellicoe lay down for a few hours in all his clothes on a settee in the small house on the bridge . . . in which his tactical plot was kept.[107]

Thus, having reached his decision, he seems to have succumbed to fatigue (his staff may have allowed him to sleep undisturbed until dawn approached, since nothing more was heard from the Admiralty until 1.48am). Sub-Lieutenant Antony de Salis of *Moresby* wrote perceptively of how the excitement and noise of such a prolonged sea-fight had by midnight induced in him, a much younger man, an 'overmastering mental fatigue'.

For the Commander-in-Chief, the Flag and Commanding Officers, for whom there was no escape from continuous and intense mental activity and responsibility for instant action, this effect may be expected to have been at least correspondingly powerful.[108]

What of Jellicoe's assertion that, except from *Active*, no enemy ship was seen from the battlefleet? After the battle, the despatch from each battleship's captain was, as the hierarchy of the Service demanded, sent to the Admiral commanding his squadron. In the case of the 2BS and 4BS, these individual

---

[106] *GSB 1915*, pp. 35–51.   [107] Dreyer, p. 151.   [108] S&H, p. 343. Roskill, p. 182 agreed.

despatches were apparently not forwarded to the flagship. Instead, Jerram and Sturdee submitted tabular summaries, but the former's table included the sightings of enemy cruisers from *Thunderer* and *Boadicea*.[109] Burney submitted his own despatch, which refers to the night attacks crossing astern and to the large ship that was seen from *Marlborough* and also from *Revenge*, though neither definitely identified her as hostile; *Revenge*'s despatch was forwarded with others to the C-in-C, on his express orders, on 11 June 1916. The reports from *Fearless* were two of many enclosures that accompanied Beatty's despatch to the C-in-C on 12 June. From the 5BS, Evan-Thomas submitted his own despatch dated 9 June directly to the C-in-C and enclosed the despatches of *Valiant* and *Malaya* with their clear descriptions of German battleships.[110] It seems inconceivable that Jellicoe did not read these reports, which leads to the disquieting conclusion that the statement about enemy ships in his narrative was deliberately misleading. It seems likely that he wished to obscure the failures in reporting by the battlefleet, which denied him confirmation that his light forces were in action with German heavy ships and that the latter were indeed crossing astern.

Table 9.18. Lützow *reports 11.55pm–4.24am*

Time of receipt	From	To	System	Message	Time of origin
pm, 31 May					
11.55	G40	C-in-C AC Scouting Forces		Lützow can only steam at slow speed. Only a few of her navigational appliances are still serviceable. Position 016ε. Course S. Only one-third of armament serviceable	2305
am, 1 June					
0.31	S52	C-in-C		Position 016ε. Enemy is interfering with W/T. Destroyers in sight steering S	0030
0.47	G40	C-in-C		To AC Scouting Forces; Position of Lützow at 0.00, 010ε. Course S. Speed 7 knots	0017
4.24	Regensburg	C-in-C		From G38 to AC Scouting Forces and Fleet: Lützow blown up and abandoned at 1.45 – G38	

[109] *OD*, pp. 108–15 and 119–21.
[110] *OD*, pp. 68, 76, 86, 139 (where Beatty mentioned *Fearless*'s encounter with a *Kaiser*-class battleship), 192, 211, 219–20, 242 and 252.

As Jellicoe and Scheer held on respectively S and SEbyS, the badly damaged *Lützow*, making revolutions for seven knots,[111] had been falling further astern. Her forward turret was now awash and water was beginning to enter her forward boiler room. A final attempt to proceed stern-first in order to relieve the strain on her forward bulkheads had to be abandoned after her propellers came out of the water. At 1.20am, with some 8,000 tons in his ship, Captain Harder decided to abandon her and save the crew; he assembled them on the quarterdeck and then ordered the four escorting destroyers to come alongside and take them off. At 1.45, when her fore-part was already submerged as far as the bridge, two torpedoes from *G38* delivered the *coup-de-grâce*. Scheer learned of her loss from a signal received at 4.24 from *G38* via *Regensburg*: but this was not picked up by Room 40 and, even at 7.10pm on 2 June, Jellicoe did not know for certain that an enemy battlecruiser had been sunk.[112]

Later night encounters

At 10.50pm, Scheer had ordered the three destroyers of the IXTF that were close to the IBS to support *Lützow* but, for unexplained reasons, only *S52* attempted to comply. While searching on the starboard quarter of the High Seas Fleet, at 0.17am she instead encountered *Castor* and the 11DF. *S52* evaded *Castor*'s attempt to ram but was then engaged at point-blank range, after which she was not seen again. *Castor* turned S once more, while *S52* was able to report the destroyers she had seen.[113]

The furious action by the 4DF had left a trail of damaged vessels. *Tipperary* and *Sparrowhawk* were immobilised while *Broke* was heading slowly Northwards. *Elbing* was disabled and *Rostock* could proceed only slowly with frequent halts. *S32* got under way again at 0.30am and made slowly for the Danish coast, where she anchored to await a tow.[114] *Tipperary*, still burning fiercely, drifted down the German line until she passed the *Regensburg* at the rear. At 0.10, Commodore Heinrich sent out *S53, S54* and *G88* to intercept her and they may have been sighted together from *Broke*. *S54* was soon hailed by *Rostock*; she took the light cruiser in tow, after which they headed in a Southerly direction at 10 knots. (At 2.55, they were joined by *V71* and *V73*.) The British and German accounts of the actions of *S53* and *G88*, especially the times, conflict somewhat but the main sequence of events seems to have been as follows. Both destroyers continued towards *Tipperary*; *S53* closed, asked the British boat to identify herself and then, rather than opening fire, picked up nine crewmen who had already taken to a raft. Both German destroyers turned back towards their fleet before observing another vessel on the port bow. At first, she did not reply to the challenge but, just as *S53*

---

[111] Her actual speed was probably about five knots: Paschen, p. 39.
[112] *GOA*, p. 207. Tarrant, pp. 255–6. *OD*(M), p. 572.
[113] *GOA*, pp. 186–7. Tarrant, p. 206. *OD*, p. 304. F&H, p. 352.   [114] Tarrant, pp. 200 and 227.

was preparing to fire a torpedo, she flashed: 'This is the "Elbing". I am helpless, please come alongside.' Before either destroyer could comply, they sighted and illuminated a British destroyer with four funnels, the damaged *Broke*. A torpedo was fired at her but it passed underneath; a few salvos followed, which made two hits amidships, before both German destroyers sheered off. After this unexpected reprieve, *Broke* again turned N for Cromarty or Scapa Flow. But early on 2 June a strong NW breeze forced her to turn away downwind; after the wind and sea moderated, she finally reached the Tyne at 5pm on 3 June.[115]

The two German destroyers had supposed that *Broke* was in a sinking condition and *S53*'s commander was anxious to return quickly to *Elbing*. *G88* stood on but then sighted another British destroyer, apparently abandoned, which she attempted to sink by gunfire until driven off by the approach of five more unidentified British boats. (None of the survivors from *Sparrowhawk* or *Tipperary* mentioned this attack.) Soon after 1am, *S53* went alongside *Elbing* and took off 477 of the crew before, with her nine British prisoners from *Tipperary*, proceeding at full speed for the Danish coast. *Elbing*'s Captain Madlung and a small skeleton crew remained with his ship and they rigged up a sail to take advantage of the favourable wind. But, at about 2am, they sighted, but were not observed by, a line of enemy destroyers, probably the group led by *Lydiard*. Madlung then gave orders to scuttle *Elbing* with explosive charges and to abandon ship in her cutter. At the same time, *Sparrowhawk*'s crew were alarmed to see a modern three-funnelled German light cruiser about two miles to the East but after about ten minutes they saw *Elbing* turn over and sink bows first. Meanwhile, at about 1.45, *Tipperary*'s crew were ordered aft; soon, she heeled to starboard and the bows went under. Some of her company got onto her large Carley float, while other survivors had to swim – including another canine casualty, the First Lieutenant's terrier Peter; neither he nor his master were seen again. A half to an hour later, the float was passed by *Elbing*'s cutter and, in the British accounts, by her whaler. The former had already picked up *Tipperary*'s surgeon (and perhaps two ratings) but had no room for more British survivors; Madlung burned a blue flare but it did not attract any British rescuers. The occupants of *Elbing*'s boats were picked up five hours later by a Dutch trawler and taken to the Netherlands. After a further interval (the times are again uncertain), the men on *Tipperary*'s raft sighted the *Sparrowhawk* at a distance, apparently going round in circles. The crippled destroyer could do little to reach them, while they were too exhausted to paddle effectively. But a petty officer found a counterpane [*sic*] to hold up as a sail and, after about an hour and a half, the raft reached *Sparrowhawk*. Four or five men died shortly after they were picked up but about 26 survived; their rescuers wondered if the Tipperarys might be 'out of the frying pan into the fire'.[116]

[115] *GOA*, p. 186. Tarrant, pp. 205–6 and 227. *OD*, pp. 324 and 327. F&H, pp. 312–14 and 341.
[116] *GOA*, p. 186. Tarrant, pp. 205–6 and 226–7. *OD*, pp. 321–2 and 328: and pp. 234–5, 241 and 263 for some of *Lydiard*'s group turning about WNW after crossing ahead of the German battle line. F&H, pp. 334–7 and 341–3.

Pommern and *V4* **blow up**

Though the order of events is unclear, shortly after *Champion* (with *Obdurate* and *Moresby*) veered away across the bows of the 12DF, both groups briefly encountered a pair of enemy light cruisers. They were *Frankfurt* and *Pillau* of the IISG which, after their brief engagement with *Castor* and the 11DF, appear to have remained to port of their battlefleet. At 11.52pm *Champion* turned further away to the NE though, in view of her obstruction of the 12DF, it seems unlikely that she turned S as early as 11.56. After further turns E and S, she steadied at 0.50am on a course SE, slightly diverging from that of the High Seas Fleet to the Southward.[117] Meanwhile, the two German cruisers had appeared close to *Menace* and *Nonsuch* at the rear of the 12DF, though too briefly for the destroyers to fire torpedoes. *Menace* had to put her helm hard over to avoid being rammed and she then rejoined the flotilla. But *Nonsuch*, in turning E at full speed, lost touch; after searching without result to the Eastward, she turned N and, at about 8.00, fell in with the immobilised *Acasta* and towed her to Aberdeen. The rest of the 12DF also turned E and then for a time to NE; the 1st Division astern of *Faulknor* reported that they had been chased in that direction, though it is uncertain whether they misidentified *Champion* or, as Stirling's 0.16 remark suggests, *Frankfurt* and *Pillau* were still dogging them. After Stirling had reduced speed to 15 knots to allow *Champion* to pass ahead, by 0.30 he was again leading the flotilla S,[118] his course converging with that of the High Seas Fleet.

Faulknor was in the lead with the 1st Division (*Obedient, Mindful, Marvel* and *Onslaught*) on her starboard quarter and the 2nd Division (*Maenad, Narwhal, Nessus* and *Noble*) on the port quarter. The remaining boats, forming the 2nd Half Flotilla, should have been led by *Marksman* (Commander Norton Sulivan) but she lost contact during the later part of the night. Command then devolved on Commander Charles Sumner in *Opal*; she was astern of the other divisions and was followed by *Menace, Munster* and *Mary Rose*.[119] At 1.43, just as the sky was beginning to lighten, enemy ships were sighted from *Obedient* (they flashed 'K', the wrong recognition code); they were also seen from *Faulknor*, who identified them as *Kaiser*-class battleships. As *Faulknor* turned onto a parallel

---

[117] Harper, pp. 100 and 101 (see also *OD*, pp. 224–5); the *Record* is the most informative source on the movements of the 13DF and 12DF, though the same movements are shown on *AN*, Diagrams 44 and 45.

[118] Harper, pp. 94–5. *AN*, p. 84 and Diagram 45. S&H, p. 348. *OD*, pp. 332 and 339.

[119] *OD*, p. 322. The orders of the three group is that in Harper, pp. 94–5 as confirmed by *OD*, p. 334, F&H p. 361(1st Divn.) and S&H, p. 349. They seem most consistent with subsequent events but are contradicted by F&H, pp. 361 (2nd Divn.) and 363 and by *OD*, p. 340. *Mischief* remained with the 2CS.

Table 9.19. *12DF signals 0.16am–5.40pm*

Time of despatch	From	To	System	Message	Time of origin
am, 1 June					
0.16	Captain D12	12DF	FL	Admiral intends to proceed at 17 knots Remarks: 0.16. Enemy Cruiser on either bow opened fire. Flotilla spread	
1.56	Captain D12	C-in-C	W/T	Urgent. Priority. Enemy's Battleships in sight. My position 10 miles astern of 1BS. (This signal was incompletely logged in Faulknor's log, and there are no records of it having been received in Iron Duke)	0152
2.08	Captain D12	C-in-C	W/T	Urgent. Am attacking. (There are no records of this signal having been received by any ship)	0207
2.13	Captain D12	C-in-C	W/T	Urgent. Course of enemy SSW. (There are no records of this signal having been received by any ship except Marksman)	0212
2.27	Maenad	Captain D12	W/T	What is your position?	0225
2.36	Onslaught	Captain D12	W/T	1st Lieut. killed. Captain seriously injured. Fore bridge gone	0230
3.20	Opal	Captain D12	W/T	Opal and eight Destroyers. Course S, 16 knots, 15 miles to Westward of your 0200 position	0315
3.20	Onslaught	Commodore F	W/T	All torpedoes fired. Gunner and 1st Lieut. killed. Commanding officer severely wounded. One gun out of action. Permission to return to base. Reply: Approved	0310 0430
4.02	Commodore F	Opal	SL	Have you seen anything of battlefleet or Cruisers? Reply: No	
4.13	Captain D12	Opal	W/T	Steer North	0410
8.36	Commodore F	Kempenfelt	Flags	Fleet ahead, inform Opal	
11.00	Captain D12	Marksman	Sem	Did you and 2nd Division attack Enemy battlefleet after me this morning? If so, with what result? Reply: My attack was spoilt by 12DF coming down in the middle of the second half. In avoiding them, I lost second half, so do not know if they attacked. Enemy then apparently turned away	
pm, 1 June					
5.40	Commodore F	Opal	SL	Report names of 12th Flotilla Destroyers present. Are there any casualties in 12th Flotilla? Reply: Opal, Menace, Munster, Noble, Mary Rose, Narwhal, Nessus, Mindful[.] Onslaught left us about 5 a.m. after we joined you. Nessus has six wounded. Onslaught and Obedient, Captain injured, 1st Lieutenant killed. Nonsuch is escorting Acasta to Newcastle	

course, *Obedient* ran alongside to report the enemy by megaphone. Stirling then ordered the 1st Division, which was nearest to the enemy, to attack but, as they turned to starboard, the enemy did the same and disappeared, after which the division rejoined the flotilla. It was fortunate that this piecemeal attack on a similar course by only four boats had to be aborted, since it would almost certainly have been driven off with heavy losses, just like the earlier British destroyer attacks. Stirling next ordered the 1st Division to form astern of *Faulknor* before he turned away to port to get ahead of the German battleships unobserved. He then led his line in succession through a large turn to starboard to bring them onto a course NW, after which the enemy were once again in sight heading SE.

The enemy was now clearly visible on our port side, dreadnought battleships leading, pre-dreadnoughts following, a long line of them. Conditions were nearly ideal for an attack, as it was too light for searchlights to be of much use to the enemy big ships, and yet, with the mist as an added cloak, it was sufficiently dark to make the laying of guns on fast-moving targets [on an opposite course] difficult.[120]

Table 9.20. *German flotilla signals 1.46–2.50am*

Time of receipt	From	To	System	Message	Time of origin
am, 1 June					
1.46	Regensburg	C-in-C		All torpedo boat flotillas are to assemble at the head of the IBS – 2nd Leader of Torpedo Boats	0159
2.01	S53	Regensburg		To C-in-C: I have almost the whole of Elbing's crew on board. My 2.00 position is 086α – IIITF	0150
	2nd Leader of Torpedo Boats	VITF and VTF		In the event of another engagement, boats with torpedoes ready for firing are to take station in the van for an attack. Boats without torpedoes are to join Regensburg	
2.50	Torpedo Boats	Fleet		V4 destroyed by explosion in fore part of ship. Captain states that it was caused by ramming a submarine. The greater part of the crew have been saved	

[120] F&H, p. 361. See also *OD*, pp. 332, 336 and 339 and F&H, pp. 360 and 363–4.

The German battleships were also uncertain about whether the destroyers in sight were friend or foe. At 1.46, Heinrich had ordered all German boats to assemble on the van of the battlefleet; by two o'clock, the boats moving into position included *V2, V4* and *V6* of the VTF, which were making their way up the starboard side of the line. When *Markgraf* and *Kronprinz* observed destroyers approaching on their port quarter, they held their fire in case they were friendly. But the next battleships in the line, *Grosser Kurfürst, König* and *Deutschland*, although their view was obscured by smoke from those ahead, did not hesitate to turn away and open fire when they sighted destroyers on their port beam.[121]

Although under fire, *Faulknor* and three of the 1st Division were able to discharge torpedoes as they raced past the enemy battleline. The reported times are, as usual, rather inconsistent but, at about 2.05, *Faulknor* fired two torpedoes, *Obedient* two and *Onslaught* four; all were set for long range and the targets were 3,000–3,500 yards distant. *Marvel* closed the range before she fired her four torpedoes, set for high speed, at ranges of 1,700–1,800 yards. *Mindful*, for unexplained reasons, had only two working boilers and she seems to have fallen behind; when she sighted the enemy on her starboard bow, she tried to go straight for them but was masked first by *Onslaught* and then by another destroyer (possibly *Maenad*) and was twice forced to turn away without firing to avoid being rammed.[122] By discharging no less than 12 torpedoes in a short time, the 12DF stood a good chance of making a hit. *Markgraf* turned away when she saw two torpedoes approaching but even so one ran underneath her. One torpedo exploded in *Kronprinz*'s wake, another ran close across the bows of *Grosser Kurfürst*, while a third was avoided by *Hessen*, by then two ships astern of *Deutschland*. But at 2.10 *Pommern*, the second predreadnought, was hit by one or possibly two torpedoes on her port side. After a succession of small explosions, dark red flames, starting on the starboard side, spread fore and aft and flared up to the mastheads before a final huge explosion broke her in two. It seems that the torpedo hit or hits set off some of her 6.7in ammunition and that the explosions then spread across the ship before reaching her propellant magazines. None of *Pommern*'s crew of 844 officers and men survived.[123]

After firing her torpedoes, *Faulknor* turned away to NNW and proceeded down the enemy line, returning the enemy fire with her 4in guns at what one officer described as point-blank range, with *Obedient* and *Marvel* following. On reaching the end of the line unharmed, she was met by three German light cruisers which opened a heavy fire; their identity is uncertain but they cannot,

---

[121] Tarrant, pp. 218–20.   [122] *OD*, pp. 339–40. *ATFJ*, pp. 12–13. *GFG&TO No. 15*, p. 52.

[123] Tarrant, pp. 220–1 (and p. 217 for *Schlesien* and *Schleswig-Holstein* having fallen astern). *OD*, p. 339. F&H, p. 362. Each of the four British boats declared a hit (*ATFJ*, pp. 12–13) but *Marvel*, whose four high-speed torpedoes would have been particularly difficult to evade, probably had the best claim to have sunk *Pommern*.

as Stirling suggested, have been of the *Rostock* class. He then turned further away to NbyE before the cruisers turned back towards their fleet; after a brief final encounter with another enemy cruiser, *Faulknor, Obedient* and *Marvel* returned to a course S. As for *Onslaught* at the rear of the 1st Division, just as she turned away by eight points after firing her four torpedoes she was caught in a German searchlight beam and hit by fire that appeared to come from the ship that had been following *Pommern*. A shell burst on *Onslaught*'s charthouse, killed the First Lieutenant and mortally wounded the Captain, started a cordite fire and wrecked the steering gear, though the after steering position was connected up smartly. She then took station astern of *Mindful* and they both joined up with the 2nd Half-Flotilla led by *Opal*.

Beginning at 1.56 and continuing while she was in action, *Faulknor* made three attempts to report the enemy to Jellicoe by wireless using what her operators believed was full power. But none of her signals was answered and only the last was received by another vessel, the nearby *Marksman*. When *Onslaught* tried to report her casualties (five killed, three wounded), *Faulknor* did not answer; thus, while interference from German wireless may have been a factor, it is probable that something was wrong with *Faulknor*'s wireless gear – Harper suggested that it may not have been properly adjusted.[124] Stirling still deserves credit for trying to report, but, even if his signals had got through, they would have made little difference since, as we shall see, the fleets were already too far apart.

As *Faulknor* turned through sixteen points to attack, Stirling ordered the flotilla 'to follow round and attack the enemy'. *Maenad*, leading the 2nd Division, received a signal to attack but her Captain, Commander John Champion, anticipating that Stirling 'intended closing and firing starboard side', had ordered that both her twin torpedo tubes should be trained to starboard. When the boats ahead turned sharply in that direction, Champion held his course, turned later and fired a single torpedo when one tube had been trained to port. *Narwhal*, which also received the order to attack, followed round and, having initially sighted three enemy ships, fired two torpedoes at 2.21 and 2.25, the second at what appeared to be the last ship in the enemy line. *Nessus* and *Noble* did not fire any torpedoes but *Nessus* was hit by a 5.9in shell at the base of the foremast; her casualties were seven killed, including her doctor, and seven or eight wounded. *Maenad*, after firing her first torpedo, did not continue in the wake of the 1st Division.

The order was . . . passed to train the tubes to starboard in preparation for another attack, which the Captain said he intended to carry out . . . We then turned a complete circle to starboard, though how we passed through the remainder of our division without collision we don't know, as *Narwhal, Nessus* and *Noble* were all astern of us.

---

[124] *OD*, pp. 333 and 337. F&H, pp. 365–6. S&H, p. 358. Harper, p. 96. *GF*, p. 241.

'A complete circle' makes no sense and a sketch by one of *Onslaught*'s officers shows *Maenad* turning through some 20 points to starboard onto a course converging with that of the German line. *Maenad* then closed to about 5,000 yards before firing two more torpedoes (one, she claimed unconvincingly, caused an explosion like that which destroyed *Pommern*) and engaging an enemy battleship with her after 4in gun.[125] Commander Champion seems to have turned about without regard to the risk of collision with the boats that had been following him; it is likely that *Nessus* and *Noble* missed their opportunity to fire torpedoes because they were forced to avoid *Maenad* as she barged through the line. A possible explanation, though not an excuse, for Champion's conduct is that, by the time *Maenad* fired her first torpedo and *Narwhal* her two, they had drawn level with the end of the enemy line and Champion decided that, to fire any more, he must reverse course (this position is also suggested by the above-mentioned sketch).

Notable omissions from the *Official Despatches* are despatches from *Nessus* and *Noble* and from *Marksman, Opal* and their half-flotilla, while the *Admiralty Narrative* states that no reports could be traced from these destroyers. However, Harper's *Record* declares that the rest of the 2nd Division and *Opal*'s half-flotilla all followed *Maenad* onto an attacking course as she first turned 16 points to starboard at 2.11. This is confirmed by the manuscript diary of *Menace*'s captain, Lieutenant-Commander Charles Poignand.

Suddenly we sighted some large [enemy] ships on the starboard bow . . . and our leading division, which was some way ahead of us, turned to starboard to attack . . . By the time it was time for us to turn, the leading boats were coming back again [being heavily shelled] and the boat ahead of us and all others following had to turn the other way to avoid collision. So none of us got a shot in.

No other boat admitted following *Maenad* while, after the attacks by the 12DF were over, nine boats – all that had taken part other than *Faulknor, Obedient, Marvel* and *Maenad* herself – remained with *Opal* under Sumner's leadership.[126] Thus most of the obstruction to the boats whose reports are missing was probably the fault of *Maenad*. It seems permissible to speculate that many of their despatches blamed either *Maenad* specifically or, like Poignand, more generally the boats ahead. Also, *Marksman*'s reply to Stirling's 11am query of 1 June implies that she did not lose contact with her half-flotilla until she was forced to avoid some unidentified boats from the 1st Half Flotilla. It seems that, rather than expose these errors and the subsequent recriminations, Stirling – or perhaps Hawksley or even the C-in-C – chose to suppress the critical reports.

---

[125] *OD*, pp. 332 and 334–5. F&H, pp. 361 (for quotation) and 369. S&H, pp. 359–60. Campbell, p. 340. *ATFJ*, p. 13. *GFG&TMs*, p. 52.
[126] *AN*, p. 85 (also *NSA*, para. 92). Harper, pp. 95–6. S&H, p. 360 (for quotation). *OD*, pp. 337 and 340.

Table 9.21. *British destroyer signals 2.20–3.05am*

Time of despatch	From	To	System	Message	Time of origin
am, 1 June					
2.20	Captain D13	Marksman	FL	Where are Enemy's ships? Reply: Suspicious ships South	
2.20	Marksman			Remarks: Engaged Enemy's Destroyers and Light Cruisers (four Destroyers and two Cruisers)	
2.25	Captain D13	Marksman	FL	Where is our battlefleet? Reply: Bearing South	
2.30	Marksman	Captain D13	FL	What are ships bearing South? Reply: Germans, I think	
2.35	Captain D12	Marksman	W/T	Work round to South. (Passed to Champion)	0220
2.35	Marksman	Captain D13	FL	Shall I join you? Reply: Yes	
2.40	Marksman	Maenad	FL	Am joining Champion	
2.42	Maenad	Captain D12	W/T	What is your course and speed?	0238
2.55	Captain D13	Destroyers in Company	Flags	Alter course in succession to WNW ... speed 19 knots	
3.05	Captain D13	Marksman	Sem.	Do you know where the rest of your flotilla is? Reply: I think to the Southward	

As the 12DF began their attacks, Farie in *Champion*, accompanied by *Obdurate* and *Moresby*, was still heading SE, a course that, even if not intentionally, maintained his distance from the High Seas Fleet. But, at 2.15, on hearing their guns firing, he turned W, and soon sighted the straying *Marksman*. In an exchange of signals (the third pair at 2.30 was probably also initiated by *Champion*), Farie was told that both the enemy and British fleets bore S. In his 1976 memoir, H P K Oram, at Jutland a sub-lieutenant in *Obdurate*, wrote: '*Champion*, thinking we had overtaken the rear ships of the Grand Fleet, turned away to avoid confusion'; she altered course to S at 2.25, SE at 2.30 and E at 2.34. However, unless *Champion*'s reckoning was wildly different from *Faulknor*'s, Oram's suggestion seems no more than an excuse for Farie's second withdrawal on meeting the enemy. Lieutenant-Commander Roger Alison of *Moresby* was determined not to follow his Captain (D).

About 2.35 a.m. four 'Deutschland' Class Ships were seen bearing West, 4,000 yards [steaming 18 knots S.E.]. I considered action imperative, hoisted Compass West [to draw attention in that direction], hauled out to port, firing a H.S Torpedo at 2.37 G.M.T.

Unfortunately, only this one torpedo was ready to fire and the opportunity was over very quickly. But, two minutes later, though the enemy could no longer be seen through the mist and smoke, both *Moresby* and *Obdurate* felt a distinct concussion. According to Oram:

Despite *Moresby*'s aggressive action *Champion* remained convinced that the ghostly forms we had seen were friendly and remained silent.

Alison reported: 'At 2.47 a.m. the "Champion" was rejoined and her orders obeyed' – which seems to imply that earlier he would have ignored any orders that interfered with his attack. By 2.40, *Marksman* (which did not follow *Moresby*'s example) was also in visual contact with *Maenad* as she withdrew after her second attack. Both vessels from the 12DF joined *Champion* as she altered course N at 2.50 in conformance with Jellicoe's recent order to the battlefleet (of which more shortly).[127]

The concussion felt by *Moresby* and *Obdurate* was not, as hoped, a battleship blowing up. Apart from *Pommern*, the only other German loss at about this time was the destroyer *V4*, which sank after an explosion tore off her bows. But, according to the German accounts, this occurred at 2.15 when she was on the starboard beam of *Westfalen* and *Rheinland* in the van, whereas *Von der Tann* turned away to avoid a torpedo at 2.42. British histories attribute *V4*'s loss to *Moresby*'s torpedo but, if the German time and position are correct, it seems more likely that she succumbed to a stray torpedo fired by the 12DF or even to an accidental explosion of one of her own torpedoes.[128]

Picking up the pieces

After joining forces, *Garland* and *Contest* sighted a number of German destroyers, though none attempted an attack. Then, at 2.20, soon after first light, the two British boats and a group of four German destroyers sighted each other on opposite courses in a position that, by German reckoning, was about 35 miles NW of the Horns Reef light vessel. *V45, G37, G38* and *G40* had taken off *Lützow*'s crew and were now steaming SSE at full speed. They evaded an attempt by *Contest* and *Garland* to cross their bows and, both sides having reverted to their initial courses, a brief but ineffective gun action followed at ranges down to 1,300 yards; only *V45* had time to fire a torpedo but it missed by several hundred yards. Both groups then continued on their respective ways, *Garland* and *Contest* soon shaping a course for the Tyne.

---

[127] Harper, p. 101. Oram, p. 171. *OD*, pp. 225 and 239.
[128] *GOA*, p. 203. Tarrant, pp. 221–2. Harper, p. 101. *AN*, pp. 82–3. Corbett, p. 411.

Later, they intercepted signals asking for assistance from the damaged *Porpoise* and, after a search, found her at 11am. *Porpoise* was only able to make about six knots; when the Tyne was eventually reached next day, *Garland* took her up the river to Palmer's yard.[129]

The four German destroyers, crowded with the 1,040 officers and men from the *Lützow*, were not yet out of danger. At 3.20, when they were about 15 miles NW of Horns Reef, they sighted *Champion* and her four destroyers approaching from ahead at a distance of 4,400 yards, steaming N. *Champion* observed four destroyers some five minutes later but, due to the mist, did not make them out as hostile until 3.30. Another brief action on opposite courses then began at ranges falling to 2,400 yards. Perhaps because they had already been thoroughly alerted by their previous action, *G40* was able to fire one torpedo and *V45* two. All three passed close to *Champion* and *Moresby*, forcing them both to take avoiding action; by the time they steadied on their previous course, the enemy had disappeared. But *G40* had been hit and, after ten minutes, the damage to her after turbine forced her to stop; she was then taken in tow by *G37*, though they could make only 10 knots.[130] Farie in *Champion* probably did not know of this success, nor could he have known that the two destroyers were carrying half of *Lützow*'s crew. But, if only he had turned his more powerful force about in pursuit, he might have caught and sunk them; by holding on, he missed an opportunity to inflict a grievous loss on the enemy.

Table 9.22. Dublin *signals 4.31–8.16am*

Time of despatch	From	To	System	Message	Time of origin
am, 1 June					
4.31	Dublin	SO BCF C-in-C	W/T	Urgent. One Cruiser and two Destroyers, probably hostile, in sight. Bearing E, Course S ...	0430
4.51	Dublin	SO 2LCS	W/T	... Dublin steering North, 17 knots	0445
8.00	C-in-C	Dublin	SL SL	Where is Cruiser and two TBDs you reported in your 0430? Reply: German Armoured Cruiser was lost sight of in fog ...	0755
	C-in-C	Dublin		Was she disabled or steaming? Reply: As far as I could see she was not disabled and appeared to be steaming fast	0816

---

[129] *OD*, p. 315. F&H, pp. 319–20. Tarrant, pp. 227–8.
[130] Tarrant, p. 228. *OD*, p. 225. Oram, p. 172. S&H, pp. 365–6.

Dublin, having lost touch with the rest of the 2LCS, continued Southwards in the hope of rejoining them at daybreak. But at first light, the visibility was low and no other vessels were in sight. At 4.00, having seen nothing in the persistent mist, she turned N. Meanwhile, the damaged *Rostock* had been struggling Southwards towed by *S54* and screened by *V71* and *V73*. About ten minute after *Dublin* altered course to N, the two light cruisers sighted each other passing starboard to starboard. The German times tend to be earlier that the British and neither vessel described the other correctly, but there are no other candidates on either side for this encounter. *Dublin* made out indistinctly a supposed armoured cruiser resembling the *Roon* steaming S at high speed with only two destroyers in company. They quickly disappeared in the fog and, although *Dublin* turned S, she could not find them again. She reported the sighting at 4.31 and by 4.45 she was once more heading N. In *Rostock*, Michelsen believed he had sighted two hostile light cruisers and his alarm was increased after he picked up a report from the Zeppelin *L11* at 3.30 that a large enemy force was approaching his position. Rather than sacrifice his ship's company in a hopeless engagement, he summoned the destroyers alongside to take them off, meanwhile making the British recognition signal and laying smoke, though neither precaution was noticed by any British vessel. *Rostock* was then scuttled with explosive charges; she sank at 4.25 after *V71* and *V73* finished her off with torpedoes. The three destroyers then made good their escape without further incident.[131]

Ambuscade joined *Castor* and the 11DF at 3am – or perhaps later since she was not ordered to form astern of *Kempenfelt*'s division until 4.32. After the 12DF's torpedo attack, the group led by *Faulknor* headed S and at 3.30 passed *Marlborough* steering N. Burney in *Revenge* was only about five miles to the South and at 3.45 he ordered *Faulknor* to close. Stirling took station on *Agincourt*'s quarter and thereafter remained with *Revenge*'s division.[132] Information about the nine boats led by *Opal* is sparse but at 4.02 *Opal* was in touch with Commodore (F) in *Castor* and the signal record suggests that they then joined forces to concentrate no less than twenty-four destroyers under Hawksley's command – though it appears that he did not inform Jellicoe about the presence of the 12DF boats until 7.33. At 5.01, Hawksley had received a report of the C-in-C's position at 4.45 but it was 7.04 before he was given a specific rendezvous position, to be reached by 8.15. He finally sighted the fleet at 8.36 and at 8.45 ordered his destroyers to form the screen for the battle squadrons.[133]

---

[131] *OD*, p. 182. F&H, pp. 300–1 (though signal to *Champion*'s group was later). *GOA*, p. 210. Tarrant, p. 227, which states *Rostock* sighted one enemy cruiser. GSM, 3.30 and 5.05am.

[132] *OD*, pp. 68, 310, 333 and 340.

[133] Jellicoe's despatch (*OD*, p. 32) states that at 7.33 Commodore (F) reported that all the 11DF and 12DF were with him but the signal for 7.16 mentions only the 11DF and *Ambuscade*. F&H, pp. 352–3. *OD*, p. 118.

Table 9.23. *British destroyer signals 3.45–8.45am*

Time of despatch	From	To	System	Message	Time of origin
am, 1 June					
3.45	SO 1BS	Faulknor	Flags	Close	
4.02	Commodore F	Opal	SL	Have you seen anything of battlefleet or Cruisers?	
				Reply: No	
4.12	Commodore F	12DF	SL	Alter course together eight points to port	
4.13	Commodore F	12DF	SL	Alter course together four points to starboard	
4.32	Commodore F	Ambuscade	SL	Form astern of Kempenfelt division. Were flotilla in action last night?	
				Reply: Enemy's Battleships cut through 4th Flotilla. We had one Cruiser and, I think, our other torpedo got home	
5.01	C-in-C	Commodore F	W/T	My position at 4.45 is 55°29 N, 6°02E steering N at 17 knots. What is your position, course and speed?	0455
7.04	C-in-C	SO 1BS	W/T	Join me 8.15 55°56 N, 6°13E	0638
		Commodore F		Reply from SO 1BS: cannot reach rendezvous before 8.45	0805
7.16	C-in-C	Commodore F	W/T	Are all your Destroyers in company or in communication? . . .	0658
				Reply: All Destroyers of 11DF present, also Ambuscade	0733
8.36	Commodore F	Kempenfelt	Flags	Fleet ahead, inform Opal	
8.45	Commodore F	Destroyers	SL	Screen in accordance with No. 9 diagram . . .	

After crossing the bows of the High Seas Fleet, the boats led by *Lydiard* headed SW and W until daylight. At 4.20, she intercepted *Lion*'s signal giving Beatty's position at 4am and set course N77°E to rejoin. Already, at 4.00, Goldsmith had sent *Laurel* on ahead with the survivors of *Queen Mary*. At about 5.30, he detached *Narborough* with *Nerissa* and *Pelican* to rejoin the BCF, but it would be 8.56 before *Gloucester* (3LCS) sighted *Narborough* on the port bow and 10.08 before the three destroyers were ordered to close

Table 9.24. *13DF signals 3.25–10.48am*

Time of despatch	From	To	System	Message	Time of origin
am, 1 June					
3.25	Narborough	Captain D13	W/T	Submit I have Pelican, Nicator, Nerissa, Petard, in company with me. Petard can only go 28 knots. Nicator reports serious accident. Request instructions	0305
4.20	SO BCF	SO 2CS	SL	My position at 4am 55°26 N, 6° 15E …	0419
4.50	SO BCF	Captain D13 Narborough	W/T	My position at 4am was 55°26 N, 6° 15E, course N½E, speed 20 knots. What is your position, course and speed? – join me with destroyers	0440
9.10	Gloucester	SO 3LCS	FL	Narborough, Pelican, Nerissa port bow (Repeated to SO BCF.)	0856
10.08	SO BCF	13DF	Flags	Close the Admiral	
10.10	SO BCF	Narborough	Sem	Where is rest of 13DF?	1008
10.48	SO BCF	Captain D13	W/T	Can you account for all your flotilla? Narborough, Nerissa and Pelican are with me. Reply: No	1045

Lion.[134] By 6am, both *Nicator* and the damaged *Petard* were getting short of oil and they were ordered to return to Rosyth; at 7.00, *Nicator*'s surgeon was transferred to *Petard* to treat her wounded. In the afternoon, at 3.30pm, *Nicator* spotted a torpedo approaching from abaft the starboard beam but she turned in time so that the torpedo passed ahead before it exploded harmlessly under water; the firing submarine, *U52*, was not seen. The two destroyers reached the Forth during the evening of 1 June. At 5.45am, *Unity* also parted company but after searching fruitlessly for *Achates*, her oil ran low and she made for Aberdeen, arriving at 10pm.[135] At 6.10am, Goldsmith ordered *Termagant* to rejoin the 13DF but she was unable to find them before, with oil running low, she turned for Rosyth, arriving there at midnight. *Lydiard* waited until 7.30am before, with only enough oil to get back to base, she proceeded with *Liberty* and *Landrail* to the Forth.[136]

[134] *OD*, pp. 230, 234, 236, 255–6 and 259.
[135] *OD*, pp. 233, 241–2 and 313. F&H, pp. 355–6.
[136] *OD*, pp. 255, 258–9 and 263. Campbell, p. 322. *Morris* is unaccounted for, but Goldsmith's despatch stated that he put ' "Narborough" in charge of all the "M.'s" '.

Table 9.25. *British light forces' signals 4.20–10.30am*

Time of despatch	From	To	System	Message	Time of origin
am, 1 June					
4.20	Marksman	SO 1BS	SL	Marksman, Maenad with Champion, remainder lost touch with after engaging Enemy. Told them to steer South after me, and at 3.40 on meeting Revenge told them to steer North and try to pick up fleet	
4.50	SO BCF	Captain D13 Narborough	W/T	My position at 4am was 55°26 N, 6° 15E, course N½E, speed 20 knots. What is your position, course and speed? – join me with destroyers	0440
4.51	Dublin	SO 2LCS	W/T	My 0432. Dublin steering North, 17 knots	0445
5.30	Dublin	Marksman	SL	Have you seen battlefleet or anyone? Reply: No. Champion is with us	
5.46	Captain D13	Destroyers in Company	Flags	Alter course in succession to N . . . 23 knots	
6.45	Dublin	Marksman	Sem.	I have picked up a man belonging to Tipperary. Can you tell me what happened to Tipperary and Sparrowhawk? Reply: Tipperary was sunk	
6.57	Captain D13	Marlborough	W/T	My position at 0615 56°9 N, 6°5E, course N½W, 20 knots. Please give me yours	0621
6.58	Captain D13	SO BCF	W/T	Joining Marlborough	0640
7.36	Marksman	C-in-C Captain D11	W/T	Am endeavouring to tow Sparrowhawk stern first	0731
8.04	Marksman	C-in-C	W/T	Priority. Hawser parted. Shall I sink Sparrowhawk? . . .	0801 0855
	Marksman	C-in-C		Reply: Is salvage possible?	0915
			W/T	Reply: Sparrowhawk has been sunk having received orders from SO 1BS	
8.14	Captain D13	SO BCF	W/T	My position, course and speed at 8am 56°42 N, 5°47E, South, 20 knots. Request instructions	0800
				Reply: Collect your flotilla and rejoin	0828
8.24	C-in-C	Dublin	SL	Close	
8.45	SO 1BS	Marksman	SL	Proceed and sink Sparrowhawk	
9.55	C-in-C	Dublin	SL	Join Battle Cruiser fleet bearing South from Barham, steering North, 20 knots	0945
10.30	Captain D12	Marksman	Flags	Close	

Following their final brushes with the enemy, *Dublin* and the group led by *Champion* resumed courses that would eventually bring them together. At 4.30am, the latter reached the location of the final attack by the 4DF, where *Marksman* and *Obdurate* picked up *Ardent*'s three survivors. *Moresby* and *Maenad* saw many dead bodies from *Ardent* covered in oil and at 5.00 rescued eighteen survivors of *Fortune* clinging to two rafts. At 5.30, *Dublin* and *Marksman* first exchanged signals by searchlight but it would be 6.45 before they were close enough to communicate by semaphore. Meanwhile at about six o'clock both had been distracted by other sightings. By great good fortune, an alert signalman in *Dublin* saw a hand waving from a spar, enabling them to save Stoker 1st Class George Thomas Augustus Parker of the *Tipperary*. At about the same time, *Champion* detached *Marksman* to examine what appeared to be a disabled destroyer to the Westward. *Champion* and the other three destroyers continued Northwards, despite Beatty's orders at 4.50 and 8.14 that the 13DF should rejoin; according the Farie's despatch:

Nothing further occurred, and I returned to base, by your [Beatty's] orders, arriving at 3.30 p.m., 2nd June 1916.[137]

No record of this order has been found, nor an explanation of why *Champion* took so long to reach Rosyth, though the signals despatched at 6.57 and 6.58 suggest that some time may have been spent searching for *Marlborough*.

The disabled destroyer was the *Sparrowhawk*, which had also been sighted by *Dublin*. By this time, the wreck's bow section had broken away but *Marksman* was able to take off from the stern the survivors of both *Sparrowhawk* and *Tipperary*. *Marksman* then attempted to tow the remains stern first, with *Dublin*, at least at first, giving a lee. But both hawsers broke under the strain so that, at 8.04, *Marksman* asked the C-in-C for permission to sink *Sparrowhawk*. By the time *Iron Duke* replied, *Marksman* was communicating by searchlight with *Revenge* and at 8.45 received Burney's order to proceed with the sinking, which was effected by gunfire.[138] Meanwhile, at 8.00 *Dublin* was in contact with the flagship by searchlight and at 8.24 was ordered to join the C-in-C's flag. But it would be 10.30 before *Faulknor* in company with *Revenge* signalled *Marksman* to close.

Scheer's return

At 9.06pm on 31 May, Scheer had made an urgent request for airship reconnaissance off Horns Reef at dawn. His signal was picked up and decrypted by Room 40 but it was not passed by the Operations Division to Jellicoe, nor was it

---

[137] *OD*, p. 225. Also *OD*, pp. 182–3, 311 and 336; F&H, 301, 347 and 370 and Oram, p. 173.
[138] *OD*, pp. 68 and 182–3. F&H, pp. 301 and 348–9.

Table 9.26. *German signals 9.06pm–5.05am*

Time of receipt	From	To	System	Message	Time of origin
pm, 31 May					
	C-in-C	Naval Airship Division		Morning reconnaissance off Horns Reef urgently required	2106
am, 1 June					
1.55	L24	3rd Entrance		To C-in-C … Under ineffective fire from several vessels in 069α IV	
	C-in-C	General		Position of battle fleet at [2.30] 101α right, centre. Course SEbyS. Speed 16 knots	0231
2.47	L24	3rd Entrance		To C-in-C … Further enemy light forces in 115ε IV …	
2.55	G39	C-in-C		Derfflinger and von der Tann have only two heavy gun serviceable. Moltke has 1,000 tons of water in the ship, and Seydlitz is also damaged – AC Scouting Forces	
3.02	G39	C-in-C		Moltke at 2.30 in 117α, left. Course SE½S. Speed 18 knots – AC Scouting Forces	0250
3.03	Oldenburg	General	Visual	Submerged enemy submarine in sight to starboard	
3.08	F. der Grosse	General	Visual	Turn together 4 points to starboard	
3.19	L24	3rd Entrance		To Fleet: 3.00 numerous enemy vessels in 036δ VII, at least 12 units. My position is 016δ. Course S	0300
3.20	Moltke	C-in-C	Visual	Moltke has joined up with IBS – AC Scouting Forces	
	C-in-C	AC Scouting Forces		ISG: Return to harbour	0324
3.30	L11	C-in-C		12 British battleships and many smaller enemy vessels in sight in 033β, steering NNE at high speed	0310
3.33	L24	C-in-C		Reported enemy vessels appear to be proceeding S at high speed. Am being chased by two cruisers in 029δ. Course NbyW	0315
3.35	C-in-C	Regensburg		To G40: Report Lützow's position	0314
	C-in-C	General		IISG take station astern. IVSG take station ahead. Leader of Torpedo Boats is to distribute torpedo boats to screen fleet against submarines. IIBS is to proceed into harbour	0338
	C-in-C	General		Course SE. Proceed into harbour eastward of Amrun Bank	0354

Table 9.26. (*cont.*)

Time of receipt	From	To	System	Message	Time of origin
4.08	F. der Grosse	General		Proceed into harbour by squadrons	
4.24	Regensburg	C-in-C		From G38 to AC Scouting Forces and Fleet: Lützow blown up and abandoned at 1.45 – G38	
4.33	L11	3rd Entrance		028α, three enemy battle cruisers steering W. Weather very misty. Difficult to maintain touch	0400
4.35	L11	C-in-C		043β VII, six more enemy dreadnought-type ships, steering N, altering course to W. Am being driven off by gunfire. Am in touch with enemy battle fleet	0340
4.47	L11	3rd Entrance		Reported enemy vessels are steering N. Several enemy vessels in 047α, now out of sight in the haze. Own course N; position uncertain. Visibility low	0410
5.05	V71	Regensburg		To C-in-C: Rostock sunk in 080α VII right, top, on approach of enemy vessels from the westward. Crew on board torpedo boats	0412

received by the German Naval Airship Division. However, in accordance with the original plan for the operation, five Zeppelins were sent up shortly after midnight. *L24* headed Northwards along the Jutland coast; at daylight, the visibility was poor but she made four reports, her final two signals, timed at 3.00 and 3.15am, describing numerous enemy vessels (they were actually a British convoy) proceeding Southwards at high speed near Jammer Bay at the Northern tip of Jutland. *L11* passed NW'wards over a fog-bound Heligoland before at 3.10 sighting what she identified as twelve British battleships accompanied by many smaller vessels, steering NNE. They were in fact Beatty's four battlecruisers in company with Heath's five armoured cruisers.[139] The reference position reported by *L11* placed them some 83 miles WSW of the Horns Reef lightship, a considerable distance from the High Seas Fleet (on British charts the BCF was shown only 57 miles in the same direction).[140]

---

[139] Hines, pp. 1141 and 1151. *GOA*, pp. 212–13. Scheer, pp. 164–5 for *L11's* report. Tarrant, pp. 229–31; the identity of the light vessels first reported by *L24* remain unknown.

[140] *Cf. OD*, Plate 2a ('Track of [British] Operations during the Night') and German Plan VII ('Return of the Main [German] Fleet').

Scheer's despatch stated that:

At daybreak the Main Fleet itself saw nothing of the enemy. The weather was so thick that one could hardly see the length of a squadron [about two miles].

His accompanying chart shows his position at 2.30 as 17 miles WNW of the Horns Reef lightship while his general signal giving his position confirmed that he was still steering SEbyS at 16 knots. By 3.10, the High Seas Fleet had advanced further on the same course to pass 10 miles WbyS of the light vessel.[141] Meanwhile *Seydlitz*, despite her damage, had made her way independently to the Horns Reef North Buoy by 2.40. At 2.55 Hipper informed Scheer that none of the ISG was fit for action; *Derfflinger* and *Von der Tann* each had only two working heavy guns and even *Moltke* had 1,000 tons of water in the ship. At 3.20, *Moltke* rejoined the battlefleet but Scheer had no recent news of *Lützow*. He also assumed that the van ships of the IIIBS 'must also have lost in fighting value' while he had only three fast light cruisers for scouting. His despatch concluded:

Owing to the bad visibility, further scouting by airships could not be counted on. It was, therefore, hopeless to try to force a regular action on the enemy reported to the South [by *L11*]. The consequences of such an encounter would have been a matter of chance. I therefore abandoned any further operations and gave the order to return to base.[142]

At 3.14, Scheer asked for a report of *Lützow*'s position but, before he received a reply, at 3.38 he ordered the IIBS to proceed into harbour and his light forces to form a screen for the dreadnoughts; the latter's return Eastward of the Amrun Bank was ordered at 3.54. Only at 4.24 did Scheer learn that *Lützow* had been abandoned at 1.45.

Scheer's memoirs differ from his despatch in claiming that:

On arriving at Horns Reef at [3am] I decided to remain there and await the *Lützow*. I had not then heard her fate ... At [3.30] came a message that the *Lützow* had been abandoned at [2am].

After that I had no difficulty in drawing my own conclusions. As the enemy did not come down from the North ... it was evident that he was retiring

But his chart tells a different story, since it shows an increase in average speed from 15 knots before three o'clock to 18 knots afterwards.[143] Furthermore, Scheer was hardly likely to reduce speed just at a time when (albeit imaginary)

---

[141] Scheer's despatch, *OD*, p. 598 and German Plan VII. Room 40 intercepted Scheer's signal and converted the reference position into longitude and latitude (Hines, p. 1153 citing signal 20456 in 'Intercepts of German Signals' – see note 31); the 6°50′E agrees with Scheer's chart but the 55°33′N is 5 miles further to the South.

[142] Scheer's despatch, *OD*, p. 598. Tarrant, p. 230 for *Seydlitz*.

[143] Scheer, pp. 163–4. *OD*, German Plan VII (speeds from distances run 2–3 and 3–4am).

submarines were being sighted and he was ordering large turns together. Even so, he added that:

the ships in a south-westerly direction as reported by 'L 11' could only just have come from the Channel to try ... to join up with their Main Fleet ... There was no occasion for us to shun an encounter with this group

However, he then repeated the same reasons as he had given in his despatch for abandoning further operations.[144] The German official history elaborated on this version of events. It declared that Scheer had been 'determined to await developments off Horns Reef' and that he had ordered the battlefleet to return to harbour after he had been informed of the sinking of *Lützow*. It suggested that the C-in-C believed that the ships sighted by *L24* to the North were the main British battlefleet and that the force sighted by *L11* was perhaps the Harwich Force. As had Scheer himself, the history implied that he had been attracted to the idea of attacking this southern group, though it then accepted that, as justified in his despatch, it was a risk that Sheer did not feel justified in incurring.[145] Despite these later assertions, it seems unlikely that, given Scheer's single-minded determination to return to his bases as quickly as possible, he waited off Horns Reef or that he delayed until he learned of *Lützow*'s fate – not least since the signal record shows that he ordered the battlefleet to proceed into harbour before not after he knew that she had been lost. Nor is it credible that he gave any consideration to deviating far from his course to attack the British ships seen by *L11*. Three further reports of more British ships in the same vicinity were received from this Zeppelin between 4.33 and 4.47, but these can only have reassured him that he had been right to press on.

The three British submarines lying on the bottom Westwards from the Vyl lightship could do nothing to impede the passage of the High Seas Fleet, although *E55*, four miles from the light vessel, heard a series of eleven explosions between 2.15 and 5.30. While most must have been the result of German firing at imagined submarines, one of the last was probably the sound of an exploding British mine. The Germans had not discovered the mines laid by *Abdiel* on 4 May; the IVSG and seven battleships of the IBS went through this line unharmed but at 5.20 the rear battleship, *Ostfriesland*, was struck on her starboard side. The explosion hurled part of the mine onto her quarterdeck (it was identified as of the British 'Striker' type); four outer watertight compartments were breached but, for the moment, the torpedo bulkhead held. When *Ostfriesland* sheered out of line, the IIIBS turned sharply to port and, in closing up, some of the IIBS were forced to stop. Scheer's determination to get home was again confirmed by his repeated order to keep straight on regardless of the

---

[144] Scheer, p. 166. For submarines, see signals at 3.03 and 3.08.
[145] Tarrant, pp. 231–3 quoting *GOA*, pp. 216–17.

Table 9.27. *German signals 5.25–8.45am*

Time of receipt	From	To	System	Message	Time of origin
am, 1 June					
5.25	Ostfriesland	General	Visual	Have struck a mine	
	Ostfriesland	F. der Grosse	Visual	Part of a mine has been found on the quarterdeck	
5.28	F. der Grosse	IIIBS	Visual	The present course is to be maintained	
5.35	Ostfriesland	F. der Grosse	Visual	Revolving striker mine, 1915	
5.56	C-in-C	Fleet		In the event of danger from mines, ships are to keep straight on	
	C-in-C	Naval Airship Division		Airship reconnaissance is no longer necessary	0608
7.55	Neumünster	C-in-C		Flagship of British Battle Fleet to Flagship of Battle Cruiser Fleet: If nothing sighted by [7.30] turn about and search to the northward	0655
8.45	Hamburg	C-in-C		Please arrange for Bruges and Nauen to send out following signal at next routine time for communicating:- As there is expectation of damaged ships returning from the Skagerrak, the patrol off East Coast is to be maintained, if at all possible, for another day. U24 and U32 are to patrol off the Tyne during this period – Leader of Submarines	0720

mine danger, and from his signal of 6.08 that he no longer needed airship reconnaissance. *Ostfriesland* was soon able to get under way again at slow speed and, screened by *V3* and *V5* (VTF), formed astern of the IIIBS.[146]

At 7.55, Scheer was doubtless reassured by news of an intercepted British signal indicating that the British were heading away from him, searching to the Northward. By 8.45, the High Seas Fleet was safely inside the Amrun Bank channel. *Regensburg* and three boats of the IXTF were able to turn back towards the Graa Dyb lightship to meet the boats (including *G40* under tow) that had embarked *Lützow*'s crew, while *G39* (previously with *Moltke*) with *V73* and *G88* proceeded up the Danish coast to tow in *S32*. Even as *Seydlitz* approached Horns Reef, the flooding forward was getting worse and she twice

[146] *OD*, p. 343. Tarrant, p. 234.

grounded slightly, though, by going astern, she had freed herself. At 6am, she briefly rejoined the battlefleet but she was unable to maintain the fleet speed of 15 knots as water spread to midships compartments. At 8.45, *Pillau* took station ahead but at 9.00 the battlecruiser ran aground at the southern end of Sylt with a draught forward of 43–44 feet; she got off only by flooding compartments amidships and aft. Her list to port increased to 8° and, with 5,300 tons of water in the ship, at times her keel was scraping along the bottom. During the day, *Pillau* made unsuccessful attempts to tow her and *Seydlitz* also tried to steer stern first for a time. At 6.30pm, two pumping ships made fast alongside and, as well as beginning to pump her out, they also gave her more steerage way. During the night, she was joined by several tugs but her draft forward increased to 46 feet and she went aground near the Weser lightship as the wind increased to Force 8. At last, at 7.30am on 2 June, she was piloted by *Pillau* past the Outer Jade lightship before anchoring off the Jade bar. Once the wounded had been taken off, at high water (11am) she was towed stern-first across the bar into Jade Roads. After this outstanding feat of seamanship, on 13 July she was taken into the Wilhelmshaven floating dock for three months of extensive repairs.

The main body of the High Seas Fleet reached the mouths of the Jade and the Elbe between midday and 1.45pm on 1 June, five battleships of the IBS then taking up guard duties in the Jade roadstead and four of the IIIBS outside the Wilhelmshaven locks. After passing through the Amrun Bank channel, the damaged *Ostfriesland* went West of Heligoland. But at 11.20am, her escorting seaplane dropped two bombs on what was thought to be an enemy submarine. When *Ostfriesland* turned sharply away to port, her already weakened torpedo bulkhead failed and she took in enough water to cause a five-degree list to starboard. Although she asked for a pumping ship, at 2.45pm she reached the North Lock at Wilhelmshaven without assistance.[147] Thus Scheer's determined withdrawal had achieved its purpose. *Lützow, Elbing* and *Rostock* had been lost but most of their crews had been saved. And, after the destruction of *Pommern*, the rest of the fleet had returned to harbour, despite the mining of *Ostfriesland* and the extensive damage to *Seydlitz*. The only remaining hope of damaging the enemy now lay with any U-boats that might have maintained their positions for one more day off the British bases.

Searching in vain

Jellicoe may have been woken from his nap on the receipt just before first light of the Admiralty's signal of 1.48am. Its wording was more definite than the version in the *Official Despatches*.

---

[147] Tarrant, pp. 235–7 with extended quotation from Captain von Egidy's report. S&H, pp. 369–70.

Table 9.28. *Grand Fleet signals 1.48–4.43am*

Time of despatch	From	To	System	Message	Time of origin
am, 1 June					
1.48	Admiralty	C-in-C	W/T	At 1.48 the Admiralty informed the C-in-C that enemy submarines were apparently coming out from German ports, and that a damaged enemy ship, probably Lutzow, was in 56°26 N, 5°41E at Midnight	0148
2.15	C-in-C	General	FL	At 2.30 2BS alter course to starboard to North. 4BS will follow round. B.F. will form single line-ahead in 5th organisation	0200
2.22	C-in-C	SO BCF, SO 4LCS, SO 2CS, SO 1CS, All Captains D	W/T	Priority. My position 2.30 55°07 N, 6° 21E, altering course N, conform and close	0212
2.27	Nottingham	SO 2LCS	FL	Barham NE	0225
2.28	SO 5BS	5BS	FL	Indicate bearing of battlefleet	
				Reply: 2BS South two miles	
2.30	King George V	C-in-C	FL	Shall I go on? Reply: Wait a minute	
2.33	Benbow			Remarks: Iron Duke opened fire	
2.35	C-in-C	King George V	SL	Carry on when you are a bit straight	
2.44	SO 5BS	5BS	Flags	Alter course in succession 16 points to starboard . . . 19 knots	
2.50	C-in-C	General	SL	King George V take Guide of fleet	
3.12	Admiralty	C-in-C	W/T	German light Cruiser in 55°45 N, 6° 25E, damaged, crew taken off, Destroyers standing by 3 a.m.	0312
3.20	Admiralty	C-in-C	W/T	Five Light Cruisers, 13 Destroyers ordered from Harwich towards Lat. 55°30 N, 6°0E to join you and replace vessels requiring fuel	0320
3.29	Admiralty	C-in-C	W/T	Urgent. At 2.30 German Main Fleet in 55°33 N, 6°50E, course SEbyS, 16 knots	0329
3.30	Oak	C-in-C	SL	Report of guns WSW	
3.36	C-in-C	SO 2BS	SL	Look out for damaged Enemy Battle Cruisers ahead or on either bow, probably with large number of TBDs	0330
3.38	SO 5BS	C-in-C	W/T	Barham, Malaya, Valiant two miles ahead of 2BS	0335
3.40	Benbow	C-in-C	Sem.	Heavy firing heard WSW from Benbow	0335
3.42	C-in-C	General	Flags	Divisions separately alter course in succession to West preserving their formation . . . 15 knots	

Table 9.28. (*cont.*)

Time of despatch	From	To	System	Message	Time of origin
3.50	Commodore T	General	Flags	Slip	
3.52	C-in-C	General	Flags	Alter course leading ships together the rest in succession to North ... 17 knots	
3.52	Collingwood	C-in-C	W/T	Urgent. Enemy Airship SSE	0350
3.55	C-in-C	General	Flags	Engage Enemy Airship	
3.58	C-in-C	General	Flags	Cease fire	
4.05	Marlborough			Remarks: Enemy Airship in sight, 4.07 open fire, 4.12 cease fire	
4.08	C-in-C	5BS	SL	Take station three miles ahead	
4.13	C-in-C	General	Flags	Form divisions in line-ahead, columns disposed abeam, ships turning to port	
4.30	C-in-C	General	Flags	Resume original course together	
4.31	Dublin	SO BCF and C-in-C	W/T	Urgent. One Cruiser and two Destroyers, probably hostile, in sight. Bearing E, Course S. My position 55° 30 N, 6°33E	0430
4.43	King George V	C-in-C	SL	Battle Cruiser fleet in sight NNW	0435

Position of Lützow at midnight 56°26′[N]-5°41′E, course S. Speed 7 knots, damaged. All German submarines are being hurried from German ports to attack. One flotilla returning round Skaw.[148]

By firmly locating the damaged *Lützow* some 40 miles almost due North from *Iron Duke*, this report can only have helped to keep Jellicoe's attention focussed astern, where, he chose to believe, the enemy fleet was still following him Southwards. At 2.15, he warned the battlefleet to prepare to alter course to North and at the same time to form single line-ahead in Organisation No. 5; the 2BS would turn to starboard and the 4BS follow round. The weather was misty with visibility at best only two to four miles. The signal record does not contain the actual orders by which the fleet turned about into single line, though it seems that a 'forming and disposing' signal was used. However, there appears to have been some delay while *Iron Duke* opened fire, possibly at a cruiser that did not respond to her challenge;[149] the manoeuvre was probably completed at

[148] Hines, p. 1153. For the intercepted signals concerning submarines and the flotilla, see 'Jutland Signals' sheets 5–7 in 'Actions and Operations', ADM 137/4067. Distance from position plotted on *Iron Duke*'s track chart, *OD*, Pl. 6a.

[149] *OD*, pp. 26, 81, 100 and 277. *Colossus*'s despatch noted: '2.30 a.m. Course, N. 1pdt. A. BD 5.' *GSB 1915* (p. 71) defines 'BD' (without a numeral) as 'I mean to pass on the Port side of the Enemy'.

about 2.50 when *King George V* took Guide of the Fleet. The 5BS, which had been following astern, also turned N and by 3.35 were two miles ahead of the 2BS. In his preliminary despatch of 2 June, Jellicoe stated that his object in turning North was 'to collect the fleet and Destroyers in readiness to renew the action'. In his full despatch, he added:

I deemed it advisable to disregard the danger from submarines due to a long line of ships and to form line of battle at once in case of meeting the enemy battlefleet before I had been able to get in touch with my cruisers and destroyers.[150]

Although columns of divisions was tactically more flexible, Jellicoe perhaps feared that, in the pre-dawn light and poor visibility, he would not have time to form line if the German fleet suddenly emerged from the mist on their supposed course S.

At 2.22, Jellicoe had ordered all his forces, including the BCF, to 'conform and close' the battlefleet on its new course N. At 3.20 the Admiralty informed the C-in-C that at last they had ordered the Harwich Force to join him to replace ships running short of fuel; Tyrwhitt's five light cruisers and eighteen destroyers slipped their moorings at 3.50,[151] though they were much too late to be of any use to the Grand Fleet itself. A slightly earlier Admiralty signal timed at 3.12 had reported that, at 3am, a damaged German light cruiser was in a position some 34 miles NNE of *Iron Duke*. As decrypted by Room 40, the intercepted German signal identified her as *Elbing* and gave her position at 2am but the Operations Division did not pass on her name and wrongly converted the time. Soon, Jellicoe's hopes of finding the enemy ahead were shattered at 3.29 by an urgent Admiralty signal (based on an intercepted signal from Scheer)[152] which placed the High Seas Fleet at 2.30 in a position that was 29 miles NEbyE from *Iron Duke* and only 16 miles W½N from the Horns Reef lightship; their course was given as SEbyS, speed 16 knots. Jellicoe must have been gratified to see that this was directly towards *Abdiel*'s two minefields, although at 16 knots the last German battleship would pass over the mines by 5am. The C-in-C's staff would also have been able to calculate that, even if the British battlefleet increased to 19 knots, it could not reach the same vicinity until just after 6am.[153] The battlefleet itself, except for Burney's 6th Division, remained together. But the BCF was still closing, so Jellicoe's scouting force was reduced to three light cruisers of the 2LCS; worse, since he had not found any of his flotillas, the fleet could depend for defence against torpedo attacks

---

[150] *OD*, p. 26, also *OD*(M), p. 575.   [151] *OD*, p. 341.

[152] Hines, p. 1153. 'Jutland Signals' (see note 148) Sh. 6 confirms *Elbing*'s position was for 4am German time, 2am GMT.

[153] *OD*, p. 22. These and subsequent distances, times and bearings have been obtained by plotting positions on *OD*, Pl. 2a.

only on the five ships of the 4LCS. As he wrote after the War in *The Grand Fleet*:

The difficulties in collecting the Fleet (particularly the destroyers) ... rendered it undesirable for the Battle Fleet to close the Horn Reef at daylight, as had been my intention when deciding to steer southward during the night. It was obviously necessary to concentrate the Battle Fleet and the destroyers before renewing action.[154]

Thus, without his destroyer screen, Jellicoe was not prepared to expose the Grand Fleet to the massed torpedo attacks that he had anticipated the night before, nor to the mine traps or lurking submarines that, as he had feared for so long, might lie in the wake of the retreating German fleet.

After receiving the Admiralty's signal, Jellicoe held his course N while warning the leading 2BS to look out ahead for damaged enemy battle-cruisers escorted by destroyers. But, even before this signal was des-patched, the destroyer *Oak* reported gunfire to the WSW. Probably in the hope of finding at least some German ships to port, at 3.42 Jellicoe ordered the battlefleet to turn by 9 Pendant to W but almost immediately *Falmouth* reported that the sounds came from the BCF firing at a Zeppelin. Ten minutes later, the battlefleet turned back to N in line-ahead, just as they too sighted the airship and briefly opened fire with their main and second-ary armaments.[155] No hits were made but, although *L11* was driven off, Jellicoe correctly anticipated that she would report his ships. The Zeppelin was also seen from *Marlborough*, while *Malaya* had an unpleasant surprise when a salvo of shells from the battlefleet dropped out of the sky near her. Although it was still misty,[156] a sudden appearance by the High Seas Fleet was no longer in prospect and, at 4.13, Jellicoe ordered the fleet to reform in columns of divisions, the evolution being completed when they turned N again at 4.30. But, a minute later, *Dublin* reported her encounter with *Rostock* in a position on the starboard beam, some 20 miles EbyS between the British battlefleet and Horns Reef; the obvious conclusion was that this straggler at least was attempting to follow in Scheer's wake towards the area S of Horns Reef. At 4.43, the BCF was first sighted from the battle-fleet to the NNW.

At 2.30, the damaged light cruiser *Chester*, with many dead and wounded, was detached from the 2CS to return to the Humber, though her departure may have been hastened by a wrongly received report that she was short of oil. At 2.50–52, Beatty and Heath turned their forces (six battlecruisers, the 2CS and *Duke of Edinburgh*, 1 and 3 LCSs and the 1DF) Northwards in accordance with Jellicoe's order to 'conform and close'. In his despatch, Beatty claimed that he

---

[154] *GF*, p. 244.   [155] *OD*, pp. 56–7, 63, 75, 86, 90, 93, 100, 114, 129, 364–5, 367 and 376.
[156] *OD*, pp. 101, 182, 220 and 277. S&H, p. 363.

Table 9.29. *BCF signals 2.15–4.40am*

Time of despatch	From	To	System	Message	Time of origin
am, 1 June					
2.15	Chester	SO 2CS	W/T	Oil will last several days. Dead now 28, seriously wounded 36 … Request instructions (Received by SO 2CS as – oil will last several hours.)	0205
2.30	SO 2CS	Chester	Sem.	Make the best of your way to the Humber	0228
2.50	SO 2CS	SO BCF	SL	Have detached Chester to Humber. She had only oil to 3 p.m.	0250
2.50	SO 2CS	2CS	Flags	Alter course in succession to N	
2.52	SO BCF	General	Flags	Alter course in succession to NNE	
3.05	SO BCF	SO 2CS	SL	Did you get signal from C-in-C to close?	0306
				Reply: Yes, am proceeding at 20 knots	
3.10	Falmouth			Remarks: Zeppelin bearing SE	
3.28	SO BCF	General	SL	Alter course in succession to NbyE	
			Flags		
3.35	C-in-C	SO BCF	W/T	Did you get Admiralty telegram 0148?	0326
4.04	SO BCF	C-in-C	W/T	When last seen Enemy was seen to the W steering SW and proceeding slowly. Zeppelin has passed astern of me steering W. Submit I may sweep SW to locate Enemy	0350
4.07	SO BCF	Light Cruisers	SL	Spread well to westward and endeavour to locate Enemy. Keep linking ships in visual touch and pass to 3LCS. My course NNW, 20 knots	0407
4.14	SO BCF	General	Flags	Alter course in succession to NNW. Ships in column to keep close order	
4.25	SO BCF	General	Flags	Alter course in succession to N½E	
4.30	SO BCF	Battle Cruisers	Sem. SL	Damage yesterday was heavy on both sides, we hope to-day to cut off and annihilate the whole German Fleet. Every man must do his utmost. Lutzow is sinking and another German Battle Cruiser expected to have sunk	
4.36	SO BCF	SO 2LCS	SL	Close nearer the Admiral	
4.40	C-in-C	SO BCF	W/T	Enemy fleet has returned to harbour. Try to locate Lutzow	0440

had intended to ask permission to sweep SW at daylight but, according to the signal record, he did not actually originate a signal making this proposal until 3.50. This signal stated that he last saw the enemy to the W, steering slowly SW – though in fact his last enemy report, for 9.00pm the previous evening, gave a bearing of NbyW and a course WSW.[157] Even so, he had been steaming NNE and NbyE for the previous hour; so, if the enemy ships had continued Southwesterly during the night and early morning, they could have been somewhere on his port beam or quarter by 3.50, in which case a search to the SW might have found them. There is no record that Jellicoe responded to Beatty's submission; the signal to Beatty at 3.35 asking if *Lion* had received the Admiralty's 1.48 signal suggests that the C-in-C still hoped that *Lützow* might be found. Meanwhile, from 3.10 onwards, several of the ships with Beatty had sighted *L11*;[158] her apparent course W seems to have added to Beatty's impression that the enemy lay in that general direction. At 4.07, he ordered his light cruisers to spread Westwards and at 4.14 the battlecruisers turned NNW: though they soon altered back to N½E at 4.25. At 4.30, Beatty encouraged his crews by declaring 'We hope today to cut off and annihilate the whole German Fleet'.[159] But, only ten minutes later, he was informed by Jellicoe that the 'Enemy fleet has returned to harbour' – a considerable exaggeration of their progress when, according to the Admiralty intelligence, they were approaching *Abdiel*'s minefields.

Jellicoe's subsequent signals show that he had not yet given up hope of encountering *Lützow*. After Heath's armoured cruisers sighted the battlefleet, they formed ahead, where they remained until they were detached at 4.33pm to search (without success) for *Warrior*. In approaching the battlefleet, Beatty made several large turns that caused Jellicoe to enquire where he was going. After an exchange of signals, Jellicoe accepted Beatty's proposal that the BCF should try to locate the unidentified enemy cruiser reported by *Dublin*, though Beatty seems to have concluded that she was the *Lützow*. Having been joined once more by the three light cruisers of the 2LCS, at 5.40am he turned the BCF SE, then at 6.15 S towards the position reported by *Dublin*.[160] In the meantime, Jellicoe continued N until 6.03 when he too turned SE and then SEbyS at 6.43. These courses took him in the general direction of the position for *Elbing* first reported by the Admiralty at 3.11 and recently confirmed by a second signal sent at 5.30. But having arrived about five miles W of this position, at 7.15 (or perhaps 7.24) the battlefleet turned N once more. Beatty continued S past *Dublin*'s supposed position. Then, having corrected his dead-reckoning by observation, at either 7.25 or 7.32 he turned NNE to return close to *Dublin*'s

---

[157] In his despatch (*OD*, pp. 138–9), Beatty gave an enemy course at 9pm of SWbyS but the signal record and '*Shannon* . . . record of W/T Traffic' (in ADM 137/2142) both give it as WSW.

[158] *OD*, pp. 166, 187, 275, 277–8 and 281. *OD*(M), 3.10–.42.

[159] This signal mentioning the damaged *Lützow* suggests that Beatty received the Admiralty signal of 1.48 but not that of 3.39.

[160] *OD*, p. 273 and Pl. 11; unlike Pl. 2a, this BCF chart shows them far enough to the East to pass close to *Dublin*'s position. *OD*(M), pp. 491–3.

Table 9.30. *British signals 4.45–10.07am*

Time of despatch	From	To	System	Message	Time of origin
am, 1 June					
4.45	C-in-C	General	SL	Leading ships of divisions look out for Lutzow, damaged, ahead	0430
4.52	SO BCF	SO 2CS	SL	Our battlefleet bearing NE. My course is E	0450
5.01	C-in-C	Commodore F	W/T	My position at 4.45 is 55°29 N, 6°2E, steering N at 17 knots. What is your position, course and speed?	0455
5.03	C-in-C	SO 5BS	Flags	Take station on the starboard beam of Colossus, 11 cables distance	
5.03	SO BCF	General	Flags	Alter course in succession eight points to starboard	
5.05	SO BCF	BCF	Flags	Alter course in succession six points to port	
5.10	SO BCF	BCF	Flags	Alter course in succession eight points to port . . . 18 knots	
5.20	C-in-C	SO BCF	SL	Where are you going? Reference position at 4.45 . . .	0520
				Reply: I have closed you in accordance with your orders. Am I to locate Cruiser reported by Dublin, probably one of two in sinking condition last night?	0525
				Further reply: Yes, I will take a cast to southward and eastward and then come North again, as I think Lutzow must be to eastward	0535
5.28	SO 1LCS	SO 3LCS	SL	Course of Battle Cruisers North, 18 knots. I have rejoined	
5.30	Admiralty	C-in-C	W/T	Elbing still afloat at 3.47, without crew. Position 3 a.m. 55°45 N, 6°25E	0530
5.40	Commodore F	C-in-C	W/T	My position approximately at 5am 55°48 N, 6°22E, course N, speed 20 knots	0535
5.43	SO BCF	General	Flags	Alter course in succession to SE	
5.54	SO BCF	SO 2LCS	SL	I am casting to the SE to endeavour to pick up a wounded Battle Cruiser sighted by Dublin. Screen ahead of me. I shall alter course to the southward at 6.15	0550

Table 9.30. (*cont.*)

Time of despatch	From	To	System	Message	Time of origin
5.57	Commodore F	C-in-C	W/T	My position 56°9 N, 6°15E, course W, speed 20 knots	0600
6.00	Commodore T	C-in-C	W/T	Am proceeding ... with five Light Cruisers and 18 Destroyers. Request instructions ...	0540
				Reply: Detach four TBDs to screen Marlborough proceeding to Rosyth via 'M' channel does not require any help. Her position at 4.30 a.m. ...	0700
6.03	C-in-C	General	Flags SL	Alter course leading ships together the rest in succession to SE	
6.14	C-in-C	SO BCF, SO 1BS, SO 2CS, all Captains D	W/T	My course SE. Speed 17 knots	0602
6.15	SO BCF	General	Flags	Alter course in succession to South	
6.43	C-in-C	General	Flags	Alter course leading ships together the rest in succession to SEbyS	
7.00	C-in-C	SO BCF	W/T	Abdiel has laid mines 12 mile W of her last mine field. I will sweep N on a five-mile front from 55°35 N, 6°23E. Keep to Eastward of me	0652
7.00	SO BCF	C-in-C	W/T	If nothing is sighted by 7.30, propose altering and sweep NE	0655
7.04	C-in-C	SO 1BS Commodore F	W/T	Join me 8.15 55°56 N, 6°13E	0638
				Reply from SO 1BS: Cannot reach rendezvous before 8.45	0805
7.16	C-in-C	General	Flags	Alter course leading ships together the rest in succession to N	
7.20	C-in-C	SO BCF, SO 1BS, SO 7CS [*sic*], Captains D4, 11,12	W/T	My course N	0715
7.25	SO BCF	General	Flags W/T	Alter course in succession to NNE	0726
7.38	SO BCF	SOs 1, 2 and 3 LCS	W/T	Course will be altered at 8am to N	0735

Table 9.30. (*cont.*)

Time of despatch	From	To	System	Message	Time of origin
8.00	SO BCF	General	Flags	Alter course in succession to N	
8.32	C-in-C	SO 5BS, SO 1BS, SO 2CS, Revenge, all Captains D	W/T	My position at 8.15 55°54 N, 6° 10E, steering N at 17 knots	0815
8.45	SO 2BS	C-in-C	SL	Castor and flotilla bear from me S50°W	0839
9.17	Admiralty	C-in-C	W/T	At 6.20 Enemy Submarines ordered to close Elbing, position now given 55°51 N, 5°55E	0917
10.07	C-in-C	SO BCF	W/T	Consider light cruiser must have been sunk. I want to ascertain if all disabled ships are on their way ... Sweep up to 57°30 N, 5°45E on your present line. I will prolong sweep to westward to ensure no disabled ships being there	0907

true position. Having found nothing, at 8.00 he altered course to N to follow the battlefleet.[161]

Jellicoe and Beatty had been told that the two reported German positions towards which they steered on their Southeasterly sweeps had been occupied at 3.00 and 4.30 respectively. Both commanders were aware that the main German fleet was already much further East and South; thus, unless both enemy ships had been completely immobilised, by seven o'clock they were most likely to have moved SE'wards in an attempt to follow the High Seas Fleet to safety. Yet, rather than press on to the SE in pursuit of what might be a damaged enemy battlecruiser, both British admirals veered away to the North. Why this shared reluctance to go any further in Scheer's wake? In the same signal at 1.48 that gave *Lützow*'s position at midnight, the Admiralty warned Jellicoe: 'All German submarines are being hurried from German ports to attack.' This was based on a German signal made the previous evening by the Officer Commanding Submarines at 7.50pm, which read: 'All submarines ready for service and U. 67 at once advance to the North'; it was transmitted again later from Heligoland and Room 40 supplied decrypts of both signals to

---

[161] *OD*, Pls. 2a and 11.

OD.[162] This intelligence can only have sharpened the apprehensions of the commanders afloat that they might be lured into a submarine trap. To make matters worse for Jellicoe, even by 7.30am he had still not found any of his flotillas. In contrast, Beatty now had all three of his light cruiser squadrons to scout ahead, plus ten destroyers for his screen, though they would soon begin to run short of oil.[163] But these light forces were evidently insufficient to make him any less reluctant than Jellicoe to head further SE. Once they turned N, both commanders abandoned their search for any stragglers (including a possible battlecruiser) that might be following Scheer; all that remained was that *Lützow* might still be somewhere ahead. Jellicoe received one more enemy report from the Admiralty; at 9.17, he was informed that at 6.20 *Elbing* was in a different position altogether from that given previously. But nothing had been seen when the battlefleet had been in the same vicinity around six o'clock and by 9.07 Jellicoe had already correctly concluded that *Elbing* had sunk (though he had not been told that *Sparrowhawk* had seen her founder).

Table 9.31. *British destroyer signals 3.05–8.47am*

Time of despatch	From	To	System	Message	Time of origin
am, 1 June					
3.05	Kempenfelt	Commodore F	SL	I do not think we made our speed on southern course	
5.40	Commodore F	C-in-C	W/T	My position approximately at 5am 55°48 N, 6°22E, course N, speed 20 knots	0535
5.57	Commodore F	C-in-C	W/T	My position 56°9 N, 6°15E, course W, speed 20 knots	0600
6.10	Kempenfelt	Commodore F	Sem.	I make my position at 6am 56°4 N, 5°30E.	
7.04	C-in-C	SO 1BS	W/T	Join me 8.15 55°56 N, 6°13E	0638
		Commodore F		Reply from SO 1BS: cannot reach rendezvous before 8.45	0805
8.32	C-in-C	SO 5BS, SO 1BS, SO 2CS, Revenge, all Captains D	W/T	My position at 8.15 55°54 N, 6°10E, steering N at 17 knots	0815
8.36	Commodore F	Kempenfelt	Flags	Fleet ahead, inform Opal	
8.47	Benbow			Remarks: Sighted our Destroyers off starboard bow	

[162] Signals 20400 and 20438 in 'Intercepts of German Signals' and *NSA*, pp. 168 and 171, which give times sent out in BST. The Admiralty did not know that the U-boats' course would take them about 40 miles N of Terschelling, so they would be no threat to the main British fleet: Tarrant, pp. 241–2.
[163] *OD*(M), 1 June, 8.20, 8.37, 9.20 and 9.30am.

Hawksley and his flotillas did not rejoined the battlefleet until shortly before nine o'clock. *Kempenfelt*'s signals at 3.05 and 6.10 suggest that *Castor*'s navigation was faulty, perhaps because of the damage to her fore bridge sustained during her action with the IVSG. Hawsley's course orders in the signals record between 2.29 and 8.33,[164] if they are correct and complete, also indicate that he was well North of the battlefleet until about five o'clock and that his reported positions at 5am and 6am (though reasonably consistent with his reported speed of 20 knots) were too far to the East. After six o'clock the flotillas were probably fairly close to the battlefleet but, in the misty conditions, they missed sighting each other until 8.36 or a little later.

Even after regaining his destroyer screen, Jellicoe's next turn at 8.52 was not SE'ward but SSW, while he did not respond to the 2LCS's report of gunfire a long way off to the East (perhaps the High Seas Fleet still firing at imaginary submarines). His main concern seems to have been to 'ascertain that all disabled ships are on the way'. After turning NbyW at 10.00am, at 11.08 Jellicoe advised the Admiralty that he no longer required the Harwich Force (except for four destroyers to screen *Marlborough*) and that he was returning to base. *Revenge*'s division, which Jellicoe believed had been 'broad on the eastern flank of the fleet during the day', finally joined him at 7.25pm. Before turning towards Scapa, Jellicoe had already ordered Beatty to sweep up to a position well to the North of the positions the latter had already reported for the wrecks of the three sunken battlecruisers; after turning NNE at 11.05am, Beatty's courses took him close the wreck locations and then towards the position given by Jellicoe, though nothing was seen. At 2.20/22pm, Jellicoe ordered that the undamaged *Valiant* should proceed independently to Rosyth with a screen of two destroyers: but that *Barham* and *Malaya* should return with the battlefleet to Scapa Flow and thence to Invergordon for repairs.[165] At 4.15pm, the BCF altered course to S89°W towards Rosyth, where they anchored at 8.24am the next morning, 2 June. The battlefleet returned to Scapa Flow between 10.30am and midday. At 9.45pm that evening, the C-in-C informed the Admiralty: 'Battlefleet at four hours' notice and ready for action.'[166]

Final encounters

The last actions of the Battle of Jutland were submarine attacks on *Warspite* and *Marlborough*. In their original orders, the U-boats stationed in the approaches to the British fleet bases had been instructed to leave their patrol areas on the

---

[164] *OD*(M) contains 15 course alterations by Commodore F between these times.

[165] *OD*(M), 1 June, 2.20, 2.22, 2.28, 3.39 and 3.50pm.

[166] *OD*, pp. 26, 28 and 68 and *OD*(M), 2 June, 8.24am and 9.45pm. The 2CS continued its unsuccessful search for *Warrior* and then for *Broke* before returning to base at 6.30pm on 3 June: *OD*, pp. 29–30.

Table 9.32. *British signals 8.52am–7.26pm*

Time of despatch	From	To	System	Message	Time of origin
am, 1 June					
8.52	C-in-C	General	Flags	Alter course leading ships together rest in succession to SSW	
9.15	SO 2LCS	SO BCF	SL and W/T	Priority. Birmingham reports have heard reports of guns from the East a long way off	0915
				(Received in Iron Duke 9.31.)	
9.36	Admiralty	SO 3BS	W/T	3BS and 3CS return to harbour and revert to usual notice	0936
9.55	C-in-C	Dublin	SL	Join Battle Cruiser fleet bearing South, steering North, 20 knots	0945
10.00	C-in-C	General	Flags	Alter course leading ships together rest in succession to NbyW	
10.01	SO BCF	C-in-C	W/T	Position of wreck of Queen Mary very approximate 56°44 N, 5°49E … Invincible 57°7 N, 6°25E … Indefatigable 56°49 N, 5°32E	0956
11.05	SO BCF	General	Flags	Alter course in succession to NNE … 16 knots	
11.08	C-in-C	Cyclops (for Admiralty)	W/T	Priority. Harwich force not required except for Destroyers to screen Marlborough. Weather very misty. Am ascertaining no disabled ships are left and returning to base. Whole area swept for disabled Enemy Cruisers without result	1044
pm, 1 June					
4.15	SO BCF	General	Flags SL	Alter course leading ships together the rest in succession to S89°W	
7.25	Revenge			Remarks: 5BS sighted	
7.26	SO 5BS	C-in-C	SL	Revenge bearing East from Barham	1725 [*sic*]

evening of 1 June. However, at about 9am that day, the wireless stations at Bruges and Nauern broadcast a message from the Leader of Submarines:

As there is expectation of damaged ships returning from Skagerrak, the patrol off East Coast is to be maintained, if at all possible, for another day. *U24* and *U32* are to patrol off the Tyne during this period.[167]

---

[167] Tarrant, pp. 244 and 293, also p. 54.

With *U52* off Berwick,[168] this left four U-boats off the Forth for the rest of the day. By the morning of 1 June, repairs to *Warspite* had enabled her to zigzag at 19 knots. At 9.35am, when she was about 100 miles ENE of May Island, without warning two torpedoes passed close on either side. The attacker was *U51*; despite the heavy swell, she had kept at periscope depth and approached to within 650 yards before attempting to fire both bow tubes – though, contrary to *Warspite*'s reports, only one torpedo was discharged. *Warspite* zigzagged away at 21 and then 22 knots, reason enough, particularly in a heavy sea, for *U51* not to give chase;[169] having seen nothing more, she started for home the following night. At 10.17, *Warspite* reported the attack to the C-in-C, Rosyth, and belatedly informed him that she was returning without escort. Six destroyers (of which five were Fisher's 'oily wads')[170] were despatched, the first two being sighted from the battleship at 11.42. Just at that moment, a periscope was seen close under the bows but the order to increase speed and ram was frustrated by the delay in conveying it to the engine room steering position. The periscope belonged to *U63* which, like *U51*, had not received the order to remain in position and was already returning with one engine disabled. In diving, she hit the bottom and was then depth-charged by the British destroyers before continuing on her way home. *Warspite*'s violent manoeuvring had dislodged some of her shores but she was able to proceed at reduced speed to arrive at Rosyth, after being cheered as she passed under the Forth Bridge, at 3.15pm. The other U-boats off the Forth, *U66* and *U70*, also did not pick up the broadcast order and they left their positions on the evening of 1 June.[171] Thus the approaches were clear of U-boats when the BCF returned the next morning. However, by the next day, their reception was much less friendly than *Warspite*'s; after the Admiralty's first blunt *communiqué* appeared in the newspapers on 3 June, a midshipman from *Valiant* encountered a small but hostile crowd at South Queensferry sneering: 'The Germans beat you, didn't they?'; and there were even reports in the press of the wounded being jeered by dockside workers.[172]

Marlborough, with *Fearless* in company, proceeded at 4.30am on 1 June to the South of the Dogger Bank with the intention of turning later towards the Forth. At 9.30 she saw two submarines about eight miles to the West and, when they dived with what looked like hostile intent, she altered away immediately some eight points to port. In fact, they were the British submarines *G3* and *G5*. At 4.00, they had been detached by *Talisman* towards the Lister Deep to seek out damaged enemy ships. They had indeed begun an attack but on recognising

---

[168] Campbell, pp. 328–9 for *U52*.
[169] *U51* mistook *Warspite* for a *Canopus*-class predreadnought: Tarrant, p. 243.
[170] *OD*(M), 1 June, 10.17am, 12.25, 12.40, 1.00 and 1.10pm.
[171] *OD*, pp. 203–4. Tarrant, p. 244. F&H, p. 156. S&H, pp. 396–7. Campbell, p. 328.
[172] S&H, pp. 420–1.

Fearless had continued on their way. (They were too late to find any German surface ships but, while returning on 3 June, *G5* joined *G2* and *G4* in an unsuccessful attack on a German submarine, probably *U46*.)[173] At 10.50 *Marlborough* turned back to a Southwesterly course, zigzagging at 10–12 knots; only two minutes later, she observed an oily patch astern and the track of a torpedo overhauling her on the port side, though it passed two cables off.[174] She had been attacked by *U46*, which at the end of a long patrol was about 65 miles North of Terschelling. *U46*'s commander thought that his boat had been seen and that, in the worsening sea-state, pursuit on the surface was unpromising, but the German historian regretted that 'a splendid opportunity to inflict further losses on the enemy after the battle had been lost'.[175]

At 1.45pm, *Marlborough* sighted the approaching Harwich Force. Tyrwhitt gave her an escort of four, soon increased to eight, *L*-class destroyers, while at 4.00 she was joined by *Ness* and *Albatross* from the East Coast. Although now well protected against submarines, the battleship still had a hard struggle in rising seas to prevent water rising further in the ship. After midnight, she altered course for the lee of Flamborough Head before proceeding to the Humber, where she secured to a buoy off Immingham at 10am on 2 June.[176] Thus she reached safety just before the British battlefleet began to arrive at Scapa Flow. Only two U-boats had been stationed off its approaches, but *U43* did not receive the new orders and *U44* decided that the weather was too bad to make an effective attack; both headed for home early on 2 June[177] so Jellicoe, like Beatty, returned without meeting even a single U-boat.

---

[173] Campbell, pp. 317–18 and 324 for British submarines.   [174] *OD*, p. 102 and Pl. 3.
[175] Tarrant, pp. 242–3 quoting *GOA*, p. 228.   [176] *OD*, pp. 102–3. Campbell, p. 325.
[177] Tarrant, p. 245.

10   Technology and tactics

Photographs taken during the Battle of Jutland capture the profound difference between the effects of hits on British and German battlecruisers. Each lost British vessel is shown soon after going into action at the moment of its destruction by one or more catastrophic magazine explosions. Whereas German battlecruisers survived propellant fires to suffer extensive damage and flooding caused by many hits; *Seydlitz* was photographed as she struggled home and in harbour with her bows almost awash.[1] The contrast between the casualty figures and number of ships lost by both sides is equally striking. The object of this chapter is to examine how these different outcomes were influenced by the key technologies described in the first two chapters and by the tactics adopted by both sides (issues of leadership and command will be addressed in the final chapter).

Ammunition and protection

Post-mortems

Immediately after the battle, Beatty acknowledged two main reasons for his losses. After meeting with Commander Dannreuther of *Invincible* on 3 June 1916, he wrote to the Admiralty: 'Undoubtedly loss of *Invincible* was due to magazine doors being left open' and that 'the destruction of *Queen Mary* and *Indefatigable* [was] due to exploding magazines, following shells striking ... turrets or beneath turrets.' Beatty had already given orders to the BCF that in action the magazine doors must be kept closed on one clip except when replenishing the handing room, though he still permitted four or five full charges to be kept there. For Jellicoe, this did not go far enough; *GFG&TO 158* insisted that the doors be secured with at least two clips and allowed only one full charge in the handing room. In a memorandum to the BCF of 2 July, Beatty tacitly accepted the restrictions imposed by this order but not without emphasising that 'the vital importance of

---

[1] S&H, photographs (unnumbered). Bonney, pp. 154–5, 181 and 206–7. Brown, '*Invincible*', p. 345. *Seydlitz* was also torpedoed.

maintaining the maximum rapidity of fire must not be prejudiced'.[2] Then, on 14 July, Beatty proposed that a committee of experts should investigate why German ships, despite heavy punishment and serious propellant fires, did not blow up. However, he did not mention open magazine doors or any other aspects of cordite handling by his own ships, instead placing the blame elsewhere. He concluded that 'either our methods of ship construction are seriously at fault or that the nature of the ammunition we use is not sufficiently stable to ensure safety', and he proposed that particular points for further investigation should include the protection of magazines and the abolition of the black-powder igniters that were attached to cordite charges.[3]

However, the Admiralty officers responsible for material took a different view. On 3 August, the DNO, Rear-Admiral Morgan Singer wrote:

I am convinced that the blowing up of our ships ... was caused not so much by greater flammability of our propellant as by the system of supply that we unfortunately practised i.e. magazine doors open, lids off powder cases, all cages and waiting positions loaded.

In a report of 7 October, the DNC, Eustace Tennyson d'Eyncourt, concurred and insisted that there was only one reported case (in *Barham*) where splinters penetrated a magazine. However, he admitted that war experience showed that 'heavy gun positions in Battle Cruisers should be as well protected as ... in Battleships'.[4] After reading the DNC's report, the Third Sea Lord, Rear-Admiral Frederick Tudor, concluded that the 'somewhat severe criticism of our ship construction' was not justified, and he laid 'great stress on the undoubted improper exposure of cordite during this action'. On 4 November, Beatty was informed (in milder words than those used by Tudor) that Their Lordships 'are forced to the conclusion that in some of the ships engaged in the action of the 31st May the precautions essential to the safety of cordite cartridges were to a certain extent subordinated to the great desire necessarily felt to achieve a rapid rate of fire'.[5] On 16 November, Tudor minuted that: 'There is no evidence ... that any enemy shell penetrated the magazines of our ships' whereas 'the amount of cordite about the ships was enormous'. On 19 December, after a detailed examination of the principal hits on surviving British ships, d'Eyncourt insisted that the losses were due to 'a direct train of cordite from the turret to the magazine' and that he had found nothing to substantiate the 'impression in the Fleet that these three ships were lost because enemy shell penetrated the lower protective deck and exploded either in the magazine or so close to it as to ignite the contents'. He again mentioned the shell fragment that reached *Barham*'s

---

[2] *BP I*, p. 318 and also p. 320 for Admiralty instruction on cordite handling of 5 June. *GFG&TOs*, 158 printed 7 June 1916. Memo, 2 July 1916, ff. 499–500, ADM 137/2134.
[3] *JP II*, pp. 28–31 and in 'Cause of Explosions in British Warships ...', ADM 1/8463/176.
[4] The DNC had expressed similar views in a minute of 22 June: *FDSF III*, pp. 266–7.
[5] Also *JP II*, p. 95.

magazine, adding that 'there were very few cases where fragments . . . penetrated the protective deck over the machinery spaces'.[6]

Meanwhile, on the day that he received the Board's letter, Beatty responded by submitting that 'there is no evidence that, in the ships lost, the "precautions essential to the safety of cordite charges" (so far as the Admiralty at that time had defined them) were neglected'. In forwarding this to the Admiralty, Jellicoe entirely concurred, adding that:

The drill and custom then in force was to keep all cages and waiting positions loaded and the magazine doors open, and all the evidence seems to show that if a turret was pierced by a shell which exploded inside it, the magazine was almost certain to blow up.[7]

Yet he still requested that Their Lordships should reconsider their conclusion. Soon after Jellicoe's return to the Admiralty as First Sea Lord on 4 December,[8] on the 16th, Tudor found it politic to assure him that the Admiralty's letter to Beatty was never intended to convey the impression that censure was implied; next day, Jellicoe insisted, with perhaps a significant qualification that: 'So far as I know the drill for turrets was carried out correctly & therefore the implication that this was not so should be withdrawn' (this was done in a letter to Beatty, now C-in-C, on 23 December). However, on 22 December, Jellicoe refused permission for d'Eyncourt's recent report to be circulated to the Fleet. This denied 'that enemy shells can penetrate the lower protective decks of modern Battle Cruisers, and Battle-ships, before they burst, no[r] that they burst so far beyond the point of entry as to explode in the immediate vicinity of the magazines': but Jellicoe insisted that this 'does not at all represent the views of officers at sea & I do not agree with it'.

Despite Jellicoe and Beatty taking umbrage at the Admiralty's censure, both sides eventually accepted that the regulations in force and the actual handling of cordite during the battle were such that, if a British turret was pierced by a shell, its magazine was all too likely to blow up. But the Admiralty rejected Beatty's request for an expert committee and, although on 17 December Jellicoe expressed his support for further investigation, nothing more was done. And no consensus emerged on whether any of the British losses were due to enemy shells bursting in or close to a magazine.

Even so, there could be no doubt that the German AP shell had behaved as it should, often bursting only after penetrating the plate. Whereas, even before the battle, British commanders were not unaware of the limited effectiveness of their AP shell; broadly, the overall expenditure at Jutland followed the

---

[6] The sources quoted in this and the next three paragraphs are in ADM 137/2027, 1/8463/176, 1/8477/ 308 and 116/1484, transcribed by Simon Harley at www.dreadnoughtproject.org/tfs/index.php/A_ Direct_Train_of_Cordite. See also N Lambert, 'Our Bloody Ships . . .', pp. 47–52 and Harley's rebuttal of Lambert's implication (pp. 32 and 52) that, because of his criticism of cordite handling in the Fleet, Tudor was shipped off to command the dilapidated cruisers of the China Squadron.

[7] Also *JP II*, pp. 96–7.   [8] *ODNB*, Andrew Lambert, 'Jellicoe, John Rushworth'.

Table 10.1. *Shell expenditures*

Calibre	British				German	
	APC	CPC	HE	Unknown	APC	SAP
15in	516	211	Not carried	512		
14in	42	Not carried				
13.5in	643	207		533		
12in	549	400	567		~1,987	437
11in					1,173	Not carried
Totals	1,750	818	567	1,045	~3,160	437

recommendations of the *GFBOs* with the 12in-gunned ships firing a lower proportion of 12in APC.[9] In August 1916, Chatfield was told by a Swedish naval officer that the Germans were describing the British shells as 'laughable' since they had broken to pieces on striking armour. Even before this, on 25 July, Jellicoe, prompted by Dreyer, had demanded that experiments should be initiated immediately 'with A.P. shell filled trotyl [TNT] using an exact copy of the German delay action fuse'; the C-in-C insisted that 'the Germans successfully reach the vitals of our ships with their shell'.[10] A Projectile Committee was appointed in August with a limited remit to investigate what projectiles and fuses should be used against enemy ships.[11] It was succeeded in March 1917 by the Shell Committee which, under its President, the DNO Captain Frederic Dreyer, by 1918 had developed a new APC shell designed for oblique attack. In comparison with the old shell, it had a heavier, hard cap; a less brittle body with a blunter point; an insensitive filler called Shellite that did not explode on impact; and a fuse that was derived from the previous British type but which gave a consistent delay after passing through the plate (fuse manufacture was entrusted to Armstrong Whitworth rather than as previously to Woolwich Arsenal, where there had been 'carelessness on manufacture and lack of proper independent inspection'). Proof firing was at 20° to normal, the shells (which were named 'Green Boys' after their paint colour) being required to penetrate the test plates intact (see Table 4.2 for plate thicknesses) and to burst 20–40 feet in rear.[12] The committees found that the old APC was certain to explode on impact when striking a one-third calibre plate even at normal; that, while a 15in weighted (inert-filled) shell could hole a

---

[9] Campbell, pp. 345–9, though the expenditures are unknown for a few ship. Of *Lützow*'s total of about 380, probably some 200 were SAP.

[10] *JP II*, p. 28 (and p. 31 for Admiralty view that the German fuse had 'obvious defects'). Dreyer, pp. 203–4.

[11] *Final Report of the President, Projectile Committee, 1917*, p. 2, ADM 186/166.

[12] *Projectile Committee* (see note 11). *Reports of the Shell Committee, 1917 and 1918*, ADM 186/169 (p. 27 for proof tests). *Technical History, TH29, Ammunition for Naval Guns*, AL (p. 55 for fuses). Chatfield, pp. 154–7 and 167. Dreyer, p. 234.

Table 10.2. *APC penetration*

Gun and shell	Striking velocity (feet/second)	Equivalent range (yards)	Plate thickness	
			New APC proof	Perforation diagrams 1915
12in Mk X	1,500	13,500	6in	8.3in
12 in Mk XI	1,500	14,900	6in	8.3in
13.5in Light	1,500	14,700	8in	9.4in
13.5in Heavy	1,500	15,500	8in	10.2in
15in	1,550	15,500	10in	

6in plate at 20° at an equivalent range of 16,800 yards, it broke up completely in doing so, with only some fragments going through the plate; and that the old APC had no distinct advantages over CPC under any action conditions. Scathingly, the Shell Committee concluded that: 'The old A.P.C. shells hardly merited the name of "armour-piercing projectiles" at all'.[13] Table 10.2 also includes a final column derived from the perforation diagrams in the *Manual of Gunnery 1915* for impact at 30°. Of course, these predictions were only for a reasonable expectation that the plate would be perforated, not that the projectiles could go through and burst far behind the plate. Even so, if the old 15in APC could not perforate a plate much more than 6in thick, it is likely that these thicknesses were overestimates by at least 4in.

Effectiveness in battle

Although it is clear that the British APC shell in use at Jutland had multiple deficiencies, 65.4% of the APC and CPC shells fired by British ships were of calibres greater than 12in, the maximum available to their opponents. How far did this greater weight of metal and high explosive make up for inferior armour penetration? In *Jutland. An Analysis of the Fighting*, John Campbell provides extensive details of the hits sustained by both sides. To provide a quantified comparison, a spreadsheet-based analysis has been made of all direct hits on armour and hull plating that fall straightforwardly into the categories in Table 10.3;[14] in many cases, the type of shell making a hit is uncertain, so no breakdown by shell type has been attempted. The bold figures give percentages of each class of hit (rounded to the nearest integer), the other figures give the actual numbers of hits included in the analysis. A considerably higher

---

[13] *Projectile Committee*, pp. 22–3. *Shell Committee*, pp. 7, 24 and 161–2 and Dia. 1 and *TH29*, p. 8 (see note 12).

[14] Campbell, chapters 5, 7, 9, 11 and 13. As well as hits for which information is insufficient, this analysis omits ricochets, hits passing though masts and funnels or on guns, and the two hits by *Agincourt*'s defective TNT-filled shell.

Table 10.3. *Effects of hits by heavy shell at Jutland*

	Effect	All thicknesses				Armour ≥5in			
		German		British		German		British	
		%	No.	%	No.	%	No.	%	No.
1.	No or incomplete burst	22	11	12	8	26	5	18	7
2.	Complete burst								
2.1.	plate not holed	8	4	27	18	21	4	33	13
2.2.	plate holed								
2.2.1.	burst outside or while penetrating	8	4	34	23	5	1	36	14
2.2.2.	burst behind plate	63	32	27	18	47	9	13	5
	Total hits on armour ≥ 5in thickness	37	19	58	39		19		39
	Total hits		51		67				

proportion of British than German hits were made on armour (taken here to be plate 5in or more in thickness); however, even when the analysis is restricted to these hits, the same general conclusions apply. First, a greater proportion of German shell did not burst properly, probably mainly due to failures of the delayed-action fuses. Second, German shell was much more likely to go right through the plate that was first struck and, when the fuse worked properly, to burst well behind it; where the distance behind was given, it ranged from 3 feet to 53 feet with an average of 17 feet. British shell behaved much as had been expected, both CPC and APC being more likely to burst outside the impacted plate or while going through it. Nonetheless, heavy British shells, even those that did not penetrate at all, could do considerable damage, progressively degrading the offensive power and buoyancy of German ships.

Shells that penetrated deep into the ship before bursting were most likely to set off a propellant explosion, particularly if the shell or its fragments could penetrate the armoured (protective) deck that protected the magazines and machinery. British shells made two (perhaps three) hits of this type, the German no more than three on surviving British ships (though, as we shall see, there was very probably at least one more on the lost battlecruisers). Of the British hits, one struck the *Von der Tann* at 4.23pm and, after going through the side, the main deck and two bulkheads, burst above the armoured deck close to the after barbette, where the latter was only 1.2in thick. The barbette was extensively holed (though no propellant was ignited) and four small holes were made in the armoured deck. The other hit pierced a German battleship magazine with fragments; at 6.35, a CPC shell from *Iron Duke* passed intact through the 7in lower edge of *König*'s belt and hence under the armoured deck; it then burst while going through the longitudinal bulkhead next inboard; fragments flew through the coal in the bunker behind the bulkhead to hole the 40mm (1.6in) torpedo bulkhead and completely destroyed a secondary magazine behind it. Fifteen charges were ignited but the fire was smothered by the inrush of coal and seawater. According to *Lützow*'s Paschen, the hit between C and D turrets at about 7.15 tore up the armoured deck, though without affecting the magazines underneath; however, the damage to the deck does not seem to be corroborated by the German damage analysis.[15] Of the three German hits, just one resulted in a shell fragment piercing a magazine. At about 4.58, a shell went through *Barham*'s upper deck to burst 15 feet from impact on the main deck. It caused serious damage, including a cordite fire in a 6in casement, though flash did not reach the magazine. Part of the shell head went through the hole in the main deck to pierce the 1in protective (middle) deck; a smaller fragment punched through not only the protective deck but the ⅜in lower deck where it formed the roof of the forward 6in magazine (though it did not ignite any cordite). However, in battlecruisers the protective decks (called the lower decks) formed the roofs of almost all the turret magazines – other than the Q magazines in the *Lions* and *Queen Mary*, which were a deck lower. Thus if this hit had been on a battlecruiser it could have sent two hot fragments, one large, into a magazine.[16] The other two German hits pierced protective decks, though not directly above magazines. That on *Tiger* at 3.55 went clean through the upper 6in belt, burst above and holed the ⅜in main deck 22 feet from impact, and sent two fragments through the 1in protective deck; the larger, once again the base of the shell, came close to severing the main steam pipe in the port engine room. The other hit was on *Warspite*, between X and Y turret; the shell went through the upper deck, burst above and riddled the main deck, the base plug then continuing through the 1in protective deck to strike the X magazine cooler.[17]

The parts of turrets above the decks – that is, the gunhouses and the upper barbettes – were directly exposed to hits which, if they penetrated, could ignite propellant charges as they were being moved within the turret from the magazines to the guns; this was the second type of hit that could then lead to a magazine explosion. There were ten direct hits by British ships on German turret armour. Five did not penetrate, though one bowed a roof plate and two sent armour fragments into the turret. Of the five hits that pierced turret armour: from two, shell fragments entered the turret, one causing a small propellant fire; one burst going through the plate and also started a small fire; one struck and ruptured the joint between horizontal and sloping roof plates and one went

[15] Campbell, pp. 91–4, 189–92 and 219–20. Paschen, p. 38. Staff, *World War One*, p. 280.

[16] Campbell, pp. 126–8. Brown, *Grand Fleet*, pp. 158–9. Roberts, *Battlecruisers*, pp. 99–105 and 108.

[17] Campbell, pp. 74–5 and 176–7. F&H, pp. 89–90. *Tiger* would have been crippled if her steam pipe had been cut, as would *Von der Tann* if the hit at 4.09 had permanently damaged her steering gear: Campbell, pp. 88–90.

through 10¼in barbette armour – the last two both burst inside and started major propellant fires.[18] In surviving British ships, there were six hits on turrets. The most dangerous, because of the subsequent fire, was that on the joint between the face and roof of *Lion*'s Q turret. Two hits on turret roofs bowed the plates but did not penetrate. Of the remaining three, one went through *Tiger*'s X barbette but fortunately did not burst properly: while the other two, on the X barbettes of *New Zealand* and *Princess Royal*, burst outside but each drove a large armour fragment into the turret.[19] If the German fuse had worked properly, *Tiger* might well have been lost, while the other two battlecruisers could have gone the same way if their hits had sent hot shell fragments into the turrets.

Of the three British battlecruisers that blew up, *Invincible*'s midship magazines exploded almost immediately after the hit on Q turret that 'bursting inside, blew the roof off'. The first hits on *Indefatigable* struck 'about outer edge of upper deck in line with after turret. A small explosion followed and she swung out of line, sinking by the stern.' A second salvo hit in the vicinity of A turret, *New Zealand*'s torpedo officer recalling that there was then a delay of about 30 seconds before *Indefatigable* 'completely blew up, commencing apparently from for'ard'.[20] It seems that, after the first hits, only some of the cordite in X magazine exploded, with sufficient downward force to blow out the bottom near the stern but with limited upward effect; this small explosion could well have been initiated by splinters penetrating directly into the magazine. Whereas the second huge explosion resembled what had happened in *Invincible* (and nearly in *Lion*), viz. a turret hit igniting cordite, the fire then spreading through the turret to set off most of the cordite in the magazine. In the wreck of *Queen Mary*, the hull is shattered in the vicinity of A and B turrets and the forward boiler rooms. At Jutland, British observers noticed hits only near Q turret (which remains largely intact). But from *Derfflinger* von Hase saw flame and an explosion forward before a much heavier explosion amidships before the masts collapsed inwards.[21] The final explosion of the forward magazines appears to have vented aft through the adjacent boiler rooms, though there is not enough evidence to decide whether the hits just beforehand penetrated the fore turrets, their magazines directly or even both.

d'Eyncourt had very little information about the destruction of *Queen Mary* but, although Pakenham's despatch describing the small explosion in the vicinity of *Indefatigable*'s X turret was available to the DNC, he did not discuss the possibility that it could have been caused by splinters entering the magazine

---

[18] Campbell, pp. 82–3, 90–1, 138–9, 189, 220–5, 234 and 264–6.

[19] *Ibid.*, pp. 64–6, 71–3, 76, 131 and 170–1. *OD*, p. 162; *New Zealand*'s 7in barbette may well have been penetrated if the shell had not hit the towing slip secured around it.

[20] *OD*, pp. 158 and 168. F&H, pp. 38–9.

[21] von Hase, pp. 160–1 and see Burt, p. 43, *OD*, pp. 147, 150 and 155. F&H, pp. 39–40.

directly. In the report to which Jellicoe took such exception, the DNC was justified in concluding that there was little danger of enemy shells remaining intact to penetrate and burst inside British magazines. But he understated the risk of a shell bursting close enough to a magazine, especially in a battlecruiser, to pierce it with fragments large and small. Both the Third Sea Lord and the DNC opposed the demands from the fleet that magazines required better protection. However, they were overruled and an additional inch of armour plate was fitted to battleship and battlecruiser magazine roofs,[22] a measure that would have been most effective in keeping out splinters. Of the six hits on the turrets of surviving British ships, roof plates struck away from the edges had proved thick enough but the hit on *Lion*'s Q turret had shown up the weakness at the joint between roof and vertical plates. Further, three barbettes had been holed, one shell partially bursting inside the turret. It was also known that *Invincible*'s Q turret had been penetrated, while the reports available to the DNC stated that, just before the final explosions in *Indefatigable* and *Queen Mary*, both had been hit close to turrets. Faced with plenty of evidence that hits on turrets, even on thick armour, were likely to cause cordite fires followed by magazine explosions, d'Eyncourt had grounds for concluding that battlecruiser turrets needed better protection. But action was limited to the addition of another 1 in of plating to turret roofs.

Of hits that directly penetrated magazines with shell fragments or had the potential to do so, two (possibly three) were British whereas, if the hit that triggered the small explosion in *Indefatigable* is counted, German ships made four such hits. These small numbers suggest that pieces of German projectiles were, albeit infrequently, more likely to reach their targets' vitals. Hits on turret armour were more numerous and the numbers made by each side were closer. In both *Lion* and *Derfflinger*, a joint with a horizontal turret roof plate was penetrated and a serious fire followed; however, hits away from these weak points (one by British, two by German ships) were kept out. Of the eight British hits on vertical turret armour, four penetrated sufficiently to cause propellant fires. The three similar German hits on surviving British ships all holed the armour but, fortuitously, none resulted in a fire; however, it is likely that *at least* another three hits of this type ignited cordite in the British battlecruisers that blew up. If only hits that actually caused a propellant fire are counted as fully effective, then for all hits on turrets, 5 of 10 British hits were effective, while the German ratio was 4:9. These simple numbers may well understate the effectiveness of the hits by the lighter German projectiles on the less well-protected British turrets. But they do support the general conclusion that, despite the deficiencies of British AP, the heavier British projectiles were not significantly less effective against the heavier German armour.

---

[22] Tudor 16 Dec. and d'Eyncourt 19 Dec. 1916 in 'Train of Cordite' (see note 6). *FDSF III*, pp. 266–8. Roberts, *Battlecruisers*, pp. 113 and 118 and *Dreadnought*, pp. 32 and 35. Watton, p. 10.

Thus British losses at Jutland were not the result of a much greater number of effective German hits leading to propellant fires but because, unlike in German ships, cordite fires so often led to the explosions of a magazine's complete contents. Why was British cordite so much more likely to blow up than the German propellant?

Propellant

Only one German ship, the predreadnought *Pommern*, was lost due to a propellant explosion. But this was the result not of gunfire but of one or even two torpedo hits which appeared to set off extensive fires in her secondary ammunition. Despite many other German ships being damaged by British gunfire, none of them blew up. In contrast, British losses due to cordite explosions, all attributable to gunfire, amounted to two obsolescent armoured cruisers, two of the older battlecruisers and one more modern vessel of the same type. To seek an explanation, we need to compare the British and German propellants and charges in some detail.

Composition   At Jutland, all British heavy ships were supplied with Cordite MD45; its composition was

30% nitrogycerine, 65% nitrocellulose (c. 13% nitrogen), 5% petroleum jelly (stabiliser).

Cordite was extruded as cord (cylindrical rods), after which the acetone employed during manufacture as a solvent was removed by drying, the cords of MD45 then shrinking to a diameter of 0.34in. German propellant at Jutland was RP C/12; for heavy guns, its composition to the nearest percent was

25% nitroglycerine, 69% nitrocellulose (12% nitrogen), 4–7% Centralite, 0.25% Stabilit, 0.25% magnesia.

Centralite was at once a non-volatile solvent (no drying required), an effective stabiliser and a flame moderator. RP C/12 was extruded as tubular grain, for the 12in gun with an outside diameter of 0.71in and inside diameter of 0.315in. When ignited in a gun, propellants burnt very rapidly to produce enormous pressures; the greater the pressure and temperature, the faster they burnt. The rate of gas production was proportional to the total area of burning surface. Thus cords burnt digressively because their surface area lessened as it burnt, whereas the total surface area of tubes, inside and out, remained more or less constant as the propellant was consumed.[23]

---

[23] Campbell, p. 377. Campbell, 'Cordite', pp. 139–40. Wikipedia, 'Centralite', 'Nitrocellulose' and 'Internal ballistics'. The % nitrogen was a measure of the level of nitration by NO_2^+ ions. The German percentages of nitroglycerine and nitrocellulose assume a ratio of 1:2.7 and 5.5% Centralite.

Like for like, British and German charges contained similar weights of propellant and had similar ratios of initial surface area to volume. Thus, if all the propellant was to be consumed in the time before the shell left the gun barrel, the burn rate per unit area of Cordite MD needed to be faster than that of RP C/12. This conclusion is confirmed by the compositions: higher nitroglycerine content resulted in hotter gas temperatures;[24] even a single percentage increase in nitration approximately doubled the burn rate of nitrocellulose;[25] and only RP C/12 contained a moderator. Furthermore, to prevent excessive pressure just after ignition, British guns had chambers (enlarged spaces behind the shell into which the cordite was loaded) almost twice as large as equivalent German pieces.[26] British post-war reports acknowledged that the German propellant was 'cooler'.[27] Admittedly, the conditions of pressure and temperature were much more extreme in a gun than in a burning turret or magazine. But more highly nitrated nitrocellulose still burnt faster even at a thirtieth of peak chamber pressure,[28] while, at all pressures, more nitroglycerine would be expected to cause more energetic burning.

Stability   Three large British warships were sunk in harbour by spontaneous explosions of their cordite magazines. The loss of *Bulwark* in November 1914 was thought to have been caused by the careless exposure of bare charges, that of *Natal* in December 1915 by questionable cordite that should have been expended or landed. But, when *Vanguard* was lost in July 1917, her magazines contained no Cordite MD manufactured before 1909, though some more recent lots made by the trade that had been ordered to be withdrawn in June were probably still on board.[29]

Propellants made by the process of nitration with concentrated nitric and sulphuric acids deteriorated with age, increasingly so if they were subjected to excessive temperatures. At first, they became more unstable and more easily ignited, and eventually they could ignite spontaneously. Deterioration was more rapid if the propellant contained impurities like iron, graphite and wood. In Britain, the problem was recognised long before the War by successive DNOs and any cordite older than 12 years was supposed to be withdrawn. However, improved manufacturing procedures – making nitrocellulose from

---

[24] Cordite MD was introduced because of the excessive temperature of its predecessor, Cordite Mark I, which contained 58% NG: Campbell, 'Cordite', pp. 138–9.

[25] Robbins and Keys, p. 9 and Fig. 3a.

[26] www.navweaps.com for British and German 12in/50 Mk XI and German 30.5cm SK L/50 guns and charges.

[27] Admiralty, Gunnery Branch, *Progress in Gunnery Material, 1921*, p. 33, ADM 186/251 and at www.admirals.org.uk.

[28] Robbins and Keys, Fig. 3a; at lower pressures, the burn-rate ratio actually increased.

[29] *Technical History and Index, TH24, Explosives*, pp. 50–4. AL. Schleihauf, pp. 66, 69–71 and 87. Campbell, p. 370.

newly carded cotton sliver rather than cotton waste, and nitrating for not less than 2½ hours – and a better stabiliser (cracked mineral jelly) were not introduced until April 1917, when the withdrawal also began of up to 6,000 tons of doubtful cordite.[30] To find substandard cordite, samples from each lot were tested on issue and, after five years, further samples were taken from ships' magazines and returned to Ordnance Laboratories ashore; suspect lots could be designated 'Fire first' or 'First use' if they were not so bad as to require immediate withdrawal. However, Captain von Schoultz of the Russian Navy thought that too few samples were tested.[31] In any case, the testing procedures would appear to have depended on ships keeping close track of all the lots in their magazines, yet magazine logs in individual ships were not instituted until 1917; the confusion in *Lion* uncovered by Grant was probably exceptionally bad but an order of 1916 refers to another ship in which the lot numbers on charges and cases did not correspond and to 'numerous instances' of first-use cordite being retained long after it should have been landed.[32]

All in all, it is probable that the British magazines at Jutland contained a significant amount of cordite that was unstable and hence more easily ignited by flash, hot fragments from shell hits, or heat from cordite already burning close by. While comparative information about the testing of German propellant is lacking, it had a superior stabiliser (especially compared with the British stabiliser that was superseded in 1917) and it is unlikely that, given the 'highly organised state of the German chemical industry',[33] the stability of RP C/12 would have been compromised by impurities or inadequate nitration. (While the light cruiser *Karlsruhe* sank in the West Indies after an explosion, it remains uncertain whether her cordite was the primary cause.)[34]

Charges and igniters   The full charge of cordite for a heavy British gun was divided into four quarter-charges, each in a single silk bag. To promote rapid ignition of the cordite on firing, a flat cloth bag containing 16oz of highly inflammable fine black powder was fixed to one end of each quarter-charge, each igniter being protected by a tear-off millboard disc.[35] Some powder percolated through the bags onto the floors of turret compartments. Also,

---

[30] *Director of Naval Ordnance for the information of His Successor*, July 1907, p. 6; 1909, p. 3 and 1912, p. 3, AL. *MoG I, 1915*, pp. 150–2, AL. Campbell, 'Cordite', p. 139. Dreyer, pp. 234–5.

[31] Grant, p. 386. Schleihauf, p. 70. von Schoultz, pp. 55–6; he suggested that simple tests of samples could be made more frequently on board (as in the Russian Navy) but he was politely rebuffed by Jellicoe.

[32] Dreyer, p. 235. *GFG&TOs*, 141 (printed March 1916); see also *GFG&TOs*, 19, 22 and 154.

[33] Hartcup, p. 197.   [34] Campbell, p. 370. Gröner I, p. 109.

[35] Campbell, p. 378. www.dreadnoughtproject/tfs/index.php/Cordite_Cartridge. According to Singer (DNO's minute of 3 August and in the Admiralty letter of 4 November) 'igniters are very little more inflammable than cordite itself', but then why fit them at all? He probably meant igniters covered by protective discs. See also Brown, *Grand Fleet*, pp. 168–9.

once the tear-off discs had been removed, the powder bags were vulnerable to damage during handling; as a result, loose powder could also get into the hoists.[36] German full charges consisted of a main charge holding three-quarters of the propellant and a fore-charge with the remaining quarter. The main charge, in a silk bag, was contained in an open-ended brass cartridge case which also sealed the sliding breech of the gun; the cartridge case covered the base of the charge and most of the sides, the rest being protected by a thin brass lid. A single 7oz igniter was placed under the charge. In the smaller fore-charge, which had no igniter, the propellant was enclosed in a double silk bag with light brass reinforcements.[37] Thus, once the tear-off discs had been removed from British charges, both cordite and black-powder igniters were covered by only single thicknesses of cloth, whereas three-quarters of German propellant and the single igniter (containing less than an eighth of the weight of black powder used by the British) were protected by a substantial brass case (albeit with a thinner lid) all the way to the guns.

Propellant handling A heavy gun turret was a large structure extending upwards from the shell room and propellant magazine deep in the ship to the revolving gunhouse above the deck. In British turrets, the cordite magazines were above the shell rooms;[38] we shall focus on the propellant handling but shells followed similar paths to the guns.[39] In the magazines, cordite was stored in cylindrical brass cases, two quarter-charges per case. From 1908, new case lids were introduced which could be set to a weakened position when in the magazines; should the cordite inside be ignited or even ignite spontaneously, the lids released the rising gas pressure before it could cause the cordite to explode. However, even in 1918, *Inflexible, Indomitable* and *Agincourt* still had unweakened lids;[40] the same was probably true of *Indefatigable* and *Invincible* at Jutland.

From the magazine, cordite quarter-charges were passed through the magazine doors – which had to be open to allow passage – into the adjacent handing room, where the charges were placed in hoppers before being tipped into the main hoists. Each hoist (one for each gun) carried four quarter-charges (accompanied by a shell) up the turret trunk to the working chamber beneath the gunhouse. In the older BVIII mountings for the Mark X 12in/45 gun, four quarter-charges were rammed directly from a main hoist into the corresponding

[36] Grant, p. 390. *Grand Fleet Orders*, 1915, Section B, 20. 'Danger from damaged igniters in cordite charges', ADM 137/4051. *GFG&TOs*, 16, 22 and 121.

[37] Campbell, pp. 377–8. *Seydlitz*, 'General Experience', ADM 137/1644, f. 274.

[38] Roberts, *Dreadnought*, pp. 216–25. Watton, pp. 94–5. Campbell, p. 371.

[39] 'No case occurred of our own shell being detonated [by] enemy fire', BCF Gunnery Committee, *BP I*, p. 365.

[40] *TH24* (see note 29), p. 3. Schleihauf, pp. 71 and 79.

gunloading cage, which took them up to the gunhouse for loading. In later mountings, the ammunition from a main cage was transferred first to a covered waiting position in the working chamber, and then from this waiting position to the gunloading cage.[41] Although hoists, waiting positions and cages were more or less closed containers and flash doors were fitted in trunks, the cordite charges in transit were not completely protected against flash from hits or hot gases from cordite already ignited. A particular deficiency was that the flash door through which a gunloading cage passed from the working chamber to gunhouse remained open when the cage was 'up'. Also, in some British ships at Jutland, the flash doors had been removed in the belief that they slowed the rate of loading.[42] Secondary hoists were also provided in case of breakdown in the primary supply route. Details differed between mountings but, in 13.5in gun mountings, the secondary hoist from handing room to working chamber held one full charge and each auxiliary hoist to the gunhouse (one per gun) also held a full charge.[43]

When action was imminent, the magazine crew began taking off the lids of the magazine cases and passing quarter-charges through the open doors to the handing room. The tear-off discs were supposed to be removed only when the charges were placed in the hoppers. Charges continued to be passed out until the guns had been loaded and all the positions in the supply chain – gunloading cages, waiting positions, main hoists and hoppers, six to eight full charges in all – had been filled. Secondary and auxiliary hoists were also filled with up to three more full charges. After the hit on *Lion*'s Q turret, the officer of the turret ordered the magazine doors to be shut but, thanks to Grant's regulations, there was no more than one full charge (possibly also some damaged quarter-charges) in the handing room[44] while, in the magazine, the lids of the magazine cases probably remained on. However, new regulations introduced after the battle imply that, in the magazines of other ships, not only were lids removed but charges were taken out of the cases before they were required in the handing room (as had been done in *Lion* at the Dogger Bank); also that the protective discs of igniters were torn off in the magazines.[45] Thus, in British ships at Jutland, there was a train of some twelve bare full charges, with igniters exposed, from the gunhouse to the handing room – albeit mostly in enclosed

[41] Hodges, pp. 51, 54, 62–5 and 70–5 (though no turrets at Jutland had a flash-tight hopper between magazine and handing room).
[42] Campbell, pp. 371–2. DNO's minute, 20 July 1916 in ADM1/8463/176 and in 'Train of Cordite'. N Lambert, 'Our Bloody Ships . . .', p. 49.
[43] Information on secondary supply from John Roberts.
[44] 'Reminiscence of Q Turret', *BP I*, p. 354.
[45] Grand Fleet report and memorandum on tear-off discs, 19 and 27 September 1916 in ADM 137/2027, ff. 275–81; the new regulations reverted to removing the tear-off discs in the handing room (except from the charges for the secondary hoists) after unsuccessful attempts to keep the discs in place until the charges were loaded.

cages and waiting positions.[46] And, in some ships, the train of naked charges extended from the handing rooms into the magazines, where magazine cases had also been opened in readiness.

German ships were more varied in their turret layouts, even within single ships. Fore and main charges were stored in separate magazines and transported to the hoists in magazine cases. However, it seems that, in *Seydlitz* at the Dogger Bank, some cases were opened in the magazines; in all, 62 full charges burnt (but did not explode) in the two after turrets and their magazines. After this chastening experience, 'the principal step taken was drastically to reduce the number of charges out of their magazine cases or in opened cases'.[47] In German working chambers and gunhouses, charges were not covered as they were transferred between troughs and trays, often by hand.[48] At Jutland, although there were three major fires in turrets, none spread to the magazines. But fore and main charges proved equally likely to be ignited if exposed to flash from shell hits or to heat and gases from charges already burning. In *Seydlitz*'s after superfiring turret, only two full charges ignited in the immediate vicinity of the hit, though, in the magazine hoist room, a main charge was blackened and its silk bag singed, and paper labels on fore-charge cases were partly burnt. But both hits on *Derfflinger*'s gunhouses started propellant fires which then spread to charges in her working chambers and handing rooms. After the first hit, four full charges burnt in hoists and trays but also three main charges being transferred to the hoists and nine fore-charges in open magazine cases; clearly, the new regulations were not being observed. After the second hit, seven full charges ignited in the turret supply paths[49] – a quantity not much less than that which burnt in *Lion*'s Q turret.

Venting   British and German observers reported that, at both the Dogger Bank and Jutland, the flames from the propellant fires in the German battlecruisers rose as high as a house or to the masthead.[50] These reports seem to confirm that German turrets had effective venting arrangements to limit the pressure rise due to the gas released from burning propellant.

---

[46] *Pace* N Lambert, 'Our Bloody Ships', p. 55, ready-use lockers for a few charges were fitted only in the working chambers of ships with 12in/50 guns, which did not include *Indefatigable*. Apart from Sir Victor Shepheard's memory of *Agincourt*, no other source has been found suggesting that bare charges were stacked in working chambers: see Brown, *Grand Fleet*, p. 168 and N Lambert, 'Our Bloody Ships', pp. 43 and 49.

[47] Campbell, pp. 372–4. Naval Staff, Intelligence Department, *Report on Interned German Vessels. Gunnery Information*, February 1919, pp. 5 (*Goeben*) and 16 (*Markgraf* class), ADM 186/240 and at www.admirals.org.uk.

[48] Hodges, pp, 57–8.

[49] Campbell, pp. 82–3 and 220–3. *Seydlitz* (see note 37) f. 274, which translated 'paper shields' literally rather than as 'paper labels'.

[50] Report from *Birmingham*, ADM 137/305, f. 182. Scheer, p. 84. Staff, *1914–18*, p. 24. von Hase, pp. 198 and 207.

The hits at Jutland on the Q turrets of both *Lion* and *Invincible* blew off the roofs, giving unrestricted venting from the gunhouses. In *Lion*, the hit was followed immediately by only a small fire. By the time of the main cordite fire, which quickly consumed as many as twelve full charges, the magazine doors had been closed and the magazines flooded. Yet, despite the open gunhouse, the pressure in the handing room rose sufficiently to buckle the magazine bulkheads, even against the water pressure, and flame entered the magazine through an unmodified venting plate – these plates were intended to allow gas to vent from magazine to handing room.[51] It is evident that the pressure rise, though not enough to trigger an explosion, was considerable: and, therefore, that venting from the handing room was restricted. *Invincible*'s gunnery officer confirmed that her magazine doors were open and that Q magazine blew up almost immediately after the hit.[52] Unlike in *Lion*, the hit must have ignited sufficient cordite for the fire to propagate quickly through the supply train to the handing room. At the time of the hit, *Invincible* was firing as rapidly as possible, which makes it more likely that bare charges were being stacked in the handing room and that there were more bare charges in the magazine, where cases may also have been opened. Very probably, many more charges were exposed than in *Lion*; once they ignited, the restricted venting from the handing room, through which gas from the magazines also passed, resulted in the pressure rising to the point of explosion.

* * *

As the conflagrations in German ships and in *Lion* establish, a propellant fire in a turret could reach an equilibrium in which the pressure and temperature were sufficient to sustain a steady rate of burning but without provoking an explosion. But, alternatively, after the propellant ignited, the pressure and temperature could continue to increase. As a result, the propellant already ignited burnt faster and the fire propagated to more charges more quickly; each increase in pressure and temperature caused a further increase as the fire accelerated into an explosion. This is an example of positive feedback, a property found in many so-called chaotic systems. It is characteristic of such systems that even very small differences in initial conditions can result in drastically different outcomes:[53] in this case either a steady fire or an explosion.

---

[51] *GFG&TMs*, 'Jutland', pp. 40–1. Campbell, pp. 64–6. *BP I*, p. 351.
[52] Dannreuther to Post-War Questions Committee, ADM 116/2060, f. 440. Tudor to Jellicoe, 16 December 1916 in ADM1/8463/176. *OD*, p. 168.
[53] Francis Heylighen, 'Complexity and Self-Organization' in M J Bates and M N Maack (eds.) *Encyclopedia of Library and Information Services* (Taylor & Francis, 2008) and at http://pesp mc1.vub.ac.be/Papers/ELIS-Complexity.pdf, pp. 4–5. See also Wikipedia, 'Positive feedback', 'Chaos theory' and 'Complexity'. Bill Jurens warned (e-mail to FCG 28 January 2010) that propellant fires are 'phenomena [which] are very chaotic and unpredictable at best'.

In fact, we can identify six distinct, and in most cases not small, differences between British and German charges, though the data are lacking to place them in order of importance. Cordite MD was a 'hotter' propellant, i.e. once ignited, it burnt faster at a higher temperature. Cordite MD was less stable; it incorporated an inferior stabiliser and, probably due to a higher level of impurities, it deteriorated more rapidly. All British propellant was in silk bags whereas only a quarter of German propellant was in silk bags, the rest in brass cartridge cases – these brass cases partly protected the propellant against ignition by flash, while their thermal inertia reduced the rate at which the temperature of the propellant could increase. The single 7oz igniter for a full German charge was safe at the bottom of the cartridge case, underneath the charge; each British quarter-charge had a 16oz igniter attached to one end, from which the protective disc was removed in the handing room or even in the magazine – also there was loose powder on the floors of turret compartments and perhaps in the hoists too. In most German ships at Jutland, main and fore charges were kept in unopened magazine cases until they were loaded into the hoists; whereas it is probable that, in many British ships, magazine lids were removed and charges taken out of the magazine cases to be stacked in readiness in the handing room and magazine aisles.[54] While venting from German turrets proved effective, the venting from British magazines and handing rooms was restricted even without the additional obstructions to gases escaping through an intact gunhouse.

Any one of these differences need not have been decisive. But their effects were mutually reinforcing and together they ensured that British charges ignited more readily and burnt faster, and that a propellant fire, once started, propagated more rapidly through British turrets and even into magazines.[55] Taken together, they constitute a more than sufficient explanation of why, if a propellant fire was started by a hit on a British ship, it was so much more likely to develop chaotically into a catastrophic explosion.

Ships

Buoyancy

Even if a ship escaped spectacular destruction by the explosion of its propellant, its survival still depended on remaining afloat. Table 10.4 lists those capital ships that were not sunk by explosions but received four or more hits by heavy shell or were struck by torpedo or mine.[56] It is evident that the ability

---

[54] If the magazine cases of *Indefatigable* and *Invincible* had unweakened lids, the cases were more likely to explode once fire reached their magazines.

[55] Brown, *Grand Fleet*, p. 169: 'It seems quite possible that magazine explosions had more than a single cause'. See also Roberts, *Battlecruisers*, p. 118.

[56] Campbell, pp. 354–5; this book is the principal source for this section.

Table 10.4. *Hits on capital ships*

		Hits received				
	German			British		
Ship	Shell	Torpedo	Mine	Ship	Shell	Torpedo
Lützow	24			*Warspite*	15	
Seydlitz	22	1		*Tiger*	15	
Derfflinger	21			*Lion*	13	
König	10			*Princess Royal*	9	
Grosser Kurfürst	8			*Malaya*	7	
Markgraf	5			*Barham*	6	
Von der Tann	4					
Ostfriesland			1	*Marlborough*		1

to stay afloat even after extensive damage was tested most severely in the three German battlecruisers. As well as receiving more hits, the hits were by the heavier British projectiles, which caused severe damage to the plating that kept out the sea. Also, whereas British heavy ships received just over 10% of hits forward of A turret, the proportion for surviving German ships was about 20% and as high as 33% in *Lützow*.[57] This concentration of hits would expose a vulnerability in German ships; in addition to the usual forward broadside torpedo flat extending from side to side just forward of A turret, they also had a bow tube in a separate flat just under the bows.[58] The flooding of these two large compartments would play a major part in the loss of *Lützow*.

At 4.00pm, the battlecruiser received two hits on the forecastle which together made a large hole that would later admit much water above the armoured deck. At about 6.30pm, two hits struck below the waterline near the forward broadside torpedo flat and another two close to the bow flat; although the details are uncertain, both flats quickly flooded with 740 tons of water. Water also spread below the armoured deck through damaged bulkheads and voice pipes and also through ventilation trunks that either lacked cut-off valves or had valves that could not be reached; by these same paths, water that entered above the armoured deck also began to leak below it. Very soon, *Lützow* had shipped over 2,000 tons of water, increasing her draught forward by nearly eight feet. Her forward leak pumps were inoperable while, due to inadequate drainage to the midships pumps, they could not prevent the water

---

[57] *Ibid.*, pp. 355 and 381; the proportions were 7:68 (British) and 15–16:78–79 (German, except *Lützow*, 8:24).

[58] Gröner I, pp. 23–30 and 53–7. Staff, *1914–18*, Fig. D. *CAWFS 1906–21*, pp. 21–35. Roberts, *Dreadnought*, p. 236 and Watton, pp. 1–13 and 101.

from spreading. As the draft forward increased to 28½ feet, all compartments below the armoured deck and forward of the conning tower were flooded while, above the armoured deck, the water reached A barbette. At the end, with over 8,300 tons of water in the fore part and more in the foremost boiler room, the upper edge of B barbette was level with the sea and her propellers were out of the water. In Campbell's words, 'her torpedoing ... did not much hasten her sinking'.[59]

While *Lützow* foundered, *Seydlitz* survived almost as many shell hits and also a torpedo hit. She too received multiple hits on the forecastle which made holes in the decks and sides that enabled water to enter and spread above the armoured deck. At 4.57, the torpedo struck near the forward end of the internal torpedo bulkhead abreast of A turret; although the side plating was holed and the armour driven in, the bulkhead held, though it was bulged and leaking. Both forward torpedo flats were kept free of water but water continued to spread to other bow compartments above and below the armoured deck through damaged voice pipes, ventilation ducts and leaky cable glands and as a result of further hits. By 6 o'clock, the ship had no buoyancy forward and a large hole on the starboard side was not far above the waterline. Because speeds of 22 and then 20 knots were maintained, more water flooded in and, by the time *Seydlitz* reached Horns Reef, she was in a dangerous condition. As she struggled on, the flooding spread further until her bow escutcheon was in the water. At worst, after counter-flooding to correct her list, there were over 5,300 tons of water in her when, at 5.30pm on 1 June, two pumping steamers reached her (though one proved to have a defective pump).[60]

Derfflinger was also holed forward so that water poured in when she steamed at high speed. At 5.55pm, one or more probably two more hits struck on the waterline forward of the hawse pipes; although the bow torpedo flat was kept drained, by 7.30 the nearby compartments had flooded. When she reached harbour, the calculated amount of water in her was 3,350 tons, though 1,020 tons had been deliberately admitted to flood the after magazines beneath the burnt-out turrets and to keep her on a more even keel. Similarly, *Grosser Kurfürst* received two heavy hits about 75 feet from the bows; water entered above the armoured deck and then spread below it so that the whole fore part of the ship, except for the torpedo flats and trimming tanks, gradually flooded. At 2.25am, she reported about 800 tons of water in the ship but this continued to increase as more water entered through the holes near the bow, eventually reaching over 3,000 tons. The hit on *König* that struck the lower edge of the armoured belt holed the torpedo bulkhead; it let in almost 500 tons of water although the resultant list was corrected by counter-flooding with some 360

---

[59] Campbell, pp. 79, 183–4 and 306–7.
[60] *Ibid.*, pp. 80, 83–5, 138–42, 272, 306 and 322–3. Tarrant, pp. 235–6.

tons. However, to extinguish propellant fires caused by this and other hits, the magazines of the whole forward group were also flooded, but flash and gas prevented them from being isolated. Hence the water spread through the flooding system and also, as in other ships, through ventilation trunks and cable glands; by 11.51pm, the weight of water had increased to 1,630 tons. *Von der Tann*'s hit aft at 4.09pm flooded compartments above and below the armoured deck, half filling the stern torpedo flat; after the battle, she had over 1,000 tons of water aft.[61] The other German capital ship that survived significant flooding was the *Ostfriesland*, which hit a British mine at 5.20am on 1 June. The explosion, which was below the starboard forward wing turret, flooded many outer compartments but the torpedo bulkhead was breached at only one point, admitting water to a magazine; Scheer claimed that she shipped only 400 tons. However, when she veered sharply away from an imaginary submarine, the torpedo bulkhead opened further and she had taken on a list of 4¾° before the flow of water was stopped.[62]

Thus, notwithstanding the reputation of German capital ships for close compartmentalisation, in the bows water was able to spread too easily above, below and through the armoured deck, in part through ventilation trunks, voice pipes and leaky cable glands. Pumping systems proved insufficiently resilient. The continuous torpedo bulkheads were breached in some cases, though not seriously, but, once weakened, were not able to withstand the stresses of violent manoeuvring.

Comparatively, British capital ships received fewer hits from lighter shell, with a smaller proportion striking ahead of the fore barbette; apart from a brief crisis in *Marlborough*, none of the ships listed in Table 10.4 were in danger of foundering. Nonetheless, it was fortunate that the only one to be torpedoed was the *Marlborough*, since she had better torpedo protection than the six battleships of the 1909–10 programme and all the battlecruisers.[63] The torpedo struck outboard of the starboard 6in magazine that was just forward of A boiler room, i.e. near the point where the forward longitudinal torpedo bulkhead met the coal bunkers protecting the boiler rooms. Twenty-eight feet of hull plating was destroyed and many outer compartments flooded. But the torpedo bulkhead, though dented, protected the magazine; apart from a badly leaking watertight door to a bunker, the longitudinal bulkhead of A boiler room remained intact and water was largely confined to this compartment. *Marlborough* listed 7–8° but this was controlled by trimming coal and oil, without resort to counter-flooding. At 10pm on 1 June, the water in the boiler room began to rise due to a choked pump and a failed

[61] Campbell, pp. 135–7, 237–45, 191–2 and 88–90 respectively.
[62] *Ibid.*, pp. 320 and 334–5. Scheer, p. 166.
[63] Burt, pp. 138–9, 195, 197, 211 and 214. Roberts, *Battlecruisers*, p. 109.

steam ejector; the level almost reached the tops of the boilers before the problems were overcome.[64]

Of the British ships heavily hit by shell, some of the flooding in *Tiger* was self-inflicted. After the hit at 3.55pm ignited two cordite charges at the top of the hoist from the 6in after magazine, the magazine was flooded as a precaution. But, when a valve in a ventilation pipe failed, water was able to spread from this magazine to Q turret's port magazine and from there to the after 6in and Q turret shell rooms. Water continued to pour from severed mains and by 7.55 *Tiger* reported that every time the helm was put over, she shipped considerable quantities of water through two large holes in the port side. It appears that her pumps were able to control this continuing influx but not to clear the water from the magazines and shell rooms.[65] In *Warspite*, a hit pierced the 6in side armour and, although it did not explode, holed the ventilation trunk to the middle engine room, allowing water to pour in until the holes were plugged. The hit that went through the top of the main belt exploded in the port feed-water tank and riddled the port wing engine room's ventilation trunk; this too let in water until the holes were plugged, as before with large rubber sheets. At 8.50, *Warspite* signalled that she could steam 16 knots but concern remained that the port wing engine room might flood. The flow through the feed-tank was eventually stopped by filling the compartment with hundreds of hammocks, though not until late that night. *Warspite* was also holed astern below the waterline; when she docked, she was drawing 35½ feet aft, almost two feet more than her deep-load draught.[66] Due to hits at two points below the waterline, *Malaya* experienced some flooding in wing compartments and to some extent above the armoured (middle) deck but the torpedo bulkhead, though bulged, was not perforated. She developed a list of about 4° to starboard, but this was corrected without counter-flooding by pumping oil from the starboard to the port bunkers.[67]

Thus, as in German heavy ships, ventilation trunks, either damaged themselves or with defective sealing valves, provided paths for water to flood below. But British capital ships were more successful in limiting the spread of water away from the vicinities of hits, which perhaps suggests both better design for resilience to damage and better damage-control procedures; however, they suffered fewer hits overall by lighter shell, and fewer still in inaccessible bow compartments.

The modern light cruisers on both sides proved very difficult to sink. *Wiesbaden* was immobilised by a 12in shell but she did not founder until

[64] Campbell, pp. 179–80. *OD*, pp. 100 and 102–7.
[65] Campbell, pp. 73–5. *OD*(M) 31 May, 7.55pm; 1 June, 5.15, 7.45 and 8.27am.
[66] Campbell, pp. 174–6 (hits 8, 10 and 13). F&H, pp. 143, 145–6 and 156. *OD*(M), 8.50pm. Burt, p. 281 for draughts.
[67] Campbell, pp. 131 and 133 (hits at 1720 and 1735).

early on 1 June, despite a torpedo hit and being targeted by so many of the passing Grand Fleet. The old *Frauenlob* capsized rapidly after being torpedoed. But *Rostock*, similarly hit, remained afloat even with about 930 tons of water in her boiler rooms and bunkers, while *Elbing* was not in immediate danger of sinking after *Posen* collided with her; both light cruisers were scuttled later after they had lost their motive power. No British light cruiser was torpedoed but *Dublin, Chester* and *Southampton* were hit repeatedly by gunfire without loss of buoyancy or serious damage to engines. However, in the last two there were many casualties because of the inadequate protection given by their gun shields.

Eight British destroyers (including *Tipperary*) and five German sank, all of them after severe damage. The German *V29* and possibly the *V4* were lost to torpedoes though *V29* remained awash for about 30 minutes; the crippled *Shark* and *Turbulent* were finally sunk with torpedoes. *S35* was struck by a salvo of heavy shells and broke in two. After their engines had been damaged, *V48* was sunk by fire from the 12DF and *V27* was finished off by *V26*. *Nestor* and *Nomad*, which had also been immobilised, were sunk by the secondary batteries of the High Seas Fleet as it passed them. As they attacked during the night, *Tipperary, Turbulent, Ardent* and *Fortune* succumbed to the withering fire from the van German battleships. *Sparrowhawk* did not survive being rammed by *Broke* and *Contest* but they got home, as, remarkably, did *Spitfire* after her head-on collision with the battleship *Nassau*.[68] No destroyer could withstand a hit from a torpedo or heavy shell, nor survive for long against the fire from the secondary armament of capital ships on a similar course. The main danger from the fire of their own kind was of damage to the engines. But, whereas *V27* was crippled solely by hits with 4in shell from *Nestor* and *Nomad*, the same result was only achieved against those two British boats and *Shark* when the 3.5in fire of German destroyers was supported by the 4.1in guns of *Regensburg*. This outcome suggests, though perhaps less than conclusively, that the British were right to adopt the heavier 4in gun for their modern destroyers.

Machinery

To be present at an action in the first place, a ship had to be serviceable; its availability depended to a great extent on the reliability of its machinery when subjected to the day-to-day stresses of wartime service. For Jellicoe, the War began badly when recurring machinery problems added to his concerns about his margin of superiority over the High Seas Fleet. Up to the end of 1914, no less that five of his more modern battleships – *Orion, Iron Duke, Ajax, King*

---

[68] Summarises Campbell, pp. 388–400: see also p. 50.

George V and *Thunderer* – were afflicted with 'condenseritis', that is, leaks in the condenser tubes through which sea water was pumped to condense the exhaust steam from the turbines. In October 1914, Jellicoe asked for the Northern bases to be supplied with spare tubes and for dockyard fitters to assist the artificers of the Fleet in retubing. In his memoir, he did not mention the problem again after January 1915; thus it appears that thereafter the Fleet was able to keep the problem under control by regular inspection and maintenance.[69] However, in December 1914 another type of defect appeared in the small-tube boilers of the light cruiser *Liverpool* and it would recur in many other ships with this type of boiler. In 1904, the Boiler Committee had recommended the adoption for smaller vessels of the Yarrow small-tube boiler, in which straight water-tubes connected the single cylindrical steam drum at the top with two water drums on either side of the grate. The water drums were D-shaped in section, with the tubes secured in the flat upper plate. However, these plates tended to bulge outwards, weakening the joints with the tubes and causing what was known as 'wrapperitis'. The solution for completed ships was to replace the original water drums with drums having a more rounded cross section. But this substantial modification required a ship to be laid up for two or three months; Jellicoe recorded that usually one, occasionally two, light cruisers were under refit for this purpose.[70]

With the ships of the Grand Fleet continually at sea, wear and tear, particularly on machinery, was greater than had been experienced in peacetime, making regular repairs a necessity. Jellicoe had to allow for at least two battleships and perhaps a battlecruiser being under routine refit at any time, much as was the case on the eve of Jutland – *Emperor of India, Queen Elizabeth* and *Dreadnought* were in dockyard hands, while *Australia* had had to go to Devonport for repairs to collision damage.[71] Yet all the light cruisers of the 1, 2, 3 and 4 LCSs took part in the battle. Destroyers, lightly built with high-speed machinery, were especially liable to damage and breakdowns. On 30 April 1916, the nominal strength of the six Grand Fleet flotillas in the North Sea – including flotilla leaders as well as destroyers and also *Oak* – was 127 boats. Of these, 101 put to sea between 30 and 1 June, an availability of 80%. This figure is probably not untypical; in his memoirs, Jellicoe, who apparently did not count the destroyers in the Southern North Sea, reckoned that seventy of the

[69] *GF*, pp. 74, 90, 95, 98, 104, 107, 116–17, 123 and 125. Brown, *Dreadnought*, pp. 165–6 and *Grand Fleet*, pp. 93–4.

[70] *GF*, pp. 34, 117, 125 and 149. Denys Griffiths, *Steam at Sea* (London: Conway, 1997), p. 128. Brown, *Dreadnought*, pp. 165–6 and *Grand Fleet*, pp. 93–4. https://en.wikipedia.org/wiki/Yarrow_boiler; wrapperitis was caused by deforming of the flat plate, not because the tubes were straight.

[71] *GF*, p. 34. *CAWFS 1906–21*, pp. 22 and 34. Burt, pp. 40, 226 and 294. *Dreadnought* appears typical in that, in the first four years of the war, she was under refit for 155 days out, 1,461, an 'unavailability' of 10.6%: Roberts, *Dreadnought*, pp. 21–3.

eighty destroyers belonging to the Grand Fleet (88%) were available and described this as 'an unusually high proportion'.[72]

Under the stresses of battle, British engines had few breakdowns unrelated to action damage. An exception was the destroyer *Mindful*, one of her three Yarrow boilers being unserviceable when she went into action. *Birmingham* and *Nottingham*, which were not hit, declared that they had sustained high speeds without difficulty. Steering machinery was more troublesome if the helm was put over too quickly. At about 6.15pm *Invincible*'s rudder jammed briefly. Then *Warspite*'s steering gear failed for long enough to force her to turn through two complete circles under the enemy guns; subsequently, she could no longer be steered from the conning tower.[73]

Condenseritis was and would remain a problem for all navies[74] but the German fleet, which spent more time in harbour, was less successful than the Royal Navy in minimising its impact on operations. *Seydlitz*'s departure for the Heligoland Bight action was delayed by condenser defects. These continued to plague German ships large and small, while the small-tube boilers in modern battleships and battlecruisers were proving to be unreliable.[75] After the Lowestoft Raid in April 1916, there were seven cases of damaged condensers in the IIIBS, while the *König Albert* had to be left behind on 30 May after developing condenser trouble a few days previously. During the Battle of Jutland itself, three ships suffered from leaking condensers: *Kaiserin* had to stop her centre engine for a little over an hour but its condenser was repaired just before the IIIBS engaged the 5BS; from 7.15pm, the light cruiser *Elbing* was unable to proceed at high speed; and *Grosser Kurfürst* had to stop her centre engine between 0.03 and 1.47am, although by then she had received seven heavy hits so they may have been at least partly to blame.[76] To keep in touch with the 5BS during the Run to the North, *Grosser Kurfürst* and her consorts in the IIIBS must have forced their engines, though apparently without any immediately adverse consequences. Instead, the effects of maintaining high speeds were felt more by the battlecruisers and destroyers. The principal cause seems to have been poor-quality fuel. However, compared with British boilers, the total grate areas of the German battlecruisers were some 20% less, so for the same power output the temperatures and rate of burning per unit area would have been higher; with inferior coal, this was likely to result in a more rapid accumulation of slag and clinker in the grates. Perhaps for this reason,

[72] *Monthly Return, May 1916* (corrected to 30 April), pp. 5–7 in ADM 186/23. *GF*, p. 254.

[73] *OD*, pp. 164, 167, 184, 203 and 339.

[74] Brown, *Grand Fleet*, p. 94. W J Fox and S C McBirnie, *Marine Steam Turbines and Engines* (London: George Newnes, 1952), pp. 207–8.

[75] Goldrick, *Before Jutland*, pp. 121, 132, 166 and 201.

[76] Scheer, pp. 134, 140 and 148. Campbell, pp. 36, 145, 246 and 298. Tarrant, p. 191 and GSM, 7.15pm.

von Hase stated that the German battlecruisers could not maintain a speed of 25 knots for any length of time.[77] In *Seydlitz*, the build-up of slag required frequent cleaning while in the intense heat the grate bars burnt through and their supporting beams buckled. By the evening of 31 May, *Von der Tann's* fires were so dirty that she could not make more than 18 knots. To make matters worse, unless given constant attention the supplementary oil firing failed in some ships due to sediment clogging the feed-pipes and filters.[78] The small destroyers of the V and VII TFs also depended on mixed coal and oil firing; by nightfall their fires were very dirty so that, even at 15 knots, they were throwing out sparks and clouds of smoke. Before she was hit, *G42* had problems with newly fitted feed pumps that reduced her speed to 25 knots.[79]

Once battle was joined, machinery was also at risk from enemy fire but the larger British ships, including those that were heavily hit, had few problems. *Warrior's* reciprocating engines, despite her extensive damage, kept going long enough for her to withdraw. *Princess Royal* and *Barham* remarked that their main engines and boilers were unaffected by hits, though in *Malaya*, there was some leakage of water into the oil fuel.[80] However, *Tiger* narrowly escaped being brought to a halt by a hit on her main steam pipe. *Chester*, despite slight damage to boiler tubes from shell splinters, was able to maintain station while *Southampton* and *Dublin*, which were hit repeatedly (the former by one 11in), did not mention engine problems in their despatches.[81] Destroyer machinery proved much more vulnerable. Of British boats lost, *Nestor, Nomad* and *Shark* were brought rapidly to a halt by hits from 4.1in and 3.5in shells in their engine rooms.[82] In the course of the night-time destroyer attacks, *Tipperary* was stopped by a hit on a main steam pipe and one of *Turbulent's* boilers exploded.[83] Of the damaged boats that survived, engine-room hits completely immobilised *Acasta* and *Onslow* while some boilers were put out of action in *Broke, Defender, Porpoise* and *Spitfire*.[84]

The machinery of German capital ships was largely immune to the effects of hits, although, as well as the possible condenser leak in *Grosser Kurfürst*, the bearing of *Markgraf's* port propeller shaft ran hot, either because the shaft was bent by a near miss or the bearing itself failed; in 1915, the shaft bearings in most of the ships of the IIIBS had to be replaced because they moored so

---

[77] British and German grate widths were similar (Staff, *1914–18*, p. 8) but the lengths of German boiler rooms were about 80% of the British (Roberts, *Battlecruisers*, p. 73). von Hase, p. 172. In the War, poor coal may have limited German battlecruisers to no more than 24 knots: Goldrick, *Before Jutland*, pp. 54 and 264.

[78] Kapitän zu See von Egidy, 'Jutland: A German View' at www.gwpda.org/naval/jut01.htm. Looks, pp. 311–12. Rahn, pp. 235–8. *GOA*, p. 168. Tarrant, pp. 109–10.

[79] *GOA*, p. 165. Campbell, p. 399.   [80] *OD*, pp. 153, 198, 221–2, 289, 292 and 339.

[81] F&H, pp. 89–90. *OD*, pp. 31, 175–7, 180–3 and 190.   [82] *OD*, pp. 317, 346 and 350.

[83] *OD*, pp. 311 and 327. Campbell, pp. 289 and 293.

[84] *OD*, pp. 228, 238, 250, 307, 312, 324 and 330.

regularly in the sandy waters of the Jade basin. However, *Von der Tann* would have been in danger if her steering gear had been permanently damaged by the hit at 4.09pm.[85] Compared with their British counterparts, German light cruisers suffered more damage to their engines, even though *Southampton, Wiesbaden* and *Pillau* were each hit once by heavy shell. All six of *Pillau*'s coal-fired boilers were put out of action, three permanently, but her four oil-fired boilers remained intact and subsequently she was able to make 24 knots. Both of *Wiesbaden*'s engines were disabled immediately. A 6in shell bursting inside *München*'s after funnel damaged the casings of her larger boilers so that she had difficulty in maintaining full speed. The torpedo that struck *Rostock* at about 11.50pm caused two of her five boiler rooms to flood but she was able to steam at 13 knots for a time until her speed was drastically reduced by salt water contaminating her boilers.[86] Of the five German destroyers that were lost, *V27* was first disabled by a hit on a main steam pipe, while *V48*'s machinery was also hit. Of the survivors, a turbine in *G40* was damaged by a 6in hit. The shocks from near misses by heavy shell caused leaks in *G42*'s condensers that further reduced her speed to 15 knots. *S32* had to stop for a time after an engine-room steam pipe was riddled and she also had to resort to seawater feed to reach the Danish coast. Some damage to boilers, steam pipes, oil tanks and feed-pipes occurred in *S36, S50, S51* and *G86*.[87]

While permanent breakdowns in turret machinery were not fatal, they certainly reduced a ship's offensive power, some for the remainder of the battle. Of this category, the breech of one gun in *Princess Royal* broke in the closed position, the casting of a run-out valve fractured in *Tiger* and *Malaya* had recurrent problems with the alignment of the X-turret main cage and the shell bogie. Also, one of *Marlborough*'s guns failed when the inner A tube cracked all round and a large piece of the jacket broke off; although the damage to the rifling was small, it was thought a 'premature' must have occurred.[88] On the German side, most of the turret problems were concentrated in *Von der Tann*, the run-out gear failing in both wing turrets; although later repaired, it was expected that the faults would recur. But the power training of *Seydlitz*'s C (superfiring) turret also failed, just before it was burnt out.[89]

In summary: at the beginning of the War, both sides suffered from condenseritis; the Royal Navy was eventually more successful at getting the problem under control, though once the British had a numerical superiority they could afford to have more ships under refit. The initial problem

---

[85] Campbell, pp. 90, 195 and 384. Scheer, p. 94.   [86] Campbell, pp. 393–5.
[87] Campbell, pp. 50 and 398–9. For *V48*, see also Chapter 8.
[88] *OD*, pp. 69 and 152. *Tiger*'s gunnery report in BTY 6/6. Campbell, pp. 77 and 134.
[89] Campbell, pp. 83, 94, 143 and 364.

with British small-tube boilers was also overcome, though only by the replacement of the water drums. The advantages of small-tube boilers in the German capital ships were partly offset by their being more unreliable and less suitable for the available coal. The engines of light cruisers on both sides suffered little damage from gunfire, except in the case of the heavy hits on German vessels. But destroyer machinery was generally vulnerable to hits from shell of 4in and greater calibres. Mostly, the turret guns and machinery on both sides worked well, the British having more problems with guns and fittings, the Germans with run-out and training gear.

Secondary armament

The serious fire in *Malaya* during the Run to the North emphasised that the charges stored in the secondary batteries of capital ships, which could be protected only by lighter armour, were potentially a major hazard. Also, the secondary guns proved to be largely ineffective against similar opponents (although a 5.9in hit may have disabled a gun in *Warspite*'s Y turret).[90] But, although there were fires of secondary propellant in other battleships and battlecruisers – six British and three German – they did not seriously endanger the ships. And British and German secondary armaments proved their value by their large part in driving off torpedo attacks, both by day and by night. German 5.9in hits were made during the day on *Moorsom* (1), *Onslow* (3) and *Acasta* (at least 2) and also on *Falmouth* (1 at c. 6.30pm) and *Calliope* (5 at c. 8.30). (German secondaries also sunk *Nestor* and *Nomad* but they had already been immobilised by German light forces.) During the night attacks by the 4DF and 11DF on similar courses, four boats (*Tipperary, Ardent, Fortune* and *Turbulent*) were sunk mainly by 5.9in fire, while 5.9in hits were also made on *Broke* (probably 1 or 2), *Garland* (1), *Porpoise* (at least 1) and *Petard* (4 hits, some 3.5in). While no destroyers were lost when the 12DF attacked at daybreak on opposite courses, hits were made on *Nessus* (1–5.9in) and *Onslow* (1–6.7in).

The main daylight attack by German destroyers occurred after 7.15pm and was directed mainly at the 4BS and 1BS, of which nine battleships of sixteen had 4in secondary armaments. Yet Campbell's analysis of hits mentions only 6in hits, five in all, one each on *V28, G41, V48, S51* and *G87*;[91] it seems that British 4in secondaries were of little use by day. By night, the British battlefleet was untroubled by German destroyers. But it is quite possible that, at the short night-time ranges, these less unwieldy guns, despite their lighter shell, would have been more effective.

---

[90] Brown, *Grand Fleet*, pp. 44–5. Campbell, p. 178.
[91] Campbell, pp. 178, 380, 388, 390 and 396–400.

Signals

Volumes

In describing the second encounter between the battlefleets at around 7.15pm, the *Naval Staff Appreciation* criticises 'the mass of [British] signals made at this stage of the battle' and the 'numberless signals' that were made in manoeuvring the fleet. This passage clearly influenced Churchill's assertion in *The World Crisis* that 'A ceaseless stream of signals from the flagship was required to regulate the movement of the fleet.'[92] These are, however, vague and subjective judgements and the intention here is to provide, so far as the records allow, a numerical analysis of the categories and volumes of signals made during the battle. The compilers of the British record of signals, which became Appendix II to the *Official Despatches*, declared that 'every message bearing on the operation has been included, and the record having been carefully checked is believed to be correct'. There are no reasons to doubt this claim for *Iron Duke*. As for *Lion*, the BCF's track chart shows many course changes for which there are no corresponding signals.[93] However, while Beatty expected his ships to follow his movements without explicit orders, some signals may not have been recorded or some records lost; thus the number of *Lion*'s signals is either correct or an underestimate. A comparison of British and German signal traffic would also be instructive but the German record provides only 'A Summary of the More Important Wireless Messages and Visual Signals';[94] while all of Scheer's manoeuvring signals would be expected to fall into this category, a few may have been omitted.

Tables 10.5 and 10.6 show the numbers of recorded signals made by *Iron Duke, Lion* and *Friedrich der Grosse* in the final three hours of daylight, beginning at six o'clock as the two battlefleets were about to make contact.[95] The analysis is concerned principally with manoeuvring signals, i.e. those specifying course, speed or disposition; they are divided into 'General' signals – those addressed to all the forces under a flagship's command – and 'Specific' – those addressed to individual squadrons, flotillas or even ships. The 'Other' category mainly contains signals requesting or reporting positions of own or enemy ships.[96] Table 10.5 gives the total number of signals in the three-hour period. In

---

[92] *NSA*, p. 106. Churchill, *World Crisis I*, p. 136 cited in Gordon, p. 566.

[93] Naval Staff, Communications Division, *Battle of Jutland. Record of Messages Bearing on the Operation*, 1919, p. 1, JMSS 49021 and ADM 186/625. *OD*, Pl. 10.

[94] GSM, p. 272.

[95] Since *Lützow* was crippled shortly after 6.30, the signals from Hipper's force are too fragmentary to be comparable.

[96] Signals from *OD*(M), 6.01–9.00pm (times of despatch) and GSM, 6.17–9.00pm (times of receipt).

Table 10.5. *Signals by flagships*

31 May 1916	Manoeuvring signals		Other	Total	Average interval
6.01–9.00pm	General	Specific	Signals		between signals
Iron Duke	28	14	7	49	3.7 mins
Lion	8	5	18	31	5.8 mins
Friedrich der Grosse	16	8		24	7.5 mins

Table 10.6. *Signals by category and time*

31 May 1916	General signals			Specific signals		
pm	Jellicoe	Beatty	Scheer	Jellicoe	Beatty	Scheer
6.01–6.30	7	1	3	1		
6.31–7.00	4	1	4		4	1
7.01–7.30	6	2	5	7		4
7.31–8.00	6	1	2	5	1	1
8.01–8.30	5	3		1		1
8.31–9.00			2			1
Total	28	8	16	14	5	8

comparing the three flagships, note that Beatty made more signals in the 'Other' category and that he was commanding a much smaller and less diverse force; also, he was leading his line and could alter course without signal if he wished. Whereas the flagships of Jellicoe and Scheer were near the centre of their lines, so concerted movements by all their ships had to be controlled by signal. And the total for Scheer may be an underestimate if signals in the 'Other' category were omitted from the record as unimportant. Nonetheless, there is little doubt that *Iron Duke* made the greatest number of signals. But a total of forty-nine in three hours at an average interval of 3.7 minutes is hardly a 'ceaseless stream'.

Table 10.6 shows how the manoeuvring signals, general and specific, were distributed in the half-hourly intervals from 6.01 to 9.00pm. Of the general signals, Beatty made the fewest and Jellicoe the most, though it should be recognised that five of Jellicoe's signals were to confirm previous orders. Also that the seven after 6.00 were at the time of the all-important deployment, whereas Scheer's battlefleet were already in single line. Between 6.31 and 8.00, all three admirals made significant numbers of additional specific manoeuvring signals; thus they chose to control directly the forces commanded by some of their subordinates, rather than leaving them to use their own initiative. Between 6.31 and 7.00, Beatty insisted that the 3BCS turn away to prolong his line astern, and he also gave explicit orders for the destroyers that remained with him to form a submarine screen ahead. From 7.01 to 7.30, Scheer, in order to cover the action-turn-about by the High Seas Fleet, ordered attacks by both the ISG and the flotillas; subsequently, he made few signals and allowed the battlecruisers to remain in an exposed position on his port flank. Between 7.01 and 8.00, Jellicoe made twelve specific signals: to the 1BS to form astern; to the 2BS urging them to take station ahead and then to turn away; to send the 4LCS and destroyers to attack the German destroyers and then to recall the destroyers and the straying *Castor*; and finally to reform all three battle squadrons in line-ahead. However, in the most critical half-hour from 7.01 to 7.30, the numbers of Jellicoe's to Scheer's manoeuvring signals – 13:9 – were not greatly different and it would have been even closer but for Jerram's delay in drawing ahead. In that period, the average intervals between the signals in the two flagships fell to 2.3 and 3.3 minutes respectively and in *Iron Duke* there were three instances of pairs of signals with the same time-of-despatch. This was undoubtedly a busy period for the signallers on both sides.

For the critical three-hour period, the complete sequence of British signals in the *Official Despatches* runs over fifteen closely printed pages; if not 'numberless', they were certainly numerous. In fact, the total number of all signals sent by the ships of the battlefleet number 211; of these, 49 – just over 23% – originated from *Iron Duke*. Of the 211, 34 were made by wireless, either alone or to repeat signals also made by flags (and, in one case, by searchlight). Only 10 of the 34, urgent signals often concerning damaged ships, were not made by *Iron Duke*; thus, during the fleet encounters, wireless was mainly reserved for the C-in-C. Of all the signals, 120 (almost 57%) were made by flags alone, many being signals from senior officers to large or small units under their direct command; these signals were thus of significance to only a limited number of ships and could be ignored by all others. Two examples are the signals, almost all by flags, made to the destroyers and light cruisers leading the van of the battlefleet. Note that Commodore

Table 10.7. *Signals by Commodore (F) and SO 4LCS*

6.01–9.00	Commodore (F)	SO 4LCS
Total	47	38
by flags	43	32
course and/or speed	32	26

Hawksley in *Castor* made almost as many signals as Jellicoe. In both examples, about two-thirds of the signals were the simple changes of course and/or speed necessary to reach and maintain position ahead of the van battleships; it will be recalled that both these forces also mounted attacks during this period.

In general, Scheer was more prepared than Jellicoe to allow the battleship at the head of his line to set the course, though Jerram showed little appetite for taking the initiative; Jellicoe was also more inclined to control the movements of individual formations. But this numerical analysis of signals, which compares Jellicoe's volumes with those of other British commanders and Scheer, shows that the Dewars' unquantified claim of a 'mass of signals which was such a feature of British tactics at Jutland'[97] is greatly exaggerated.

Manoeuvring signals

Until Jellicoe's encounter with the enemy fleet soon after 6pm, he manoeuvred his battlefleet almost entirely by general flag signals, including the major turns by 9 Pendant at 5.00am and at 3.00, 6.02 and 6.06pm; however, a warning of the 5.00am turn was also given by wireless. To zigzag the fleet, he also made frequent general signals with the Blue Pendant for two-point turns together.[98] The signal record does not indicate how any of these signals were repeated to the armoured cruisers and the 3BCS; it was probably by searchlight, the method used for specific orders from the flagship to the cruisers.[99] With action imminent, *Iron Duke* made the 6.15pm deployment signal by both flags and W/T before, in accordance with *GFBO* VI.3, turning at once with two blasts on her siren. Thereafter while daylight lasted, Jellicoe manoeuvred the battlefleet and its attached cruiser mainly by flags and wireless signals together, though, if the record is correct, there were two instances each of flags alone and W/T alone.[100] The C-in-C's specific orders to individual formations or ships were sent by either flags or searchlight. On the general signals by both flags and W/T, Jellicoe's statements are contradictory. After the War, he claimed that the time for a manoeuvring wireless signal to reach the whole fleet 'rarely exceeded two or three minutes'. But, in a letter to Beatty on 4 June 1916, he regretted that

I found signals difficult to get through in the mist, although W.T. interference was very small, to my surprise. But it took an appalling time to get course alterations through the fleet for closing.[101]

---

[97] *NSA*, p. 106.   [98] *E.g. OD*(M). 10.00, 10.20, 10.30 and 10.50am.
[99] *OD*(M), 6.05am to 3.58pm for thirteen searchlight signals from C-in-C to cruisers.
[100] *OD*(M), 6.33, 7.25, 7.36 and 8.21pm.   [101] *GF*, p. 48. *BP I*, p, 319.

It is not clear what course alterations he was referring to – possibly the turns towards the enemy at 6.44 and 6.55 – while the wording suggests the delays may have been while waiting for visual acknowledgements to be seen through the mist. Burney reported that, throughout the 1BS

wireless telegraphy communication ... were [sic] entirely satisfactory and invaluable for manoeuvring and action signals, especially in the case of the repeating ship ('Bellona'), who was often unable to distinguish the flag signals.[102]

In the battlefleet as a whole, only one general signal may not have been received and acted upon correctly, the order to slow to 14 knots with a time-of-despatch of 6.26, although it is unclear what exactly went wrong. And of the specific signals, a few may not have been received during the flurry of signals from *Iron Duke* between 7.16 and 7.28.

After two wireless signals to his screening forces early on 31 May, Scheer's next manoeuvring signals at 11.53am and at 3.10 and 3.40pm were made visually – though the German record does not indicate whether 'visual' signals by flags were repeated by searchlight. Beginning at 4.05 when the BCF and ISG were already in action but the BCF had not yet sighted the German battlefleet, Scheer appears to have started using the procedure for signalling in action, in which the signals were made by flags and auxiliary wireless simultaneously.[103] In the main, for the remainder of the day he continued with this method with which, he declared, 'I ... was able to signal with great rapidity in both directions' along the line; however (again assuming the record is correct) a few manoeuvring signals were made only visually.[104] According to orders, Hipper and Hartog manoeuvred the ISG by visual signals only. The German system appears to have malfunctioned only once; *König* missed the flag and wireless signals ordering Scheer's first action-turn-together at 6.36, no doubt because she had just been under a heavy fire from *Iron Duke* that also put her wireless out of action.

Thus manoeuvring signals were made in both battlefleets using similar systems, with very few failures. In contrast, there were too many errors in the handling of signals in Beatty's flagship, especially with orders intended for the 5BS.

Signalling in the BCF

By 1920, Jellicoe was writing that Beatty's flag lieutenant Ralph Seymour 'throughout disobeyed my Battle Instructions that when in the face of the

---

[102]   *OD*, p. 67.
[103]   'Signal Orders during and after an Action' in *German Tactical Orders. January 1915*, p. 11 in 'German Fleet Orders', ADM 186/17.
[104]   Scheer, p. 146. GSM, 4.36, 4.42, 5.30, 6.28 and 7.45pm, though the last was repeated by wireless at 7.52pm.

enemy all signals were to be made by flag, searchlight and wireless. Had these instructions been carried out and the 5th Battle Squadron had been closed up I think Hipper would have been annihilated'. Historians have accepted that Seymour was chiefly responsible for the inefficiency of Beatty's signalling organisation and for the delays in turns by the 5BS – though, for their turn N after 4.48pm, Gordon also points to Evan-Thomas's over-punctilious adherence to signalling protocol.[105] Seymour's competence was indeed questionable. He was not a fully qualified signals officer, having taken only the short signals course in February 1913. During the Scarborough Raid, a vital signal from *Lion* to the light cruisers had been wrongly addressed;[106] however, as explained in Chapter 2, it is less certain that the unsatisfactory end to the Dogger Bank action was the consequence of a signalling mistake. After Jutland, Seymour continued as flag-lieutenant even after Beatty became C-in-C and when the War ended Seymour was retained for a time as one of Beatty's naval assistants. But in 1920 Seymour was cast out of the Beatty circle after he became engaged briefly to a niece of Ethel Beatty; he suffered a nervous breakdown and, rather than meet Beatty again, committed suicide in 1922. As Gordon suggests, it was probably after this break that Beatty complained that Seymour had 'lost three battles for me'.[107] As Beatty himself came under fire during the Jutland Controversy, Seymour became a convenient scapegoat.

In action the task of a flag lieutenant was to ascertain his admiral's precise intentions, even when they were expressed informally or even unclearly, and translate them into terse 'signalese'.[108] He was also responsible for ensuring that signals were repeated and acknowledged by all addressees; normally, having received the acknowledgements, he could inform the admiral and wait for the order to make the signal executive. During the morning of the 31st, Seymour had ensured that signals were repeated by searchlight to the 5BS, though after 2.15pm, almost all Beatty's general manoeuvring signals were made only by flags (the delayed repeat to the 5BS after 2.35 being an exception). If, as seems probable, the 5BS did not receive the 2.32 general signal to turn SSE, *Barham* could not have acknowledged it. Thus, although Seymour should be held responsible for the lack of a searchlight repeat, Beatty must have made the decision to execute the turn without confirmation that the 5BS would alter course with him. Then, after the 5BS eventually turned to follow some ten miles astern of the battlecruisers, nothing was done in *Lion* to ensure that her signals were repeated by searchlight. Again, while Seymour was primarily

[105] Roskill, pp. 156–7 (quote) and 167. *FDSF III*, p. 57. Gordon, p. 149.
[106] *FDSF II*, pp. 139 and 140 n. 9. Gordon, pp. 95–6 and 385. Chalmers, pp. 170–1. Goldrick, pp. 205–6.
[107] Gordon, pp. 96 and 540 and 542–3 citing *FDSF II*. p. 140 for quote.
[108] *FDSF II*, p. 140 n. 9. Dreyer, p. 146 for the exchange between Jellicoe and his Fleet Signal Officer about the deployment signal.

responsible, Beatty was now aware that at least one important order had not reached *Barham*, yet he apparently ignored the continuing indications that his signals were not reaching Evan-Thomas.

Just before 3.47, when firing began, the tactical situation demanded that Beatty's battlecruisers should be formed on a line-of-bearing NW heading ESE, as ordered in the two last-minute flag signals hoisted by *Lion*.[109] Perhaps Beatty belatedly stated his requirements in terms of the course and formation he wanted after the manoeuvre had been completed and that Seymour expressed his admiral's wishes in the two signals that translated them literally, i.e. first form the line-of-bearing, then turn together to ESE. But there was no longer sufficient time to form the line-of-bearing by an unequal-speed manoeuvre while, in carrying it out, some rear turrets would not bear on the enemy. At the time, Beatty – and probably Seymour too – was preoccupied with the signal to the C-in-C. The flag-captain, Chatfield, on whom Beatty relied for gunnery advice, was not on hand to warn that the signals chosen by Seymour were inappropriate, but the gunnery commander, Sydney Bailey, was with Beatty on the admiral's bridge.[110] The larger tactical and gunnery consequences of the flagship's signals were not the responsibility solely of the flag-lieutenant but of the admiral and his whole staff; so, while Seymour chose unsuitable signals, it would be unjust to blame him for not doing Beatty's job for him.

It appears that, at 4.40, *Lion* ordered all Beatty's forces to turn through 16 points to starboard (away from the enemy) by means of a general Compass Pendant signal. It is inconceivable that Beatty intended to preserve the relative bearings of the 5BS and light cruiser squadrons before the turn; if the signal is recorded correctly, it must have been made in error by Seymour and his signallers, though it had no immediate consequences.[111] The general situation demanded that the 5BS should continue Southwards until they could turn about into the single line that permitted mutual support, while both admirals almost certainly assumed without question that the battlecruisers would take the lead. Beatty's turn from NW to N at 4.45 indicated that he wanted the 5BS on his disengaged side when he passed them; this ensured that his own line-of-fire to the ISG was not obstructed and it could also provide the battleships with some protection from enemy fire as they turned. As Gordon proposes, Beatty could have stated his intention simply by ordering the 5BS to prolong the line astern. This was expressed directly by the familiar action signal '71: Prolong the Line by taking Station Astern';[112] this had already been used to order the 2BCS into line at 3.34 and it would be used again at 5.01 (to the 5BS) and at 6.50 (to the 3BCS). The signal could have been made, acknowledged and made executive

---

[109] See Chapter 5.　　[110] Chatfield, p. 140.　　[111] See Chapter 6.
[112] Gordon, p. 131. *GSB 1915*, p. 65.

while the two flagships were approaching each other, after which Evan-Thomas could execute the manoeuvre as he saw fit.[113] Instead, *Lion* used flags to order the turn by Compass Pendant (correctly this time), specifying that the turn be made to starboard; she also took control of the timing of the 5BS's turn since it commenced only when the signal was made executive. If *Barham* were to haul into line within a few cables of *New Zealand*, Evan-Thomas needed to begin the turn about a minute before his flagship passed Beatty's; then there would have been time to turn and regain speed just as *New Zealand* overhauled *Barham*. As it was, the signal was probably hauled down between one and two minutes after the flagships passed. Yet, before Seymour could give the necessary order to his signallers, signalling procedure required that, if he had not done so already, he had to obtain permission to haul it down. Thus, at a particularly hectic moment, either Beatty or Seymour or both could have contributed to the delay; there can be no certainty that Seymour alone was responsible. As for Evan-Thomas, when he was approaching the battlecruisers he may not even have sighted the German battlefleet for himself; yet, to avoid falling astern after turning about, he had both to disregard the clear import of the signal flying in *Lion* and to turn well before he passed her. Such a decision would have required exceptional boldness and prescience. It seems fairer to conclude that the principal fault lay not with him but with the choice and timing of the signal.

So why was the 5BS's turn ordered by Compass Pendant rather than action signal 71? As Gordon points out, of the two only the Compass Pendant signal allowed the direction of the turn to be specified, and he suggests that Beatty wanted the 5BS to turn to starboard because VAC BCF intended to turn to *port* across their wake as soon as they had passed.[114] However, no such turn is shown on the BCF track chart that accompanied Beatty's despatch, while his narrative mentions only a one-point turn to *starboard* at 4.51; on the other hand, large turns to port are implied by *Lion*'s target bearings and they are shown on Corbett's and Marder's charts.[115] Yet, even if the track chart and narrative are correct, Beatty may still have wanted to impose a turn to starboard on the 5BS: either because he considered that there was not enough searoom between the two columns (perhaps as little as half a mile) for a turn to port; or because he wanted to avoid unfavourable comparisons with his own 16-point turn-away from the enemy. Another possibility is that, rather than explicitly insisting that Seymour order the 5BS's turn by Compass Pendant, Beatty may have expressed himself less formally by simply telling Seymour to order the battleships to haul into line astern, perhaps adding that they should do so by turning

---

[113] He could even have turned his ships together rather than in succession; in his 'Errors made in Jutland Battle', Jellicoe criticised Beatty for not ordering the turn by Blue Pendant: *JP II*, p. 449.

[114] Gordon, pp. 131–3.

[115] *OD*, Pl. 10 and also Pl. 8a. VNE, 4.51. REL, 4.50–4.56. *FDSF III*, Chart 6. Corbett, Map 26.

to starboard. Then Seymour, already under pressure and with the previous Compass Pendant signal fresh in his mind (perhaps with the previously used pendant and numeral flags still to hand), may have jumped at the chance to use the same signal again. But in that case Beatty may not have realised until prompted that he had to authorise the signal being hauled down. With so many possibilities, it is impossible to determine whether Beatty or Seymour decided on the Compass Pendant signal. But we cannot be certain the faulty choice was Seymour's alone.

Seymour must be held responsible for the failures to repeat signals to the 5BS during the approach to the Run to the South. But it was Beatty's decision, despite there being no immediate urgency, to turn SSE at 2.32pm without an acknowledgement from the fast battleships, while the vice-admiral seems to have remained indifferent to Seymour's continuing omissions. Just before fire opened, Seymour chose inappropriate signals but the delay in forming the line-of-bearing was due to Beatty's tactical misjudgements. Lastly, we cannot be certain that Beatty did not contribute to the delay in turning the 5BS about at the start of the Run to the North. Seymour made mistakes; but Beatty appointed and retained him and was far from blameless for the BCF's signalling failures in action.

Reporting signals

Goaded by criticism in the *Naval Staff Appreciation* and the *Admiralty Narrative*, in an unpublished draft Jellicoe was scathing about the 'absence of even approximately correct information from the Battle Cruiser Fleet and its attendant light cruisers regarding the position, formation and strength of the High Sea Fleet'.[116] But we should also ask whether the reports from the battlefleet were any better and how the British reports compared in number and accuracy with those sent to Scheer. To make timely decisions on tactics, each Commander-in-Chief depended on early reports by wireless of his opponent's movements, so we shall concentrate on this type of report. The British signal record establishes that *Iron Duke*'s wireless picked up not only those reports addressed directly to the C-in-C but also many that were made to formation commanders, notably SO BCF.[117] Similarly, in addition to German signals addressed to the C-in-C, others were 'General' reports to the whole fleet while others, though addressed to subordinate commanders, were headed for the attention of the C-in-C.[118] Thus, to compare the readiness of both sides to report sightings of the enemy, the totals in Table 10.8 are of *all* wireless reports of enemy vessels, plus those sent by visual means that were addressed explicitly to the Commanders-in-Chief.

[116] *BP II*, p. 470.
[117] *E.g.* the 11 signals from *Galatea* to SO BCF between 2.20 and 3.59pm in *OD*(M).
[118] *E.g.* GSM, 3.30, 3.35 and 3.54pm (from *Lützow*) and 6.02pm (from *Frankfurt*).

Table 10.8. *Enemy reports to the Commanders-in-Chief*

Times	Phase	To Scheer from		To Jellicoe from	
		Vessels	Airships	Vessels	Admiralty
2.20–3.59pm	First encounters to battlecruisers opening fire	17		16	1
4.20–6.25pm	Run to the South to meeting of battlefleets	6		19	2
6.45–9.10pm	Battlefleet engagements until nightfall	6		18	
9.30pm–5.30am	Night and morning	12	9	9	7
	Totals	41	9	62	10

In his memoirs, Frederic Dreyer declared:

the Commander-in-Chief must be given full information about the enemy by his advance forces, including the number of each type of ship, their formation, position, course and speed. We had practised and developed this for years … especially in countless naval manoeuvres before 1914.[119]

Both navies reported positions in terms of grids of reference squares, each square having a unique and supposedly secure code. German practice was usually to give the estimated position of the enemy ship and, sometimes, the estimated course: but not the position of the reporting ship. Of the forty-one reports from surface vessels, twenty-five gave enemy position and of these eleven also gave the enemy course. In contrast, the positions supplied in British reports were normally those of the reporting ships; consequently, the enemy position could only be determined accurately if the report also gave the enemy bearing and distance.[120] Of the sixty-two British reports, just five met this standard, with only three also giving the enemy course.[121] Less usefully, a further thirty-two specified only the position of the reporting ship, although fifteen of these included enemy bearing and course. Thus, while direct comparison between the reports is not possible, in broad terms the German were fewer but more informative.

At the beginning of the battle, the scouting forces on both sides made regular enemy reports. But, once they were in action during the Run to the South, their reporting almost ceased, although this may be excused in part by damage to wireless installations. After Hipper joined Scheer, only the IISG made a few

---

[119] Dreyer, pp. 155–6.
[120] Exceptions were submarine reports which gave the enemy's position: *OD*(M), 6.54, 8.33 and 8.51pm.
[121] Two were from *Southampton* and two from *Lion* so their usefulness was compromised by the BCF's errors in dead-reckoning.

reports. Hipper, who continued to be heavily engaged, perhaps assumed that the C-in-C could see as much as he could; it was Bödicker in *Frankfurt* who informed Scheer at 5.10pm that only four British battlecruisers were left. The IISG on *Lützow*'s disengaged starboard bow was not in a position to sight the advanced forces of the Grand Fleet until they encountered *Chester* and the 3BCS, mistaking Hood's battlecruisers for battleships. Even after the battle-fleets were in touch, very few enemy reports were sent to Scheer during the remaining daylight hours; the most useful was that from *Moltke* at 6.45 that gave the bearing (though not distance) of the enemy van. One reason for this dearth must have been the further damage inflicted on both *Lützow* and *Derfflinger*; a second was that, after the third action-turn-together, the IVSG and the IISG formed ahead of the battle squadrons; thus they were in no position to report on British movements until they encountered British light forces at about 8.20. During the night, Scheer received rather more reports than Jellicoe,[122] several providing welcome confirmation that the British courses were Southerly. Beginning at daybreak, Scheer also received nine reports of enemy ships from *L24* and *L11*, though the former's information served only to confuse his appreciation of the British dispositions.

The enemy reports to Jellicoe were particularly deficient when he needed them most to inform his decision on the deployment, but, while he had good cause to criticise the BCF, he also received little useful information from the battlefleet. Of the BCF, *Southampton* was of course an exception, despite errors in her dead-reckoning and a wrong bearing of the German battle-cruisers from their battleships – though this may have been due to wireless interference. But between 4.45 and 6.06pm, Jellicoe received no information from Beatty, Evan-Thomas or from the other two light cruiser squadrons, except indirectly from *Falmouth* through *Black Prince*. And, when they did report, *Lion* and *Barham* gave only the enemy's bearing. From the battlefleet, only the armoured cruisers actually sighted vessels approaching from the Southward but neither *Defence* nor, it seems, *Black Prince* identified them as friend or foe; however, *Black Prince* did supply her position and the battle-cruisers' bearing and distance. The other reports from the battlefleet were only of the approximate direction of the sound and flashes of gunfire. Once the battlefleets were in action, hardly any reports were made by ships in either of the lines. Dreyer acknowledged that:

Many experienced officers in . . . our Fleet at Jutland, when they sighted enemy ships, did not realise that Jellicoe could not see them and that they were withholding priceless information from him.

---

[122] The total of nine includes the three failed attempts by *Faulknor* to report the 12DF's attack on the German line.

Dreyer included himself among these officers, admitting that, from his station in *Iron Duke*'s conning tower, he had seen *König* turn away but had not informed Jellicoe on the manoeuvring platform. Jellicoe would tell the Tactical School: 'Never imagine that your C.-in-C. sees what you see.'[123] Evidently the officers of the High Seas Fleet had made the same mistake. At Jutland, neither side came anywhere close to the reporting standards that Dreyer claimed had been usual in peacetime exercises.

Intercepts

In addition to the reports from their own ships, both Commanders-in-Chief also received intelligence derived from signals intercepted by shore-based stations. During the morning of the 31 May, Scheer received two reports based on intercepts though he disregarded them. Thereafter, according to the German signal record, he was sent a partially decrypted British signal at 8.00pm, then nothing more until 7.55am the next morning. However, after the War both Jellicoe and his critics believed that Scheer had been informed that at 9.27pm Jellicoe had ordered his flotillas to take station five miles astern.[124] A signal from Neumünster to this effect – 'Destroyers have taken up position five miles astern of enemy main Fleet' – can be found in two British lists of German signals with a time-of-origin of 2130, though that implies that it was decrypted almost immediately.[125] Yet it is not in the German signal record; it is not mentioned in Birch and Clarke's history of Room 40; and the German official history declared:

> The German shore wireless stations had carefully monitored the British wireless traffic during the battle, but it had taken them much longer to decipher and digest the inter-cepted messages than had been the case at the British Admiralty. That Jellicoe had stationed all his destroyer flotillas astern of the battlefleet ... remained unknown to Scheer until after his return to harbour.[126]

In any case, the time-of-origin of Scheer's *Durchhalten* signal to steer for Horns Reef was 2114, before Jellicoe disposed his destroyers. If Scheer had learnt later of Jellicoe's signal, it would only have reinforced his determination to press on should his battleships encounter the British flotillas.

Jellicoe and the Admiralty's intelligence   Thanks to the British signals intelligence operation centred on Room 40, Admiralty Old Building, Jellicoe received many more reports of enemy movements than did Scheer. Even so, after the War Jellicoe claimed that a good part of the intelligence he received from the Admiralty derived from direction-finding and that he had

---

[123] Dreyer, pp. 168–9.   [124] GSM. *JP II*, p. 437. *AN*, pp. 73–4 and 112–13.
[125] *NSA*, App. G, p. 170 (signal 20421). 'Jutland Signals', Sh. 6 in ADM 137/4067.
[126] *GOA*, p. 193. Tarrant, p. 213.

Table 10.9. *The Admiralty's intelligence reports to Jellicoe*

Time of despatch	From	To	System	Message	Time of origin
pm, 31 May					
3.10	Admiralty	C-in-C	W/T	At 2.31pm directionals placed Enemy Light Cruiser at 56°57 N, 6°9E, and Enemy Destroyers at 56°57 N, 5°43E. (Received in Lion 3.29pm)	1510
5.00	Admiralty	C-in-C	W/T	At 4.9 Enemy battlefleet 56°27 N, 6°18E, course NW, 15 knots	1700
5.45	Admiralty	C-in-C	W/T	Enemy main force at 4.30pm 56°31 N, 6° 5E, steering N, 15 knots (Received in Iron Duke 5.53)	1745
9.55	Admiralty	C-in-C	W/T	Three Destroyer flotillas have been ordered to attack you during the night	2105 [*sic*]
9.58	Admiralty	C-in-C	W/T	At 9.00, rear ships of Enemy B.F. in 56°33 N, 5°30E on southerly course. (Received in Iron Duke 10.23)	2158
10.41	Admiralty	C-in-C	W/T	At 10.41 the Admiralty informed the C-in-C that the enemy was believed to be returning to its base as its course was SSE¾E and speed 16 knots	2241
am, 1 June					
1.48	Admiralty	C-in-C	W/T	At 1.48 the Admiralty informed the C-in-C that enemy submarines were apparently coming out from German ports, and that a damaged enemy ship, probably Lutzow, was in 56°26 N, 5°41E at Midnight.	0148
3.12	Admiralty	C-in-C	W/T	German light Cruiser in 55°45 N, 6°25E, damaged, crew taken off, Destroyers standing by at 3 a.m.	0312
3.29	Admiralty	C-in-C	W/T	Urgent. At 2.30 German Main Fleet in 55° 33 N, 6°50E, course SEbyS, 16 knots	0329
5.30	Admiralty	C-in-C	W/T	*Elbing* still afloat at 3.47, without crew. Position 3 a.m. 55°45 N, 6°25E	0530
9.17	Admiralty	C-in-C	W/T	At 6.20 Enemy Submarines ordered to close *Elbing*, position now given 55°51 N, 5°55E	

been right to prefer the reports of his own ships in sight of the enemy. And, as we shall see, during the night, much of the signals intelligence gathered by Room 40 was not passed on to Jellicoe by the Operations Division (OD). For the rest of this section only, a 24-hour clock set for GMT is used for identifying both British and German signals by their times-of-origin, and for times in the text (except that quotations are unaltered).[127]

On the 31 May, the 1230 signal from the Admiralty informed Jellicoe that 'directional wireless places flagship in Jade at 11.10 G.M.T.'. As Captain Hope noted: 'As far as Room 40 was concerned, there was nothing to actually show that the Fleet was at sea until 2.40 p.m.' when directionals located *Lützow* and *Elbing* in 'about 57°N, 6°E'.[128] In fact, Hope sent out a handwritten note giving the 1431 positions of *Elbing* and *B109* as determined by direction-finding and this information was repeated exactly to Jellicoe in the Admiralty's signal of 1510. (The position of *Lützow*'s new call sign was not established until some time between 1455 and 1530.)[129] However, directionals are not mentioned in any of the Admiralty's subsequent signals to the C-in-C; as we now know, the information in all these later signals was obtained from intercepts of Scheer's own signals, though their source was not given explicitly. The Admiralty's signals of 1700 and 1745 gave *verbatim* the courses and speeds in the German signals timed for 1609 and 1630, and positions that had been converted from the German reference squares.[130] There was then a long gap, reflecting Scheer's own silence, until what may have been a delayed signal from the Admiralty about expected flotilla attacks during the night. This was quickly followed at 2158 by a position for the rear German battleship at 2100, the 'southerly' course being that given in the original signal from *Regensburg* to the II and VI TFs.[131] The final Admiralty signal of the 31st was the definitive report at 2241 stating:

German battlefleet ordered home at 9.14 p.m. Battle cruisers in rear. Speed 16 knots. Course S.S.E. ¾ E.

This signal brought together most of the information in three of Scheer's signals timed at 2114, 2129 and 2146, the course being that ordered in the last signal (the first specified SSE¼E).[132]

After the 2241 signal, Jellicoe received nothing more from the Admiralty for more than three hours, until the signal timed at 0148 informed him, again in different words from those in the *Official Despatches*:

---

[127] In the original German signals, on the Room 40 forms and in 'Jutland Signals', the German 'time-group' (time-of-origin) was two hours ahead of GMT (but in GSM, one hour ahead).

[128] Captain H W Hope, 'Notes on Action of May 31 – June 1 1916', f. 2 in ADM 137/4168 and 'Diary ... Apr May 1916', section headed 'Operation 30th, 31st, 1st' in ADM 137/4169.

[129] 'Jutland. Telegraphic Record (C.O.S)', ADM 137/1642, ff. 24–7.

[130] Signals 20372 and 20379 passed to OD at 4.35 and 5.00.

[131] Signal 20406 (time-group from 'Jutland Signals' 2103) passed to OD 9.25. Birch and Clarke gave the positional time as 4pm instead of 9pm.

[132] Signals 20410, 20411 (passed to OD 9.55) and 20413 (10.10). These forms show how Room 40 recorded times in both GMT and British Summer Time (BST), though inconsistently. 20413 is one of several forms in which the time-of-receipt is in GMT and the time passed in BST. The times in GMT by Birch and Clarke (except 20406) appear to be correct.

Position of LÜTZOW at midnight 56°26′ – 5°41′E, course S. speed 7 knots, damaged. All German submarines are being hurried from German ports to attack. One flotilla returning around Skaw.

The alarming intelligence about submarines appears to have been based on the German signal first transmitted at 1950 the previous evening. But, despite a report of 2207 announcing that just three U-boats 'were leaving the Ems for the North at high speed', only the earlier information was added to more recent intelligence about *Lützow* and the IITF.[133] The next Admiralty signal to Jellicoe, timed at 0310, omitted *Elbing*'s name and wrongly converted the German time. Then Jellicoe was informed in the 0329 signal that at 0230, the High Seas Fleet was already out of reach in the vicinity of Horns Reef.[134]

In his dissenting appendix of 'General Remarks' to the *Admiralty Narrative* (published in 1924), Jellicoe was dismissive of the enemy reports that he had received from the Admiralty.

I should not for a moment have relied on Admiralty information in preference to reports from ships which actually sighted him, or even have attached equal weight to such reports. It would be assumed that the Admiralty report [*sic*] relied on directional wireless, as was stated to be the case in the signal made at 1510.[135]

He might also have added that the thoroughly misleading report of the German Fleet still being in the Jade at 1110 was also based on directionals though, on the other hand, he tacitly accepted that the method was not mentioned again. Yet he also understood the limited accuracy of direction-finding.

At this time this method of position finding was still more or less in its infancy, and seeing that the High Seas Fleet was some 250–300 miles from the wireless stations, the accuracy of the report was problematical.[136]

Patrick Beesly considered that, even after further development in World War I: 'Based on World War II experience, it is unlikely that fixes were accurate to within a smaller radius than twenty miles from a central point even in the North Sea'.[137] Since this radius was about equal to the distance a ship would travel in one hour, two cross-bearings separated by many hours would have been needed to determine even approximate speed and course, though only in the unlikely

---

[133] Signals 20400 and 20438 (both timed at 1950, not in Hines's table), 20426 (2207), 20439 (2352) and 20440 (0017).

[134] German signal 20456 (0230) passed to OD 3.00.

[135] *AN*, p. 108; unlike the *NSA*, the *AN* did not mention the Admiralty's 1230 signal.

[136] Unpublished 1922 appendix to *The Grand Fleet* in *JP II*, p. 423.

[137] Beesly, p. 254 n. 1. ±20 miles equates to ±0.33° of latitude, ±0.76° of longitude. After the war in peacetime conditions, cross-bearing error of ±1–2° were common with occasional errors of ±5° and upwards: R Keen, *Wireless Direction Finding*, (London: Wireless World, 3rd edn., 1938) p. 553. At 250 miles, ±2–5° equates to 8.7–21.8 miles.

event that both remained constant.[138] Furthermore, Jellicoe was well aware that German signals were being intercepted and deciphered. As early as November 1914, he knew of the capture of German codebooks and had pressed for copies so that enemy signals could be read in the flagship: but his request had been refused on security grounds. By April 1916, the C-in-C pronounced himself 'in mortal terror' that the German deciphering of British signals might reveal that their own messages were being read routinely.[139] Thus he would have expected the Admiralty to hold back any less vital information that could reveal the source of a report as an intercepted signal – the obvious candidates being the identities of the sender and recipient(s) of the German original. These were routinely omitted by the Admiralty but usually the rest of the signal content was sent without alteration – except that the German reference positions were translated into latitude and longitude. The first two Admiralty signals of 1230 and 1510 doubtless planted the idea of directionals in Jellicoe's mind. But then he received three reports (of 1700, 1745 and 2241) with precise speeds and courses; not only was the course in the third report accurate to a quarter of a point but the wording left no doubt that it was based on an actual German order. Given Jellicoe's evident appreciation of both the problematical accuracy of direction-finding and the need for signals security, it is hard to credit that he did not recognise that all three signals derived from intercepted German signals.

In stating his preference for reports from ships, Jellicoe implied that they were often at variance with those from the Admiralty. He cited the specific case of the Admiralty signal of 1510 'giving the position of an enemy light cruiser, which position appeared to be at least 16 miles in error, by the *Nottingham*'s 1522 report'.[140] But he failed to mention that the 1510 signal gave positions at 1431 not only of a cruiser but also of destroyers: or that *Nottingham*'s 1522 report described 'five columns of smoke' – it was made from a position close to that of *Lion*, which at 1535 reported sighting five enemy battlecruisers.[141] The Admiralty's signal of 1510 clearly related not to *Nottingham*'s of 1522 but to the two signals from *Galatea* originated at 1430, both of which were received in *Iron Duke*. One reported that *Galatea* was chasing two destroyers (previously described as cruisers); the other gave her position and stated that an enemy cruiser bore E, steering ESE. From this position and those in the Admiralty's signal, it could be deduced that the distances and bearings from *Galatea* of the enemy destroyers and cruiser were, respectively, 14.9 miles EbyN and 28.2

---

[138] E.g. after a four-hour steady run at 20 knots, errors of ±20 miles in positions would result in worst-case errors of ±10 knots in speed, ±30° in course (though not simultaneously).

[139] Oliver, 'Recollections, Vol. II' (1946), pp. 103, 116, 143 and 175, OLV/12. Beesly, pp. 41–3. Hines, p. 1131 citing *JP I*, p. 231.

[140] *AN*, p. 108 and also *JP II*, p. 423.

[141] In his 1922 appendix (*JP II*, p. 423), Jellicoe cited *Falmouth*'s 1500 rather than *Nottingham*'s 1522 to suggest that 'it seemed very improbable that the Admiralty [1510] signal gave correct information'. Here too he mentioned neither the time (1431) nor the destroyers' position.

miles E. Thus the bearings agreed within a point. If the visibility was about 12 miles, the error in the cruiser's distance could well have been about 16 miles; but, in that case, the error for the destroyers was no more than three miles. Whether deliberately or not, by confusing the reports and omitting important details, Jellicoe was able to avoid the admission that, at least for the destroyers, the reports from *Galatea* at sea and from the Admiralty were in quite good agreement.

The next two Admiralty signals referred to the German battlefleet at 1609 and 1630. In his published appendix, Jellicoe seemed to accept that these were after all based on intercepts but, even so, he still insisted that they were not as reliable as reports from ships; he alleged, though without being specific, that 'one might be misled if trusting too much to Intercepts *e.g.* the different courses assigned to the enemy by the Admiralty and the *Southampton*'.[142] In fact, the Admiralty reported courses of NW at 1609 and N at 1630; *Southampton* N at 1638, 1648 and 1700 (and NNW at 1740). Thus both sets of reports were consistent with a German course N by 1630 that was held until some time after 1700. But while the report for 1609 provided the useful intelligence that the German fleet speed was 15 knots, its position was not consistent with *Southampton*'s at 4.38, since it implied a distance of only 7.1 miles between the two; however, at five o'clock there was no way of telling where the error lay.

Despite Jellicoe's declared preference for reports from ships in touch with the enemy, he was prepared to admit – though only in his unpublished appendix for *The Grand Fleet* – that they were sometimes less than accurate. He noted that from *Lion*'s 1550 signal it appeared that she had reversed course in the previous five minutes, while *Southampton*'s reports between 1630 and 1700 implied that she had been steaming at speeds between 35 and more than 60 knots.[143] Nonetheless, Goodenough's reports were used to predict that at 1800 the High Seas Fleet would be 30 miles right ahead of *Iron Duke*. After a 40-minute gap, *Southampton* next reported her position at 1740 – which was NWbyN from her position at 1700 – and an enemy course of NNW. Then, at 1745, a new Admiralty signal gave the enemy's position, course and speed at 1630. Since it did not reach *Iron Duke*'s bridge until about 1800, the signal was not immediately relevant. But it did provide an alternative starting position for plotting the German course Northwards. As Jellicoe acknowledged in the appendix to the *Admiralty Narrative*:

The Admiralty 1745 message and *Southampton*'s 5.40 signal agreed fairly well if one assumed that ... the enemy bore East 10 to 11 miles from *Southampton* as in the previous message ... (5 p.m.).[144]

---

[142] *AN*, p. 113.   [143] *JP II*, p. 422.   [144] *AN*, p. 110.

In fact, if the enemy positions for 1740 inferred from these two reports are plotted, they almost coincide. Furthermore, whereas the same plot confirms that the position for the High Seas Fleet at 1800 as predicted from *Southampton*'s reports up to 1700 was 30 miles ahead (SEbyS) from *Iron Duke*, the German position as predicted from the Admiralty's 1745 was only 20 miles from *Iron Duke*, one point (SE) on the starboard bow. The true position was actually West of South but, even so, the Admiralty's data gave a better prediction than *Southampton*'s reports up to 1700, though there was much better agreement with *Southampton*'s 1740 report. It is not known whether the full implications of the Admiralty's 1745 were worked out during the battle itself. But it is clear that, despite Jellicoe's attempts after the War to demonstrate otherwise, he had no good reasons for dismissing the information in this or the two preceding Admiralty reports as misleading.

In his post-war appendices, Jellicoe did not mention the Admiralty 2105 signal, despatched at 2155, perhaps because its report of orders to the enemy destroyers could only have been based on intercepts. The next Admiralty signal of 2158 was not received in *Iron Duke* until 2223, by which time there were signs on the starboard quarter of the first engagement between light forces. The signal implied that at 2100 the rear German battleships had borne WSW from *Iron Duke*, but Jellicoe would dismiss it as obviously inaccurate, preferring instead a bearing of NWbyN deduced from Jerram's false report. Nowhere did he mention that at about 2115 enemy firing had been observed to the Westward of his flagship; thus he avoided the question of how, in the next hour, enemy forces had moved from abeam to the starboard quarter, and subsequently astern and onto the port quarter. Jellicoe could not and did not deny that the information in the final Admiralty signal of 31 May, describing the order for the High Seas Fleet to return past Horns Reef, was obtained by interception. But he had deployed selective, even specious, arguments to denigrate the accuracy of most of the previous Admiralty reports. This reasoning had prepared the ground for him to claim that the final unambiguous signal was not conclusive, and to accept that *Birmingham* had correctly reported (despite a most unlikely position) that the German course was still South. (We shall return in the final chapter to why he found it necessary to justify his decisions by these questionable means.)

Up to the signal of 2241 Jellicoe received nearly all the essential intelligence obtained from intercepted German signals, apart from the identity of the senders and recipients. But thereafter, although Room 40 continued to provide the OD with decrypts confirming that Scheer was indeed maintaining his course for Horns Reef, none of this intelligence was passed to Jellicoe. Probably the most informative was the intercept of Scheer's urgent request of 2106 to the Airship Division for early air reconnaissance at Horns Reef. This was handed to the OD at 2210 at the same time as the signal ordering course

SSE¾E[145] yet was omitted from the composite Admiralty signal of 2241. Subsequently, at least six more signals giving Scheer's course were picked up. The first two – the second also gave a position indicating that Scheer was about to cross Jellicoe's wake – were passed to OD at 2315 and 2350,[146] the other four between midnight and 0120.[147] An equally conclusive signal of 2232 ordered all German flotillas not returning around The Skaw to assemble off Horns Reef at 2am; this was passed to OD at 2315.[148] When Jellicoe eventually discovered how much intelligence had been kept from him, he justifiably declared:

These errors were *absolutely fatal*, as the information if passed to me would have clearly shown me that Scheer was making for the Horn Reef [and] would have led me to alter course during the night.[149]

No satisfactory explanation has been unearthed for why, after the 2241 signal, the OD sent no more intelligence on Scheer's movements for almost five hours. In Oliver's recollection:

We had all been busy for about 30 hours before the battle began and the night of the battle I borrowed Capt. Everett the 1st Sea Lord[']s Naval Assistant to help and Jackson the D.O.D. and Grant [Assistant D.O.D.] had a rest and relieved me at 5 a.m. next day. Everett knew the Room 40 business.[150]

Everett was 'the Royal Navy's most authoritative signalling expert' and he had been Captain of the Fleet under Callaghan and then Jellicoe until May 1915.[151] Thus, knowing of Jellicoe's unsuccessful bid for his own decrypting service and of the current work of Room 40, Everett would have understood better than most the danger that, if the Germans managed to read the Admiralty's signals, they would discover that their codes were compromised. Thus either Oliver or Everett could have decided that the 2241 signal was a clear indication that Scheer was returning to base via Horns Reef and that further reports of almost identical German courses would be a security risk not worth taking[152] – though that does not excuse the holding back of other important intelligence.

---

[145] Signals 20414 and 20413.

[146] Signals 20422 and 20428. The latter reported course SE¾E, position 56°15N, 5°42E at 2306; the position, if plotted on *Iron Duke*'s track (*OD*, Pl. 3a), placed *Friedrich der Grosse* 11.7 miles about NNW.

[147] Signals, 20430, 20433, 20444 and 20445. The first two were not listed by Birch and Clarke but it has been assumed that the times at which they were passed to OD were given on the forms in BST.

[148] Signal 20423.   [149] 'Errors made in Jutland Battle' (1932) in *JP II*, 452.

[150] Oliver (see note 139), p. 175.

[151] Hines, p. 1112. Gordon, pp. 301, 321 and 357. Black, p. 163. Kent, pp. 23 and 245. *GF*, pp. 18 and 144. *FDSF III*, p. 177 (though Marder supposed that Everett had little knowledge of German signalling and procedures).

[152] See also Corbett, p. 402.

Furthermore, the errors and omissions in the signals of 0148 and 0312 may suggest that the decrypts still being received in the OD from Room 40 were no longer being handled efficiently, perhaps because Oliver was more tired than he realised. Something went seriously wrong while he and Everett were on watch, but what it was, and who was responsible, still remains hidden.

Gunnery and fire control

For effective fire control, both the British and German systems depended on good visibility for precise ranging, aiming and spotting. But such conditions were only experienced by both sides during the first phase of the Run to the South though, even then, the patches of mist were a greater inconvenience to the British ships. Yet, although the British ranging errors were greater, the opening ranges of both sides were inaccurate. von Hase of *Derfflinger* thought that initially his range-takers had been overwhelmed by their first view of the enemy. However, he claimed that subsequently 'there was seldom a variation of more than 300 metres. between any of the range-finders even at the longest ranges';[153] this spread ($\pm1\%$ at 15,000 yards) was only half that expected from German range-takers. After an uncertain start, it appears that the actual spread of German ranges was small enough for the 'Mittlungs Apparat' to give good mean ranges and range-rates. During the Run to the South, the conditions were easy enough for *Seydlitz* to fire by the range clock; subsequently 'the movements of the ship were so frequent and sudden' that firing had to continue using the mean range-finder range.[154] Because the ISG's range errors were smaller, they needed less time to correct them by spotting and they began hitting at least three minutes before the BCF. They were also in the lee position so did not suffer from interference from their own smoke.

At the moment when Hipper opened fire, Beatty's tactical direction had placed his battlecruisers under several gunnery disadvantages. They were still altering course as they tried to form the line-of-bearing that would free them from interference from their own smoke. The 2BCS were still struggling to get into line. Not all the British turrets were bearing and none of the British ships had selected *Derfflinger* as a target. Yet, while the British smoke interfered with their own ranging, it did not much inconvenience their opponents, whose stereoscopic range-finders could still range provided that the range-takers 'could see the smallest speck of the mast-heads'.[155] Unlike those astern of her, *Princess Royal* must have kept out of *Lion*'s smoke, since the ranges from her coincidence range-finders were outstandingly accurate, bettered only by

[153] von Hase, pp. 147–8. In 1930, Mahrholz (p. 53) claimed that initially *Von der Tann*'s range-finders measured within 100 metres but, if he remembered correctly, this must have been exceptional.
[154] *Seydlitz* (see note 37), f. 272.   [155] von Hase, p. 154.

Moltke's. In contrast, *Lion* obtained ranges which were few in number and notably imprecise. Since she cannot have suffered from smoke interference, the fault would appear to have been with her range-takers, the result of poor training and insufficient practice. To make matters worse, her fire controllers did not recognise, even in the few ranges that were obtained, how quickly the enemy was approaching; the consequences were serious not only for *Lion*'s gunnery but also for Beatty's tactical appreciation. By the end of the first phase of the Run to the South, his battlecruisers had scored only 6 hits but received at least 22.

At the conclusion of this phase, the visibility was deteriorating, particularly for the British. After *Indefatigable* blew up and *Lion*'s Q turret was hit, the flagship veered away for a time before regaining the head of the line and leading a new approach. But again smoke interference was a problem and gunnery and tactics were compromised by *Lion*'s ranges being too high and her range-rate too small. Also, 'we were being led by the Flagship on a snake-like course, to reduce the chances of being hit'. Throughout the Run to the South, this compromised range-finding and, after opening fire, aiming as well; it was far from Chatfield's 'steady course which is so important for gunnery'.[156] Nonetheless, by 4.25 *Princess Royal*'s ranges were once again close to those in use in German ships. The British battlecruisers probably made three hits early in the second phase, but none subsequently. In contrast, despite the worsening visibility and ranges as high as 19,000 yards, the 5BS were able to concentrate on *Moltke* and *Von der Tann*, while their 15-feet range-finders were sufficiently accurate to enable them to make as many as seven hits. Hipper's battlecruisers scored another thirteen hits, including one on *Barham*.

Because *Lion* had been out of line, *Derfflinger* mistook *Queen Mary*'s position in the line and sank her in a concentration with *Seydlitz*. von Hase tabulated *Derfflinger*'s final salvos in his book, noting that 'the training angles of the turrets remained practically unchanged and that ... during these vital minutes, the ship steered an admirable course'. On first opening fire, the salvo rates of the British and German battlecruisers were quite similar; for example, the first five or six salvos from *Lion, Princess Royal, Lützow* and *Derfflinger* were fired with average intervals of 38, 55, 45 and 48 seconds respectively. When engaging a new target, in general both sides spotted each salvo until they crossed the target and then worked a 'bracket' or 'fork' in which each correction was half the preceding one. As von Hase described it:

Each time we had to wait for the splashes. When these were observed new orders had generally to be given for deflection, rate and elevation.

---

[156] F&H, p. 39, Chatfield, p. 142 and also pp. 109 and 134.

Table 10.10. Derfflinger's *gunnery log against* Queen Mary

GUNNERY LOG DURING THE DESTRUCTION OF 'QUEEN MARY'						
Time			Training angle	Range in m.	Deflection		Orders for elevation telegraph, etc.
h.	m.	s.					
4	22	–	52°	14,000	left	10	E-U-3!
4	22	40	51°	13,900	„	16	2 short!
4	23	45	52°	13,700	„	14	1 short!
4	24	20	52°	13,500	„	14	Good, Rapid!
4	24	40	52°	13,400	„	14	
4	25	–	52°	13,400	„	14	
4	25	20	52°	13,200	„	14	
4	25	45	52°	13,100	„	14	
4	26	10	52°	13,200	„	10	2 short! Heavy explosion in our enemy! Change of target to the second battle-cruiser from the left!

But, as can be seen in Table 10.10, once the target had been consistently straddled, 'Good, Rapid!' ordered rapid fire with a salvo interval of 20 seconds.

While the firing was going on any observation was out of the question ... Naturally such furious rapid fire could only be maintained for a limited time ... It was not long before our salvoes fell over or short, as a result of the enemy altering course ... Each salvo was then directed afresh and this continued until the target was again straddled.[157]

These bursts of rapid fire, so crucial to the German gunnery successes, made such an impression that, after Jutland, the Royal Navy wrongly assumed that their opponents had fired rapid salvos even when finding the target; this led to the introduction of the 'ladder' system in which, in order to bracket the target more quickly, double salvos were fired and spotted together before firing the next double, all salvos being separated by a fixed amount.[158]

Those British ships that hit repeatedly employed the same control principles as the Germans: first straddle consistently with single spotted salvos to obtain a good range and range-rate; then break into rapid fire until the target threw out the rate by taking evasive action. Thus *Barham* waited to straddle before she 'fired four more salvoes rapid and straddled again' and from *Valiant* 'on four or five occasions rapid bursts were carried out when it was seen that hitting was

---

[157] von Hase, pp. 145, 147–9, 160 and 163–4. For other salvo intervals: REL; *OD*, p. 387 and Campbell, pp. 40 and 364.
[158] *DGBJ*, pp. 248 and 268.

established';[159] more examples will follow. But, of the British battlecruisers, only *New Zealand* (and *Tiger* intermittently after she resorted to two-gun salvos) came close to the rate of German rapid fire. When *New Zealand* opened fire at 3.51pm, she broke immediately into rapid salvos fired mostly at 30-second intervals; from this wild fusillade – undoubtedly another case where 'the rapidity ideas were carried to excess' – she made not one hit. Uniquely, the record from *Lion*'s transmitting station gives the spotting corrections ordered after nearly every salvo; unfortunately the salvo times are given to the nearest half-minute so it is only possible to give average salvo intervals. The spotting corrections themselves seem almost random; they show no sign of systematic bracketing to obtain straddles, nor even of the scheme proposed by Chatfield after the Dogger Bank – large DOWN corrections until SHORT, then small UP corrections. Perhaps, in the hope of straddling quickly, the spotter was trying to estimate how far each salvo fell from the target. It took until just on 4 o'clock to obtain two straddles, when rapid fire was ordered, but then *Lion* was hit on Q turret and her rate of fire slowed rather than increased.[160]

During the Run to the North, the visibility continued to deteriorate, the advantage being at first with the German but later with the British squadrons. Beatty's battlecruisers made no definite hits before they drew out of range by 5.10, but on re-engaging *Lion* made the BCF's only hit of this phase. At 5.44½, she spotted a straddle, one short; without waiting for a second straddle she immediately broke into rapid fire, five salvos following at half-minute intervals to secure a hit on *Lützow*. This was her only sustained burst of rapid fire to the clock range (except for a single UP 200 spotting correction).[161] The 5BS remained in action throughout and, despite having to divide their fire and contend at the start with long ranges, probably made eighteen hits. This was almost as many as the twenty-one hits scored by the ISG and the IIIBS: five on the BCF and sixteen on the 5BS. After the battlefleets met, the visibility became even worse, especially for the German ships, though, for both sides, there were occasional clear views of the enemy through the murk. Just before six o'clock, the 3BCS sighted the light cruisers of the IISG at a range of only 8,000 yards on opposite courses; even though the battlecruisers probably had only simple manually worked fire control systems, they succeeded in disabling *Wiesbaden* and damaging *Pillau*. Hood's ships then encountered the ISG at ranges between 8,000 and 9,500 yards. Just before *Invincible*'s end, she had broken into rapid fire and was hitting repeatedly. But at that moment the mist that had hidden her from *Lützow* and *Derfflinger* lifted. At such short ranges,

---

[159] Diary for 31 May 1916 in Peter Hore (ed.) *Patrick Blackett. Sailor, Scientist, Socialist* (London: Frank Cass, 2003), p. 5 (times in BST). *OD*, p. 214.

[160] REL; *Lion* fired 19 salvos between 3.47½ and 4.00, an average interval of 42 seconds. *BP I*, p. 356.

[161] REL.

both ships quickly straddled; once again von Hase ordered rapid salvos, while *Lützow* claimed that she fired only three salvos before *Invincible* blew up. At almost the same time *Iron Duke* provided a further demonstration that the way to repeated hitting was to straddle consistently with spotted salvos and then to break into rapid fire; however, she was able to spot her rapid salvos and make UP corrections as the *König* turned away to escape further hits. One more instance of effective rapid fire is found when, beginning at 7.12 with a range-finder range of 10,750 yards, *Marlborough* fired fourteen rapid salvos in six minutes to score three (perhaps more) of the seven hits on *Grosser Kurfürst* at this time. However, no other British battleships had opportunities to develop extended bursts of rapid salvos or to fire at the long ranges that had featured in their gunnery practices. Jellicoe accepted that

the use of distribution of gunfire signals was out of the question, only three or four ships being in sight at a time from the van and centre, though more were visible from the rear. Ships fired at what they could see, when they could see it.

Thunderer found that

Objects came into view and disappeared again in about 3 minutes. A quick R.F. reading, used immediately, was the only practicable method.[162]

The Dreyer Tables

Of the British ships that shot well, those of the 5BS and *Iron Duke* were equipped with automatic Dreyer Tables Mark IV and IV*. Yet apparently none of them made a bearing plot during the battle; *Malaya* definitely stated that she did not, while only *Lion* is known to have sent in a bearing plot afterwards.[163] Neither *Invincible* nor *Marlborough* was equipped to plot bearings automatically. In principle, the Dumaresqs in all these ships (provided their settings were reasonably accurate) could indicate the changes of range-rate and deflection due to alterations of own course, though only some were adjusted automatically. But, in the fleeting visibility with which they all contended, they could only fire in fairly short bursts; the 5BS found, even during the Run to the South, that 'firing was intermittent due to the great difficulty in seeing the enemy' while, although *Valiant* obtained sufficient ranges to give a rate, her opening range was an estimate.[164] Also, apart from the brief period when *Von der Tann* engaged *Barham* and in *Invincible's* final moments, none of

---

[162] *OD*, pp. 18 and 376.
[163] Memoranda by Jellicoe and Chatfield (24 Sep. and 1 Oct. 1916) in BTY 6/6 and from *Revenge, Ajax, Malaya* and *Monarch* (also from *Tiger, Warspite, Centurion* and *King George V* which sent in single plots, presumably of range) in ADM 116/1487.
[164] *OD*, pp. 193 and 213.

these British ships was under fire during the short spells of effective firing, so they were able to hold steady courses. In these conditions, fire often had to be opened with estimates of target range, speed and inclination and hence of range-rate and deflection. At best, there would have been time before firing commenced to plot a few ranges and correct the initial estimates of range and range-rate. Thereafter, spotting became the principal sources of further corrections. Refinements such as the bearing plot and the gyro-compass connection were hardly needed.

The British battlecruisers were equipped with a variety of fire control system but all could keep the range-rate and deflection during course changes by own ship, though some, including *Queen Mary*'s Dreyer Table Mark II, depended on manually set target bearings.[165] Thus at first sight it might seem that the BCF fire control systems, especially those with Dreyer Tables Mark III and IV, could correct for their frequent course alterations. Indeed, after the Battle of the Dogger Bank, Beatty concluded that, at high speed, one-point turns with small helm 'will in no way interfere with our gunnery', though his range-takers, gunlayers and turret-trainers may have been less sanguine. But, in any case, adjustments to the rates in use were only of value if the rates themselves had already been determined with reasonable accuracy. Whereas, with the usual exception of *Princess Royal*, the other battlecruisers underestimated the range-rate – including *Lion*, so even if she obtained an accurate bearing-rate from her bearing-plot, it alone was not enough to refine the setting of her Dumaresq. Thus the fire control systems of the BCF had the potential to compensate for some of the disadvantages arising from Beatty's 'snake-like course': but, because they were not supplied with even the minimum of necessary data, *viz.* reasonably accurate ranges, that potential could not be exploited.

Though for different reasons, the refinements of the later Dreyer Tables were of little benefit to any British capital ships at Jutland, whether or not they shot well. Thus, apart from the actual method for obtaining mean range and range-rate, the fire control methods of British and German ships at Jutland were similar in principle. In a different action fought in better visibility, engagements would have been more protracted and, in many cases, course alterations would have been necessary as they progressed. Then, whether or not firing continued through such turns, the gyro-compass connections of the Dreyer Tables Mark III–IV* would have enabled them to adjust the rates in use automatically so that, at worst, firing could recommence as soon as the course steadied.[166] In better visibility these more elaborate tables could also have made bearing plots

---

[165] *DGBJ*, pp. 97–8 and 286–7.
[166] The rates after the turn were correct only if the target held its course but, even if it did not, it would still have been helpful to know the changes in rate due to own ship's turn.

though, because accuracy was limited by the coarse steps of ¼° in which bearings were transmitted, their utility would probably have been marginal. But, after the transmission step size had been reduced to four minutes of arc at the end of the War, the principle of bearing plotting was incorporated in the Gyro Director Training (GDT) gear that replaced the old bearing-plot on the Dreyer Tables, and in the bearing-plots of the new Admiralty Fire Control Tables.[167]

Assessments

Beatty and Chatfield were quick enough to criticise the quality of their armour-piercing shells for the ineffectiveness of their gunnery but the BCF's gunnery committee concluded that, despite the poor visibility and light, 'the British system of fire control ... on the whole ... stood the test successfully'. While exaggerating how frequently their opponents altered course, the committee also noted that

The action ... appears to show that more value was obtained from rangefinders by some ships than by others, and that at such times as the enemy was on a steady course undoubted assistance was received from the plot.

It is again strongly emphasised that the enemy system of continuously altering course defeats any system of fire control based on rate-finding, for the reason that by the time the plot has established a rate it is no longer applicable.

The Committee also recommended that every capital ship should be supplied with one 15-foot range-finder and, apparently recognising failings in the BCF itself, that the 'training of [range-finder] operators must be intensive and on standardised lines'.[168] The equivalent Dreadnought Battlefleet Committee also concluded that 'Generally our [fire control] arrangements worked well' and that 'The Director system [of firing] worked better than any other.' But both committees acknowledged the difficulties in poor visibility of getting spotters aloft and the director onto the same target, since the spotter's stereoscopic binoculars did not have a target indicator. This deficiency was not corrected until after the battle by the supply of 'aid-to-spotter' instruments, either with electric bearing receivers or, in older dreadnoughts, mechanical coupling to the director.

The Battlefleet Committee was impressed by the rapidity of German fire and that half the armament (one gun per turret) fired in each salvo. 'This shows great precision in drill and accuracy of arrangements', the committee admitting that 'we still require to improve our accuracy of drill, to enable us to fire four- or

---

[167] Brooks, 'AFCTs', pp. 71–4 and 79–82.
[168] *BP I*, p. 349; the committee hoped that 'a fully developed rangefinder [control] system will give quicker information than any other, as to the movements of the enemy'. *DGBJ*, pp. 267–9.

five-gun salvos in rapid firing' (emphasis in original).[169] However, German ships may not have been able to sustain such precision, especially after hits; C turret in *Seydlitz* was burnt out early in the battle but the ammunition consumptions of the other turrets differed significantly. *Lützow* was alone in preferring salvos fired alternatively by all four guns of the fore turrets and then of the after turrets; but the view in her sister *Derfflinger* was that 'four separate impacts are easier to observe than two double impacts'.[170]

On the whole the highly trained German range-takers, their stereoscopic range-finders and the 'Mittlungs Apparat' gave accurate mean ranges and range-rates. Captain Harder of *Lützow* reported that 'The electrical fire control equipment functioned excellently', apart from experimental gyro-firing gear in the turrets, which was not used in the battle because of earlier failures at practice.[171] More important exceptions were the unreliable time-of-flight indicators, *Derfflinger*'s requiring repair just before the action and *Seydlitz*'s breaking down soon after the start. The German training director (*Rw*) concentrated in one instrument the functions of target designation, turret training and spotting. Thus there was no danger, as in the British system, of the spotter mistaking the target. In *Derfflinger*, the spotting officer aloft could also indicate the bearing of the target if it could not be seen from the training director on the conning tower. But this was not possible with the older-model director fitted in *Seydlitz*, and the monocular eyepiece provided for the director trainer also proved useless; thus the control officer had to train the director as well as observe the effects of his fire.[172] The Germans were well aware of the British advantage of being able to aim and fire from aloft, whereas, once the visibility worsened, their gunlayers found it difficult or impossible to get on their targets. Training could also be compromised due to the lower position of the *Rw*; *Derfflinger* found that, at times, 'smoke from the forward turret group drifted aft and made it impossible to keep the RW [*sic*] telescopes on the target'.[173]

* * *

The British and German gunnery and fire control systems were quite similar in principle; at Jutland, both showed that, when courses were steady, they were capable of accurate shooting. Even so, each had distinct advantages. The British range plots could easily identify and discount individual anomalous ranges and graphically compare observed and predicted ranges. The Dreyer fire

---

[169] 'Report of Dreadnought Battlefleet Committee' and correspondence on aid-to-spotter in ADM 1/8460/149. See also *Description of Mechanical Aid to Spotter* in Ja011, AL.

[170] Staff, *World War One*, pp. 172, 234, 275 and 282. Paschen, p. 33.

[171] Staff, *World War One*, pp. 272 and 282.

[172] von Hase, pp. 134, 145, 155–6 and 159. *Seydlitz*, f. 271. Rahn, p. 241.

[173] Hipper, 'Lessons from the Skagerrak Battle', p. 4, translation in DRYR 6/10. von Hase, p. 158. Staff, *World War One*, p. 234.

control tables had integral Dumaresqs which permitted manual or automatic adjustment of the clock rates in response to any changes of own ship's course. The British director could lay, train and fire the guns from an aloft position largely free from smoke and spray, but until after Jutland the spotter's glasses were not part of the system and had no instruments to indicate the target.

German stereoscopic range-finders could cope better with partially obscured targets. Although precise comparative figures are lacking, it can be assumed that on average their 3-metre instruments, in part due to their better-trained operators, were more accurate and had smaller spreads than the British 9-foot coincidence range-finders. This gave two benefits. First, the German system did not need range plotting to eliminate individual anomalous ranges; instead, the 'Mittlungs Apparat' automatically averaged all ranges (though any range-finder giving poor results could be switched out entirely). Second, it could use a form of range-finder control to follow the range as its rate changed due to an alteration of course: either by the target; or, as *Seydlitz* described, by one's own ship. The latter made up, at least to some extent, for the German system's lack of a means to adjust the rate of the range clock automatically for alterations of own course. The German training director integrated target indication, training and spotting but the guns were laid and fired from the turrets. With both the director and especially the turret sights lower in the ship, German shooting was more liable to interference from smoke and spray.

Torpedoes and tactics

Torpedo expenditure, especially by the German destroyers during the day, was considerable but resulted in few sinkings. Contrary to Jellicoe's apprehensions before the battle, not one British ship under way was sunk by torpedo, though *Shark* and *Turbulent* were finished off with torpedoes after they had been immobilised by gunfire. *Marlborough* was the only British capital ship to be hit but she survived. British torpedoes were more successful; *V29, Frauenlob*

Table 10.11. *Torpedo expenditure*

Fired by:	Daytime		Night and dawn	
	British	German	British	German
Battleships	5	1		
Battlecruisers	8	7		
Light cruisers	8	?4	2	3
Destroyers	33	?78	38	19
Totals	54	?90	40	22

and *Pommern* (and perhaps *V4*) sank quickly after being hit, while *Rostock* was crippled and had to be scuttled later. *Onslow*'s torpedo probably contributed to *Wiesbaden*'s foundering during the following night. *Seydlitz* was also hit but her torpedo bulkhead held and she was able to get back to harbour. Neither *Elbing* nor *Sparrowhawk* were struck by torpedoes but both had to be abandoned after collisions that were induced by the torpedo attack at night by the 4DF. Some torpedo attacks had important tactical consequences, whether or not they also resulted in sinkings. The British attacks at the end of the Run to the South accounted for *V29* and damaged *Seydlitz* but they also played their part in forcing Hipper to break off the action by turning away together by a full eight points. *Shark*'s division made no hits but disrupted the German flotilla attacks on the 3BCS. Most important of all, even though all the torpedoes fired by the German IXTF and VITF after 7.15pm were avoided by the battleships in the British rear, Jellicoe turned the whole British line away by up to four points, thereby permanently losing touch with the enemy battlefleet.

Successful torpedo attacks were the result, in varying degrees, of sound tactical direction; of sufficient numbers, both of attackers and of torpedoes fired; and of determined leadership and support. An admiral needed to locate his flotillas relative to his line so that they could quickly move out into favourable attacking positions on the enemy's bows. At the start of the Run to the South, Beatty ordered his destroyers ahead and (except for the *L*-class boats) they were assembled in readiness by Farie in *Champion*. When ordered to attack, Bingham in *Nestor* led them into a good position before he turned to attack from ahead of the enemy. The British boats were also able to break up the simultaneous attack by the smaller number of destroyers that had remained with Hipper, though, unlike Heinrich in *Regensburg*, Farie gave them no effective support. *Petard*, by firing at a group of German destroyers with a torpedo set for HS, maximised her chances of hitting and accounted for *V29*. And, as a whole, the British destroyers fired sufficient torpedoes to ensure that too many approached *Seydlitz* for her to avoid them all. During the Run to the North, only Tovey in *Onslow* remained in an attacking position on *Lion*'s engaged bow, though a single destroyer could achieve only so much. Forceful leadership by Loftus Jones inspired the successful defensive action by *Shark*'s division, while Ramsey in *Acheron* led the 1DF ahead to form a destroyer screen for the BCF (though they had no opportunity for a subsequent attack). For the German covering attack after 7.15pm, only the equivalent of one-and-a-half flotillas were in position near the ISG to attack promptly. But they advanced opposite the centre of the British line, so they were well positioned both for attacking the British rear and for remaining out of reach of the defending light forces positioned at the van and rear. In the main, these German boats were able to fire three torpedoes each; no hits were made but the tactical effect was decisive.

For the night, Jellicoe placed his flotillas five miles astern between the two battlefleets, while the 2LCS fell back with them. Whatever he may have thought about the enemy's later movements, this disposition achieved the desirable end of putting his flotillas in touch with the enemy. But, as they followed the battlefleet S, they lay across the SSE'ly course of the High Seas Fleet as it approached them from to starboard on gently converging courses. Thus the first three actions began in the same way, with the leading German ships looming out of the darkness at short ranges, leaving the British vessels with no time to do anything other than attack on similar courses; with their bearings from the German ships changing only slowly, they were easy gunnery targets. During the 4DF's encounter, both the British leaders were hesitant about opening fire; both were quickly knocked out by gunfire and there was little coordination of the flotilla's attacks. Yet *Spitfire* and *Ambuscade* each fired a pair of torpedoes, individual boats attacked with determination and, despite heavy losses, their efforts eventually resulted in the loss of *Rostock* and *Elbing*. It should also be mentioned here that the Germans were also better equipped for defence against night attacks. First, their star shell illuminated their attackers but not themselves.[174] Second, with their recognition system, previously unknown to the British, unless a vessel responded at once in kind with a string of coloured lights, it was certainly hostile. In contrast, by nightfall, the Germans had established that the British recognition system relied on the exchange of challenge and response codes – and, unlike their opponents, they had shared information on what had been observed. Thus, by flashing codes, even when these were incorrect, the Germans often induced British commanders to delay opening fire. Third, the Germans had superior searchlights with iris shutters, which enabled them to illuminate their targets instantly.[175] Without these German advantages, the 4DF might well have achieved more at less cost.

When the 12DF encountered the enemy fleet just before daybreak, Stirling's first intention was to attack with just one division on a converging course, which would probably have been driven off with the same heavy losses suffered by the 4DF. Fortunately, the German battleships turned away, which gave Stirling the opportunity to reorganise, draw ahead and then turn to lead a determined attack by his 1st Division on an opposite course; in the poor light, his boats were particularly difficult gunnery targets. *Onslaught* and *Marvel* each fired salvos of four torpedoes, the latter with HS settings, while the other two boats in the first attack fired two each, i.e. twelve in all, eight from positions 50–60° on the targets' bows.[176] This was an almost textbook attack made on

---

[174] *GFG&TO 167*, 7(ii).
[175] Their arcs could be kept burning continuously behind the iris shutters: Hezlett, p. 81.
[176] *ATFJ*, pp. 12–13; *Marvel's* inclination was 90A, i.e. on her target's beam.

opposite course with a large number of torpedoes fired mostly from optimal positions ahead of the targets; the reward was the blowing up of *Pommern* (and perhaps a stray torpedo also found *V4*). But Champion in *Maenad* leading the 2nd Division turned back after she fired her first torpedo and she probably disrupted the approaches of the boats following her; whatever the reason, there was no attack by the rest of the flotilla.

If successful torpedo attacks were the result of sound tactical positioning, sufficient numbers and effective leadership, conversely the limited effectiveness of the torpedo weapon at Jutland can be explained by many instances of inadequacies in these same factors. Torpedoes fired singly with LR and ER settings by battleships and battlecruisers on both sides proved to be wasted shots. The only way of increasing the probability of hits by torpedoes fired from one line at the other would have been to fire concerted salvos from a group of ship (perhaps each firing several torpedoes as rapidly as possible) at a quite short section of the enemy line. But apparently neither side had arrangements to coordinate torpedo fire in this way; in their absence, it must be doubted whether the torpedo armaments of capital ships were worth the risks arising from their high explosive heads and from flooding of the large torpedo 'flats'.[177]

Hipper had begun the battle with a significant superiority in destroyers over Beatty but, by the end of the Run to the South, his advantage had been lost because too many of his destroyers had remained with his straying light cruisers. Thus he was unable to mount a strong counter-attack while he was also at a positional disadvantage with Beatty further ahead. During the Run to the North, almost all the destroyers on both sides were left on the disengaged flanks; thus Beatty did not take advantage of his position ahead and the destroyers on both sides remained out of action until the leading German light cruisers and flotillas encountered the 3BCS on their starboard bows. Also Beatty's orders for his light cruisers to attack came too late. After the British deployment, too many of the Grand Fleet's destroyers were out of position at the rear of their line while, on the German side, some flotillas were caught inside the curving German line. The IIITF was better placed for an attack but, rather than urge them on to cover the first action-turn-about, Michelsen cancelled the attack, which made little impression in the British line. The attack that covered the third action-turn-about was led out in a timely manner by Heinrich in *Regenburg* but, although it forced Jellicoe to turn away and came close to scoring hits on the 1BS, it was made by only one-and-a-half of the six-and-a-half German flotillas present. The follow-on attacks ordered by Michelsen were too little and too late to threaten the British battle line.

By about 7.30pm, the 4LCS and half the 11DF had moved out from their positions in the British van but the German attack had been abeam of the British

---

[177] For risks, see Brown, *Grand Fleet*, p. 46.

centre so Le Mesurier and Hawksley were too late to disrupt the German torpedo firings. Only the light cruisers were able to engage some of the attackers and to hit *V28*. If the 11DF and Hawksley had not been recalled by Jellicoe, they might have pressed on to encounter the German battlefleet in considerable disorder after its third action-turn-about; however, half a flotilla would not have provided the numbers for a decisive attack. From their positions in the rear, both the 2LCS and a division of the 12DF also belatedly engaged a few enemy destroyers and sank one of them, probably the damaged *V48*. At 8.11pm, the 11DF and 4LCS were well positioned to intercept approaching German destroyers of the VTF, although the advance was again by no more than half of the 11DF, supported by the 1st Division of the 4LCS. Only the latter engaged the enemy destroyers before continuing towards the German battle-fleet while Hawksley withdrew to rejoin the rest of his flotilla and the 4DF in the van. Between them, the three light cruisers were able to fire only one torpedo before they were driven off by German gunfire; without support from the destroyers, they were too few to have any chance of success. At 9.00, *Caroline* and *Royalist* made their own attack on the approaching German IBS; they did better than the 1st Division by firing three torpedoes and, although none hit, two tracks passed close to the *Nassau*. Yet, even when Jerram withdrew his objection, Hawksley held back the 11DF, despite the ships in sight being clearly hostile and favourably positioned on his starboard quarter.

Apart from the brief encounter between the VIITF and the 4DF at 9.47pm, none of the German flotillas were able to attack British ships during the night, even though three flotillas and two half-flotillas still had sufficient torpedoes. Michelsen and Heinrich had little idea of the enemy's position and they resorted to searching in sectors radiating from reference points astern of the German line. The first searches, by the IITF and the XIIHF in the sectors between ENE and SE, were ordered prematurely by Heinrich; they found the rear of the British line but too soon, while it was still twilight. This was the most difficult part of the line to attack and there was no shortage of defenders following just astern; the German boats were easily driven off by gunfire from the 2LCS. The smaller destroyers of the VII and V TFs were allocated sectors from SE to SSW but their searches were hampered by dirty fires; the VTF also split into four groups so, if one of these had encountered a British force, it would have been too weak to attack effectively. At 10.30pm, Michelsen ordered the flotillas to assemble at Horns Reef by 2am and the searches appear to have abandoned soon after midnight. First Heinrich and then Michelsen granted permission for the IITF to return around The Skaw, which gave Captain Schuur[178] the excuse to withdraw, despite his torpedo comple-ment being almost intact. As events turned out, this retreat had no

---

[178] Named by Scheer, p. 138.

consequences but, had the battlefleets met again at dawn near Horns Reef, Scheer would have been deprived of his most potent flotilla.

As the boats of the 4DF hurled themselves at the IBS, three more British flotillas to the Eastward – the 13DF, 9DF and 12DF – were still heading S in sight of each other; they could also see the 4DF in action with what both Farie and Stirling identified as enemy ships. Thus they were well placed to attack in their turn, even (since they were forewarned of the enemy's approach) from ahead. Yet this, the best opportunity for a massed British night-time attack, was thrown away. When enemy shells fell among the 9DF, Farie in *Champion* suddenly increased speed and veered away to the Eastward, leaving all but *Moresby* and *Obdurate* behind and pushing the 12DF to the NE so that they lost contact with the enemy fleet until daybreak. Command of the remaining destroyers of the 13DF and 9DF (plus three boats from the 10DF) now devolved on Commander Goldsmith of the 9DF, who led the (probably disorganised) line of destroyers SW across the bows of the big ships in sight. But he and some other commanders persisted in believing that the battleships were British, so there was no attempt to exploit their ideal position for attacking from ahead on both sides of the enemy lines.

Command of flotillas and destroyers undoubtedly required exceptional qualities and some officers coped better than others. On the British side, we should recognise the outstanding conduct of Bingham, Tovey, Loftus Jones, Ramsey and, despite an initial misjudgement, Stirling. Whereas, while Farie marshalled the destroyers for their attack at the end of the Run to the South, *Champion* gave them no support once they engaged the enemy. Then, in the Run to the North, Farie did not act on Beatty's orders to move the destroyers ahead into better positions for attack or for the meeting with the Grand Fleet. However, these were small failings compared with his conduct during the night. Farie's flight Eastward at 11.30pm – there seems to be no other appropriate description – broke up the strong concentration of three flotillas that might otherwise have seriously disrupted the High Seas Fleet's steady withdrawal towards Horns Reef. And, at daybreak, when Alison of *Moresby* 'considered action imperative', Farie once again shied away from the enemy. After Farie's earlier withdrawal, Goldsmith may not have appreciated the size of the force he was now leading but, even so, it must be regretted that he did not seize the opportunity for attack that was so obvious to Thomson of *Petard* and even to Captain Redlich of *Westfalen*. Another destroyer officer whose conduct fell short was Champion of *Maenad*, whose inept leadership of the 2nd Division of the 12DF prevented the boats astern from attacking in their turn.

The most senior British destroyer commander was the recently appointed Commodore (F) Hawksley in *Castor*. Having brought the 11DF, which he also commanded, to its correct deployment position, at 7.26pm he led out only half the flotilla towards the German destroyers before pushing on with the apparent intention of attacking the disorganised German battlefleet. But Jellicoe then peremptorily ordered Hawksley's own destroyers to 'Tell Castor to come back.' The commodore could well have read this signal as a public rebuke for seeking out the enemy too far from his normal position at the head of the line; thereafter, he was much more cautious. He did not support the 4LCS in their attack on the German dreadnoughts. And at 9.15pm, even though he recognised the ships in sight as German, he failed to attack despite his favourable position. The excuse in his despatch that he had to wait for supporting fire from the Fleet receives no justification from the *GFBOs*, which demanded that in poor visibility opportunities to attack should be seized immediately. In the first night action, Hawksley's 11DF briefly engaged the IVSG but, once contact was lost, Hawksley did no more than return to the ordered course S so as not to stray further from the battlefleet.

Of the German torpedo-boat leaders, Heinrich gave effective support to his flotillas with *Regensberg*'s gunfire. He also positioned and in good time led out the IXTF and some of the VITF for the attack that had such decisive tactical consequences by forcing Jellicoe to turn away. Whereas both daytime arracks ordered by Michelsen (the first leader) were in insufficient strength, while the first was cancelled and the second was too late. The German scheme of searching in sectors was almost completely ineffective, while it spread the destroyer forces over too wide an area for mutual support if they had found any British forces. Both leaders gave their permission for the IITF to return around The Skaw but this in no way justified Schuur's decision to withdraw from the battle rather than to make for Horns Reef to join Scheer at daybreak.

Evasive turns

A further reason why few torpedo hits were made, especially during the day, was the use by both sides of evasive turns-away. Hipper's succession of turns from 4.27pm succeeded in evading the torpedoes fired earlier in the British attack (though *Seydlitz* was hit later); but the turns broke off the action while the ISG still enjoyed gunnery superiority and may well have saved the BCF from further losses. Likewise, Jellicoe's two Preparative turns at 7.22 and 7.25pm by the whole battlefleet were only partly successful since, although no torpedoes reached his two leading battle squadrons, Burney reckoned that at least twenty-one passed through the 1BS.[179] There was also a serious tactical cost; by turning all his squadrons away, Jellicoe lost touch with Scheer for good. We shall end this section by asking whether Jellicoe had any alternative.

When the IXTF and VITF were first sighted from *Iron Duke* at 7.18pm as they began their covering attack, they bore abaft or at worst on the beam from

[179] *OD*, p. 67.

Iron Duke's 3rd Division, posing no significant threat to them or to the 2BS trying to overtake to port. From the 4th Division, the destroyers were 'a little before the beam' so their torpedoes could be avoided by turning away by one or at most two points; since the 4th Division was, or would soon be, in line with the 3rd Division, the latter was not in the way of such turns. However, to the exposed 1BS the enemy flotillas were a serious threat which could only be avoided by immediate turns-away of a full four points. These turns would also close the gap between them and the 4th Division so that they could haul into line astern of *Vanguard*.[180] Jellicoe's straightforward option was to turn the whole battlefleet away using the simple and familiar Preparative signal. The extent of the turns had to be sufficient for the 1BS in the rear to evade the main torpedo attack, although the turns by the 2BS and 4BS would then be too large and they would risk losing touch with the enemy's big ships, which were already withdrawing into the mist. Also, there was a difficulty that was local to the flagship: that the 2nd Division was so close to *Iron Duke*'s port bow that they would need to turn sharply away together before the 4BS could turn by subdivisions. But, by turning equally, the fleet could keep together.

However, Jellicoe had a second option if he could find a means to order the first three divisions to hold their course and the divisions astern to turn away by as much as was necessary. This would avoid any risk of collisions between the 2nd and 3rd Divisions; allow the 2BS more time to form in line-ahead; improve the chances of keeping in touch with the enemy, especially since the leading divisions would be able to follow any further turns-away by the enemy; but unavoidably the British line would have been divided. Furthermore, at this critical moment, there was no time for anything other than a single, simple signal. One such signal was the hoist of Flag O and a tack-line superior to the Preparative; the superior part signified that 'it is optional for the Ships addressed to carry out the purport of the Signal'.[181] But this would have handed control of the timing and extent of the turns-away to Jellicoe's divisional admirals.

Jellicoe allowed little time to consider his options or to discuss them with his staff; at 7.21 he ordered the 2BS to turn away together by four points. This opened the way for the 3rd Division to turn away by subdivisions but it also severed contact between the 2BS and the enemy fleet; until she turned four points to port, *Orion*, leading the 2nd Division, could still see an enemy battleship at a range of 14,800 yards. At 7.22 and 7.25, *Iron Duke* twice hauled down the Preparative, though many battleships (including even the flagship herself) seem to have turned by less than four points; this would prove to be a

---

[180] The 5BS could keep out of trouble by turning with the 1BS.

[181] The tack-line separated the two flags by 6ft. Alternatively, the Preparative signal could have been addressed to the 1BS (Flag 0 superior to Pendant 1) though this might have inhibited the 4th Division from turning away. *GSB 1915*, pp. 6–7, 20, 23, 26 and 329.

mistake for those in the 1BS, where the many near misses leave no doubt that their turns-away were necessary but insufficient. According to Jellicoe in *The Grand Fleet*, the second turn in particular was made on the advice of Commander Bellairs working the Bunbury Enemy Torpedo Calculator. This instrument was able to calculate turns-away not only for the ship using it but also for ships ahead and astern in the line, so, if it was worked correctly, it should have confirmed that only the 1BS needed to make a second turn; however, Jellicoe's account gives the impression that Bellairs's recommendation applied to the whole fleet. Jellicoe declared that these turns had moved the fleet less than 2,000 yards further from the enemy. Thus, unaware of the extent of Scheer's action-turn-about and knowing that he had a two to three-knot speed advantage, Jellicoe could reasonably have expected that he would soon be able to re-establish contact, rather than that he would lose touch for good. We shall return in the final chapter to the questions of whether Jellicoe considered the second option and how he justified his fateful decision to turn the whole battlefleet away.

11   An unpalatable result

In his secret despatch of 18 June 1916, Jellicoe wrote of the Run to the South:

The disturbing feature of the battle-cruiser action is the fact that five German battle-cruisers engaging six British vessels of this class, supported after the first twenty minutes, although at great range, by the fire of four battleships of the 'Queen Elizabeth' class, were yet able to sink the 'Queen Mary' and 'Indefatigable.' It is true that the enemy suffered very heavily later, and that one vessel, the 'Lützow' was undoubtedly destroyed, but even so the result cannot be other than unpalatable.

Quite how unpalatable is apparent from Table 11.1 for ships that suffered casualties,[1] though of course the full extent of the German losses (including, it seems, the sinking of *Pommern*) were not known to Jellicoe at the time. As would be expected, the most serious casualties on both sides were in ships that blew up, though the Germans also lost 910 men in two light cruisers, the *Wiesbaden*, utterly wrecked by gunfire from the whole British line, and the obsolete *Frauenlob*, which foundered immediately on being torpedoed. Yet the weaker side inflicted much greater losses, while the stronger, although left in control of the battleground, was unable to prevent the enemy fleet from regaining its bases largely intact. In this final chapter, we turn to the qualities of command and leadership displayed by the four senior commanders (and, on the British side, other senior officers) and their influence on the battle's outcome.

Hipper

After the first contact between the British and German light forces, Hipper's confidence may have been briefly shaken by the misread report that he was about to encounter twenty-four to twenty-six enemy battleships. But, once the error had been corrected, he pressed on in a Northwesterly direction with the IISG and its screening destroyers some eight miles ahead. He received no definite warning of the presence of British battlecruisers until they were sighted

---

[1] Figures from Campbell, pp. 338–41.

Table 11.1. *Ships with casualties*

Ship type		British			German	
		Number of ships	Killed or wounded	Prisoners	Number of ships	Killed or wounded
Battleships	blown up				1	844
	survived	6	263		12	246
Battlecruisers	blown up	3	3,316	4		
	sunk				1	165
	survived	3	323		4	422
Armoured Cruisers	blown up	2	1,760			
	sunk	1	107			
Light Cruisers	sunk				4	946
	survived	6	277		5	147
Destroyers	sunk	8	554	173	5	240
	survived	11	168		9	48
Totals			6,768	177		3,058

from the ISG. Then, as soon as Beatty turned E with the evident purpose of cutting across the German line of retreat, Hipper deftly reversed course so that he could both engage from a favourable position and lead the BCF towards the High Seas Fleet – though this left many of his light forces trailing a long way astern. Hipper kept the wind advantage, enjoyed somewhat better initial visibility and was able to proceed at an easy speed before turning inwards just before he opened fire, thereby throwing out any rates that Beatty's ships might have obtained. Since Beatty held his fire, Hipper was able to do likewise until the range taken in *Lützow* fell to 16,800 yards. Thanks to Hipper's superior tactical leadership during the approach, the ISG quickly gained gunnery superiority to sink *Indefatigable* in the first phase of the Run to the South and *Queen Mary* in the second, even though the German battlecruisers were outnumbered throughout. But, at the moment of the latter triumph, a heavy fire from the 5BS was descending on *Moltke* and *Von der Tann*, while Beatty's destroyers were advancing to make a torpedo attack. Faced with this dual threat, Hipper began a series of turns-away totalling eight points that, for the moment, ended the action. His own destroyer attack, which was largely ineffective, was made from a less favourable position by only a part of his full force.

Hipper continued to withdraw Eastwards until he sighted the advancing High Seas Fleet. He then turned back to engage the 5BS and, after turning N, the BCF as well, until they vanished into the murk. But the ISG continued to be hit by the 5BS at ranges that made it difficult to reply effectively. To Scheer, it seemed that the fire from his battlecruisers was slackening and, at 5.17pm, he openly chided Hipper by ordering him to 'Take up the chase'. Hipper's caution proved to have been justified; when he obeyed Scheer by turning NW, in worsening visibility he received fire to which he could not reply, not only from the 5BS but once more from the BCF. This fire, difficulty in maintaining full speed and the first signs of the 3BCS's action with the IISG probably all contributed to Hipper's decision to turn E at about 5.55. But then enemy cruisers and destroyers appeared to the N, apparently threatening a torpedo attack. Although his own destroyers were already in action with the 3BCS, Hipper turned about to fall back on the battlefleet van some seven miles astern. This retreat enabled the ISG to take up its designated position for a decisive fleet action ahead of the leading battle squadron,[2] but it prevented Hipper from identifying the enemy forces to the N and E; thus he added nothing to Bödicker's report that the IISG was in action with enemy battleships.

Briefly, Hipper led the German line NE before being pushed E and S as he came under fire from Beatty's and then from Hood's battlecruisers. At first, little could be seen of the 3BCS from the ISG, *Lützow* receiving eight hits, most if not all by *Invincible*. But, as the ISG turned further away, the mist parted to reveal Hood's flagship on *Lützow*'s starboard quarter; *Invincible* was quickly straddled and then blew up. But *Lützow* was now crippled and forced to withdraw, so that the leadership of the remainder of the ISG devolved upon Captain Hartog of *Derfflinger*. His courage and determination during their attack to cover the High Seas Fleet's third action-turn-about was a credit both to him and to the inspiration of his admiral. Not for want of trying, Hipper himself was unable to shift his flag to *Moltke* until after dark, by which time she was the only German battlecruiser even partly fit to fight. He tried to reach the van but succeeded only in cutting across the bows of the IVSG without giving them any support in their actions with British light forces. Thereafter his movements are uncertain until 3.24am, when Scheer ordered the survivors of the ISG to return to harbour, though *Seydlitz* made her own way to safety by the narrowest of margins.

* * *

At the start of the Run to the South when Beatty turned E, Hipper easily countered the move by turning about. It was the best possible response; he then coolly exploited Beatty's mistakes, seizing and retaining gunnery superiority as he led Beatty towards Scheer. However, by the time *Queen Mary* blew up, the pressure from both the accurate fire of the 5BS and the imminent destroyer attack was becoming unbearable. Thus it was Hipper rather than Beatty who broke off what had been a spectacularly successful action by turning sharply away when he still had gunnery superiority. During the Run

---

[2] *German Tactical Orders, January 1915*, pp. 4 and 10 in 'German Fleet Orders', ADM 186/17.

to the North, Beatty's battlecruisers withdrew out of reach for half an hour but Hipper did not close the 5BS until urged on by Scheer. Hipper's subsequent turn E was made partly to escape the British fire to which he could not reply, though also to support the IISG. But he then fell back on the van of the battlefleet before he could observe and report on the presence of the Grand Fleet. He was withdrawing yet again when a chance shift in visibility created the opportunity to sink *Invincible*. At the beginning of the battle, Hipper took the initiative against superior forces and inflicted two serious losses on the BCF. But thereafter, when threatened by torpedo attacks or under damaging fire in worsening visibility, he was less determined, responding to rather than controlling events. Even so, the loss of a third British battlecruiser demonstrated yet again the outstanding accuracy of the ISG's gunnery, a further testament to Hipper's leadership of the German scouting groups.

Scheer

Due to the delays while waiting for the weather and because Jellicoe and Beatty put to sea at night, the submarine traps set by Scheer outside the British bases achieved little. Also, he chose to continue with the operation despite the reports, a few from the submarines, that substantial enemy forces had left harbour at much the same time as he had. As the German forces debouched from the minefields in the Bight, the ISG proceeded some 50 miles directly ahead of the battlefleet. This large separation, though it might entice a similarly detached force of British battlecruisers to attack, had its risks; if a strong enemy force had been able to cut across Hipper's wake – as the BCF was not far from doing – it would have taken up to three hours for the battlefleet to come up in support. Initially, Scheer's single line was in open order, though he closed up when ordering action stations.[3] Briefly, he veered NW and then W with the object of catching Beatty between two fires but, once Bödicker reported the sighting of five enemy battleships, Scheer recognised that he must turn N again in order to join the ISG as quickly as possible. His battleships were still in single line when they sighted the British ships; despite its tactical inflexibility, this formation was no disadvantage in the subsequent stern chase, since it allowed the faster van battleships to forge ahead. But unavoidably the battlefleet became strung out, with only the ISG and the IIIBS engaging the enemy. Dissatisfied with the battlecruisers' rate of fire, Scheer insisted that Hipper 'Take up the chase', though later the C-in-C may have regretted this implied

---

[3] There were only sufficient destroyers for a screen of four boats along each flank of a squadron of eight battleships. By cruising in a rectangular formation of columns of divisions, the British fleet had a much denser screen on the flanks and ahead. Compare *GOA*, p. 40 and Tarrant, p. 61 with *GFBOs III*, pp. 3 and 5.

reprimand. Hipper obeyed but only to suffer more damage; it would have been better if he had been allowed by Scheer to make his own decision.

During the Run to the North, Scheer and his staff apparently failed to recognise that Beatty's course was towards a rendezvous with a larger supporting British force. Whatever their appreciation, they never had an opportunity to adopt a more flexible preparatory formation. As the head of Scheer's line veered Eastwards, all he could do was make Behncke in *König* the guide of the battlefleet and reduce speed to allow the slower ships to close up. It appears that the German commanders did not realise that they were about to meet the Grand Fleet until the first shots between battleships were exchanged as Jellicoe deployed. Nothing could then be done to prevent the ISG and the IIIBS, caught in the jaws formed by the bent British line, from coming under a damaging fire to which they could reply only occasionally – as when the visibility shifted to reveal the *Invincible*. Scheer, seeing his van's predicament and the danger that Jellicoe might soon turn Southwards to envelop it, prudently ordered his first action-turn-about. The High Seas Fleet, thanks to its training in the manoeuvre and also to the initiative shown by Captain Redlich of *Westfalen*, disengaged rapidly to head Westwards out of trouble.

At 6.45pm, *Moltke* reported the enemy van bearing EbyS, though the ISG was not then under fire. Three minutes later, Scheer turned his columns together in succession from W to WNW, but this did not renew contact with the enemy and at 6.55 he ordered his second action-turn-about. His leading ships soon ran headlong into the British centre. Yet his mistake was not in the turn itself but in making it too soon. If he had continued W or even WNW, then after Jellicoe turned S as Scheer had anticipated, most or all of the British line would have passed well clear across the German rear.[4] An action-turn-together made later would then either have missed the British line altogether or have created an opportunity for a concentration on the British rear ('underlining the I', as it were). Howsoever Jellicoe reacted to the move, Scheer would have regained the better position for light and visibility, the Grand Fleet would no longer have blocked his return route to the Bight[5] and he might even have been able to send assistance to *Wiesbaden*. Yet Scheer himself does not seem to have acknowledged these possibilities. Instead in his memoirs he declared that 'in spite of "crossing the T" the acknowledged purpose was to deal a blow at the centre of the enemy line', even though both he and his Chief-of-Staff accepted elsewhere that this had been an elementary tactical blunder. Perhaps Scheer hinted at an explanation in his book: 'our action in retaining the direction taken after turning the line [W] would partake in the

[4] Scheer, pp. 154 and 157 (charts) show his appreciation of the positions of the two sides at 6.35 and 7.17pm.

[5] Dreyer, p. 134 proposed, though without discussing the timing, that Scheer was 'obviously hoping to pass under the stern of the Grand Fleet and make for the Horns Reef'.

nature of a retreat'.[6] Did his martial pride cloud his judgement, pushing him into a premature turn-about that could have led to disaster? In the event, he was forced to retreat anyway by means of a third action-turn-about, during which the ISG had to be hurled regardless of damage and casualties at the enemy line. This second withdrawal was made with considerable difficulty, during which *Friedrich der Grosse*, despite the risk of even further confusion, had to turn the wrong way. And, after the two previous action-turns-about, only one and a half German destroyer flotillas were in position to mount the covering torpedo attack ordered by Scheer; this made no hits but succeeded in forcing Jellicoe to turn away. After scrambling out of trouble, Scheer swung his ships from W to S; the dreadnoughts, led by *Westfalen*, were in single line-ahead with the predreadnoughts of the IIBS to starboard and the ISG on the port flank. Thus Scheer, who seems to have underestimated his opponents' determination to re-engage, left his battered battlecruisers exposed to Beatty's new attack; they received further hits but Scheer's mistake did not lead to anything worse because, when his columns turned away, Beatty did not pursue them.

As early as 8.15pm, Scheer gave general orders for destroyer attacks during the night, though he left the details to Michelsen and Heinrich; somehow, in allocating flotillas to search sectors, they anticipated his intention to turn towards Horns Reef. At 9.14, Scheer ordered the High Seas Fleet to turn SSE¼E and to maintain the course for Horns Reef come what may; he then sent his predreadnoughts to the rear, leaving the redoubtable Captain Redlich in *Westfalen* to lead the van through the night. The brief attacks by the BCF at about 8.30 and by British light forces after nine o'clock had both come from the general direction in which Scheer was now turning; thus he must have realised that the new course might lead to a short-range, uncertain and bloody night action between the two fleets. Yet he was determined to reach Horns Reef by dawn and did not consider any alternative to the direct route. Perhaps he persuaded himself that, given the greater British losses during the day, his own battlefleet might suffer less in such an encounter – but in any case he accepted the risk. His tactical judgement was vindicated when he encountered not the British battlefleet but the destroyers and light cruisers positioned five miles astern. During the night, two German light cruisers were lost to torpedo attacks and one to a collision but the British flotillas were unable to mount concerted attacks from ahead on the German van. The single successful attack was made at daybreak by only one division of the 12DF but it still succeeded in sinking the *Pommern*. In the course of Scheer's withdrawal towards Horns Reef, his low losses were in part the fortunate consequence of British mistakes, but his

---

[6] Scheer, pp. 155–6.

attackers were also facing very effective defensive fire, especially that from *Westfalen* and her consorts in the van.

After Scheer had pressed on with such determination towards Horns Reef, it must be doubted whether, on arriving there, he even slowed down, let alone that he contemplated a large deviation towards the British force reported by *L11*. Doubtless he wanted to give the impression that he and the battlefleet were eager for further action. But the enemy forces reported by *L11* and *L24* were too far away and, despite later rationalisations, the possibility remained that, at any moment, the main British force might emerge from the mist. Scheer had fought his way almost to safety; he had no need later to disavow his intention to bring in the High Seas Fleet without delay.

* * *

Until Scheer met the Grand Fleet as it deployed, he had been constrained by events to remain in his unwieldy in-line formation while he pursued Beatty and Evan-Thomas Northwards, apparently without recognising the immediate danger into which he was being led. But, as soon as it became apparent that the German van was at risk of envelopment, Scheer confidently made use of the well-practised action-turn-about to withdraw. Unfortunately for his reputation as a tactician, this success was followed by his greatest tactical error, the premature second action-turn-about by which he crossed his own T. Yet, by ordering a third *Gefechtskehrtwendung*, he extracted his ships from their predicament; the covering attacks by the battlecruisers and by destroyers, though with only a fraction of his flotillas, were enough to ensure that the British fleet turned away so that, as well as losing touch, it was unable to exploit the considerable confusion in the German line. Having evaded Jellicoe, Scheer left the battered ISG in an exposed position and he was lucky that Beatty made little of the opportunity to damage them further. Once darkness had fallen, Scheer showed an iron determination to return to his bases by the most direct route. Although he implicitly accepted the risk of a night fleet action, the High Seas Fleet instead encountered the British light forces, through which they forced their way with few losses.

Scheer enjoyed a measure of good fortune and he made misjudgements and mistakes, one serious. But, when the dangers were greatest, he acted coolly and promptly to extricate his forces. He engaged a stronger enemy force, inflicted considerably greater casualties than he suffered and brought most of his ships safely to their havens.

Jellicoe

Even before his appointment as C-in-C, Jellicoe was concerned that German capital ships might be superior fighting machines. Once he took up his appointment, he also worried about inadequate numbers, especially of battle-cruisers, light cruisers and destroyers. His lack of the last two types led him to insist that their commanders must give primacy to defending against enemy destroyer attacks rather than acting offensively. Also, early in the War, he was troubled by frequent machinery breakdowns. But, as 1915 progressed, his relative strength in all types of vessel steadily improved, though it was not until the beginning of 1916 that the *GFBOs* ceased to warn that his destroyers might be outnumbered by as much as 2:1; even so, on the eve of Jutland, and despite the pleas from Beatty and Hood, the destroyers' priorities were still largely defensive. This was only one example of Jellicoe's willingness to assume the worst, even when, as Balfour protested, the C-in-C's fears were not corroborated by the intelligence returns. Jellicoe also supposed that German availabilities would be close to 100% and he ignored their commitments in Flanders and the Baltic. He also attributed to their light forces capabilities that he was not prepared to entertain for his own vessels, notably that German submarines would operate closely with their battlefleet and that their destroyers and light cruisers would carry mines into a fleet action. His fears about underwater weapons were a major concern of the tactical exercises conducted by the Grand Fleet; even though they demonstrated that such attacks were not easily delivered, Jellicoe continued to emphasise the dangers.

In 1912, Admiral Bridgeman warned Fisher that Jellicoe was 'so extremely anxious ... He must learn to work his captains and staff more and himself less ... and if they don't fit, he must kick them out!'[7] After he became C-in-C, these characteristics became even more marked. Despite serious reservations, Jellicoe did nothing to replace his three battle squadron commanders, notably Jerram who would lead the line if the deployment went as hoped. These anxieties and Jellicoe's reluctance to decentralise command led to the development of the *GFBOs* in which he and his staff attempted to provide for all conceivable eventualities. In defence of the *GFBOs*, it should be recognised that as many as twenty-one of the thirty sections are concerned with routine matters that needed to be carefully specified – as, for example, organisations, cruising formations and special signals and procedures. Nonetheless, nine crucial sections provide for the deployment of the fleet (though only in good visibility) and the conduct in action of its squadrons and flotillas. It was accepted that the opposing fleets might deploy initially on opposite courses but even then that the main action would take place on similar courses, in good visibility at the long range that favoured the heavier British guns. The commanders of the battle squadrons, including the 5BS, were given only limited permission to act independently, although the commander of the van of the battlefleet was expected to close the enemy gradually as the action

---

[7] *FGDN II*, pp. 418–19 quoted in Andrew Lambert, 'Jellicoe, John Rushworth', *ODNB*.

progressed. As a guide, the *GFBOs* included a deployment diagram which showed the 5BS and particularly the BCF well ahead and inclining inwards towards the enemy van. But there were no orders on how these two powerful forces should exploit this overlap – the British battle array was like a huge snake poised over its prey but lacking the instinct to strike. Jellicoe recognised that the enemy fleet might not stand but turn away, and he persisted in his belief that it would cover its retreat with mines and torpedoes. He declared that he would not follow such a move 'shortly after deployment', though he was unclear on what he intended later in an action. But the only other recommendation was that, if the enemy flotillas attacked in these or other circumstances, the British battle line must turn away in subdivisions by Preparative. The battle orders say little of the need for enemy reporting prior to action, while, in action, only the cruisers were explicitly ordered to report what they could see if the probability was that it could not be seen by the C-in-C. Similarly, the orders for the fleet after action, including an indecisive action broken off as darkness fell, did not insist that the C-in-C be informed of enemy sightings. Thus Jellicoe's own *GFBOs* must be held in part responsible for the paucity of enemy reports that he was sent during the battle.

As the British ships slipped their moorings late on 30 May, most of their officers and men were confident that, if only they could catch the High Seas Fleet, they could win a great Nelsonic victory. But many of the anxieties that had weighed on Jellicoe since or even before August 1914 had been given expression in the *GFBOs*, so those officers who had read them attentively may well have shared the doubts of their Commander-in-Chief that the enemy could be defeated decisively. Even so, the British forces now enjoyed a substantial superiority in numbers of capital ships and even more in the weight of their fire, which should have been enough to allay Jellicoe's long-held concerns about his ships' inferior protection and the known deficiencies of British AP shell,[8] though he probably still believed that his destroyers (and perhaps his light cruisers) would be outnumbered. Despite being naturally cautious to the point of pessimism, he could hope for success should Scheer oblige him by fighting a prolonged gun action at long range. But, even with Sturdee's assistance, Jellicoe had been unable to find a solution to the tactical problem of an enemy turn-away; hence the *GFBOs* gave no guidance on how to prevent the enemy from running out of range, especially if the retreat was also covered by a flotilla attack. The battle orders were primarily about how to avoid serious losses, even defeat, but not about how to win a victory, especially against a reluctant opponent.

On 30 May, the Admiralty had informed Jellicoe that next day the Germans would leave via the route past Horns Reef. With no further intelligence to go

---

[8] Jellicoe, like all British commanders, was unaware of the dangerous nature of British cordite.

on, during the morning of the 31st, the British forces proceeded towards their rendezvous on converging courses at the easy speeds that would conserve their destroyers' fuel. The Admiralty's signal at 12.30pm that the enemy fleet was still in harbour correctly reflected the intelligence then available but it left the impression that only the meeting of the Grand Fleet and the BCF was imminent. When Beatty turned NbyE at 2.15, he was some 70 miles from Jellicoe, much the same as the gap that separated Hipper from Scheer, and with the same risks. As soon as *Iron Duke* received the first enemy reports from the BCF's light cruisers, Jellicoe ordered the Grand Fleet to raise steam for full speed and, at 3.59, to proceed at an unprecedented 20 knots. Then, as he had already intimated he might do, he ordered Hood to support Beatty; this left the armoured cruisers as his only advanced force, one which, despite his subsequent order, was unable to increase its distance ahead by more than 12 miles. Since Beatty had been given the massive firepower of the 5BS and had so far engaged only five enemy battlecruisers, Jellicoe might have concluded that he himself had the greater need of the 3BCS as his fast advanced guard; his generosity would have unintended and tragic consequences not only for Hood but for the 1CS as well.

From four to six o'clock, Jellicoe pressed on SEbyS at 20 knots. After the reports from the BCF ceased at five o'clock, he was left to assume that the High Seas Fleet would cross his bows an hour later, some 30 miles ahead. But from 5.40pm onwards, new reports from *Southampton* suggested that at six o'clock the enemy would be 20 miles distant to the SSE, while the first reports from his own ships indicated that ships were in action to the West of South and closer still. By 6.00, there was firing from ahead round to the starboard beam, though nothing of the enemy could be seen from *Iron Duke*. However, it was already clear to Jellicoe that he would soon have to deploy from columns into line with, since he had disposed the 2BS as the port columns, a port deployment as his preferred option. Jellicoe's brief turn S at 6.01 is best explained if it is assumed that, even then, he had decided to deploy to port – despite his later sop to his critics, it must be doubted whether he ever seriously considered a deployment to starboard. But, as he turned his columns back to SE at 6.06, he still had to decide on the deployment method and course. Both the visibility and the wind favoured a Southeasterly course and the Equal Speed Pendant was appropriate for any course between ENE and SE; however, the closer the deployment course was to SE, the greater would be the resultant bend in the line. At 6.14, Jellicoe was at last informed that from *Lion* (which he could see heading ESE) the enemy battlefleet bore SSW, though no one thought to inform him of the enemy's course or distance. After some 20 seconds of silent reflection, he ordered, 'Equal Speed, SE', which, after a onepoint adjustment to avoid any ambiguity, was hoisted as 'Equal Speed, Charlie London'. This simple three-flag signal was enough to gain most of the objectives of deployment: seizing the wind and light gages; positioning the 2BS in the van; and threatening the enemy's line-of-retreat. Jellicoe also judged rightly that, in the poor visibility, there would be no enemy concentration on the turning point at the bend in his own line. However, despite his earlier efforts to gain ground to starboard, the enemy ships remained at or beyond the limits of visibility. Nonetheless, he had continued to close until the last possible moment; as it was, his starboard division came under fire from the German line as they began to deploy, but their seven-point turn to port soon took them out of range once more. At this decisive moment of the battle, under enormous pressure and with little information to go on, Jellicoe calmly chose the best option that was available to him. Whatever might happen later in the day, he had secured his place among outstanding naval commanders.

However, by permitting the 3BCS to go on ahead, Jellicoe had denied himself an earlier warning that he would meet the High Seas Fleet sooner than he was expecting.[9] While his quick thinking brought the British battlefleet through unscathed, there was no time for Arbuthnot's 1CS to extricate itself. When deployment was imminent, the 1CS and Heath's 2CS were supposed to turn outwards, to starboard and port respectively, towards the flanks of the battlefleet.[10] The 2CS had plenty of room, though Heath made an excessively wide sweep before eventually reaching his position in the van. But Arbuthnot's three inner ships were just to the East of the shrinking wedge of sea formed between the heads of the battleship columns and Beatty's line, with the chaos of Windy Corner at its Western point. As Arbuthnot bore down on the immobilised *Wiesbaden*, he had no clear indication that he was so close to the enemy battlefleet until heavy shells first descended on the 1CS at 6.07pm. If he had had the sea-room, he might have turned immediately to starboard to pass between the BCF and the column guides of the starboard divisions of the battlefleet. But with Beatty approaching on the beam and the confusion of light craft astern of the battlecruisers, this move would have been difficult at best. Arbuthnot was not an officer who would have readily let go of *Wiesbaden*, but he probably had no other option than to keep on across *Lion*'s bow before turning to starboard in an attempt to withdraw down the engaged side of the BCF. It is easy to caricature Arbuthnot[11] but his unbending character is at most a partial explanation for his death in action. He was caught in a tight corner created

---

[9] If Hood's force had remained some 20 miles in advance of the armoured cruisers, he might have joined forces with Beatty so that, when they met the ISG, they would have been in close order.

[10] *Pace* Chatfield (p. 146), during the approach, the armoured cruisers were not on the wings of the battlefleet but ahead; in the absence of the BCF, they were necessarily between the opposing fleets; none needed to move to the opposite flank on deployment; but they had to move to a flank by passing down between the fleets. In good visibility, this move could be made without much danger as soon as the enemy was sighted at long range but, at Jutland, the 1CS turned too late.

[11] Geoffrey Lowis, *Fabulous Admirals* (London: Putman, 1957), Ch. XIV.

inadvertently by Jellicoe and Beatty; he did his duty but could not save *Defence* and *Warrior*.

After the deployment, Jellicoe ordered a reduction in speed to 14 knots though he could not prevent his ships from bunching together. The enemy remained on the edge of visibility; only a few battleships, most notably Jellicoe's own flagship, were able to fire more than a few salvos, while the crippled *Wiesbaden* distracted fire from more worthwhile targets. Jellicoe appears to have intended that, once in line, the battlefleet should turn three points to SSE. But the anticipatory hoist was negatived and instead Jellicoe ordered a turn of only one point to SE. As the officer leading the line, Jerram in *King George V* was charged in the *GFBOs* (VII.7) with adjusting course and speed to the best advantage. Yet, although he had lost sight of the enemy, he failed to take the initiative by closing the enemy on a more Southerly course than SE – even when the BCF ahead itself turned SSE and then further S. But, as *Lion* continued turning to make a complete circle, it was left to Jellicoe to signal a 9 Pendant turn S at 6.55pm, though it is possible that Jerram just anticipated the order. In 1932, Jellicoe acknowledged that it would have been better if ten minutes earlier he had altered course gradually to South. Even so, without his knowing anything of Scheer's two action-turns-about, his turn S put the Grand Fleet in the right place to cross the German T for a second time.

Although the 9 Pendant turn had allowed all the divisions to alter course quickly to S, the fire from the rear ships of the leading four divisions was masked by the ships on their starboard beams and quarters. After Jellicoe ordered brief turns together by Blue Pendant to close the range, he reverted to course S while driving off the first small German destroyer attack. When the enemy battlecruisers and leading battleships emerged from the mist, the battlecruisers attacked resolutely before they and the battleships withdrew under fire from the British line, Scheer's third action-turn-about being covered by the next destroyer attack. These were definitely not the circumstances that since 1914 had so troubled Jellicoe, namely an enemy withdrawal shortly after deployment with the object of leading the British fleet over previously prepared submarine and mine traps. After chasing the BCF at utmost speed since 4.30pm, the High Seas Fleet could not possibly have anticipated being in their present position. However, Jellicoe seems to have taken the pessimistic view that some of their submarines had managed to keep pace, writing in his despatch that 'there was no time for [the enemy] to lay a prepared mine area, and not much time for him to place his submarines, although many submarines were present'.[12] His apprehensions about submarines were doubtless

---

[12] *OD*, p. 3. Here Jellicoe also drew specific attention to his letter to the Admiralty of 30 October 1914 (*OD*, App. IV) in which he stated that he would not follow an enemy withdrawal *shortly after deployment* (my emphasis).

heightened by the recent torpedoing of *Marlborough* and by the reports of (imagined) submarines by *Lion, King George V* and *Duke of Edinburgh*. Yet, even if he had taken a more realistic view of the capabilities of the German U-boats, he still faced the problem for which he had no satisfactory counter, an enemy withdrawal under cover of destroyer attacks, while he probably still feared that at least some of the destroyers were equipped to drop mines as they retired. To evade the torpedoes and keep away from any mines, he ordered all his battle squadrons to turn away.

Prior to the covering German destroyer attack, Jellicoe's immediate concern had been to unmask his own fire by reforming the battle squadrons in single line-ahead. If a more alert admiral than Jerram had been leading the van, he would have realised, as soon as he resumed the course S at 7.09pm, that he should increase speed and then bring his two divisions into line-ahead of the 4BS while steering well clear of *Iron Duke*. Instead, at 7.16 Jellicoe had to order the 2BS to take station ahead, though he did not reduce the speed of the rest of the battlefleet until 7.20. Thus, when the second destroyer attack commenced, the rear ships of the 2BS were still on the flagship's port bow, so that Jellicoe's own 3rd Division could not turn away unless the 2BS did the same. To resolve this problem, which was in part of his own making, Jellicoe opted for one simple, familiar signal that allowed him to continue manoeuvring the fleet as a whole and to keep its squadrons together. But his turns-away were insufficient to prevent many torpedoes running through the rear divisions, yet they were enough to lose touch permanently with the enemy fleet.

Jellicoe was facing the situation that he had long dreaded and he may well have decided at once on the response that was mandated by the *GFBOs*, namely to turn the whole fleet away by Preparative. But perhaps he considered an alternative, by which the leading divisions could hold their course and maintain contact, while those in the rear could turn away as far as was necessary. If so, he gave himself only about a few minutes' thought before rejecting it, though even in that time his natural caution and centralising instincts would probably have prompted several objections. First, to order the manoeuvres simply, he would have had to use an unfamiliar signal that might be misunderstood. (However, he claimed later that 'Such a movement was provided for in the Battle Orders';[13] confirmation has not been found in the *GFBOs* though, as we have seen, there were suitable signals in the *Signal Book*.) Second, until the 2BS drew ahead, the 3rd Division was blocked from turning away should more destroyers attack from forward bearings (a real possibility given the modest scale of the attacks so far). Third, he would have to leave the turns-away by the rear divisions to Sturdee and Burney (though, from the sounding of their sirens, he probably knew that both admirals had already ordered Preparative turns on their own

[13] *GF*, p. 259.

initiatives). Last, the different courses must result in a gap in the line, even to the point that the leading divisions could not hold on to the enemy without becoming dangerously outnumbered.

These objections, especially when taken together, could have persuaded Jellicoe to order the simple Preparative turn-away. Yet, when in *The Grand Fleet* he 'asked whether it was necessary to turn the whole line of battle away from the attack', he mentioned none of them. Instead, he referred solely to the first small flotilla attack, declaring no less than four times that it had approached from G60 while omitting the fact that only the first destroyer sighted from *Iron Duke* had been on this dangerous bearing. He made the same assertion in his despatch and even stated that the two Preparative turns had been in response to this first attack; however, he did accept that the bearing of the second attack had been about G120 from the flagship. This last admission was omitted from *The Grand Fleet*, which claimed that it had been necessary to turn the whole battlefleet away because 'the leading Battle Squadron was as open to attack by torpedoes as was the centre or rear squadron'.[14] However, in his 'Errors made in Jutland Battle' of 1932, Jellicoe accepted that the 2BS 'was not nearly as much exposed to the destroyer attack at 7.22 as was the rest of the Battle Fleet'.[15] Why had Jellicoe previously resorted to what appears to be deliberate misrepresentation, rather than cite at least some of the real objections to the leading divisions holding on? No doubt he preferred to keep to himself his lack of confidence in his subordinate admirals but there was nothing discreditable about the other objections. A plausible explanation is that he was not prepared to admit that there had been a better alternative but that, under considerable pressure, either he (or his staff) did not think of it or excessive caution led him to reject it.

Jellicoe's turns-away may also have further delayed the 11DF and 4DF in reaching their van positions. But, in any event, his disposition of light forces at the ends of his line put them too far from the German attacks opposite his centre squadron; thus the German flotillas were able to fire their torpedoes undisturbed. The 4LCS did not counter-attack until ordered to do so by Jellicoe, whereas Hawksley in *Castor* led out half the 11DF on his own initiative. But, when he and Le Mesurier pressed forward to attack the German battlefleet as it withdrew in considerable disorder, Jellicoe actively discouraged them; he instructed the 4LCS not to go too near the enemy battlefleet, quickly recalled the destroyers and peremptorily ordered *Castor* to come back when she did not return promptly. However, since Hawksley advanced with only a quarter of the boats available in the van, he was probably mindful of the defensive emphasis of the destroyer orders even before Jellicoe's rebuke. When the German VTF

---

[14] *GF*, pp. 228 (though 'S. 50 W.' was equivalent to Green 50), 230 and 259. *OD*, p. 19.
[15] *JP II*, p. 450.

were sighted, Hawksley again led out only half of the 11DF (a sufficient force only if no other enemy vessels were encountered) but, as soon as the VTF turned away, Hawksley rejoined the destroyers that had remained at the head of the line rather than support Le Mesurier. After 9 o'clock, Hawksley followed *Caroline* and was urged by her captain to attack what Crooke was convinced were enemy ships. Yet, although Hawksley seems to have agreed, he held back, his despatch failing to give even a half-convincing justification for his conduct. Thus on three occasions, Hawksley advanced with apparently offensive intentions, although the defensive priorities of the *GFBOs* may have discouraged him from detaching adequate forces for his first two attacks. Yet Jellicoe himself ordered the end of the first attack and openly reprimanded Hawksley when he did not obey at once. This can only have sapped Hawksley's resolution, which was further undermined by Jerram's vacillation about the identity of the targets. It is still difficult to excuse Hawksley's failure to attack the IBS but Jellicoe and Jerram must bear some of the responsibility; undamaged, the IBS would reform for the night as the German van and play the major part in fighting off the British destroyer attacks.

Returning now to the British battlefleet, after the two turns-away by Preparative, Jellicoe waited until 7.35pm to turn SbyW by 9 Pendant, though it may have taken until about 7.53 before all the ships were in line on a course SW. By that time, Jellicoe knew that at 7.30, when the BCF's course was already SW, the enemy was still visible from *Lion* bearing NWbyW at 10–11 miles. Beatty did not tell the C-in-C when the BCF, which was no longer visible from the battlefleet, turned WSW, while the important information that the enemy's course was SW did not reach *Iron Duke* until 7.59; this was at about the same time that Jellicoe read Beatty's signal urging that the van battle squadron should follow the BCF so that: 'We can cut off whole of enemy's battlefleet'. To Jellicoe, this must have seemed at best a distant prospect since, as far as he knew, both the BCF and the High Seas Fleet were still heading SW (though actually the latter had already turned S). Rather than continuing SW, at 8.00 Jellicoe turned all his battleships by 9 Pendant to W. Since he enjoyed the better visibility, he could expect that there would be time to turn back to SW in line-ahead between sighting the enemy and opening fire. Thus, as Jellicoe would later declare, he was indeed 'steering the better course to intercept the enemy'.

However, Jellicoe did not hold his course W for long enough to make contact. Perhaps he was fretting about the criticism that might come his way if, albeit with justification, he did not respond to Beatty's urgings. At about 8.10pm, he ordered Jerram's 2BS to 'follow our battlecruisers', though their precise bearing remained unknown to him and to Jerram until the BCF opened fire at 8.21. The flashes and sound of the battlecruisers' gunfire explain Jellicoe's turn-away by 9 Pendant to WSW at the same nominal time. But he then seemed briefly to regret his decision, turning back once more to W at 8.25 before at 8.28 forming single line-ahead, course SW – a heading he would maintain until 9.01. In his 1932 note on 'Errors made in Jutland Battle', Jellicoe admitted that he should have ordered the 4LCS to search for the enemy when he turned SW at 7.42, though this would have been contrary both to his recent admonition not to go too near to the enemy battlefleet and to the *GFBOs'* insistence that the chief duty of the 4LCS was to defend the fleet against enemy destroyers. Jellicoe also acknowledged that he should have closed when *Comus* reported at 8.38 that she had been firing at the enemy battlefleet bearing W.[16] In fact, it was then too late since the German columns had already turned away Westwards. Yet if he had followed his instinct by holding his course W at 8.21 or even at 8.28, by about 8.35 his port divisions would probably have sighted the IIIBS (now the rear German battle squadron) on forward bearings.[17] While hastening their withdrawal, there might also have been a brief opportunity to inflict further damage on these German battleships – although that is probably the most that could have been achieved.

At 9.01pm, Jellicoe turned S while by about 9.15 enemy firing was heard and seen to Westward from his battleships, including *Iron Duke*. Thus at that time, the Grand Fleet was, as he declared, between the enemy and the three possible routes to his bases. Jellicoe had no wish for a night action between the fleets but the possibility remained that at dawn he would be able to intercept the High Seas Fleet before it reached the protection of one of the swept channels through the minefields. He disposed his battle squadrons for the night in a tactically inflexible formation which inhibited further manoeuvring. He then ordered his flotillas to positions five miles to the rear; from there, they could act defensively or offensively against enemy forces following astern towards Heligoland or the Ems or attempting to cross his wakes towards Horns Reef. This disposition was sound and later it could have resulted in a joint attack by the more Easterly flotillas had Farie not broken up their concentration. As it was, Stirling's dawn attack showed what more might have been accomplished during the dark hours.

Jellicoe received no enemy reports from the Admiralty between 5.45 and 9.55pm. Then at 10.23 he was informed that at 9.00 the enemy rear had been WSW from him on a southerly course. This intelligence was soon followed by the Admiralty's 10.41 signal stating categorically that at 9.14 the German fleet had been ordered home on a course SSE¾E, the heading for Horns Reef. When the signal was received, enemy forces could be heard and seen from *Iron Duke*'s 4BS firing on the starboard quarter, evidently in action with the British light forces, while by 11.30 the firing had moved astern and, after

[16] *JP II*, p. 451. *GFBO* XXIV, p. 11.

[17] Alternative courses plotted on Corbett, Map 41; the relative positions of the German squadrons are similar to those on *OD*, German Plan VI, which accompanied Scheer's despatch.

midnight, onto the port quarter. Also at 11.30, *Birmingham* reported that she had sighted battlecruisers, 'probably hostile' on a course S; her reported position implied a bearing almost astern of the flagship, which was consistent with the firing then being observed, but her distance of 30 miles was suspiciously great. Apart from this signal and two inconclusive reports of actions with enemy cruisers, Jellicoe received nothing from the ships of the Grand Fleet that had sighted the enemy. Furthermore, despite Room 40's interception of several German signals that confirmed that the High Seas Fleet was making for Horns Reef, the Admiralty's Operations Division sent no more intelligence to Jellicoe until 1.48am, when they informed him that at midnight *Lützow* was almost astern and, with considerable exaggeration, that all German submarines were being hurried to the attack. Prior to this signal, Jellicoe took a much needed rest while his battle squadrons continued passively Southwards. Nothing was done to prepare for any renewal of action until 2.15 when Jellicoe signalled his intention to turn N; however, after the turn-about was completed at about 2.45, his hopes of quickly picking up his flotillas would be disappointed.

At 3.26am, the Admiralty advised Jellicoe that at 2.30 the High Seas Fleet was approaching the Horns Reef lightship. Thus the main enemy force was already beyond his reach; he would have needed to alter course towards the lightship by about 0.30 to have crossed the enemy bows with some margin.[18] When *Iron Duke* received the signal, the lightship bore ENE but, instead of turning in that general direction, in which enemy stragglers were most likely to be found, Jellicoe continued N.[19] After the BCF rejoined the battlefleet, Beatty turned the battlecruisers SE at 5.43 and then S at 6.15 towards the position reported by *Dublin*. Jellicoe (still without his destroyers) waited until 6.02 before he too turned SE; he then continued towards Horns Reef until about 7.16 before turning N again. Beatty ended his sweep S at about 7.25 by altering course NNE and then N to follow in the battlefleet's wake. It is a striking feature of Jellicoe's chart[20] that neither admiral crossed the N-S line lying 30 miles W of the Horns Reef lightship and that they swept mainly N and S to the W of this line. While there is no evidence that they were following a preconcerted plan, there is a strong echo of Jellicoe's letter to Beatty of April 1916 in which the C-in-C insisted that 'our policy should be to engage them *not* in a position close to their minefields and ... to their SM, TBD and aircraft bases'.[21]

By the Spring of 1922, Jellicoe was aware that he was being severely criticised in the *Naval Staff Appreciation* for making no attempt to intercept the High Seas Fleet at daybreak near Horns Reef; the Dewars declared that

---

[18] *NSA*, p. 129. Plotting *Iron Duke*'s course from OD, Plan 2a on *OD*, German Plan VII shows that, if the turn had been delayed until 1.00am, there would have been no margin left.

[19] This critical point is also made in *NSA*, p. 129. Only *Lützow* and an enemy light cruiser had been reported on Northerly bearings.

[20] *OD*, Pl.2a and *GF*, p. 247.   [21] *BP I*, p. 302 with original emphasis.

'pursuing the enemy ... was an irredeemable charge that was not done'. Until then, Jellicoe had written little on this final phase of the battle. Now he had to explain why he had not acted on the Admiralty's clear intelligence that the enemy fleet was returning home past Horns Reef.[22] Jellicoe's rebuttals were set out in two appendices, one published with the *Admiralty Narrative*, the other an appendix for a new edition of *The Grand Fleet* which, despite his wishes, remained unpublished.[23] But, as we have seen, Jellicoe's explanations were fallacious and incomplete. The reports of the enemy received from the Admiralty earlier in the day were not greatly at variance with the reports from his own ships, while the precise positions, courses and speeds could not have been obtained from direction-finding.[24] Jellicoe never mentioned the many observations of enemy fire and a starshell on his starboard beam at about 9.15pm, while his own preferred enemy position at about that time implied that their fleet speed in the next hour had exceeded his own by an infeasible 6.4 knots. Thus he provided no satisfactory explanation for the change of enemy bearing that had been visible from *Iron Duke*, which was consistent with the enemy course for Horns Reef as reported by the Admiralty. Furthermore, Jellicoe did not even attempt to explain his dismissal of the Horns Reef route, which was clearly the best for the High Seas Fleet if it could evade the Grand Fleet.

The very inadequacy of Jellicoe's attempted self-justification for not intercepting the High Seas Fleet suggests that he could not bring himself to acknowledge the true reason, perhaps even to himself. But the subsequent reluctance of both Beatty and Jellicoe to go anywhere near Horns Reef points to what was behind his inaction – a deep and long-standing aversion to approaching any area near the German coast where his ships might be exposed to threats from underwater weapons, that is, to prepared mine and submarine traps and to massed attacks by destroyers and torpedo boats. Perhaps these apprehensions, aggravated by extreme fatigue, were so strong that, without recognising their influence, Jellicoe subconsciously rejected any intelligence that demanded that he should lead the Grand Fleet towards Horns Reef; then, having persuaded himself that the High Seas Fleet was still following Southwards, he could assume that nothing more needed to be done until daybreak, when he would turn about, pick up his destroyers and renew the action. However, there is a second possibility: that he had already taken a conscious

---

[22] *JP II*, p. 413. *NSA*, p. 129.

[23] *JP II*, p. 403. Despite their obvious agenda, these appendices contain some information that can be found nowhere else.

[24] He was no longer constrained to use direction-finding as a cover for Room 40's interception and deciphering of enemy signals; the majority of the Admiralty's signals had already appeared more or less *verbatim* with the *Official Despatches* of 1920 and the Admiralty itself gave the exact wording of the crucial 10.41pm signal in *AN*, p. 72.

decision that, come what may, he would not be drawn towards Horns Reef; that he understood the implications of the Admiralty's intelligence but decided to ignore it; and therefore that he knew that he need make no preparations for renewing the action at dawn.

By early 1922, Jellicoe was under attack for failing to pursue a damaged and fleeing enemy. He could have claimed, not without reason, that the risks of underwater attack were too great and that the consequent British losses would not have compensated for the damage he might have been able to inflict. Furthermore, even though, when he took the decision to continue Southwards, he did not know that his flotillas would soon be widely scattered, he could also have pointed out that, if he had intercepted the High Seas Fleet, he, unlike Scheer, would have engaged without any destroyers whatsoever. But instead, Jellicoe concocted an unconvincing, even specious, explanation for rejecting both the clear implication in the Admiralty's signal and other strong indications that Scheer was heading for Horns Reef. Because Jellicoe attempted to explain away his conduct rather than to admit the truth, the question remains: was his judgement, which had served him well during the day, undermined by a subconscious dread of underwater attack and by tiredness; or did he decide deliberately, contrary to his own battle orders, not to make 'every effort to damage the enemy'?

* * *

As Jellicoe led the Grand Fleet towards Jutland, he was burdened by anxieties about material, tactics and the calibre of his senior officers. But, as soon as Jellicoe knew that the enemy was at sea, he advanced at full speed. With little information to go on, his deployment achieved all that could be hoped for, even though the enemy remained at the limits of visibility. Perhaps Jellicoe should then have turned S earlier but nonetheless his tactical intuition again served him well, enabling him to cross the German T for the second time. When Scheer ordered some of his flotillas to attack as cover for his third action-turn-about, the rather ragged formation of the Grand Fleet added to Jellicoe's tactical dilemma; he chose simply to turn the whole battlefleet away by Preparative but thereby lost touch with the enemy for good. At eight o'clock, he turned W, a course that would have found the German rear if only he had held on a little longer. But towards the end of the day and into the night, Jellicoe's apprehensions weighed more heavily. The few British torpedo attacks in daylight were ineffective, as much because of Jellicoe's orders, especially those to Hawksley, but also to the defensive emphasis of the *GFBOs*. After dark, Jellicoe was badly let down by the reporting failures of his own ships and the Admiralty's Operations Division. Nonetheless, despite clear indications that Scheer was making for Horns Reef, Jellicoe continued S, ruling out any possibility of renewing the action in that vicinity at daybreak.

Jellicoe's own accounts of the battle are most misleading where he exaggerated the threat from the torpedo attacks after 7.15pm and the unreliability of the enemy reports that he had received from the Admiralty. These distortions suggest that he recognised but would not admit that he had been wrong to turn the whole battlefleet away from the torpedoes and that he should have altered course in time to intercept the High Seas Fleet at dawn. The first decision was finely balanced and he may well have judged himself too harshly. As for the second, while an action at daybreak undoubtedly had its risks, it was, in Nelson's words, the 'business of an English Commander-in-Chief . . . to bring an Enemy's Fleet to battle'.[25] Yet, in view of the resolve that Jellicoe had shown during the gun actions, it seems fair to conclude that, if he did not during the night live up to the Nelsonic ideal, it was due to the subconscious effects of an overmastering fatigue and a profound anxiety about underwater threats.

Beatty

Beatty was no less ready than Jellicoe to believe unlikely rumours about bigger guns for existing German ships, while at the Dogger Bank he proved just as anxious about imagined enemy submarines and destroyers that might drop mines in their wakes. But, unlike the C-in-C, he was quick to recognise that, as more destroyers joined the Grand Fleet, they could be used offensively and that the British had gained a decisive superiority in numbers of light cruisers. The *GFBOs* gave VAC BCF the freedom to act as he considered necessary in engaging his primary objective, the German battlecruisers. But, although the BCF had been temporarily augmented by the four fast battleships of the 5BS, the battlecruisers of the 2BCS and 3BCS would still have to face opponents that were much better protected. In the *BCOs*, Beatty demanded that his senior officers (not least those commanding the light cruisers) must display initiative. However, once the battlecruisers were in line, the scope for independent action by their commanders was mainly limited to avoiding smoke interference and following *Lion*'s unsignalled turns.

While Jellicoe would not rid himself of senior commanders in whom he lacked confidence, Beatty retained officers who were less than competent. His flag lieutenant, Ralph Seymour, made a serious error during the Scarborough Raid, though his handling of *Lion*'s signals at the end of the Dogger Bank action, whether in error or not, made little difference to the outcome. Lieutenant-Commander Gerald Longhurst was *Lion*'s gunnery officer at the Dogger Bank; yet despite Beatty's dissatisfaction with her gunnery and the later discovery of the chaotic state of her cordite magazines, Longhurst retained his post and Beatty even pressed for his promotion.[26] Beatty also knew that

---

[25] Mackay and Duffy, p. 189.   [26] Roskill, p. 136.

Captain Henry Pelly of *Tiger* had not properly supported his gunnery lieutenant while the ship was working up and that her shooting continued to be unsatisfactory, yet Pelly still commanded her at Jutland. Although *Tiger*'s gunnery was unusually bad, that of the other battlecruisers seems to have been little better. Because they were based at Rosyth, practices were more difficult to arrange but, when Jellicoe criticised the BCF's bad range-taking and excessively rapid fire, Beatty showed scant concern. The emphasis on rapidity of fire also suggests that, despite Grant's reforms in *Lion*, the other battlecruisers probably continued to expose more cordite and leave more magazine doors open than most other ships in the Fleet.

At 1.30pm on 31 May, Beatty disposed his forces for his expected meeting with the Grand Fleet, with the 5BS five miles NNW of *Lion*; then, at 2.15 he ordered all his forces to turn NbyE towards the rendezvous. Shortly afterwards, *Galatea* confirmed that she had sighted two hostile cruisers to the ESE and, in accordance with the *BCOs*, both the 1LCS and 3LCS turned without orders to engage them. Beatty reacted by instructing his destroyers to prepare for a turn to the SSE that was intended to place his whole force between the small enemy unit and its base. The general flag signal to turn was made executive at 2.32 but had not then been received or acknowledged by Evan-Thomas. Until the order to turn was somehow repeated, SO 5BS was understandably hesitant about whether Beatty wanted him to follow the battlecruisers as they charged off SSE'wards – they hardly needed the support of the fast battleships against a few cruisers or destroyers. Thus there had been no immediate urgency; if Beatty had wanted to keep the 5BS as close as possible, he had time enough for his signallers to hoist the turn signal, repeat it by searchlight (*Lion* was best placed to do this) and wait for an acknowledgement. Although Seymour must be held responsible for the failure to make the searchlight repeat, only Beatty could have taken the decision to turn about without acknowledgement from *Barham*. Thus Beatty's unnecessary haste was as much to blame as Evan-Thomas's hesitation for doubling the separation between the two flagships from five to about ten miles.

At about the same time as the 5BS eventually turned SSE, *Galatea* reported 'smoke as from a fleet'. Beatty, only now aware that a substantial enemy force was in his vicinity, swung from SSE to E to NE in his effort to cut them off, but he did nothing to reform his squadrons in readiness for action. His course changes were ordered by general signals made only by flags that would not have been readable from the 5BS; until Beatty confirmed his course by wireless, Evan-Thomas attempted to close the gap by 'cutting the corners'. Yet, during a meeting at the Admiralty on 26 July 1916, Beatty, while accepting that this had been the right thing to do, claimed that Evan-Thomas, unlike other squadron commanders, failed to seize the opportunity;[27] this was the very

[27] *BP II*, pp. 367–8.

opposite of what had occurred. Meanwhile, the 1LCS and 3LCS turned N and NNW with the object of leading the German IISG, followed by the ISG, towards the Grand Fleet, movements that separated both Beatty and Hipper from most of their light cruisers. The immediate effect was more serious for Beatty because, without cruisers to scout well ahead, he turned too far North of East and was unable to cut across his opponent's line of retreat. However, Beatty's despatch gives an entirely different impression by claiming that the 1LCS and 3LCS had formed a screen in advance of his heavy ships.

Prior to sighting the ISG, Beatty had done nothing to help the 5BS close the gap or to pull back the 2BCS from their advanced position. At 3.30pm, general flag signals ordered all squadrons to turn E before the 2BCS was commanded to prolong the line astern; the restricted space between their course and that of the 1BCS forced them to make two large, tight turns, after which they had to force their engines to make up the speed lost. The 5BS could not read the general flag signal but they were then given specific orders by searchlight to turn onto a parallel course E; clearly, Beatty did not wish them even to try to join his line. Hipper easily countered the attempt to cut him off by turning about at 3.35 onto a course SE, so that Beatty found himself on a steep approach with the enemy on forward bearings. But he pressed on until, just before the ISG opened fire, he ordered the formation of a line-of-bearing NW on a course ESE. This was too little and too late, though Seymour's choice of signals compounded the gunnery problems. The fire distribution signal was also made at the last minute. Beatty's 3.45 report of the enemy's course was quite accurate and was consistent with the range-rate recorded a little earlier in *Lion*'s transmitting station; thus Beatty and his staff should have been aware that the range was falling at 300–400 yards per minute. But *Lion*'s range-takers, then and later, obtained ranges that were misleadingly high. When Hipper opened fire, already well within his effective range, Beatty's conduct of the approach had inflicted serious disadvantages on his battlecruisers: they were still changing course and formation; *Queen Mary*'s and *Tiger*'s target selection, ranging and aiming were compromised by smoke interference so that they missed out *Derfflinger*; *Queen Mary*'s rear turrets were probably not bearing; and the 2BCS were struggling to catch up. Yet once again Beatty's despatch gave a quite different and more favourable impression; it claimed that he turned ESE and formed the line-of-bearing when the range was as high as 23,000 yards,[28] that the smoke had cleared and that the tactical situation was good.

When firing began, the ISG quickly seized and retained gunnery superiority; in the first phase of the Run to the South, they made twenty-two hits for only six received. Beatty led the 1BCS in unsignalled turns-away but was already too close to the enemy to escape repeated hits, especially on *Tiger*. To keep clear of

---

[28] This was the range recorded in *Lion*'s TS at 3.30: REL.

the smoke from the ships ahead, Pakenham continued E for longer before turning the 2BCS to SSE; his initiative, though in the spirit of the *BCOs*, took his two vulnerable battlecruisers closer to the ISG, with fatal consequences for *Indefatigable*. Just before she blew up, a shell penetrated *Lion*'s Q turret so the flagship had good reasons for veering away for a time; however, she remained out of line, hidden from the ships astern of *Lützow*, so that *Derfflinger* concentrated with *Seydlitz* on *Queen Mary*. In visibility that was now distinctly worse for the British ships, Beatty turned back to re-engage but with the same mistakes as in the first approach: *Lion*'s ranges were too high and rates too low; the approach was too rapid so that he was soon within the German's effective range; and smoke interference was again a problem, not least because he made no order for a line-of-bearing. In this second phase of the action, Beatty's battlecruisers probably made only three hits, all at the start before the German fire again began to tell; in return, they received at least twelve hits and lost the *Queen Mary* to a second cordite explosion. They might well have suffered even greater damage had it not been for the effective fire from the 5BS on Hipper's two rear battlecruisers which, at very long range, scored as many as seven hits. It is to Beatty's credit that, despite the German successes, it was Hipper not Beatty who broke off the action. Shortly after the ISG had been first sighted, Beatty, in accordance with his conviction that the best defence against enemy destroyer attacks was a pre-emptive attack by his own flotillas, had ordered his screening destroyers to move ahead in readiness. Thus they were able to threaten the ISG and help to force Hipper's withdrawal; to drive back an attack by the German destroyers before they could get within torpedo range; and to make the attacks that ended with the torpedo hit on *Seydlitz*.

Having sighted the High Seas Fleet, Beatty's first though not exclusive duty was to lead them under the guns of the Grand Fleet. While turning all his forces Northwards, he had the opportunity to form the single line that would enable his battlecruisers and battleships to provide mutual support, but, due to the delay in hauling down the 'Compass 16' signal, the 5BS were left trailing about three miles astern. Seymour must have played a part in both the choice of signal and the delay in making it executive, but Beatty cannot with certainty be held blameless. Just before the 5BS turned about, Beatty ordered a speed of 25 knots, which could be made only by the battlecruisers, while Evan-Thomas turned through 17 points to take a position on the battlecruisers's starboard quarter. The position of the 5BS became even more exposed once Beatty had turned away NNW; since *Lion* was then being hit, this was excusable, but to leave the 5BS unsupported for almost half an hour was not. The 5BS had no choice but to divide their fire between the ISG and the IIIBS, while *Warspite* and particularly *Malaya* at the rear were hit repeatedly; if either had suffered damage to her machinery, she would almost certainly have been lost. Although

Beatty was aware that the 5BS were 'still firing hard', he pushed on at 24 knots ('utmost speed' for the 5BS) and the battlecruisers only re-engaged the ISG from 5.34pm. During this firing, *Lion* scored the only probable hit by the battlecruisers in this phase, though there was another 'possible' earlier.

The 1LCS and 3LCS were able to form ahead of the battlecruisers for the Run to the North but they were not far enough in advance to give effective warning of the approach of the Grand Fleet, while Beatty's order to attack the enemy came too late. Beatty's few orders to his flotillas to form ahead were made only by flags and a delayed wireless repeat and they were not acted upon; except for *Onslow*, they remained without further urging on his disengaged side, making no attempt to threaten the pursuing German forces (a little later, they would be out of position for reaching their correct deployment positions). Thus there was no sign of the offensive spirit that had been shown during the Run to the South.

In part because *Iron Duke* did not give the correct time for her position at 5.00pm, Beatty probably believed that he and the enemy fleet would cross well ahead of the Grand Fleet. Until he sighted British armoured cruisers at 5.50, he had been closing cautiously on the ISG but, as the visibility deteriorated, they found it increasingly difficult to return the British fire. This was one reason for Hipper's large turn E between 5.53 and 5.55, though another was the sound of the IISG's action with Hood's 3BCS. Beatty did not himself turn E until 6.00, when he was in danger of losing touch with Hipper and he also needed to turn away from the advancing British 1BS. Thus Beatty's movements, which were more a reaction to than a cause of Hipper's large turn-away, played no more than a small part in preventing the leading German ships from sighting the Grand Fleet before the moment of deployment.

At the start of the Run to the North, the 5BS's delayed turn-about left them in a dangerous position but this has rather obscured the fact that the 5BS's situation became even more perilous after Beatty left them unsupported to face the whole German battle array. Yet for this phase of the action, Beatty's despatch once again gives an account which is seriously at variance with all other accounts and records. He declared that, rather than withdrawing out of range, the battlecruisers remained in action at a range of about 14,000 yards; that they inflicted 'severe punishment'; that he saw an enemy battlecruiser quit the line (neither *Princess Royal* nor *Tiger* provided corroboration, as he claimed);[29] and that he turned the enemy van at about six o'clock.

After turning E, Beatty was on course for his position ahead of the 2BS when the battlefleet deployed to port. But, while this may have been clear to him, he

---

[29] The despatch (*OD*, p. 135) mentions a report from *Fearless* of a heavy enemy ship on fire and apparently blowing up as corroboration of a hit by *Moresby*'s torpedo. What *Fearless* saw remains a mystery.

should have realised that the C-in-C urgently needed to know the positions and courses of the enemy battlecruisers and battleships, information which Beatty (and Evan-Thomas) had failed to supply. Yet Jellicoe found it necessary to demand, twice: 'Where is the Enemy's B.F?' and he had to wait before *Lion* reported only the enemy's bearings, of the ISG at 6.06 and the battlefleet at 6.14pm. During this critical period, the enemy forces may well have been visible only intermittently to Beatty, but this was no reason for not at once giving a full report of their last-seen positions; fortunately, the C-in-C's tactical judgement made up for VAC BCF's reporting failures.

After Beatty's battlecruisers were forced to veer away to avoid *Defence* and *Warrior*, he turned back to continue his effort to overhaul the 2BS. Before he could do so, he met and formed astern of Hood's 3BCS, though there is no reason to believe that he ordered Hood to take station ahead; in the ensuing action with the ISG, Beatty's four ships then provided some support, though they had ceased firing before it ended with the loss of *Invincible*. After she blew up, Beatty drew ahead of *King George V*, initially with *Inflexible* and *Indomitable* leading the now united BCF. But he refused to follow *Inflexible* when she turned to close the ISG, instead ordering her and *Indomitable* to prolong his line astern. At this moment, Beatty seemed to be more concerned to reach his position on the Deployment Diagram than to keep in touch with his principal objective, the enemy's battle-cruisers. He had already lost sight of the ISG when *Falmouth* reported at 6.45pm that they had turned W while still engaged with the 3BCS; though the 6.20 time for this turn was too early, *Falmouth* was alone in reporting the first German action-turn-about. Beatty then delayed passing on this important intelligence to Jellicoe, though as a bearing only, until 7.00, by which time it was of little use. By about 6.50, Beatty had lost touch with *King George V* as well as with all enemy ships; *Lion* then turned some eight points to starboard with the object of regaining contact. There is little doubt that this turn then continued through a full 32 points. Then at 7.05–06, by which time Jellicoe's order to turn S had been received, *Lion* turned gradually from SSE to SW; she crossed the bow of *King George V* at about 7.12, some of the battlecruisers then firing a few ineffective salvos between 7.13 and 7.20. Yet Beatty's despatch misled Jellicoe into assuming that the battlecruisers had continued to engage the enemy van and that they had inflicted considerable punishment; the despatch at least acknowledged that the BCF lost sight of the enemy at 7.45.

Beatty always vehemently denied that he had led his battlecruisers around in a circle, despite much evidence to the contrary and the conspicuous lack of support from *Lion*'s officers. Beginning after the battle and continuing post-War, he went to considerable and discreditable lengths to impose his version of events.[30] Why was he prepared to risk his reputation in this way? He admitted

[30] Roskill, pp. 176 and 326–7. *FDSF III*, pp. 148–50. *JP II*, pp. 458–90 for Harper's narrative.

that the reason for the initial turn to starboard had been that he had lost touch with both friend and foe but, since Bentinck was the first to mention the failure of the gyro compass, this was probably the actual reason for the turn continuing beyond 8 to about 16 points, after which it would have been easier and quicker to continue through 32 points rather than to reverse *Lion's* helm.[31] In the middle of a battle, steaming round in a circle looked rather ridiculous and distinctly unheroic, but was it so shameful that it had to be denied at all costs? The real problem for Beatty seems to have been that he had to deny the circle so that he could insist that by 7.05pm he had been ahead of *King George V*, not three points on her disengaged bow. He was not prepared to admit that, as the battleships were once more coming into action, he had led the battlecruisers into a position from which they could neither see nor engage the enemy. This also explains why, yet again, his despatch was misleading in that it falsely implied that, when he eventually re-engaged, his ships had fired to good effect. Furthermore, the controversy about the 32-point turn has also distracted attention from two more of Beatty's failures. First, by ignoring Heaton-Ellis's lead and pushing on towards a deployment position that in the bad visibility was too far ahead, he lost contact with the enemy battlecruisers; and, second, he did not pass on immediately *Falmouth's* report that the ISG had turned about.

By 7.40pm, Beatty had reduced speed to 18 knots, only one knot more than the British battlefleet. This ensured that the BCF would not draw much further ahead but at 7.45 he lost sight of the enemy. Then or shortly afterwards he turned towards the enemy although by only two points to WSW; assuming that the High Seas Fleet maintained its course SW at 16 knots, 52 minutes would have passed before the distance between them halved.[32] Just before eight o'clock, Jellicoe received Beatty's report of the enemy's last observed bearing (NWbyW) and course (SW) and his urgent submission that the van battleships should follow the battlecruisers. Yet Jellicoe alone recognised that a decisive turn W was needed to give at least some chance of finding the High Seas Fleet before dark and he at once informed Beatty of his change of course. However, the battlecruisers continued WSW, although Beatty ordered the 3LCS to sweep to the Westward and they soon sighted enemy vessels at 8.09. Only then did Beatty turn W and soon, beginning at 8.18, his battlecruisers were able to open fire. At about 8.20 and 8.25 respectively, he turned away to WSW and SW, thereby bringing his targets onto bearings about 20° abaft the beam and reducing the rate of approach. Nonetheless, the BCF was able to keep in touch with enemy battlecruisers and battleships to fight the final action between

---

[31] Beatty claimed that: 'We could not have turned 32 points without colliding with the rear ships' but *New Zealand's* log recorded that the turn had been gradual – *BP II*, pp. 435 and 437.

[32] Ninety-four minutes would pass before the BCF crossed 3.1nm ahead of the German ships.

heavy ships, making six hits on battlecruisers and one or two on predreadnought battleships. The visibility prevented the German ships from replying effectively and they were forced to turn away Westwards but, to their surprise, Beatty did not follow to make more of his positional and gunnery advantages. Earlier, Beatty's urgent 'follow me' signal gave no guidance to Jellicoe or Jerram on his course or position. But, once the battlecruisers' position became clear as they began firing, not only the 2BS but all the battle squadrons followed the battlecruisers. Yet, by doing as Beatty had urged, the British battlefleet gave up its last chance of a further encounter with the High Seas Fleet.

When the BCF lost sight of the enemy bearing NWbyW at 7.45pm, Beatty and Napier seem to have forgotten the *BCOs'* insistence that 'an enemy once sighted must never escape us' and that light cruisers 'must keep touch tenaciously with any enemy sighted'.[33] Given his own observations of the enemy's position and course, Beatty's turn WSW at an easy 18 knots was too tentative to re-establish contact, let alone 'cut off whole of enemy's battlefleet'. What was needed was the immediate despatch of the light cruisers Westward with the battlecruisers following at high speed in support. Instead, Beatty took no further action other than to compose what Jellicoe considered his 'rather insubordinate' signal urging that the van battleships should follow him.[34] When Beatty eventually followed Jellicoe in turning W, he was able promptly to re-engage: not because he had actively sought out the enemy forces but because, in turning S, they had inadvertently found him. If Beatty had turned W at eight o'clock or at the earlier time when he actually turned WSW, he would probably have been able to engage the ISG five or ten minutes earlier.[35] Given the fading light (sunset was at 8.07),[36] this would have significantly assisted the BCF's shooting; even a few more hits on *Seydlitz* might well have ensured that she foundered before reaching harbour.

To explain the 'follow-me' signal, both admirals Chatfield and Drax declared that Beatty had seen the 2BS turn away from the enemy to port and wanted the battleships to follow him while he was still in touch with the enemy.[37] But the 2BS had last turned away to port at 7.25pm; after 7.35, they turned progressively to starboard, even to WSW for a time, in order to regain their position in the van. Since wireless signals could take several minutes from despatch to reaching the admiral's bridge, it is possible that Beatty did not know that the battlefleet's course was SW when he composed his 'follow-me' signal, in which case it may not have had a deliberately tendentious intent. Even so, after the battle Beatty wanted Jerram court-martialled for not following

---

[33] BCO 6 in DRAX 1/3.   [34] *FDSF III*, p. 145 n. 81.
[35] *Lion*'s alternative courses also plotted on Corbett, Map 41.   [36] Harper, p. 2. *AN*, p. 60 n. 1.
[37] *FDSF III*, pp. 141–4. Roskill, pp. 177–8.

him – as we have seen, there was no substance to this accusation – while the signal became another bone of contention during the post-war Jutland Controversy.[38] Whatever Beatty's original intention, the furore over his signal is another instance of a controversy that, conveniently for Beatty, distracted attention from his own failings, namely: that he disregarded his own precepts about keeping touch tenaciously; that, given his own observation of the enemy course, his course WSW could not have regained touch while some daylight remained; and that, after the enemy came to him, he did not press his gunnery advantage but continued passively SW.

After ceasing fire, Beatty must have sighted the enemy at least once more, since he was able to inform Jellicoe, though rather belatedly, that at 9.00pm they bore NbyW, course WSW. Beatty, whose appreciation of the situation was very close to Jellicoe's, was equally reluctant to seek a night action and he decided that he would be carrying out the C-in-C's wishes if he too turned S. However, like Jellicoe, Beatty did not explain their belief that British forces would remain between the enemy and the German bases and that the enemy would certainly be located at daybreak. Nor did he justify his concern that the enemy's fleet, even though hampered by slower predreadnoughts, might pass round the Southern flank of the British forces. Beatty's despatch stated that at daybreak, he had obeyed Jellicoe's order to conform and close rather than, as he had intended, ask permission to make a sweep SW. It is uncertain how this claim related to his unanswered signal at 4.04am proposing the same thing – but, as we now know, any sweep in that direction would have been fruitless. Beatty closed the battlefleet at 5.20, when he took the opportunity to remind Jellicoe that he had done so in accordance with the C-in-C's orders. Only then did Beatty propose that he should try to locate the enemy vessels reported by *Dublin* at 4.31. However, even though Beatty now had almost all his light cruisers to scout ahead and an adequate submarine screen, he was no more prepared than Jellicoe to proceed any further towards Horns Reef, the most likely direction in which to pick up enemy stragglers. Instead, he followed Jellicoe Northwards before shaping a course for Rosyth.

* * *

In their despatches and later writings, both Scheer and Jellicoe were not above some misrepresentations of their actions during the battle.[39] But these were minor compared with Beatty's concerted efforts in his despatch to cover up his mistakes, and with his part in the controversies that began after the battle and continued into the 1920s. Contrary to his despatch:

---

[38] *Ibid.*   [39] Only Hipper remained silent after the War.

- he failed to retain his cruiser screen while he was trying to make his first contact with Hipper
- during the approach to the Run to the South, he did not turn ESE on a line-of-bearing in good time
- he did not remain in action throughout the Run to the North
- as the High Seas Fleet executed its third action-turn-about, the BCF was too distant to inflict any significant punishment.

Then the later controversies effectively distracted attention *from* Beatty's errors:

- Evan-Thomas's delayed turn SSE after 2.35pm *from* Beatty's subsequent failure to concentrate all his squadrons and form a suitable approach formation
- Evan-Thomas's quite short delay in turning about at 4.48pm *from* Beatty's leaving the 5BS unsupported for nearly half an hour
- Beatty's denial of his 32-point turn at seven o'clock *from both* his refusal to pursue the ISG *and* then completely losing touch with the enemy just as the battle was approaching its climax
- the 'follow-me' signal *from both* his tentative movements (less bold than Jellicoe's) to regain touch with the enemy before dark *and*, after the enemy came to him, his failure to follow their withdrawal.

While no evidence has been found that these controversies were fomented deliberately, the correlation between them and some of Beatty's greater mistakes is certainly striking. But, even if this is no more than coincidence, the controversies and his mendacious despatch are clear pointers to the actions and decisions which Beatty himself knew were most open to criticism and which, by whatever means, had to be denied or covered up.

Captain Roskill memorably called Beatty 'for better or worse ... The Last Naval Hero'.[40] While the terrible, anonymous slaughter continued on land, the nation (and the Navy) needed heroes and Beatty undoubtedly looked the part, a handsome officer in his non-regulation jacket, his cap at a jaunty angle. He knew the value of his public reputation; from before his appointment to command the battlecruisers, he had been supported by influential sections of the press while, after he became C-in-C, Grand Fleet, he was adept at using his dashing image to sustain morale despite long periods of inactivity.[41] In the Battle of Jutland, Beatty lived up to his image in his initial handling of his destroyers, ordering them forward in good time so that they could act offensively. But he had not demanded and did not inspire the highest professional standards in key departments like gunnery and signalling. His approaches in the Run to the South were rash and careless, and the crews of *Indefatigable* and

---

[40] Roskill, subtitle and p. 375.
[41] Bryan Ranft, 'Beatty, David', *ODNB*. Andrew Lambert, *Admirals*, pp. 349 and 360.

Queen Mary paid the price. He bore their loss (and that of *Invincible*) with fortitude but, after he encountered the High Seas Fleet, rashness gave way to caution. During the Run to the North, he drew out of range, leaving the 5BS to receive the full weight of enemy fire; also he neglected to position his destroyers for an attack or in preparation for his meeting with the battlefleet. After the deployment, Beatty seemed intent solely on reaching a position well ahead of the van battleships; thus the BCF was barely engaged when Jellicoe crossed the enemy T for the second time and then turned away from their destroyers. At the end of the day, Beatty closed with excessive caution and then did not keep hold of the enemy when they withdrew. Beatty blamed Jellicoe for turning away and allowing the enemy to elude the British fleet. Yet Beatty gave Jellicoe no significant support at this critical moment and was more tentative in trying to renew contact in the final period of daylight. By criticising Jellicoe and encouraging his supporters to do likewise,[42] Beatty invites us to judge him by no less exacting standards. The conclusion is unavoidable; he did not live up to his own image – there was little that was truly heroic in Beatty's leadership at Jutland.

Missed opportunities

The battle ended with the Royal Navy still dominant in the North Sea and with the High Seas Fleet retreating to the safety of its bases. But strategic victory had been gained at a disconcertingly high cost. The higher British losses were in part due to inadequacies in British material – especially in the explosive hazards inherent in cordite charges. But throughout the battle, British commanders (knowingly or not) missed opportunities to inflict more damage on enemy ships, to limit losses to their own ships, or even both at once. The list must begin with the Run to the South. If Beatty had formed his battlecruisers and the 5BS in one line and then made a less precipitate approach, each German battlecruiser would have been under fire from two British ships. Even though the concentrated fire of the battlecruisers would probably have been less accurate than that of the battleships, the effect on the ISG would have been overwhelming, especially on *Moltke* and *Von der Tann*. Most probably *Indefatigable* would have survived, there would have been no German concentration on *Queen Mary* and, even if no German battlecruisers were actually lost, the ISG would have been finished as a fighting force even before Beatty encountered the High Seas Fleet. Yet, however the Run to the South ended, Beatty would then have turned about to lead Scheer to Jellicoe. Whether or not the 5BS was trailing a few miles astern, it would have been in an exposed position. However, if Beatty had remained in action with his fire directed at the

---

[42] *BP II*, pp. 443–4 and 455. Chatfield, p. 149.

ISG, the 5BS would have been free to bring its formidable firepower to bear on the leading German battleships, so that the damage and casualties would have been less severe in *Warspite* and *Malaya* and more serious in the IIIBS. Also, if Beatty had kept in sight of the enemy, he might have seized the opportunity to press his destroyers to attack, either during the Run to the North or as the Grand Fleet deployed – an attack at the latter time might well have disrupted the already curved German line and its fire at *Defence, Warrior, Warspite* and even *Invincible*. As a separate possibility, *Defence* and *Warrior* might also have survived if Jellicoe had kept the 3BCS as his advanced scouting line, but there are too many imponderables to guess whether or not, in that event alone, *Invincible* would have been lost.

After Jellicoe's deployment had enveloped the head of the German line, Scheer made his first action-turn-about; this caused some confusion in his line, while the ISG (less *Lützow*) was forced to stop while *Derfflinger* cut away her torpedo nets. These opportunities to attack while the enemy was vulnerable could not be seen from the British battle line. But they could have become visible: if Jerram had turned towards the enemy as soon as he lost sight of the enemy; if Jellicoe had not delayed until 6.55pm before turning S; or if Beatty had allowed *Inflexible* to lead the BCF in pursuit of the ISG after the sinking of *Invincible*. The opportune moment passed but then Scheer made his premature second action-turn-about, only to find Jellicoe crossing the T once again. After Scheer's third action-turn-about, his battlefleet was in greater confusion than it had been previously and even more vulnerable to attack by gunfire and torpedoes. But once again this could not be seen from the British line, whereas the covering attack by some of the German flotillas was a clear threat, at least to the rear divisions. Jerram's hesitancy in leading the line had already added to Jellicoe's tactical dilemmas, which the C-in-C resolved by turning all his divisions away. At the time, it probably did not enter his mind that the Germans had executed a manoeuvre as drastic as the action-turn-about directly away from him; therefore his most likely assumption would have been that they would soon turn back into line on a course not much different from his own. The *Naval Staff Appreciation* roundly criticised Jellicoe for not turning his fleet by divisions (or even sub-divisions) Westwards in order to envelop and destroy the enemy fleet.[43] But to him such an idea would, with justification, have seemed foolhardy since it ignored both the torpedo threat to his rear and the risk that his divided divisions might run head-on into an unbroken German battle line. However, as we have seen, there was another alternative, that only the rear British divisions turned away and that those in the lead formed line before turning towards and re-engaging the retreating enemy squadrons while they were still in some disorder. It is even possible that Jellicoe himself saw this

[43] *NSA*, pp. 106–7.

as one of the missed opportunities of Jutland although, if he did, he was not prepared to admit it.

Even after Jellicoe turned the battlefleet away, an opportunity remained of a bold advance by the two flotillas ahead of the British van, which might have found the enemy fleet still in disarray, an ideal target for a massed attack. Instead, Hawksley moved out with only half a flotilla and, while he was still searching for the enemy, was recalled by Jellicoe. In the final action between heavy ships, Beatty did not pursue the Germans when they turned away; thus *Seydlitz* escaped further damage that might have caused her to sink. Then, just as night was falling, Hawksley and the 11DF missed another opportunity when they failed to follow up the attack on the IBS by *Caroline* and *Royalist*. Hawksley's own explanation for holding back was not credible but his determination can only have been undermined by Jerram's confusing signals and by Jellicoe's earlier reprimand.

During the night, Farie's flight from the enemy disrupted the British destroyers' best opportunity to deliver a massed attack from ahead on the advancing German line. Even then, those destroyers that remained with Goldsmith were favourably positioned to attack but he would not, or perhaps could not, accept that he was crossing ahead of the enemy line. At daybreak, the attack on opposite courses by the 1st Division of Stirling's 12DF torpedoed the *Pommern* but opportunities for further successes were obstructed by Champion's *Maenad*. The High Seas Fleet was clearly seen moving across the wakes of the 1BS and 5BS in the direction of Horns Reef but neither Burney not Evan-Thomas reported these sightings to Jellicoe; had they done so, it is possible that the C-in-C would then have accepted that he must turn all his forces in the same direction in order to intercept Scheer at daybreak. But would this have been a final opportunity to damage the enemy further? Apart from *Marlborough* and *Warspite*, the British battlefleet was almost unharmed. But it would have been without nearly all its destroyers in an action that, in the poor visibility, would have been at short ranges. If the Grand Fleet had sighted the enemy, for a time its superior firepower might have inflicted more damage than it received, though there would always have been a risk that a German hit might cause another cordite explosion. But in any event Scheer would quickly have ordered a destroyer attack to cover a withdrawal, while Jellicoe, made doubly apprehensive by his lack of destroyers and by his fears of underwater attack, would not have dared to follow. Thus a dawn encounter would very probably have been no more decisive than the previous day's actions.

This catalogue of missed opportunities epitomises the character of British tactical leadership during the battle. As many historians have emphasised, Andrew Gordon most recently, the Grand Fleet's senior officers were formed during the long Victorian and Edwardian heyday of the Royal Navy. However, it should be recognised that most were well qualified to understand the many technological changes that had punctuated their careers; of the eleven officers of flag rank in the fleet at Jutland, eight had specialised as gunnery or torpedo officers – Beatty and Jerram were the conspicuous exceptions.[44] Nevertheless, in the years of peace, the Navy had never been able to test equipment or men in the crucible of a fleet action. Unsurprisingly, promotion came to depend on technical competence, on those leadership qualities that made for efficiency as the Fleet followed its peacetime routines, and on occasional actions ashore that allowed young officers to display bravery and initiative. Ability, though also due deference to senior officers, was rewarded but mediocre officers could still climb, though more slowly, up the ladder of promotion. Jellicoe was one of the outstanding officers of his generation and the progress of his early career, though unusually rapid, was in many ways typical. He was wounded during the Boxer Rebellion; his mathematical ability enabled him to specialise in gunnery and in time to become Director of Naval Ordnance and Torpedoes and then Controller – though perhaps his lesser expertise in torpedoes and mines led him to overestimate the capabilities of these weapons. After his appointment as Commander-in-Chief, Jellicoe could not shake off his initial pessimism about the enemy's material superiority and numbers. He continued to find delegation difficult, a tendency that was made worse by a lack of confidence in his squadron commanders, especially Jerram.[45] As C-in-C, Jellicoe bore a daunting responsibility for most of Britain's naval strength. His strategic object was to preserve the Grand Fleet so that its ships continued to dominate the North Sea so that it could quickly contain and drive back any foray by the weaker High Seas Fleet; inflicting major losses on the enemy was a lesser priority.[46] The pre-war naval race had created 'grand fleets of battle' of unprecedented size and destructive power but the technical advances had not been matched by tactical innovation. Jellicoe, but also Scheer, still preferred the single line, which maximised broadside weight of fire and mutual support but was tactically unwieldy.

Jellicoe, a man of precise, analytical intelligence, responded to the challenges he faced by working with his staff to produce what were intended as comprehensive battle orders. However, even on their own terms, they were incomplete. Although they assumed that the C-in-C would retain control of the whole fleet at least until the fleet was deployed and battle was joined, they did not emphasise sufficiently that, in bad visibility and at night, he depended on complete and frequent enemy reports. As in the tactical exercises conducted in the Grand Fleet, the *GFBOs* were most concerned with cruising, the approach and the formation of the battle line; they provided little guidance on how, even

---

[44] *ODNB. Australian Dictionary of Biography* (adb.anu.edu.au) for Gaunt.

[45] For a judicious assessment of Jellicoe's character, see Andrew Lambert, 'Jellicoe, John Rushworth' in *ODNB*.

[46] *JP I*, p. 232.

if the enemy chose to stand and fight, the battle might then be won. However, it was accepted that the weaker German battlefleet was much more likely to withdraw while covering its retreat with torpedoes and mines. Yet, while Jellicoe and Sturdee had studied this scenario intensively, they had not found a means to keep hold of the enemy without risking what they feared might be serious losses.

During the Battle of Jutland, Jellicoe was at his best as he decided how to deploy and at eight o'clock when he recognised that only a bold turn W would have at least a chance of regaining touch. Both decisions were reached with only limited information and neither depended on exhaustive prior analysis. Also, while Jellicoe was reaching his deployment decision, he could not see any enemy ships, so he was not disturbed by visible threats of attack by underwater weapons. He waited cooly until at last Beatty reported the bearing of the enemy battleships; Jellicoe's deployment by the unfamiliar Equal Speed Pendant was as inspired as it was unexpected by his staff. However, for the remainder of the battle, he was faced repeatedly with the long-anticipated and unresolved problem of a retiring enemy, to which was added the difficulty that, in the poor visibility, the enemy ships quickly disappeared once they had turned away. Without a safe counter-move, Jellicoe refused to follow immediately and, by also keeping his destroyers on a tight rein, he missed opportunities to inflict further damage on the enemy. But he had already determined that he must resist '[c]onsiderations of moral effect [that might] force the stronger fleet to follow the weaker and play into the hands of the enemy'.[47] Even the spectacular explosions in *Defence* and *Invincible*[48] did not push Jellicoe, armoured by quiet self-confidence, into taking risks; the enemy's withdrawals were already enough to achieve Britain's strategic aims. For Jellicoe, that and the avoidance of any further unnecessary losses were sufficient.

Beatty was very different in personality and career, though he too made his reputation fighting in China and also in the Sudan. He had boundless self-confidence, avoided all technical specialisations and held a succession of successful captaincies. But his appointment to command the battlecruiser squadron in 1913 was also due to Churchill's patronage and to Beatty's cultivation of press support. In the *Battle Cruiser Orders*, Beatty endeavoured to define the battlecruisers' roles and his expectations of his senior officers, though their scope for using their individual initiative was limited when, as at Jutland, they were fighting in line. After the disappointing Battle of the Dogger Bank, in early 1915 Beatty took command of the newly formed Battle Cruiser Fleet based at Rosyth. There they had limited opportunities for essential

---

[47] *GF*, p. 257.
[48] Jellicoe would not learn of the loss of *Indefatigable* and *Queen Mary* until the following morning: *OD*(M), 1 June, 10.01am and 11.04am.

practice but Beatty was insouciant about their evident inefficiency in gunnery. At Jutland prior to the Run to the South, his excessive self-assurance led to the elementary military blunder of not bringing the full force at his disposal to bear upon the enemy. And during the approach, without Chatfield to guide him, Beatty's own knowledge of gunnery was insufficient for him to recognise the disruptive effects of his tactical orders. Having initially engaged the enemy with careless overconfidence, for the remainder of the battle Beatty's leadership was cautious to a fault, especially for the commander of the British scouting forces. As his despatch suggests, he was well aware that, after the destruction of two battlecruisers under his direct command, his reputation was on the line and that he could not risk any more disasters. But it is also possible that his catastrophic losses (which through no fault of his would soon extend to the *Invincible*) undermined his self-belief more severely than he ever admitted.

After the battle, the guileful fabrications of Beatty's despatch and the controversies that conveniently diverted attention from his mistakes ensured that his reputation remained largely intact. He was soon appointed Commander-in-Chief and successfully 'maintained the fighting spirit of his men throughout the years of frustration that lay ahead', while, after the war, he was a highly effective First Sea Lord and Chief of the Defence Staff.[49] That his remarkable career continued to flourish after Jutland is a testament to Beatty's exceptional political skills. Despite his carefully promoted image, he was in his true element not in action at sea but in the committee rooms of Whitehall.

Both Jellicoe and Beatty retained the gentlemanly peacetime tolerance of mediocre or even incompetent officers. Beatty kept on Seymour, Longhurst and Pelly and Jellicoe's reservations about Jerram proved justified. But this is at most a partial explanation of the less satisfactory aspects of British leadership, while it should also be recognised that other officers did very well. Characteristically, the C-in-C valued Burney's caution; yet, Burney, and also Sturdee, took the tactical initiative by turning away from enemy destroyers, though Jellicoe denied them any further opportunities to do the same again. But during the night Burney and Evan-Thomas were unable to overcome their deference to a supposedly omniscient Commander-in-Chief, so neither reported the enemy ships passing astern of their squadrons. On the other hand, Evan-Thomas bears at most limited responsibility for the delayed turns by the 5BS after 2.35pm and 4.48pm; Beatty was chiefly responsible for the fast battleships' late engagement during the Run to the South and for their exposure to the undivided German fire during the Run to the North. Hood was free to lead the 3BCS with distinction until he was killed. The other rear-admirals and the captains of both battleships and battlecruisers were required to do little more than maintain their positions in line, though in the BCF they had to be alert to

[49] Bryan Ranft, 'Beatty, David', *ODNB*.

Beatty's unsignalled alterations of course. Among the commanders of light forces, Goodenough distinguished himself by his readiness to seek out the enemy, though unfortunately *Southampton*'s inaccurate dead-reckoning reduced the value of his reports. Bingham, Loftus Jones, Tovey, Ramsey and Stirling all displayed aspects of the aggressive determination expected of destroyer leaders but Hawksley, Goldsmith and especially Farie fell well short of this standard.

After Jutland, Beatty found it expedient to blame Jerram for not joining him at once after the 'follow-me' signal; when Beatty became C-in-C, Jerram left the Grand Fleet and retired in 1917. Pelly, as had been intended before the battle, went ashore as commodore of the Portsmouth barracks. Though Hawksley and Farie continued to serve, they were not promoted further; both attained flag rank only on retirement in 1922 at the time of the drastic reductions in naval manpower. But this was also an opportunity to retain the best officers; of those whose conduct during the battle had been outstanding, Goodenough, Stirling and Ramsey all reached flag rank in service, while Tovey went on to command the Home Fleet and to be appointed Admiral of the Fleet. Two other officers who reached the highest rank after commanding at sea in World War II were also present at Jutland – Sir Charles Forbes (flag commander in *Iron Duke*) and Sir Philip Vian (in the destroyer *Morning Star*).[50] But, as well as these direct experiences of the Battle of Jutland, its unsatisfactory outcome led to the self-criticism and doctrinal reforms of the inter-war years. Consequently, in 1939 the Royal Navy was much better prepared than it had been in 1914 to face the dire challenges of the next conflict with Germany.

---

[50] Summaries of service records of Ramsey, Hawksley and Farie (in ADM 196) at www .dreadnoughtproject.org. Other biographies from *ODNB*; Captain Dudley Pound commanded *Colossus* at Jutland.

Bibliography

I   Abbreviated sources

AN   Admiralty, *Narrative of the Battle of Jutland* (London: HMSO, 1924)

ATFJ   Admiralty, Gunnery Branch, *Analysis of Torpedo Firing in the Battle of Jutland*, January 1918, ADM 186/586

BP I   Ranft, Bryan (ed.) *The Beatty Papers, Volume I 1902–1918* (Aldershot: Scholar Press for Navy Records Society, 1989)

BP II   Ranft, Bryan (ed.) *The Beatty Papers, Volume II 1916–1927* (Aldershot: Scholar Press for the Navy Records Society, 1993)

CAWFS
1860–1905   Chesnau, R and Kolensik, E (eds.) *Conway's All the World's Fighting Ships 1860–1905* (London: Conway Maritime Press, 1979)

CAWFS
1906–21   Grey, Randal (ed.) *Conway's All the World's Fighting Ships 1906–1921* (London: Conway Maritime Press, 1985)

DGBJ   Brooks, John, *Dreadnought Gunnery and the Battle of Jutland. The Question of Fire Control* (London: Routledge, 2005)

FCBD   Brooks, John, 'Fire Control for British Dreadnoughts. Choices in Technology and Supply' (University of London: PhD Thesis, 2001) – at http://ethos.bl.uk/OrderDetails.do?uin=uk.bl.ethos.274933

F&H   Fawcett H W and Hooper G W (eds.) *The Fighting at Jutland* (Rochester: Chatham, 2001 – first published 1921)

FDSF   Marder, Arthur, *From the Dreadnought to Scapa Flow. The Royal Navy in the Fisher Era, 1904–1919* (Oxford University Press)
Vol. I. *The Road to War, 1904–1914* (London: 1961)
Vol. II. *The War Years: To the Eve of Jutland* (London: 1966)
Vol. III. *Jutland and After* (May 1916–December 1916) (Oxford: 1978 – 2nd edition)

GF   Jellicoe, Viscount, *The Grand Fleet 1914–1916. Its Creation, Development and Work* (Ringshall: Ad Hoc Publications, 2006 – first published 1919)

GFBOs I   Grand Fleet Battle Orders Vol. I 1914–1916, ADM 116/1341 and 186/595 (A further collection for 1914–15 is in ADM 137/288)

GFBOs III	Grand Fleet Battle Orders Vol. III in force at Jutland, ADM 116/134 and 186/597 – reproduction by Brad Golding (Mitcham, Victoria: AAD Services, 1997)
GFG&TMs	*Grand Fleet Gunnery and Torpedo Memoranda on Naval Actions 1914–1918*, 1922, ADM 188/615
GFG&TOs	*Grand Fleet Gunnery and Torpedo Orders*, 1915–1918, ADM 137/293
GMS	'Summary of the More Important German Wireless Messages and Visual Signals Relating to the Battle of Jutland', Tarrant, App. 10, pp. 272–303
GOA	Groos, Captain O (trans. Bagot, Lieut-Cmdr. W T) *The Battle of Jutland (The German Official Account)*, Naval Staff, Admiralty, 1 May 1926 and typed draft Ca889, both AL. Also ADM 186/626
GSB 1915	*General Signal Book 1915*, ADM 186/699
IDNS	Sumida, Jon, *In Defence of Naval Supremacy. Finance, Technology and British Naval Policy 1889–1914* (London: Unwin Hyman, 1989)
JMSS	The Jellicoe Papers, Add. 48989–49057, BL. View at www.bl.uk/manuscripts/FullDisplay.aspx?ref=Add_MS_[number]
JP I	Patterson, A Temple (ed.) *The Jellicoe Papers. Volume I, 1893–1916* (Navy Records Society, 1966)
JP II	Patterson, A Temple (ed.) *The Jellicoe Papers. Volume II, 1916–1935* (Navy Records Society, 1968)
MoG I 1915	Admiralty, *Manual of Gunnery (Volume I) for His Majesty's Fleet*, Ja254, AL
MoG III 1915	Admiralty, Gunnery Branch, *Manual of Gunnery (Volume III) for His Majesty's Fleet*, Ja254, AL
NSA	Naval Staff, Training and Staff Duties Division, *Naval Staff Appreciation of Jutland with Appendices and Diagrams* (Admiralty, 1922)
	JMMS 49042 for Jellicoe's annotated copy
	Schleihauf, William (ed.) *Jutland. The Naval Staff Appreciation* (Barnsley: Seaforth, 2016)
OD	*Battle of Jutland 30th May to 1st June 1916. Official Despatches with Appendices*, Cmd.1068 (London: HMSO, 1920). https://archive.org/download/battleofjutland300grearich/battleofjutland300grearich.pdf
OD(M)	'Record of Messages Bearing on the Operation', *OD*, App. II, pp. 398–586
ODNB	Goldman, Lawrence (ed.) *Oxford Dictionary of National Biography* (Oxford: Oxford University Press, 2009)
REL	'Record of Events during Action of 31st May from Records kept in Control Position and Transmitting Station. H.M.S. Lion', BTY 6/6 and JMSS 49014 and transcription at: www.dreadnoughtproject.org/tfs/index.php/H.M.S._Lion_at_the_Battle_of_Jutland
S&H	Steel, N and Hart, P, *Jutland 1916. Death in the Grey Wastes* (London: Cassell, 2003)
VNE	'VABCF's Personal Records. Battle of 31st May. Narrative of Events' in BTY 6/3 and DRAX 1/57

II   Archives

Admiralty Historical Library [AL]

British Library [BL]

Churchill College, Cambridge [CC]

DRAX   Admiral Sir Reginald Plunkett-Ernle-Erle-Drax
DRYR   Admiral Sir Frederic Dreyer
FISR   Admiral of the Fleet Lord Fisher

Imperial War Museum [IWM]

National Maritime Museum [NMM]

BTY   Admiral of the Fleet Earl Beatty
CHT   Admiral of the Fleer Lord Chatfield
OLV   Admiral of the Fleet Sir Henry Oliver

The National Archive [TNA]

ADM   Admiralty
HW   Government Code and Cypher School and Predecessors: Personal Papers, Unofficial Histories [etc.]

III   Sources by author

Bacon, Admiral Sir Reginald, *From 1900 Onwards* (London: Hutchinson, 1940).
Beeler, John, *Birth of the Battleship. British Capital Ship Design, 1870–1881* (London: Chatham Publishing, 2001).
Beesly, Patrick, *Room 40. British Naval Intelligence 1914–18* (London: Hamish Hamilton, 1982).
Bell, Christopher, *Churchill and Sea Power* (Oxford: Oxford University Press, 2013).
Bennett, Geoffrey, *The Battle of Jutland* (Barnsley: Pen & Sword, 2006).
Bingham, Barry, *Falklands, Jutland and the Bight* (London: John Murray, 1919).
Black, Nicholas, *The British Naval Staff in the First World War* (Woodbridge: Boydell, 2009).
Blyth, R, Lambert, A and Rüger, J (eds.) *The Dreadnought and the Edwardian Age* (Farnham: Ashgate, 2011).
Brooks, John, 'The Admiralty Fire Control Tables' in Antony Preston (ed.) *Warship 2002–2003* (London: Conway Maritime Press, 2003) pp. 69–93.
  '*Dreadnought*: Blunder or Stroke of Genius', *War in History* 14, 2, (2007), pp. 157–78.
  'Grand Battle-Fleet Tactics: From the Edwardian Age to Jutland' in Blyth *et al.* pp. 183–211.
  'The Mast and Funnel Question' in John Roberts (ed.) *Warship 1995* (London: Conway Maritime Press, 1995) pp. 40–60.

'Percy Scott and the Director' in David McLean and Antony Preston (eds.) *Warship 1996* (London: Conway Maritime Press, 1996) pp. 150–70.

'Preparing for Armageddon. Gunnery Practices and Exercises in the Grand Fleet Prior to Jutland', *Journal of Strategic Studies*, 38, 7 (2015), pp. 1006–23. dx.doi.org/10.1080/01402390.2015.1005446.

Brown, David K, *The Grand Fleet. Warship Design and Development 1906–1922* (London: Chatham Publishing, 1999).

'HMS *Invincible*. The Explosion at Jutland . . .', *Warship International*, XL, 4 (2003), pp. 339–49.

Warrior to Dreadnought. Warship Development 1860–1905 (London: Chatham Publishing, 1997).

Burt, R A, *British Battleships of World War One* (Barnsley: Seaforth, new edition 2012)

Campbell, N J M, 'Cordite' in Antony Preston (ed.) *Warship 6* (London: Conway Maritime Press, April 1978) pp. 138–40.

Jutland, an Analysis of the Fighting (London: Conway Maritime Press, 1986) – referenced as 'Campbell'.

Warship Special 1. Battlecruisers (London: Conway Maritime Press, 1978).

Chalmers, Rear-Admiral R S, *The Life and Letters of David, Earl Beatty* (London: Hodder and Stoughton, 1951).

Chatfield, Lord, *The Navy and Defence* (London: Heinemann, 1942).

Corbett, Sir Julian, *Naval Operations Vol. I to . . . December 1914* (London: Longmans, Green, 1920).

Naval Operations Vol. III (London: Longmans, Green, 1923) – referenced as 'Corbett'.

Dreyer, Admiral Sir Frederic, *The Sea Heritage. A Study of Maritime Warfare* (London: Museum Press, 1955).

Epkenhans, Michael, 'Dreadnought: A "Golden Opportunity" for Germany's Naval Aspirations' in Blyth *et al.* pp. 79–91.

Tirpitz: Architect of the German High Seas Fleet (Washington, DC: Potomac Books, 2008).

'Etienne' (Stephen King-Hall), *A Naval Lieutenant 1914–1918* (London: Methuen, 1919).

Fremantle, Sydney, *My Naval Career 1880–1928* (London: Hutchinson, 1949).

Friedman, Norman, *British Destroyers. From Earliest Days to the Second World War* (Barnsley: Seaforth, 2009).

Godfrey, Captain J H, 'Jutland', lectures to Royal Navy Staff College, Greenwich, 1930, AL.

Goldrick, James, *Before Jutland* (Annapolis, MD: Naval Institute Press, 2015).

The King's Ships Were at Sea (Annapolis, MD: Naval Institute Press, 1984) – referenced as 'Goldrick'.

Goodenough, Admiral Sir William, *A Rough Record* (London: Hutchinson, 1943).

Gordon, Andrew, *The Rules of the Game. Jutland and British Naval Command* (London: John Murray, 1996).

Grant, Alexander, 'H.M.S. *Lion*, 1915–16' in Susan Rose (ed.) *The Naval Miscellany Vol. VII* (NRS, 2008) pp. 379–406.

Gröner, Erich (rev. Jung, Dieter and Maass, Martin), *German Warships 1815–1945* (London: Conway). Vol. I, Major Surface Vessels (1990) and Vol. II, U-Boats and Mine Warfare Vessels (1991).

Halpern, Paul, *A Naval History of World War I* (London: UCL Press, 1994).

Harper, Captain J E T, *Reproduction of the Record of the Battle of Jutland prepared. . .in 1919–1920*, Cmd. 2870 (London: HMSO, 1927).

Hartcup, Guy, *The War of Invention. Scientific Developments, 1914–18* (London: Brassey's Defence Publishers, 1988).

Herwig, Holger, 'German Reaction to the *Dreadnought* Revolution', *International History Review*, XIII, 2 (May 1991), pp. 273–83.

    'Luxury Fleet'. The Imperial German Navy, 1888–1918 (London: Ashfield Press, revised edition 1987) – referenced as 'Herwig'.

Hezlett, Arthur, *The Electron and Sea Power* (London: Peter Davies, 1975).

Hines, Jason, 'Sins of Omission and Commission: A Reassessment of the Role of Intelligence in the Battle of Jutland', *Journal of Military History*, 72 (October 2008), pp. 1117–53.

Hodges, Peter, *The Big Gun* (London: Conway Maritime Press, 1981).

James, Admiral Sir William, *A Great Seaman. The Life of Admiral of the Fleet Sir Henry Oliver* (London; Witherby, 1956).

Kelly, Patrick, *Tirpitz and the Imperial German Navy* (Bloomington, IL: Indiana University Press, 2011).

Kent, Captain Barrie, *Signal! A History of Signalling in the Royal Navy* (East Meon, Hants: Hyden House, 2004).

Kerr, Admiral Mark, *The Navy in My Time* (London: Rich & Cowan, 1933).

King-Hall, Louise (ed.) *Sea Saga being the Naval Diaries of. . .the King-Hall Family* (London: Gollancz, 1935).

Lambert, Andrew, *Admirals. The Naval Commanders Who Made Britain Great* (London: Faber & Faber, 2008).

    (ed.) *Steam, Steel & Shellfire. The Steam Warship 1815–1905* (London: Conway Maritime Press, 1992).

Lambert, Nicholas, '"Our Bloody Ships" or "Our Bloody System"?', *Journal of Military History*, 62, 1 (January, 1998), pp. 29–55.

    Sir John Fisher's Naval Revolution (Columbia, SC: University of South Carolina Press, 1999).

Lautenschläger, Karl, 'The Dreadnought Revolution Reconsidered' in Daniel Masterson (ed.) *Naval History, The Sixth Symposium of the U.S. Naval Academy* (Wilmington, DE: Scholarly Resources, 1987) pp. 121–43.

Layman, R D, *Naval Aviation in the First World War. Its Impact and Influence* (London: Chatham Publishing, 1996).

Liddle, Peter, *The Sailor's War 1914–18* (Poole: Blandford Press, 1985).

Looks, Otto, 'Engineer-Commander of *Seydlitz*, "The Engine Room Staff in the Battle of the Skagerrack"', *The Naval Review*, X, 2 (May 1922), pp. 307–17.

Lyon, David, *The First Destroyers* (London: Chatham Publishing, 1996).

Mackay, Ruddock, *Fisher of Kilverstone* (Oxford: Clarendon Press, 1973).

Mackay, Ruddock and Duffy, Michael, *Hawke, Nelson and British Naval Leadership, 1747–1805* (Woodbridge: The Boydell Press, 2009).

Mahrholz, Konteradmiral a. D. *Der Artillerieoffizier eines Grosskampfschiffes im Kriege 1914/18* (Berlin: Reichswehrministerium, 1930).

March, Edgar, *British Destroyers. A History of Development 1892–1953* (London: Seeley Service, 1966).

Marder, Arthur, *The Anatomy of British Sea Power* (London: Frank Cass, 1940, 3rd impression 1972).
  Fear God and Dread Nought. The Correspondence of Admiral of the Fleet Lord Fisher of Kilverstone. Vols. I and II (London: Cape, 1952 and 1955).
  Portrait of an Admiral (London: Cape, 1952).
McBride, K D, 'On the Brink of Armageddon' in John Roberts (ed.) *Warship 1995* (London: Conway Maritime Press, 1995) pp. 61–73.
  'The Royal Navy "Scout" Class of 1904–05', *Warship International*, XXXI, 3 (1994), pp. 260–81.
McCartney, Innes, 'The Armoured Cruiser *Defence* ...', *International Journal of Nautical Archaeology*, 41, 1 (2012), pp. 56–66.
McLaughlin, Stephen, 'Battle Lines and Fast Wings. Battle Fleet Tactics in the Royal Navy, 1900–1914', *Journal of Strategic Studies*, 38, 7 (2015), pp. 985–1005. dx. doi.org/10.1080/01402390.2015.1005444.
  'Equal Speed Charlie London: Jellicoe's Deployment at Jutland' in *Warship 2010* (London: Conway, 2010) pp. 122–39.
  Russian and Soviet Battleships (Annapolis: Naval Institute Press, 2003).
Oram, H P K, *Ready for Sea* (London: Futura, 1976).
Padfield, Peter, *Guns at Sea* (London: Evelyn, 1974).
Parkes, Oscar, *British Battleships* (London: Leo Cooper, reprinted 1990).
Paschen, Commander G, 'S.M.S. "Lützow at Jutland"', *Journal of the Royal United Services Institution*, LXXII, 485 (February, 1927), pp. 32–41.
Patterson, A Temple, *Jellicoe. A Biography* (London: Macmillan, 1969).
Pelly, Admiral Sir Henry, *300,000 Sea Miles* (London: Chatto & Windus, 1938).
Rahn, Werner, 'The Battle of Jutland from the German Perspective' in M Epkenhans, J Hillman and F Nägler, *Jutland. World War I's Greatest Naval Battle* (Lexington, KY: University Press of Kentucky, 2015) pp. 143–281.
Ramsay, Captain B H, lectures on Jutland Royal Navy Staff College, Greenwich, 1929, JMSS, Add. 49030.
Rasor, Eugene, *The Battle of Jutland. A Bibliography* (Westport, CT: Greenwood Press, 1992).
Robbins, F W and Keys, T, *The Burning Behaviour of Pure Nitrocellulose Propellant Samples* (US Army Research Laboratory, ARL-TR-82, March 1993).
Roberts, John, *Battlecruisers* (London: Chatham Publishing, 1997).
  The Battleship Dreadnought (London: Conway Maritime Press, 1992).
Roskill, Stephen, *Admiral of the Fleet Earl Beatty. The Last Naval Hero: An Intimate Biography* (New York: Athenium, 1981).
Rüger, Jan, *The Great Naval Game. Britain and Germany in the Age of Empire* (Cambridge: Cambridge University Press, 2007).
Scheer, Admiral, *Germany's High Sea Fleet in the World War* (London: Cassell, 1920).
Schleihauf, William, 'Disaster in Harbour. The Loss of HMS *Vanguard*', *The Northern Mariner/Le Marin du nord*, X, 3 (2000), pp. 57–89.
Seligmann, Matthew, 'A German Preference for a Medium Range Battle? British Assumptions about German Naval Gunnery, 1914–1915', *War in History*, 19, 1 (2012), pp. 33–48.
  (ed.) *Naval Intelligence from Germany. The Reports of the British Naval Attachés in Berlin 1906–1914* (Aldershot: Ashgate for the Navy Records Society, 2007).

The Royal Navy and the German Threat 1901–1914 (Oxford: Oxford University Press, 2012).

'Switching Horses. The Admiralty's Recognition of the Threat from Germany', *International History Review*, 30, 2 (2008), pp. 239–58.

Seligmann, M, Nägler, F and Epkenhans, M (eds.), *The Naval Route to the Abyss. The Anglo-German Naval Race 1895–1914* (Farnham: Ashgate for Naval Records Society, 2015).

Sondhaus, Lawrence, *Naval Warfare 1815–1914* (London: Routledge, 2001).

Staff, Gary, *German Battlecruisers 1914–18* (Oxford: Osprey, 2006).

German Battlecruisers of World War One. Their Design, Construction and Operation (Barnsley: Seaforth, 2014).

Stevenson, David, *Armaments and the Coming of War. Europe, 1904–1914* (Oxford: Clarendon Press, 2000).

Sumida, Jon, 'Expectation, Adaptation and Resignation. British Fleet Tactical Planning, August 1914–April 1916', *Naval War College Review*, 60, 3 (Summer 2007), pp. 101–22.

'A Matter of Timing: The Royal Navy and the Tactics of Decisive Battle, 1912–1916', *Journal of Military History*, 67 (January 2003), pp. 85–136.

Tarrant, V E, *Jutland. The German Perspective* (London: Arms and Armour Press, 1997).

von Hase, Commander Georg (trans. A Chambers and F A Holt), *Kiel and Jutland* (London: Skeffington & Son, 1921) and at https://archive.org/details/kieljutland00haseuoft.

von Schoultz, Commodore Gustav, *With the British Battle Fleet* (London: Hutchinson, 1925).

von Waldeyer-Hartz, Hugo (trans. F Appleby Holt), *Admiral von Hipper* (London: Rich & Cowan, 1933).

Watton, Ross, *The Battleship Warspite* (London: Conway, 1986).

Williams, M W, 'The Loss of HMS *Queen Mary* at Jutland' in D McLean and A Preston (eds.) *Warship 1996* (London: Conway, 1996) pp. 111–32.

Winton, John, *Jellicoe* (London: Michael Joseph, 1981).

Index of Warships and Formations

These indexes refer to the names of warships, classes and formations in the text. See also the tables appended to Chapter 1 and in Chapter 4.

German (including Zeppelins)

Formations

British

German

General Index

The titles and naval ranks of officers and men who served at Jutland are those held at the time of the battle.